Fodor's 2003

San Francisco

The Guide
for All Budgets

Completely
Updated

Where to Stay, Eat,
and Explore

On and Off
the Beaten Path

When to Go,
What to Pack

Maps, Travel Tips,
and Web Sites

Fodor's Travel Publications • New York, Toronto, London, Sydney, Auckland
www.fodors.com

Fodor's San Francisco 2003

EDITOR: Mary Beth Bohman

Contributors: Denise M. Leto, Andy Moore, Marty Olmstead, Sharon Silva, John Andrew Vlahides, Sharron S. Wood

Editorial Production: Tom Holton

Maps: David Lindroth, *cartographer*; Bob Blake and Rebecca Baer, *map editors*

Design: Fabrizio La Rocca, *creative director*; Guido Caroti, *art director*; Jolie Novak, *senior picture editor*; Melanie Marin, *photo editor*

Cover Design: Pentagram

Production/Manufacturing: Colleen Ziemba

Cover Photo (View of Coit Tower and Telegraph Hill): Peter Guttman

Copyright

ISBN 1–4000–1051–9

ISSN 1525–1829

Important Tip

Although all prices, open times, and other details in this book are based on information supplied to us at press time, changes occur all the time in the travel world, and Fodor's cannot accept responsibility for facts that become outdated or for inadvertent errors or omissions. So **always confirm information when it matters,** especially if you're making a detour to visit a specific place.

Special Sales

Fodor's Travel Publications are available at special discounts for bulk purchases for sales promotions or premiums. Special editions, including personalized covers, excerpts of existing guides, and corporate imprints, can be created in large quantities for special needs. For more information, contact your local bookseller or write to Special Markets, Fodor's Travel Publications, 280 Park Avenue, New York, NY 10017. Inquiries from Canada should be directed to your local Canadian bookseller or sent to Random House of Canada, Ltd., Marketing Department, 2775 Matheson Blvd., East, Mississauga, Ontario L4W 4P7. Inquiries from the United Kingdom should be sent to Fodor's Travel Publications, 20 Vauxhall Bridge Road, London SW1V 2SA, England.

PRINTED IN THE UNITED STATES OF AMERICA

10 9 8 7 6 5 4 3 2 1

CONTENTS

On the Road with Fodor's   vi

Don't Forget to Write *vii*

Smart Travel Tips A to Z   viii

1   **Destination San Francisco**   *1*

Splendor in the Fog 2
What's Where 4
Pleasures and Pastimes 6
Fodor's Choice 7
Great Itineraries 8

2   **Exploring San Francisco**   **10**

Union Square Area 11
CLOSE-UP: *How Cable Cars Spared the City's Hills and Horses 18*
South of Market (SoMa) and the Embarcadero 20
The Heart of the Barbary Coast 25
Chinatown 29
North Beach and Telegraph Hill 33
Nob Hill and Russian Hill 37
Pacific Heights 42
Japantown 44
Civic Center 46
Northern Waterfront 49
The Marina and the Presidio 53
Golden Gate Park 57
Lincoln Park and the Western Shoreline 63
Mission District 66
Noe Valley 70
The Castro 72
CLOSE-UP: *Sweet Painted Ladies 73*
The Haight 76

3   **Dining**   **79**

4   **Lodging**   **105**

5   **Nightlife and the Arts**   **130**

Nightlife 131
The Arts 146

6   **Outdoor Activities and Sports**   **153**

Participant Sports and the Outdoors 154
Spectator Sports 161
Beaches 163

7   **Shopping**   **165**

CLOSE-UP: *Antiquing Around Town 188*

8   **Side Trips from San Francisco**   *191*

Marin County *192*
The East Bay *207*
CLOSE-UP: *Berkeley in the 1960s 211*
The Inland Peninsula *218*
San Mateo County Coast *223*
On and Around the Bay *227*

9   **The Wine Country**   *230*

Carneros Region *237*
The Napa Valley *238*
The Sonoma Valley *255*
CLOSE-UP: *Wine Tasting 101 256*
Elsewhere in Sonoma County *262*
CLOSE-UP: *Spa Treatment in the Wine Country 269*

Books and Movies   *273*

Index   *274*

Maps

San Francisco *12–13*

Downtown San Francisco *16–17*

Fisherman's Wharf/ Marina and the Presidio *51*

Golden Gate Park *60*

Lincoln Park and Western Shoreline *64*

The Mission District/ Noe Valley *69*

The Castro and the Haight *75*

Downtown San Francisco Dining *82–83*

Fisherman's Wharf/ Marina Dining *91*

The Mission District/The Castro/ Noe Valley Dining *94*

Downtown San Francisco Lodging *108–109*

Downtown San Francisco Nightlife and the Arts *134–135*

The Mission District/ Castro Nightlife and the Arts *138*

Downtown San Francisco Shopping *170–171*

The Mission District/ Noe Valley Shopping *179*

The Castro and the Haight Shopping *184*

Northern California *194–195*

The Bay Area *196*

Marin County *197*

Berkeley *209*

Oakland *215*

The Wine Country *234–235*

Napa and Sonoma Dining *240–241*

Napa and Sonoma Lodging *242–243*

ON THE ROAD WITH FODOR'S

A TRIP TAKES YOU OUT OF YOURSELF. Concerns of life at home completely disappear, driven away by more immediate thoughts—about, say, what marvels will beguile the next day, or where you'll have dinner. That's where Fodor's comes in. We make sure that you know all your options, so that you don't miss something that's around the next bend just because you didn't know it was there. Mindful that the best memories of your trip might have nothing to do with what you came to San Francisco to see, we guide you to sights large and small all over town. You might set out to ride a cable car over Nob Hill, but back at home you find yourself unable to forget the bay views as framed by the flowers of Macondray Lane. With Fodor's at your side, serendipitous discoveries are never far away.

About Our Writers

Our success in showing you every corner of San Francisco is a credit to our extraordinary writers. Although there's no substitute for travel advice from a good friend who knows your style, our contributors are the next best thing—the kind of people you would poll for travel advice if you knew them.

Berkeley-based writer and editor **Denise M. Leto** left no stone unturned in her quest to discover the latest in San Francisco sights. When she's not working, she can be found roaming the city's backstreets in search of the perfect gin gimlet or squeezing *zampanos* at her favorite Berkeley haunt, the Cheese Board.

Lodgings expert **Andy Moore** has lived on a hilltop in San Francisco for over 20 years but has evaluated so many hostelries here that he often feels like a traveler in his own town. A frequent Fodor's contributor, Andy is also active in the independent film scene as a filmmaker and as a staff member of Film Arts Foundation's *Release Print* magazine.

Marty Olmstead moved to the Sonoma Valley from San Francisco in 1989. She updated the Side Trips and Wine Country chapters for this book. She covers the wine-country region for her weekly column in the *Marin Independent Journal* and other publications.

Dining updater **Sharon Silva,** a writer and editor specializing in food books, lives in San Francisco. She is a longtime Fodor's contributor.

John Andrew Vlahides, the Smart Travel Tips and Outdoor Activities and Sports updater, is an essayist and former Clefs díOr concierge. He also plays the local cult celebrity Kathy Barra on Cubby Vision, an absurdist public-access television series.

Frequent contributor to Fodor's, **Sharron Wood** has been happy to call the Bay Area home for 12 years. Updating the Shopping and the Nightlife and the Arts chapters for this book allowed her to indulge in two of her favorite pastimes: shopping for books and searching for the perfect sidecar.

You can rest assured that you're in good hands—and that no property mentioned in the book has paid to be included. Each has been selected strictly on its merits, as the best of its type in its price range.

How to Use This Book

Up front is Smart Travel Tips A to Z, arranged alphabetically by topic and loaded with tips, Web sites, and contact information. Destination: San Francisco helps get you in the mood for your trip. The Exploring chapter is divided into neighborhood sections arranged in logical geographical order; each recommends a good tour and lists local sights alphabetically. The chapters that follow Exploring are arranged alphabetically. At the end of the book you'll find Background and Essentials, including the Books and Movies section that suggests enriching reading and viewing.

Icons and Symbols

★   Our special recommendations
✕   Restaurant
🏠   Lodging establishment
⚿   Campgrounds
☺   Good for kids (rubber duck)
☞   Sends you to another section of the guide for more information
✉   Address
☎   Telephone number

Opening and closing times

Admission prices (those we give apply to adults; substantially reduced fees are almost always available for children, students, and senior citizens)

Numbers in white and black circles ③ ❸ that appear on the maps, in the margins, and within the tours correspond to one another.

Don't Forget to Write

Your experiences—positive and negative—matter to us. If we have missed or misstated something, we want to hear about it. We follow up on all suggestions. Contact the San Francisco editor at editors@fodors.com or c/o Fodor's at 280 Park Avenue, New York, New York 10017. And have a fabulous trip!

Karen Cure

Karen Cure
Editorial Director

ESSENTIAL INFORMATION

ADDRESSES

San Francisco is built on the grid system, with Market Street running diagonally and dividing several neighborhoods. If a street begins at Market, that's where the numbering of its addresses begins.

Throughout the city, as you move from one block to the next, the addresses on most streets increase by 100. To find the block number you're in, look at the top of the white street signs at intersections. You'll see a multiple of 100, with an arrow pointing to the next highest block.

When a road is numbered, it's important to determine whether it is called an avenue or a street. "The Avenues" begin west of Arguello Boulevard and run north–south through the Richmond and Sunset districts in the western part of the city. Numbered streets, however, begin downtown, south of Market Street, and continue south and west through Potrero Hill, the Mission, the Castro, and Noe Valley.

AIR TRAVEL TO AND FROM SAN FRANCISCO

Heavy fog is infamous for causing chronic delays in and out of San Francisco. If you're heading to the East and South Bay make every effort to fly into either the Oakland or San Jose airport. The Oakland airport, which is easy to navigate and is accessible by public transit, is a good alternative to San Francisco's airport.

BOOKING

When you book **look for nonstop flights** and **remember that "direct" flights stop at least once.** Try to avoid connecting flights, which require a change of plane. Two airlines may operate a connecting flight jointly, so ask if your airline operates every segment of the trip; you may find that the carrier you prefer flies you only part of the way. To find more booking tips and to check prices and make on-line flight reservations, log on to www.fodors.com.

CARRIERS

Airlines from around the world and the nation fly into the San Francisco area, so you'll likely have many flights from which to choose. Northwest flies into San Francisco. Alaska, America West, American, Continental, Delta, Southwest, United, and US Airways fly into both Oakland and San Francisco.

➤ MAJOR AIRLINES: **Alaska** ☎ (800/426–0333). **America West** (☎ 800/235–9292). **American** (☎ 800/433–7300). **Continental** (☎ 800/523–3273). **Delta** (☎ 800/221–1212). **Northwest** (☎ 800/225–2525). **Southwest** (☎ 800/435–9792). **United** (☎ 800/241–6522). **US Airways** (☎ 800/428–4322).

➤ SMALLER AIRLINES: **Midwest Express** (☎ 800/452–2022) to San Francisco. **Frontier Airlines** (☎ 800/432–1359) to San Francisco.

CHECK-IN AND BOARDING

Always **ask your carrier about its check-in policy.** Plan to arrive at the airport about two hours before your scheduled departure time for domestic flights and 2½ to 3 hours before international flights. Assuming that not everyone with a ticket will show up, airlines routinely overbook planes. When everyone does, airlines ask for volunteers to give up their seats. In return, these volunteers usually get a certificate for a free flight and are rebooked on the next flight out. If there are not enough volunteers, the airline must choose who will be denied boarding. The first to get bumped are passengers who checked in late and those flying on discounted tickets, so **get to the gate and check in as early as possible,** especially during peak periods.

Always **bring a government-issued photo I.D. to the airport**; even when it's not required, a passport is best.

CUTTING COSTS

The least expensive airfares to San Francisco are priced for round-trip travel and must usually be purchased in advance. Airlines generally allow you to change your return date for a fee; most low-fare tickets, however, are nonrefundable. Depending on the price difference, you might **consider flying into Oakland or San Jose.** It's smart to **call a number of airlines,** and when you are quoted a good price, **book it on the spot**—the same fare may not be available the next day. Always **check different routings** and look into using alternate airports. Also, price off-peak flights, which may be significantly less expensive than others. Travel agents, especially low-fare specialists (☞ Discounts and Deals, *below*), are helpful.

Consolidators are another good source. They buy tickets for scheduled international flights at reduced rates from the airlines, then sell them at prices that beat the best fare available directly from the airlines. Sometimes you can even get your money back if you need to return the ticket. Carefully read the fine print detailing penalties for changes and cancellations, purchase the ticket with a credit card, and **confirm your consolidator reservation with the airline.**

When you **fly as a courier,** you trade your checked-luggage space for a ticket deeply subsidized by a courier service. There are restrictions on when you can book and how long you can stay. Some courier companies list with membership organizations, such as the Air Courier Association and the International Association of Air Travel Couriers; these require you to become a member before you can book a flight.

➤ CONSOLIDATORS: **Cheap Tickets** (☎ 800/377–1000 or 888/922–8849, WEB www.cheaptickets.com). **Discount Airline Ticket Service** (☎ 800/576–1600). **Unitravel** (☎ 800/325–2222, WEB www.unitravel.com). **Up & Away Travel** (☎ 212/889–2345, WEB www.upandaway.com). **World Travel Network** (☎ 800/409–6753).

➤ COURIER RESOURCES: **International Association of Air Travel Couriers** (☎ 352/475–1584, WEB www.courier.org).

ENJOYING THE FLIGHT

State your seat preference when purchasing your ticket, and then repeat it when you confirm and when you check in. For more legroom, you can request one of the few emergency-aisle seats at check-in, if you are capable of lifting at least 50 pounds—a Federal Aviation Administration requirement of passengers in these seats. Seats behind a bulkhead also offer more legroom, but they don't have under-seat storage. Don't sit in the row in front of the emergency aisle or in front of a bulkhead, where seats may not recline.

If you have dietary concerns, **ask for special meals when booking.** These can be vegetarian, low-cholesterol, or kosher, for example. It's a good idea to pack some healthy snacks and a small (plastic) bottle of water in your carry-on bag. On long flights, try to maintain a normal routine, to help fight jet lag. At night, **get some sleep.** By day, **eat light meals, drink water** (not alcohol), and **move around the cabin** to stretch your legs. For additional jet-lag tips consult *Fodor's FYI: Travel Fit & Healthy* (available at bookstores everywhere).

Smoking policies vary from carrier to carrier. Many airlines prohibit smoking on all of their international flights; others allow smoking only on certain routes or certain departures. Ask your carrier about its policy.

FLYING TIMES

Flying time is 6 hours from New York, 4 hours from Chicago, 1 hour from Los Angeles, 3½ hours from Dallas, 10 hours from London, and 15 hours from Sydney.

HOW TO COMPLAIN

If your baggage goes astray or your flight goes awry, complain right away. Most carriers require that you **file a claim immediately.** The Aviation Consumer Protection Division of the Department of Transportation publishes *Fly-Rights*, which discusses airlines and consumer issues and is available on-line. At PassengerRights.com, a

Web site, you can compose a letter of complaint and distribute it electronically.

➤ AIRLINE COMPLAINTS: **Aviation Consumer Protection Division** (✉ U.S. Department of Transportation, Room 4107, C-75, Washington, DC 20590, ☎ 202/366–2220, WEB www.dot.gov/airconsumer). **Federal Aviation Administration Consumer Hotline** (☎ 800/322–7873).

RECONFIRMING

Check the status of your flight before you leave for the airport. You can do this on your carrier's Web site, by linking to a flight-status checker (many Web booking services offer these), or by calling your carrier or travel agent.

AIRPORTS AND TRANSFERS

The major gateway to San Francisco is **San Francisco International Airport (SFO)**, just south of the city, off U.S. 101. Several domestic airlines serve **Oakland Airport (OAK)**, which is across the Bay but not much farther away from downtown San Francisco (via I–880 and I–80), although rush-hour traffic on the Bay Bridge may make travel times longer. Several domestic airlines serve **San Jose International Airport (SJC)**, which is about 40 mi south of San Francisco.

➤ AIRPORT INFORMATION: **San Francisco International Airport** (☎ 650/761–0800). **Oakland International Airport** (☎ 510/577–4000). **San Jose International Airport** (☎ 408/277–4759).

AIRPORT TRANSFERS

FROM SAN FRANCISCO INTERNATIONAL AIRPORT: A taxi ride from SFO to downtown costs about $30. Airport shuttles are inexpensive and efficient. The SFO Airporter ($12) picks up passengers at baggage claim (lower level) and serves selected downtown hotels. SuperShuttle stops at the upper-level traffic islands and takes you from the airport to anywhere within the city limits of San Francisco. It costs from $12 to $17 depending on your destination. Inexpensive shuttles to the East Bay (among them Bayporter Express) also depart from SFO's upper-level traffic islands; expect to pay around $30.

The cheapest way to get from the airport to San Francisco is via Sam-Trans Bus 292 (55 minutes; $2.20) and KX (35 minutes; $3; only one small carry-on bag permitted) to San Francisco or Bus BX to the Colma BART train station. Board the Sam-Trans buses at the north end of the lower level. A new BART extension will connect SFO to downtown San Francisco directly. When the line is completed, which is scheduled to happen in 2003, the trip from the new International Terminal at SFO to downtown will take just 29 minutes. Check at airport information kiosks, or the SFO website, for the latest information.

To drive to downtown San Francisco from the airport, take U.S. 101 north to the Civic Center (9th Street), 7th Street, or 4th Street exit. If you're headed to the Embarcadero or Fisherman's Wharf, take Interstate 280 north (the exit is to the right, just past 3Com Park) and get off at the 4th Street/King Street exit. King Street becomes the Embarcadero a few blocks east of the exit. The Embarcadero winds around the waterfront to Fisherman's Wharf.

FROM OAKLAND INTERNATIONAL AIRPORT: A taxi from Oakland's airport to downtown San Francisco costs between $30 and $35. America's Shuttle, Bayporter Express, and other shuttles serve major hotels and provide door-to-door service to the East Bay and San Francisco. Marin Door to Door serves Marin County for a flat $50 fee. The best way to get to San Francisco via public transit is to take the AIR BART bus ($2) to the Coliseum/Oakland International Airport BART station (BART fares vary depending on where you're going; the ride to downtown San Francisco costs $2.75).

If you're driving from Oakland International Airport, take Hegenberger Road east to Interstate 880 north to Interstate 80 west over the Bay Bridge.

FROM SAN JOSE INTERNATIONAL AIRPORT: A taxi from the airport to downtown San Jose costs about $12 (a taxi to San Francisco costs about $100). South & East Bay Airport

Shuttle transports you to the South Bay and East Bay. A shuttle to downtown San Jose costs $16. VIP Shuttle provides service from the airport in San Jose to downtown San Francisco for $89.

To drive to downtown San Jose from the airport, take Airport Boulevard east to Route 87 south. To get to San Francisco from the airport, take Airport Boulevard east to Route 87 south to Interstate 280 north.

➤ TAXIS AND SHUTTLES: In San Francisco, pick up shuttles on the upper level center islands. In Oakland and San Jose, look outside baggage claim exits. **American Airporter** (☎ 415/202–0733). **Bayporter Express** (☎ 415/467–1800). **East Bay Express Airporter** (☎ 510/547–0404). **Laurie's** (☎ 415/334–9000). **Marin Door to Door** (☎ 415/457–2717). **SamTrans** (☎ 800/660–4287). **South & East Bay Airport Shuttle** (☎ 408/559–9477). **SFO Airporter** (☎ 800/532–8405). **SuperShuttle** (☎ 415/558–8500 or 800/258–3826). **VIP Airport Shuttle** (☎ 408/885–1800 or 800/235–8847).

BIKE TRAVEL

San Francisco's famous hills present a big challenge for bike riders, but you'll still see plenty of residents riding through the city. The Embarcadero, Marina Green, and Golden Gate Park are popular cycling areas.

➤ BIKE MAPS: **S.F. Biking/Walking Guide** ($2.50) is an excellent biking map that shows street grades and routes. It's available at most bike shops and select city bookstores. You can also buy it on-line for $5 at WEB www.reineckandreineck.com.

➤ BIKE RENTALS: **Adventure Bicycle Co.** (☎ 415/771–8735 or 888/544–2453). **Vision Cyclery** (☎ 415/221–9766).

BOAT AND FERRY TRAVEL

Several ferry lines run out of San Francisco. Blue and Gold Fleet operates a number of lines, including a Bay cruise, service to Alcatraz and Angel Island, and ferries to Sausalito and Tiburon. Tickets for the Bay cruise can be purchased at Pier 39; all other tickets are sold at Pier 41. Golden Gate Ferry runs seven days a week to and from Sausalito and Larkspur, leaving from behind the San Francisco Ferry Building on the Embarcadero. The Oakland/Alameda Ferry operates seven days a week between Alameda's Main Street Ferry Building and Oakland's Jack London Square and San Francisco's Pier 39 and the Ferry Building; some ferries only go to Pier 39, so ask when you board. Tickets may be purchased on board.

➤ BOAT AND FERRY INFORMATION: **Blue and Gold Fleet** (☎ 415/705–5555). **Golden Gate Ferry** (☎ 415/923–2000). **Oakland/Alameda Ferry** (☎ 510/522–3300).

BUSINESS HOURS

MUSEUMS AND SIGHTS

Most museums are open daily from 9 or 10 in the morning until 5 or 6, and are closed one day of the week (usually Monday or Wednesday). Most stay open late one day of the week, and many offer free admission once a month.

PHARMACIES

Most pharmacies are open weekdays 9:30–8, and weekends 9:30–5. Two **Walgreens Drug Stores** have 24-hour pharmacies (✉ 498 Castro, at 18th St., ☎ 415/861–3136; ✉ 3201 Divisadero St., at Lombard St., ☎ 415/931–6417). The downtown Walgreens pharmacy (✉ 135 Powell St., near Market St., ☎ 415/391–7222) is open weekdays 8–9, Saturday 9–5.

SHOPS

Store hours vary slightly, but standard shopping times are between 10 AM and 5 or 6 PM on Monday, Tuesday, Wednesday, Friday, and Saturday; between 10 and 8 or 9 Thursday; and from noon to 5 on Sunday. Stores on and around Fisherman's Wharf often have longer hours in summer. Most airport shops are open daily.

BUS TRAVEL TO AND
FROM SAN FRANCISCO

Greyhound, the only long-distance bus company in San Francisco, operates buses to and from most major cities in the country. Smoking is prohibited on all buses in California.

FARES AND SCHEDULES

Call Greyhound or visit their Web site for fare and schedule information.

PAYING

Cash, travelers checks, and credit cards are accepted.

RESERVATIONS

Reservations are not accepted on Greyhound. Seating is on a first-come, first-served basis.

➤ BUS INFORMATION: **Greyhound** (✉ 425 Mission St., ☎ 415/495–1569 or 800/231–2222, WEB www.greyhound.com).

BUS AND TRAIN TRAVEL
WITHIN SAN FRANCISCO

The San Francisco Muni Transit and Street Map ($2.50) is a useful map and guide to the extensive transportation system. You can buy it at most bookstores and at the San Francisco Visitors Center on the lower level of Hallidie Plaza at Powell and Market streets.

BART

You can use Bay Area Rapid Transit (BART) trains to reach Oakland, Berkeley, Concord, Richmond, Fremont, Martinez, and Dublin/Pleasanton. Trains also travel south from San Francisco as far as Daly City and Colma. The BART-SFO Extension Project, which at press time was scheduled for completion in 2003, will connect downtown San Francisco to the San Francisco International Airport. Fares range from $1.10 to $4.70; trains run until midnight.

➤ BART: **Bay Area Rapid Transit** (☎ 650/992–2278, WEB www.bart.gov).

CALTRAIN

CalTrain connects San Francisco to Palo Alto, San Jose, Santa Clara, and many smaller cities en route. In San Francisco, trains leave from the main depot at 4th and King streets, and a rail-side stop at 22nd St. and Pennsylvania streets. One-way fares run $1.25–$6.75. Trips last 1–1½ hours.

➤ CALTRAIN: **CalTrain** (☎ 800/660–4287, WEB www.caltrain.com).

MUNI

The San Francisco Municipal Railway, or Muni, operates light-rail vehicles, the historic streetcar line along Fisherman's Wharf and Market Street, trolley buses, and the world-famous cable cars. Light rail travels along Market Street to the Mission District and Noe Valley (J line), the Ingleside district (K line), and the Sunset District (L, M, and N lines). Muni provides 24-hour service on selected lines to all areas of the city.

On buses and streetcars, the fare is $1. Exact change is required, and dollar bills are accepted in the fare boxes. For all Muni vehicles other than cable cars, 90-minute transfers are issued free upon request at the time the fare is paid. Transfers are valid for two additional transfers in any direction. Cable cars cost $2 and include no transfers. For more information on cable cars, *see below.*

A $6 pass good for unlimited travel all day on all routes can be purchased on the cable cars. Also, one-day ($6), three-day ($10), or seven-day ($15) Passports can be purchased at several outlets, including the cable car ticket booth at Powell and Market streets and the Visitors Information Center downstairs in Hallidie Plaza. A monthly ticket, called a Fast Pass, is available for $35 and can be used on all Muni lines (including cable cars) and on BART within city limits.

➤ BUS AND TRAIN INFORMATION: **AC Transit** (☎ 510/839–2882) serves the East Bay. **Golden Gate Transit** (☎ 415/923–2000) serves Marin County. **San Francisco Municipal Railway System (Muni;** ☎ 415/673–6864, WEB www.sfmuni.com) operates many routes within San Francisco.

CABLE CARS

Don't miss the sensation of moving up and down some of San Francisco's steepest hills in a clattering cable car. As it pauses at a designated stop, **jump aboard and wedge yourself into any available space.** Then just hold on!

The fare (for one direction) is $2. You can buy tickets on board (exact change is not necessary) or at the kiosks at the cable car turnarounds located at Hyde and Beach streets and Powell and Market streets.

The heavily traveled Powell-Mason and Powell-Hyde lines begin at Powell and Market streets near Union Square and terminate at Fisherman's Wharf; lines for these routes can be long, especially in summer. The California Street line runs east and west from Market and California streets to Van Ness Avenue; there is often no wait to board this route.

CAMERAS
AND PHOTOGRAPHY

Early afternoon is the best time to avoid the fog in your photos—though you may want a few shots of the fog blanketing the city. The views from Coit Tower, Ocean Beach, and Fisherman's Wharf will inspire any shutterbug. Of course, don't miss a shot of the Golden Gate Bridge and a cable car.

Film is readily available throughout the city, from photo centers, drugstores, supermarkets, and many corner markets.

The *Kodak Guide to Shooting Great Travel Pictures* (available at bookstores everywhere) is loaded with tips.
➤ PHOTO HELP: **Kodak Information Center** (☎ 800/242–2424, WEB www. kodak.com).

EQUIPMENT PRECAUTIONS

Don't pack film and equipment in checked luggage, where it is much more susceptible to damage. X-ray machines used to view checked luggage are becoming much more powerful and therefore are much more likely to ruin your film. Try to **ask for hand inspection of film,** which becomes clouded after repeated exposure to airport X-ray machines, and **keep videotapes and computer disks away from metal detectors.** Always **keep film, tape, and computer disks out of the sun.** Carry an extra supply of batteries, and **be prepared to turn on your camera, camcorder, or laptop** to prove to airport security personnel that the device is real.

CAR RENTAL

Unless you plan on making excursions into Marin County, the East Bay, the South Bay, or the Wine Country, **avoid renting a car.** First see how well suited the cable cars are to this city of hills, how quickly the

Muni buses and streetcars get you around every neighborhood, and how efficiently BART trains deliver you to the East Bay.

Rentals in San Francisco begin at $38 a day and $194 a week for an economy car with air-conditioning, automatic transmission, and unlimited mileage. This does not include tax on car rentals, which is 8.25%. If you dream of driving the coast with the top down, or heading out of town to ski the Sierra, consider renting a specialty vehicle. Most major agencies have a few on hand, but the locally owned SpecialtyRentals.com features them; they will also arrange for airport pick-up and drop-off.
➤ MAJOR AGENCIES: **Alamo** (☎ 800/ 327–9633; WEB www.alamo.com). **Avis** (☎ 800/331–1212; 800/879– 2847 in Canada; 02/9353–9000 in Australia; 09/526–2847 in New Zealand; 0870/606–0100 in the U.K.; WEB www.avis.com). **Budget** (☎ 800/ 527–0700; 0870/156–5656 in the U.K.; WEB www.budget.com). **Dollar** (☎ 800/800–4000; 0124/622–0111 in the U.K.; where it's affiliated with Sixt; 02/9223–1444 in Australia; WEB www.dollar.com). **Hertz** (☎ 800/654– 3131; 800/263–0600 in Canada; 020/ 8897–2072 in the U.K.; 02/9669– 2444 in Australia; 09/256–8690 in New Zealand; WEB www.hertz.com). **National Car Rental** (☎ 800/227– 7368; 020/8680–4800 in the U.K.; WEB www.nationalcar.com).
➤ LOCAL AGENCIES: **SpecialtyRentals. com** (☎ 415/701–1600 or 800/400– 8412).

CUTTING COSTS

For a good deal, **book through a travel agent who will shop around.** Also, **price local car-rental companies**— whose prices may be lower still, although their service and maintenance may not be as good as those of major rental agencies—and **research rates on-line.** Remember to ask about required deposits, cancellation penalties, and drop-off charges if you're planning to pick up the car in one city and leave it in another. If you're traveling during a holiday period, also make sure that a confirmed reservation guarantees you a car.

➤ LOCAL AGENCIES: **City Rent-a-Car** (☎ 415/928–4414).

INSURANCE

When driving a rented car you are generally responsible for any damage to or loss of the vehicle. You may also be liable for any property damage or personal injury that you may cause while driving. Before you rent, see what coverage you already have under the terms of your personal auto-insurance policy and credit cards.

For $9 a day, rental companies sell protection, known as a collision- or loss-damage waiver (CDW or LDW), that eliminates your liability for damage to the car; it's always optional and should never be automatically added to your bill. In most states you don't need a CDW if you have personal auto insurance or other liability insurance. Some states, including California, have capped the price of the CDW and LDW. However, **make sure you have enough coverage to pay for the car.** If you do not have auto insurance or an umbrella policy that covers damage to third parties, purchasing liability insurance and a CDW or LDW is highly recommended.

Rental agencies in California are not required to include liability insurance in the price of the rental. If you cause an accident, you may expose your assets to litigation. When in doubt, **take the liability coverage that the agency offers.** If you plan to take the car out of California, **ask if the policy is valid in other states or countries.** Most car rental companies will not insure a loss or damage that occurs outside of their coverage area—particularly in Mexico.

REQUIREMENTS AND RESTRICTIONS

In San Francisco you must be 21 to rent a car, and rates may be higher if you're under 25. Some agencies will not rent to those between 21 and 24; check when you book.

SURCHARGES

Before you pick up a car in one city and leave it in another, **ask about drop-off charges or one-way service fees,** which can be substantial. Note, too, that some rental agencies charge extra if you return the car before the time specified in your contract. To avoid a hefty refueling fee, **fill the tank just before you turn in the car,** but be aware that gas stations near the rental outlet may overcharge. It's almost never a deal to buy the tank of gas in the car when you rent it; the understanding is that you'll return it empty, but some fuel usually remains. Surcharges may apply if you're under 25. You'll pay extra for child seats (about $6 a day), which are compulsory for children under five, and for additional drivers (about $5 per day).

CAR TRAVEL

Driving in San Francisco can be a challenge because of the hills, one-way streets, and traffic. Take it easy, remember to **curb your wheels** when parking on hills (turn wheels away from the curb when facing uphill, toward the curb when facing downhill). Do **use public transportation** or **cab it** whenever possible.

EMERGENCY SERVICES

Dial 911 to report accidents on the road and to reach police, the highway patrol, or the fire department.

PARKING

This is a great city for walking and a terrible city for parking. On certain streets, parking is forbidden during rush hours. **Look for the warning signs;** illegally parked cars are towed. Downtown parking lots are often full and most are expensive. (The city-owned Sutter-Stockton, Ellis-O'Farrell, and 5th-and-Mission garages have the most reasonable rates in the downtown area.) Finding a spot in North Beach at night can be exceedingly difficult; try the five-level 766 Vallejo Garage. Larger hotels often have parking available, but it doesn't come cheap; many charge as much as $30 a day for the privilege.

➤ GARAGES: **Ellis-O'Farrell Garage** (✉ 123 O'Farrell St., at Stockton St., ☎ 415/986–4800). **Embarcadero Center Garage** (✉ 1–4 Embarcadero Center, between Battery and Drumm Sts., ☎ 800/733–6318). **5th-and-Mission Garage** (✉ 833 Mission St., at 5th St., ☎ 415/982–8522). **Opera**

Plaza Garage (⊠ 601 Van Ness Ave., at Turk St., ☎ 415/771–4776). **Pier 39 Garage** (⊠ 2550 Powell St., at the Embarcadero, ☎ 415/705–5418). **Portsmouth Square Garage** (⊠ 733 Kearny St., at Clay St., ☎ 415/982–6353). **766 Vallejo Garage** (⊠ 766 Vallejo St., at Powell St., ☎ 415/989–4490). **Sutter-Stockton Garage** (⊠ 444 Stockton St., at Sutter St., ☎ 415/982–7275). **The Wharf Garage** (⊠ Fisherman's Wharf, 350 Beach St., at Taylor St., ☎ 415/921–0226).

ROAD CONDITIONS

Although "rush hour" is 7 to 10 in the morning and 4 to 7 in the evening, you can hit gridlock on any day at any time, especially over the Bay Bridge, and leaving and/or entering the city from the south. Sunday afternoon traffic can be heavy as well, especially over the bridges.

Market Street runs west from the Ferry Building to Twin Peaks. The major east–west streets north of Market are Geary Boulevard (it's called Geary Street until Van Ness Avenue), which runs to the Pacific Ocean; Fulton Street, which begins at the back of the Opera House and continues along the north side of Golden Gate Park to Ocean Beach; Oak Street, which runs east from Golden Gate Park toward down-town, then flows into north-bound Franklin Street; and Fell Street, the left two lanes of which cut through Golden Gate Park and empty into Lincoln Boulevard, which continues to the ocean.

Among the major north–south streets are Divisadero, which becomes Castro Street at Duboce Avenue and contin-ues past Cesar Chavez Street; Van Ness Avenue (it becomes South Van Ness Avenue when it crosses Market Street); and Park Presidio Boulevard, which empties into 19th Avenue.

RULES OF THE ROAD

The use of seat belts is required in California. The speed limit on city streets is 25 mph unless otherwise posted. A right turn on a red light after stopping is legal unless posted otherwise, as is a left on red at the intersection of two one-way streets.

Always **strap children under 40 pounds or age 4 into approved child-safety seats.** If you are renting a car, don't forget to **arrange for a car seat.**

CHILDREN IN SAN FRANCISCO

The City by the Bay is made for kids—from the awesome hills to the ferries to the cable cars. Wherever you go in San Francisco, you're bound to find kid-friendly activities. *Fodor's Around San Francisco with Kids* (available in bookstores every-where) can help you plan your days together.

The San Francisco Convention and Visitors Bureau operates a telephone line and a Web site, where you can find information on family activities and calendars of events.

If you are renting a car, don't forget to **arrange for a car seat** when you reserve. For general advice about traveling with children, consult *Fodor's FYI: Travel with Your Baby* (available in bookstores everywhere).

➤ LOCAL INFORMATION: **San Francisco Convention and Visitors Bureau** (⊠ ☎ 415/283–0177, WEB www. sfvisitor.org.

BABY-SITTING

Many agencies specialize in on- and off-site group and individual child care for conventions, tourists, and special events. Hotel concierges can usually recommend a reliable baby-sitting service.

➤ AGENCIES: **Bay Area Child Care** (☎ 650/991–7474).

FLYING

Experts agree that it's a good idea to use safety seats aloft for children weighing less than 40 pounds. Air-lines set their own policies: U.S. carriers usually require that the child be ticketed, even if he or she is young enough to ride free, since the seats must be strapped into regular seats. Do **check your airline's policy about using safety seats during takeoff and landing.** Safety seats are not allowed everywhere in the plane, so get your seat assignments as early as possible.

When reserving, **request children's meals or a freestanding bassinet** (not available at all airlines) if you need them. But note that bulkhead seats, where you must sit to use the bassinet, may lack an overhead bin or storage space on the floor.

FOOD

Many San Francisco restaurants make at least some accommodation for kids: child-size portions, seats for children, or amusements such as crayons and coloring paper. The most family-friendly establishments tend to be in tourist areas like Fisherman's Wharf and the Embarcadero. Check Dining (☞ Chapter 3) for restaurants that welcome kids.

LODGING

Most hotels in San Francisco allow children under a certain age to stay in their parents' room at no extra charge, but others charge for them as extra adults; be sure to **find out the cutoff age for children's discounts.** Some hotels charge extra for a roll-away bed, usually $10–$30.

Not surprisingly, given the range of lodgings available in San Francisco, there are many great hotels for families. The family suites at the Hotel Del Sol help kids to feel at home with child-friendly furnishings and games, plus there is an outdoor pool and hammock. The Radisson Fisherman's Wharf has an outdoor pool and easy access to all of the family attractions at the Wharf. The glass elevators at the Hyatt Regency entertain both young and old.

➤ BEST CHOICES: **Hotel Del Sol** (⊠ 3100 Webster St., 94123, ☎ 415/921–5520 or 877/433–5765). **Radisson Hotel at Fisherman's Wharf** (⊠ 250 Beach St., 94133, ☎ 415/392–6700 or 800/333–3333). **Hyatt Regency** (⊠ 5 Embarcadero Center, 94111, ☎ 415/788–1234 or 800/233–1234).

SIGHTS AND ATTRACTIONS

Most of San Francisco's major attractions, from Golden Gate Park to Fisherman's Wharf, are as fun for children as they are for adults. Places that are especially appealing to children are indicated by a rubber-duckie icon (🐤) in the margin.

The Zeum is a high-tech interactive arts and technology center geared to children ages eight and over. The Exploratorium, a "museum of science, art, and human perception," has more than 650 exhibits that focus on sea and insect life, computers, electricity, the weather, and much more. Lawrence Hall of Science, a dazzling hands-on science center, lets kids look at insects under microscopes, solve crimes using chemical forensics, and explore the physics of baseball.

CONCIERGES

Concierges, found in many hotels, can help you with theater tickets and dinner reservations: a good one with connections may be able to get you seats for a hot show or prime-time dinner reservations at the restaurant of the moment. You can also turn to your hotel's concierge for help with travel arrangements, sightseeing plans, services ranging from aromatherapy to zipper repair, and emergencies. Always, **always tip** a concierge who has been of assistance (☞ Tipping, *below*).

CONSUMER PROTECTION

Whether you're shopping for gifts or purchasing travel services, **pay with a major credit card** whenever possible, so you can cancel payment or get reimbursed if there's a problem (and you can provide documentation). If you're doing business with a particular company for the first time, **contact your local Better Business Bureau and the attorney general's offices** in your state and (for U.S. businesses) the company's home state as well. Have any complaints been filed? Finally, if you're buying a package or tour, always **consider travel insurance** that includes default coverage (☞ Insurance, *below*).

➤ BBBs: **Council of Better Business Bureaus** (⊠ 4200 Wilson Blvd., Suite 800, Arlington, VA 22203, ☎ 703/276–0100, FAX 703/525–8277, WEB www.bbb.org). **Better Business Bureau** (⊠ 510 16th St., Suite 550, 94612-1584, Oakland, ☎ 510/238–1000, WEB www.oakland.bbb.org).

CUSTOMS AND DUTIES

IN AUSTRALIA

Australian residents who are 18 or older may bring home A$400 worth of souvenirs and gifts (including jewelry), 250 cigarettes or 250 grams of tobacco, and 1,125 ml of alcohol (including wine, beer, and spirits). Residents under 18 may bring back A$200 worth of goods. Prohibited items include meat products. Seeds, plants, and fruits need to be declared upon arrival.

► INFORMATION: **Australian Customs Service** (Regional Director, ⊠ Box 8, Sydney, NSW 2001, ☎ 02/9213–2000, FAX 02/9213–4043, WEB www. customs.gov.au).

IN CANADA

Canadian residents who have been out of Canada for at least seven days may bring in C$750 worth of goods duty-free. If you've been away fewer than seven days but more than 48 hours, the duty-free allowance drops to C$200; if your trip lasts 24 to 48 hours, the allowance is C$50. You may not pool allowances with family members. Goods claimed under the C$750 exemption may follow you by mail; those claimed under the lesser exemptions must accompany you. Alcohol and tobacco products may be included in the seven-day and 48-hour exemptions but not in the 24-hour exemption. If you meet the age requirements of the province or territory through which you reenter Canada, you may bring in, duty-free, 1.5 liters of wine *or* 1.14 liters (40 imperial ounces) of liquor *or* 24 12-ounce cans or bottles of beer or ale. If you are 19 or older you may bring in, duty-free, 200 cigarettes and 50 cigars. Check ahead of time with the Canada Customs and Revenue Agency or the Department of Agriculture for policies regarding meat products, seeds, plants, and fruits.

You may send an unlimited number of gifts (only one gift per recipient, however) worth up to C$60 each duty-free to Canada. Label the package UNSO-LICITED GIFT—VALUE UNDER $60. Alcohol and tobacco products are excluded.

► INFORMATION: **Canada Customs and Revenue Agency** (⊠ 2265 St. Laurent Blvd. S, Ottawa, Ontario K1G 4K3, ☎ 204/983–3500; 506/636–5064; 800/461–9999, WEB www. ccra-adrc.gc.ca/).

IN NEW ZEALAND

All homeward-bound residents may bring back NZ$700 worth of souvenirs and gifts; passengers may not pool their allowances, and children can claim only the concession on goods intended for their own use. For those 17 or older, the duty-free allowance also includes 4.5 liters of wine or beer; one 1,125-ml bottle of spirits; and either 200 cigarettes, 250 grams of tobacco, 50 cigars, *or* a combination of the three up to 250 grams. Meat products, seeds, plants, and fruits must be declared upon arrival to the Agricultural Services Department.

► INFORMATION: **New Zealand Customs** (⊠ Head Office, The Customhouse, 17–21 Whitmore St., Box 2218, Wellington, ☎ 09/300–5399, WEB www.customs.govt.nz).

IN THE U.K.

From countries outside the European Union, including the United States, you may bring home, duty-free, 200 cigarettes or 50 cigars; 1 liter of spirits or 2 liters of fortified or sparkling wine or liqueurs; 2 liters of still table wine; 60 ml of perfume; 250 ml of toilet water; plus £145 worth of other goods, including gifts and souvenirs. Prohibited items include meat products, seeds, plants, and fruits.

► INFORMATION: **HM Customs and Excise** (⊠ Portcullis House, 21 Cowbridge Rd. E, Cardiff CF11 9SS, ☎ 029/2038–6423, WEB www.hmce. gov.uk).

DINING

San Francisco restaurants are regularly rated among the best in the world. Out-of-towners planning a visit should **make reservations well in advance** at popular eateries like Aqua, Boulevard, Delfina, Jardinière, Masa's, and Zuni Café. Unless you call weeks, or in some cases months, ahead you won't get a table. And it's just as essential to book ahead at the top spots in Wine Country like French Laundry, Auberge du Soleil, and Tra Vigne.

The restaurants we list are the cream of the crop in each price category. Properties indicated by a ✕🅃 are lodging establishments whose restaurant warrants a special trip. Unless otherwise noted, the restaurants listed in this guide are open daily for lunch and dinner.

RESERVATIONS AND DRESS

Reservations are always a good idea; we mention them only when they're essential or not accepted. Book as far ahead as you can, and reconfirm as soon as you arrive. (Large parties should always call ahead to check the reservations policy.) We mention dress only when men are required to wear a jacket or a jacket and tie.

SPECIALTIES

San Francisco is the birthplace of sourdough bread, and you'll find pungent, chewy loaves of it everywhere, particularly along Fisherman's Wharf. San Francisco is also noted for its wide range of international cuisines, from authentic *taquerias* in the Mission district to superb Asian restaurants. Another Bay Area hallmark is California cuisine, unique dishes created entirely out of fresh, organic produce and meats. This concept was first developed at the famed Chez Panisse restaurant across the Bay in Berkeley, and many San Francisco restaurants serve their own versions of California cuisine.

WINE, BEER, AND SPIRITS

Wine, beer, and spirits are readily available throughout the city, in supermarkets, liquor stores, and corner markets. The legal age to buy alcoholic beverages in California is 21. Alcohol may be served in bars, clubs, and restaurants between the hours of 6 AM and 2 AM.

The proximity of the Napa and Sonoma valleys, just north of San Francisco, means you'll find excellent and moderately priced California wines just about everywhere. Look also for the excellent Anchor Steam beer, which is brewed locally.

DISABILITIES
AND ACCESSIBILITY

California is a national leader in making attractions and facilities accessible to travelers with disabilities. Since 1982, the state building code has required that all construction for public use include access for people with disabilities. State laws more than a decade old provide special privileges, such as license plates allowing special parking spaces, unlimited parking in time-limited spaces, and free parking in metered spaces. Identification from states other than California is honored.

The Independent Living Resource Center of San Francisco can provide information and referrals for people with all types of disabilities. Access Northern California has a Web site that travelers with disabilities can visit to find information on the accessibility of lodgings, attractions, transportation services, recreation facilities, and outdoor activities.

The California State Coastal Conservancy distributes the free booklet *Wheelchair Riders Guide to San Francisco Bay and Nearby Shorelines.*

➤ LOCAL RESOURCES: **Independent Living Resources** (✉ 649 Mission St., 3rd floor, 94105, ☎ 415/543–6222). **Access Northern California** (1427 Grant St., Berkeley, 94703, ☎ 510/524–2026, WEB www.accessnca.com). **California State Coastal Conservancy** (✉ Publications Dept., 1330 Broadway, Suite 1100, Oakland 94612, ☎ 510/286–1015).

LODGING

Despite the Americans with Disabilities Act, the definition of accessibility seems to differ from hotel to hotel. Some properties may be accessible by ADA standards for people with mobility problems but not for people with hearing or vision impairments, for example.

If you have mobility problems, ask for the lowest floor on which accessible services are offered. If you have a hearing impairment, check whether the hotel has devices to alert you visually to the ring of the telephone, knock at the door, and a fire/emergency alarm. Some hotels provide these devices without charge. Discuss your needs with hotel personnel if this equipment isn't available, so that a staff member can personally alert you in the event of an emergency.

If you're bringing a guide dog, get authorization ahead of time and write down the name of the person you spoke with.

The San Francisco Convention and Visitors Bureau publishes a free *San Francisco Lodging Guide* that spells out which hotels are up to ADA requirements.

➤ BEST CHOICES: **Hotel Palomar** (✉ 12 4th St., 94103, ☎ 415/348–1111 or 877/294–9711). **Hyatt at Fisherman's Wharf** (✉ 555 N. Point St., 94133, ☎ 415/563–1234 or 800/233–1234).

➤ LOCAL RESOURCES: **San Francisco Convention and Visitors Bureau** (✉ Box 429097, San Francisco 94142-9097, ☎ 415/974–6900; 415/392–0328 TTY).

PARKS

The National Park Service provides a Golden Access Passport for all national parks free of charge to those who are medically blind or have a permanent disability; the passport covers the entry fee for the holder and anyone accompanying the holder in the same private vehicle as well as a 50% discount on camping and various other user fees. Apply for the passport in person at a national recreation facility that charges an entrance fee; proof of disability is required.

RESERVATIONS

When discussing accessibility with an operator or reservations agent, **ask hard questions.** Are there any stairs, inside *or* out? Are there grab bars next to the toilet *and* in the shower/tub? How wide is the doorway to the room? To the bathroom? For the most extensive facilities meeting the latest legal specifications, **opt for newer accommodations.** If you reserve through a toll-free number, consider also calling the hotel's local number to confirm the information from the central reservations office. Get confirmation in writing when you can.

SIGHTS AND ATTRACTIONS

Major attractions in San Francisco are wheelchair accessible, including the elevator to Coit Tower, Alcatraz, ferries, and the museums.

TRANSPORTATION

All Bay Area Rapid Transit (BART) stations are equipped with elevators, as well as wheelchair-accessible rest rooms, phones, and drinking fountains. (It's a good idea to call the day of travel, though, as elevators are frequently out of service.) Travelers with disabilities are entitled to a Bay Region Transit Discount Card, which offers savings of up to 75% off BART fares. Muni trains are wheelchair accessible, but not all Muni buses are.

➤ LOCAL RESOURCES: **BART Passes Office** (☎ 510/464–7133).

➤ COMPLAINTS: **Aviation Consumer Protection Division** (☞ Air Travel, *above*) for airline-related problems. **Departmental Office of Civil Rights** (for general inquiries, ✉ U.S. Department of Transportation, S-30, 400 7th St. SW, Room 10215, Washington, DC 20590, ☎ 202/366–4648, FAX 202/366–3571, WEB www.dot.gov/ost/docr/index.htm). **Disability Rights Section** (✉ U.S. Department of Justice, Civil Rights Division, 950 Pennsylvania Ave. NW, Washington, DC 20530, ☎ ADA information line 202/514–0301, 202/514–0383 TTY; WEB www.usdoj.gov/crt/ada/adahom1.htm).

TRAVEL AGENCIES

In the United States, the Americans with Disabilities Act requires that travel firms serve the needs of all travelers. Some agencies specialize in working with people with disabilities.

➤ TRAVELERS WITH MOBILITY PROBLEMS: **Access Adventures** (✉ 206 Chestnut Ridge Rd., Scottsville, NY 14624, ☎ 716/889–9096, dltravel@prodigy.net), run by a former physical-rehabilitation counselor. **Accessible Vans of America** (✉ 9 Spielman Rd., Fairfield, NJ 07004, ☎ 877/282–8267; 888/282–8267 reservations, FAX 973/808–9713, WEB www.accessiblevans.com). **CareVacations** (✉ No. 5, 5110–50 Ave., Leduc, Alberta T9E 6V4, Canada, ☎ 780/986–6404 or 877/478–7827, FAX 780/986–8332, WEB www.carevacations.com), for group tours and cruise vacations. **Flying Wheels Travel** (✉ 143 W. Bridge St., Box 382, Owatonna, MN 55060, ☎ 507/451–5005, FAX 507/451–1685, WEB www.flyingwheelstravel.com).

➤ TRAVELERS WITH DEVELOPMENTAL DISABILITIES: **New Directions** (✉ 5276 Hollister Ave., Suite 207, Santa Barbara, CA 93111, ☎ 805/967–2841 or 888/967–2841, FAX 805/964–7344, WEB www.newdirectionstravel.com).

DISCOUNTS AND DEALS

Discount coupons for area restaurants and hotels are available at the San Francisco Visitors Information Center in the lower level of Hallidie Plaza at Powell and Market streets. You can pick up same-day discount tickets to performing arts events at the TIX Bay Area booth in Union Square.

Be a smart shopper and **compare all your options** before making decisions. A plane ticket bought with a promotional coupon from travel clubs, coupon books, and direct-mail offers or purchased on the Internet may not be cheaper than the least expensive fare from a discount ticket agency. And always keep in mind that what you get is just as important as what you save.

DISCOUNT RESERVATIONS

To save money, **look into discount reservations services** with Web sites and toll-free numbers, which use their buying power to get a better price on hotels, airline tickets, even car rentals. When booking a room, always **call the hotel's local toll-free number** (if one is available) rather than the central reservations number—you'll often get a better price. Always ask about special packages or corporate rates.

➤ AIRLINE TICKETS: ☎ **800/AIR–4LESS.**

➤ HOTEL ROOMS: **Accommodations Express** (☎ 800/444–7666, WEB www.accommodationsexpress.com). **Central Reservation Service** (CRS; ☎ 800/548–3311, WEB www.roomconnection.net). **Hotel Reservations Network** (☎ 800/964–6835, WEB www.hoteldiscount.com). **Quikbook** (☎ 800/789–9887, WEB www.quikbook.com). **RMC Travel** (☎ 800/245–5738, WEB www.rmcwebtravel.com). **Steigenberger Reservation Service** (☎ 800/223–5652, WEB www.srs-worldhotels.com). **Travel Interlink** (☎ 800/888–5898, WEB www.travelinterlink.com). **Turbotrip.com** (☎ 800/473–7829, WEB www.turbotrip.com).

PACKAGE DEALS

Don't confuse packages and guided tours. When you buy a package, you travel on your own, just as though you had planned the trip yourself. Fly/drive packages, which combine airfare and car rental, are often a good deal. In cities, ask the local visitor's bureau about hotel packages that include tickets to major museum exhibits or other special events.

DIVERS' ALERT

Do not fly within 24 hours of scuba diving.

GAY AND LESBIAN TRAVEL

San Francisco's reputation as a gay-friendly destination is well deserved. The Castro has long been thought of as ground zero for the gay community, but today gay men and lesbians have enclaves all over the city and in the surrounding communities like Oakland and Berkeley. Gay-owned shops and nightlife are sprinkled throughout the area as well.

For details about the gay and lesbian scene, consult *Fodor's Gay Guide to the USA* (available in bookstores everywhere).

➤ GAY RESOURCES: The *Bay Area Reporter* (☎ 415/861–5019) is a weekly gay paper.

➤ GAY- AND LESBIANFRIENDLY TRAVEL AGENCIES: **Different Roads Travel** (✉ 8383 Wilshire Blvd., Suite 902, Beverly Hills, CA 90211, ☎ 323/651–5557 or 800/429–8747, FAX 323/651–3678, lgernert@tzell.com). **Kennedy Travel** (✉ 314 Jericho Turnpike, Floral Park, NY 11001, ☎ 516/352–4888 or 800/237–7433, FAX 516/354–8849, WEB www.kennedytravel.com). **Now, Voyager** (✉ 4406 18th St., San Francisco, CA 94114, ☎ 415/626–1169 or 800/255–6951, FAX 415/626–8626, WEB www.nowvoyager.com). **Skylink Travel and Tour** (✉ 1006 Mendocino Ave., Santa Rosa, CA 95401, ☎ 707/546–9888 or 800/225–5759, FAX 707/546–9891), serving lesbian travelers.

BOOKSTORES

A Different Light, the city's most extensive gay bookstore, has books by, for, and about lesbians, gay men, bisexuals, and the transgendered. It has a rack in front that is chock-full of flyers for local events.

➤ BOOKSTORES: **A Different Light** (✉ 489 Castro St., between Market and 18th Sts., ☎ 415/431–0891).

COMMUNITY CENTERS

In 2002, the San Francisco Lesbian, Gay, Bisexual, and Transgender Community Center opened at the corner of Market and Octavia Streets, with facilities including offices for local nonprofit organizations, a performance space, and meeting halls. The Lavender Youth Recreation & Information Center offers lesbian, gay, bisexual, and transgender people under 24 various social, educational, and recreational programs. The Pacific Center is a lesbian, gay, bisexual, and transgender community service center in the East Bay.

➤ COMMUNITY CENTERS: **The Center (San Francisco Lesbian/Gay/Bisexual/ Transgender Community Center)** (✉ 1800 Market St., ☎ 415/437–2257). **Community United Against Violence (CUAV)** ✉ 160 14th St., ☎ 415/777– 5500). **The Lavender Youth Recreation & Information Center** (✉ 127 Collingwood St., ☎ 415/703–6150; 415/863–3636 hot line). **The Pacific Center** (✉ 2712 Telegraph Ave., Berkeley, CA 94705, ☎ 510/548– 8283).

GUIDEBOOKS

Plan well and you won't be sorry. Guidebooks are excellent tools—and you can take them with you. You may want to check out color-photo-illustrated *Fodor's Exploring San Francisco* and *Compass American Guide: San Francisco,* thorough on culture and history, and pocket-size *Citypack San Francisco,* with a supersize city map. *Flashmaps San Francisco* is loaded with theme maps, and *Fodor's CITYGUIDE San Francisco,* for residents, with colorful listings. All are available at on-line retailers and bookstores everywhere.

HOLIDAYS

Major national holidays include New Year's Day (Jan. 1); Martin Luther King, Jr., Day (3rd Mon. in Jan.); President's Day (3rd Mon. in Feb.); Memorial Day (last Mon. in May); Independence Day (July 4); Labor Day (1st Mon. in Sept.); Thanksgiving Day (4th Thurs. in Nov.); Christmas Eve and Christmas Day (Dec. 24 and 25); and New Year's Eve (Dec. 31).

Many attractions in San Francisco are closed on these days, so it's best to call ahead.

INSURANCE

The most useful travel-insurance plan is a comprehensive policy that includes coverage for trip cancellation and interruption, default, trip delay, and medical expenses (with a waiver for preexisting conditions).

Without insurance you will lose all or most of your money if you cancel your trip, regardless of the reason. Default insurance covers you if your tour operator, airline, or cruise line goes out of business. Trip-delay covers expenses that arise because of bad weather or mechanical delays. Study the fine print when comparing policies.

U.K. residents can buy a travel-insurance policy valid for most vacations taken during the year in which it's purchased (but check preexisting-condition coverage).

Always **buy travel policies directly from the insurance company**; if you buy them from a cruise line, airline, or tour operator that goes out of business you probably will not be covered for the agency or operator's default, a major risk. Before making any purchase, **review your existing health and home-owner's policies** to find what they cover away from home.

➤ TRAVEL INSURERS: In the U.S.: **Access America** (✉ 6600 W. Broad St., Richmond, VA 23230, ☎ 800/284–8300, FAX 804/673–1491 or 800/346–9265, WEB www.accessamerica.com). **Travel Guard International** (✉ 1145 Clark St., Stevens Point, WI 54481, ☎ 800/ 826–1300; 715/345–0505, FAX 800/ 955–8785, WEB www.travelguard.com).

FOR INTERNATIONAL TRAVELERS

For information on customs restrictions, see Customs and Duties, *above*.

CAR RENTAL

When picking up a rental car, non-U.S. residents need a reservation voucher for any prepaid reservations that were made in the traveler's home country, a passport, a driver's license, and a travel policy that covers each driver.

CAR TRAVEL

In San Francisco gasoline costs $1.78–$1.83 a gallon (unleaded). Stations are plentiful. Most stay open late (24 hours along large highways and in big cities), except in rural areas, where Sunday hours are limited and where you may drive long stretches without a refueling opportunity. Highways are well paved. Interstate highways—limited-access, multilane highways whose numbers are prefixed by "I–"—are the fastest routes. Interstates with three-digit numbers encircle urban areas, which may have other limited-access expressways, freeways, and parkways as well. Tolls may be levied on limited-access highways. So-called U.S. highways and state highways are not necessarily limited-access but may have several lanes.

Along larger highways, roadside stops with rest rooms, fast-food restaurants, and sundries stores are well spaced. State police and tow trucks patrol major highways and lend assistance. If your car breaks down on an Interstate, pull onto the shoulder and wait for help, or have your passengers wait while you walk to an emergency phone. If you carry a cell phone, dial *55, noting your location on the small green roadside mileage markers.

Driving in the United States is on the right. Do **obey speed limits** posted along roads and highways. Watch for lower limits in small towns and on back roads. California requires passengers to wear seat belts. Always **strap children under 40 pounds or four years into approved child-safety seats.**

In California you may turn right at a red light after stopping if there is no oncoming traffic, unless a sign forbids you to do so. The same goes for a left on red at two adjoining one-way streets. When in doubt, wait for the green. Be alert for one-way streets, "no left turn" intersections, and blocks closed to car traffic. On weekdays between 6 and 10 AM and again between 4 and 7 PM **expect heavy traffic.** To encourage carpooling, some freeways have special lanes for so-called high-occupancy vehicles (HOV)—cars carrying more than one or two passengers.

Book stores, gas stations, convenience stores, and rest stops sell maps (about $3) and multiregion road atlases (about $10).

CONSULATES AND EMBASSIES

➤ AUSTRALIA: (⊠ 625 Market St., Suite 200, ☎ 415/536–1970).

➤ CANADA: (⊠ 555 Montgomery St., Suite 1288, ☎ 415/834–3180, WEB www.cdntrade.com).

➤ NEW ZEALAND: (⊠ 1 Maritime Plaza, ☎ 415/399–1255).

➤ UNITED KINGDOM: (⊠ 1 Sansome St., Suite 850, ☎ 415/981–3030).

CURRENCY

The dollar is the basic unit of U.S. currency. It has 100 cents. Coins include the copper penny (1¢); the silvery nickel (5¢), dime (10¢), quarter (25¢), and half-dollar (50¢); and the golden $1 coin, replacing a now-rare silver dollar. Bills are denominated $1, $5, $10, $20, $50, and $100, all green and identical in size; designs vary. The exchange rate at press time was US$1.43 per British pound, 63¢ per Canadian dollar, 53¢ per Australian dollar, and 44¢ per New Zealand dollar.

ELECTRICITY

The U.S. standard is AC, 110 volts/60 cycles. Plugs have two flat pins set parallel to each other.

EMERGENCIES

For police, fire, or ambulance, **dial 911** (0 in rural areas).

INSURANCE

Britons and Australians need extra medical coverage when traveling overseas.

➤ INSURANCE INFORMATION: In the U.K.: **Association of British Insurers** (✉ 51 Gresham St., London EC2V 7HQ, ☎ 020/7600–3333, FAX 020/7696–8999, WEB www.abi.org.uk). In Australia: **Insurance Council of Australia** (✉ Level 3, 56 Pitt St., Sydney, NSW 2000, ☎ 02/9253–5100, FAX 02/9253–5111, WEB www.ica.com.au). In Canada: **RBC Insurance** (✉ 6880 Financial Dr., Mississauga, Ontario L5N 7Y5, ☎ 905/816–2400 or 800/668–4342, FAX 905/813–4704, WEB www.rbcinsurance.com). In New Zealand: **Insurance Council of New Zealand** (✉ Level 7, 111–115 Cust018house Quay, Box 474, Wellington, ☎ 04/472–5230, FAX 04/473–3011, WEB www.icnz.org.nz).

MAIL AND SHIPPING

You can buy stamps and aerograms and send letters and parcels in post offices. Stamp-dispensing machines can occasionally be found in airports, bus and train stations, office buildings, drugstores, and the like. You can also deposit mail in the stout, dark blue, steel bins at strategic locations everywhere and in the mail chutes of large buildings; pickup schedules are posted.

For mail sent within the United States, you need a 37¢ stamp for first-class letters weighing up to 1 ounce (23¢ for each additional ounce) and 23¢ for domestic postcards. For overseas mail, you pay 80¢ for 1-ounce airmail letters, 70¢ for airmail postcards, and 35¢ for surface-rate postcards. For Canada and Mexico you need a 60¢ stamp for a 1-ounce letter and 50¢ for a postcard. For 70¢ you can buy an aerogram—a single sheet of lightweight blue paper that folds into its own envelope, stamped for overseas airmail.

To receive mail on the road, have it sent c/o General Delivery at your destination's main post office (use the correct five-digit ZIP code). You must pick up mail in person within 30 days and show a driver's license or passport.

PASSPORTS AND VISAS

When traveling internationally, **carry your passport** even if you don't need one (it's always the best form of I.D.) and **make two photocopies of the data page** (one for someone at home and another for you, carried separately from your passport). If you lose your passport, promptly call the nearest embassy or consulate and the local police.

Visitor visas are not necessary for Canadian citizens, or for citizens of Australia and the United Kingdom who are staying fewer than 90 days.

➤ AUSTRALIAN CITIZENS: **Australian State Passport Office** (☎ 131–232, WEB www.passports.gov.au). **United States Consulate General** (✉ MLC Centre, 19–29 Martin Pl., 59th floor, Sydney, NSW 2000, ☎ 02/9373–9200, 1902/941–641 fee-based visa-inquiry line, WEB www.usis-australia.gov/index.html).

➤ CANADIAN CITIZENS: **Passport Office** (☎ 819/994–3500 or 800/567–6868, WEB www.dfait-maeci.gc.ca/passport).

➤ NEW ZEALAND CITIZENS: **New Zealand Passport Office** (☎ 04/474–8100, WEB www.passports.govt.nz). **Embassy of the United States** (✉ 29 Fitzherbert Terr., Thorndon, Wellington, ☎ 04/462–6000, WEB usembasssy.org.nz). **U.S. Consulate General** (✉ Citibank Center, 3rd floor, 23 Customs St. E, Auckland, ☎ 09/303–2724, WEB usembassy.org.nz).

➤ U.K. CITIZENS: **London Passport Office** (☎ 0870/521–0410, WEB www.passport.gov.uk). **U.S. Consulate General** (✉ Queen's House, 14 Queen St., Belfast BT1 6EQ, Northern Ireland, ☎ 028/9032–8239, WEB www.usembassy.org.uk). **U.S. Embassy** (enclose a SASE to ✉ Consular Information Unit, 24 Grosvenor Sq., London W1 1AE, for general information; ✉ Visa Branch, 5 Upper Grosvenor St., London W1A 2JB, to submit an application via mail; ☎ 09068/200–290 recorded visa information or 09055/444–546 operator service, both with per-minute charges; WEB www.usembassy.org.uk).

TELEPHONES

All U.S. telephone numbers consist of a three-digit area code and a seven-digit local number. Within most local calling areas, you dial only the seven-digit number. To call between area-code regions, dial "1" then all 10 digits; the same goes for calls to numbers prefixed by "800," "888," and "877"—all toll-free. For calls to numbers preceded by "900" you must pay—usually dearly.

For international calls, dial "011" followed by the country code and the local number. For help, dial "0" and ask for an overseas operator. The country code is 61 for Australia, 64 for New Zealand, 44 for the United Kingdom. Calling Canada is the same as calling within the United States. Most local phone books list country codes and U.S. area codes. The country code for the United States is 1.

For operator assistance, dial "0". To obtain someone's phone number, call directory assistance, 555–1212 or occasionally 411 (free at public phones). To have the person you're calling foot the bill, phone collect; dial "0" instead of "1" before the 10-digit number.

At pay phones, instructions are usually posted. Usually you insert coins in a slot (10¢–50¢ for local calls) and wait for a steady tone before dialing. When you call long-distance, the operator tells you how much to insert; prepaid phone cards, widely available in various denominations, are easier. Call the number on the back, punch in the card's personal identification number when prompted, then dial your number.

LODGING

The lodgings we list are the cream of the crop in each price category. We always list the facilities that are available—but we don't specify whether they cost extra. When pricing accommodations, always ask what's included and what costs extra. Properties indicated by a ✕⊡ are lodging establishments whose restaurant warrants a special trip.

Assume that hotels operate on the **European Plan** (EP, with no meals) unless we specify that they use the **Continental Plan** (CP, with a Continental breakfast), **Modified American Plan** (MAP, with breakfast and dinner), or the **Full American Plan** (FAP, with all meals).

The hotel tax in San Francisco is 14%.

APARTMENT RENTALS

If you want a home base that's roomy enough for a family and comes with cooking facilities, **consider a furnished rental.** These can save you money, especially if you're traveling with a group. Home-exchange directories sometimes list rentals as well as exchanges.

➤ INTERNATIONAL AGENTS: **Hideaways International** (⊠ 767 Islington St., Portsmouth, NH 03801, ☎ 603/430–4433 or 800/843–4433, FAX 603/430–4444, WEB www.hideaways.com; membership $129).

➤ LOCAL AGENTS: **Absolutely Accommodations** (⊠ Box 330298, San Francisco, 94133, ☎ 415/732–7959.

BED-AND-BREAKFASTS

San Francisco's bed-and-breakfast inns run the gamut from the traditional room to let in a residential home to palatial digs like the Archbishop's Mansion or the Sherman House.

➤ RESERVATION SERVICES: **Bed and Breakfast California** (☎ 408/867–9662, WEB www.bbintl.com). **Bed and Breakfast San Francisco** (☎ 415/899–0060 or 800/452–8249, WEB www.bbsf.com).

HOME EXCHANGES

If you would like to exchange your home for someone else's, **join a home-exchange organization,** which will send you its updated listings of available exchanges for a year and will include your own listing in at least one of them. It's up to you to make specific arrangements.

➤ EXCHANGE CLUBS: **HomeLink International** (⊠ Box 47747, Tampa, FL 33647, ☎ 813/975–9825 or 800/638–3841, FAX 813/910–8144, WEB www.homelink.org; $106 per year). **Intervac U.S.** (⊠ Box 590504, San Francisco, CA 94159, ☎ 800/756–4663, FAX 415/435–7440, WEB www.intervacus.com; $93 yearly fee includes one catalog and on-line access).

HOSTELS

No matter what your age, you can **save on lodging costs by staying at hostels.** In some 4,500 locations in more than 70 countries around the world, Hostelling International (HI), the umbrella group for a number of national youth-hostel associations, offers single-sex, dorm-style beds and, at many hostels, rooms for couples and family accommodations. Membership in any HI national hostel association, open to travelers of all ages, allows you to stay in HI-affiliated hostels at member rates; one-year membership is about $25 for adults (C$35 for a two-year minimum membership in Canada, £13 in the U.K., A$52 in Australia, and NZ$40 in New Zealand); hostels run about $10–$30 per night. Members have priority if the hostel is full; they're also eligible for discounts around the world, even on rail and bus travel in some countries.

➤ ORGANIZATIONS: **Hostelling International—American Youth Hostels** (✉ 733 15th St. NW, Suite 840, Washington, DC 20005, ☎ 202/783–6161, FAX 202/783–6171, WEB www.hiayh.org). **Hostelling International—Canada** (✉ 400–205 Catherine St., Ottawa, Ontario K2P 1C3, ☎ 613/237–7884; 800/663–5777, FAX 613/237–7868, WEB www.hihostels.ca). **Youth Hostel Association of England and Wales** (✉ Trevelyan House, Dimple Rd., Matlock, Derbyshire DE4 3YH, U.K., ☎ 0870/870–8808, FAX 0169/592–702, WEB www.yha.org.uk). **Youth Hostel Association Australia** (✉ 10 Mallett St., Camperdown, NSW 2050, ☎ 02/9565–1699, FAX 02/9565–1325, WEB www.yha.com.au). **Youth Hostels Association of New Zealand** (✉ Level 3, 193 Cashel St., Box 436, Christchurch, ☎ 03/379–9970, FAX 03/365–4476, WEB www.yha.org.nz).

HOTELS

Most of the major chains have properties in or near San Francisco. It's a good idea to **reserve ahead from July through October.** All hotels listed have private bath unless otherwise noted. We always list the amenities that are available, but we don't specify whether they cost extra. When pricing accommodations, always **ask what's included and what costs extra.**

➤ TOLL-FREE NUMBERS: **Best Western** (☎ 800/528–1234, WEB www.bestwestern.com). **Choice** (☎ 800/424–6423, WEB www.choicehotels.com). **Clarion** (☎ 800/424–6423, WEB www.choicehotels.com). **Comfort Inn** (☎ 800/424–6423, WEB www.choicehotels.com). **Days Inn** (☎ 800/325–2525, WEB www.daysinn.com). **Doubletree and Red Lion Hotels** (☎ 800/222–8733, WEB www.hilton.com). **Embassy Suites** (☎ 800/362–2779, WEB www.embassysuites.com). **Fairfield Inn** (☎ 800/228–2800, WEB www.marriott.com). **Four Seasons** (☎ 800/332–3442, WEB www.fourseasons.com). **Hilton** (☎ 800/445–8667, WEB www.hilton.com). **Holiday Inn** (☎ 800/465–4329, WEB www.sixcontinentshotels.com). **Howard Johnson** (☎ 800/654–4656, WEB www.hojo.com). **Hyatt Hotels & Resorts** (☎ 800/233–1234, WEB www.hyatt.com). **Inter-Continental** (☎ 800/327–0200, WEB www.intercontinental.com). **La Quinta** (☎ 800/531–5900, WEB www.laquinta.com). **Marriott** (☎ 800/228–9290, WEB www.marriott.com). **Nikko Hotels International** (☎ 800/645–5687, WEB www.nikkohotels.com). **Omni** (☎ 800/843–6664, WEB www.omnihotels.com). **Quality Inn** (☎ 800/424–6423, WEB www.choicehotels.com). **Radisson** (☎ 800/333–3333, WEB www.radisson.com). **Ramada** (☎ 800/228–2828; 800/854–7854 international reservations, WEB www.ramada.com or www.ramadahotels.com). **Renaissance Hotels & Resorts** (☎ 800/468–3571, WEB www.renaissancehotels.com). **Ritz-Carlton** (☎ 800/241–3333, WEB www.ritzcarlton.com). **Sheraton** (☎ 800/325–3535, WEB www.starwood.com/sheraton). **Sleep Inn** (☎ 800/424–6423, WEB www.choicehotels.com). **Westin Hotels & Resorts** (☎ 800/228–3000, WEB www.starwood.com/westin).

MAIL AND SHIPPING

Post offices are conveniently located throughout the city. Most post offices are busiest at lunchtime and just before closing, and long lines are the norm at these times. The post office in the Macy's department store in Union Square is open on Sundays 11–5, in addition to its regular weekday hours.

➤ POST OFFICES: **Sutter Post Office** (✉ 150 Sutter St., 94104-9991, ☎ 415/765–1761 or 800/275–8777). **Federal Building Post Office** (✉ 450 Golden Gate Ave., 94102-3400,

☎ 415/931–1053 or 800/275–8777).
Macy's Union Square Post Office
(✉ 170 O'Farrell St., 94108-9991;
☎ 415/956–0131 or 800/275–8777).

OVERNIGHT SERVICES

Most major overnight service carriers,
including Federal Express and DHL
Worldwide Express, have drop-off
points throughout the city.

➤ MAJOR SERVICES: **Federal Express**
(✉ 120 Bush St. or 1150 Harrison
St., ☎ 800/463–3339). **DHL Worldwide Express** (✉ 345 California St. or
330 Newhall St., ☎ 800/225–5345).

MEDIA

NEWSPAPERS AND MAGAZINES

The story of San Francisco's two main
papers, the *San Francisco Chronicle*
and the *San Francisco Examiner,* is the
stuff of legends. It reached a crescendo
of sorts in 2000, when the Hearst
Corporation, owner of the *Examiner,*
bought the *Chronicle,* but had the
deal blocked by an antitrust suit filed
by a recently defeated mayoral candidate. Hearst then agreed to pay a
third publisher—who happened to be
a staunch supporter of the winning
mayoral candidate—a whopping $6
million to take the *Examiner* off its
hands, so it could keep the *Chronicle.*
Bad blood and some high-profile
blunders by the "new" *Examiner* have
fueled the cross-city snipping. In the
latest twist, the editor and publisher
of the *Examiner* was fired from his
job in 2001 by his mother, the chair-
woman of the *Examiner's* parent
company. The fact remains that neither paper is considered a top-tier
paper, and San Francisco remains
conspicuously lacking in that regard.
Both papers are published in the
morning and include extensive local
listings and coverage; the *Chronicle*
also publishes an afternoon edition
called the *Chronicle PM.*

The two free weekly papers are the
San Francisco Bay Guardian and the
SF Weekly. They are published every
Wednesday and can be found in
kiosks throughout the city. Both offer
a liberal spin on local politics and
have reviews and listings of restaurants, bars, and events throughout
the Bay Area.

Bay Area Reporter is a weekly gay
newspaper available free at shops and
restaurants all over the city.

San Francisco magazine is a glossy
monthly periodical that covers arts,
style, dining, and shopping in the city.
Wired magazine, published nationally, is based in San Francisco and
covers the computer scene.

RADIO AND TELEVISION

San Francisco has more than 75 radio
stations, covering a wide range of
music from classic rock to jazz to soul
and hip-hop. **KQED** (88.5 FM) and
KALW (91.7 FM) are the National
Public Radio affiliates, and **KDFC**
(102.1 FM) is the leading classical
music station. For regular updates on
the latest news and traffic, tune into
KCBS (740 AM) or **KGO** (810 AM),
both owned by local television affiliates. **KFOG** (104.5 FM) is one of the
most popular classic rock and pop
stations in town, with a strong fan
base of local listeners. **KMEL** (106.1
FM) is the funky soul and hip-hop
station.

The four major television affiliates
have stations in the Bay Area. **KGO**
(Channel 7) is the ABC affiliate; **KPIX**
(Channel 5) is the CBS affiliate; and
KTVU (Channel 2), based in Oakland, is part of the Fox TV Network.
KNTV (Channel 11) is the NBC
affiliate, but it is located in San Jose,
so reception without cable in San
Francisco can be poor. **KQED** (Channel 9) is the local PBS station.

MONEY MATTERS

Prices throughout this guide are given
for adults. Substantially reduced fees
are almost always available for children, students, and senior citizens.
For information on taxes, *see* Taxes,
below.

ATMS

ATMs are widely available throughout San Francisco.

➤ ATM LOCATIONS: **Cirrus** (☎ 800/
424–7787). **Plus** (☎ 800/843–7587)
for locations in the United States and
Canada, or visit your local bank.

CREDIT CARDS

Throughout this guide, the following
abbreviations are used: **AE,** American

Express; **D**, Discover; **DC**, Diners Club; **MC**, MasterCard; and **V**, Visa.

➤ REPORTING LOST CARDS: **American Express** (☎ 800/441–0519); **Diners Club** (☎ 800/234–6377); **Discover Card** (☎ 800/347–2683); **MasterCard** (☎ 800/622–7747); and **Visa** (☎ 800/847–2911).

NATIONAL PARKS

Look into discount passes to save money on park entrance fees. For $50, the National Parks Pass admits you (and any passengers in your private vehicle) to all national parks, monuments, and recreation areas, as well as other sites run by the National Park Service, for a year. (In parks that charge per person, the pass admits you, your spouse and children, and your parents, when you arrive together.) Camping and parking are extra. The $15 Golden Eagle Pass, a hologram you affix to your National Parks Pass, functions as an upgrade, granting entry to all sites run by the NPS, the U.S. Fish and Wildlife Service, the U.S. Forest Service, and the Bureau of Land Management (BLM). The upgrade, which expires with the parks pass, is sold by most national-park, Fish-and-Wildlife, and BLM fee stations. A percentage of the proceeds from pass sales funds National Parks projects.

Both the Golden Age Passport ($10), for U.S. citizens or permanent residents who are 62 and older, and the Golden Access Passport (free), for those with disabilities, entitle holders (and any passengers in their private vehicles) to lifetime free entry to all national parks, plus 50% off fees for the use of many park facilities and services. (The discount doesn't always apply to companions.) To obtain them, you must show proof of age and of U.S. citizenship or permanent residency—such as a U.S. passport, driver's license, or birth certificate—and, if requesting Golden Access, proof of disability. The Golden Age and Golden Access passes, as well as the National Parks Pass, are available at any NPS-run site that charges an entrance fee. The National Parks Pass is also available by mail and via the Internet.

➤ INFORMATION: **National Park Foundation** (✉ 1101 17th St. NW, Suite 1102, Washington, DC 20036, ☎ 202/785–4500, WEB www.nationalparks.org). **National Park Service** (✉ National Park Service/Department of Interior, 1849 C St. NW, Washington, DC 20240, ☎ 202/208–4747, WEB www.nps.gov). **National Parks Conservation Association** (✉ 1300 19th St. NW, Suite 300, Washington, DC 20036, ☎ 202/223–6722, WEB www.npca.org.)

➤ PASSES BY MAIL AND ON-LINE: **National Park Foundation** (WEB www.nationalparks.org). **National Parks Pass** (✉ 27540 Ave. Mentry, Valencia, CA 91355, ☎ 888/GO–PARKS or 888/467–2757, WEB www.nationalparks.org); include a check or money order payable to the National Park Service for the pass, plus $3.95 for shipping and handling.

PACKING

When packing for a vacation in the San Francisco Bay Area, **prepare for temperature variations.** An hour's drive can take you up or down many degrees, and the variation from daytime to nighttime in a single location is often marked. Make sure to **take along sweaters, jackets, and clothes for layering** as your best insurance for coping with variations in temperature. Include shorts or cool cottons for summer, and always tuck in a bathing suit, since many lodgings have pools and hot tubs. Bear in mind, though, that the city can be chilly at any time of the year, especially in summer, when the fog is apt to descend and stay.

Although casual dressing is a hallmark of the California lifestyle, men will need a jacket and tie for many of the more expensive restaurants in the evening, and women will be more comfortable in something dressier than regulation sightseeing garb.

In your carry-on luggage, **pack an extra pair of eyeglasses or contact lenses and enough of any medication** you take to last the entire trip. You may also ask your doctor to write a spare prescription using the drug's generic name, since brand names may vary from country to country. In luggage to be checked, **never pack prescription drugs or valuables.** And don't forget to carry with you the addresses of offices that handle refunds of lost traveler's checks. Check *Fodor's How to Pack* (available in bookstores everywhere) for more tips.

To avoid customs and security delays, carry medications in their original packaging. Don't pack any sharp objects in your carry-on luggage, including knives of any size or material, scissors, manicure tools, and corkscrews, or anything else that might arouse suspicion.

CHECKING LUGGAGE

You are allowed one carry-on bag and one personal article, such as a purse or a laptop computer. Make sure that everything you carry aboard will fit under your seat or in the overhead bin. Get to the gate early, so you can board as soon as possible, before the overhead bins fill up.

If you are flying internationally, note that baggage allowances may be determined not by piece but by weight—generally 88 pounds (40 kilograms) in first class, 66 pounds (30 kilograms) in business class, and 44 pounds (20 kilograms) in economy.

Airline liability for baggage is limited to $2,500 per person on flights within the United States. On international flights it amounts to $9.07 per pound or $20 per kilogram for checked baggage (roughly $640 per 70-pound bag) and $400 per passenger for unchecked baggage. You can buy additional coverage at check-in for about $10 per $1,000 of coverage, but it excludes a rather extensive list of items, shown on your airline ticket.

Before departure, **itemize your bags' contents** and their worth, and label the bags with your name, address, and phone number. (If you use your home address, cover it so potential thieves can't see it readily.) Inside each bag, **pack a copy of your itinerary.** At check-in, **make sure that each bag is correctly tagged** with the destination airport's three-letter code. If your bags arrive damaged or fail to arrive at all, file a written report with the airline before leaving the airport.

REST ROOMS

Public facilities are located in forest-green kiosks at Pier 39, on Market Street at Powell Street, at Castro and Market streets, and at the Civic Center. The fee to use the facilities is 25¢. Most of the public garages have rest rooms, and there are usually lobby-level facilities in large hotels.

SAFETY

San Francisco is generally a safe place for travelers who observe all normal precautions. First, **avoid looking like a tourist.** Dress inconspicuously, remove badges when leaving convention areas, and know the routes to your destination before you set out. Use common sense and **steer clear of certain neighborhoods late at night.** The Tenderloin, Civic Center plaza, parts of the Mission (around 14th Street, for example, or south of 24th to Cesar Chavez Street), and the Lower Haight should be avoided, especially if you're walking alone.

Like many larger cities, San Francisco has many homeless people. While most are no threat to the traveler, some are more aggressive and can persist in their pleas for cash until it feels like harassment. If you feel uncomfortable, don't reach for your wallet.

SENIOR-CITIZEN TRAVEL

To qualify for age-related discounts, **mention your senior-citizen status up front** when booking hotel reservations (not when checking out) and before you're seated in restaurants (not when paying the bill). Be sure to have identification on hand. When renting a car, ask about promotional car-rental discounts, which can be cheaper than senior-citizen rates.

➤ EDUCATIONAL PROGRAMS: **Elderhostel** (✉ 11 Ave. de Lafayette, Boston, MA 02111-1746, ☎ 877/426–8056, ℻ 877/426–2166, 📠 www.elderhostel.org).

SIGHTSEEING TOURS

In addition to bus and van tours of the city, most tour companies run excursions to various Bay Area and Northern California destinations such as Marin County and the Wine Country, as well as farther-flung areas such as Monterey and Yosemite. City tours generally last 3½ hours and cost $28–$32. Golden Gate Tours offers bay cruises ($38) as well as standard city bus tours. In addition to bay cruises, Gray Line offers city tours in motor coaches and motorized cable cars ($15–$37); Great Pacific Tours conducts the city tours (starting at $37).

➤ TOUR COMPANIES: **Golden Gate Tours** (☎ 415/788–5775). **Gray Line Tours** (☎ 415/558–9400, WEB www.graylinesanfrancisco.com). **Great Pacific Tour** (☎ 415/626–4499, WEB www.greatpacifictour.com). **Tower Tours** (☎ 415/434–8687, WEB www.towertours.com).

WALKING TOURS

The best way to see San Francisco is to hit the streets. The San Francisco Convention and Visitors Bureau publishes a brochure that includes self-guided walking tours of popular neighborhoods—Chinatown, Fisherman's Wharf, North Beach, and Union Square. Brochures are available at the San Francisco Visitors Center on the lower level of Hallidie Plaza, at Powell and Market streets. City Guides, a free service sponsored by the San Francisco Public Library, offers a variety of guided walks, including Chinatown, North Beach, Coit Tower, Pacific Heights mansions, Japantown, Haight-Ashbury, Market Street, the Palace Hotel, and downtown roof gardens and atriums. Schedules are available at the visitor center and at library branches.

Tours of various San Francisco neighborhoods generally cost $15–$40. Some tours have culinary themes: lunch and snacks are often included. Trevor Hailey leads a popular "Cruising the Castro" tour focusing on the history and development of the city's gay and lesbian community. Cookbook author Shirley Fong-Torres and her team lead a tour through Chinatown—"Chinatown with the Wok Wiz," with stops at Chinese herbal markets and art studios. The Chinese Culture Center leads a Chinatown heritage walk and a culinary walk for groups of four or more only. "Javawalk" explores the San Francisco's historic ties to coffee while visiting a few of San Francisco's more than 300 cafés. "Victorian Home Walk" is a low-impact amble through some of the city's less traveled neighborhoods. Learn about the different styles of Victorian buildings while exploring Pacific Heights and Cow Hollow.

➤ TOUR OPERATORS: **San Francisco Convention and Visitors Bureau's Visitor Information Center** (☎ 415/974–6900, WEB www.sfcvb.org). **City Guides** (☎ 415/557–4266, WEB www.sfcityguides.org). **"Chinatown with the Wok Wiz"** (☎ 415/981–8989, WEB www.wokwiz.com). **Chinese Culture Center** (☎ 415/986–1822, WEB www.c-c-c.org). **"Javawalk"** (☎ 415/673–9255, WEB www.javawalk.com). **Trevor Hailey** (☎ 415/550–8110, WEB www.webcastro.com/castrotour). **"Victorian Home Walk"** (☎ 415/252–9485, WEB www.victorianwalk.com).

STUDENTS IN SAN FRANCISCO

➤ I.D.s AND SERVICES: **Travel Cuts** (✉ 187 College St., Toronto, Ontario M5T 1P7, Canada, ☎ 416/979–2406 or 888/838–2887, FAX 416/979–8167, WEB www.travelcuts.com).

TAXES

The sales tax in San Francisco is 8.25%. The tax on hotel rooms is 14%.

TAXIS

Taxi service is notoriously bad in San Francisco, and hailing a cab can be frustratingly difficult in some parts of the city, especially on the weekends. Popular night spots like the Mission, SoMa, North Beach, Haight, and the Castro have a lot of cabs, but a lot of people, too. Midweek, and during the day, you shouldn't have much of a problem—unless it's raining. In a pinch, hotel taxi stands are an option, as is calling ahead for a pick-up. But be forewarned: taxi companies frequently don't answer the phone in peak periods.

Taxis in San Francisco charge $2.50 for the first ⅙ of a mile, $1.80 for each additional mile, and 40¢ per minute in stalled traffic. There is no charge for additional passengers, there is no surcharge for luggage.

➤ TAXI COMPANIES: **City Wide Cab** (☎ 415/920–0700; San Francisco). **DeSoto Cab** (☎ 415/970–1300; San Francisco). **Veteran's Taxicab** (☎ 415/552–1300; San Francisco). **Yellow Cab** (☎ 415/626–2345; San Francisco).

➤ COMPLAINTS: **San Francisco Police Department Taxi Detail** (☎ 415/553–1447).

TIME

San Francisco is on Pacific Time. Chicago is 2 hours ahead of San Francisco, New York is 3 hours ahead, and depending on the time of year (daylight savings), London is either 8 or 9 hours ahead, and Sydney is 17 or 18 hours ahead.

TIPPING

At restaurants, a 15% tip is standard for waiters; up to 20% may be expected at more expensive establishments. The same goes for taxi drivers, bartenders, and hairdressers. Coat-check operators usually expect $1, while bellhops and porters should get $1–$2 per bag. Maids should receive at least 4%–5% of the room-rate total, before taxes, for rooms that cost $100 a night or more. If the room is less than $100 per night, then 3%–4%. If the hotel charges a service fee, be sure to ask what it covers, as it may include this gratuity. A concierge typically receives a tip of $5–$10, with an additional gratuity for special services or favors.

On package tours, conductors and drivers usually get $10 per day from the group as a whole; check whether this has already been figured into your cost. For local sightseeing tours, you may individually tip the driver-guide $2 if he or she has been helpful or informative. Ushers in theaters do not expect tips.

TOURS AND PACKAGES

Because everything is prearranged on a prepackaged tour or independent vacation, you spend less time planning—and often get it all at a good price.

BOOKING WITH AN AGENT

Travel agents are excellent resources. But it's a good idea to collect brochures from several agencies, as some agents' suggestions may be influenced by relationships with tour and package firms that reward them for volume sales. If you have a special interest, **find an agent with expertise in that area**; the American Society of Travel Agents (ASTA; ☞ Travel Agencies, *below*) has a database of specialists worldwide.

Make sure your travel agent knows the accommodations and other services of the place being recommended. Ask about the hotel's location, room size, beds, and whether it has a pool, room service, or programs for children, if you care about these. Has your agent been there in person or sent others whom you can contact?

Do some homework on your own, too: local tourism boards can provide information about lesser-known and small-niche operators, some of which may sell only direct.

BUYER BEWARE

Each year consumers are stranded or lose their money when tour operators—even large ones with excellent reputations—go out of business. So **check out the operator.** Ask several travel agents about its reputation, and try to **book with a company that has a consumer-protection program.** (Look for information in the company's brochure.) In the United States, members of the National Tour Association and the United States Tour Operators Association are required to set aside funds to cover your payments and travel arrangements in the event that the company defaults. It's also a good idea to choose a company that participates in the American Society of Travel Agents' Tour Operator Program (TOP); ASTA will act as mediator in any disputes between you and your tour operator.

Remember that the more your package or tour includes the better you can predict the ultimate cost of your vacation. Make sure you know exactly what is covered, and **beware of hidden costs.** Are taxes, tips, and transfers included? Entertainment and excursions? These can add up.

➤ TOUR-OPERATOR RECOMMENDATIONS: **American Society of Travel Agents** (☞ Travel Agencies, *below*). **National Tour Association** (NTA; ✉ 546 E. Main St., Lexington, KY 40508, ☎ 859/226–4444 or 800/682–8886, WEB www.ntaonline.com). **United States Tour Operators Association** (USTOA; ✉ 275 Madison Ave., Suite 2014, New York, NY 10016, ☎ 212/599–6599 or 800/468–7862, FAX 212/599–6744, WEB www.ustoa.com).

TRAIN TRAVEL TO AND FROM SAN FRANCISCO

Amtrak trains travel to San Francisco and the Bay Area from different cities in California and the United States. The *Coast Starlight* travels north from Los Angeles to Seattle, passing the Bay Area along the way. Amtrak also has several inland routes between San Jose, Oakland, and Sacramento. The *California Zephyr* route travels from Chicago to the Bay Area. There is no Amtrak station in San Francisco. Instead, there is one Amtrak station in Emeryville, just over the Bay Bridge, and one in Oakland. A free shuttle operates between these two stations and the Ferry Building and CalTrain station in San Francisco.

Smoking is prohibited entirely on short-distance train trips. On long-distance train routes, smoking is allowed only in one section of the train. (The one exception is the long-distance *Coast Starlight,* where smoking is prohibited entirely.)

➤ TRAIN INFORMATION: **Amtrak** (☎ 800/872–7245, WEB www.amtrak.com).

TRANSPORTATION AROUND SAN FRANCISCO

Within San Francisco it's easy to get around by foot, bus, cable car, or taxi. You'll need a car to get to Marin County, the East Bay, the Wine Country, and beyond.

TRAVEL AGENCIES

A good travel agent puts your needs first. Look for an agency that has been in business at least five years, emphasizes customer service, and has someone on staff who specializes in your destination. In addition, **make sure the agency belongs to a professional trade organization.** The American Society of Travel Agents (ASTA)—the largest and most influential in the field with more than 24,000 members in some 140 countries—maintains and enforces a strict code of ethics and will step in to help mediate any agent-client disputes involving ASTA members if necessary. ASTA (whose motto is "Without a travel agent, you're on your own") also maintains a Web site that includes a directory of agents. (If a travel agency is also acting as your tour operator, *see* Buyer Beware *in* Tours and Packages, *above*.)

➤ LOCAL AGENT REFERRALS: **American Society of Travel Agents** (ASTA; ✉ 1101 King St., Suite 200, Alexandria, VA 22314, ☎ 800/965–2782 24-hr hot line, FAX 703/739–3268, WEB www.astanet.com). **Association of British Travel Agents** (✉ 68–71 Newman St., London W1T 3AH, ☎ 020/7637–2444, FAX 020/7637–0713, WEB www.abtanet.com). **Association of Canadian Travel Agents** (✉ 130 Albert St., Suite 1705, Ottawa, Ontario K1P 5G4, ☎ 613/237–3657, FAX 613/237–7052, WEB www.acta.ca). **Australian Federation of Travel Agents** (✉ Level 3, 309 Pitt St., Sydney, NSW 2000, ☎ 02/9264–3299, FAX 02/9264–1085, WEB www.afta.com.au). **Travel Agents' Association of New Zealand** (✉ Level 5, Tourism and Travel House, 79 Boulcott St., Box 1888, Wellington 6001, ☎ 04/499–0104, FAX 04/499–0827, WEB www.taanz.org.nz).

VISITOR INFORMATION

TOURIST INFORMATION

The San Francisco Convention and Visitors Bureau can mail you brochures, maps, and festivals and events listings; or try the bureau's 24-hour fax-on-demand service (☎ 800/220–5747). For information about the Wine Country, redwood groves, and northwestern California, contact the Redwood Empire Association Visitor Information Center. For $3 they'll send you a visitor's guide within five days, but if you can wait three to five weeks, they'll send it for free; or pick one up for no charge at the center or at the California Welcome Center on Pier 39. You can get information about the South Bay from the San Jose Visitor Information Center.

➤ CITY: **San Francisco Convention and Visitors Bureau's Visitor Information Center** (✉ Box 429097, San Francisco 94142-9097, or ✉ lower level of Hallidie Plaza, ☎ 415/391–2000 or 415/974–6900, 🕸 www.sfvisitor.org).

➤ METRO AREA: **Berkeley** (✉ 2015 Center St., 1st floor, Berkeley 94704, ☎ 800/847–4823 or 510/549–7040; 510/549–8710 for recorded information, 🕸 www.berkeleycvb.com). **Oakland** (✉ 475 14th St., Oakland 94612, ☎ 510/839–9000 or 800/262–5526, 🕸 www.oaklandcvb.com). **San Jose** (✉ 333 W. San Carlos St., Suite 1000, San Jose 95110, ☎ 408/295–9600 or 800/726–5673, 🕸 www.sanjose.org). **Santa Clara** (✉ 1850 Warburton Ave., Santa Clara 95050, ☎ 800/272–6822 or 408/244–9660, 🕸 www.santaclara.org).

➤ WINE COUNTRY: **Redwood Empire Association** (✉ 1925 13th Ave., Suite 103, Oakland 94606, ☎ 510/536–8808 or 800/200–8334, FAX 510/536–8824, 🕸 www.redwoodempire.com).

➤ STATE: **California Division of Tourism** has free visitor's information and itinerary planners (✉ 801 K St., Suite 1600, Sacramento 95814 ☎ 916/322–2881 or 800/862–2543). Also try the **California Welcome Center** (✉ Lobby Area, Great San Francisco Adventure, Pier 39, 2nd level, San Francisco 95814, ☎ 800/862–2543 or 415/956–3493, 🕸 www.gocalif.com.)

WEB SITES

Do check out the World Wide Web when planning your trip. You'll find everything from weather forecasts to virtual tours of famous cities. Be sure to **visit Fodors.com** (www.fodors.com), a complete travel-planning site. You can research prices and book plane tickets, hotel rooms, rental cars, vacation packages, and more. In addition, you can post your pressing questions in the Travel Talk section. Other planning tools include a currency converter and weather reports, and there are loads of links to travel resources.

For more specific information on San Francisco, visit:

ACCESS

The Access-Able Travel Source site (🕸 www.access-able.com) carries information about attractions and restaurants, lodgings, and other establishments that are accessible to travelers with disabilities.

NEWS AND LISTINGS

The *Gate* is an excellent Bay Area resource (🕸 www.sfgate.com), with local headline news, daily weather updates, entertainment listings, classified ads, and much more.

If you're hunting for a restaurant, movie, or club listings, or even a new job, be sure to browse the *Guardian*, the on-line version (🕸 www.sfbg.com) of San Francisco's popular weekly newspaper, the *San Francisco Bay Guardian*.

The smart features on *MetroActive*, the on-line version (🕸 www.metroactive.com) of *San Jose Metro*, include guides to nightlife, the arts, dining, and entertainment in the Bay Area, including Silicon Valley and Santa Cruz.

A must-visit for gay and lesbian visitors, the Q San Francisco site (🕸 www.qsfmagazine.com) provides nightlife and entertainment listings, accommodation tips, and links to Bay Area gay and lesbian organizations.

The colorful and easy-to-navigate site of *SF Weekly* (🕸 www.sfweekly.com) carries news and feature reports plus complete arts and entertainment listings and reviews.

Yahoo!, the popular World Wide Web search engine, maintains an exhaustive site (🕸 http://sfbay.yahoo.com) on San Francisco and the Bay Area, with links to hundreds of local businesses and community organizations.

OFFICIAL SITES

In addition to its own travel tips, events calendars, and other resources, the California Division of Tourism Web site (🕸 gocalif.ca.gov) will link you—via the Regions icon—to the

Web sites of city and regional tourism offices and attractions.

The National Park Service site (www.nps.gov), which lists national parks and other lands administered by the park service, has extensive historical, cultural, and environmental information. Another site (WEB www.reserveusa.com) can be used to make camping reservations.

The Visitor Information Center's Web site (WEB www.sfvisitor.org) of the San Francisco Convention and Visitors Bureau has calendar listings and good maps.

WHEN TO GO

You can **visit San Francisco comfortably any time of year.** The climate here always feels Mediterranean and moderate—with a foggy, sometimes chilly bite. The temperature rarely drops lower than 40°F, and anything warmer than 80°F is considered a heat wave. Be prepared for rain in winter, especially December and January. Winds off the ocean can add to the chill factor, so pack warm clothing. North, east, and south of the city, summers are warmer. Shirt-sleeves and thin cottons are usually fine for the Wine Country.

CLIMATE

The weather in San Francisco is remarkably consistent throughout the year. The average high is 63°F, while the average low is 51°F. Summer comes late in San Francisco, which sees its warmest days in September and October. Of the 20 inches of rain that falls on average each year, most of it comes from December through March.

➤ FORECASTS: **Weather Channel Connection** (☎ 900/932–8437), 95¢ per minute from a Touch-Tone phone.

The following chart lists the average daily maximum and minimum temperatures for San Francisco.

Jan.	56F	13C	May	64F	17C	Sept.	70F	21C
	46F	8C		51F	10C		56F	13C
Feb.	60F	15C	June	66F	19C	Oct.	69F	20C
	48F	9C		53F	11C		55F	13C
Mar.	61F	16C	July	66F	19C	Nov.	64F	18C
	49F	9C		54F	12C		51F	10C
Apr.	63F	17C	Aug.	66F	19C	Dec.	57F	14C
	50F	10C		54F	12C		47F	8C

FESTIVALS AND SEASONAL EVENTS

➤ JAN.: The **Shrine East-West All-Star Football Classic** takes place at Stanford Stadium (☎ 800/227–8881, WEB www.shrinegame.com), 25 mi south of San Francisco in Palo Alto.

➤ JAN.–APR.: Whale-watching can be enjoyed throughout the winter, when hundreds of gray whales migrate along the coast. Contact the **Oceanic Society** (☎ 415/441–1104 or 800/326–7491, WEB www.oceanic-society.org) for details.

➤ FEB.: The **Chinese New Year** celebration in San Francisco's Chinese community, North America's largest, lasts for two weeks, culminating with the Golden Dragon Parade. Contact the **Chinese Chamber of Commerce** (☎ 415/982–3071, WEB www.chineseparade.com).

➤ MAR.: On the Sunday closest to March 17, San Francisco's **St. Patrick's Day** celebration includes snake races and a parade through downtown.

➤ APR.: The **Cherry Blossom Festival** (☎ 415/563–2313), an elaborate presentation of Japanese culture and customs, winds up with a colorful parade through Japantown.

➤ APR.–MAY: The **San Francisco International Film Festival** (☎ 415/561–5000, WEB www.sfiff.org) draws scads of film buffs eager to catch the premieres the festival brings to theaters across town.

➤ MAY: Thousands sign up to run the *San Francisco Examiner* **Bay to Breakers Race** (☎ 415/359–2600, WEB www.baytobreakers.com), a 7½-mi route from bay side to ocean side that's a hallowed San Francisco tradition.

➤ MAY: The **Cinco de Mayo Festival** (☎ 415/826–1401), held on the Sunday closest to May 5, is celebrated in the Mission District with much fanfare, including a vibrant parade, Mexican music, and dancing in the streets.

➤ MAY–JUNE: **Carnaval** (☎ 415/826–1401), held in the Mission District over Memorial Day weekend, includes a parade and street festival.

➤ JUNE: The **Haight Street Fair** (☎ 415/661–8025, WEB www.haightstreetfair.org) turns this neighborhood into even more of an outdoor party than it usually is, with live music, crafts and food booths, and crowds of revelers.

➤ JUNE: The **North Beach Festival** (☎ 415/989–2220), held every Father's Day weekend, transforms Washington Square Park and Grant Avenue into an Italian marketplace with food, music, and entertainment.

➤ JUNE: **The Lesbian, Gay, Bisexual, and Transgender Pride Parade and Celebration** (☎ 415/864–3733 or 415/677–7959, WEB www.sfpride.com) winds its way from the Embarcadero to the Civic Center on the third or fourth Sunday of the month.

➤ JUNE–SEPT.: The **Stern Grove Festival** (☎ 415/252–6252, WEB www.sterngrove.org), held over 10 weekends, hosts free concerts (from classical to jazz to blues) in a lush, shaded grove of redwood and eucalyptus trees with a natural amphitheater.

➤ JULY: The **Fourth of July** celebration, at Crissy Field in the Presidio, includes family festivities beginning in mid-afternoon and a fireworks display at 9.

➤ JULY: The **Cable Car Bell-Ringing Championship** (☎ 415/673–6864, WEB www.sfmuni.com) is on the third Thursday of July at noon in Union Square.

➤ SEPT.: **A La Carte A La Park** (☎ 415/383–9378, WEB www.sfgate.com) is an opportunity to taste food from the city's best restaurants in the lush environs of Golden Gate Park.

➤ SEPT.: The **San Francisco Comedy Day Celebration** (☎ 415/831–2700) brings the Bay Area's top comedians to Golden Gate Park for a riotous afternoon of laughs, puns, and one-liners.

➤ SEPT.: **Opera in the Park** (☎ 415/864–3330, WEB www.sfopera.com) hits the high notes in Golden Gate Park on the Sunday after Labor Day.

➤ SEPT.: The **San Francisco Blues Festival** (☎ 415/979–5588, WEB www.sfblues.com), on the Great Meadow at Fort Mason, is held on the third weekend of September.

➤ SEPT.: Celebrate the Bard during the **San Francisco Shakespeare Festival** (☎ 415/422–2222, WEB www.sfshakes.org) with free Shakespeare performances in Golden Gate Park starting on the Saturday of Labor Day weekend and continuing for five weekends.

➤ SEPT.–OCT.: More than 700 San Francisco artists open their studios to the public during **San Francisco Open Studios** (☎ 415/861–9838, WEB www.artspan.org), held over a series of weekends.

➤ OCT.: Beginning the second weekend of the month, **Fleet Week** celebrates the navy's first day in the port of San Francisco with a Blue Angels air show over the bay.

➤ OCT.: On the Sunday closest to Columbus Day, a parade through North Beach kicks off the **Columbus Day** celebration (☎ 415/434–1492).

➤ OCT.: The always popular **Reggae in the Park** (☎ 415/383–9378) draws spirited crowds of reggae lovers to Golden Gate Park for two days of music in the outdoors.

➤ OCT.: On the 31st, San Francisco celebrates **Halloween** with a flair all its own, when boisterous, bedecked crowds parade through the Castro and Civic Center until the wee hours of the morning.

➤ OCT.–NOV.: Jazz artists from around the country perform all over the city in the **San Francisco Jazz Festival** (☎ 415/398–5655, WEB www.sfjazz.org).

➤ DEC.: The San Francisco Ballet's rendition of *The Nutcracker* (☎ 415/865–2000, WEB www.sfballet.org) is an elaborate, memorable production.

➤ DEC.: The annual **Sing-It-Yourself Messiah** (☎ 415/864–6000) takes place at Davies Symphony Hall during the first week of the month.

1 DESTINATION: SAN FRANCISCO

Splendor in the Fog

What's Where

Pleasures and Pastimes

Fodor's Choice

Great Itineraries

SPLENDOR IN THE FOG

THAT VISITORS WILL ENVY San Franciscans is a given—at least, so say Bay Area residents, who tend to pity anyone who did not have the foresight to settle here. (There's probably never been a time when the majority of the population was native born.) Their self-satisfaction may surprise some, considering how the city has been battered by fires and earthquakes from the 1840s onward, most notably in the 1906 conflagration and again in 1989, when the Loma Prieta earthquake rocked the city's foundations and caused serious damage to the Marina District as well as to numerous local freeways. Since its earliest days San Francisco has been a phoenix, the mythical bird that periodically dies in flame to be reborn in greater grandeur.

Its latest rebirth has occurred in SoMa, the neighborhood south of Market Street, where the Yerba Buena Gardens development has taken shape with the world-class SFMOMA (San Francisco Museum of Modern Art) at its heart—transforming a formerly seedy neighborhood into a magnet of culture. As a peninsula city, surrounded on three sides by water, San Francisco grows from the inside out. Its blighted areas are improved, not abandoned. The museum development's instant success—measured by a huge influx of residents, suburban commuters, and international visitors—perfectly exemplifies this tradition.

In its first life San Francisco was little more than a small, well-situated settlement. Founded by Spaniards in 1776, it was prized for its natural harbor, so commodious that "all the navies of the world might fit inside it," as one visitor wrote. Around 1849 the discovery of gold at John Sutter's sawmill in the nearby Sierra foothills transformed the sleepy little settlement into a city of 30,000. Millions of dollars' worth of gold was panned and blasted out of the hills, the impetus for the development of a western Wall Street. Fueled by the 1859 discovery of a fabulously rich vein of silver in Virginia City, Nevada, San Francisco became the West Coast's cultural fulcrum and major transportation hub, and its population soared to 342,000. In 1869 the transcontinental railway was completed, linking the once-isolated western capital to the East. San Francisco had become a major city of the United States. Of course the boom was not without its price. Gambling and violent crime were rampant, destructive fires flared up on an almost daily basis, and immigrant railroad workers suffered cruelly under multifarious anti-Chinese laws.

San Francisco has long been a bastion of what it likes to refer to as "progressive politics." The Sierra Club, founded here in 1892 by John Muir, has its national headquarters on Polk Street. The turn-of-the-20th-century "yellow journalism" of William Randolph Hearst's *San Francisco Examiner* gave way to such leftist publications as *Mother Jones* magazine and today's left-of-center weekly newspapers. Political contentiousness has sometimes led to violence, most notably in 1978 when the city's liberal mayor, George Moscone, and its first gay supervisor, Harvey Milk, were assassinated by a vindictive right-wing ex-supervisor.

However, despite a boomtown tendency toward raucousness and a sad history of anti-Asian discrimination, the city today prides itself on its tolerance. Consider the makeup of the city's chief administrative body, the 11-member Board of Supervisors. Chinese, Hispanics, gays, blacks, and women have all been representatives. The mix, everybody knows, is what makes San Francisco.

Loose, tolerant, and even licentious are words that are used to describe San Francisco. Bohemian communities thrive here. As early as the 1860s the Barbary Coast—a collection of taverns, whorehouses, and gambling joints along Pacific Avenue close to the waterfront—was famous, or infamous. North Beach, the city's Little Italy, became the home of the Beat movement in the 1950s (Herb Caen, the city's best-known columnist, coined the term "beatnik"). Lawrence Ferlinghetti's City Lights, a bookstore and publishing house that still stands on Columbus Avenue, brought out, among other titles, Allen Ginsberg's *Howl* and *Kaddish*. Across Broadway a plaque identifies the Condor as the site of the nation's first topless and bottomless performances. In the '60s the Free Speech Movement began at the University of California at Berkeley, and Stanford's David Harris, who went to prison for defying the draft, numbered among the nation's most famous student leaders. In October 1965 Allen Ginsberg introduced the term "flower power," and the Haight-Ashbury district became synonymous with hippiedom, giving rise to such legendary bands as Jefferson Airplane and the Grateful Dead. Today the Haight's history and its name still draw neo-hippies, as well as new wavers with black lips and blue hair, and some rather menacing skinheads. Transients make panhandling one of Haight Street's major business activities, and the potential for crime and violence after dark has turned many of the liberal residents into unlikely law-and-order advocates. Still, most remain committed to keeping the Haight the Haight.

SOUTHWEST OF THE HAIGHT is the onetime Irish neighborhood known as the Castro, which during the 1970s became identified with gay and lesbian liberation. Castro Street is dominated by the elaborate Castro Theatre, a 1922 vision in Spanish baroque style, which presents first-run art and independent films with occasional revivals of Hollywood film classics. (The grand old pipe organ still plays during intermissions, breaking into "San Francisco" just before the feature begins.) There's been much talk, most of it exaggerated, about how AIDS has "chastened" and "matured" the Castro. The disease *has* spawned the creation of AIDS education, treatment, and caregiving networks that have served as models for the rest of the nation. The Castro is still an effervescent neighborhood, and—as housing everywhere has become more and more scarce—an increasingly mixed one. But because of its historical importance, the Castro still draws gays from around the world.

In terms of both geography and culture, San Francisco is about as close as you can get to Asia in the continental United States. The first great wave of Chinese immigrants came as railroad laborers. Chinese workers quickly became the target of race hatred and discriminatory laws. Chinatown—which began when the Chi-

nese moved into old buildings that white businesses seeking more fashionable locations had abandoned—developed as a refuge, as much as anything else. It is still a fascinating place to wander and a good bet for late-night food, but it's not the whole story by any means. The Asian community, which now accounts for 35%– 40% of San Francisco's population, reaches into every San Francisco neighborhood and particularly into the Sunset and Richmond districts, west toward the ocean. There was heavy Japanese immigration earlier in the 20th century, but most of it went to Southern California, where organized labor had less of a foothold and where there were greater opportunities for Asian workers. Still, San Francisco has its Japantown, with the Japan Center complex and a handful of shops and restaurants. Working hard to establish themselves over the decades, today Asian-Americans of every persuasion are at the highest levels of the city's elected and appointed government and in leadership positions in San Francisco's business, medical, and educational communities.

Geographically, San Francisco is the thumbnail on a 40-mi thumb of land, the San Francisco Peninsula, which stretches northward between the Pacific Ocean and San Francisco Bay. Hemmed in on three sides by water, its land area (less than 50 square mi) is relatively small. The population, at about 789,000, is small, too. Technically speaking, it's only California's fourth-largest city, behind Los Angeles, San Diego, and nearby San Jose. But that statistic is misleading: the Bay Area, extending from the bedroom communities north of Oakland and Berkeley south through the peninsula and the San Jose area, is really one continuous megacity, with San Francisco as its heart.

Not so many centuries ago the area that was to become San Francisco was a windswept, virtually treeless, and, above all, sandy wasteland. Sand even covered the hills. The sand is still there, but—except along the ocean—it's well hidden. The beautifully renovated City Hall is built on 80 ft of it. The westerly section of the city seems flat only because sand has filled in the contours of the hills.

The hills that remain are spectacular. They provide vistas all over the city. Nothing is more common than to find yourself staring out toward Angel Island or Alcatraz, or across the bay at Berkeley and Oakland. The hills also made cable cars a necessity early on. The city's two bridges, which are almost as majestic as their surroundings, had their 50th birthdays in 1986 and 1987. The Golden Gate Bridge, which crosses to Marin County, got a bigger party, but the San Francisco–Oakland Bay Bridge got a better present: a necklace of lights along its spans. They were supposed to be temporary, but the locals were so taken with the glimmer that bridge boosters started a drive to make them permanent. Radio DJs and newspaper columnists put out daily appeals, drivers gave extra quarters to the toll takers, various corporations put up shares, and now—nearly $1 million later—the lights on the Bay Bridge shine nightly.

First-time visitors to San Francisco sometimes arrive with ideas about its weather gleaned from movie images of sunny California or from a misinformed 1967 song that celebrated "a warm San Franciscan night." Sunny, perhaps. Warm—not likely. That's *Southern* California. (A perennially popular T-shirt quotes Mark Twain's alleged remark: "The coldest winter I ever spent was a summer in San Francisco.") Still, it almost never freezes here, and heat waves are equally rare. Most San Franciscans come to love the climate, which is genuinely temperate—sufficiently welcoming for the imposing row of palms down the median of Dolores Street but seldom warm enough for just a T-shirt at night. The coastal stretch of ocean may look inviting, but the surfers you sometimes see along Ocean Beach are wearing wet suits (though the beach can be fine for sunning). And, of course, there's the famous fog—something that tourists tend to find more delightful than do the residents. It's largely a summer phenomenon: San Francisco's real summer begins in September, when the fog lifts and the air warms up for a while. November brings on the rains.

Victorian architecture is as integral to the city as fog and cable cars. Bay-windowed, ornately decorated Victorian houses—the historical, multicolor paint jobs that have become popular make them seem even more ornate—are the city's most distinguishing architectural feature. They date mainly from the latter part of Queen Victoria's reign, 1870 to the turn of the 20th century. In those three decades San Francisco more than doubled in population (from 150,000

to 342,000); the transcontinental railway, linking the once-isolated western capital to the East, had been completed in 1869. That may explain the exuberant confidence of the architecture.

Another measure of the city's exuberance is its many festivals and celebrations. The Lesbian, Gay, Bisexual, and Transgendered Pride Parade and Celebration, held each June, vies with the Chinese New Year's Parade, an annual February event, as the city's most elaborate. They both get competition from Japantown's Cherry Blossom Festival, in April; the Columbus Day and St. Patrick's Day parades; Carnaval, held in the Hispanic Mission District in May; and the May Day march, a labor celebration in a labor town. The mix of ethnic, economic, social, and sexual groups can be bewildering, but the city's residents—whatever their origin—face it with aplomb and even gratitude. Nearly everyone smiles on the fortunate day they arrived on this windy, foggy patch of peninsula.

WHAT'S WHERE

The Neighborhoods

San Francisco is a city of neighborhoods, each with its own unique flavor. Visitors are most likely to stay, eat, and shop in the Union Square area, so that's where we start. From this central point, we go on to explore the rest of downtown—SoMa, the Barbary Coast, North Beach, Chinatown, and Civic Center—and the city's central residential neighborhoods: Nob Hill, Russian Hill, and Pacific Heights. Then we head north to Fisherman's Wharf, the Marina, and the Presidio, before moving on to neighborhoods a bit farther afield, from the Mission to Ocean Beach.

Union Square

Classy Union Square attracts countless visitors with its fine department stores, hotels, and nearby theater row. Two of the city's three cable car lines start here.

South of Market (SoMa) and the Embarcadero

The San Francisco Museum of Modern Art and the Center for the Arts at Yerba Buena Gardens have transformed the once-seedy area called SoMa into one of San Francisco's most important areas. Nearby attractions are the Moscone Center and several noteworthy art galleries. Along the waterfront boulevard known as the Embarcadero are Embarcadero Center—a huge complex of offices, shops, and a Hyatt hotel—and the Ferry Building.

The Barbary Coast
In the northeastern corner of the city is San Francisco's Financial District, dominated by the towering Bank of America and Transamerica buildings. Its northern neighbor is Jackson Square, a tiny but tony district of antiques stores in former town houses. During the latter half of the 19th century these areas formed the heart of the brawling, boozing boomtown once called the Barbary Coast.

Chinatown
Buddhist temples, Chinese restaurants, ginseng and root stores, and throngs of people make this crowded, ever-expanding miniature city one of San Francisco's liveliest neighborhoods. With Grant Avenue as the heart of the gastronomical and retail activity, Chinatown stretches from Bush Street to Broadway.

North Beach and Telegraph Hill
With its mix of Italian cafés and beatnik landmarks, the area just north of the Financial District and Chinatown evokes a mood of distant places and long-ago eras. The smell of garlic wafts in the streets, which are lined with pint-size antiquarian shops; and Coit Tower rises, beaconlike, from the top of Telegraph Hill. At the heart of the neighborhood is Columbus Avenue, with its landmark City Lights bookstore.

Nob Hill and Russian Hill
California Street rises west from the Financial District to Nob Hill. In this classy neighborhood, the very exclusive Pacific Union Club, the Gothic Grace Cathedral, and the landmark Fairmont Hotel all stand as beacons of Old San Francisco. Due north of Nob Hill, the more low-key Russian Hill is full of small parks, historic houses, quiet lanes, and stairways with spectacular views of the bay.

Japantown
Just south of Pacific Heights, tiny Japantown is centered on the 5-acre Japan Center complex. Here you'll find a handful of stores and restaurants, and the modern, multiscreen AMC Kabuki cinema.

Civic Center
The Civic Center includes City Hall, the War Memorial Opera House, the Louise M. Davies Symphony Hall, a new public library, and the new Asian Art Museum (scheduled to reopen in 2003). Dignified and imposing, this area north of Market Street between 7th and Gough streets is relatively quiet by day but rather unsavory—and sometimes downright dangerous—after dark.

The Northern Waterfront
Fisherman's Wharf and Pier 39 aren't the only draws along this stretch of piers, whose bayside views draw masses of tourists. You'll also find Ghirardelli Square, the Cannery, and Fort Mason, which is known for its ethnic museums, Greens restaurant, and the Magic Theatre.

The Marina and the Presidio
Known for its yacht club and marina jammed with boats, its elegant waterfront homes with views of the Golden Gate Bridge, and its 1915 Palace of Fine Arts, this waterfront neighborhood is one of San Francisco's yuppiest. Its main thoroughfare, Chestnut Street, is filled with art deco buildings and myriad coffee bars, eateries, movie houses, and markets. The nearby Presidio, with its 1,500 acres of hills, woods, and former army barracks, was a military base for more than 100 years. Today parts of the national park land are being developed to help the Presidio become financially self-sustaining.

Golden Gate Park
Between the Richmond and Sunset districts on the western side of the city, this 1,000 acre swath of grassy fields, trees, lakes, and ponds contains such attractions as the California Academy of Sciences, Strybing Arboretum, and a Japanese tea garden.

Lincoln Park and the Western Shoreline
This windswept stretch of shoreline is dotted with attractions: the Cliff House, the ruins of the Sutro Baths, and the San Francisco Zoo. At the northwestern tip of the city, the elegant Palace of the Legion of Honor rises above Lincoln Park,

surrounded by cypress-lined walking trails and an 18-hole golf course.

The Mission District

A mix of ethnic groups lives in this neighborhood, whose heart is at Mission and Valencia streets between 16th and 24th streets. The main attractions are Mission Dolores, myriad outdoor murals, the Galería de la Raza (a gallery of Hispanic art), and a slew of inexpensive ethnic eateries.

The Castro/Noe Valley

Where Castro and Market streets intersect, the vintage Castro Theatre is the main landmark of the gay-friendly Castro, where a mixed crowd lives among Victorian houses, alternative shops, and a handful of cafés. South of the Castro along 24th Street, Noe Valley teams with mom-and-pop shops, bakeries, and sidewalk activity.

The Haight

Three decades after the flower-power era, the Haight still feels slightly stuck in the spirit of the '60s. At the heart of the neighborhood is the section of Haight Street between Masonic Avenue and Stanyan Street, where vintage clothing and record stores conjure up days gone by.

Side Trips

Marin County

North of the Golden Gate Bridge lies some of the most desirable real estate in all of California. Beyond Sausalito, Tiburon, and Mill Valley—all villagelike towns famous for their bay views—outdoors attractions abound: the Marin Headlands, Muir Woods, Mt. Tamalpais, and Point Reyes offer a virtually limitless choice of hiking trails.

The East Bay

Across the Bay Bridge, Berkeley is a university town whose liberal, bohemian spirit persists from its glory days as the center of the magical, mythical '60s. To the south is Oakland, a port city whose grand historical sites and vibrant ethnic communities outshine its rough-and-tumble reputation.

The Inland Peninsula and San Mateo County Coast

Along the southern half of the San Francisco Bay, the Peninsula is home to Stanford University and several major high-tech corporations. The rugged Pacific coastline of San Mateo County, stretching south from San Francisco, is a series of quaint towns with bed-and-breakfast inns, lighthouses, and quiet beaches.

The Wine Country

North of San Francisco and Marin County, Napa and Sonoma counties are known as the undisputed American capital of wine production. The region's hilly landscapes, redolent of the ripe smells and rich colors of the vines, also foster a multitude of outstanding restaurants and resorts.

PLEASURES AND PASTIMES

The Bay and Its Bridges

The sight of a suit-clad stockbroker unloading a Windsurfer from his Land Rover is not uncommon in San Francisco, where the bay perpetually beckons to pleasure seekers of every stripe. On sunny weekends the bay teems with sailboats, and when the surf's up, daredevils in wet suits line the beaches. For those not inclined to get wet, various ferries, tour boats, and dinner cruises give participants a fish's-eye view of all three bridges—the Golden Gate Bridge, the Richmond, and the Bay—as well as Angel Island, Treasure Island, and the legendary Alcatraz.

The Fog

Every summer morning a white shroud of mist rolls down from the Marin Headlands, often obliterating all but the tops of the towers of the Golden Gate Bridge from view, and then it evaporates by noon. To native San Franciscans, summer fog is a part of life, as dependable as the sunrise. It's part of what makes San Francisco feel like a living, breathing city exposed to the whims of nature.

Hidden Lanes and Stairways

Though it does have its share of major boulevards, San Francisco is a city of small side streets—many one-way-only hidden lanes and out-of-the-way stairways. Whether you're in Chinatown, Nob Hill, North Beach, Pacific Heights, Potrero Hill, or Russian Hill, there's always a quiet lane or stairway nearby. A few of the most scenic hidden corners are in Nob Hill, Russian Hill, and North Beach—but if you look carefully, you'll find them where they're least expected.

The Hills

Anyone who's afraid of heights would do well to stay away from San Francisco, where almost everything worth getting to lies at the top of or just beyond a steep hill. Driving the city feels like riding a roller coaster, but don't worry: Your stomach catches up to the rest of you at the base of each extreme dip. But for all the challenges they present to drivers and walkers, the hills are what give San Francisco its distinctly European look and its dazzling bay views, as well as its cable cars and landmark hilltop hotels and monuments. It's a city of hills: Nob Hill, Russian Hill, Telegraph Hill, Potrero Hill, the smaller hills within neighborhoods, and the larger hills across the bay.

Patches of Green

With its hills and fresh air, its myriad parks and waterfront promenades, San Francisco is an outdoor person's dream. Golden Gate Park, with its 1,000 acres of trails and fields, is deservedly popular, but the choices don't end there. The Presidio, a former military base, offers 2,500 acres of hilly, wooded trails interspersed with old army barracks. The Marina, which stretches from the Presidio to the northern waterfront, is the turf of choice for a stylishly outfitted crowd of runners and skaters. Along the western shore there's the 275-acre Lincoln Park; the 6-mi loop around Lake Merced; and the Great Highway, a 3-mi ocean-side stretch with a paved jogging path. Across the Bay, Muir Woods and the Marin Headlands attract legions of nature lovers.

Wining and Dining

Europhiles who bemoan the lack of a sophisticated food and wine culture in America will have nothing to complain about in San Francisco. As the birthplace of nouvelle cuisine—cooking that combines fresh, locally grown ingredients in visually stunning ways—and as the next-door neighbor of Napa Valley, the city has been attracting notable chefs—Alice Waters, Bradley Ogden, Jeremiah Tower, and Traci des Jardins, to name just a few—for years.

FODOR'S CHOICE

Even with so many special places in San Francisco, Fodor's writers and editors have their favorites. Here are just a few.

For more information about each entry, refer to the appropriate chapters within this guidebook.

Dining

Gary Danko. Usually solidly booked six weeks in advance, Gary Danko gets rave reviews for its contemporary cuisine, making it a must for visiting foodies. $$$$

Jardinière. One of the city's most talked-about restaurants is a serious pre-theater event, thanks in large part to the incredible cooking of chef-owner Traci Des Jardins. $$$

B44. A casual, very smart Catalan restaurant in restaurant-lined Belden Alley serves tapas and paellas to satisfy the fussiest matador. $$

Fringale. The Gallic classics come at neighborhood prices in this touch of France in South of Market. $$

Rose Pistola. This large, lively spot, with its mix of Ligurian and neighborhood specialties, is a magnet for North Beach residents and visitors alike. $–$$

Lodging

Ritz-Carlton, San Francisco. The opulent lobby and elegant rooms have earned the Ritz its rating as one of the top hotels in the world. $$$$

Sherman House. A landmark mansion in Pacific Heights is San Francisco's most luxurious small hotel. $$$$

Hotel Monaco. Whimsical travel theme decor and a devotion to pampering are combined in a surefire hit. $$$–$$$$

Hotel Rex. The richly decorated rooms and literary soirées evoke the spirit of salon society in the 1920s. $$$

Union Street Inn. This romantic getaway has an old-fashioned English garden, elaborate complimentary breakfast, and personable owners. $$–$$$

Memorable Views

Harry Denton's Starlight Room. Drink in the city views along with your martini at this glamorous nightspot on the 21st floor of the Sir Frances Drake Hotel.

Walk Across the Golden Gate Bridge. You can see all that the city has to offer—the bay, Alcatraz, Angel and Treasure Islands, the Pacific Ocean crashing against the rocks, the city skyline—and to the north, the majestic Marin Headlands.

Coit Tower. Glowing at night atop Telegraph Hill, Coit Tower is a beacon of western individualism, inspired by Lily Coit, one of early San Francisco's great originals.

Take a Nighttime Ferry on the Bay. The city's lighted bridges look like celestial creations.

Chinatown. Crates of brightly colored vegetables line the bustling markets in the shadow of pagoda-topped roofs in one of the city's most distinctive neighborhoods.

Special Moments

Ride on a Cable Car. The cable cars are the best way to appreciate the steepness of the city's hills and still have enough breath left to appreciate the views from the top.

California Palace of Fine Arts. Feed the ducks on the shores of the lagoon and enjoy one of San Francisco's most historic landmarks.

San Francisco Museum of Modern Art. Crossing the sky bridge in the atrium, you'll appreciate the cutting-edge designs of architect Mario Botta.

A Classic Double-Feature at the Castro Theater. Arrive early to hear the organ player's repertoire at the grandest of San Francisco's few remaining movie palaces.

PacBell Park. For a dose of team spirit, watch the Giants beat the Dodgers in a day game at the city's new, retro baseball stadium.

Lombard Street. The "crookedest street in the world," with its winding brick paths and its well-tended flowerbeds, is worth the queue.

Beach Blanket Babylon. The city's longest-running cabaret revue offers a hilarious musical salute to "Baghdad by the Bay" in all its eccentric and campy splendor.

GREAT ITINERARIES

San Francisco in 5 Days

Much of San Francisco's appeal springs from the distinct personalities of its neighborhoods, so allow as much time as possible to soak up the city's ambience. Five days is enough to see highlights of the city by the bay: Fisherman's Wharf, Union Square, Alcatraz, North Beach, Chinatown, and the Golden Gate Bridge.

Day One. Spend the day checking out San Francisco's bustling centers of commercial activity. In the morning explore Fisherman's Wharf and its jumble of tourist shops, street performers, and artists. Pier 39 is a consumer extravaganza; a double-decker carousel shares space with touristy shops and Aquarium of the Bay, a fascinating walk-through glimpse of ocean life. Don't miss the antics of the hundreds of sea lions basking in the sun. Jump a cable car (the Powell-Hyde line is the most dramatic) at the wharf and take in sweeping views of the bay, Alcatraz, and the Golden Gate Bridge as you rattle your way to Union Square, ground zero for sophisticated shopping. Maiden Lane's charming galleries and boutiques are worth a look. After a few hours of browsing swank shops, take in an evening of culture on Geary Street's theater row or quaff a cocktail and watch the sun set at one of the square's sky-view lounges.

🕑 Best on weekdays.

Day Two. Devote the day to two of the most important cultures in the city's history. Head to North Beach, the Italian quarter, and join locals from the old country for breakfast Italian-style: an espresso and pastry at an outdoor café along Columbus Avenue. Allow an hour or two to wander this small area filled with tempting delis, bakeries, and pasta houses. You'll see beat-era landmarks like City Lights Bookstore and reminders of the city's bawdy past in the steamy shops and clubs of Broadway. Be sure to walk up Telegraph Hill to Coit Tower. You'll be rewarded with breathtaking views of the bay and the city's tightly stacked homes. Spend the afternoon exploring labyrinthine Chinatown, where tea and herb shops, live fish markets, and exotic-produce stalls spill onto the street.

Then take the California Street cable car up blue-blood Nob Hill and top off the evening with a tropical concoction at the Tonga Room, the Fairmont Hotel's kitschy-chic Polynesian lounge, or take in the quirky musical revue of San Francisco, *Beach Blanket Babylon*, back in North Beach.

☉ If *Beach Blanket Babylon* is on your list, this won't work on Monday or Tuesday.

Day Three. Today you'll hit the city's outdoor highlights. Take a morning ferry from Pier 41 to the infamous prison Alcatraz. When the boat docks back at the pier, head toward the Marina neighborhood, home to young professionals and exclusive boutiques and bistros. Along the way, catch a glimpse of San Francisco's nautical history at the National Maritime Museum. If you love chocolate, stop off at Ghirardelli Square, which includes a shopping center and the tempting Ghirardelli Chocolate Factory. Make a beeline for the end of the Marina and the stunning Palace of Fine Arts. Don't miss the Palace's wacky and wonderful hands-on science museum, the Exploratorium. Before dusk, bundle up and head to the Golden Gate Bridge to catch the sunset.

☉ The Exploratorium is closed on Monday in winter (Labor Day to Memorial Day).

Day Four. Dedicate the morning to art and the rest of the day to funk. Start south of Market at the San Francisco Museum of Modern Art to take in works by local, Mexican, and European masters. While you're in the area, don't miss Yerba Buena Gardens and its Center for the Arts. Then take the antique-streetcar "F"-line down Market Street to the colorful, gay-friendly Castro, brimming with shops and cafés. A double feature at the Castro Theatre makes for a great afternoon diversion. Head to the mural-filled Mission District, a neighborhood of twentysomething hipsters and working-class Latino families. Simple Mission Dolores, built in 1776, is San Francisco's oldest standing structure. In the evening check out some of the Mission's trendy watering holes and restaurants.

☉ Avoid Wednesday, when the Museum of Modern Art is closed.

Day Five. Step back into San Francisco's hippie days and explore its most glorious green space. Start out in the Haight, the epicenter of 1960s counterculture, whose streets are lined with excellent music and book shops and groovy vintage-clothing stores. In the afternoon join in-line skaters, joggers, and walking enthusiasts in picnic-perfect Golden Gate Park—more than 1,000 acres of greenery stretching from the Haight to the Pacific. Among the botanical gardens and playing fields, you'll find the serene Japanese Tea Garden. Then either take a swing through the California Academy of Sciences, the city's famed natural-history museum, or spend the rest of the afternoon strolling the park, around Stow Lake and all the way to the Dutch Windmill on the park's coastal edge. Head up to the Cliff House for dinner or a drink and a view of the Pacific sunset.

☉ Never on Monday, when the museums are closed.

☉ *So that you don't show up somewhere and find the doors locked, shuffle the itinerary segments with closing days in mind.*

If You Have More Time

Drive over the Golden Gate Bridge to the dramatic coastline of the Marin Headlands or to redwood-rich Muir Woods. Or head across the Bay Bridge and explore formerly radical, still-offbeat Berkeley. A visit to diverse Oakland also makes a great afternoon; don't miss waterfront Jack London Square and the gorgeous art deco Paramount Theatre. The wineries of Napa and Sonoma counties are also within reach.

If You Have 3 Days

If it's your first visit, follow the suggestions for the first day: See Fisherman's Wharf and Pier 39 in the morning and Union Square in the afternoon, then head to the San Francisco Museum of Modern Art. On the second day, begin with a walk on the Golden Gate Bridge, then explore North Beach and Chinatown in the afternoon. Begin the third day with a ferry to Alcatraz. Spend the rest of the day in the neighborhood most appealing to you, either the Castro, the Mission, or the Haight.

2 EXPLORING SAN FRANCISCO

Brace yourself for the brilliant colors of ornately painted, bay-window Victorians; the sounds of foghorns and cable car lines; and the crisp, salty smell of the bay. San Francisco's world-famous landmarks—the Golden Gate Bridge, Alcatraz, the Transamerica Pyramid—provide an unforgettable backdrop for its eclectic neighborhoods, from bustling Chinatown and bacchanalian North Beach to the left-of-center Castro district and the city's cultural and new-media center, SoMa.

Y OU COULD LIVE IN SAN FRANCISCO a month and ask no greater entertainment than walking through it," wrote Inez Hayes Irwin, author of *The Californiacs*, an effusive 1921 homage to the state of California and the City by the Bay. Her claim remains true today: As in the 1920s, touring on foot is the best way to experience this diverse metropolis.

Revised by
Denise M. Leto

San Francisco is a relatively small city. About 800,000 residents live on a 46½-square-mi tip of land between San Francisco Bay and the Pacific Ocean. San Franciscans cherish the city's colorful past; many older buildings have been spared from demolition and nostalgically converted into modern offices and shops. Longtime locals rue the sites that got away—railroad- and mining boom–era residences lost in the 1906 earthquake, the baroque Fox Theater, and Playland at the Beach. Despite acts of nature, the indifference of developers, and the mixed record of the city's planning commission, much of the architectural and historical interest remains. Bernard Maybeck, Julia Morgan, Willis Polk, and Arthur Brown Jr. are among the noteworthy architects whose designs endure.

San Francisco's charms are great and small. You wouldn't want to miss Golden Gate Park, the Palace of Fine Arts, the Golden Gate Bridge, or a cable car ride over Nob Hill. But a walk down the Filbert Steps or through Macondray Lane or a peaceful hour spent gazing east from Ina Coolbrith Park can be equally inspiring.

The neighborhoods of San Francisco retain strong cultural, political, and ethnic identities. Locals know this pluralism is the real life of the city. Experiencing San Francisco means visiting the neighborhoods: the colorful Mission District, the gay Castro, countercultural Haight Street, swank Pacific Heights, lively Chinatown, and ever bohemian North Beach.

Exploring by car involves navigating a maze of one-way streets and restricted parking zones. San Francisco's famed 40-plus hills can also be a problem for drivers who are new to the terrain. Cable cars, buses, and trolleys can take you to or near many attractions.

UNION SQUARE AREA

Much of San Francisco may feel like a collection of small towns strung together, but the Union Square area bristles with big-city bravado. The city's finest department stores—including Bloomingdale's, scheduled to open in spring 2003—do business here, along with exclusive emporiums like Tiffany & Co., Prada, and Coach and big-name franchises like Niketown, the Original Levi's Store, and Virgin Megastore. Several dozen hotels within a three-block walk of the square cater to visitors. The downtown theater district and many fine arts galleries are nearby.

Numbers in the text correspond to numbers in the margin and on the Downtown San Francisco map.

A Good Walk

Begin three blocks south of Union Square at the **San Francisco Visitor Information Center** ①, on the lower level of Hallidie Plaza at Powell and Market streets. Up the escalators on the east side of the plaza, where Powell dead-ends into Market, lies the **cable car terminus** ② for two of the city's three lines. Head north on Powell from the terminus to Geary Street, make a left, and walk west 1½ blocks into the

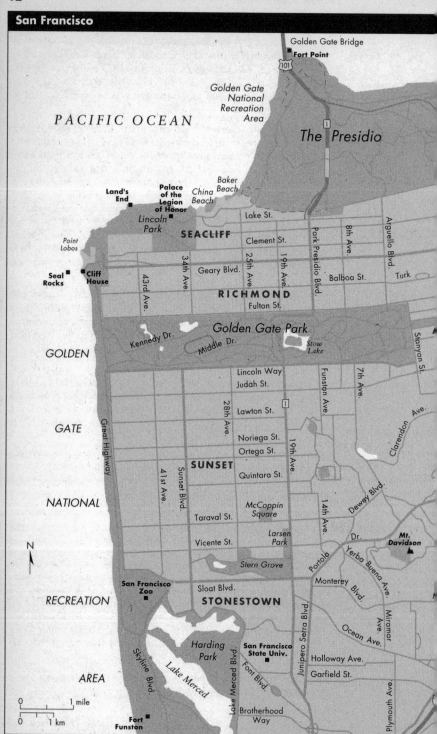

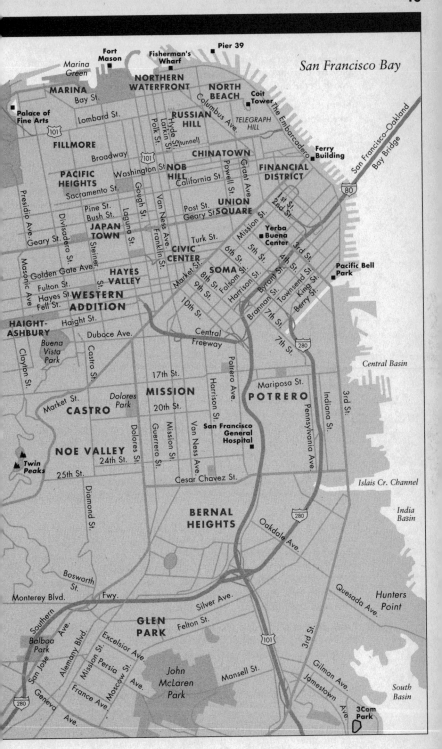

San Francisco Bay

theater district for a peek at the **Geary Theater** ③. Backtrack on the north side of Geary Street, where the sturdy and stately **Westin St. Francis Hotel** ④ dominates Powell between Geary and Post streets. **Union Square** ⑤ is across Powell from the hotel's main entrance. You can pick up discount and full-price event tickets at the **TIX Bay Area** ⑥ booth in the square.

From the square head south on Stockton Street to O'Farrell Street and take a spin through **F.A.O. Schwarz** ⑦ (also south on Stockton is Virgin Megastore; the Original Levi's Store is north). Walk back toward Union Square past Geary Street and make a right on **Maiden Lane** ⑧, a two-block alley directly across Stockton from Union Square that runs east parallel to Geary. When the lane ends at Kearny Street, turn left, walk 1½ blocks to Sutter Street, make a right, and walk a half block to the **Hallidie Building** ⑨. After viewing this historic building, reverse direction and head west 1½ blocks up Sutter to the fanciful beaux-arts–style **Hammersmith Building** ⑩, on the southwest corner of Sutter Street and Grant Avenue. In the middle of the next block of Sutter stands a glorious Art Deco building at **No. 450** ⑪. From here, backtrack a half block east to Stockton Street and take a right. In front of the the Grand Hyatt hotel sits **Ruth Asawa's Fantasy Fountain** ⑫. Union Square is a half block south on Stockton.

TIMING

Allow two hours to see everything around Union Square. Stepping into the massive Macy's or Bloomie's or browsing in boutiques can eat up countless hours. If you're a shopper, give yourself extra time.

Sights to See

❧ ❷ **Cable car terminus.** San Francisco's signature red cable cars were declared National Landmarks—the only ones that move—in 1964. Two of the three operating lines begin and end their runs in Union Square. The more dramatic Powell–Mason line climbs up Nob Hill, then winds through North Beach to Fisherman's Wharf. The Powell–Hyde line also crosses Nob Hill but then continues up Russian Hill and down Hyde Street to Victorian Park, across from the Buena Vista Café and near Ghirardelli Square. Buy your ticket ($2 one-way) on board, at nearby hotels, or at the police/information booth near the turnaround.

Depending on your disposition, you'll find the panhandlers, street preachers, and other regulars at the Powell and Market terminus daunting or diverting. Either way you'll wait longer here to board a cable car than at any other stop in the system. If it's just the experience of riding a cable car you're after, board the less-busy California line at Van Ness Avenue and ride it down to the Hyatt Regency Hotel. ⊠ *Powell and Market Sts., Union Square.*

❧ ❼ **F.A.O. Schwarz.** This upmarket, three-floor playland ignites the imaginations of children and adults alike with 6-ft-tall stuffed animals and elaborate fairy-tale sculptures. Among the wares are a large Barbie section, an astounding supply of stuffed animals (the priciest is a whopping $15,000), and just about every other toy out there. ⊠ *48 Stockton St., Union Square,* ☎ *415/394–8700,* WEB *www.faoschwarz.com.* ☉ *Mon.–Sat. 9:30–7, Sun. 11–6.*

❶ **450 Sutter Street.** Handsome Maya-inspired designs adorn the exterior and interior surfaces of this 1928 Art Deco skyscraper, a masterpiece of terra-cotta and other detailing. ⊠ *Between Stockton and Powell Sts., Union Square.*

3 **Geary Theater.** The American Conservatory Theater (ACT), one of North America's leading repertory companies, uses the 1,035-seat Geary as its main venue. Built in 1910, the Geary has a serious neoclassic design lightened by colorful carved terra-cotta columns depicting a cornucopia of fruits. Damaged heavily in the 1989 earthquake, the Geary has been completely restored to gilded splendor. ☒ *415 Geary St. (box office at 405 Geary St.), Union Square,* ☏ *415/749–2228.*

9 **Hallidie Building.** Named for cable car inventor Andrew S. Hallidie, this 1918 structure is best viewed from across the street. Willis Polk's revolutionary glass-curtain wall—believed to be the world's first such facade—hangs a foot beyond the reinforced concrete of the frame. The reflecting glass, decorative exterior fire escapes that appear to be metal balconies, and Venetian Gothic cornice are worth noting. Ornamental bands of birds at feeders stretch across the building on several stories. ☒ *130 Sutter St., between Kearny and Montgomery Sts., Union Square.*

10 **Hammersmith Building.** Glass walls and a colorful design distinguish this four-story beaux-arts–style structure, built in 1907. The Foundation for Architectural Heritage once described the building as a "commercial jewel box." Appropriately, it was originally designed for use as a jewelry store. ☒ *301 Sutter St., at Grant Ave., Union Square.*

NEED A BREAK?	You can nibble on sampler plates or have a full meal at the **E&O Trading Co.** (☒ 314 Sutter St., Union Square, ☏ 415/693–0303). The ambience at this upscale microbrewery is late-19th-century Asian trading post, but the chow is strictly modern pan-Asian.

8 **Maiden Lane.** Known as Morton Street in the raffish Barbary Coast era, this former red-light district reported at least one murder a week during the late 19th century. After the 1906 fire destroyed the brothels, the street emerged as Maiden Lane, and it has since become a semichic pedestrian mall stretching two blocks, between Stockton and Kearny streets. Traffic is prohibited most days between 11 and 5, when the lane becomes a patchwork of umbrella-shaded tables. Masses of daffodils and balloons lend a carnival mood during the annual spring festival, when throngs of street musicians, arts-and-crafts vendors, and spectators emerge.

With its circular interior ramp and skylights, the handsome brick 1948 structure at **140 Maiden Lane,** the only Frank Lloyd Wright building in San Francisco, is said to have been his model for the Guggenheim Museum in New York. **Xanadu Tribal Arts** (☏ 415/392–9999), a gallery showcasing Baltic, Latin American, and African folk art, occupies the space. ☒ *Between Stockton and Kearny Sts., Union Square.*

12 **Ruth Asawa's Fantasy Fountain.** Local artist Ruth Asawa's sculpture, a wonderland of real and mythical creatures, honors the city's hills, bridges, and architecture. Children and friends helped Asawa shape the hundreds of tiny figures from baker's clay; these were assembled on 41 large panels from which molds were made for the bronze casting. ☒ *In front of Grand Hyatt at 345 Stockton St., Union Square.*

1 **San Francisco Visitor Information Center.** A multilingual staff operates this facility below the cable car terminus. They answer questions and provide maps and pamphlets. You can also pick up discount coupons—the savings can be significant, especially for families—and hotel brochures here. ☒ *Hallidie Plaza, lower level, Powell and Market Sts., Union Square,* ☏ *415/391–2000 or 415/283–0177,* WEB *www.sfvisitor.org.* ☉ *Weekdays 9–5, weekends 9–3.*

Downtown San Francisco

Alta Plaza Park **64**

Asian Art Museum . . **76**

Broadway
and Webster
Street estates **63**

Cable Car
Museum **55**

Cable car
Terminus **2**

California
Historical Society . . . **19**

Cartoon Art
Museum **20**

Center for the
Arts **14**

Chinatown Gate . . . **32**

Chinese–American
National Museum and
Learning Center **39**

Chinese Culture
Center **35**

City Hall **77**

City Lights
Bookstore **41**

Coit Tower **46**

Embarcadero
Center **22**

F.A.O. Schwarz **7**

The Fairmont **52**

Ferry Building **24**

Feusier House **57**

450 Sutter Street . . **11**

Franklin Street
buildings **69**

Geary Theater **3**

Golden Gate
Fortune
Cookies Co. **38**

Grace Cathedral . . **50**

Haas-Lilienthal
House **68**

Hallidie Building . . . **9**

Hammersmith
Building **10**

Hyatt Regency
Hotel **23**

Ina Coolbrith
Park **56**

Jackson Square . . . **30**

Japan Center **71**

Japan Center
Mall **73**

Julius' Castle **47**

Kabuki Springs
& Spa **72**

Kong Chow
Temple **40**

Lafayette Park **66**

Levi Strauss
headquarters **48**

Lombard Street . . . **59**

Louise M. Davies
Symphony Hall **80**

Macondray Lane . . **58**

Magnes Museum . . **26**

Maiden Lane **8**

Mark Hopkins
Inter-Continental
Hotel **53**

Masonic
Auditorium **49**

Metreon **15**

Moscone
Convention
Center **16**

Noteworthy
Victorians **70**

Octagon House **61**

Old Chinese
Telephone
Exchange **36**

Old St. Mary's
Cathedral **33**

Pacific Stock
Exchange **27**

Pacific Union
Club **51**

Palace Hotel **21**

Portsmouth
Square **34**

Renaissance
Stanford Court
Hotel **54**

Rincon Center **25**

Rooftop@Yerba
Buena Gardens . . .**17**

Ruth Asawa's
Fantasy Fountain . . .**12**

St. Francis of
Assisi Church **42**

Saints Peter
and Paul
Catholic Church . . .**44**

San Francisco
Art Institute **60**

San Francisco
Brewing
Company **31**

San Francisco Museum
of Modern Art
(SFMOMA) **13**

San Francisco
Public Library **75**

San Francisco
Visitor Information
Center **1**

Seymour Pioneer
Museum **18**

Spreckels
Mansion **67**

Telegraph Hill **45**

Tin How Temple . . .**37**

TIX Bay Area **6**

Transamerica
Pyramid **29**

Union Square **5**

United Nations
Plaza **74**

Vedanta Society . . .**62**

Veterans
Building **78**

War Memorial
Opera House **79**

Washington
Square **43**

Wells Fargo
Bank History
Museum **28**

Westin St.
Francis Hotel **4**

Whittier Mansion . . .**65**

HOW CABLE CARS SPARED THE CITY'S HILLS AND HORSES

GAZE UP FROM THE BASE of Nob Hill or Russian Hill, and you won't have trouble figuring out why the ASPCA became an early supporter of Andrew Smith Hallidie's proposal to add cable cars to San Francisco's mass transit mix. Conductors of horse-drawn streetcars heading up these and other peaks in the 1850s and 1860s screamed at and fiercely whipped the animals, vainly encouraging them to muster the strength to halt their slides back *down* to the base.

The "sorrowful plight" of the horses may have been one of Hallidie's inspirations, but he was also in the business of selling wire cable. He was the first person to manufacture it in California, beginning during the gold rush. Hallidie, a Scotsman, had come to California seeking gold. He didn't find much, but he did strike it rich selling his cable and building suspension bridges and mine conveyances. The technology for cable cars had been used for decades in mines, but it was Hallidie who successfully applied it to an urban environment.

Drop by the Cable Car Museum on Nob Hill, and you'll see how breathtakingly simple Hallidie's system, eventually employed by more than a dozen cities around the world, is. Four sets of cables—one for each of the streets (Powell, Hyde, Mason, and California) on which the cars now travel—spin on huge powerhouse wheels, making a continuous circuit beneath city streets. When the conductor wants to put a car in motion, he or she operates a handgrip, the end of which grabs the cable, allowing the car to move along with the cable. When the conductor releases the grip, the car comes to a halt. Brakes are also involved when the vehicle is on an incline.

San Francisco's system dates from 1873, when Hallidie demonstrated his first car on Clay Street. It's said that no one was brave enough to operate the car back down Nob Hill, so the inventor took the helm himself, guiding the car safely back to the base of Portsmouth Plaza (now Square) at Kearny Street. Historians have pointed out that without cable cars the city's hills might well have been leveled, or at least reduced in height, as happened in Manhattan and other urban areas that expanded before the cars were invented. As it turned out, the cars made previously uninhabited or sparsely populated crests a magnet for the wealthy. The rich folk on Nob Hill built their own line, the California Street leg, in operation to this day, to convey them between the Financial District and their mansions.

The heyday of cable cars was the two decades after their introduction. At the dawn of the 20th century, 500 cable cars zipped along a network of more than 100 mi. Today a few dozen cars travel on three lines, and the network covers just 9½ mi. Most of the cars date from the 1800s, though the cars and lines had a complete overhaul during the early 1980s and the cables are replaced every three to six months. Hallidie, who was considered a civic hero in his day, fittingly has his name on the Hallidie Building, an innovative skyscraper built in 1918.

— Daniel Mangin

❻ TIX Bay Area. This excellent service provides half-price day-of-performance tickets (cash or traveler's checks only) to all types of performing arts events, as well as regular full-price box office services for theater, concerts, clubs, and sporting events (credit cards accepted). Telephone reservations are not accepted for half-price tickets. Half-price tickets for Sunday and Monday events are sold on Saturday. Also sold at the booth are Muni Passports and adult Fast Passes for use on the transit system. ✉ *Stockton St. between Geary and Post Sts., Union Square,* ☎ *415/433–7827,* WEB *www.theatrebayarea.org.* ⊙ *Tues.–Thurs. 11– 6, Fri.–Sat. 11–7.*

❺ Union Square. The heart of San Francisco's downtown since 1850, the 2½-acre square takes its name from the violent pro-union demonstrations staged here prior to the Civil War. At center stage, the *Victory Monument,* by Robert Ingersoll Aitken, commemorates Commodore George Dewey's victory over the Spanish fleet at Manila in 1898. The 97-ft Corinthian column, topped by a bronze figure symbolizing naval conquest, was dedicated by Theodore Roosevelt in 1903 and withstood the 1906 earthquake. After the earthquake and fire of 1906, the square was dubbed "Little St. Francis" because of the temporary shelter erected for residents of the St. Francis Hotel. Actor John Barrymore, the grandfather of actress Drew Barrymore and a notorious carouser, was among the guests pressed into volunteering to stack bricks in the square. His uncle, thespian John Drew, remarked, "It took an act of God to get John out of bed and the United States army to get him to work."

Completely renovated in 2002, the once dowdy square now has an open-air stage and central plaza, an outdoor café, gardens, and a visitor information booth. Four sculptures by the artist R. M. Fischer preside over the space, which fills daily with a familiar kaleidoscope of characters: office workers sunning and brown-bagging, street musicians, the occasional preacher, and a fair share of homeless people. Union Square covers a convenient but costly four-level underground garage. For cheaper parking try the nearby Sutter-Stockton Garage. ✉ *Between Powell, Stockton, Post, and Geary Sts., Union Square.*

❹ Westin St. Francis Hotel. The second-oldest hotel in the city, established in 1904, was conceived by railroad baron and financier Charles Crocker and his associates as a hostelry for their millionaire friends. Swift service and sumptuous surroundings—glass chandeliers, a gilt ceiling, and marble columns—have always been hallmarks of the property. After the hotel was ravaged by the 1906 fire, a larger, more luxurious Italian Renaissance–style residence was opened in 1907 to attract loyal clients from among the world's rich and powerful. The hotel's checkered past includes the ill-fated 1921 bash in the suite of the silent-film comedian Fatty Arbuckle, at which a woman became ill and later died. Arbuckle endured three sensational trials for rape and murder before being acquitted, by which time his career was kaput. In 1975 Sara Jane Moore, standing among a crowd outside the hotel, attempted to shoot then-president Gerald R. Ford. As might be imagined, no plaques in the lobby commemorate these events. The ever-helpful staff will, however, direct you to tea (daily from 3 to 5) or champagne and caviar in the **Compass Rose** (☎ 415/774–0167) lounge. Elaborate Chinese screens, secluded seating alcoves, and soothing background music make this an ideal rest stop after frantic shopping or sightseeing. Reservations are not required, but walk-ins should expect a wait during December and on weekends. ✉ *335 Powell St., at Geary St., Union Square,* ☎ *415/397–7000,* WEB *www.westin.com.*

SOUTH OF MARKET (SOMA) AND THE EMBARCADERO

Key players in San Francisco's arts scene migrated to the area south of Market Street along the waterfront and west to the Mission District in the 1990s. At the heart of the action in this area, known as SoMa, are the San Francisco Museum of Modern Art (SFMOMA) and the Center for the Arts at Yerba Buena Gardens.

SoMa was once known as South of the Slot, in reference to the cable car slot that ran up Market Street. Ever since gold-rush miners set up their tents in 1848, SoMa has played a major role in housing immigrants to the city; except for a brief flowering of elegance during the mid-19th century, these streets were reserved for newcomers who couldn't yet afford to move to another neighborhood. Industry took over most of the area when the 1906 earthquake collapsed most of the homes into their quicksand bases.

SoMa's emergence as a focal point of San Francisco's cultural life was more than three decades in the making. Huge sections of the then industrial neighborhood were razed in the 1960s to make way for an ambitious multiuse redevelopment project, but squabbling over zoning and other issues delayed construction well into the 1970s. In the meantime, alternative artists and the gay leather crowd set up shop. A dozen bars frequented by the latter group existed alongside warehouses, small factories, and art studios. Although many artists moved farther southwest within SoMa or to the Mission District when urban renewal began in earnest, they still show their work at the Center for the Arts at Yerba Buena Gardens and other galleries.

Today the gentrified South Park area, not long ago the buzzing epicenter of new-media activity, has lost much of its new-economy luster, but the recent influx of money from the cyber heyday has changed the face of SoMa forever. Despite the dot-com meltdown, the construction of pricey live-work lofts and major new commercial ventures continues apace, causing many to scratch their heads in wonder. Glitzy projects like the Four Seasons Hotel and residential complex coexist uneasily with still-gritty stretches of Mission and Market streets. This juxtaposition creates a friction that keeps the neighborhood interesting.

Numbers in the text correspond to numbers in the margin and on the Downtown San Francisco map.

A Good Walk

The **San Francisco Museum of Modern Art** ⑬ dominates a half block of 3rd Street between Howard and Mission streets. Use the crosswalk near SFMOMA's entrance to head across 3rd Street into Yerba Buena Gardens. To your right after you've walked a few steps, a sidewalk leads to the main entrance of the **Center for the Arts** ⑭. Straight ahead is the East Garden of Yerba Buena Gardens and beyond that, on the 4th Street side of the block, is the **Metreon** ⑮ entertainment, retail, and restaurant complex. A second-level walkway in the southern portion of the East Garden, above the Martin Luther King Jr. waterfall, arches over Howard Street, leading to the main (south) entrance to **Moscone Convention Center** ⑯ and the **Rooftop@Yerba Buena Gardens** ⑰ facilities. Exit the rooftop near Folsom Street, cross 4th Street, turn left, walk half a block to Folsom Street, turn right, and go one block to the **Seymour Pioneer Museum.** ⑱.

Head back up 4th Street to Mission Street and walk east on Mission (toward SFMOMA) past the monolithic San Francisco Marriott, also known as the "jukebox" Marriott because of its exterior design. Just before St. Patrick's Catholic Church, which hosts a notable chamber-music series, turn left onto the pedestrian walkway Yerba Buena Lane, due to open late in 2002, past a water course, shops, and restaurants to the plaza on Market Street at the foot of Grant Avenue. (Also scheduled to open on this block of Mission Street in late 2003 are the new Mexican Museum and Magnes Museum.) Head east up Market Street to where 3rd, Market, Kearny, and Geary streets converge. In the traffic triangle here stands historic **Lotta's Fountain.** Walk south on 3rd Street to Mission Street; a half block east on Mission is the headquarters of the **California Historical Society** ⑲. Across the street and a few steps farther east is the **Cartoon Art Museum** ⑳.

Continue east on Mission Street and turn left up New Montgomery Street to Market Street and the **Palace Hotel** ㉑. Enter via the Market Street entrance, checking out the Pied Piper Bar, Garden Court restaurant, and main lobby. Exit via the lobby onto New Montgomery Street and make a left, which will bring you back up to Market Street. Turn right and you'll see several unusual **Market Street buildings** as you walk to the waterfront. Toward the end of Market a three-tier pedestrian mall connects the five buildings of the **Embarcadero Center** ㉒ office-retail complex. Embarcadero 5, at the very end of Market Street, houses the **Hyatt Regency Hotel** ㉓. On the waterfront side of the hotel is Justin Herman Plaza, home in winter to the Kristi Yamaguchi Embarcadero Center Ice Rink.

Across the busy Embarcadero roadway from the plaza stands the port's trademark, the **Ferry Building** ㉔. Near here slithers a portion of the 5-ft-wide, 2½-mi-long glass-and-concrete Promenade Ribbon, which spans the waterfront from the base of Telegraph Hill past the Ferry Building to the South Beach area.

The ground floor of the ornate 1889 Audiffred Building, on the southwest corner of the Embarcadero and Mission Street, houses Boulevard restaurant. Head west on Mission Street along the side of Boulevard and cross Steuart Street. In the middle of the block is the entrance to the historic sections of **Rincon Center** ㉕, worth seeing for the famous murals and the old Rincon Annex Post Office. Continue south within the center to its newer portions and make a left as you exit through the doors near Chalkers Billiards. Across Steuart Street you'll see the Jewish Community Federation Building, which houses the **Magnes Museum** ㉖.

If you need a drink after all this walking, pop into the plush but welcoming bar at the Harbor Court Hotel at 165 Steuart, a few doors south of the Magnes Museum, or continue south on Steuart and then the Embarcadero to Harrison Street and the cheerily postmodern Gordon Biersch Brewing Co. restaurant and microbrewery, perched under the Bay Bridge. In the center island of the Embarcadero across from Gordon Biersch you can catch the N–Judah light-rail train, which winds around the Embarcadero and up Market Street.

OFF THE
BEATEN PATH
F-LINE TROLLEYS – Giving the cable cars a run for their money as San Francisco's best-loved mode of transportation is the F-line, the city's system of vintage electric trolleys. The F-line sends beautifully restored streetcars—some dating from the 19th century—from the Castro all the way down Market Street to the Embarcadero, and since 2000, north to Fisherman's Wharf. Each car is unique, restored to the original colors of the cities that operated them, from New Orleans and Philadelphia, Moscow and Milan. These charming trolleys of long ago have become so popular that there's talk of extending the line all the way to Fort Mason. Purchase tickets ($1) onboard. For information visit WEB www.streetcar.org.

TIMING

The walk above takes a good two hours, more if you visit the museums and galleries. SFMOMA merits about two hours; the Center for the Arts and the Cartoon Art Museum, 45 minutes each.

Sights to See

⑲ California Historical Society. The society, founded in 1871, administers a vast repository of Californiana—500,000 photographs, 150,000 manuscripts, thousands of books, periodicals, and paintings as well as gold-rush paraphernalia. The airy sky-lit space has a central gallery, two adjacent galleries, the North Baker Research Library (accessible by appointment only), and a well-stocked bookstore. ⊠ *678 Mission St., South of Market,* ☎ *415/357–1848,* WEB *www.californiahistoricalsociety.org.* ▨ *$3, free 1st Tues. of month.* ⊙ *Tues.–Sat. 11–5 (galleries close between exhibitions).*

⑳ Cartoon Art Museum. Krazy Kat, Zippy the Pinhead, Batman, and other colorful cartoon icons greet you at the Cartoon Art Museum. In addition to a 12,000-piece permanent collection (only a small selection of which is on display), a 3,000-volume library, and a CD-ROM gallery, changing exhibits examine everything from the impact of underground comics to the output of women and African-American cartoonists. The museum store carries many books on popular and underground strips and animated movies and a tempting selection of toys and gifts. ⊠ *655 Mission St., South of Market,* ☎ *415/227–8666,* WEB *www.cartoonart.org.* ▨ *$5 (pay what you wish 1st Thurs. of month).* ⊙ *Tues.–Fri. 11–5, Sat. 10–5, Sun. 1–5.*

⑭ Center for the Arts. The dance, music, theater, visual arts, films, and videos presented at this facility in Yerba Buena Gardens range from the community-based to the international and lean toward the cutting edge. At the outdoor performance stage there's often music at midday from April through October. ⊠ *701 Mission St., South of Market,* ☎ *415/978–2787,* WEB *www.yerbabuenaarts.org.* ▨ *Galleries $6, free 1st Tues. of month 5 PM–8 PM.* ⊙ *Galleries and box office Tues.–Wed. and weekends 11–6, Thurs.–Fri. 11–8.*

㉒ Embarcadero Center. John Portman designed this five-block complex built during the 1970s and early 1980s. Shops and restaurants abound on the first three levels; there's ample office space on the floors above. Louise Nevelson's 54-ft-high black-steel sculpture, *Sky Tree,* stands guard over Building 3 and is among 20-plus artworks throughout the center. ⊠ *Clay St. between Battery St. (Embarcadero 1) and the Embarcadero (Embarcadero 5), Embarcadero,* ☎ *415/772–0734,* WEB *www.embarcaderocenter.com.*

NEED A
BREAK?

On sunny days **Justin Herman Plaza** (⊠ Market St. and the Embarcadero, east of Embarcadero 5) is a nice place to enjoy a snack from one of Embarcadero Center's dozen or so take-out shops. The plaza plays host to arts-and-crafts shows, street performers, and skateboarders on weekends year-round (almost daily in summer). The Kristi Yamaguchi Embarcadero Center Ice Rink, named for the Olympic gold medalist from San Francisco, is set up during winter.

㉔ Ferry Building. The beacon of the port area, erected in 1896, has a 230-ft clock tower modeled after the campanile of the cathedral in Seville, Spain. On April 18, 1906, the four great clock faces on the tower, powered by the swinging of a 14-ft pendulum, stopped at 5:17—the moment the great earthquake struck—and stayed still for 12 months. Renovated in 2002 to the tune of $70 million, the Ferry Building now has a skylit market hall on street level bustling with restaurants, cafés, and local-food purveyors. A waterfront promenade that extends from the piers on the north side of the building south to the Bay Bridge is great for jogging, in-line skating, watching sailboats on the bay, or enjoying a picnic. Ferries behind the building sail to Sausalito, Larkspur, Tiburon, and the East Bay. ⊠ *The Embarcadero at the foot of Market St., Embarcadero.*

㉓ Hyatt Regency Hotel. John Portman designed this hotel noted for its 17-story hanging garden. Christmas is the best time to see it, when strands of tiny white lights hang down above the lobby starting at the 12th floor. The four glass elevators facing the lobby are fun to ride, unless you suffer from vertigo. Head all the way up to the hotel's revolving restaurant, Equinox, for the best show in town—the 360° view. The Hyatt played a starring role in the 1970s disaster movie *The Towering Inferno.* ⊠ *Embarcadero 5, Embarcadero,* ☎ *415/788–1234,* WEB *www.hyatt.com.*

OFF THE BEATEN PATH	**SS JEREMIAH O'BRIEN –** A participant in the D-Day landing in Normandy during World War II, this Liberty Ship freighter is one of two such vessels (out of 2,500 built) still in working order. To keep the 1943 ship in sailing shape, the steam engine (which appears in the film *Titanic*) is operated dockside seven times a year on special "steaming weekends." Cruises take place twice a year, in May and October. The ship is docked at Pier 45. ⊠ *Pier 45, Embarcadero,* ☎ *415/441–3101,* WEB *www.ssjeremiahobrien.com.* ☒ *$6.* ☉ *Daily 9–5.*

Lotta's Fountain. San Franciscans gather each April 18, the anniversary of the 1906 earthquake, at this quirky monument, given in 1875 to the city by entertainer Lotta Crabtree. The exploits of this Madonna prototype so enthralled San Francisco's early population of miners that they were known to shower her with gold nuggets and silver dollars after her performances. The fountain, whose peculiar and a bit clunky design she had a hand in, was her way of saying thanks to her fans. After years of neglect, the fountain has finally been restored to its original condition. Lotta Crabtree is depicted in one of the Anton Refregier murals in Rincon Center. ⊠ *Traffic triangle at intersection of 3rd, Market, Kearny, and Geary Sts., Union Square.*

㉖ The Magnes Museum. The exhibits at this small museum survey Jewish art, history, and culture. Call ahead before visiting; the museum sometimes closes between exhibits. In late 2003 the museum plans to move into its new, state-of-the-art, Daniel Libeskind–designed quarters South of Market, on Mission Street between 3rd and 4th streets. ⊠ *121 Steuart St., Embarcadero,* ☎ *415/788–9990,* WEB *www.magnesmuseum.org.* ☒ *$5, free 1st Mon. of month.* ☉ *Sun.–Thurs. noon–5.*

Market Street buildings. Market Street, which bisects the city at an angle, has consistently challenged San Francisco's architects. One of the most intriguing responses to this challenge sits diagonally across Market Street from the Palace Hotel. The tower of the **Hobart Building** (⊠ 582 Market St., Financial District) combines a flat facade and oval sides and is considered one of Willis Polk's best works in the city. East on Market Street is another classic solution, Charles Havens's triangular **Flatiron Building** (⊠ 540–548 Market St., Financial District). Farther on at **388 Market** is a sleek modern variation on the flatiron theme by Skidmore, Owings, and Merrill. Holding its own against the skyscrapers that tower over this intersection is the **Donahue Monument** (⊠ Market and Battery Sts., Financial District). This homage to waterfront mechanics, which survived the 1906 earthquake (a famous photograph shows Market Street in ruins around the sculpture), was designed by Douglas Tilden, a noted California sculptor who was hearing impaired. The plaque below the monument marks the spot as the location of the San Francisco Bay shoreline in 1848. ☒ *Market St. between New Montgomery and Beale Sts., Financial District.*

🐚 ⓭ **Metreon.** Child's play meets the 21st century at this Sony entertainment center with interactive play areas based on books like Maurice Sendak's *Where the Wild Things Are* and a three-screen, three-dimensional installation that illustrates principles discussed in architect David Macauley's *The Way Things Work.* In the Digital Solutions shop you can access the Internet for free. There are also a 15-screen multiplex, an IMAX theater, retail shops, and outposts of some of the city's favorite restaurants. ☒ *4th St. between Mission and Howard Sts., South of Market,* ☎ *800/638–7366,* WEB *www.metreon.com.*

⓰ **Moscone Convention Center.** The site of the 1984 Democratic convention, Moscone is distinguished by a contemporary glass-and-girder lobby at street level (all convention exhibit space is underground) and a column-free interior. An expansion of the center is scheduled for completion in late 2003. ☒ *Howard St. between 3rd and 4th Sts., South of Market.* WEB *www.moscone.com.*

⓴ **Palace Hotel.** The city's oldest hotel, a Sheraton property, opened in 1875. Fire destroyed the original Palace following the 1906 earthquake despite the hotel's 28,000-gallon reservoir fed by four artesian wells; the current building dates from 1909. President Warren Harding died at the Palace while still in office in 1923, and the body of King Kalakaua of Hawaii spent a night chilling here after he died in San Francisco in 1891. The managers play up this ghoulish past with talk of a haunted guest room. San Francisco City Guides offers free **guided tours** (☎ 415/557–4266) of the hotel's grand interior. You'll see the glass-dome Garden Court restaurant, mosaic-tile floors in Oriental rug designs, and Maxfield Parrish's wall-size painting *The Pied Piper,* the centerpiece of the Pied Piper Bar. Glass cases off the main lobby contain memorabilia of the hotel's glory days. ☒ *2 New Montgomery St., South of Market,* ☎ *415/512–1111,* WEB *www.sfpalace.com.* ☉ *Tours Tues. and Sat. at 10* AM, *Thurs. at 2* PM.

㉕ **Rincon Center.** A sheer five-story column of water resembling a minirainstorm is the centerpiece of the indoor arcade at this mostly modern office-retail complex. The lobby of the streamline moderne–style former post office on the Mission Street side contains a Works Project Administration **mural by Anton Refregier.** The 27 panels depict California life from the days when Native Americans were the state's sole inhabitants through World War I. Completion of this significant work was interrupted by World War II and political infighting. The latter led to some alteration in Refregier's "radical" historical interpretations; they exuded too much populist sentiment for some of the politicians who opposed the artist. A permanent exhibit below the murals contains photographs and artifacts of life in the Rincon area in the 1800s. ☒ *Between Steuart, Spear, Mission, and Howard Sts., South of Market.*

★ 🐚 ⓱ **Rooftop@Yerba Buena Gardens.** Fun is the order of the day among these brightly colored concrete and corrugated-metal buildings atop Moscone Convention Center South. The historic **Looff carousel** ($2 for two rides) that originally graced San Francisco's beloved Playland at the Beach twirls from Sunday through Friday between 10 and 6, Saturday between 10 and 8. South of the carousel is **Zeum** (☎ 415/777–2800, WEB www. zeum.org), a high-tech interactive arts and technology center ($7) geared to children ages eight and over. Kids can make Claymation videos, work in a computer lab, and view exhibits and performances. Zeum is open in summer from Wednesday through Sunday between 11 and 5, in winter on weekends and school holidays from 11 to 5. Also part of the rooftop complex are gardens, an ice-skating rink, and a bowling alley. ⊠ *4th St. between Howard and Folsom Sts., South of Market.*

OFF THE BEATEN PATH	**SEA CHANGE** – The 10-ton, 70-ft-tall *Sea Change* sculpture, a bright red steel work with a crown that moves gracefully in the wind, soars above South Beach Park. The artist, Mark di Suvero, came to San Francisco in 1941 as an eight-year-old immigrant from Shanghai—his father was a naval attaché for the Italian government—and later worked as a welder on the city's waterfront. A half block southwest of the sculpture is Pacific Bell Park, opened in April 2000 as the new home of the San Francisco Giants baseball team. ⊠ *The Embarcadero near Townsend St., South of Market.*

★ ⑬ **San Francisco Museum of Modern Art (SFMOMA).** Mario Botta designed the striking SFMOMA facility, completed in early 1995, which consists of a sienna brick facade and a central tower of alternating bands of black and white stone. Inside, natural light from the tower floods the central atrium and some of the museum's galleries. A black-and-gray stone staircase leads from the atrium to four floors of galleries. Works by Matisse, Picasso, O'Keeffe, Kahlo, Pollock, and Warhol form the heart of the diverse permanent collection. The photography holdings are also strong. The adventurous programming includes traveling exhibits and multimedia installations. The café, accessible from the street, provides a comfortable, reasonably priced refuge for drinks and light meals. ⊠ *151 3rd St., South of Market,* ☎ *415/357–4000,* WEB *www.sfmoma.org.* ⌦ *$10, free 1st Tues. of each month, ½-price Thurs. 6–9.* ◷ *Memorial Day–Labor Day, Fri.–Tues. 10–6, Thurs. 10–9; Labor Day–Memorial Day, Fri.–Tues. 11–6, Thurs. 11–9.*

⑱ **Seymour Pioneer Museum.** Opened in 2000, this small museum brings California history to life through exhibits focusing on landmark events in the state's history, such as the Panama-Pacific Exhibition of 1915. Displays include photographs, film, and paintings belonging to the Society of California Pioneers, which founded the museum. A research library and photography archives are available by appointment. The museum closes between exhibits, mid-December–March. ⊠ *300 4th St., South of Market,* ☎ *415/957–1849,* WEB *www.californiapioneers.org.* ⌦ *$3.* ◷ *Mar.–mid-Dec., Tues.–Fri. and the 1st Sat. of the month 10–4.*

★ **Yerba Buena Gardens.** The centerpiece of the SoMa redevelopment area, these two blocks encompass the Center for the Arts, Metreon, Moscone Center, and the Rooftop@Yerba Buena Gardens. A circular walkway lined with benches and sculptures surrounds the East Garden, a large patch of green amid this visually stunning complex. The waterfall memorial to Martin Luther King Jr. is the focal point of the East Garden. Powerful streams of water surge over large, jagged stone columns, mirroring the enduring force of King's words that are carved on the stone walls and on glass blocks behind the waterfall. Above the memorial are two restaurants and an overhead walkway to Moscone Convention Center's main entrance. ⊠ *Between 3rd, 4th, Mission, and Folsom Sts., South of Market.* ◷ *Daily sunrise–10 PM.* WEB *www. yerbabuena.org.*

THE HEART OF THE BARBARY COAST

"The slums of Singapore at their foulest, the dens of Shanghai at their dirtiest, the waterfront of Port Said at its vicious worst—none of these backwaters of depravity and vice . . . achieved the depths of utter corruption that typified the 'Barbary Coast.' " So screamed the breathless dust jacket of Herbert Asbury's 1933 account of San Francisco's days as a brawling, extravagant upstart of a town in the latter half of the 19th century.

It was on Montgomery Street, in the Financial District, that Sam Brannan proclaimed the historic gold discovery that took place at Sutter's Mill on January 24, 1848. The gold rush brought streams of people from across America and Europe, transforming the onetime frontier town into a cosmopolitan city almost overnight. The population of San Francisco jumped from a mere 800 in 1848 to more than 25,000 in 1850 and to nearly 150,000 in 1870. Along with the prospectors came many other fortune seekers. Saloon keepers, gamblers, and prostitutes all flocked to the so-called Barbary Coast (now Jackson Square and the Financial District). Underground dance halls, casinos, bordellos, and palatial homes sprung up as the city grew into a world-class metropolis. Along with the quick money came a wave of violence. In 1852 the city suffered an average of two murders and one major fire each day. Diarists commented that hardly a day would pass without bloodshed in the city's estimated 500 bars and 1,000 gambling dens, and "houses of ill repute" proliferated.

By 1917 the excesses of the Barbary Coast had fallen victim to the Red-Light Abatement Act and the ire of church leaders—the wild era was over, and the young city was forced to grow up. Since then the redlight establishments have edged upward to the Broadway strip of North Beach, and Jackson Square evolved into a sedate district of refurbished brick buildings decades ago. Only one remnant of the era remains. Below Montgomery Street between California Street and Broadway, underlying many building foundations along the former waterfront area (long since filled in), lay at least 100 ships abandoned by frantic crews and passengers caught up in gold fever.

Numbers in the text correspond to numbers in the margin and on the Downtown San Francisco map.

A Good Walk

Bronze sidewalk plaques mark the street corners along the 50-sight, approximately 3¾-mi Barbary Coast Trail. The trail begins at the Old Mint, at 5th and Mission streets, and runs north through downtown, Chinatown, Jackson Square, North Beach, and Fisherman's Wharf, ending at Aquatic Park. For information about the sites on the trail, pick up a brochure at the San Francisco Visitor Information Center (☞ Union Square Area, *above*).

To catch the highlights of the Barbary Coast Trail and a glimpse of a few important Financial District structures, start at Montgomery and Market streets (above the Montgomery BART/Muni station). Walk east on Market Street toward the Ferry Building to Sansome Street and turn left. At 155 Sansome Street is the Stock Exchange Tower. Around the corner (to the left) on Pine Street is the **Pacific Stock Exchange** ㉗ building. Continue north on Sansome. Turn left on California and right on Montgomery Street. Between California and Sacramento streets is the **Wells Fargo Bank History Museum** ㉘.

Two blocks north on Montgomery from the Wells Fargo museum stands the **Transamerica Pyramid** ㉙, between Clay and Washington streets. A tranquil redwood grove graces the east side of the pyramid. Walk through it, and you'll exit on Washington Street, across which you can see Hotaling Place to your left. Walk west (left) to the corner, cross Washington Street, and walk back to Hotaling. This historic alley is your entrance to **Jackson Square** ㉚, the heart of the Barbary Coast.

Of particular note here are the former A. P. Hotaling whiskey distillery, on the corner of Hotaling Place, and the 1850s structures around the corner in the **700 block of Montgomery Street.** To see these buildings, walk west on Jackson from the distillery and make a left on Montgomery. Continue south on Montgomery to Washington Street, make a right, and cross Columbus Avenue. Head north (to the right) up Columbus to the **San Francisco Brewing Company** ㉛, the last standing saloon of the Barbary Coast era and a place overflowing with freshly brewed beers and history.

TIMING

Two hours should be enough time to see everything on this tour—unless you plan on trying all the homemade beers at the San Francisco Brewing Company. The Wells Fargo museum (open only on weekdays) deserves a half hour. Evenings and weekends are peaceful times to admire the area's distinctive architecture. If you want to see activity, go on a weekday around lunchtime.

Sights to See

㉚ **Jackson Square.** Here was the heart of the Barbary Coast of the Gay '90s. Though most of the red-light district was destroyed in the 1906 fire, old redbrick buildings and narrow alleys recall the romance and rowdiness of the early days. Some of the city's earliest business buildings, survivors of the 1906 quake, still stand in Jackson Square, between Montgomery and Sansome streets.

By the end of World War II most of the 19th-century brick structures had fallen on hard times. But in 1951 a group of preservation-minded designers and furniture wholesale dealers selected the area for their showrooms, turning Jackson Square into the interior design center of the West. In 1972 the city officially designated the area—bordered by Columbus Avenue on the west, Broadway and Pacific Avenue on the north, Washington Street on the south, and Sansome Street on the east—San Francisco's first historic district. When property values soared, many of the fabric and furniture outlets fled to Potrero Hill. Advertising agencies, attorneys, and antiques dealers now occupy the Jackson Square–area structures. Restored 19th-century brick buildings line Hotaling Place, which connects Washington and Jackson streets. The lane is named for the head of the **A. P. Hotaling Company whiskey distillery** (✉ 451 Jackson St., at Hotaling Pl., Financial District), which was the largest liquor repository on the West Coast in its day. The Italianate Hotaling building reveals little of its infamous past, but a plaque on the side of the structure repeats a famous query about its surviving the quake: IF, AS THEY SAY, GOD SPANKED THE TOWN FOR BEING OVER FRISKY, WHY DID HE BURN THE CHURCHES DOWN AND SAVE HOTALING'S WHISKEY?

The **Ghirardelli Chocolate Factory** once occupied 415 Jackson Street. Domenico Ghirardelli moved his growing business and his family into this property in 1857 (it was quite common for the upper floors of these buildings to be used as flats by owners and tenants). By 1894 the enterprise had become large enough to necessitate the creation of what's now **Ghirardelli Square,** near Fisherman's Wharf.

With the gentrification, it takes a bit of conjuring to evoke the Barbary Coast days when viewing the gold-rush–era buildings in the **700 block of Montgomery Street.** But much happened here. Writer Bret Harte wrote his novel *The Luck of Roaring Camp* at No. 730. He toiled as a typesetter for the spunky *golden-era* newspaper, which occupied No. 732 (now part of the building at No. 744). The late ambulance-chaser extraordinaire, lawyer Melvin Belli, had offices in Nos. 722–728. The lawyer's headquarters were in the former Melodeon Theater at No. 722, where Lotta Crabtree—she of Lotta's Fountain fame—performed. ⊠ *Jackson Square district: between Broadway and Washington and Montgomery and Sansome Sts., Financial District.*

㉗ Pacific Stock Exchange. Ralph Stackpole's monumental 1930 granite sculptural groups, *Earth's Fruitfulness* and *Man's Inventive Genius,* flank this imposing structure, which dates from 1915. The Stock Exchange Tower, around the corner at 155 Sansome Street, is a 1930 modern classic by architects Miller and Pfleuger, with an art deco gold ceiling and a black marble wall entry. ⊠ *301 Pine St., Financial District,* WEB *www.pacificex.com.*

㉛ San Francisco Brewing Company. Built in 1907, this pub looks like a museum piece from the Barbary Coast days. An old upright piano sits in the corner under the original stained-glass windows. Take a seat at the mahogany bar and look down at the white-tile spittoon. In an adjacent room look for the handmade copper brewing kettle used to produce a dozen beers—with names like Pony Express—by means of old-fashioned gravity-flow methods. ⊠ *155 Columbus Ave., North Beach,* ☏ *415/434–3344,* WEB *www.sfbrewing.com.*

㉙ Transamerica Pyramid. The city's most photographed high-rise is the 853-ft Transamerica Pyramid. Designed by William Pereira and Associates in 1972, the initially controversial icon has become more acceptable to most locals over time. A fragrant redwood grove along the east side of the building, replete with benches and a cheerful fountain, is a placid patch in which to unwind. Inside, the tony Redwood Park restaurant offers respite of a more luxurious kind. ⊠ *600 Montgomery St., Financial District,* WEB *www.tapyramid.com.*

㉘ Wells Fargo Bank History Museum. There were no formal banks in San Francisco during the early years of the gold rush, and miners often entrusted their gold dust to saloon keepers. In 1852 Wells Fargo opened its first bank in the city, and the company established banking offices in the mother-lode camps, using stagecoaches and pony express riders to service the burgeoning state. (California's population boomed from 15,000 to 200,000 between 1848 and 1852.) The museum displays samples of nuggets and gold dust from mines, a mural-size map of the Mother Lode, original art by western artists Charles M. Russell and Maynard Dixon, mementos of the poet bandit Black Bart ("Po8," as he signed his poems), and an old telegraph machine on which you can practice sending codes. The showpiece is the red Concord stagecoach, the likes of which carried passengers from St. Joseph, Missouri, to San Francisco in three weeks during the 1850s. ⊠ *420 Montgomery St., Financial District,* ☏ *415/396–2619.* 🎟 *Free.* ☺ *Weekdays 9–5.*

OFF THE BEATEN PATH | **BANK OF AMERICA BUILDING –** This 52-story polished red granite–and-marble building takes up nearly an entire downtown block. A massive, abstract black-granite sculpture designed by the Japanese artist Masayuki commands the corner of the complex at Kearny and California streets. The work has been dubbed "The Banker's Heart" by local wags. On top of the building is the **Carnelian Room** (☏ 415/433–7500), a chic cocktail lounge and restaurant—open weekdays from 3 to 11, weekends from 3 to midnight, and for Sunday brunch from 10 to 2—with a view of the city and the bay. This is a perfect spot for a sunset drink; until mid-afternoon the room is the exclusive Banker's Club, open only to members or by invitation. ⊠ *Between California, Pine, Montgomery, and Kearny Sts., Financial District.*

CHINATOWN

Prepare to have your senses assaulted in Chinatown. Pungent smells waft out of restaurants, fish markets, and produce stands. Good-luck banners of crimson and gold hang beside dragon-entwined lampposts, pagoda roofs, and street signs with Chinese calligraphy. Honking cars chime in with shoppers bargaining loudly in Cantonese or Mandarin. Add to this the sight of millions of Chinese-theme goods spilling out of the shops along Grant Avenue, and you get an idea of what Chinatown is all about.

Bordered roughly by Bush, Kearny, and Powell streets and Broadway, Chinatown has one of the largest Chinese communities outside Asia. The area is tightly packed, mostly because housing discrimination in the past kept residents from moving outside Chinatown. There was nowhere to go but up and down—thus the many basement establishments in the neighborhood. The two main drags of Chinatown are Grant Avenue, jammed with kitschy tourist shops, and Stockton Street, where the locals do business.

Many of Chinatown's earliest residents came from southern China, and they brought their cuisine with them. Nowadays Cantonese cooking exists alongside spicier Szechuan, Hunan, and Mandarin specialties. In the windows of markets on Stockton Street and Grant Avenue you can see roast ducks hanging, fish and shellfish swimming in tanks, and strips of Chinese-style barbecued pork shining in pink glaze.

Merely strolling through Chinatown and its many bazaars, restaurants, and curio shops yields endless pleasures, but you'll have a better chance of experiencing an authentic bit of one of the world's oldest cultures by venturing off the beaten track. You needn't be shy about stepping into a temple or an herb shop: Chinatown has been a tourist stop since the late 1800s, and most of its residents welcome guests.

You may find the noisy stretches of Grant Avenue and Stockton Street difficult to navigate, especially by car. Park outside the area, as a spot here is extremely hard to find and traffic is impossible.

Numbers in the text correspond to numbers in the margin and on the Downtown San Francisco map.

A Good Walk

The Bus 30–Stockton, which travels north and south on Stockton Street, will get you from downtown or Fisherman's Wharf to Chinatown. While wandering through Chinatown's streets and alleys, don't forget to look up. Above street level, many older structures—mostly brick buildings that replaced rickety wooden ones destroyed during the 1906 earthquake—have ornate balconies and cornices. The architecture in the 900 block of Grant Avenue (at Washington Street) and Waverly Place (west of and parallel to Grant Avenue between Sacramento and Washington streets) is particularly noteworthy, though some locals decry it and similar examples as inauthentic adornment meant to make their neighborhood seem "more Chinese."

Enter Chinatown through the green-tile **Chinatown Gate** ㉜, on Grant Avenue at Bush Street. Shops selling souvenirs, jewelry, and home furnishings line Grant north past the gate. Pop into Dragon House, at No. 455. A veritable museum, the store sells centuries-old antiques rather than six-month-old goods made in Taiwan. **Old St. Mary's Cathedral** ㉝ towers over the corner of Grant Avenue and California Street. Continue on Grant to Clay Street and turn right. A half block down on your left is **Portsmouth Square** ㉞. A walkway on the eastern edge of the park leads over Kearny Street to the third floor of the Holiday Inn, where you'll find the **Chinese Culture Center** ㉟.

Backtrack on the walkway to Portsmouth Square and head west up Washington Street a half block to the **Old Chinese Telephone Exchange** ㊱ (now the Bank of Canton), and then continue west on Washington Street. Cross Grant Avenue and look for Waverly Place a half block up on the left. One of the best examples of this alley's traditional architecture is the **Tin How Temple** ㊲. After visiting Waverly Place and Tin How, walk back to Washington Street. Several herb shops do business in this area. Two worth checking out are Superior Trading Company at No. 839 and the Great China Herb Co. at No. 857. These Chinese pharmacies carry everything from tree roots and bark to over-the-counter treatments for impotence.

Across Washington Street from Superior is Ross Alley. Head north on Ross toward Jackson Street, stopping along the way to watch the bakers at the **Golden Gate Fortune Cookies Co.** ㊳. Turn right on Jackson. When you get to Grant Avenue, don't cross it. For some of Chinatown's best pastries, turn left and stop by No. 1029, the Golden Gate Bakery, where the moon cakes are delicious. The markets in the 1100 block of Grant Avenue carry intriguing delicacies, such as braised pig noses and ears, eels, and all manner of live game birds and fish.

Head west on Pacific Avenue to Stockton Street, turn left, and walk south past Stockton Street's markets. At Clay Street make a right and head halfway up the hill to the **Chinese-American National Museum and Learning Center** ㊴. Return to Stockton Street and make a right; a few doors down is the **Kong Chow Temple** ㊵, and next door is the elaborate **Chinese Six Companies** building.

TIMING

Allow at least two hours to see Chinatown. Brief stops will suffice at the cultural center and temples. The restaurants don't invite lingering, so if you're lunching, a half hour should be adequate unless you choose one of the higher-end places.

Sights to See

㉜ **Chinatown Gate.** The official entrance to Chinatown is a symbolic and literal transition from standard downtown scenes to what sometimes seems like another country altogether. Stone lions flank the base of the pagoda-topped gate. The male lion's right front paw rests playfully on a ball; the female's left front paw tickles a cub lying on its back. The lions and the glazed clay dragons atop the largest of the gate's three pagodas symbolize, among other things, wealth and prosperity. The fish whose mouths wrap tightly around the crest of this pagoda also symbolize prosperity. The four Chinese characters immediately beneath the pagoda represent the philosophy of Sun Yat-sen (1866–1925), the leader who unified China in the early 20th century. Sun Yat-sen, who lived in exile in San Francisco for a few years, promoted the notion of friendship and peace among all nations based on equality, justice, and goodwill. The vertical characters under the left pagoda read "peace" and "trust," the ones under the right pagoda "respect" and "love." ✉ *Grant Ave. at Bush St., Chinatown.*

NEED A BREAK?

Tea belongs to the fabric of Chinese daily life, and some of Chinatown's most delightful (and most accessible) shops proffer the elixir. In the heart of Grant Avenue, step into the **Ten Ren Tea Company** (✉ 949 Grant Ave., near Washington St., Chinatown, ☎ 415/362–0656) for a sample of hot green tea and to browse walls lined with mammoth metal canisters of tea by the pound. They'll even perform a traditional Chinese tea ceremony at a table in the back upon request. Straddling the border of North Beach, the **Imperial Tea Court** (⌧ 1411 Powell St., at Broadway, Chinatown, ☎ 415/788–6080) serves such rare teas as Monkey-Picked Tekuanyin with elegance. Take a seat at one of the heavy wooden tables and check out the gilded Chinese birdcages hanging from the ceiling.

㊴ Chinese-American National Museum and Learning Center. This airy, light-filled gallery has displays about the Chinese-American experience from 19th-century agriculture to 21st-century food and fashion trends, including a poignant collection of racist games and toys. A separate room hosts rotating exhibits by contemporary Chinese-American artists; another describes the building's time as the Chinatown YWCA, which served as a meeting place and residence for Chinese women in need of social services. Julia Morgan, the architect known for the famous Hearst Castle and the first woman in California to be licensed as an architect, designed this handsome redbrick building. ⌧ *965 Clay St., Chinatown,* ☎ *415/391–1188,* WEB *www.chsa.org.* ⌧ *$3.* ☉ *Tues.– Fri. 11–4, weekends noon–4.*

㉟ Chinese Culture Center. The San Francisco Redevelopment Commission agreed to let Holiday Inn build in Chinatown if the chain provided room for a Chinese culture center. Inside the center are the works of Chinese and Chinese-American artists as well as traveling exhibits relating to Chinese culture. Walking tours ($12; make reservations one week ahead) of historic points in Chinatown take place on most days at 10 AM. ⌧ *Holiday Inn, 750 Kearny St., 3rd floor, Chinatown,* ☎ *415/986–1822,* WEB *www.c-c-c.org.* ⌧ *Free.* ☉ *Tues.–Sun. 10–4.*

Chinese Six Companies. Several fine examples of Chinese architecture can be spotted along Stockton Street, but this is the most noteworthy. With its curved roof tiles and elaborate cornices, the imposing structure's oversize pagoda cheerfully calls attention to itself. The business leaders who ran the six companies, which still exist today, dominated Chinatown's political and economic life for decades. ⌧ *843 Stockton St., Chinatown.*

㊳ Golden Gate Fortune Cookies Co. Walk down Ross Alley and you'll likely be invited into this small cookie factory. The workers sit at circular motorized griddles and wait for dollops of batter to drop onto a tiny metal plate, which rotates into an oven. A few moments later out comes a cookie that's pliable and ready for folding. It's easy to peek in for a moment, and hard to leave without a few free samples. A bagful of cookies—with mildly racy "adult" fortunes or more benign ones—costs $2 or $3; personalized fortunes are also available. ⌧ *56 Ross Alley (west of and parallel to Grant Ave. between Washington and Jackson Sts.), Chinatown,* ☎ *415/781–3956.* ☉ *Daily 10–7.*

㊵ Kong Chow Temple. The god to whom the members of this temple pray represents honesty and trust. You'll often see his image in Chinese stores and restaurants because he's thought to bring good luck in business. Chinese immigrants established the temple in 1851; its congregation moved to this building in 1977. Take the elevator up to the fourth floor, where incense fills the air. Your party can show its respect by placing a dollar or two in the donation box. Amid the statuary, flowers, and richly colored altars (red wards off evil spirits and signifies virility, green symbolizes longevity, and gold majesty) are a couple of plaques announcing that MRS. HARRY S. TRUMAN CAME TO THIS TEMPLE IN JUNE 1948 FOR A PREDICTION ON THE OUTCOME OF THE ELECTION . . . THIS FORTUNE CAME TRUE. The temple's balcony has a good view of Chinatown. ⌧ *855 Stockton St., Chinatown,* ☎ *no phone.* ⌧ *Free.* ☉ *Mon.–Sat. 9–4.*

36 **Old Chinese Telephone Exchange.** Most of Chinatown burned down after the 1906 earthquake, and this building set the style for the new Chinatown. The intricate three-tier pagoda was built in 1909. The exchange's operators were renowned for their prodigious memories, about which the San Francisco Chamber of Commerce boasted in 1914: "These girls respond all day with hardly a mistake to calls that are given (in English or one of five Chinese dialects) by the name of the subscriber instead of by his number—a mental feat that would be practically impossible to most high-schooled American misses." ✉ *Bank of Canton, 743 Washington St., Chinatown.*

NEED A BREAK? Dim sum is the Chinese version of a smorgasbord. In most dim sum restaurants women navigating stacked food-service carts patrol the premises. Customers choose dishes and the cost is stamped on the bill. Dim sum is served at the garishly fancy **New Asia** (✉ 772 Pacific Ave., Chinatown, ☎ 415/391–6666) weekdays from 9 AM to 3 PM, weekends from 8:30 AM to 3 PM. More down-to-earth and inexpensive than New Asia, **Kay Cheung Seafood Restaurant** (✉ 615 Jackson St., Chinatown, ☎ 415/989–6838) serves dim sum from 9 AM to 2:30 PM. It's best to arrive at both restaurants before 1 PM for the best selection.

33 **Old St. Mary's Cathedral.** This building, whose structure includes granite quarried in China, was dedicated in 1854 and served as the city's Catholic cathedral until 1891. The church needs to undergo seismic retrofitting or be demolished and is in the process of raising funds for the procedure. Across California Street in **St. Mary's Park,** the late local sculptor Beniamino (Benny) Bufano's 12-ft-tall stainless-steel and rose-color granite statue of Sun Yat-sen towers over the site of the Chinese leader's favorite reading spot during his years in San Francisco. ✉ *Grant Ave. and California St., Chinatown,* WEB *www.oldstmarys.org.*

34 **Portsmouth Square.** Captain John B. Montgomery raised the American flag here in 1846, claiming the area from Mexico. The square—a former potato patch—was the plaza for Yerba Buena, the Mexican settlement that was renamed San Francisco. Robert Louis Stevenson, the author of *Treasure Island,* lived on the edge of Chinatown in the late 19th century and often visited the square, chatting up the sailors who hung out here. Some of the information he gleaned about life at sea found its way into his fiction. Bruce Porter designed the bronze galleon that sits on top of a 9-ft granite shaft in the northwestern corner of the square in honor of the writer. With its pagoda-shape structures, Portsmouth Square is a favorite spot for morning tai chi. By noon dozens of men huddle around Chinese chess tables, engaged in not-always-legal competition. Undercover police occasionally rush in to break things up, but this ritual, like tai chi, is an established way of life. Children scamper about two playgrounds within the square, which has rest room facilities. ✉ *Bordered by Walter Lum Pl. and Kearny, Washington, and Clay Sts., Chinatown.*

★ 37 **Tin How Temple.** Day Ju, one of the first three Chinese to arrive in San Francisco, dedicated this temple to the Queen of the Heavens and the Goddess of the Seven Seas in 1852. Climb three flights of stairs—on the second floor is a mah-jongg parlor whose patrons hope the spirits above will favor them. In the temple's entryway, elderly ladies can often be seen preparing "money" to be burned as offerings to various Buddhist gods or as funds for ancestors to use in the afterlife. Red-and-gold lanterns adorn the ceiling—the larger the lamp the larger its donor's contribution to the temple—and the smell of incense is usually thick. Oranges and other offerings rest on altars to various gods. The gold-leaf wood carving suspended from the ceiling depicts the north and east sides of the sea, which Tin How (Tien Hau or Tien Hou in Cantonese) and other gods protect. A statue of Tin How sits in the middle of the back of the temple, flanked by a red lesser god and by a green one. Photography is not permitted, and visitors are asked not to step onto the balcony. ⊠ *125 Waverly Pl., Chinatown*, ☎ *no phone.* ✉ *Free (donations accepted).* ⊘ *Daily 9–4.*

NORTH BEACH AND TELEGRAPH HILL

Novelist and resident Herbert Gold calls North Beach "the longest-running, most glorious American bohemian operetta outside Greenwich Village." Indeed, to anyone who's spent some time in its eccentric old bars and cafés or wandered the neighborhood, North Beach evokes everything from the Barbary Coast days to the no-less-rowdy beatnik era. Italian bakeries appear frozen in time, homages to Jack Kerouac and Allen Ginsberg pop up everywhere, and the modern equivalent of the Barbary Coast's "houses of ill repute," strip joints, do business on Broadway.

More than 125,000 Italian-American residents once lived in North Beach, but now only about 2,000, most of them elderly, do. Today the neighborhood is largely Chinese, and as neighborhood real-estate prices have escalated, a number of young professionals have moved in as well. But walk down narrow Romolo Place (off Broadway east of Columbus) or Genoa Place (off Union west of Kearny) or Medau Place (off Filbert west of Grant) and you can feel the immigrant Italian roots of this neighborhood. North Beach is still the number one place for cappuccino and biscotti, after which you can pop into that icon of the Beat era, the City Lights Bookstore.

Like Chinatown, this is a neighborhood where eating is unavoidable. Several Italian restaurants specialize in family-style multicourse meals at reasonable prices; other eateries serve pricey nuovo-Italian dishes. Try the focaccia, sold fresh from the oven at places like **Liguria Bakery** (⊠ 1700 Stockton St., at Filbert St., North Beach, ☎ 415/421–3786). Eaten warm or cold, it's the perfect walking food. Many other aromas fill the air: coffee beans, deli meats and cheeses, Italian pastries, and—always—the pungent smell of garlic.

Seafood is usually associated with nearby Fisherman's Wharf, but fishing was North Beach's first industry. The neighborhood truly was a beach at the time of the gold rush—the bay extended into the hollow between Telegraph and Russian hills. Among the first immigrants to Yerba Buena during the early 1840s were young men from the northern provinces of Italy. The Genoese started the fishing industry in the newly renamed boomtown of San Francisco, as well as a much-needed produce business. Later, Sicilians emerged as leaders of the fishing fleets and eventually as proprietors of the seafood restaurants lining Fisherman's Wharf. Meanwhile, their Genoese cousins established banking and manufacturing empires. Less than a square mile, North Beach is the most densely populated district in the city—and among the most cosmopolitan.

Numbers in the text correspond to numbers in the margin and on the Downtown San Francisco map.

A Good Walk

Stand on the northwest corner of Broadway and Columbus Avenue to get your bearings. To the southwest is Chinatown—the Chinatown portion of Grant Avenue intersects Broadway a few steps west of Columbus before changing character completely after it crosses Broadway and

Columbus in North Beach. The Financial District skyscrapers loom overhead to the south of the intersection of Columbus and Broadway, though one of the earliest and shortest examples, the triangular Sentinel Building, where Kearny Street and Columbus Avenue meet at an angle, grabs the eye with its unusual shape and mellow green patina. (The building's owner, filmmaker Francis Ford Coppola, has the penthouse office.)

East across Columbus is the Condor, where in 1964 local celeb Carol Doda became the nation's first dancer at a nightclub to go topless. (These days Doda runs a lingerie shop at 1850 Union Street and the Condor is a sports bar.) Around the same time, North Beach was a nexus of comedy. Bill Cosby, Phyllis Diller, Dick Gregory, the Smothers Brothers, and other talents cut their teeth at clubs like the hungry i and the Purple Onion.

To the north of Broadway and Columbus is the heart of Italian North Beach. A few doors north of the Condor, **Grant Avenue** heads to the north, toward Telegraph Hill. Columbus shoots northwest past Washington Square to Fisherman's Wharf.

Walk southeast across Columbus to **City Lights Bookstore** ㊶, where you can pick up a book by one of the Beat writers. Three of the most atmospheric bars in San Francisco are near here: Vesuvio, across Jack Kerouac Alley from City Lights; Specs, across Columbus from City Lights at 12 William Saroyan Place; and, a few steps south of Specs at 242 Columbus, Tosca, where opera tunes stock the jukebox. For joltingly caffeinated espresso drinks, also to the tune of opera, head north on Columbus a block and a half on the same side of the avenue as City Lights to Caffè Puccini, at No. 411. By now, you've been in North Beach for a couple of hours and hardly gone anywhere. There are sights to see, but relaxing and enjoying life is what North Beach is all about.

Head up the east side of Columbus Avenue (the same side as the Condor) past Grant Avenue. On the northeast corner of Columbus and Vallejo Street is the Victorian-era **St. Francis of Assisi Church** ㊷. Go east on Vallejo Street to Grant Avenue and make another left. Check out the eclectic shops and old-time bars and cafés between Vallejo and Union streets.

Turn left at Union Street and head west. Pick up a delectable, Italian-style treat at **Gelato Classico Italian** (✉ 576 Union St., at Stockton St., North Beach, ☎ 415/391–6667) and continue west to **Washington Square** ㊸, an oasis of green amid the tightly packed streets of North Beach. At Union and Stockton streets is San Francisco's oldest Italian restaurant, Fior d'Italia, which opened in 1886. After the 1906 earthquake and fire, the restaurant operated out of a tent until its new quarters were ready. On the north side of the park, on Filbert, stands the double-turreted **Saints Peter and Paul Catholic Church** ㊹.

After you've had your fill of North Beach, head up **Telegraph Hill** ㊺ from Washington Square. Atop the hill is **Coit Tower** ㊻. People in poor health will not want to attempt the walk up the steep hill; Coit Tower can be reached by car (though parking is very tight) or public transportation—board Muni Bus 39–Coit at Washington Square. To walk, head east up Filbert Street at the park; turn left at Grant Avenue and go one block north, then right at Greenwich Street and ascend the steps on your right. Cross the street at the top of the first set of stairs and continue up the curving stone steps to Coit Tower.

On the other side of Coit Tower, the Greenwich steps take you down the east side of Telegraph Hill, with stunning views of the bay en route. At Montgomery Street, perched on the side of the hill, is **Julius' Castle** ㊼ restaurant. A block to the right at **1360 Montgomery Street,** where the Filbert steps intersect, is a brilliant art deco apartment building. Descend the Filbert steps amid roses, fuchsias, irises, and trumpet flowers—courtesy of Grace Marchant, who labored for nearly 30 years to transform a dump into one of San Francisco's hidden treasures in the 1900s. At the foot of the hill is the serene **Levi Strauss headquarters** ㊽.

TIMING

It takes a little more than an hour to walk the tour, but the point in both North Beach and Telegraph Hill is to linger—set aside at least a few hours.

Sights to See

★ ㊶ **City Lights Bookstore.** Finally designated a city landmark in 2001, the hangout of Beat-era writers—Allen Ginsberg and Lawrence Ferlinghetti among them—remains a vital part of San Francisco's literary scene. Still leftist at heart, in 1999 the store unveiled a replica of a revolutionary mural destroyed in Chiapas, Mexico, by military forces. ✉ *261 Columbus Ave., North Beach,* ☎ *415/362–8193,* WEB *www.citylights.com.*

NEED A BREAK?

Filmmaker Francis Ford Coppola has expanded his wine business to include a North Beach wine bar. Drop by triangular **Café Niebaum-Coppola** (✉ 916 Kearny St., at Columbus Ave., North Beach, ☎ 415/291–1700, WEB www.cafecoppola.com), on the ground floor of Coppola's landmark Sentinel Building, for wines from the Niebaum-Coppola winery in Napa, simple Italian dishes, and gourmet gifts. The man himself can sometimes be spotted at a sidewalk table in the evening.

★ ㊻ **Coit Tower.** Among San Francisco's most distinctive skyline sights, the 210-ft-tall Coit Tower stands as a monument to the city's volunteer firefighters. During the early days of the gold rush, Lillie Hitchcock Coit (known as Miss Lil) was said to have deserted a wedding party and chased down the street after her favorite engine, Knickerbocker No. 5, while clad in her bridesmaid finery. She was soon made an honorary member of the Knickerbocker Company and after that always signed her name as "Lillie Coit 5" in honor of her favorite fire engine. Lillie died in 1929 at the age of 86, leaving the city $125,000 to "expend in an appropriate manner . . . to the beauty of San Francisco."

Inside the tower, 19 depression-era murals depict economic and political life in California. The government commissioned the murals, and the 25 artists who painted them were each paid $38 a week. Some were fresh from art school; others had found no market for art in the early 1930s. The radical Mexican painter Diego Rivera inspired the murals' socialist-realist style, with its biting cultural commentary, particularly about the exploitation of workers. At the time the murals were painted, clashes between management and labor along the waterfront and elsewhere in San Francisco were widespread.

Ride the elevator to the top of the tower to enjoy the view of the San Francisco–Oakland Bay Bridge and the Golden Gate Bridge; due north is famous Alcatraz Island. Artists are often at work in Pioneer Park, at the foot of the tower. For a modest price you can often pick up a small painting of the view you're witnessing. *Discoverer of America,* the impressive bronze statue of Christopher Columbus, was a gift from the local Italian community in 1957. ✉ *Telegraph Hill Blvd., at Greenwich St. or Lombard St., North Beach,* ☎ *415/362–0808.* ✑ *$3.75.* ☉ *Daily 10–6.*

OFF THE
BEATEN PATH

TATTOO ART MUSEUM – Possibly the lowest-brow museum in the city, legendary tattoo artist and historian Lyle Tuttle's collection of tattoo memorabilia fills half his crowded tattoo parlor on the edge of North Beach. Exhibits, including equipment, photographs, newspaper clippings, and a stuffed bat, range from primitive tattooing in Somoa (where the bat comes in) to tattooing in San Francisco in the 1960s. ⊠ *841 Columbus Ave., near Lombard St., North Beach,* ☎ *415/775–4991.* 🎟 *Free.* ☉ *Daily noon–9.*

Grant Avenue. Originally called Calle de la Fundación, Grant Avenue is the oldest street in the city. Here you'll find dusty bars such as the Saloon, odd curio shops, unusual import stores, atmospheric cafés, and authentic Italian delis. The North Beach Festival, the city's oldest street fair, celebrates the area's Italian culture here each June. ⊠ *Between Columbus Ave. and Filbert St., North Beach.*

NEED A
BREAK?

Cafés are a way of life in North Beach. A must-visit spot is **Caffe Trieste** (⊠ 601 Vallejo St., at Grant Ave., North Beach, ☎ 415/392–6739), where the Giotta family presents a weekly musical (patrons are encouraged to participate) every Saturday at 2 PM; arrive by 1 or 1:15 to secure seats. The program ranges from Italian pop and folk music to operas. A neighborhood favorite since 1956, this was once the headquarters of the area's Beat poets, artists, and writers. If you want to be surrounded by the sights and smells of Sicily, try **Caffe Sport** (⊠ 574 Green St., near Columbus Ave., North Beach, ☎ 415/981–1251), where bright artifacts from the old country decorate the walls.

㊸ Julius' Castle. Every bit as romantic as its name implies, this contemporary Italian restaurant commands a regal view of the bay from its perch high up Telegraph Hill. An official historic landmark whose founder, Julius Roz, had his craftsmen use materials left over from the 1915 Panama-Pacific International Exposition, the restaurant has a dark-paneled Victorian interior. Ask for a table on the upper floor's outside terrace, where the views are especially dazzling. ⊠ *1541 Montgomery St., North Beach,* ☎ *415/392–2222,* WEB *www.juliuscastlerestaurant.com.* ☉ *Daily 5 PM–10 PM.*

㊽ Levi Strauss headquarters. This carefully landscaped complex appears so collegiate it is affectionately known as LSU (Levi Strauss University). Grassy knolls complement the redbrick buildings, providing a perfect environment for brown-bag and picnic lunches. ⊠ *Levi's Plaza, 1155 Battery St., North Beach.*

㊷ St. Francis of Assisi Church. This 1860 building stands on the site of the frame parish church that served the Catholic community during the gold rush. Its solid terra-cotta facade complements the many brightly colored restaurants and cafés nearby. ⊠ *610 Vallejo St., North Beach,* ☎ *415/983–0405,* WEB *www.shrinesf.org.* ☉ *Daily 11–5.*

㊹ Saints Peter and Paul Catholic Church. Camera-toting tourists focus their lenses on the Romanesque splendor of what's often called the Italian Cathedral. Completed in 1924, the cathedral has Disneyesque stone-white towers that are local landmarks. On the first Sunday of October a mass followed by a parade to Fisherman's Wharf celebrates the Blessing of the Fleet. Another popular event is the Columbus Day pageant in North Beach, with a parade that ends at the church. ⊠ *666 Filbert St., at Washington Square, North Beach,* ☎ *415/421–0809,* WEB *www.stspeterpaul.san-francisco.ca.us/church.*

㊺ Telegraph Hill. Telegraph Hill got its name from one of its earliest functions—in 1853 it became the location of the first Morse Code Signal

Station. Hill residents have some of the best views in the city, as well as the most difficult ascents to their aeries (the flower-lined steps flanking the hill make the climb more than tolerable for visitors, though). The Hill rises from the east end of Lombard Street to a height of 284 ft and is capped by Coit Tower. ⊠ *Between Lombard, Filbert, Kearny, and Sansome Sts., North Beach.*

OFF THE
BEATEN PATH

1360 MONTGOMERY STREET – In the 1947 film *Dark Passage,* Humphrey Bogart plays an escaped prisoner from San Quentin convicted of killing his wife. His real-life wife, Lauren Bacall, befriends him and lets him hole up in her apartment, inside this fantastic art deco building. From the street you can view the etched-glass gazelles and palms counterpointing a silvered fresco of a heroic bridge worker. ⊠ *Montgomery St., between Union and Filbert Sts. (near the top of the Filbert Steps)., North Beach.*

43 **Washington Square.** Once the daytime social heart of Little Italy, this grassy patch has changed character numerous times over the years. The Beats hung out in the 1950s, hippies camped out in the 1960s and early 1970s, and nowadays you're just as likely to see kids of Southeast Asian descent tossing a Frisbee as Italian men or women chatting about their children and the old country. In the morning elderly Asians perform the motions of tai chi, but by mid-morning groups of conservatively dressed Italian men in their seventies and eighties begin to arrive. Lillie Hitchcock Coit, in a show of affection for San Francisco's firefighters, donated the statue of two firemen with a child they've rescued. ⊠ *Bordered by Columbus Ave. and Stockton, Filbert, and Union Sts., North Beach.*

NOB HILL AND RUSSIAN HILL

Once called the Hill of Golden Promise, this area was officially dubbed Nob Hill during the 1870s when "the Big Four"—Charles Crocker, Leland Stanford, Mark Hopkins, and Collis Huntington, who were involved in the construction of the transcontinental railroad—built their hilltop estates. The lingo is thick from this era: those on the hilltop were referred to as "nabobs" (originally meaning a provincial governor from India) and "swells," and the hill itself was called Snob Hill, a term that survives to this day. By 1882 so many estates had sprung up on Nob Hill that Robert Louis Stevenson called it "the hill of palaces." But the 1906 earthquake and fire destroyed all the palatial mansions, except for portions of the Flood brownstone. Though Nob Hill lacks the quirky flavor of other San Francisco neighborhoods, it exudes history.

Just nine blocks or so from downtown and a few blocks north of Nob Hill, the old San Francisco families of Russian Hill were joined during the 1890s by bohemian artists and writers that included Charles Norris, George Sterling, and Maynard Dixon. Several stories explain the origin of Russian Hill's name, though none are known to be true. One legend has it that during San Francisco's early days, the steep hill (294 ft) was the site of a cemetery for unknown Russians; in another version Russian farmers raised vegetables here for Farallon Islands seal hunters; and a third attributes the name to a Russian sailor of prodigious drinking habits who drowned when he fell into a well on the hill. Today, simple studios, spiffy pieds-à-terre, Victorian flats, Edwardian cottages, and boxlike condos rub elbows on the hill. The bay views here are some of the city's best.

Numbers in the text correspond to numbers in the margin and on the Downtown San Francisco map.

A Good Walk

The Van Ness–California cable car line runs up to Nob Hill. If you're not up for a strenuous walk, this is the best way to get here from the Financial District or the Embarcadero (from downtown take any of the Powell Street cars). Begin on California and Taylor streets at the **Masonic Auditorium** ㊽. Across California Street is the majestic **Grace Cathedral** ㊾. From the cathedral walk east (toward Mason Street and downtown) on California Street to the **Pacific Union Club** ㊿. Across Mason Street from the Pacific Union Club is the lush hotel **The Fairmont** ㊾, with its quirky Tonga Room tiki bar. Directly across California Street from the Fairmont is the **Mark Hopkins Inter-Continental Hotel** ㊾, famed for panoramic views from its Top of the Mark lounge. Head east down the hill one block to Powell Street to the **Renaissance Stanford Court Hotel** ㊾. From here walk north on Powell Street three blocks to Washington Street and then west one block to Mason Street to the **Cable Car Museum** ㊾.

From the Cable Car Museum continue four blocks north on Mason Street to Vallejo Street, turn west, and start climbing the steps that lead to the multilevel **Ina Coolbrith Park** ㊾. At the top, you can see the **Vallejo steps area** across Taylor Street. The Flag House, one of several brown-shingle prequake buildings in this area, is to your left at Taylor Street. Cross Taylor Street and ascend the Vallejo steps; the view east takes in downtown and the Bay Bridge. Continue west from the top of the Vallejo steps to two secluded Russian Hill alleys. Down and to your left is Florence Place, an enclave of 1920s stucco homes, and down a bit farther on your right is Russian Hill Place, with a row of 1915 Mediterranean town houses designed by Willis Polk. After reemerging on Vallejo Street from the alleys, walk north (right) on Jones Street one short block to Green Street. Head west (left) halfway down the block to the octagonal **Feusier House** ㊾. Backtrack to Jones Street, and head north to **Macondray Lane** ㊾. Walk west (to the left) on Macondray and follow it to Leavenworth Street. Head north (to the right) on Leavenworth to the bottom of **Lombard Street** ㊾, the "Crookedest Street in the World." Continue north one block on Leavenworth and then east one block on Chestnut Street to the **San Francisco Art Institute** 60.

TIMING

The tour above covers a lot of ground, much of it steep. If you're in reasonably good shape you can complete this walk in 3½ to 4 hours, including 30-minute stops at Grace Cathedral and the Cable Car Museum. Add time for gazing at the bay from Ina Coolbrith Park or enjoying tea or a cocktail at one of Nob Hill's grand hotels.

Sights to See

★ ㊾ **Cable Car Museum.** San Francisco once had more than a dozen cable car barns and powerhouses. The only survivor, this 1907 redbrick structure, is an engaging stopover between Russian Hill and Nob Hill. Photographs, old cable cars, signposts, ticketing machines, and other memorabilia dating from 1873 document the history of these moving landmarks. The massive powerhouse wheels that move the entire cable car system steal the show; the design is so simple it seems almost unreal. You can also go downstairs to the sheave room and check out the innards of the system. A 15-minute video describes how it all works—cables must be replaced every three to six months—or you can opt to read the detailed placards. The gift shop sells cable car paraphernalia. ✉ *1201 Mason St., at Washington St., Nob Hill,* ☎ *415/474–1887,* WEB *www.cablecarmuseum.com.* ✇ *Free.* ☉ *Oct.–Mar., daily 10–5; Apr.–Sept., daily 10–6.*

52 The Fairmont. The Fairmont's dazzling opening was delayed a year by the 1906 quake, but since then the marble palace has hosted presidents, royalty, movie stars (Valentino, Dietrich), and local nabobs. Things have changed since its early days, however: on the eve of World War I you could get a room for as low as $2.50 per night, meals included. Nowadays, prices go as high as $8,000, which buys a night in the eight-room, Persian art–filled penthouse suite that was showcased regularly in the 1980s TV series *Hotel*. Swing through the opulent lobby on your way to tea (served daily from 3 to 6) at the **Laurel Court** restaurant. Don't miss an evening cocktail (the situation demands that you order a mai tai) in the kitschy **Tonga Room,** complete with tiki huts, a sporadic tropical rainstorm, and a floating bandstand.

Across from the Fairmont, **Brocklebank Apartments,** on the northeast corner of Sacramento and Mason streets and viewable only from a distance, is also a media star. In 1958 it was a major location in Alfred Hitchcock's *Vertigo* and in the 1990s popped up in the miniseries *Tales of the City,* Armistead Maupin's homage to San Francisco. ⊠ *950 Mason St., Nob Hill,* ☎ *415/772–5000,* WEB *www.fairmont.com.*

57 Feusier House. Octagonal houses were once thought to make the best use of space and enhance the physical and mental well-being of their occupants. A brief mid-19th-century craze inspired the construction of several in San Francisco. Only the Feusier House, built in 1857 and now a private residence surrounded by lush gardens, and the Octagon House remain standing. Across from the Feusier House is the **1907 Firehouse** (⊠ 1088 Green St., Russian Hill). Mrs. Ralph K. Davies, a local art patron, bought it from the city in 1956. It's closed to the public, so view from outside. ⊠ *1067 Green St., Russian Hill.*

NEED A
BREAK?

Take a break from walking the hills at the original **Swensen's Ice Cream** (⊠ 1999 Hyde St., at Union St., Russian Hill, ☎ 415/775–6818). A neighborhood favorite, it opened in 1948.

50 Grace Cathedral. The seat of the Episcopal Church in San Francisco, this soaring Gothic structure, erected on the site of Charles Crocker's mansion, took 53 years to build. The gilded bronze doors at the east entrance were taken from casts of Ghiberti's Gates of Paradise, which are on the baptistery in Florence, Italy. A black-and-bronze stone sculpture of St. Francis by Beniamino Bufano greets you as you enter.

The 35-ft-wide labyrinth, a large, purplish rug, is a replica of the 13th-century stone labyrinth on the floor of the Chartres cathedral. All are encouraged to walk the ¼-mi-long labyrinth, a ritual based on the tradition of meditative walking. There's also a terrazzo outdoor labyrinth on the church's north side. The AIDS Interfaith Chapel, to the right as you enter Grace, contains a sculpture by the late artist Keith Haring and panels from the AIDS Memorial Quilt. Especially dramatic times to view the cathedral are during Thursday-night evensong (5:15) and during special holiday programs. ⊠ *1100 California St., at Taylor St., Nob Hill,* ☎ *415/749–6300,* WEB *www.gracecathedral.org.* ☉ *Weekdays 7–5:45, weekends 7–5.*

56 Ina Coolbrith Park. This attractive park is unusual because it's vertical—that is, rather than being one open space, it's composed of a series of terraces up a very steep hill. A poet, Oakland librarian, and niece of Mormon prophet Joseph Smith, Ina Coolbrith (1842–1928) introduced Jack London and Isadora Duncan to the world of books. For years she entertained literary greats in her Macondray Lane home near the park. In 1915 she was named poet laureate of California. ⊠ *Vallejo St. between Mason and Taylor Sts., Russian Hill.*

★ ⑤⑨ **Lombard Street.** The block-long "Crookedest Street in the World" makes eight switchbacks down the east face of Russian Hill between Hyde and Leavenworth streets. Residents bemoan the traffic jam outside their front doors, and occasionally the city attempts to discourage drivers by posting a traffic cop near the top of the hill, but the determined can find a way around. If no one is standing guard, join the line of cars waiting to drive down the steep hill, or avoid the whole morass and walk down the steps on either side of Lombard. You'll take in super views of North Beach and Coit Tower whether you walk or drive—though if you're the one behind the wheel, you'd better keep your eye on the road lest you become yet another of the many folks who ram the garden barriers. ⊠ *Lombard St. between Hyde and Leavenworth Sts., Russian Hill.*

⑤⑧ **Macondray Lane.** Enter this "secret garden" under a lovely wooden trellis and walk down a quiet cobbled pedestrian street lined with Edwardian cottages and flowering plants and trees. A flight of steep wooden stairs at the end of the lane leads down to Taylor Street—on the way down you can't miss the bay views. If you've read any of Armistead Maupin's *Tales of the City* or sequels, you may find the lane vaguely familiar. It's the thinly disguised setting for part of the series's action. ⊠ *Jones St. between Union and Green Sts., Russian Hill.*

⑤③ **Mark Hopkins Inter-Continental Hotel.** Built on the ashes of railroad tycoon Mark Hopkins's grand estate (which was built at his wife's urging; Hopkins himself preferred to live frugally), this 19-story hotel went up in 1926. A combination of French château and Spanish Renaissance architecture, with noteworthy terra-cotta detailing, it has hosted statesmen, royalty, and Hollywood celebrities. From the 1920s through the 1940s, Benny Goodman, Tommy Dorsey, and other top-drawer entertainers appeared here regularly. The 11-room penthouse was turned into a glass-walled cocktail lounge in 1939: the **Top of the Mark** is remembered fondly by thousands of World War II veterans who jammed the lounge before leaving for overseas duty. Wives and sweethearts watching the ships depart gave the room's northwest nook its name—Weepers' Corner. With its 360° views, the lounge is a wonderful spot for a nighttime drink. ⊠ *1 Nob Hill, at California and Mason Sts., Nob Hill,* ☎ *415/392–3434,* WEB *www.hotels.san-francisco.interconti.com.*

④⑨ **Masonic Auditorium.** Formally called the California Masonic Memorial Temple, this building was erected by Freemasons in 1957. A selection of brochures by the entrance explains the beliefs of Freemasonry: only men can join, atheists are forbidden, patriotism and love of family are central tenets, and so on. (Readers of Tolstoy will remember Pierre's painful ambivalence about Freemasonry in *War and Peace*.) The auditorium is the site of occasional musical events (Van Morrison, Natalie Cole), as well as lectures (Desmond Tutu), conventions, and seminars. The impressive lobby mosaic, done mainly in rich greens and yellows, depicts the Masonic fraternity's role in California history and industry. There's also an intricate model of King Solomon's Temple in the lobby. ⊠ *1111 California St., Nob Hill,* ☎ *415/776–4702,* WEB *www.masonicauditorium.com.* ☉ *Lobby weekdays 8–5.*

⑤① **Pacific Union Club.** The former home of silver baron James Flood cost a whopping $1.5 million in 1886, when even a stylish Victorian like the Haas-Lilienthal House cost less than $20,000. All that cash did buy some structural stability. The Flood residence (to be precise, its shell) was the only Nob Hill mansion to survive the 1906 earthquake and fire. The Pacific Union Club, a bastion of the wealthy and powerful, purchased the house in 1907 and commissioned Willis Polk to redesign it; the architect added the semicircular wings and third floor. (The ornate fence design dates from the mansion's construction.) Art shows frequently take place in Huntington Park, west of the house. ⊠ *1000 California St., Nob Hill.*

54 **Renaissance Stanford Court Hotel.** In 1876 Leland Stanford, a California governor and founder of Stanford University, was the first to build an estate on Nob Hill. The only part that survived the earthquake was a basalt-and-granite wall that's been restored; it can be seen on the eastern side of the hotel. In 1912 an apartment house was built on the site of the former estate, and in 1972 the present-day hotel was constructed from the shell of that building. The lobby has a stained-glass dome and sepia-tone murals depicting scenes of early San Francisco. ⊠ *905 California St., Nob Hill,* ☏ *415/989–3500,* WEB *www.renaissancehotels.com.*

NEED A BREAK?
A harpist plays the classics and other tunes during afternoon tea at the **Ritz-Carlton, San Francisco** (⊠ 600 Stockton St., at California St., Nob Hill, ☏ 415/296–7465, WEB www.ritzcarlton.com). Hours vary throughout the year, but tea is generally served from 2:30 to 4:30 on weekdays and from 1:30 to 4:30 on weekends.

60 **San Francisco Art Institute.** A Moorish-tile fountain in a tree-shaded courtyard immediately draws the eye as you enter the institute. The highlight of a visit is Mexican master Diego Rivera's *The Making of a Fresco Showing the Building of a City* (1931), in the student gallery to your immediate left once inside the entrance. Rivera himself is in the fresco—his back is to the viewer—and he's surrounded by his assistants. They in turn are surrounded by a construction scene, laborers, and city notables such as sculptor Robert Stackpole and architect Timothy Pfleuger. *The Making of a Fresco* is one of three Bay Area murals painted by Rivera.

The older portions of the Art Institute were erected in 1926. Ansel Adams created the school's fine-arts photography department in 1946, and school directors established the country's first fine-arts film program. Notable faculty and alumni have included painter Richard Diebenkorn and photographers Dorothea Lange, Edward Weston, and Annie Leibovitz. The **Walter & McBean Galleries** (☏ 415/749–4563) exhibit the often provocative works of established artists. ⊠ *800 Chestnut St., North Beach,* ☏ *415/771–7020,* WEB *www.sanfranciscoart.edu.* ⊠ *Galleries free.* ⊙ *Walter & McBean Galleries Mon.–Sat. 11–6, student gallery daily 9–9.*

Vallejo steps area. Several Russian Hill buildings survived the 1906 earthquake and fire and remain standing. Alert firefighters saved what's come to be known as the **Flag House** (⊠ 1652–56 Taylor St., Russian Hill) when they spotted the American flag on the property and doused the flames with seltzer water and wet sand. The owner, a flag collector, fearing the house would burn to the ground, wanted it to go down in style, with "all flags flying."

The Flag House, at the southwest corner of Ina Coolbrith Park, is one of a number of California Shingle–style homes in this neighborhood, several of which were designed by Willis Polk. Polk also laid out the Vallejo steps, which climb the steep ridge across Taylor Street from the Flag House. Polk designed the **Polk-Williams House** (⊠ Taylor and Vallejo Sts., Russian Hill) and lived in one of its finer sections, and **1034– 1036 Vallejo,** across the street. ⊠ *Taylor and Vallejo Sts. (steps lead up toward Jones St.), Russian Hill.*

PACIFIC HEIGHTS

Some of the city's most expensive and dramatic real estate—including mansions and town houses priced in the millions—is in Pacific Heights. Grand Victorians line the streets, and from almost any point in this neighborhood you get a magnificent view.

Old money and new, personalities in the limelight, and those who prefer absolute media anonymity live here. Few outsiders see anything other than the pleasing facades of Queen Anne charmers, English Tudor imports, and baroque bastions, but that's reason enough for a stroll. You'll notice that few of the homes in Pacific Heights have large gardens. Space has always been at a premium in San Francisco, even in such a wealthy neighborhood.

Numbers in the text correspond to numbers in the margin and on the Downtown San Francisco map.

A Good Walk

Pacific Heights lies on an east–west ridge along the city's northern flank from Van Ness Avenue to the Presidio and from California Street to the Marina, but a few important sights are in the lowlands (still technically Pacific Heights). The first stop is the **Octagon House** ⑥, at the corner of Gough (rhymes with "cough") and Union streets. Stroll west through the upscale shopping district of Union Street. The modest **Wedding Houses** sit on the north side of Union Street just before Buchanan Street. Continue one block farther to Webster Street and then one block north to Filbert Street. You can't miss the elaborately styled **Vedanta Society** ⑥②, on the southwest corner of Filbert and Webster streets.

Prepare for a steep climb as you head south up Webster Street. At the crest of the hill, four notable **Broadway and Webster Street estates** ⑥③ stand within a block of each other. Two are on the north side of Broadway to the west of the intersection, one is on the same side to the east, and the last is south a half block on Webster Street. After viewing the estates, continue south on Webster to Pacific Avenue and turn right (west). You'll pass some apartment buildings in the first block and a half, then single-family homes. The Italianate gem at 2475 Pacific Avenue sat on a 25-acre farm in the 1850s. Several Queen Anne homes stand tall on the south side of the 2500 block (between Steiner and Pierce streets); a three-story circular glass-walled staircase distinguishes the more modern home at No. 2510, on the north side. Continue west on Pacific to Scott Street, and walk south into **Alta Plaza Park** ⑥④.

Catch your breath at the park, and then walk east on Jackson Street several blocks to the **Whittier Mansion** ⑥⑤, on the corner of Jackson and Laguna streets. Make a right on Laguna and a left at the next block, Washington Street. The patch of green that spreads southeast from here is **Lafayette Park** ⑥⑥. Walk on Washington along the edge of Lafayette Park past the formal French **Spreckels Mansion** ⑥⑦, at the corner of Octavia Street, and continue east two more blocks to Franklin Street. Turn left (north); halfway down the block stands the handsome **Haas-Lilienthal House** ⑥⑧. Head back south on Franklin Street, stopping to view several **Franklin Street buildings** ⑥⑨. At California Street, turn right (west) to see more **noteworthy Victorians** ⑦⓪ on that street and Laguna Street.

TIMING

Set aside about two hours to see the sights mentioned here, not including the tours of the Haas-Lilienthal House and the Octagon House. Unless you're in great shape, it'll be a slow walk up extremely steep Webster Street from the Union Street sights, and although most of the attractions are walk-bys, you'll be covering a good bit of pavement.

Sights to See

64 Alta Plaza Park. Landscape architect John McLaren, who also created Golden Gate Park, designed Alta Plaza in 1910, modeling its terracing on the Grand Casino in Monte Carlo, Monaco. From the top you can see Marin to the north, downtown to the east, Twin Peaks to the south, and Golden Gate Park to the west. ✉ *Between Clay, Steiner, Jackson, and Scott Sts., Pacific Heights.*

63 Broadway and Webster Street estates. Broadway uptown, unlike its garish North Beach stretch, does have some prestigious addresses. At **2222 Broadway** is a three-story palace with an intricately filigreed doorway built by Comstock silver mine heir James Flood and later donated to a religious order. The Convent of the Sacred Heart purchased the Grant House at **2220 Broadway**. These two buildings, along with a Flood property at **2120 Broadway**, are used as school quarters. A gold mine heir, William Bourn II, commissioned Willis Polk to build the nearby mansion at **2550 Webster St.**

69 Franklin Street buildings. Don't be fooled by the **Golden Gate Church** (✉ 1901 Franklin St., Pacific Heights)—what at first looks like a stone facade is actually redwood painted white. A Georgian-style residence built in the early 1900s for a coffee merchant sits at **1735 Franklin.** On the northeast corner of Franklin and California streets is a **Christian Science church**; built in the Tuscan Revival style, it's noteworthy for its terra-cotta detailing. The **Coleman House** (✉ 1701 Franklin St., Pacific Heights) is an impressive twin-turreted Queen Anne mansion built for a gold-rush mining and lumber baron. Don't miss the large stained-glass window on the house's north side. ✉ *Franklin St. between Washington and California Sts., Pacific Heights.*

68 Haas-Lilienthal House. A small display of photographs on the bottom floor of this elaborate 1886 Queen Anne house, which cost a mere $18,500 to build, makes clear that it was modest compared with some of the giants that fell victim to the 1906 earthquake and fire. The Foundation for San Francisco's Architectural Heritage operates the home, whose carefully kept rooms provide an intriguing glimpse into late-19th-century life. Volunteers conduct one-hour house tours two days a week and an informative two-hour tour of the eastern portion of Pacific Heights on Sunday afternoon. ✉ *2007 Franklin St., between Washington and Jackson Sts., Pacific Heights,* ☎ *415/441–3004,* WEB *www.sfheritage.org/house.html.* 🎫 *$5.* ☉ *Wed. noon–4 (last tour at 3), Sun. 11–5 (last tour at 4). Pacific Heights tours ($5) leave the house Sun. at 12:30.*

66 Lafayette Park. Clusters of trees dot this four-block-square oasis for sunbathers and dog-and-Frisbee teams. During the 1860s a tenacious squatter, Sam Holladay, built himself a big wooden house in the center of the park. Holladay even instructed city gardeners as if the land were his own and defied all orders to leave. The house was finally torn down in 1936. On the south side of the park, **2151 Sacramento**, a private condominium, is the site of a home occupied by Sir Arthur Conan Doyle in the late 19th century. ✉ *Between Laguna, Gough, Sacramento, and Washington Sts., Pacific Heights.*

70 Noteworthy Victorians. Two Italianate Victorians (✉ 1818 and 1834 California St., Pacific Heights) stand out on the 1800 block of California. A block farther is the Victorian-era **Atherton House** (✉ 1990 California St., Pacific Heights), whose mildly daffy design incorporates Queen Anne, Stick-Eastlake, and other architectural elements. The oft-photographed **Laguna Street Victorians,** on the west side of the 1800 block of Laguna Street, cost between $2,000 and $2,600 when they were built in the 1870s. ⊠ *California St. between Franklin and Octavia Sts., and Laguna St. between Pine and Bush Sts., Pacific Heights.*

⑥ **Octagon House.** This eight-sided home sits across the street from its original site on Gough Street. White quoins accent each of the eight corners of the pretty blue-gray exterior, and a Colonial-style garden completes the picture. Inside, it's full of antique American furniture, decorative arts (paintings, silver, rugs), and documents from the 18th and 19th centuries. A deck of revolutionary-era hand-painted playing cards takes an anti-monarchist position: in place of kings, queens, and jacks, the American upstarts substituted American statesmen, Roman goddesses, and Indian chiefs. ⊠ *2645 Gough St., Pacific Heights,* ☎ *415/441–7512.* ☜ *Free (donations encouraged).* ⊙ *Feb.–Dec., 2nd Sun. and 2nd and 4th Thurs. of each month noon–3; group tours weekdays by appointment.*

⑥⑦ **Spreckels Mansion.** This estate was built for sugar heir Adolph Spreckels and his wife, Alma. Mrs. Spreckels was so pleased with her house that she commissioned George Applegarth to design another building in a similar vein: the California Palace of the Legion of Honor. One of the city's great iconoclasts, Alma Spreckels was the model for the bronze figure atop the Victory Monument in Union Square. ⊠ *2080 Washington St., at Octavia St., Pacific Heights.*

⑥② **Vedanta Society.** A pastiche of Colonial, Queen Anne, Moorish, and Hindu opulence, with turrets battling onion domes and Victorian detailing everywhere, this 1905 structure was the first Hindu temple in the West. The highest of the six Hindu systems of religious philosophy, Vedanta maintains that all religions are paths to one goal. Although the Vedanta Society's main location is the temple at Vallejo and Fillmore streets (closed Tuesday), the Webster Street temple (open only on Friday evening) is the organization's heart. ⊠ *2963 Webster St., Pacific Heights,* ☎ *415/922–2323,*

Wedding Houses. These identical white double-peak homes (joined in the middle) were erected in the late 1870s or early 1880s by dairy rancher James Cudworth as wedding gifts for his two daughters. These days, the buildings house businesses and an English-style pub. ⊠ *1980 Union St., Pacific Heights.*

⑥⑤ **Whittier Mansion.** This was one of the most elegant 19th-century houses in the state, with a Spanish-tile roof and scrolled bay windows on all four sides. An anomaly in a town that lost most of its grand mansions to the 1906 quake, the Whittier Mansion was built so solidly that only a chimney toppled over during the disaster. ⊠ *2090 Jackson St., Pacific Heights.*

JAPANTOWN

Around 1860 a wave of Japanese immigrants arrived in San Francisco, which they called Soko. After the 1906 earthquake and fire, many of these newcomers settled in the Western Addition. By the 1930s they had opened shops, markets, meeting halls, and restaurants and established Shinto and Buddhist temples. Known as Japantown, this area was virtually deserted during World War II when many of its residents, including second- and third-generation Americans, were forced into so-called relocation camps. Today Japantown, or "Nihonmachi," is centered on the southern slope of Pacific Heights, north of Geary Boulevard between Fillmore and Laguna streets. The Nihonmachi Cherry Blossom Festival is celebrated on two weekends in April.

Japantown doesn't feel much different from other parts of the city. Most shops and restaurants are Japanese-oriented, but the majority are tidily lined up in the Japan Center rather than spilling out onto the streets. And though it contains Japanese touches, the architecture in the area is fairly generic. That said, there are plenty of authentic treasures to be found in the shops and restaurants of Japantown. About three dozen restaurants serve Japanese, Chinese, and Korean food. Following the practice in Japan, plastic replicas of the various dishes are on view.

Though Japantown is a relatively safe area, the Western Addition, which lies to the south of Geary Boulevard, can be dangerous; after dark also avoid straying too far west of Fillmore Street just north of Geary.

Numbers in the text correspond to numbers in the margin and on the Downtown San Francisco map.

A Good Walk

Several key components of San Francisco's history intersect at Geary Boulevard and Fillmore Street. The three-block **Japan Center** ⑦ sits on a portion of the area settled by Japanese and Japanese-Americans in the early 20th century. The stretch of Fillmore on either side of Geary Boulevard was a center of African-American culture during the mid-20th century. The part to the south remains so today, though the many blues and other music clubs that once thrived here have closed. One notable exception is blues legend John Lee Hooker's Boom Boom Room.

Near the southwest corner of Geary and Fillmore is the entrance to the legendary Fillmore Auditorium, where 1960s bands like Jefferson Airplane and the Grateful Dead performed. Two doors west of the Fillmore was the People's Temple (since demolished), the headquarters of the cult run by the Reverend Jim Jones, whose flock participated in a mass suicide in Guyana in November 1978.

Kabuki Springs & Spa ⑦ is on the northeast corner of Geary and Fillmore. Head north on Fillmore to Post Street and make a right. Pass the entrance to the eight-screen AMC Kabuki theater and enter the Japan Center mid-block, in the Kinokuniya Building. Among the shops of note are the Kinokuniya Bookstore and Ma-Shi'-Ko Folk Craft, both on the second floor.

A second-level bridge spans Webster Street, connecting the Kinokuniya and Kintetsu buildings. Make a right after you cross the bridge and then a left. There are usually several fine ikebana arrangements in the windows of the headquarters of the Ikenobo Ikebana Society of America. A few doors farther along at May's Coffee Stand you can pick up a lemonade and a tasty fish-shape waffle filled with red-bean paste. If you're hungrier, make two more lefts (heading back toward the bridge) to the noodle shop Mifune.

After exiting the Kintetsu Building, pop across Post Street to the open-air **Japan Center Mall** ⑦, a short block of shoji-screened buildings on Buchanan Street between Post and Sutter streets.

TIMING

The distance covered in the tour is extremely short, and apart from the worthwhile Kabuki Springs & Spa there isn't much to see here. Not including a visit to the Kabuki Springs, an hour will probably suffice.

Sights to See

❼ Japan Center. The noted American architect Minoru Yamasaki created this 5-acre complex, which opened in 1968. The development includes a hotel (the Radisson Miyako, at Laguna and Post streets); a public garage with discounted validated parking; shops selling Japanese furnishings, clothing, cameras, tapes and records, porcelain, pearls, and paintings; an excellent spa; and a multiplex cinema.

Between the Miyako Mall and Kintetsu Building are the five-tier, 100-ft-tall **Peace Pagoda** and the Peace Plaza, where seasonal festivals are held. The pagoda, which draws on the 1,200-year-old tradition of miniature round pagodas dedicated to eternal peace, was designed by Yoshiro Taniguchi to convey the "friendship and goodwill" of the Japanese people to the people of the United States. ⊠ *Bordered by Geary Blvd. and Fillmore, Post, and Laguna Sts., Japantown,* ☎ *415/922–6776.*

NEED A
BREAK?

At **Isobune** (☎ 415/563–1030), between street level and the second floor of the Kintetsu Building, "sushi boats" float by customers, who take what they want and pay per dish at the end of the meal.

🅷 **Japan Center Mall.** The buildings lining this open-air mall are of the shoji school of architecture. Seating in this area can be found on local artist Ruth Asawa's twin origami-style fountains, which sit in the middle of the mall; they're squat circular structures made of fieldstone, with three levels for sitting and a brick floor. ⊠ *Buchanan St. between Post and Sutter Sts., Japantown.*

★ 🅷 **Kabuki Springs & Spa.** Japantown's house of tranquillity got a complete makeover in 1999. The feel is less Japanese than before. Balinese urns decorate the communal bath area, and you're just as likely to hear soothing flute or classical music as you are Kitaro. The massage palette has also expanded well beyond the traditional shiatsu technique. The experience is no less relaxing, however, and the treatment regimen includes facials, salt scrubs, and mud and seaweed wraps. You can take your massage in a private room with a bath or in a curtained-off area. The communal baths ($15 before 5 PM, $18 after 5 and all weekend) contain hot and cold tubs, a large Japanese-style bath, a sauna, a steam room, and showers. The baths are open for men only on Monday, Thursday, and Saturday and for women only on Wednesday, Friday, and Sunday. Bathing suits are required on Tuesday, when the baths are co-ed. Men and women can reserve private rooms daily. A 90-minute massage-and-bath package with a private room costs $95. A package that includes a 50-minute massage and the use of the communal baths costs $75. ⊠ *1750 Geary Blvd., Japantown,* ☎ *415/922–6000,* WEB *www.kabukisprings.com.* ◷ *Daily 10–10.*

OFF THE
BEATEN PATH

ST. MARY'S CATHEDRAL – Affectionately known as Our Lady of the Maytag for its resemblance to a washing-machine agitator, this Catholic house of worship was designed by a team of local architects and Pierre Nervi of Rome; it was dedicated in 1971. The interior is as unusual as the exterior: seven thousand aluminium ribs cascade powerfully above the marble altar, which is backed by purple and blue cloth partitions and brightly colored lights. Four stained-glass windows cross in the massive dome and represent the four elements. ⊠ *1111 Gough St., at Geary Blvd. (from Japan Center head east on Geary), Japantown,* ☎ *415/567–2020.*

CIVIC CENTER

The Civic Center—the beaux-arts complex between McAllister and Grove streets and Franklin and Hyde streets that includes City Hall, the War Memorial Opera House, the Veterans Building, and the old Public Library (slated to become the Asian Art Museum and Cultural

Center in early 2003)—is a product of the "City Beautiful" movement of the early 20th century. City Hall, completed in 1915 and renovated in 1999, is the centerpiece. The new main library on Larkin Street between Fulton and Grove streets, completed in 1996, is a modern variation on the Civic Center's architectural theme.

The Civic Center area may have been set up on City Beautiful principles, but illusion soon gives way to reality. The buildings may be grand, but there's a stark juxtaposition of the powerful and the powerless here. On the streets and plazas of Civic Center, many of the city's most destitute residents eke out an existence.

Despite the evidence of social problems, there are areas of interest on either side of City Hall. East of City Hall is United Nations Plaza, a carnival of bright colors during the twice-weekly farmers' market. The handsome new main library is just a block west of the plaza. On the west side of City Hall are the opera house, the symphony hall, and other cultural institutions. A few upscale restaurants in the surrounding blocks cater to the theater-symphony crowd.

Numbers in the text correspond to numbers in the margin and on the Downtown San Francisco map.

A Good Walk

Start at **United Nations Plaza** ㉔, set on an angle between Hyde and Market streets. BART and Muni trains stop here, and the Bus 5–Fulton, Bus 21–Hayes, and other lines serve the area. Walk west across the plaza toward Fulton Street, which dead-ends at Hyde Street, and cross Hyde. Towering over the block of Fulton between Hyde and Larkin streets is the Pioneers Monument. The new main branch of the **San Francisco Public Library** ㉕ is south of the monument. North of it is the old library, in 2003 slated to become the **Asian Art Museum** ㉖. The patch of green west of the museum is Civic Center Plaza, and beyond that is **City Hall** ㉗. If City Hall is open, walk through it, exiting on Van Ness Avenue and turning right. If the building's closed, walk around it to the north—to the right as you're facing it—and make a left at McAllister. Either way you'll end up at McAllister Street and Van Ness Avenue. Looking south (to the left) across the street on Van Ness, you'll see three grand edifices, each of which takes up most of its block. On the southwestern corner of McAllister and Van Ness Avenue is the **Veterans Building** ㉘. A horseshoe-shape carriage entrance on its south side separates the building from the **War Memorial Opera House** ㉙. In the next block of Van Ness Avenue, across Grove Street from the opera house, is **Louise M. Davies Symphony Hall** ㉚. From Davies, head west (to the right) on Grove Street to Franklin Street, turn left (south), walk one block to Hayes Street, and turn right (west). A hip strip of galleries, shops, and restaurants lies between Franklin and Laguna streets. Like Japantown, the Civic Center borders the Western Addition; it's best not to stray west of Laguna at night.

TIMING

Walking around the Civic Center shouldn't take more than about 45 minutes. The Asian Art Museum merits an hour; another half hour or more can be spent browsing in the shops along Hayes Street. On Wednesday or Sunday allot some extra time to take in the farmers' market in United Nations Plaza.

Sights to See

★ ㉖ **Asian Art Museum.** In early 2003 the Asian Art Museum, one of the largest collections of Asian art in the world, opens in its new home. Holdings include more than 12,000 sculptures, paintings, and ceramics from 40 countries, illustrating major periods of Asian art. Though the bulk of the art and artifacts come from China, treasures from Korea, Iran, Turkey, Syria, India, Tibet, Nepal, Pakistan, India, Japan, Afghanistan, and Southeast Asia are also on view. ✉ *200 Larkin St., between McAllister and Fulton Sts., Civic Center,* ☎ *415/668–8921 or 415/379–8801,* WEB *www.asianart.org.*

⓱ City Hall. This masterpiece of granite and marble was modeled after St. Peter's cathedral in Rome. City Hall's bronze and gold-leaf dome, which is even higher than the U.S. Capitol's version, dominates the area. Arthur Brown Jr., who also designed Coit Tower and the War Memorial Opera House, was trained in Paris; his classical influences can be seen throughout the structure. The building was spruced up and seismically retrofitted in the late 1990s, but the sense of history remains palpable. Some noteworthy events that have taken place here include the marriage of Marilyn Monroe and Joe DiMaggio (1954); the hosing—down the central staircase—of civil-rights and freedom-of-speech protesters (1960); the murders of Mayor George Moscone and openly gay supervisor Harvey Milk (1978); the torching of the lobby by angry members of the gay community in response to the light sentence (8 years for manslaughter, eventually reduced to 5½ years) given to the former supervisor who killed them (1979); and the weddings of scores of gay couples in celebration of the passage of San Francisco's Domestic Partners Act (1991). The palatial interior, full of grand arches and with a sweeping central staircase, is impressive. Free tours are available weekdays at 10, noon, and 2 and weekends at 12:30. Inside City Hall, the **Museum of the City of San Francisco** (☎ 415/928–0289, WEB www.sfmuseum.org) displays historical items, maps, and photographs, as well as the 500-pound head of the Goddess of Progress statue, which crowned the City Hall building that crumbled during the 1906 earthquake. Admission to the museum is free. Across Polk Street is **Civic Center Plaza,** with lawns, walkways, seasonal flower beds, a playground, and an underground parking garage. ✉ *Between Van Ness Ave. and Polk, Grove, and McAllister Sts., Civic Center,* ☎ *415/554–6023.* WEB *www.ci.sf.ca.us/cityhall.*

⓳ Louise M. Davies Symphony Hall. Fascinating and futuristic looking, this 2,750-seat hall is the home of the San Francisco Symphony. The glass wraparound lobby and pop-out balcony high on the southeast corner are visible from the outside. Henry Moore created the bronze sculpture that sits on the sidewalk at Van Ness Avenue and Grove Street. The hall's 59 adjustable Plexiglas acoustical disks cascade from the ceiling like hanging windshields. Concerts range from typical symphonic fare to more unusual combinations, such as pop-rock singer Elvis Costello accompanied by a string quartet, and performers like Al Green and Arlo Guthrie. San Francisco Symphony leader Michael Tilson Thomas is one of the few U.S.-born music directors of a major American orchestra. Scheduled tours (75 minutes), which meet at the Grove Street entrance, take in Davies and the nearby opera house and Herbst Theatre. ✉ *201 Van Ness Ave., Civic Center,* ☎ *415/552–8338.* ▦ *Tours $5.* ☉ *Tours Mon. on the hr 10–2.*

NEED A
BREAK?

For a quick sandwich or reasonably priced salad, dash over to **Parco Coffee and Tea** (✉ 350 Hayes St., Hayes Valley, ☎ 415/621–1348), open Monday–Wednesday 8–7, Thursday–Sunday 8–8.

⓯ San Francisco Public Library. The main library, which opened in 1996, is a modernized version of the old beaux-arts library that sits just across Fulton Street. Specialty rooms include centers for the hearing and visually impaired, a gay and lesbian history center, and African-American and Asian centers. Also here are an auditorium, an art gallery, a café, and a rooftop garden and terrace. The San Francisco

History Room and Archives contains historic photographs, maps, and other city memorabilia. At the library's core is a five-story atrium with a skylight, a grand staircase, and murals painted by local artists. Tours of the library are conducted Wednesday and Friday at 2:30 PM. ✉ *100 Larkin St., between Grove and Fulton Sts., Civic Center,* ☎ *415/557–4400,* W̅E̅B̅ *www.sfpl.lib.ca.us.* ⊙ *Mon. and Sat. 10–6, Tues.–Thurs. 9–8, Fri. noon–6, Sun. noon–5.*

㉔ United Nations Plaza. Brick pillars listing various nations and the dates of their admittance into the United Nations line the plaza, and its floor is inscribed with the goals and philosophy of the United Nations charter, which was signed at the War Memorial Opera House in 1945. On Wednesday and Sunday a farmers' market fills the space with homegrown produce and plants. ✉ *Fulton St. between Hyde and Market Sts., Civic Center.*

㉘ Veterans Building. Performing and visual arts organizations occupy much of this 1930s structure. The **Herbst Theatre** (☎ 415/392–4400) hosts classical ensembles, dance performances, and City Arts and Lectures events. Past City Arts speakers have included author Salman Rushdie and veteran anchor Ted Koppel. Also in the building are two galleries that charge no admission. The street-level **San Francisco Arts Commission Gallery** (☎ 415/554–6080), open from Wednesday through Saturday between 11 and 5:30, displays the works of Bay Area artists. The **San Francisco Performing Arts Library and Museum** (☎ 415/255–4800) occupies part of the fourth floor. A small gallery hosts interesting exhibitions, though the organization functions mainly as a library and research center, collecting, documenting, and preserving the San Francisco Bay Area's rich performing arts legacy. The gallery is open Wednesday 11 to 7 and Thursday through Saturday 11 to 5. ✉ *401 Van Ness Ave., Civic Center.*

㉙ War Memorial Opera House. During San Francisco's Barbary Coast days, operagoers smoked cigars, didn't check their revolvers, and expressed their appreciation with "shrill whistles and savage yells," as one observer put it. All the old opera houses were destroyed in the 1906 quake, but lusty support for opera continued. The opera didn't have a permanent home until the War Memorial Opera House was inaugurated in 1932 with a performance of *Tosca.* Modeled after its European counterparts, the building has a vaulted and coffered ceiling, marble foyer, two balconies, and a huge silver art deco chandelier that resembles a sunburst. The San Francisco Opera performs here from September through December and during the summer; the opera house hosts the San Francisco Ballet from February through May, with December *Nutcracker* performances. ✉ *301 Van Ness Ave., Civic Center,* ☎ *415/621–6600.*

THE NORTHERN WATERFRONT

For the sights, sounds, and smells of the sea, hop the Powell–Hyde cable car from Union Square and take it to the end of the line. The views as you descend Hyde Street down to the bay are breathtaking—tiny sailboats bob in the whitecaps, Alcatraz hovers ominously in the distance, and the Marin Headlands form a rugged backdrop to the Golden Gate Bridge. Once you reach sea level at the cable car turnaround, Aquatic Park and the National Maritime Museum are immediately to the west, and the commercial attractions of the Fisherman's Wharf area are to the east. Bring good walking shoes and a jacket or sweater for mid-afternoon breezes or foggy mists.

Years pass for most San Franciscans between visits to Fisherman's Wharf, though a handful of new destination restaurants has increased the area's interest to locals. While most diversions here are decidedly tourist-oriented, the area is not without cultural and historical points of interest (it is the departure point for the ferry ride to the deservedly popular Alcatraz Island). Even if you abhor schlock you can have a good time here if you pay attention.

Each day street artists—jewelers, painters, potters, photographers, and leather workers—and others offer their wares for sale. Beauty, of course, is always in the eye of the beholder, but some of the items may be over-priced and of questionable quality. Bargaining is always possible.

Numbers in the text correspond to numbers in the margin and on the Northern Waterfront/Marina and the Presidio map.

A Good Walk

Begin at Polk and Beach streets at the **National Maritime Museum** ①. (Walk west from the cable car turnaround; Bus 19 stops at Polk and Beach streets, and Bus 47–Van Ness stops one block west at Van Ness Avenue and Beach Street.) Across Beach from the museum is **Ghirardelli Square** ②, a complex of shops, cafés, and galleries in an old chocolate factory. Continue east on Beach to Hyde Street and make a left. At the end of Hyde is the **Hyde Street Pier** ③. South on Hyde a block and a half is the former Del Monte **Cannery** ④, which holds more shops, cafés, and restaurants. Walk east from the Cannery on Jefferson Street to **Fisherman's Wharf** ⑤. A few blocks farther east is **Pier 39** ⑥.

TIMING

For the entire Northern Waterfront circuit, set aside three or four hours, not including boat tours, which will take from one to three hours or more. All the attractions here are open daily.

Sights to See

★ **Alcatraz Island.** The boat ride to the island is brief (15 minutes) but affords beautiful views of the city, Marin County, and the East Bay. The audio tour, highly recommended, includes observations of guards and prisoners about life in one of America's most notorious penal colonies. A separate ranger-led tour surveys the island's ecology. Plan your schedule to allow at least three hours for the visit and boat rides combined. Reservations, even in the off-season, are recommended. ⊠ *Pier 41, Fisherman's Wharf,* ☎ *415/773–1188 boat schedules and information; 415/705–5555; 800/426–8687 credit-card ticket orders; 415/705–1042 park information.* ☎ *$13.25, $9.25 without audio ($20.75 evening tours, including audio); add $2.25 per ticket to charge by phone.* ☉ *Ferry departures Sept.–late May, daily 9:30–2:15 (4:20 for evening tour Thurs.–Sun. only); late May–Aug., daily 9:30–4:15 (6:30 and 7:30 for evening tour).* WEB *www.nps.gov/alcatraz.*

Angel Island. For an outdoorsy adventure, consider a day at Angel Island, northwest of Alcatraz. Discovered by Spaniards in 1775 and declared a U.S. military reserve 75 years later, the island was used from 1910 until 1940 as a screening ground for Asian immigrants, who were often held for months, even years, before being granted entry. In 1963 the government designated Angel Island a state park. Today people come for picnics and hikes—a scenic 5-mi path winds around the perimeter of the island—as well as guided tours that explain the park's history. Twenty-five bicycles are permitted on the regular ferry on a first-come, first-served basis, and you can rent mountain bikes for $10 per hour or $30 per day at the landing. ⊠ *Pier 41, Fisherman's Wharf,* ☎ *415/435–1915 park information and ferry schedules; 415/705–5555; 800/426–8687 tickets,* WEB *www.angelisland.org or www.angelisland.com.*

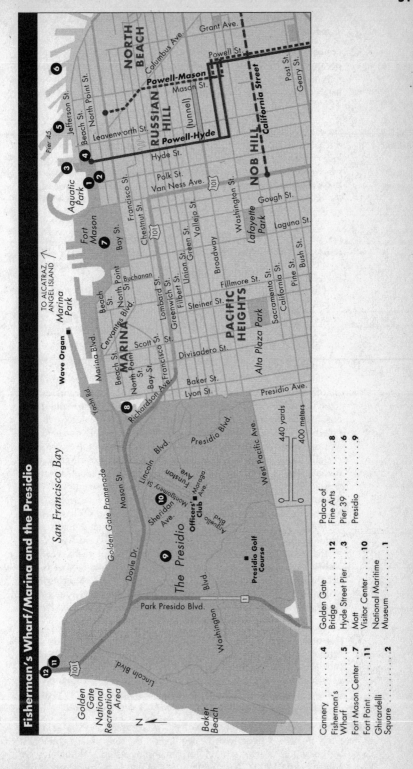

Fisherman's Wharf/Marina and the Presidio

51

Cannery 4
Fisherman's
Wharf 5
Fort Mason Center . .7
Fort Point 11
Ghirardelli
Square 2

Golden Gate
Bridge 12
Hyde Street Pier 3
Mott
Visitor Center 10
National Maritime
Museum 1

Palace of
Fine Arts 8
Pier 39 6
Presidio 9

☎ *$10.50.* ⊙ *Ferry sailing days and departure times vary; call for schedule.*

❹ Cannery. This three-story structure was built in 1894 to house what became the Del Monte Fruit and Vegetable Cannery. Today the Cannery has shops, art galleries, a comedy club (Cobb's), and some unusual restaurants. ⊠ *2801 Leavenworth St., Fisherman's Wharf,* ☎ *415/771–3112.*

....

NEED A
BREAK?

The mellow **Buena Vista Café** (⊠ 2765 Hyde St., Fisherman's Wharf, ☎ 415/474–5044) claims to be the first U.S. establishment to have served Irish coffee. The late San Francisco columnist Stan Delaplane is credited with importing the Celtic concoction. The café opens at 9 AM weekdays, 8 AM weekends, and serves a great breakfast. It is always crowded, but try for a table overlooking nostalgic Victorian Park with its cable car turntable.

....

Ferries. Alcatraz Island and Angel Island are just two of the destinations served by the **Blue and Gold Fleet** (⊠ Pier 41, Fisherman's Wharf, ☎ 415/705–5555). Alcatraz is the best deal—you get all the fun of a bay cruise and a great tour of the prison. But the boats are a fine way to day-trip to Sausalito and Tiburon. Blue and Gold also runs ferries to Oakland, Alameda, Sausalito, Tiburon, and Vallejo. The Vallejo boat docks near Six Flags Marine World. The **Red and White Fleet** (⊠ Pier 43½, Fisherman's Wharf, ☎ 415/447–0591 or 800/229–2784) operates bay and other cruises.

❺ Fisherman's Wharf. Ships creak at their moorings; seagulls cry out for a handout. By mid-afternoon the fishing fleet is back to port. The chaotic streets of the wharf have numerous seafood restaurants, among them sidewalk stands where shrimp and crab cocktails are sold in disposable containers. T-shirts and sweats, gold chains galore, redwood furniture, acres of artwork (precious little of it original), and generally amusing street artists also beckon visitors. Everything's overpriced, especially the so-called novelty museums, which can provide a diversion if you're touring with antsy kids. The best of the lot, though mostly for their kitsch value, are **Ripley's Believe It or Not! Museum** (⊠ 175 Jefferson St., Fisherman's Wharf, ☎ 415/771–6188, WEB www.ripleysf.com) and the **Wax Museum** (⊠ 145 Jefferson St., Fisherman's Wharf, ☎ 415/439–4305), rebuilt in the late 1990s. For an intriguing if mildly claustrophobic glimpse into life on a submarine during World War II, drop by the USS *Pampanito* (⊠ Pier 45, Fisherman's Wharf, ☎ 415/775–1943). The sub, open Thursday–Tuesday 9–8, Wednesday 9–6 (October through Memorial Day open Sunday–Thursday 9–6, Friday–Saturday 9–8), sank six Japanese warships and damaged four others. Admission is $7. ⊠ *Jefferson St. between Leavenworth St. and Pier 39, Fisherman's Wharf.*

❷ Ghirardelli Square. Most of the redbrick buildings in this early 20th-century complex were part of the Ghirardelli chocolate factory. Now they house name-brand emporiums, tourist-oriented restaurants, and galleries that sell everything from crafts and knickknacks to sports memorabilia. Placards throughout the square describe the factory's history. ⊠ *900 N. Point St., Fisherman's Wharf,* ☎ *415/775–5500.*

❸ Hyde Street Pier. The pier, one of the wharf area's best bargains, always crackles with activity. Depending on the time of day, you might see boatbuilders at work or children manning a ship as though it were still the early 1900s. The highlight of the pier is its collection of historic vessels, all of which can be boarded: the *Balclutha,* an 1886 full-rigged three-masted sailing vessel that sailed around Cape Horn 17 times;

the *Eureka,* a side-wheel ferry; the *C. A. Thayer,* a three-masted schooner; and the *Hercules,* a steam-powered tugboat. ⊠ *Hyde and Jefferson Sts., Fisherman's Wharf,* ☏ *415/556–3002 or 415/556–0859,* WEB *www.maritime.org.* ⊡ *$6.* ☉ *May 15–Sept. 15, daily 9:30–5:30, Sept. 16–May 14, daily 9:30–5.*

❶ **National Maritime Museum.** You'll feel as if you're out to sea when you step inside this sturdy, rounded structure. Part of the San Francisco Maritime National Historical Park, which includes Hyde Street Pier, the museum exhibits ship models, maps, and other artifacts chronicling the development of San Francisco and the West Coast through maritime history. ⊠ *Aquatic Park at the foot of Polk St., Fisherman's Wharf,* ☏ *415/556–3002,* WEB *www.nps.gov.* ⊡ *Donation suggested.* ☉ *Daily 10–5.*

🖑 ❻ **Pier 39.** This is the most popular—and commercial—of San Francisco's waterfront attractions, drawing millions of visitors each year to browse through its dozens of shops. Ongoing free entertainment, accessible validated parking, and nearby public transportation ensure crowds most days. Check out the **Marine Mammal Store & Interpretive Center** (☏ 415/289–7373), a quality gift shop and education center whose proceeds benefit Sausalito's Marine Mammal Center, and the **National Park Store** (☏ 415/433–7221), with books, maps, and collectibles sold to support the National Park Service. Brilliant colors enliven the double-decker **Venetian Carousel,** often awhirl with happily howling children ($2 a ride). The din on the northwest side of the pier comes courtesy of the hundreds of sea lions that bask and play on the docks. At **Aquarium of the Bay** (☏ 415/623–5300 or 888/732–3483), moving walkways transport you through a space surrounded on three sides by water filled with indigenous San Francisco Bay marine life, from fish and plankton to sharks. The **California Welcome Center** (☏ 415/956–3493), inside the Citibank Cinemax Theater, is open from 10 to 6 daily. Parking is at the Pier 39 Garage, off Powell Street at the Embarcadero. ⊠ *Beach St. at the Embarcadero, Fisherman's Wharf,* WEB *www.pier39.com.*

THE MARINA AND THE PRESIDIO

The Marina district was a coveted place to live until the 1989 earthquake, when the area's homes suffered the worst damage in the city—largely because the Marina is built on landfill. Many homeowners and renters fled in search of more solid ground, but young professionals quickly replaced them, changing the tenor of this formerly low-key neighborhood. The number of upscale coffee emporiums skyrocketed. A bank became a Williams-Sonoma, and the local grocer gave way to a Pottery Barn. On weekends, a fairly homogeneous well-to-do crowd frequents these and other establishments. One unquestionable improvement was the influx of contemporary cuisine in this former bastion of coffee shops and outdated Italian fare. Even before the quake, though, the Marina Safeway, at Laguna Street and Marina Boulevard, was a famed pickup place for young heterosexual singles.

West of the Marina is the sprawling Presidio, a former military base. In 1996 President Clinton signed a bill placing the Presidio in the hands of a trust corporation as part of a novel money-generating experiment. The trust is leasing buildings and allowing limited development in hopes of making enough money to cover some of the Presidio's operating costs. Whether this arrangement is a worthy model for national parks of the future—or the first step in the crass commercialization of a public resource—remains to be seen. Whatever the outcome, the Presidio will still have superb views and the best hiking and biking areas in San Francisco; a drive through the area can also be rewarding.

Numbers in the text correspond to numbers in the margin and on the Northern Waterfront/Marina and the Presidio map.

A Good Drive

Though you can visit the sights below using public transportation, this is the place to use your car if you have one. You might even consider renting one for a day to cover the area, as well as Lincoln Park, Golden Gate Park, and the western shoreline.

Start at **Fort Mason Center** ⑦, whose entrance for automobiles is off Marina Boulevard at Buchanan Street. If you're coming by bus, take Bus 30–Stockton heading north (and later west); get off at Chestnut and Laguna streets and walk north three blocks to the pedestrian entrance at Marina Boulevard and Laguna. To get from Fort Mason to the **Palace of Fine Arts** ⑧ by car, make a right on Marina Boulevard. The road curves past a small marina and the Marina Green. Turn left at Divisadero Street, right on North Point Street, left on Baker Street, and right on Bay Street, which passes the palace's lagoon and dead-ends at the Lyon Street parking lot. Part of the palace complex is the **Exploratorium,** a hands-on science museum. (If you're walking from Fort Mason to the palace, the directions are easier: Follow Marina Boulevard to Scott Street. Cross to the south side of the street—away from the water—and continue past Divisadero Street to Baker Street, and turn left; you'll see the palace's lagoon on your right. To take Muni, walk back to Chestnut and Laguna streets and take Bus 30–Stockton continuing west; get off at North Point and Broderick streets and walk west on North Point.)

The least confusing way to drive to the **Presidio** ⑨ from the palace is to exit from the south end of the Lyon Street parking lot and head east (left) on Bay Street. Turn right (south) onto Baker Street, and right (west) on Francisco Street, taking it across Richardson Avenue to Lyon Street. Turn south (left) on Lyon and right (west) on Lombard Street, and go through the main gate to Presidio Boulevard. Turn right on Presidio, which becomes Lincoln Boulevard. Make a left at Montgomery Street; a half block up on the right is the Presidio's **Mott Visitor Center** ⑩. (To take the bus to the Presidio, walk north from the palace to Lombard Street and catch Bus 28 heading west; it stops on Lincoln near the visitor center.)

From the visitor center head north a half block to Sheridan Avenue, make a right, and make a left when Sheridan runs into Lincoln Boulevard. Lincoln winds through the Presidio past a large cemetery and some vista points. After a couple of miles you'll see a parking lot marked FORT POINT on the right. Park and follow the signs leading to **Fort Point** ⑪, walking downhill through a lightly wooded area. To walk the short distance to the **Golden Gate Bridge** ⑫, follow the signs from the Fort Point parking lot; to drive across the bridge, continue on Lincoln Boulevard a bit and watch for the turnoff on the right. Bus 28 serves stops fairly near these last two attractions; ask the driver to call them out.

TIMING

The time it takes to see this area will vary greatly depending on whether you'll be taking public transportation or driving. If you drive, plan to spend at least three hours, not including a walk across the Golden Gate Bridge or hikes along the shoreline—each of which will take a few hours. A great way to see the area is on bicycle; the folks at the Mott Visitor Center will help you find the closest rental outfit. With or without kids, you could easily pass two hours at the Exploratorium.

Sights to See

★ ⟳ **Exploratorium.** The curious of all ages flock to this fascinating "museum of science, art, and human perception" within the Palace of Fine Arts. The more than 650 exhibits focus on sea and insect life, computers, electricity, patterns and light, language, the weather, and much more. "Explainers"—often high school students on their days off from school—provide help and demonstrate scientific principles (lasers, dissection of a cow's eye). Reservations are required to crawl through the pitch-black, touchy-feely **Tactile Dome**, an adventure of 15 minutes. The object is to crawl and climb through the space relying solely on the sense of touch. ⊠ *3601 Lyon St., at Marina Blvd., Marina,* ☏ *415/561–0360 general information; 415/561–0362 Tactile Dome reservations,* WEB *www.exploratorium.edu.* ⊡ *$10, free 1st Wed. of month; Tactile Dome $4 extra.* ⊙ *Memorial Day–Labor Day, Sun.–Tues. and Thurs.–Sat. 10–6, Wed. 10–9; Labor Day–Memorial Day, Tues. and Thurs.–Sun. 10–5, Wed. 10–9.*

OFF THE
BEATEN PATH

WAVE ORGAN – Fashioned by stonecutters George Gonzales and Thomas Lipps, this unusual instrument gives off harmonic sounds produced by the seawater that passes through its three stone chambers. ⊠ *North of the Marina Green at the end of the jetty by Yacht Rd. (park in lot north of Marina Blvd. at Lyon St.), Marina.*

❼ **Fort Mason Center.** Originally a depot for the shipment of supplies to the Pacific during World War II, Fort Mason was converted into a cultural center in 1977. In business here are the popular vegetarian restaurant Greens and shops, galleries, and performance spaces, most of which are closed on Monday.

Two interesting small museums are in Building C. The **Museo Italo-Americano** (☏ 415/673–2200) mounts impressive exhibits of the works of Italian and Italian-American artists—paintings, sculpture, etchings, and photographs. It's closed Monday and Tuesday. The exhibits at the **San Francisco African-American Historical and Cultural Society** (☏ 415/441–0640) document past and contemporary black arts and culture.

In Building A is the **San Francisco Craft and Folk Art Museum** (☏ 415/775–0990), an airy space with exhibits of American folk art, tribal art, and contemporary crafts. The museum is open daily; its shop is a sure bet for whimsical gifts from around the world. Next door to the Craft and Folk Art Museum is the **SFMOMA Artists Gallery** (☏ 415/441–4777), where the art is available for sale or rent. The gallery is closed Sunday and Monday. Most of the museums and shops at Fort Mason close by 6 or 7. The museum admission fees range from pay-what-you-wish to $4. ⊠ *Buchanan St. and Marina Blvd., Marina,* ☏ *415/979–3010 event information.*

NEED A
BREAK?

Greens to Go (⊠ Fort Mason, Bldg. A, Marina, ☏ 415/771–6330), the take-out wing of the famous Greens restaurant, carries mouthwatering salads, sandwiches, and soups.

⓫ **Fort Point.** Designed to mount 126 cannons with a range of up to 2 mi, Fort Point was constructed between 1853 and 1861 to protect San Francisco from sea attack during the Civil War—but it was never used for that purpose. It was, however, used as a coastal defense fortification post during World War II, when soldiers stood watch here. This National Historic Site is a museum filled with military memorabilia. The building has a gloomy air and is suitably atmospheric. On days when Fort Point is staffed, guided group tours and cannon drills take place. The top floor affords a unique angle on the bay. Take care when walking along the front side of the building, as it's slippery and the waves have a dizzying effect. Just north of this structure is the cluster of buildings known as **Fort Point Mine Depot,** an army facility that functioned as the headquarters for underwater mining operations throughout World War II. ⊠ *Marine Dr. off Lincoln Blvd., Presidio,* ☎ *415/556–1693,* WEB *www.nps.gov/fopo.* ⊡ *Free.* ☾ *Thurs.–Mon. 10–5.*

★ ⑫   **Golden Gate Bridge.** The suspension bridge that connects San Francisco with Marin County has long wowed sightseers with its rust-color beauty, 750-ft towers, and simple but powerful art deco design. At nearly 2 mi, the Golden Gate, completed in 1937 after four years of construction, was built to withstand winds of more than 100 mph. Though frequently gusty and misty (walkers should wear warm clothing), the bridge offers unparalleled views of the Bay Area. The east walkway yields a glimpse of the San Francisco skyline as well as the islands of the bay. The view west takes in the wild hills of the Marin Headlands, the curving coast south to Land's End, and the majestic Pacific Ocean. A vista point on the Marin side affords a spectacular view of the city. On sunny days sailboats dot the water, and brave windsurfers test the often-treacherous tides beneath the bridge. Muni Buses 28 and 29 make stops at the Golden Gate Bridge toll plaza, on the San Francisco side. ⊠ *Lincoln Blvd. near Doyle Dr. and Fort Point, Presidio,* ☎ *415/ 921–5858,* WEB *www.goldengatebridge.org.* ☾ *For pedestrians: In winter daily 6–6; in summer daily 5* AM*–9* PM.

⑩   **Mott Visitor Center.** National Park Service employees at the William P. Mott Jr. Visitor Center dispense maps, brochures, and schedules for guided walking and bicycle tours, along with information about the Presidio's past, present, and future. The building also houses the **Presidio Museum,** under renovation at press time, which focuses on the role played by the military in San Francisco's development. ⊠ *Montgomery St. between Lincoln Blvd. and Sheridan Ave., Presidio,* ☎ *415/561–4323.* ⊡ *Free.* ☾ *Daily 9–5.*

★ ⑧   **Palace of Fine Arts.** San Francisco's rosy rococo Palace of Fine Arts is at the western end of the Marina. The palace is the sole survivor of the many tinted plaster buildings (a temporary classical city of sorts) built for the 1915 Panama-Pacific International Exposition, the world's fair that celebrated San Francisco's recovery from the 1906 earthquake and fire. The expo lasted for 288 days and the buildings extended about a mile along the shore. Bernard Maybeck designed this faux Roman Classic beauty, which was reconstructed in concrete and reopened in 1967. The massive columns, great rotunda (dedicated to the glory of Greek culture), and swan-filled lagoon have been used in countless fashion layouts and films. ⊠ *Baker and Beach Sts., Marina,* ☎ *415/561–0364 palace tours,* WEB *www.exploratorium.edu/palace.*

⑨   **Presidio.** Part of the Golden Gate National Recreation Area, the Presidio was a military post for more than 200 years. Don Juan Bautista de Anza and a band of Spanish settlers first claimed the area in 1776. It became a Mexican garrison in 1822 when Mexico gained its independence from Spain; U.S. troops forcibly occupied the Presidio in 1846. The U.S. Sixth Army was stationed here until October 1994, when the coveted space was transferred into civilian hands. Today, after much controversy, the area is being transformed into a self-sustaining national park with a combination of public, commercial, and residential projects. After fierce bidding, Bay Area filmmaker George Lucas won the right to build his digital studio "campus" on a corner of the land. The battle continues over the fate of the rest of the Presidio. It may remain in its current state, or a new entertainment and commercial complex may transform the park into the city's latest tourist destination. Today the more than 1;400 acres of hills, majestic woods, and redbrick army barracks present an air of serenity on the edge of the city. There are two beaches, a golf course, a visitor center, and picnic sites, and the views of the bay, the Golden Gate Bridge, and Marin County are sublime. ⊠ *Between the Marina and Lincoln Park, Presidio,* WEB *www. nps.gov/prsf.*

<table>
<tr><td>OFF THE
BEATEN PATH</td><td>**PRESIDIO OFFICERS' CLUB** – A remnant of the days when the Presidio was an army base, this mission-style clubhouse now hosts temporary art exhibitions that explore the unique cultural identity of the American West and the Pan-Pacific, such as Japanese woodblocks prints. Part of the Presidio's transition to self-sustaining national park, the club also offers dance performances, lectures, and theater. And a bonus rare in San Francisco—ample free parking. ⊠ *50 Moraga Ave., Presidio,* ☎ *800/ 965–4827.* ☞ *$9.* ☉ *Mon. and Thurs.–Sun. 10–5, Wed. 10–8.* WEB *www.atthepresidio.org.*</td></tr>
</table>

GOLDEN GATE PARK

William Hammond Hall conceived one of the nation's great city parks and began in 1870 to put into action his plan for a natural reserve with no reminders of urban life. Hammond began work in the Panhandle and eastern portions of Golden Gate Park, but it took John McLaren the length of his tenure as park superintendent, from 1890 to 1943, to complete the transformation of 1,000 desolate brush- and sand-covered acres into a rolling, landscaped oasis. Urban reality now encroaches on all sides, but the park remains a great getaway. On Sunday John F. Kennedy Drive is closed to cars and comes alive with joggers, cyclists, and in-line skaters. In addition to cultural and other attractions there are public tennis courts, baseball diamonds, soccer fields, and trails for horseback riding. **Friends of Recreation and Parks** (☎ 415/263–0991) conducts walking tours of Golden Gate Park year-round. The fog can sweep into the park with amazing speed; always bring a sweatshirt or jacket.

Because the park is so large, a car will come in handy if you're going to tour it from one end to the other—though you'll still do a fair amount of walking. You can make the jump between the attractions on the eastern edge of the park and the ones near the ocean on public transportation.

Muni also serves the park. Buses 5–Fulton and 21–Hayes stop along its northern edge, and the N–Judah light-rail car stops a block south of the park between Stanyan Street and 9th Avenue, then two blocks south and the rest of the way west.

Numbers in the text correspond to numbers in the margin and on the Golden Gate Park map.

A Good Walk

Begin on the park's north side at Fulton Street and 6th Avenue, where the Bus 5–Fulton and Bus 21–Hayes from downtown stop. Walk south into the park at 6th Avenue. The road you'll come to is John F. Kennedy Drive. Turn left on the blacktop sidewalk and head east. Across the drive on your right is the Rhododendron Dell. (If it's springtime and the rhododendrons are in bloom, detour into the dell and return to John F. Kennedy Drive heading east.) Past the first stop sign you'll see the exterior gardens of the **Conservatory of Flowers** ① on your left. Explore the gardens; then walk south (back toward Kennedy Drive) from the conservatory entrance. Continue east on Kennedy Drive a short way to the three-way intersection and turn right (south) at Middle Drive East.

Less than a block away at the intersection of Middle and Bowling Green drives you'll see a sign for the National AIDS Memorial Grove. Before you enter the grove, follow the curve of Bowling Green Drive to the left, past the Bowling Green to the **Children's Playground** ②. If you've got kids in tow, you'll probably be spending time here. If not, still take a peek at the vintage Herschell-Spillman Carousel.

Reverse direction on Bowling Green Drive and enter the **National AIDS Memorial Grove** ③, a sunken meadow that stretches west along Middle Drive East. At the end of the wheelchair-access ramp make a left to view the Circle of Friends; then continue west along the graded paths (ignore the staircase on the right halfway through the grove) to another circle with a poem by Thom Gunn. Exit north from this circle. As you're standing in the circle looking at the poem, the staircase to take is on your left. At the top of the staircase make a left and continue west on Middle Drive East. You'll come to the back entrance of the **California Academy of Sciences** ④.

At the end of Middle Drive East, turn right and follow the signs leading to the **Shakespeare Garden** ⑤. After touring the garden, exit via the path on which you entered and turn left (to the south). A hundred feet shy of the Ninth Avenue and Lincoln Way entrance to Golden Gate Park is the main entrance to **Strybing Arboretum & Botanical Gardens** ⑥. You could spend an afternoon here, but to sample just a bit of this fine facility take the first right after the bookstore. Follow the path as it winds north and west. Take your second right and you'll see signs for the Fragrance and Biblical gardens.

Backtrack from the gardens to the path you started on and make a right. As the path continues to wind north and west, you'll see a large fountain off to the left. Just before you get to the fountain, make a right and head toward the duck pond. A wooden footbridge on the pond's left side crosses the water. Signs on the other side identify the mallards, geese, American coots, mews, and other fowl in the pond. Stay to the right on the path, heading toward the exit gate. Just before the gate, continue to the right to the Primitive Garden. Take the looped boardwalk past ferns, gingko, cycads, conifers, moss, and other plants. At the end of the loop, make a left and then a right, exiting via the Eugene L. Friend gate. Go straight ahead on the crosswalk to the blacktop path on the other side. Make a right, walk about 100 ft, and make a left on Tea Garden Drive. A few hundred feet east of here is the entrance to the **Japanese Tea Garden** ⑦.

Tour the Japanese Tea Garden, exiting near the gate you entered. Make a left, and you'll soon pass the former Asian Art Museum and the M. H. de Young Memorial Museum; both buildings are closed for construction. A crosswalk leads south to the Music Concourse, with its gnarled trees, century-old fountains and sculptures, and the Golden Gate Bandshell. Turn left at the closest of the fountains and head east toward the bronze sculpture of Francis Scott Key.

Turn left at the statue and proceed north through two underpasses. At the end of the second underpass, you'll have traveled about 2 mi. If you're ready to leave the park, take the short staircase to the left of the blue-and-green playground equipment. At the top of the staircase is the 10th Avenue and Fulton Street stop for Bus 5–Fulton heading back downtown. If you're game for walking ½ mi more, make an immediate left as you exit the second underpass, cross 10th Avenue, and make a right on John F. Kennedy Drive. After approximately ¼ mi you'll see the Rose Garden on your right. Continue west to the first stop sign. To the left is a sign for **Stow Lake** ⑧. Follow the road past the log cabin to the boathouse.

From Stow Lake it's the equivalent of 30 long blocks on John F. Kennedy Drive to the western end of the park and the ocean. If you walk, you'll pass meadows, the Portals of the Past, the buffalo paddock, and a nine-hole golf course. You can skip most of this walk by proceeding west on John F. Kennedy Drive from the stop sign mentioned above, making the first right after you walk underneath Cross-Over Drive, and following the road as it winds left toward 25th Avenue and Fulton. On the northwest corner of Fulton Street and 25th Avenue, catch Bus 5–Fulton heading west, get off at 46th Avenue, walk one block west to 47th Avenue, and make a left. Make a right on John F. Kennedy Drive.

By foot or vehicle, your goal is the **Dutch Windmill** ⑨ and adjoining garden. A block to the south, wind up with a microbrew at the **Beach Chalet** ⑩.

TIMING

You can easily spend a whole day in Golden Gate Park, especially if you walk the whole distance. Set aside at least an hour for the Academy of Sciences. Even if you plan to explore just the eastern end of the park (up to Stow Lake), allot at least two hours.

Sights to See

⑩ **Beach Chalet.** This Spanish colonial–style structure, architect Willis Polk's last design, was built in 1925 after his death. A wraparound Federal Works Project mural by Lucien Labaudt depicts San Francisco in the 1930s; the labels describing the various panels add up to a minihistory of depression-era life in the city. A three-dimensional model of Golden Gate Park, artifacts from the 1894 Mid-Winter Exposition and other park events, a visitor center, and a gift shop that sells street signs and other city paraphernalia are on the first floor as well. On a clear day, the brewpub-restaurant upstairs (notice the carved banister on the way up) has views past Ocean Beach to the Farallon Islands, about 30 mi offshore. ⊠ *1000 Great Hwy., at west end of John F. Kennedy Dr., Golden Gate Park,* WEB *www.beachchalet.com.*

OFF THE
BEATEN PATH

BUFFALO PADDOCK – The original denizens of the paddock arrived at the park in 1894 for the Mid-Winter Exposition. The present herd, from Wyoming, was acquired in 1984. ⊠ *John F. Kennedy Dr. west of Spreckels Lake, Golden Gate Park.*

★ ⚇ ❹ **California Academy of Sciences.** A three-in-one attraction, the nationally renowned academy houses an aquarium, numerous science and natural-history exhibits, and a planetarium.

Leopard sharks, silver salmon, sea bass, and other fish loop around the mesmerizing Fish Roundabout, the big draw at **Steinhart Aquarium.** Feeding time is 1:30 PM. At the Touch Tide Pool, you can cozy up to starfish, hermit crabs, and other critters. Elsewhere at Steinhart swim dolphins, sea turtles, piranhas, manatees, and other sea life. Tropical reef sharks cruise their own tank, and there are also reptile and amphibian displays and an alligator pond. Vibrantly colored fish vie for attention with iridescent coral at the tropical coral reef. Always amusing to watch, the penguins dine at 11:30 AM and 4 PM.

The multimedia earthquake exhibit in the Earth and Space Hall at the **Natural History Museum** simulates quakes, complete with special effects. Videos and displays in the Wild California Hall describe the state's

Golden Gate Park

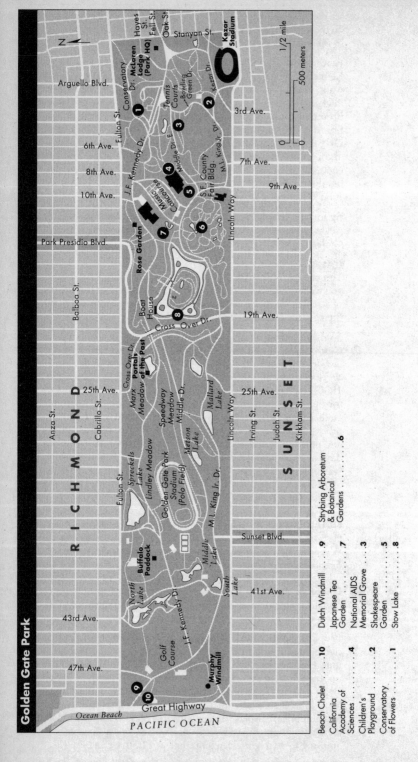

Beach Chalet **10**

California
Academy of
Sciences **4**

Children's
Playground **2**

Conservatory
of Flowers **1**

Dutch Windmill **9**

Japanese Tea
Garden **7**

National AIDS
Memorial Grove **3**

Shakespeare
Garden **5**

Stow Lake **8**

Strybing Arboretum
& Botanical
Gardens **6**

wildlife, and there's a re-creation of the environment of the rocky Farallon Islands. Dinosaur bones and a brontosaurus skull draw dinophiles to the Hall of Fossils. The African Hall contains animals (real, but stuffed) specific to Africa in their native vegetation; don't miss the sights and sounds of the African watering hole at the end of the room. The natural-history wing's other attractions include the gem and mineral hall, an insect room, Far Side of Science cartoons by Gary Larson, and an open play and learning space for small children.

There is an additional charge ($2.50) for **Morrison Planetarium** shows (☎ 415/750–7141 schedule), which you enter through the Natural History Museum. Daily multimedia shows present the night sky through the ages under a 55-ft dome, complete with special effects and music. A cafeteria is open daily until one hour before the museum closes. ⊠ *Music Concourse Dr. off South Dr., Golden Gate Park,* ☎ *415/750–7145,* WEB *www.calacademy.org.* ⊡ *$8.50 ($2.50 discount with Muni transfer), free 1st Wed. of month.* ☉ *Memorial Day–Labor Day, daily 9–6; Labor Day–Memorial Day, daily 10–5; 1st Wed. of month closes at 8:45* PM.

🐾 ❷ **Children's Playground.** Kids have been coming here to cut loose since the 1880s. The equipment has changed over the years, but the squeals and howls remain the same. A menagerie of handcrafted horses and other animals—among them cats, frogs, roosters, and a tiger—twirl on the 1912 Herschell-Spillman Carousel, inside a many-windowed circular structure. The Romanesque-style Sharon Building looms over the playground. The 1887 structure has been rebuilt twice, following the earthquake of 1906 and a 1980 fire. ⊠ *Bowling Green Dr., off Martin Luther King Jr. Dr., Golden Gate Park,* ☎ *415/753–5210 or 415/831–2700.* ⊡ *Playground free, carousel $1.* ☉ *Playground daily dawn–midnight; carousel June–Sept., daily 10–5, Oct.–May, Fri.–Sun. 9–4.*

❶ **Conservatory of Flowers.** The oldest building in the park and the last remaining wood-frame Victorian conservatory in the country, the Conservatory, which was built in the late 1870s, is a copy of the one in the Royal Botanical Gardens in Kew, England. Heavily damaged during a 1995 storm, the whitewashed facility is closed indefinitely but its architecture and gardens make it a worthy stop nonetheless. The gardens in front of the Conservatory are planted seasonally, with the flowers often fashioned like billboards—depicting the Golden Gate Bridge or other city sights. On the east side of the Conservatory (to the right as you face the building), cypress, pine, and redwood trees surround the **Fuchsia Garden,** which blooms in summer and fall. To the west several hundred feet on John F. Kennedy Drive is the **Rhododendron Dell.** The dell contains the most varieties—850 in all—of any garden in the country. It's especially beautiful in March, when many of the flowers bloom, and is a favorite spot of locals for Mother's Day picnics. ⊠ *John F. Kennedy Dr. at Conservatory Dr., Golden Gate Park.*

❾ **Dutch Windmill.** Two windmills anchor the western end of the park. The restored 1902 Dutch Windmill once pumped 20,000 gallons of well water per hour to the reservoir on Strawberry Hill. With its heavy cement bottom and wood-shingled arms and upper section the windmill cuts quite the sturdy figure. It overlooks the equally photogenic **Queen Wilhelmina Tulip Garden,** which bursts into full bloom in early spring and late summer. The **Murphy Windmill,** on Martin Luther King Jr. Drive near the Great Highway, was the world's largest windmill when it was built in 1905. Now in disrepair, its wings clipped, the Murphy Windmill also pumped water to the Strawberry Hill reservoir. ⊠ *Between 47th Ave. and the Great Hwy., Golden Gate Park.*

★ ❼ **Japanese Tea Garden.** A serene 4-acre landscape of small ponds, streams, waterfalls, stone bridges, Japanese sculptures, *mumsai* (planted bonsai) trees, perfect miniature pagodas, and some nearly vertical wooden "humpback" bridges, the tea garden was created for the 1894 Mid-Winter Exposition. Go in the spring if you can (March is particularly beautiful), when the cherry blossoms are in bloom. ⊠ *Tea Garden Dr. off John F. Kennedy Dr., Golden Gate Park,* ☎ *415/752–4227 or 415/752–1171.* ⌑ *$3.50.* ☉ *Mar.–Sept., daily 9–6; Oct.–Feb., daily 8:30–5.*

NEED A BREAK?

Rest your feet and take in the soothing sights of the Japanese Tea Garden from a seat in the covered-roof, open-air **Tea House,** a low-lit space with hanging lanterns and long wooden benches. Tea and cookies are served daily from 9 to 5.

❸ **National AIDS Memorial Grove.** San Francisco has lost many residents, gay and straight, to AIDS. This 15-acre grove, started in the early 1990s by people with AIDS and their families and friends, was conceived as a living memorial to those the disease has claimed. Hundreds of volunteers toiled long and hard raising funds and clearing this patch of green, also known as De Laveaga Dell. In 1996 Congress passed a bill granting the grove status as a national memorial. Coast live oaks, Monterey pines, coast redwoods, and other trees flank the grove, which is anchored at its east end by the stone Circle of Friends (of donors, people who have died of AIDS, and those who loved them). A 1996 poem by San Franciscan Thom Gunn in the tan fieldstone circle at the west end of the grove reads: WALKER WITHIN THIS CIRCLE PAUSE/ALTHOUGH THEY DIED OF ONE CAUSE/REMEMBER HOW THEIR LIVES WERE DENSE/WITH FINE COMPACTED DIFFERENCE. ⊠ *Middle Dr. E, west of tennis courts, Golden Gate Park,* WEB *www.aidsmemorial.org.*

OFF THE BEATEN PATH

PORTALS OF THE PAST – An evocative relic of a Nob Hill mansion that was wrecked by the 1906 earthquake and fire, the Ionic columns that once framed the mansion's entryway now stand in solitude on the edge of Lloyd Lake. ⊠ *Beside Lloyd Lake off John F. Kennedy Dr., south of 25th Ave., Golden Gate Park.*

❺ **Shakespeare Garden.** Two hundred flowers and herbs mentioned in the Bard's plays grow here. Bronze-engraved passages contain relevant floral quotations. ⊠ *Middle Dr. E at southwest corner of California Academy of Sciences, Golden Gate Park.*

❽ **Stow Lake.** One of the most picturesque spots in Golden Gate Park, this placid body of water surrounds Strawberry Hill. A couple of bridges allow you to cross over and ascend the hill (the old 19th-century stone bridge on the southwest side of the lake is especially quaint). A waterfall cascades down from the top of the hill, and panoramic views make it worth the short hike up here. Down below, rent a boat, surrey, or bicycle or stroll around the perimeter. Just to the left of the waterfall sits the elaborate Chinese Pavilion, a gift from the city of Taipei. It was shipped in 6,000 pieces and assembled on the shore of Strawberry Hill Island in 1981. ⊠ *Off John F. Kennedy Dr., ½ mi west of 10th Ave., Golden Gate Park,* ☎ *415/752–0347.*

❻ **Strybing Arboretum & Botanical Gardens.** The 55-acre arboretum specializes in plants from areas with climates similar to that of the Bay Area, such as the west coast of Australia, South Africa, and the Mediterranean; more than 8,000 plant and tree varieties bloom in gardens throughout the grounds. Among the highlights are the Biblical, Fragrance, California Native Plants, Succulents, and Primitive Plant gardens, the new- and old-world cloud forests, and the duck pond. The exhaustive reference library holds approximately 18,000 volumes, and the bookstore is a great resource. Maps are available at the main and Eugene L. Friend entrances. ⊠ *9th Ave. at Lincoln Way, Golden Gate Park,* ☎ *415/661–1316,* 🌐 *www.strybing.org.* 🎫 *Free.* ⊙ *Weekdays 8–4:30, weekends 10–5. Tours from bookstore weekdays at 1:30, weekends at 10:20 and 1:30; tours from Friend Gate Wed., Fri., and Sun. at 2.*

LINCOLN PARK AND THE WESTERN SHORELINE

Few other American cities provide a close-up view of the power and fury of the surf attacking the shore. A different breed of San Franciscan chooses to live in this area: surfers who brave the heaviest fog to ride the waves; writers who seek solace and inspiration in this city outpost; dog lovers committed to giving their pets a good workout each day.

From Land's End in Lincoln Park you'll have some of the best views of the Golden Gate (the name was originally given to the opening of San Francisco Bay, long before the bridge was built) and the Marin Headlands. From the historic Cliff House south to the sprawling San Francisco Zoo, the Great Highway and Ocean Beach run along the western edge of the city. The wind is often strong along the shoreline, summer fog can blanket the ocean beaches, and the water is cold and usually too rough for swimming. Carry a jacket and bring binoculars.

Numbers in the text correspond to numbers in the margin and on the Lincoln Park and the Western Shoreline map.

A Good Drive

A car is useful out here. There are plenty of hiking trails, and buses travel to all the sights mentioned, but the sights are far apart. Start at **Lincoln Park** ①. The park entrance is at 34th Avenue and Clement Street. Those without a car can take Bus 38–Geary—get off at 33rd Avenue and walk north (to the right) one block on 34th Avenue to the entrance. At the end of 34th Avenue (labeled on some maps as Legion of Honor Drive within Lincoln Park) is the **California Palace of the Legion of Honor** ②, a splendid art museum. From the museum, head back out to Clement Street and follow it west. At 45th Avenue, Clement turns into Seal Rock Drive. When Seal Rock dead-ends at 48th Avenue, turn left on El Camino del Mar and right on Point Lobos Avenue. After a few hundred yards, you'll see parking lots for **Sutro Heights Park** ③ and the **Cliff House** ④. (To get from the Legion of Honor to Point Lobos Avenue by public transit, take Bus 18 from the Legion of Honor parking lot west to the corner of 48th and Point Lobos avenues.) Two large concrete lions near the southeast corner of 48th and Point Lobos guard the entrance to Sutro Heights Park. After taking a quick spin through the park, exit past the lions, cross Point Lobos, make a left, and walk down to the Cliff House. From the Cliff House it's a short walk farther downhill to **Ocean Beach** ⑤.

The **San Francisco Zoo** ⑥ is a couple of miles south, at the intersection of the Great Highway and Sloat Boulevard. If you're driving, follow the Great Highway (heading south from the Cliff House, Point Lobos Avenue becomes the Great Highway), turn left on Sloat Boulevard, and park in the zoo's lot on Sloat. The hike along Ocean Beach from the Cliff House to the zoo is a flat but scenic 3 mi. To take public transportation from the Cliff House, reboard Bus 18, which continues south to the zoo.

California
Palace of
the Legion
of Honor 2

Cliff House 4

Lincoln Park ...1

Ocean
Beach 5

San Francisco
Zoo 6

Sutro Heights
Park 3

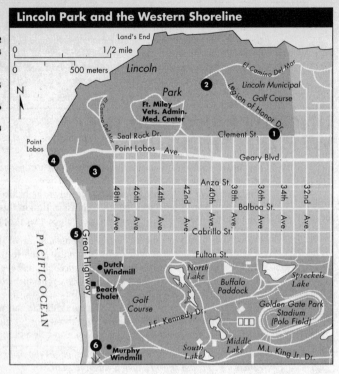

Lincoln Park and the Western Shoreline

TIMING

Set aside at least three hours for this tour—more if you don't have a car. You can easily spend an hour in the Palace of the Legion of Honor and 1½ hours at the zoo.

Sights to See

★ ② **California Palace of the Legion of Honor.** Spectacularly situated on cliffs overlooking the ocean, the Golden Gate Bridge, and the Marin Headlands, this landmark building is a fine repository of European art. A pyramidal glass skylight in the entrance court illuminates the lower-level galleries, which exhibit prints and drawings, English and European porcelain, and ancient Assyrian, Greek, Roman, and Egyptian art. The 20-plus galleries on the upper level display the permanent collection of European art (paintings, sculpture, decorative arts, tapestries) from the 14th century to the present day. The noteworthy Rodin collection includes two galleries devoted to the master and a third with works by Rodin and other 19th-century sculptors. An original cast of Rodin's *The Thinker* welcomes you as you walk through the courtyard.

The **Legion Café**, on the lower level, has a garden terrace and a view of the Golden Gate Bridge. North of the museum (across Camino del Mar) is George Segal's *The Holocaust*, a sculpture that evokes life in concentration camps during World War II. It is hauntingly eloquent at night, when backlit by lights in the Legion's parking lot. ⊠ *34th Ave. at Clement St., Lincoln Park,* ☎ *415/863–3330 information,* WEB *www.thinker.org.* ⊠ *$8 ($2 off with Muni transfer); free 2nd Wed. of month.* ⊙ *Tues.–Sun. 9:30–5.*

④ **Cliff House.** Three buildings have occupied this site since 1863. The original Cliff House hosted several U.S. presidents and wealthy locals who would drive their carriages out to Ocean Beach; it was destroyed by fire on Christmas Day 1894. The second Cliff House, the most beloved and resplendent of the three, was built in 1896; it rose eight stories with an observation tower 200 ft above sea level, but it burned down in 1907. The current building dates from 1909. The complex, which includes restaurants, a pub, and a gift shop, remains open while undergoing a gradual renovation to restore its early 20th-century look.

The upstairs brunch at the Cliff House is standard—eggs any style, good omelets, and the like—but the views enhance the experience. Lunch and dinner are nothing to write home about, but there are those vistas, which can be 30 mi or more on a clear day. The dining areas overlook Seal Rock (the barking marine mammals sunning themselves are actually sea lions).

Below the Cliff House is the splendid **Musée Mécanique** (☎ 415/386–1170), a time-warped arcade with antique mechanical contrivances, including peep shows and nickelodeons. Some favorites are the giant, rather creepy "Laughing Sal," an arm-wrestling machine, and mechanical fortune-telling figures who speak from their curtained boxes. A disturbing display is the "Opium-Den," a tiny diorama with Chinese figures clearly depicting the effects of heavy drug use. The museum opens daily from Memorial Day to Labor Day between 10 and 8 and the rest of the year on weekdays between 11 and 7 and on weekends between 10 and 8. Admission is free, but you may want to bring change to play the games.

The Musée Mécanique looks out on a fine observation deck and the **Golden Gate National Recreation Area Visitors' Center** (☎ 415/556–8642, WEB www.nps.gov/goga), which contains fascinating historical photographs of the Cliff House and the glass-roof Sutro Baths. Eccentric onetime San Francisco mayor and Cliff House owner Adolf Sutro built the bath complex in 1896—including a train out to the site—so that everyday folks could enjoy the benefits of swimming. The complex, which comprised six enormous baths (some freshwater and some seawater), more than 500 dressing rooms, and several restaurants, covered 3 acres north of the Cliff House and accommodated 25,000 bathers. Likened to Roman baths in a European glass palace, the baths were for decades the favorite destination of San Franciscans in search of entertainment. The complex fell into disuse after World War II, was closed in 1952, and burned down during demolition in 1966. You can explore the ruins on your own (they look a bit like water-storage receptacles) or take ranger-led walks on weekends. The visitor center, open daily from 10 to 5, provides information about these and other trails. ⊠ *1090 Point Lobos Ave., Lincoln Park,* ☎ *415/386–3330,* WEB *www.cliffhouse.com and www. nps.gov/goga/clho.* ☉ *Weekdays 8 AM–10:30 PM, weekends 8 AM–11 PM; cocktails served nightly until 2 AM.*

❶ **Lincoln Park.** At one time most of the city's cemeteries were here, segregated by nationality. In 1900, the Board of Supervisors voted to ban burials within city limits (two exceptions are the cemetery at Mission Dolores and the one in the Presidio). Large Monterey cypresses line the fairways at Lincoln Park's 18-hole golf course. There are scenic walks throughout the 275-acre park, with postcard-perfect views from many spots. The trail out to **Land's End** starts outside the Palace of the Legion of Honor, at the end of El Camino del Mar. Be careful if you hike here; landslides are frequent. ⊠ *Entrance at 34th Ave. at Clement St., Lincoln Park.*

❺ **Ocean Beach.** Stretching 3 mi along the western side of the city, this is a good beach for walking, running, or lying in the sun—but not for swimming. Surfers here wear wet suits year-round, as the water is extremely cold. Riptides are also very dangerous here. Paths on both sides of the Great Highway lead from Lincoln Way to Sloat Boulevard (near the zoo); the beachside path winds through landscaped sand dunes, and the paved path across the highway is good for biking and in-line skating. The **Beach Chalet** restaurant and brewpub are across the Great Highway from Ocean Beach, about five blocks south of the Cliff House. ✉ *Along the Great Hwy. from the Cliff House to Sloat Blvd. and beyond.*

☝ ❻ **San Francisco Zoo.** More than 1,000 birds and animals—220 species altogether—reside at the zoo. Among the more than 130 endangered species are the snow leopard, Sumatran tiger, jaguar, and Asian elephant. A favorite attraction is the greater one-horned rhinoceros, next to the African elephants. Another popular resident is Prince Charles, a rare white tiger and the first of its kind to be exhibited in the West.

African Kikuyu grass carpets the circular outer area of **Gorilla World,** one of the largest and most natural gorilla habitats of any zoo in the world. Trees and shrubs create communal play areas. Fifteen species of rare monkeys—including colobus monkeys, white ruffed lemurs, and macaques—live and play at the two-tier **Primate Discovery Center,** which contains 23 interactive learning exhibits on the ground level.

Magellanic penguins waddle about **Penguin Island,** splashing and frolicking in its 200-ft pool. Feeding time is 3 PM. Koalas peer out from among the trees in **Koala Crossing,** and kangaroos and wallabies headline the **Walkabout** exhibit. The 7-acre **Puente al Sur** (Bridge to the South) re-creates habitats in South America, replete with a giant anteater, tapir, and a capybaras. The **Feline Conservation Center,** a natural setting for rare cats, plays a key role in the zoo's efforts to encourage breeding among endangered felines. Don't miss the big-cat feeding—they love their horse meat—at the **Lion House** Tuesday–Sunday at 2.

The **children's zoo** has a population of about 300 mammals, birds, and reptiles, plus an insect zoo, a meerkat and prairie dog exhibit, a nature trail, a nature theater, and a restored 1921 Dentzel carousel. A ride astride one of the 52 hand-carved menagerie animals costs $2. ✉ *Sloat Blvd. and 45th Ave., Sunset (Muni L–Taraval streetcar from downtown),* ☎ *415/753–7080,* WEB *www.sfzoo.org.* ✆ *$10 ($1 off with Muni transfer), free 1st Wed. of month.* ✆ *Daily 10–5; children's zoo weekdays 11–4, weekends 10:30–4:30.*

❸ **Sutro Heights Park.** Crows and other large birds battle the heady breezes at this cliff-top park on what were the grounds of the home of eccentric mining engineer and former San Francisco mayor Adolph Sutro. Monterey cypresses and Canary Island palms dot the park, and photos on placards depict what you would have seen before the house burned down in 1896. All that remains of the main house is its foundation. Climb up for a sweeping view of the Pacific Ocean and the Cliff House below, and try to imagine what the perspective might have been like from one of the upper floors. ✉ *Point Lobos and 48th Aves., Lincoln Park.*

MISSION DISTRICT

The sunny Mission District wins out in San Francisco's system of microclimates—it's always the last to succumb to fog. Italian and Irish in the early 20th century, the Mission became heavily Latino in the late 1960s, when immigrants from Mexico and Central America began arriving. Despite its distinctive Latino flavor, in the 1980s and early 1990s the Mission saw an influx of Chinese, Vietnamese, Arabic, and other immigrants, along with a young bohemian crowd enticed by cheap rents and the burgeoning arts-and-entertainment scene. In the late 1990s gentrification led to skyrocketing rents, causing clashes between the longtime residents forced out and the wealthy yuppies moving in. With the collapse of the dot-com economy, the district is yet again in transition, as rents stabilize and the landlord-tenant wars fade into memory. The Mission, still a bit scruffy in patches, lacks some of the glamour of other neighborhoods, but a walk through it provides the opportunity to mix with a heady cross section of San Franciscans.

The eight blocks of Valencia Street between 16th and 24th streets—what's come to be known as the Valencia Corridor—typifies the neighborhood's diversity. Businesses on the block between 16th and 17th streets, for instance, include an upscale Vietnamese restaurant, a Lebanese restaurant where in the evening belly dancers writhe gracefully, the Bombay Ice Cream parlor (try a scoop of the zesty cardamom ice cream) and adjacent Indian grocery and sundries store, a tattoo parlor, the yuppie-chic Blondie's bar, pizzerias and taquerías, a Turkish restaurant, a sushi bar, bargain and pricey thrift shops, and the Puerto Allegre restaurant (a hole-in-the-wall whose pack-a-punch margaritas locals revere). With new, stylish eateries popping up all the time, this unlikely strip remains one of the city's hottest culinary destinations.

Cinco de Mayo is an important event in the Mission: music, dance, and parades commemorate the victory, on May 5, 1862, of Mexicans over French troops who had invaded their country. On Memorial Day weekend, the revelers come out in earnest, when Carnaval transforms the neighborhood into a northern Rio de Janeiro for three days. Festivities close down several blocks (usually of Harrison Street), where musicians and dancers perform and crafts and food booths are set up. The Grand Carnaval Parade, along 24th and Mission streets, caps the celebration.

Numbers in the text correspond to numbers in the margin and on the Mission District/Noe Valley map.

A Good Walk

The spiritual heart of the old Mission lies within the thick, white adobe walls of **Mission Dolores** ①, where Dolores Street intersects with 16th Street. From the mission, cross Dolores Street and head east on 16th Street. Tattooed and pierced hipsters abound a block from Mission Dolores, but the eclectic area still has room for a place like **Creativity Explored** ②, where people with developmental disabilities work on art and other projects. Cafés and bookstores tumble willy-nilly into each other in the next block, between Guerrero and Valencia streets, which contains the idiosyncratic Roxie Cinema, a great venue for art and independent films. At the intersection of 16th and Valencia streets, head south (to the right), poking your head into any shops that intrigue you. At 18th Street walk a half block west (right) to view the mural adorning the **Women's Building** ③.

Head back to Valencia Street and make a right to check out the shops and cafés on the next several blocks. A few businesses the likes of which—depending on where you live—you might not see back home include Leather Tongue Video at No. 714, the leftist Modern Times Bookstore at No. 888, and Good Vibrations, a tastefully jolly women-run erotica emporium at No. 1210.

By the time you reach 24th Street and head east (left off Valencia), the atmosphere becomes distinctly Latin American. Record stores such as Discolandia, at No. 2964, sell the latest Spanish-language hits, family groceries sell Latin-American ingredients and delicacies, shops proffer religious goods, and restaurants serve authentic dishes from several nations.

A half block east of Folsom Street, mural-lined **Balmy Alley** ④ runs south from 24th Street to 25th Street. View the murals and then head back up Balmy to 24th and continue east a few steps to the **Precita Eyes Mural Arts and Visitors Center** ⑤. From the center continue east past St. Peter's Church, where Isías Mata's mural *500 Years of Resistance,* on the exterior of the rectory, reflects on the struggles and survival of Latin-American cultures. At 24th and Bryant streets is the **Galería de la Raza/Studio 24** ⑥ art space.

Diagonally across from the Galería, on Bryant at the northeast corner near 24th Street, you can catch Bus 27–Bryant to downtown. If you want to combine tours of the Mission District and Noe Valley but save yourself a little walking, take a Muni Bus 48–Quintara/24th Street heading west (board directly across from the Galería on 24th Street) and get off at Church Street, where the Noe Valley tour begins.

TIMING

The above walk takes about two hours, including brief stops at the various sights listed. If you plan to go on a mural walk with Precita Eyes or if you're a browser who tends to linger, add at least another hour.

Sights to See

❹ **Balmy Alley.** Mission District artists have transformed the walls of their neighborhood with paintings, and Balmy Alley is one of the best-executed examples. The entire one-block alley is filled with murals. Local children working with adults started the project in 1971. Since then dozens of artists have steadily added to it, with the aim of promoting peace in Central America, as well as community spirit and AIDS awareness. (Be careful here: the other end of the street adjoins a somewhat dangerous area.) ⊠ *24th St. between and parallel to Harrison and Treat Sts. (alley runs south to 25th St.), Mission.*

❷ **Creativity Explored.** Joyous, if chaotic, creativity pervades the workshops of Creativity Explored, an art education center and gallery for developmentally disabled adults. Several dozen adults work at the center each day—guided by a staff of working artists—painting, working in the darkroom, producing videos, and crafting prints, textiles, and ceramics. On weekdays, you can drop by and see the artists at work. Five blocks east is **Creativity Explored II** (⊠ 2797 16th St., Mission, ☎ 415/863–2946), the work space for the center's adults who are more severely developmentally disabled. ⊠ *3245 16th St., Mission,* ☎ *415/ 863–2108,* WEB *www.creativityexplored.org.* ⊡ *Free.* ☉ *Weekdays 10– 3, Sat. 11–6.*

❻ **Galería de la Raza/Studio 24.** San Francisco's premiere showcase for Latino art, the gallery exhibits the works of local and international artists. Next door is the nonprofit Studio 24, which sells prints and paintings by Chicano artists, as well as folk art, mainly from Mexico. In early November the studio brims with art objects paying tribute to *Día de los Muertos* (Day of the Dead). In Mexican tradition death is not feared but seen as a part of life—thus the many colorful skeleton figurines doing everyday things like housework or playing sports. ⊠ *2857 24th St., at Bryant St., Mission,* ☎ *415/826–8009.* ☉ *Wed.–Sun. noon–6.*

NEED A
BREAK?

If you've worked up an appetite walking the Mission, consider a *panadería* (bakery) stop at **Dominguez** (⊠ 2951 24th St., at Alabama St., Mission, ☎ 415/821–1717). Latin American pastries are also available at **La Victoria** (⊠ 2937 24th St., at Alabama St., Mission,

The Mission District/Noe Valley

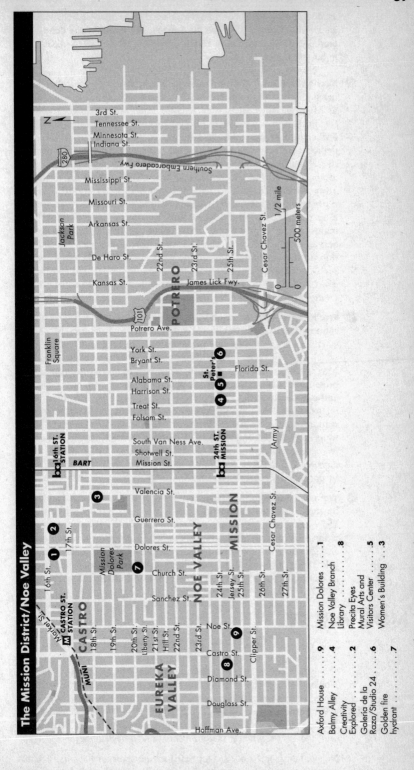

Axford House 9
Balmy Alley 4
Creativity
Explored 2
Galeria de la
Raza/Studio 24 .. 6
Golden fire
hydrant 7

Mission Dolores 1
Noe Valley Branch
Library 8
Precita Eyes
Mural Arts and
Visitors Center 5
Women's Building ... 3

☎ 415/642–7120). For an old-fashioned soda or some homemade ice cream or candy, stop into the **Saint Francis Fountain and Candy Store** (✉ 2801 24th St., at York St., Mission, ☎ 415/826–4200), in business since 1918.

❶ Mission Dolores. Mission Dolores encompasses two churches standing side by side. Completed in 1791, the small adobe building known as Mission San Francisco de Asís is the oldest standing structure in San Francisco and the sixth of the 21 California missions founded by Father Junípero Serra in the 18th and early 19th centuries. Its ceiling depicts original Ohlone Indian basket designs, executed in vegetable dyes. The tiny chapel includes frescoes and a hand-painted wooden altar; some artifacts were brought from Mexico by mule in the late 18th century. There is a small museum, and the pretty little mission cemetery (made famous by a scene in Alfred Hitchcock's *Vertigo*) maintains the graves of mid-19th-century European immigrants. (The remains of an estimated 5,000 Native Americans lie in unmarked graves.) Services are held in both the Mission San Francisco de Asís and next door in the handsome multidome basilica. ✉ *Dolores and 16th Sts., Mission,* ☎ *415/621–8203.* ▣ *Free (donations welcome), audio tour $7.* ☉ *Daily 9–4.* ᴡᴇʙ *www.sfmuseum.org/hist5/misdolor.html or www.missiondolores.citysearch.com.*

❺ Precita Eyes Mural Arts and Visitors Center. This nonprofit arts organization sponsors guided walks of the Mission District's murals. Most tours start with a 45-minute slide presentation. The bike and walking trips, which take between one and three hours, pass by several dozen murals. May is Mural Awareness Month, with visits to murals-in-progress and presentations by artists. You can pick up a map of 24th Street's murals at the center and buy art supplies, T-shirts, postcards, and other mural-related items. Bike tours are available by appointment; Saturday's 11 ᴀᴍ walking tour meets at Cafe Venice at 24th and Mission streets (all other tours meet at the Center). ✉ *2981 24th St., Mission,* ☎ *415/285–2287,* ᴡᴇʙ *www.precitaeyes.org.* ▣ *Center free, tours $8–$12.* ☉ *Center weekdays 10–5, Sat. 10–4, Sun. noon–4; walks weekends at 11 and 1:30 or by appointment; bike tours 2nd Sun. of month at 11.*

❸ Women's Building. The cornerstone of the female-owned and -run businesses in the neighborhood is the Women's Building, which since 1979 has held workshops and conferences of particular interest to women. It houses offices for many social and political organizations and sponsors talks and readings by writers like Alice Walker and Angela Davis. The building's two-sided exterior mural depicts women's peacekeeping efforts over the centuries. ✉ *3543 18th St., Mission,* ☎ *415/431–1180.* ☉ *Weekdays 9–5.*

NOE VALLEY

Noe Valley and adjacent Twin Peaks were once known as Rancho San Miguel, a parcel of land given to the last Mexican mayor of San Francisco (then known as Yerba Buena) in 1845. Mayor Don José de Jesús Noe built his ranch house at 22nd and Eureka streets, and the area continued as a bucolic farming community until 1906. Because Noe Valley was so little affected by the quake, many of the displaced headed here and decided to stay. It was predominantly working class and largely Irish until the 1970s, when it saw an influx of well-heeled liberals.

Noe Valley storefronts are modest looking, everyone seems to know each other, and the pace is fairly slow. While there's very little of official interest here, for a low-key, pleasant stroll, Noe Valley is hard to beat. Crowds slump in front of 24th Street's bagel shop and nearby coffee shops, and strollers clog the sidewalk. Resident and *Zippy the Pinhead* cartoonist Bill Griffith describes the street as "primarily an urban mall for caffeine addicts and people who have jobs that don't require them to go to an office."

Numbers in the text correspond to numbers in the margin and on the Mission District/Noe Valley map.

A Good Walk

Start at Church and 24th streets (the J–Church streetcar from downtown stops here). Walk north (back toward downtown) on Church Street. At No. 1079—between 23rd and 22nd streets—you'll see a house with a large mural of a rain forest painted on it. To the right at Nos. 1081–1089 are three Queen Anne bungalows with lacy wedding-cake trim. Continue north to the southeast corner of 20th and Church streets, where a **golden fire hydrant** ⑦ figured in the 1906 earthquake and fire.

Take a gander at 20th Street heading west. Be ready for a steep incline as you walk up 20th Street between Church and Sanchez. If the hill looks too steep, you can head back to 24th Street and have a cappuccino. Otherwise, proceed up 20th past Victorian houses of various vintages and make a left at Sanchez. As you make the turn, you'll see the meticulously maintained Spanish Mission–style residence at 701 Sanchez. Continue south on Sanchez one block to Liberty Street. Across Sanchez at this intersection a staircase leads to the upper level of Liberty Street. Walk up it, enjoy the views of Pacific Heights north from the top, then look south across Liberty Street, where you'll see another set of stairs. Take them (from the landing on a sunny day you'll have views of the Bay Bridge and Oakland) and continue south. On the northeast corner of Sanchez and 21st streets is a Tudor-style mansion; the garden was designed by John McLaren, responsible for much of Golden Gate Park. This hill is the site of a former resort spot where Californians came to soak in the healing waters of the area's many springs. The Native Americans who lived near Mission Dolores came up here for water from those springs. The same source helped extinguish fires after the 1906 quake. The dried-up springs left shaky soil that made some structures here vulnerable during the Loma Prieta quake of 1989.

It isn't hard to figure out how Hill Street, parallel to and between 21st and 22nd streets, got its name. The street was once known as Nanny Goat Hill for the goats that grazed there. Proceed downhill on Sanchez Street. Make a right at 22nd Street, where Victorian houses line both sides of the street. Make a left at Noe, walk south to 24th Street, and make a right. Continue west on 24th to Castro Street and turn left. Walk the short block to Jersey Street and head west (right). Halfway down the block is the **Noe Valley Branch Library** ⑧. From the library, backtrack east on Jersey, make a right at Noe, walk a half block to 25th Street, and make a left. As you walk down 25th Street you'll see the side of the art deco James Lick Middle School. On the northwest corner of 25th and Noe streets is the **Axford House** ⑨, a private home. Walk north from the Axford House to 24th Street; Church Street, where your walk began, is two blocks east (to the right). If you stop into the Just for Fun & Scribbledoodles card and gift shop at No. 3982, you can pick up a postcard to commemorate your Noe Valley tour.

TIMING
This loop through Noe Valley takes about an hour, not counting stops to shop or sip tea or coffee.

Sights to See

⑨ Axford House. This mauve house was built in 1877, when Noe Valley was still a rural area, as evidenced by the hayloft in the gable of the adjacent carriage house. The house is perched several feet above the sidewalk. Several types of roses grow in the well-maintained garden that surrounds the house. ⊠ *1190 Noe St., at 25th St., Noe Valley.*

NEED A
BREAK?

Lovejoy's Antiques & Tea Room (⊠ 1351 Church St., at Clipper St., Noe Valley, ☎ 415/648–5895) takes its name from the British series about a fictional antiques dealer with a penchant for mysteries. The room is homey yet stylish, its tables and couches mixing in nicely with the antiques for sale. High tea and cream tea are served, along with traditional English-tearoom "fayre," such as the Ploughman's lunch and sandwiches (oak-smoked finnan haddock is a favorite) served on soft, white, crustless triangles.

⑦ Golden fire hydrant. When all the other fire hydrants went dry during the fire that followed the 1906 earthquake, this one kept pumping. Noe Valley and the Mission District were thus spared the devastation wrought elsewhere in the city, which explains the large number of pre-quake homes here. ⊠ *Church and 20th Sts., southeast corner, across from Mission Dolores Park, Noe Valley.*

⑧ Noe Valley Branch Library. In the early 20th century philanthropist Andrew Carnegie told Americans he would build them elegant libraries if they would fill them with books. A community garden flanks part of the yellow-brick library Carnegie financed, and there's a deck (accessed through the children's book room) with picnic tables where you can relax and admire Carnegie's inspired structure. ⊠ *451 Jersey St., Noe Valley,* ☎ *415/695–5095.* ☉ *Tues. 10–9, Wed. 1–9, Thurs. and Sat. 10–6, Fri. 1–6.*

THE CASTRO

Historians are still trying to discover what drew tens of thousands of gays and lesbians to the San Francisco area during the second half of the 20th century. Some point to the libertarian tradition rooted in Barbary Coast piracy, prostitution, and gambling. Others note that as a huge military embarkation point during World War II, the city was occupied by many single men. Whatever the cause, San Francisco became the city of choice for lesbians and gay men, and in the 1970s Castro Street—nestled at the base of Twin Peaks and just over Buena Vista hill from Haight Street—became its social, cultural, and political center.

The Castro district is one of the liveliest and most welcoming neighborhoods in the city, especially on weekends. Come Saturday and Sunday, the streets teem with folks out shopping, pushing political causes, heading to art films, and lingering in bars and cafés. Cutting-edge clothing stores and gift shops predominate, and pairs of all genders and sexual persuasions (even heterosexual) hold hands.

Numbers in the text correspond to numbers in the margin and on the Castro and the Haight map.

A Good Walk

Begin at **Harvey Milk Plaza** ① on the southwest corner of 17th and Market streets; it's outside the south entrance to the Castro Street Muni station (K, L, and M streetcars stop here). Across Castro Street from the plaza is the neighborhood's landmark, the **Castro Theatre** ②. Many shops line Castro Street between 17th and 19th streets, 18th between Sanchez and Eureka streets, and Market Street heading east toward

SWEET PAINTED LADIES

BRIGHT, CHEERFUL, AND STURDILY proud, San Francisco's Painted Ladies are wooden (mostly redwood) Victorian homes built in the 19th and early 20th century. They provide the perfect grace notes of exuberance for a metropolis that burst onto the scene as capriciously as did the City by the Bay. Though viewed as picturesque antiques these days, the homes, about 15,000 of which survive today, represented the height of modernity in their time.

Made possible by the newly created streetcar and cable car lines—not to mention sewer systems and money from the gold and silver rushes of the 1800s—the Painted Ladies had indoor plumbing (the later ones electricity, too) and other modern touches like porcelain bathroom and kitchen fixtures and machine-tooled wood detailing. The older Victorians downtown perished in the 1906 earthquake and fire. But west of Van Ness Avenue, where grand mansions were dynamited to halt the fire's spread, and in the Haight, the outer Mission District, and Noe Valley, sterling examples remain.

Were the Painted Ladies always as brilliantly hued as they are today? Apparently so: various accounts in the late 1800s mention bright, even "garish" colors. Some writers attributed this to the city's carefree attitudes, others to the desire of San Franciscans to create a visual reality as different as possible from that of the more conservative East Coast cities from which many of them had come.

Three main Victorian styles emerged in San Francisco. The architecture of Re-naissance Italy's palaces informed the Italianate style, characterized by Corinthian porch columns, tall and narrow doorways, and slanted bay windows. (The bay window was invented in San Francisco, where the standard lot is only 25 ft wide, to take advantage of water views.) The Stick style employs wood strips as ornamentation—as opposed to floral and other patterns—and squared-off bay windows, which let in even more light than slanted bays. The Stick style evolved into what came to be known as the Stick-Eastlake style, with faux gables, minimansards, and other embellishments adding a playful quality to the basic Stick look. If you see a home with a rounded turret or other curvy elements, it's probably a Queen Anne, the third major San Francisco style. Angled roofs, lacy detailing, and jolly bits of froufrou—arching portals, wedding-cake trim, rounded shingling—enliven Queen Anne homes.

There's plenty of overlapping of these styles. Many Italianate houses built in the 1870s but remodeled in the 1890s, for example, acquired Queen Anne touches. The Atherton House daffily combines the Stick-Eastlake and Queen Anne styles. And you'll find Gothic, Tudor, and Greek Revival Victorians in much smaller numbers.

To view the quintessential strip of Victorians, head to Alamo Square and look east toward downtown. The Queen Anne homes—710–720 Steiner Street—in the foreground, which have been painted and photographed numerous times, are known as Postcard Row.

— Daniel Mangin

downtown. Several doors south of the Castro Theatre at Number 489 is A Different Light Bookstore, which operates as an unofficial community center.

After exploring the shops on 18th and Castro streets, head west up 19th Street to Douglass Street and turn right. On the corner of Douglass and Caselli streets sprawls **Clarke's Mansion** ③. Continue north on Douglass Street to 18th Street and make a right; head left at Castro Street. The rest of this walk becomes strenuous. If you're not up for it, park yourself at one of the myriad cafés along Castro Street or turn right on Market and walk one block to Café Flore. For an unforgettable vista, continue north on Castro Street two blocks to 16th Street, turn left, and head up the steep hill to Flint Street. Turn right on Flint and follow the trail on the left (just past the tennis courts) up the hill. The beige buildings on the left contain the **Randall Museum** ④ for children. Turn right up the dirt path, which soon loops back up Corona Heights. At the top you'll be treated to an all-encompassing view of the city. To the east is downtown. Among the rows of homes on the hills and valleys to the south are many Victorians.

You can retrace your steps back to Castro Street. To continue north and walk the Haight Street tour, follow the trail down the other side of Corona Heights to a grassy field. The gate to the field is at the intersection of Roosevelt Way and Museum Way. Turn right on Roosevelt (head down the hill) and cross Roosevelt at Park Hill Terrace. Walk up Park Hill to Buena Vista Avenue, turn left, and follow the road as it loops west and south around Buena Vista Park to the Spreckels Mansion.

TIMING

Allot an hour to an hour and a half to visit the Castro district. Set aside an extra hour to hike Corona Heights and visit the Randall Museum.

Sights to See

★ ❷ **Castro Theatre.** The neon marquee is the neighborhood's great landmark, and the 1,500-seat theater, which opened in 1922, is the grandest of San Francisco's few remaining movie palaces. Janet Gaynor, who in 1927 won the first Oscar for best actress, worked as an usher here. The Castro's elaborate Spanish baroque interior is fairly well preserved. Before many shows the theater's pipe organ rises from the orchestra pit and an organist plays pop and movie tunes, usually ending with the Jeanette McDonald standard "San Francisco" (go ahead, sing along). The crowd can be enthusiastic and vocal, talking back to the screen as loudly as it talks to them. Classics like *Who's Afraid of Virginia Woolf?* take on a whole new life, with the assembled beating the actors to the punch and fashioning even snappier comebacks for Elizabeth Taylor. Catch classics, a Fellini film retrospective, or the latest take on same-sex love here. The **San Francisco International Lesbian and Gay Film Festival** (☏ 415/703–8650) takes place in June at the Castro and other venues. ⊠ *429 Castro St., Castro,* ☏ *415/621–6120.*

❸ **Clarke's Mansion.** Built for attorney Alfred "Nobby" Clarke, this off-white baroque Queen Anne home completed in 1892 was dubbed Clarke's Folly when his wife refused to inhabit it because it was in an unfashionable part of town—at the time, everyone who was anyone lived on Nob Hill. The greenery-shrouded house is a beauty, with dormers, cupolas, rounded bay windows, and huge turrets topped by gold-leaf spheres. ⊠ *250 Douglass St., between 18th and 19th Sts., Castro.*

❶ **Harvey Milk Plaza.** An 18-ft-long rainbow flag, a gay icon, flies above this plaza named for the man who electrified the city in 1977 by being elected to its Board of Supervisors as an openly gay candidate. In the

Buena Vista
Park 5

Castro
Theatre 2

Clarke's
Mansion 3

Grateful Dead
house 8

Haight–
Ashbury
intersection . . 7

Harvey Milk
Plaza 1

Randall
Museum 4

Red Victorian
Peace Center
Bed &
Breakfast 9

Spreckels
Mansion . . . 6

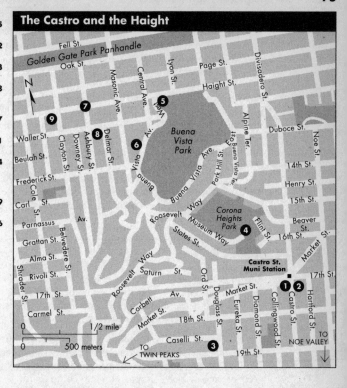

The Castro and the Haight

early 1970s, Milk had opened a camera store on the block of Castro Street between 18th and 19th streets. The store became ground zero for his campaign to gain thorough inclusion for gays in the city's social and political life. The liberal Milk hadn't served a full year of his term before he and Mayor George Moscone, also a liberal, were shot in November 1978 at City Hall. The murderer was a conservative ex-supervisor named Dan White, who had recently resigned his post and then become enraged when Moscone wouldn't reinstate him. Milk and White had often been at odds on the board, and White felt that Milk had been part of a cabal to keep him from returning to his post. Milk's assassination shocked the gay community, which became enraged when the famous "Twinkie defense"—that junk food had led to diminished mental capacity—resulted in a manslaughter verdict for White. During the so-called White Night Riot of May 21, 1979, gays and their sympathizers stormed City Hall, torching its lobby and several police cars. Milk, who had feared assassination, had left behind a videotape in which he urged the community to continue the work he began. His legacy is the high visibility of gay people throughout city government. A plaque at the base of the flagpole lists the names of past and present openly gay and lesbian state and local officials. ⊠ *Southwest corner of Castro and Market Sts., Castro.*

NEED A BREAK?	Sometimes referred to as "Café Floorshow" because it's such a see-and-be-seen place, **Café Flore** (⊠ 2298 Market St., Castro, ☎ 415/621-8579) serves coffee drinks, beer, and light meals. It's a good place to catch the latest Castro gossip.

✋ ❹ **Randall Museum.** The highlight of this facility is the educational animal room, popular with children, where you can observe birds, lizards, snakes, spiders, and other creatures that cannot be released to the wild because of injury or other problems. Also here are a greenhouse, woodworking and ceramics studios, and a theater. The Randall sits on 16 acres of public land; the hill that overlooks the museum is variously known as Red Rock, Museum Hill, and, correctly, Corona Heights. ✉ *199 Museum Way, off Roosevelt Way, Castro,* ☎ *415/554–9600,* WEB *www.randallmuseum.org.* ✆ *Free.* ◷ *Tues.–Sat. 10–5.*

OFF THE
BEATEN PATH
TWIN PEAKS – Windswept and desolate Twin Peaks yields sweeping vistas of San Francisco and the neighboring east and north bay counties. You can get a real feel for the city's layout here; arrive before the late-afternoon fog turns the view into pea soup during the summer. To drive, head west from Castro Street up Market Street, which becomes Portola Drive past Corbett Street. Turn right (north) at the intersection of Portola Drive and Twin Peaks Boulevard and follow the signs to the top. Muni Bus 37–Corbett heads west to Twin Peaks from Market Street. Catch this bus above the Castro Street Muni light-rail station on the island west of Castro at Market Street.

THE HAIGHT

East of Golden Gate Park is the neighborhood known as the Haight. Despite a fair amount of gentrification, there is still a wandering tribe of Deadheads in the area, as well as anarchist book collectives and shops selling incense and tie-dye T-shirts.

Once an enclave of large middle-class families of European immigrants, the Haight began to change during the late 1950s and early 1960s. Families were fleeing to the suburbs, and the big old Victorians were deteriorating or being chopped up into cheap housing. Young people found the neighborhood an affordable spot in which they could live according to new precepts. By 1966 the Haight had become a hot spot for rock bands like the Grateful Dead—whose members moved into a big Victorian near the corner of Haight and Ashbury streets—and Jefferson Airplane, whose grand mansion was north of the district at 2400 Fulton Street.

The Haight's famous political spirit—it was the first neighborhood in the nation to lead a freeway revolt, and it continues to host regular boycotts against chain stores—exists alongside some of the finest Victorian-lined streets in the city. The area is also known for its vintage merchandise, including clothes, records, and books, and miscellany like crystals, jewelry, and candles.

Numbers in the text correspond to numbers in the margin and on the Castro and the Haight map.

A Good Walk

Start your visit on the western edge of **Buena Vista Park** ⑤, at Haight Street and Buena Vista Avenue West. The avenue, which becomes Buena Vista Avenue East before returning to Haight Street, loops around the park. If you're up for a climb, walk a few blocks south on Buena Vista Avenue West along the edge of the park to **Spreckels Mansion** ⑥. From the mansion, backtrack on its side of the street to Central Avenue. Head down Central two blocks to Haight Street, and make a left.

The avowedly radical Bound Together Anarchist Book Collective at 1369 Haight Street has been "fighting the good fight" against capitalism for decades. Whatever your political persuasion, you may find the collection of political literature intriguing. For a 1960s flashback, cross the street to Pipe Dreams, at No. 1376. This head shop keeps the hippie era alive with merchandise like hookahs, bongs, and water pipes.

The flashbacks continue as you cross Masonic Avenue. You can't miss the brightly colored building on the southwest corner of Haight and Masonic that houses Positively Haight Street. Here you can purchase tie-dye T-shirts, dresses, and scarves, along with Grateful Dead paraphernalia.

Continue west to the fabled **Haight-Ashbury intersection** ⑦. Despite the franchise operations, you won't need to close your eyes to conjure the 1960s. A motley contingent of folks attired in retro fashions and often sporting hippie-long hair hangs here. Most of the assembled are either under 25 or over 50; many are homeless. Consider yourself hopelessly square if by now someone hasn't sidled up to you to proffer "buds" or perhaps something stronger than marijuana. One block south of Haight and Ashbury is the **Grateful Dead house** ⑧, the pad that Jerry Garcia and band inhabited in the 1960s.

The stores along Haight Street up to Shrader Street are worth checking out. You will encounter many panhandlers along this walk. At Clayton Street, you can stop in at the meditative Peace Arts Center on the ground floor of the **Red Victorian Peace Center Bed & Breakfast** ⑨.

TIMING

The distance covered here is only several blocks, and although there are shops aplenty and other amusements, an hour or so should be enough.

Sights to See

⑤ Buena Vista Park. Great city views can be had from this eucalyptus-filled park. Although it's not exactly sedate (drug deals are common), it's a very pretty park, especially on a sunny day. Don't wander here after dark. ⊠ *Haight St. between Lyon St. and Buena Vista Ave. W, Haight.*

⑧ Grateful Dead house. Nothing unusual marks the house of legend. On the outside, it's just one more well-kept Victorian on a street that's full of them—but true fans of the Dead may find some inspiration here. The three-story house (closed to the public) is tastefully painted in sedate mauves, tans, and teals (no bright tie-dye colors). ⊠ *710 Ashbury St., just past Waller St., Haight.*

⑦ Haight-Ashbury intersection. On October 6, 1967, hippies took over the intersection of Haight and Ashbury streets to proclaim the "Death of Hip." If they thought hip was dead then, they'd find absolute confirmation of it today, what with the Gap holding court on one quadrant of the famed corner.

Everyone knows the Summer of Love had something to do with free love and LSD, but the drug and other excesses of the Summer of Love have tended to obscure the residents' serious attempts to create an America more spiritually oriented, more environmentally aware, and less caught up in commercialism. The Diggers, a radical group of actors and populist agitators, for example, operated a free shop a few blocks off Haight Street. Everything really was free at the free shop; people brought in things they didn't need and took things they did. The Diggers also distributed free food in Golden Gate Park every day.

Among the folks who hung out in or near the Haight during the late 1960s were writers Richard Brautigan, Allen Ginsberg, Ken Kesey, and Gary Snyder; anarchist Abbie Hoffman; rock performers Marty Balin, Jerry Garcia, Janis Joplin, and Grace Slick; LSD champion Timothy Leary; and filmmaker Kenneth Anger.

⑨ Red Victorian Peace Center Bed & Breakfast. By even the most generous accounts the Summer of Love quickly crashed and burned, and the

Haight veered sharply away from the higher goals that inspired the fabled summer. In 1977 Sami Sunchild acquired the Red Vic, built as a hotel in 1904, with the aim of preserving the best of 1960s ideals. She decorated her rooms with 1960s themes—one chamber is called the Flower Child Room—and on the ground floor opened the Peace Art Center. Here you can buy her paintings, T-shirts, and "meditative art," along with books about the Haight and prayer flags. There's also a meditation room. ⊠ *1665 Haight St., Haight*, ☎ *415/864–1978*, WEB *www.redvic.com.*

NEED A
BREAK?

Boisterous **Cha Cha Cha** (⊠ 1801 Haight St., at Shrader St., Haight, ☎ 415/386–5758) serves island cuisine, a mix of Cajun, southwestern, and Caribbean influences. The decor is Technicolor tropical plastic, and the food is hot and spicy. Try the fried calamari or chili-spiked shrimp and wash it down with a pitcher of Cha Cha Cha's signature sangria. Reservations are not accepted, so expect a wait for dinner.

⑥ Spreckels Mansion. Not to be confused with the Spreckels Mansion of Pacific Heights, this house was built for sugar baron Richard Spreckels in 1887. Later tenants included Jack London and Ambrose Bierce. The boxy, putty-color Victorian is in mint condition. ⊠ *737 Buena Vista Ave. W, Haight.*

3 DINING

San Francisco, one of the world's great dining cities, is the culinary stomping grounds of such nationally celebrated chefs as Traci Des Jardins, Nancy Oakes, Gary Danko, and Mark Franz. San Francisco is also a highly touted capital of ethnic eating, home to a growing number of restaurants whose cooks mastered their craft in Bangkok's noodle shops or in the dim sum kitchens of Hong Kong. Diversity is the key to the city's culinary richness, and it has absolutely spoiled the locals. Whether it's the best tapas this side of Barcelona or the silkiest seared foie gras this side of Paris, San Francisco has it all—most often within convenient walking distance.

By Sharon
Silva

SAN FRANCISCO HAS MORE RESTAURANTS per capita than any
other city in the United States, and nearly every ethnic cuisine
is represented, from Afghan to Indian to Vietnamese. Select-
ing some 110 recommended restaurants is a next-to-impossible task.
Several restaurants represent each popular style of dining in various
price ranges. In most cases, the restaurants were chosen because of
the superiority of the food, but in some instances because of the view
or ambience.

The areas of town most frequented by visitors have received the greatest attention. This has meant leaving out some great places in the more
distant districts, such as the Haight, Bernal Heights, Potrero Hill, the
Sunset, and the Richmond. The outlying restaurants that are recommended were chosen because they offer an experience not available elsewhere. All listed restaurants serve lunch and dinner unless otherwise
specified. The restaurants here are organized by neighborhood, which
are listed alphabetically.

Most upper-end restaurants offer valet parking—worth considering in
crowded neighborhoods such as North Beach, Union Square, Civic Center, and the North Mission. There is often a nominal charge and a time-
length restriction on validated parking.

Smoking is banned in all Bay Area workplaces, including restaurants,
bars, and supper clubs.

Restaurants do change their policies about hours, credit cards, and the
like. Many restaurants close for Thanksgiving and Christmas. It is always best to call in advance.

The price ranges listed below are per person for a main course at dinner. Prices, like other restaurant policies, are highly fluid, however, and
most restaurants are happy to review their prices briefly with any potential diner over the phone.

CATEGORY	COST*
$$$$	over $35
$$$	$25–$34
$$	$15–$24
$	under $15

* per person for a main course at dinner

The Castro

Contemporary

$$–$$$ ✕ **Mecca.** This sleek bar and restaurant on the edge of the Castro is a
mecca for both local Armani-clad cocktailers and Bay Area foodies. If
clubbing is not your thing, reserve a seat in the dining area, away from
the always-jammed, velvet-curtained circular bar that anchors the cavernous space. The bar is also the site of live music that draws a large,
toe-tapping crowd. The menu focuses on the American Southwest and
Cajun tables—ahi tuna spring rolls, crispy sesame catfish—but delivers them with an Asian accent. ✉ *2029 Market St., Castro,* ☎ *415/
621–7000. AE, DC, MC, V. No lunch.*

$–$$ ✕ **2223.** Opened in the mid-1990s, the smart, sophisticated 2223—
the address became the name when the principals couldn't come up
with a better one—was an instant success and has continued to attract
a loyal clientele. That means you'll need strong lungs, however, as the
restaurant's popularity makes conversation difficult. Thin-crust pizzas,
dim sum dumplings, and superthick pork chops are among the kitchen's

popular dishes. Sunday brunch means such satisfying offerings as blood orange–ricotta pancakes. ⊠ *2223 Market St., Castro,* ☎ *415/431–0692. AE, DC, MC, V. No lunch Mon.–Sat.*

$ ✕ **Zao Noodle Bar.** Good prices, fresh ingredients, and generous portions have made this minichain a success. The menu items span Asia, from Vietnamese rice noodles with seared pork to wheat noodles with grilled chicken and greens to Thai green curry–coconut prawns with ramen, and salmon and napa cabbage with soba. Among the beverages are top-flight sakes served in martini glasses and Zao ginger orange cooler. The black and red decor, with plenty of wood, is as hip as the food and the diners. ⊠ *3583 16th St., Castro,* ☎ *415/864–2888;* ⊠ *2406 California St., Lower Pacific Heights,* ☎ *415/345–8088;* ⊠ *822 Irving St., Inner Sunset,* ☎ *415/682–2828;* ⊠ *2031 Chestnut St., Marina,* ☎ *415/928–3088. Reservations not accepted. MC, V.*

Chinatown

Chinese

$–$$ ✕ **Great Eastern.** Cantonese chefs are known for their expertise with seafood, and the kitchen at Great Eastern continues that venerable tradition. In the busy dining room, tanks are filled with Dungeness crabs, black bass, abalone, catfish, shrimp, and other creatures of the sea, and a wall-hung menu in both Chinese and English specifies the cost of selecting what can be pricey indulgences. In the wee hours Chinese night owls often drop in for a plate of noodles or a bowl of *congee* (rice gruel). ⊠ *649 Jackson St., Chinatown,* ☎ *415/986–2550. AE, MC, V.*

$–$$ ✕ **R&G Lounge.** The name conjures up an image of a dark bar with a cigarette-smoking piano player, but the restaurant, on two floors, is actually as bright as a new penny. Downstairs (entrance on Kearny Street) is a no-tablecloth dining room that is always packed at lunch and dinner. The classier upstairs space (entrance on Commercial Street) is a favorite stop for Chinese businessmen on expense accounts and anyone else seeking Cantonese banquet fare. A menu with photographs helps you decide among the many wonderful, sometimes pricey, dishes. ⊠ *631 Kearny St., Chinatown,* ☎ *415/982–7877 or 415/982–3811. AE, DC, MC, V.*

Civic Center/Hayes Valley

Contemporary

$$$ ✕ **Jardinière.** One of the city's most talked-about restaurants since its
★   opening in the late 1990s, Jardinière continues to be *the* place to dine before a performance at the nearby Opera House or any time you have something to celebrate. The chef-owner is Traci Des Jardins, and the sophisticated interior, with its eye-catching oval atrium and curving staircase, is the work of designer Pat Kuleto. The menu is a match for the decor, from a foie gras first course to a superb monkfish main to a berry-rich shortcake for dessert. ⊠ *300 Grove St., Hayes Valley,* ☎ *415/861–5555. Reservations essential. AE, DC, MC, V. No lunch.*

$$–$$$ ✕ **Stars.** Gone are superchef Jeremiah Tower and his famed kitchen, but a highly respectable—and sophisticated—table that mixes Eastern European, Middle Eastern, and Mediterranean flavors with a solid California tradition has taken their place. The results are such heavenly dishes as tuna *bagna cauda,* cumin-scented sweet potatoes with thick pork chops, and a spice-laden persimmon cake. Old-timers will be happy to know that the mile-long bar, a favorite hangout of the city's power brokers is still lined with locals every night. ⊠ *150 Redwood Alley, at Van Ness Ave., Civic Center,* ☎ *415/861–7827. AE, DC, MC, V. No lunch weekends.*

82

Absinthe 1
Acquerello 66
Antica Trattoria . . .63
Aqua 41
Azie 16
Beach Chalet 72
B44 33
Bizou 17
Black Cat 49
Boulevard 37
Café Claude 30
Campton Place
Restaurant 28
Capp's Corner 61
Carta 5
Chez Nous 86
Cosmopolitan
Cafe 35
Dine 25
Elisabeth Daniel . . .45
Enrico's Sidewalk
Café 51
Eos Restaurant &
Wine Bar 69
Farallon 13
Fifth Floor 22
Fleur de Lys 12
Florio 83
Fog City Diner 57
Fringale 18
Garden Court 24
Grand Café 9
Great Eastern 46
Harbor Village 39
Harris' 65
Hawthorne Lane . . .26
Hayes Street Grill . . .2
Helmand 50
Il Fornaio 58
Indian Oven 67
Jardinière 3
Jianna 55
Kabuto Sushi 81
Katia's 74
Kokkari 47
Kyo-ya 23
La Folie 64
La Vie 77
Le Central 29
Le Colonial 11
Le Soleil 79
L'Osteria del
Forno 60
LuLu 15
MacArthur Park . . .48
Masa's 31
Maykadeh 53
Mifune 75
Millennium 7
Mo's Grill 21
Momo's 19

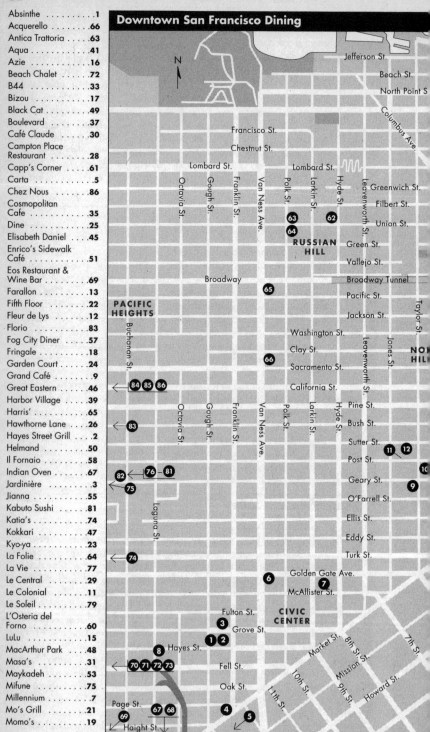

Downtown San Francisco Dining

Moose's **56**
One Market **38**
Palio d'Asti **43**
Parc Hong Kong
Restaurant **76**
Park Chow **73**
Pastis **59**
Plouf **34**
Postrio **10**
R&G Lounge **42**
Ristorante Ideale . . . **52**
Ritz-Carlton Dining
Room and Terrace . . **32**
Rose Pistola **54**
Rubicon **44**
San Tung No. 2 . . . **71**
Sanppo **82**
Scala's Bistro **14**
South Park Café **20**
Stars **6**
Straits Café **80**
Suppenkuche **8**
Tadich Grill **40**
Thep Phanom **68**
Ton Kiang **78**
Vivande Porta Via . . . **84**
Yank Sing **27, 36**
Zao Noodle
Bar **70, 85**
Zarzuela **62**
Zuni Café & Grill **4**

$$ ✕ **Carta.** Although it opened occupying only a single storefront, Carta has expanded into the space next door to create a warm, lavish dining room and comfy bar, complete with piano player. The menu of small and large plates changes every two months, moving easily from locale to locale—Tuscany, Southeast Asia, Scandinavia, Provence, Mexico—with each geographical shift. The popular Sunday brunch keeps French toast aficionados happy. ⊠ *1772 Market St., Civic Center,* ☎ *415/863–3516. AE, DC, MC, V. No lunch Sat.*

Eclectic

$$ ✕ **Absinthe.** Despite the restaurant's name, the long-banned cloudy green liqueur is not served here. The plush banquettes draw the city's social set for cold seafood platters; coq au vin; duck confit with braised cabbage; grilled rib-eye steak; thin, crisp fries piled into a paper cone; and other delicacies. Though the burgundy walls and yards of wood recall a sophisticated French brasserie, the menu shows Italian and American influences as well. A late-night bar menu is offered. ⊠ *398 Hayes St., Hayes Valley,* ☎ *415/551–1590. AE, DC, MC, V. Closed Mon.*

German

$ ✕ **Suppenkuche.** Bratwurst and braised red cabbage accompany a long list of German beers at this lively, hip outpost of simple German cooking in the trendy Hayes Valley corridor. Strangers sit down together at unfinished pine tables when the room gets crowded, which it regularly does. The food—potato pancakes with homemade applesauce, sauerbraten, cheese spaetzle, schnitzel, apple strudel—is tasty and easy on the pocketbook, and the brews are first-rate. There's also a good Sunday brunch. ⊠ *601 Hayes St., Hayes Valley,* ☎ *415/252–9289. AE, MC, V. No lunch.*

Mediterranean

$$ ✕ **Zuni Café & Grill.** Zuni's Italian-Mediterranean menu, created by
★ nationally known chef Judy Rodgers, packs in an eclectic crowd from early morning to late evening. A balcony dining area overlooks the large zinc bar, where a first-rate oyster selection and drinks are dispensed. The menu changes daily, but the superb whole roast chicken and Tuscan bread salad for two is always on it. Even the hamburgers (served until 5:30 and after 10:30) have an Italian accent—they're topped with Gorgonzola and served on focaccia. ⊠ *1658 Market St., Hayes Valley,* ☎ *415/552–2522. Reservations essential. AE, MC, V. Closed Mon.*

Seafood

$$ ✕ **Hayes Street Grill.** More than a dozen kinds of seafood are chalked on the blackboard each night at this bustling restaurant. The fish is simply grilled, with a choice of sauces ranging from tomato salsa to a spicy Sichuan peanut concoction to beurre blanc. Fresh crab slaw and superb crab cakes are regular appetizers, and for dessert, the crème brûlée is legendary. Bentwood chairs, dark-wood floors, coat hooks, and white tablecloths define the traditional look of this seafood mainstay. ⊠ *320 Hayes St., Hayes Valley,* ☎ *415/863–5545. Reservations essential. AE, D, DC, MC, V. No lunch weekends.*

Vegetarian

$–$$ ✕ **Millennium.** Tucked into the former carriage house of the venerable Abigail hotel, Millennium has a menu of "animal-free" dishes made with organic ingredients that keep vegans and their carnivore friends equally satisfied. Start your meal with a warm spinach salad and follow it with Caribbean pumpkin curry or with steak in marsala sauce made with seitan, a whole-wheat meat substitute. Come dessert, you may find the German chocolate cake hard to resist. Organic wines and beers are served. ⊠ *246 McAllister St., Civic Center,* ☎ *415/487–9800. MC, V. No lunch.*

Cow Hollow/Marina

French

$ ✕ **Cassis Bistro.** Take a seat at the tiny bar and enjoy a glass of wine while you wait for a free table in this sunny yellow, postage stamp–size operation, which recalls the small bistros tucked away on side streets in French seaside towns. The servers have Gallic accents; the food—onion tart, veal ragout, braised rabbit, tarte Tatin—is comfortingly home style; and the prices are geared toward the penurious. Bare hardwood floors make conversations a challenge on busy nights. ⊠ *2120 Greenwich St., Cow Hollow,* ☎ *415/292–0770. No credit cards. Closed Sun. and Mon. No lunch.*

Italian

$$$–$$$$ ✕ **Merenda.** This cozy, friendly combination trattoria, *enoteca* (wine bar), and take-out counter is the domain of chef Keith Luce and his wife, Raney, who oversees the front of the house. The menu is prix fixe, two, three, or four courses, and the food is sophisticated Italian—chicken liver crostini, rabbit with a tomatoey porcini sauce, duck confit, walnut torta. The take-away items run the gamut from whole roasted chickens to house-made filled pastas, and the wines are some of Italy's most intriguing bottlings. ⊠ *1809 Union St., Cow Hollow,* ☎ *415/346–7373. MC, V. Closed Tues. No lunch.*

$$ ✕ **Pane e Vino.** A long table topped with various antipasti seduces everyone who enters this very popular trattoria. Polenta with mushrooms, grilled bass, *vitello tonnato* (roasted veal in a tuna sauce and served cold), and house-made sausages are among the dishes regulars can't resist. The Italian-born owner-chef concentrates on specialties from Tuscany and the north, dishing them up in a charming room with rustic wooden furniture and bright white walls punctuated with colorful pottery. ⊠ *3011 Steiner St., Cow Hollow,* ☎ *415/346–2111. MC, V. No lunch Sun.*

$ ✕ **Rose's Café.** Chef Reed Hearon opened this more casual kin of his famed Rose Pistola in the late 1990s. Breakfast, lunch, and dinner can be taken in the dining room or outside on a heater-equipped patio. In the morning, folks line up for seductive breads and even breakfast pizzas with ham and eggs. Midday is the time for a hot hero sandwich, a grilled-chicken salad, or a pizza topped with arugula and prosciutto. Evening hours find customers working their way through hanger steak or plump mussels roasted in the pizza oven. ⊠ *2298 Union St., Cow Hollow,* ☎ *415/775–2200. AE, MC, V.*

Mediterranean

$$–$$$ ✕ **PlumpJack Café.** This clubby dining room, with its smartly attired clientele of bankers and brokers, socialites and society scions, takes its name from an opera composed by oil tycoon and music lover Gordon Getty, whose sons are two of the partners here. The regularly changing menu spans the Mediterranean; possible dishes include lamb sirloin with squash risotto and beef fillet with green peppercorn sauce. The restaurant is an offshoot of the nearby highly regarded wine shop of the same name, as reflected in the reasonably priced wine list. ⊠ *3127 Fillmore St., Cow Hollow,* ☎ *415/463–4755. AE, MC, V. Closed Sun. No lunch Sat.*

Mexican

$ ✕ **Café Marimba.** Fanciful folk art adorns the walls of this colorful Mexican café, where an open kitchen turns out contemporary renditions of regional specialties, from Oaxacan moles to Yucatecan tacos. Although the food is treated to many innovative touches, authenticity plays a strong role—even the guacamole is made to order in a *molcajete*, the classic three-legged lava-rock Mexican mortar. A cajeta sundae—thick, rich Mexican caramel sauce spooned over vanilla ice cream—makes a fine finale to any meal. ⊠ *2317 Chestnut St., Marina,* ☏ *415/776–1506. AE, MC, V. Closed Sun. No lunch Mon.*

Pan-Asian

$–$$ ✕ **Betelnut.** A pan-Asian menu and an adventurous drinks list—with everything from house-brewed rice beer to martinis—draw a steady stream of hip diners to this Union Street landmark. Lacquered walls, bamboo ceiling fans, and period posters create a comfortably exotic mood in keeping with the unusual but accessible food. Among the big and small plates are steamed dumplings, chicken satay, tea-smoked quail, Korean grilled pork, and an addictive mix of dried anchovies, chiles, peanuts, garlic, and green onions. ⊠ *2030 Union St., Cow Hollow,* ☏ *415/929–8855. D, DC, MC, V.*

Steak

$–$$ ✕ **Izzy's Steak & Chop House.** Izzy Gomez was a legendary San Francisco saloon keeper, and his namesake eatery carries on the tradition. Here, in this old-fashioned, clamorous spot, you'll find terrific steaks—especially dry-aged sirloins—chops, and seafood, plus all the trimmings, from cheesy scalloped potatoes to creamed spinach. Regulars favor the Caesar salad or Cajun fried oysters to start. Prime rib is offered on Saturday and Sunday only. A collection of Izzy memorabilia and antique advertising art covers almost every inch of wall space. ⊠ *3345 Steiner St., Marina,* ☏ *415/563–0487. AE, DC, MC, V. No lunch.*

Vegetarian

$–$$ ✕ **Greens.** This beautiful restaurant with expansive bay views is owned and operated by the Green Gulch Zen Buddhist Center of Marin County. Creative meatless dishes are served, such as Thai-style vegetable curries, thin-crust pizzas, house-made pastas, and desserts like apricot and blueberry cobbler with vanilla ice cream. Dinners are à la carte on weeknights, but only a four-course prix-fixe dinner is served on Saturday. Sunday brunch is a good time to watch local sailboat skippers take out their crafts. ⊠ *Bldg. A, Fort Mason (enter across Marina Blvd. from Safeway), Marina,* ☏ *415/771–6222. D, MC, V. No lunch Mon., no dinner Sun.*

Embarcadero

American

$–$$ ✕ **Fog City Diner.** Arguably the country's sleekest American diner, Fog City has a dining room that emulates a luxurious railroad car, with wood paneling, huge windows, chrome fixtures, and comfortable booths. The menu is both classic and contemporary and includes macaroni and gouda cheese, mu shu pork burritos, a big rib steak with fingerling potatoes, and chocolate chip ice cream sandwiches. Grumblers have complained of inconsistent service, and locals complain of too many out-of-towners, but the booths are often full at lunch and dinner. ⊠ *1300 Battery St., Embarcadero,* ☏ *415/982–2000. D, DC, MC, V.*

Chinese

$–$$$ ✕ **Harbor Village.** At lunchtime, businesspeople looking to impress their clients fill the dining room of this outpost of upmarket Cantonese cooking, all of them enjoying the extraordinary selection of dim sum. At dinnertime, fresh seafood from the restaurant's own tanks, crisp Peking duck, and various exotica—bird's nest, crab roe, shark fin—are among the most popular requests from the loyal customers who regularly fill this opulent 400-seat branch of a Hong Kong establishment. There's validated parking at the Embarcadero Center Garage. ✉ *4 Embarcadero Center, Embarcadero,* ☎ *415/781–8833. AE, DC, MC, V.*

Contemporary

$$$ ✕ **Boulevard.** Two of San Francisco's top restaurant talents—chef Nancy Oakes and designer Pat Kuleto—are responsible for this high-profile eatery in the magnificent 1889 Audiffred Building, a Parisian look-alike that was one of the few downtown structures to survive the 1906 earthquake. Oakes's menu is seasonally in flux, but you can always count on her signature juxtaposition of delicacies such as foie gras with homey comfort foods like wood oven–roasted pork loin. Save room—and calories—for one of the dynamite desserts. ✉ *1 Mission St., Embarcadero,* ☎ *415/543–6084. Reservations essential. AE, D, DC, MC, V. No lunch weekends.*

$$–$$$ ✕ **One Market.** A giant among American chefs, Bradley Ogden gained fame at Campton Place and later at his Lark Creek Inn in Marin County. This huge, bustling brasserie across from the Ferry Building is his popular San Francisco outpost. The two-tier dining room, done in mustard tones, seats 170, and a spacious bar-café serves snacks, including addictive wire-thin onion rings, beginning at noon. Fine—and homey—preparations include rabbit in mustard, cinnamon-glazed pork shank, and caramel pecan tart with bourbon ice cream. ✉ *1 Market St., Embarcadero,* ☎ *415/777–5577. AE, DC, MC, V. Closed Sun. No lunch Sat.*

French

$$ ✕ **Pastis.** At lunchtime the sunny cement bar and sleek wooden banquettes in this exposed-brick dining room are crowded with workers from nearby offices; they come to fuel up on such plates as grilled prawns marinated in pastis (anise-flavor liqueur). The evening menu may include buttery boned oxtails with *ravigote* sauce (with capers, onions, and herbs) and a thick veal chop with shallot sauce. Pastis, with its French and Basque plates, is chef-owner Gerald Hirigoyen's popular successor to his SoMa bistro Fringale. ✉ *1015 Battery St., Embarcadero,* ☎ *415/391–2555. AE, MC, V. Closed Sun. No lunch Sat.*

Italian

$$ ✕ **Il Fornaio.** An offshoot of the Il Fornaio bakeries, this tile-floored, wood-paneled complex combines a café, first-rate bakery, and upscale trattoria with a pleasant outdoor seating area. The Tuscan cuisine, laid out in a sizable menu, includes crisp, thin pizzas from a wood-burning oven; house-made pastas and gnocchi; grilled poultry, seafood, and meats, plus Italian regional specials are always offered. Il Fornaio has become as comfortable as an old shoe, which means the kitchen sometimes rests on past laurels. ✉ *Levi's Plaza, 1265 Battery St., Embarcadero,* ☎ *415/986–0100. AE, DC, MC, V.*

Financial District

American

$$$$ ✕ **Garden Court.** This quintessential Old San Francisco restaurant is in the Palace Hotel. During the daytime, light splashes through the dining room's beautiful stained-glass ceiling and against the towering Ionic columns and crystal chandeliers. The draw here is not the dinner menu, but rather the truly extravagant Sunday buffet brunch, one of the city's great traditions. If you can't make it to the Palace for breakfast, try the Saturday-afternoon high tea. ✉ *Market and New Montgomery Sts., South of Market,* ☎ *415/546–5011. Reservations essential. AE, D, DC, MC, V. No lunch weekends. No dinner Sun.–Tues.*

$–$$$ ✕ **MacArthur Park.** At happy hour, a sea of suits fills this handsomely renovated pre-1906-earthquake brick warehouse. Much of the crowd stays on for the legendary baby back ribs, but the oak-wood smoker and mesquite grill also turn out other all-American dishes, from steaks to burgers to rack of lamb to seafood. Cobb, spinach, and Caesar salads will put some greens in your meal, and enthusiasts of the skinny french fry will fill up on what's served here. ⊠ *607 Front St., Financial District,* ☎ *415/398–5700. AE, DC, MC, V. No lunch weekends.*

Chinese

$ ✕ **Yank Sing.** The city's oldest teahouse, Yank Sing began in Chinatown in the late 1950s but moved to the Financial District in the 1980s. The kitchen prepares 100 varieties of dim sum on a rotating basis, serving some 60 varieties daily. The Spear Street location is large and upmarket, while the older Stevenson Street site is far smaller, a cozy refuge for neighborhood office workers who fuel up on steamed buns and parchment chicken at lunchtime. Take-out counters in both establishments make a meal on the run a delicious compromise. ⊠ *49 Stevenson St., at Market St., Financial District,* ☎ *415/541–4949;* ⊠ *One Rincon Center, 101 Spear St., Financial District,* ☎ *415/957–9300. AE, DC, MC, V. No dinner.*

Contemporary

$$–$$$ ✕ **Rubicon.** With initial investors like Robin Williams, Robert De Niro, and Francis Ford Coppola, this sleek, cherrywood-lined restaurant, an offshoot of New York's famed Drew Nieporent restaurant empire, was destined to be a hot spot. Set in a stately stone building dating from 1908, the downstairs dining room has the air of a men's club, while the upstairs space is more ascetic. The menu—veal chop in grape leaves, salmon poached in beurre rouge, seared quail with warm chanterelle salad—suits the restaurant's understated glamour. ⊠ *558 Sacramento St., Financial District,* ☎ *415/434–4100. AE, DC, MC, V. Closed Sun. No lunch Sat.*

French

$$$$ ✕ **Elisabeth Daniel.** San Franciscans who loved the meals at Babette's in Sonoma, but dreaded the drive, were happy when Elisabeth Ramsey and Daniel Patterson decided to leave the Wine Country for the big city. This small dining room in easygoing blue and gray, with candlelight and brocade tablecloths, has been their home since 2000, and Patterson's exquisite—and costly—six-course fixed-price menu displays a high degree of finesse in the kitchen. The menu changes at least slightly every night, but the food is always elegant and eye-catching. ⊠ *550 Washington St., Financial District,* ☎ *415/397–6129. Reservations essential. MC, V Closed Sun.–Mon.*

$–$$ ✕ **Le Central.** This venerable institution is the quintessential French brasserie: noisy and crowded, with tasty but not so subtly cooked classics, such as garlicky pâtés, leeks vinaigrette, steak au poivre, cassoulet, and grilled blood sausage with crisp french fries. Local power brokers, even an occasional rock star such as Mick Jagger, snag noontime tables. Staff from the nearby French consulate dine here as well, giving the place an air of authenticity. A traditional zinc bar provides a good perch for people-watching. ⊠ *453 Bush St., Financial District,* ☎ *415/391–2233. MC, V. Closed Sun.*

$–$$ ✕ **Plouf.** This sleek spot, turned out in chrome and the colors of the sea, is a gold mine for mussel lovers, with eight generously portioned preparations from which to choose. Among them are *marinière* (garlic and parsley) and apple cider, leeks, and cream. Order a side of fries and that's all most appetites will need. Other main courses run the gamut from steak frites to *bourride* (Provençal fish soup). The appetizers maintain the seaside theme, with raw oysters on the half shell and soft-shell crab among the offerings. ✉ *40 Belden Pl., Financial District,* ☎ *415/986–6491. AE, MC, V. Closed Sun.*

$ ✕ **Café Claude.** This standout French bistro, in an alley near the French consulate, has a true Parisian interior, with a zinc bar, old-fashioned banquettes, and cinema posters that once actually outfitted a bar in the City of Light's 11th arrondissement. Order an *assiette de charcuterie* (plate of assorted meats), *croque monsieur* (grilled cheese sandwich), or duck breast with braised endives from the French-speaking staff, and you might forget what country you're in. ✉ *7 Claude La., Financial District,* ☎ *415/392–3505. AE, DC, MC, V. Closed Sun.*

Greek

$$–$$$ ✕ **Kokkari.** Sophistication is written all over this handsome taverna. In its inviting interior, complete with an outsize fireplace and a lively bar, folks sit down to a full menu of Aegean plates. Most savvy diners start off with a trio of dips—eggplant, yogurt and cucumber, *taramasalata* (fish roe pureed with olive oil and bread crumbs)—and then move on to such Athenian standards as moussaka, octopus salad, lemon chicken, braised lamb shank, and grilled whole bass. A bar menu of small plates satisfies mid-afternoon customers. ✉ *200 Jackson St., Financial District,* ☎ *415/981–0983. AE, DC, MC, V. Closed Sun. No lunch Sat.*

Italian

$$–$$$ ✕ **Palio d'Asti.** Restaurateur Gianni Fassio draws a lively crowd to this authentic spot serving dishes from Tuscany and the Piedmont. The kitchen's freshly baked breads, exquisite pastas, and carefully constructed sauces are legendary. Colorful flags decorate the elegant restaurant, each representing a neighborhood that participates in the famed Palio, a horse race that's been held annually since medieval times in Fassio's hometown of Asti. The small wine bar is a wonderful place to sit and enjoy small plates and a memorable Italian wine. Nearby, **Palio Paninoteca** (✉ 505 Montgomery St., Financial District, ☎ 415/362–6900) offers stylish takeout or eat-in lunchtime *panini* (Italian sandwiches) served on house-made bread. ✉ *640 Sacramento St., Financial District,* ☎ *415/395–9800. AE, D, MC, V. Closed weekends.*

Japanese

$$–$$$ ✕ **Kyo-ya.** Rarely replicated outside Japan, the refined experience of dining in a fine Japanese restaurant has been introduced with extraordinary authenticity at this showplace within the Palace Hotel. In Japan a *kyo-ya* is a nonspecialized restaurant that serves a wide range of food. Here, the range is spectacular, encompassing tempuras, one-pot dishes, deep-fried and grilled meats, and three dozen sushi selections. *Kaiseki* meals, multicourse seasonal dinners, are also offered, priced for an emperor. ✉ *Palace Hotel, 2 New Montgomery St., at Market St., South of Market,* ☎ *415/546–5000. AE, D, DC, MC, V. Closed Sun. No lunch Mon. or Sat.*

Seafood

$$$ ✕ **Aqua.** This quietly elegant and ultrafashionable spot, heavily mir-
★ rored and populated by a society crowd, is among the city's most lauded seafood restaurants—and among the most expensive. Chef-owner Michael Mina creates contemporary versions of French, Italian, and American classics. Mussel soufflé with a Chardonnay sauce, white anchovy terrine, and chunks of lobster alongside lobster-stuffed ravioli are all especially good. Service is as smooth as silk, desserts are showy, and the wine list is as high class as the crowd. ✉ *252 California St., Financial District,* ☎ *415/956–9662. Reservations essential. Jacket and tie. AE, DC, MC, V. No lunch weekends.*

$-$$ ✕ **Tadich Grill.** Owners and locations have changed many times since this old-timer opened during the gold-rush era, but the 19th-century atmosphere remains. Simple sautés are the best choices, or cioppino during crab season, petrale sole during sole season, and an old-fashioned house-made tartar sauce anytime. There is seating at the counter as well as in private booths, but expect long lines for a table at lunchtime on weekdays. The crusty, white-coated waiters are a reminder of good, old-fashioned service. ⊠ 240 California St., Financial District, ☎ 415/391–2373. Reservations not accepted. MC, V. Closed Sun.

Spanish

$$ ✕ **B44.** Belden Place is a restaurant gold mine, with a cluster of won-
★ derful European eateries. This spare, modern Spanish addition, with its open kitchen, draws locals who love the menu of Catalan tapas and paellas. Among the small plates are white anchovies with pears and Idiazábal cheese, sherry-scented fish cheeks, warm octopus with tiny potatoes, and blood sausage with white beans. The paellas, each serving presented in an iron skillet, bring together such inviting combinations as chicken, rabbit, and mushrooms. ⊠ 44 Belden Pl., Financial District, ☎ 415/986–6287. AE, MC, V. Closed Sun. No lunch Sat.

Fisherman's Wharf

French

$$$$ ✕ **Gary Danko.** At his late-1990s eponymous restaurant, chef Gary
★ Danko delivers the same fine food that won him a 1995 James Beard best chef award during his stint at the city's Ritz-Carlton. The cost of a meal is pegged at the number of courses, from three to five, and the plates run the gamut from horseradish-crusted salmon to quail with morels to a truly decadent chocolate soufflé with two sauces. The wine list is the size of a small-town phone book, and the look of the banquette-lined room is as high class as the food. ⊠ 800 N. Point St., Fisherman's Wharf, ☎ 415/749–2060. Reservations essential. AE, D, DC, MC, V. No lunch.

Indian

$-$$ ✕ **Gaylord's.** You'll find a vast selection of mildly spiced northern Indian food here, along with excellent meats and breads from the tandoor ovens and a range of vegetarian dishes. Although the kitchen sometimes stumbles, and the staff is occasionally overbearing, the elegantly appointed dining room goes a long way in soothing disappointments. So do the prime bay views. Validated parking is offered at the Ghirardelli Square garage. ⊠ Ghirardelli Sq., Fisherman's Wharf, ☎ 415/771–8822. AE, D, DC, MC, V.

Seafood

$-$$$ ✕ **McCormick & Kuleto's.** This seafood emporium in Ghirardelli Square is a visitor's dream come true: a fabulous view of the bay from every seat in the house; an Old San Francisco atmosphere; and dozens of varieties of fish and shellfish prepared in scores of international ways. The food has its ups and downs—stick with the simplest preparations, such as oysters on the half shell and grilled fish—but even on foggy days you can count on the view. Validated parking is available in the Ghirardelli Square garage. ⊠ Ghirardelli Sq. at Beach and Larkin Sts., Fisherman's Wharf, ☎ 415/929–1730. AE, D, DC, MC, V.

The Haight

Contemporary

$$ ✕ **Eos Restaurant & Wine Bar.** The culinary marriage of California cuisine and the Asian pantry is the specialty of chef-owner Arnold Wong, who serves an impressive East-West menu at this popular spot. Grilled

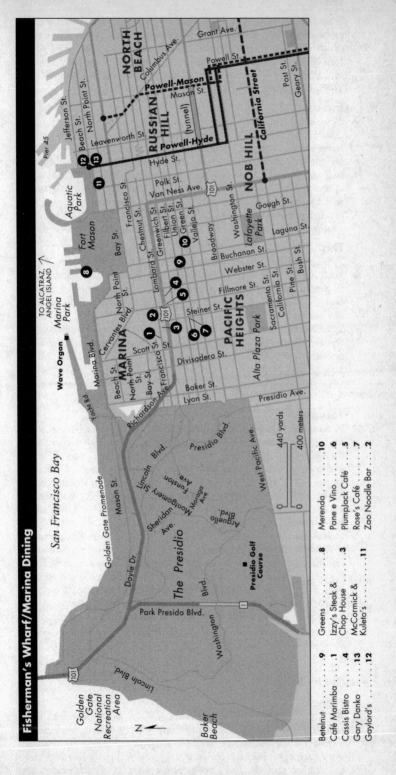

Fisherman's Wharf/Marina Dining

Betelnut **9**
Café Marimba **1**
Cassis Bistro **4**
Gary Danko **13**
Gaylord's **12**

Greens **8**
Izzy's Steak &
Chop House **3**
McCormick &
Kuleto's **11**

Merenda **10**
Pane e Vino **6**
Plumpjack Café **5**
Rose's Café **7**
Zao Noodle Bar **2**

lamb chops are marinated in a red Thai curry and served with mashed potatoes; skirt steak is treated to a Korean marinade before it is slapped on the grill; and a tea-smoked duck breast replaces the usual whole bird. The wine bar next door shelves hundreds of vintages, any of which is available at your dinner table. ⊠ *901 Cole St., Haight,* ☎ *415/566–3063. Reservations essential. AE, MC, V. No lunch.*

Indian

$–$$ ✕ **Indian Oven.** One of the Lower Haight's most popular restaurants, this cozy Victorian storefront never lacks for customers. Many of them come here to order the tandoori specialties—chicken, lamb, breads— but the *sag paneer* (spinach with Indian cheese) and *aloo gobhi* (potatoes and cauliflower with black mustard seeds and other spices) are also excellent. A complete meal, called a *thali* for the metal plate on which it is served, includes a choice of entrée, plus soup, a curried vegetable, cardamom-scented rice, nan, and chutney. ⊠ *223 Fillmore St., Lower Haight,* ☎ *415/626–1628. AE, D, DC, MC, V. No lunch.*

Thai

$ ✕ **Thep Phanom.** The fine Thai food and the lovely interior at this Lower
★   Haight institution keep local food critics and restaurant goers singing its praises. Duck is deliciously prepared in several ways—in a fragrant curry, minced for salad, resting atop a bed of spinach. Other specialties are seafood in various guises, stuffed chicken wings, fried quail, and addictive Thai curries. A number of daily specials supplement the regular menu, and a tropical mango sorbet is sometimes offered for dessert. ⊠ *400 Waller St., Lower Haight,* ☎ *415/431–2526. AE, D, DC, MC, V. No lunch.*

Japantown

Japanese

$–$$ ✕ **Sanppo.** This modestly priced, casual spot has an enormous selection of almost every type of Japanese food: yakis, *nabemono* dishes (one-pot meals), *donburi* (meat- or chicken-topped rice bowls), udon, and soba, not to mention featherlight tempura and sushi. Grilled eel on rice in a lacquered box and tempting small dishes for snacking make Sanppo a favorite. Ask for validated parking at the Japan Center garage. ⊠ *1702 Post St., Japantown,* ☎ *415/346–3486. Reservations not accepted. MC, V.*

$ ✕ **Mifune.** Thin, brown soba and thick, white udon are the specialties at this North American outpost of an Osaka-based noodle empire. A line often snakes out the door, but the house-made noodles, served both hot and cold and with more than a score of toppings, are worth the wait. Seating is at wooden tables, where diners can be heard slurping down big bowls of such traditional Japanese combinations as fish cake–crowned udon and *tenzaru* (cold noodles and hot tempura with a gingery dipping sauce) served on lacquered trays. ⊠ *Japan Center, Kintetsu Bldg., 1737 Post St., Japantown,* ☎ *415/922–0337. Reservations not accepted. AE, D, DC, MC, V.*

Lower Pacific Heights

French

$$ ✕ **Florio.** San Franciscans are always ready to fall in love with little French bistros, and this has made Florio a hit. It has all the elements: a space reminiscent of a Paris address, excellent roasted chicken, and some reasonably priced French wines. Of course, there's also duck confit, steamed mussels, and steak *pommes frites.* Forgo the pastas, but don't pass up the crème caramel or the house-made gelatos and sorbets. The room can get noisy, so don't come here hoping for a quiet

tête-à-tête. ✉ *1915 Fillmore St., Lower Pacific Heights,* ☎ *415/775–4300. MC, V. No lunch.*

Italian

$–$$ ✕ **Vivande Porta Via.** Tucked in among the boutiques on upper Fillmore Street, this pricey Italian delicatessen-restaurant, operated by well-known chef and cookbook author Carlo Middione, draws a crowd at lunch and dinner for both its take-out and sit-down fare. Glass cases holding dozens of prepared delicacies span one wall. The rest of the room is given over to seating and to shelves laden with wines, olives, and other gourmet goods. The regularly changing menu includes a half dozen pastas and risottos, as well as meat and fish mains. ✉ *2125 Fillmore St., Lower Pacific Heights,* ☎ *415/346–4430. AE, MC, V.*

Spanish

$ ✕ **Chez Nous.** The concept here is Spanish tapas, although many of the small dishes—duck leg confit with apple slices, baked goat cheese with oven-roasted tomatoes, french fries served with aioli spiked with *harissa* (Moroccan chili sauce)—cross the border into other national cuisines. Grilled asparagus with lemon zest, salad of squid with greens, and grilled quail with a scattering of wild mushrooms are among the other choices. The stylish yet casual and noisy dining room includes wood floors, zinc-topped tables, and blue walls. ✉ *1911 Fillmore St., Lower Pacific Heights,* ☎ *415/441–8044. Reservations not accepted. MC, V. Closed Mon. No lunch Tues.*

The Mission District

Cambodian

$ ✕ **Angkor Borei.** Aromatic Thai basil, lemongrass, and softly sizzling chilies lace many of the dishes at this true neighborhood restaurant. The menu includes an array of curries, plump spring rolls, and delicate crepes stuffed with vegetables and a smattering of meat and seafood. Chicken on skewers, grilled, and served with mildly pickled vegetables is a house specialty, as is the green papaya salad. The modest yet handsome space is decorated with lovely Khmer objects. ✉ *3471 Mission St., Outer Mission,* ☎ *415/550–8417. AE, D, MC, V. No lunch Sun.*

Contemporary

$$ ✕ **42 Degrees.** This industrial-style space, with its curving metal staircase and seductive view of the bay, has been a draw since the mid-1990s. The name refers to the latitude on which Provence, Tuscany, and northern Spain lie, and the menu combines the kitchens of California and the Mediterranean. Specials are scrawled on a blackboard, and there are wonderful small plates to share. Nightly jazz keeps late-night patrons—mostly a younger crowd—tapping their toes. It's noisy, so sensitive ears should beware. ✉ *235 16th St., Potrero Hill,* ☎ *415/777–5558. MC, V. Closed Sun.–Tues. No lunch.*

$ ✕ **Andalou.** The menu here includes some 30 globe-circling small plates, from duck confit spring rolls and miniature tacos filled with ceviche to a fritto misto of artichokes and potatoes and a crock of *brandade* (salt cod puree). The wine list is equally global, and many offerings come by the glass to tempt curious palates. The hip, two-level dining room in the North Mission is outfitted in tables in aquamarine and black. Don't overlook the dessert of doughnut holes and thick, hot cocoa topped with whipped cream. ✉ *3198 16th St., Mission,* ☎ *415/621–2211. MC, V. Closed Sun. No lunch.*

$ ✕ **Luna Park.** Anytime after 6:30, it's a tight and noisy fit in this wildly popular bistro in the busy North Mission. The crowd of mostly twenty- and thirtysomethings is here to sip cosmos or *mojitos* and eat steamed mussels served with a paper cone crammed with french fries;

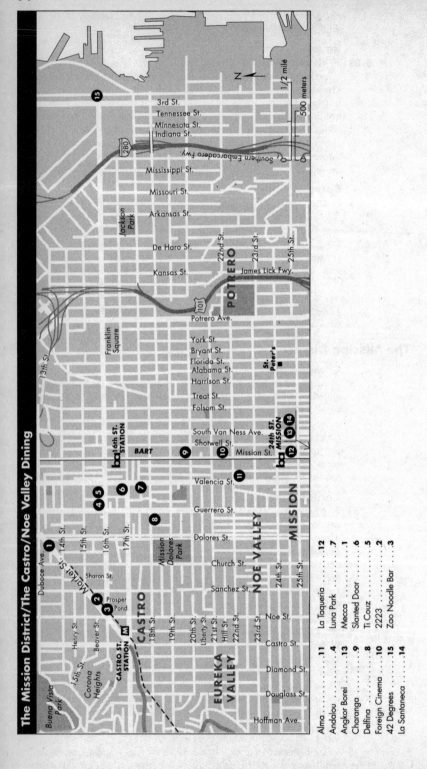

The Mission District/The Castro/Noe Valley Dining

Alma **11**
Andalou **4**
Angkor Borei **13**
Charanga **9**
Delfina **8**
Foreign Cinema ...**10**
La Santaneca **14**

La Taqueria **12**
Luna Park **7**
Mecca **1**
Slanted Door **6**
Ti Couz **5**
2223 ....**2**
Zao Noodle Bar ...**3**

poke salad (Hawaiian raw tuna partnered with wonton chips); or grilled flatiron steak. For dessert, an order of s'mores includes cups of melted chocolate and marshmallows and a handful of house-made graham crackers for constructing your own campfire classic. ✉ *694 Valencia St., Mission,* ☎ *415/553–8584. MC, V. No lunch weekends.*

French

$–$$ ✕ **Foreign Cinema.** The Bay Area is home to many of the country's most respected independent filmmakers, making this innovative spot a sure-fire hit with cinemaphiles. In the hip, loftlike space not only can you sit down to orders of crab cakes and duck confit, but you can also watch such foreign classics as Fellini's *La Dolce Vita,* plus a passel of current indie features, projected in the large courtyard. Fussy filmgoers will want to call ahead to find out what's playing and arrive early enough to get a good seat. ✉ *2534 Mission St., Mission,* ☎ *415/648–7600. MC, V. Closed Mon. No lunch.*

$ ✕ **Ti Couz.** Big, thin buckwheat crepes just like you find in Brittany are the specialty here, filled with everything from ham and Gruyère cheese to Nutella and banana ice cream. The blue-and-white European-style dining room in the North Mission is always crowded, and diners too hungry to wait for a seat can try for one next door, where the same owners operate a seafood bar with both raw and cooked choices. Although there is a full bar serving mixed drinks, the best beverage to sip in this Gallic spot is French hard cider served in pottery bowls. ✉ *3108 16th St., Mission,* ☎ *415/252–7373. MC, V. Reservations not accepted.*

Italian

$–$$ ✕ **Delfina.** Delfina is always hopping. Indeed, within several months
★ of opening in 1999, success forced chef-owner Craig Stoll to take over a neighboring storefront to accommodate the throngs. The loyal crowd comes for the simple yet exquisite Italian fare found on a daily changing menu: grilled fresh sardines; orecchiette with broccoli rabe and chickpeas; halibut riding atop olives and braised fennel. If calories are no concern, try the profiteroles packed with coffee ice cream and dressed with a lavalike chocolate sauce. ✉ *3621 18th St., Mission,* ☎ *415/552–4055. MC, V. No lunch.*

Latin

$–$$ ✕ **Alma.** Chef Johnny Alamilla has created a mix of Nuevo Latino flavors in this small, comfortably urban space of blue walls and wood floors. Hangar steak is served with hearts of palm, seared fresh fish comes with fried plantains and onions, and tuna is treated to a coconut marinade. The theme continues with sides of yucca fries; corn *arepas* (small pancakes filled with cheese, corn, and onions); and a jicama and cabbage slaw. Even the wine list carries a Latino stamp, with wines from Argentina, Chile, and Uruguay. ✉ *1101 Valencia St., Mission,* ☎ *415/401–8959. MC, V. Closed Sun. No lunch.*

$ ✕ **Charanga.** Cozy and lively, this neighborhood tapas restaurant, named for a Cuban salsa style that relies on flute and violins, serves an eclectic mix of small plates, from mushrooms cooked with garlic and sherry to *patatas bravas* (twice-fried potatoes with a roasted-tomato sauce). Asian influences show up here as well, in such dishes as shrimp and calamari with coconut rice. The small dining room, with its walls of exposed brick and soothing green, is a friendly place, so order a pitcher of sangria and enjoy yourself. ✉ *2351 Mission St., Mission,* ☎ *415/282–1813. Reservations not accepted. MC, V. Closed Sun. and Mon. No lunch.*

$ ✕ **La Santaneca.** Lots of El Salvadorans live in the Mission, and here they can find *pupusa,* a stuffed cornmeal round that is more or less the hamburger of their homeland. It usually comes filled with cheese, meat, or both and is eaten along with seasoned shredded cabbage. The cooks at La Santaneca, a plain-Jane, home-cooking place, also turn out fried plantains, tamales filled with pork and potatoes, and *chicharrones* (fried pork skins) and yucca as well as other dishes popular in Central America. ⊠ *3781 Mission St., Mission,* ☎ *415/648–1034. No credit cards.*

Mexican

$ ✕ **La Taqueria.** Although there are many taquerías in the Mission, this attractive spot, with its arched exterior and modest interior, is one of the oldest and finest. The tacos are superb: two warm corn tortillas topped with your choice of meat—*carne asada* (grilled steak) and *carnitas* (slowly cooked pork) are favorites—and a spoonful of perfectly fresh salsa. Big appetites may want to try a burrito. Chase your meal with an *agua fresca* (fresh fruit cooler). ⊠ *2889 Mission St., Mission,* ☎ *415/285–7117. No credit cards.*

Vietnamese

$$ ✕ **Slanted Door.** Behind the canted facade of this highly popular North Mission restaurant, you'll find upmarket Vietnamese food with a thick Western accent. There are fresh spring rolls packed with rice noodles, pork, shrimp, and pungent mint leaves, and fried vegetarian imperial rolls concealing bean thread noodles, cabbage, and taro. Shaking beef (seasoned beef cubes) and five-spice chicken are among the favorite dishes. The menu changes regularly, but crowd pleasers are never abandoned. Service, alas, is sometimes haphazard. ⊠ *584 Valencia St., North Mission,* ☎ *415/861–8032. MC, V. Closed Mon.*

Nob Hill

French

$$$$ ✕ **Masa's.** Although the Masa's toque has been passed to three chefs since the death of founder chef Masa Kobayashi, the restaurant continues to be one of the country's most celebrated food temples. Today, chef Ron Siegel, famous for besting Japan's Iron Chef, is at the helm, and his efforts have pleased the fussiest restaurant critics. Dinners are prix-fixe with two menus offered, a four-course menu du jour and a five-course menu, both laced with truffles and foie gras and both priced at a king's ransom. ⊠ *648 Bush St., Nob Hill,* ☎ *415/989–7154. Reservations essential. Jacket required. AE, D, DC, MC, V. Closed Sun. and Mon. No lunch.*

$$$$ ✕ **Ritz-Carlton Dining Room and Terrace.** There are two distinctly dif-
★   ferent places to eat in this neoclassic Nob Hill showplace. The Dining Room is formal and elegant and serves only three- to five-course French seasonal dinners, priced by the number of courses. The Terrace, a cheerful, informal spot with a large garden patio for outdoor dining, serves breakfast, lunch, dinner, and a Sunday jazz brunch. In both cases, executive chef Sylvain Portay, previously chef de cuisine at New York's Le Cirque, oversees the superb menus. ⊠ *600 Stockton St., Nob Hill,* ☎ *415/296–7465. AE, D, DC, MC, V. Closed Sun. No lunch.*

North Beach

Afghan

$ ✕ **Helmand.** Don't be put off by Helmand's location on a rather scruffy block of Broadway—inside you'll find authentic Afghan cooking, elegant surroundings with white table linens and Afghan carpets, and amazingly low prices. Highlights include *aushak* (leek-filled ravioli served with yogurt and ground beef), pumpkin with a yogurt and garlic sauce, and any of the lamb dishes, in particular the kabob strewn with yellow split peas and served on Afghan flat bread. There's free validated parking at 468 Broadway. ✉ *430 Broadway, North Beach,* ☎ *415/362–0641. AE, MC, V. Closed Mon. No lunch.*

Contemporary

$–$$$ ✗ **Moose's.** Ed Moose and his wife, Mary Etta, are well known in San Francisco and beyond, so local and national politicians and media types typically turn up at their restaurant. The menu is a sophisticated take on familiar preparations, such as grilled calamari salad, oven-roasted grouper with salsify-and-potato gratin, rosemary-braised lamb shank, and butterscotch pot-de-crème. The surroundings are classic and comfortable, with views of Washington Square. There's live music at night and a fine brunch on Saturday and Sunday. ✉ *1652 Stockton St., North Beach,* ☎ *415/989–7800. Reservations essential. AE, D, DC, MC, V. No lunch Sat.–Wed.*

$$ ✗ **Enrico's Sidewalk Café.** For years this historic North Beach hangout was more a drinking spot than a dining destination, but a steadier kitchen has changed all that. Diners regularly tuck into thin-crust pizzas, steamed mussels, thick and juicy burgers, and grilled fish while gently swaying to first-rate live music. Grazers will be happy to find a slew of eclectic tapas, from tuna tartare to fried oysters. An outdoor patio is outfitted with heat lamps to keep the serious people-watchers warm until closing. ✉ *504 Broadway, North Beach,* ☎ *415/982–6223. AE, MC, V.*

$$ ✗ **Jianna.** The dining room, with its copper-leaf-covered columns and open kitchen, provide a perfect frame for the stylish but unfussy food and carefully chosen wines served here. The menu, which changes with the seasons, includes such satisfying first courses as roasted baby beet salad and such delicious mains as roast pork loin with chestnuts and blue cheese–topped New York strip loin. The modestly priced sweets are served in small portions on a dessert tasting platter, which leaves room for more than one delectable treat. ✉ *1548 Stockton St., North Beach,* ☎ *415/398–0442. AE, D, MC, V. No lunch.*

French

$$ ✗ **Black Cat.** A combination restaurant and lounge—the latter called the Blue Bar—Black Cat, which opened in 1997, takes its name from a famous San Francisco café-bar that was a hangout for everyone from artists to trade unionists in the 1930s through the 1960s. Today's Black Cat has undergone menu changes and is now a fine French brasserie, complete with zinc bar, alfresco seating, and raw-seafood platters. The ambience is a spirited one, with live jazz and a bar menu served up until the wee hours in the seriously blue lounge. ✉ *501 Broadway, North Beach,* ☎ *415/981–2233. AE, DC, MC, V. Closed Sun. No lunch.*

Italian

$$ ✗ **Ristorante Ideale.** The food here is what you might sit down to in a Roman trattoria—grilled vegetables, fettuccine with porcini, ravioli filled with ricotta and spinach, pork marsala, *pesce misto* (mixed seafood for two), and tiramisu. The red tile floors, rows of wine racks, and friendly, although sometimes frazzled, staff make this one of the nicest spots in the neighborhood, a place where you appreciate just how *simpatico* North Beach can be. On weekends, expect a wait for a table. ✉ *1309 Grant Ave., North Beach,* ☎ *415/391–4129. DC, MC, V. Closed Mon. No lunch.*

$–$$ ✗ **Capp's Corner.** This is one of North Beach's last family-style trattorias, a pleasantly down-home spot where the men at the bar still roll dice for drinks and diners sit elbow to elbow at long oilcloth-covered tables. The fare is bountiful, well-prepared five-course dinners—not award winning, but a meal here will mean you'll still be able to send your children to college. The osso buco and roast lamb are good choices for the main. For calorie counters or the budget-minded, a simpler option is a tureen of minestrone, salad, and pasta. ✉ *1600 Powell St., North Beach,* ☎ *415/989–2589. AE, D, DC, MC, V.*

$–$$ ✕ **Rose Pistola.** Chef-owner Reed Hearon's busy 130-seat spot draws
  ★   huge crowds. The name honors one of North Beach's most revered barkeeps, and the food celebrates the neighborhood's Ligurian roots. An assortment of antipasti—roasted peppers, house-cured fish, fava beans dusted with pecorino shards—and pizzas from the wood-burning oven are favorites, as are the cioppino and fresh fish of the day served in various ways. A big bar area opens onto the sidewalk, and an exhibition kitchen lets you keep an eye on your order. ✉ *532 Columbus Ave., North Beach,* ☎ *415/399–0499. AE, DC, MC, V.*

$ ✕ **L'Osteria del Forno.** An Italian-speaking staff, a small and unpretentious dining area, and irresistible aromas drifting from the open kitchen make customers who pass through the door of this modest storefront operation feel as if they've just stumbled into Italy. The kitchen produces small plates of simply cooked vegetables, a few baked pastas, a roast of the day, creamy polenta, and thin-crust pizzas—including a memorable "white" pie topped with porcini mushrooms and mozzarella. At lunch try one of the delectable focaccia sandwiches. ✉ *519 Columbus Ave., North Beach,* ☎ *415/982–1124. Reservations not accepted. No credit cards. Closed Tues.*

Middle Eastern

$–$$ ✕ **Maykadeh.** Although it sits in a decidedly Italian neighborhood, this authentic Persian restaurant serves a large and faithful following. Lamb dishes with rice are the specialties, served in a setting so elegant that the modest check comes as a surprise. Various kabobs and poultry and meats marinated in olive oil with lime juice, and herbs before hitting the grill are typical choices, while anyone looking for a hearty, traditional main dish should order *ghorme sabzee,* lamb shank braised with a bouquet of Middle Eastern spices. ✉ *470 Green St., North Beach,* ☎ *415/362–8286. MC, V. No lunch.*

Richmond District

Chinese

$–$$ ✕ **Parc Hong Kong Restaurant.** This tablecloth Cantonese restaurant has long been known as a place to enjoy such classy plates as smoked black cod and Peking duck. The kitchen is especially celebrated for its seafood, which is plucked straight from tanks; in the cool months, crab and lobster are usually priced to sell. Chefs here keep up with whatever is hot in Hong Kong eateries, so check on what's new with the generally genial waiters. Midday dim sum is available. ✉ *5322 Geary Blvd., Richmond District,* ☎ *415/668–8998. AE, D, DC, MC, V.*

$–$$ ✕ **Ton Kiang.** The lightly seasoned Hakka cuisine of southern China,
  ★   rarely found in this country, was introduced to San Francisco at this restaurant, with such regional specialties as salt-baked chicken, braised stuffed bean curd, delicate fish balls, chicken in wine sauce, and various clay pots of meats and seafood. Don't overlook the other seafood offerings here—salt-and-pepper shrimp, smoked black cod, or stir-fried crab, for example—or the pea sprouts stir-fried with garlic. The dim sum is arguably the finest in the city. ✉ *5821 Geary Blvd., Richmond,* ☎ *415/387–8273. MC, V.*

Japanese

$–$$ ✕ **Kabuto Sushi.** For one of the most spectacular acts in town, head down Geary Boulevard past Japantown to Kabuto. Here, behind the sushi counter, master chef Sachio Kojima flashes his knives before an admiring crowd who can't get enough of his buttery yellowfin tuna or golden sea urchin on pads of pearly rice. In addition to fine sushi and sashimi, traditional Japanese dinners are served in the adjoining dining room. Be sure to consider the excellent selection of sakes, each one rated for dryness and labeled with its place of origin. ⊠ *5116 Geary Blvd., Richmond,* ☎ *415/752–5652. MC, V. Closed first Tues. and last Sun. each month. No lunch.*

Russian

$ ✕ **Katia's.** This bright Richmond District gem serves Russian food with considerable flair at remarkably reasonable prices. Try the beautiful purple borscht, topped with a dollop of sour cream. Small plates of smoked salmon, marinated mushrooms, and meat- or vegetable-filled piroshki are also wonderful ways to start a meal, and light chicken cutlets or delicate *pelmeni* (meat-filled dumplings in broth) are fine main courses. There is live Russian music on most evenings. The slow service may occasionally try your patience. ⊠ *600 5th Ave., Inner Richmond,* ☎ *415/668–9292. AE, D, MC, V. Closed Mon. No lunch weekends.*

Singaporean

$–$$ ✕ **Straits Café.** This highly popular restaurant serves the unique fare of Singapore, a cuisine that combines the culinary traditions of China, India, and the Malay archipelago. That mix translates into complex curries, stir-fried seafood, chewy Indian breads, fragrant satays, and seafood noodle soups. The handsome dining room includes one wall that re-creates the old shop-house fronts of Singapore. ⊠ *3300 Geary Blvd., Richmond,* ☎ *415/668–1783. AE, MC, V.*

Vietnamese

$ ✕ **La Vie.** This small Vietnamese restaurant caters to a mostly neighborhood clientele with such traditional dishes as *nep chien* (balls of sticky rice stuffed with pork, shrimp, and mushrooms). One delectable dish consists of small cakes made from shrimp, rice flour, and mung beans: You wrap the cakes in lettuce leaves and dip them in chili-laced fish sauce. The beef *la lot* (minced beef in a tropical leaf) and beef vinegar fondue are also recommended. The attentive staff is always happy to answer questions about the food. ⊠ *5380 Geary Blvd., Richmond,* ☎ *415/668–8080. AE, MC, V. No lunch weekdays.*

$ ✕ **Le Soleil.** The food of Vietnam is the specialty of this pastel, light-filled restaurant in the heart of Inner Richmond. An eye-catching painting of Saigon hangs on one wall, and a large aquarium of tropical fish adds to the tranquil mood. The kitchen prepares traditional dishes from every part of the country. Try the excellent raw-beef salad; crisp, flavorful spring rolls; a simple stir-fry of chicken and aromatic fresh basil leaves; or large prawns simmered in a clay pot. ⊠ *133 Clement St., Inner Richmond,* ☎ *415/668–4848. MC, V.*

Russian Hill

French

$$$–$$$$ ✕ **La Folie.** Long a favorite of dedicated Francophiles, this small, *très* ★ Parisian establishment is a jewel. The surroundings are lovely, but the food is the star here, especially the five-course "discovery menu" that offers a treasure trove of rarified mouthfuls, from foie gras to truffles. Much of the food is edible art—whimsical presentations in the form of savory terrines and napoleons—or such elegant accompaniments as bone-marrow flan. Save this special—and costly—place for a celebratory occasion. ⊠ *2316 Polk St., Russian Hill,* ☎ *415/776–5577. Reservations essential. AE, D, DC, MC, V. No lunch.*

Italian

$$ ✕ **Antica Trattoria.** The dining room is stark, with off-white walls, dark wood, a partial view of the kitchen, and a strong sense of restraint. The food is characterized by the same no-nonsense quality. A small menu delivers classic plates such as fennel with blood oranges and red onions, beef carpaccio, farro pasta with Bolognese sauce, monkfish wrapped in pancetta, and venison medallions matched with wilted greens. The Italian wine list is fairly priced, and the genial service is polished but not overly formal. ✉ *2400 Polk St., Russian Hill,* ☎ *415/928–5797. DC, MC, V. Closed Mon. No lunch.*

Spanish

$ ✕ **Zarzuela.** Until the mid-1990s, San Francisco lacked a great tapas restaurant, but the opening of this charming eatery changed all that. The small, crowded storefront serves nearly 40 different hot and cold tapas plus some dozen main courses. There is a tapa to suit every palate, from poached octopus atop new potatoes and hot garlic-flecked shrimp to slabs of manchego cheese with paper-thin slices of serrano ham. A menu of rice dishes and stews is also offered. Hop a cable car to get here, as parking is nightmarish. ✉ *2000 Hyde St., Russian Hill,* ☎ *415/ 346–0800. D, MC, V. No lunch.*

South of Market

American

$–$$$ ✕ **Momo's.** Many of the baseball fans spilling out of the San Francisco Giants ballpark like to stop at this former printing plant, now a serious drinking and dining hangout. A shiny stainless-steel exhibition kitchen delivers french fries with chipotle ketchup, crisp onion rings, thick steaks, and thin pizzas to crowds in the Craftsman-appointed dining room with its big banquettes and high ceilings. The large patio and long bar are gathering places for everyone from sports enthusiasts to businesspeople shaking hands on a deal. ✉ *760 2nd St., South of Market,* ☎ *415/227–8660. AE, MC, V.*

$–$$ ✕ **Cosmopolitan Cafe.** The name of this establishment reflects the style of the menu. Indeed, such plates as yellowfin tuna with olive oil mashed potatoes show off the pleasantly appointed café's worldly yet unpretentious style. The signature appetizer is the trio sampler, for which chef Steven Levine takes a single ingredient, such as shrimp, and gives it three distinct treatments on the same plate. Mama Levine's warm chocolate chip cookies, served with a vanilla shake, are as comforting as comfort food can be. ✉ *121 Spear St., South of Market,* ☎ *415/ 543–4001. AE, DC, MC, V. Closed Sun. No lunch Sat.*

$ ✕ **Mo's Grill.** The term "burger" takes on new meaning at Mo's, which is within easy walking distance of the Moscone Center and SFMOMA. This eatery is devoted to what is arguably America's favorite food, and it dresses it up in lots of ways: with Monterey Jack and avocado; with bacon; with cheese and chilies; and more. But beef burgers are not the only story here. Salmon, lamb, and turkey burgers are among the other choices also cooked over the volcanic-rock grill, and sides of fries or onion rings fill out the plates deliciously. ✉ *772 Folsom St., South of Market,* ☎ *415/957–3779. MC, V.*

Contemporary

$$$–$$$$ ✕ **Fifth Floor.** San Franciscans began fighting for tables at this topflight
★   hotel dining room within days of its opening in 1999. Chef Laurent Gras has replaced the opening chef, but the plates remain elegant, sophisticated, visually stunning—and the crowds keep coming. The 75-seat room, done in dark wood and zebra-stripe carpeting, is where such exquisite dishes as venison saddle with cherry marmalade are served. There's even

ice cream made to order—the machine churns out a creamy, cool, rich serving for one. ⊠ *Palomar Hotel, 12 4th St., South of Market,* ☎ *415/ 348–1555. Reservations essential. AE, DC, MC, V. Closed Sun. No lunch.*

$$–$$$ ✕ **Hawthorne Lane.** This stylish restaurant draws a crowd to a quiet alley
★ not far from the Yerba Buena Center. At the tables in the large, high-ceiling bar, you can order a selection of irresistible small plates—tuna tartare with nori chips, tempura green beans with mustard sauce—plus anything on the full menu. Patrons in the formal, light-flooded dining room engage in more serious eating. The bread basket, full of such house-made delights as biscuits, bread sticks, rye, and rolls, is the best in town. ⊠ *22 Hawthorne St., South of Market,* ☎ *415/777–9779. D, DC, MC, V. No lunch weekends.*

$$ ✕ **Azie.** This large, highly sophisticated yet casual space has a sleek wood-and-metal staircase, outsize red columns, curtained booths for privacy, and an open kitchen that turns out inspired French-Asian fusion fare. Begin with the signature appetizer called "Nine Bites," which is just that: nine bite-size tastes to intrigue the palate. End your meal with nine more bites: a sampler of the chef's sweets. There are plenty of choices for in-between, from butter roasted lobster to sake-braised beef short ribs. ⊠ *826 Folsom St., South of Market,* ☎ *415/538–0918. AE, D, DC, MC, V. No lunch.*

$$ ✕ **Dine.** Dine resembles many other successful South of Market restaurants: a warehouse-style space with high ceilings, exposed brick walls, metal-and-wood chairs, and classic colors. The kitchen delivers a modernist twist to an American menu of such crowd-pleasing plates as rib eye with sautéed spinach, stuffed pork chops, and crisp-skinned roast chicken. When the room is packed and the diners are exuberant, conversation in a normal tone is difficult. ⊠ *662 Mission St., South of Market,* ☎ *415/538–3463. AE, MC, V. Closed Sun. No lunch.*

French

$$ ✕ **Bizou.** Chef Loretta Keller serves a distinctive French country menu, with some Italian touches, at this comfortable corner bistro, the name of which translates as "kiss." Fans of her rustic cooking cite the thin and crisp pizzas, sautéed skate with mashed potatoes, braised beef cheeks, duck liver terrine, and rabbit cooked in pumpkin sauce as evidence of her talents. The space itself is small and unpretentious. Outsize windows mean it's sunny and bright during the typically busy lunch hour. ⊠ *598 4th St., South of Market,* ☎ *415/543–2222. AE, MC, V. Closed Sun. No lunch Sat.*

$$ ✕ **Fringale.** The bright yellow paint on this small, dazzling bistro stands out like a beacon on an otherwise ordinary street. The well-dressed clientele comes for the French-Basque–inspired creations of Biarritz-born chef Gerald Hirigoyen, whose classic *frisées aux lardons* (curly salad greens with crisp bacon cubes and a poached egg), steak frites, duck confit with tiny French lentils, and almond torte filled with custard cream are hallmarks of the regularly changing menu. ⊠ *570 4th St., South of Market,* ☎ *415/543–0573. Reservations essential. AE, MC, V. Closed Sun. No lunch Sat.*

$$ ✕ **South Park Café.** This utterly Parisian spot is open from early morning, for your caffe latte, to late at night, for a wedge of fruit tart or a flute of champagne. No place in the City of Lights itself serves a more authentic steak frites than this warm, sometimes clamorous spot overlooking a grassy square. A notable first course is the salad greens with baked goat cheese or the familiar niçoise. For an entrée try duck breast or hangar steak, and don't miss the thin, crisp fries. A good wine list will keep you happily sipping. ⊠ *108 South Park, at Bryant St., South of Market,* ☎ *415/495–7275. MC, V. Closed Sun. No lunch Sat.*

Mediterranean

$–$$ ✕ **LuLu.** The food here, prepared under the watchful eye of executive
★ chef Jody Denton, is satisfyingly uncomplicated and delectable. Beneath
a high barrel-vaulted ceiling, you can feast on mussels roasted in an
iron skillet, wood-roasted poultry, meats, and shellfish, plus pizzas and
pastas. Each day a different main course prepared on the rotisserie is
featured, such as the truly succulent suckling pig on Friday. Sharing
dishes is the custom here. A sister restaurant, Azie, serving a creative
French fusion menu, is next door. ⊠ *816 Folsom St., South of Market,* ☎ *415/495–5775. AE, D, DC, MC, V.*

Sunset District

American-Casual

$$ ✕ **Beach Chalet.** In a historic colonnaded building with handsome
Works Project Administration–produced murals depicting San Fran-
cisco in the mid-1930s, the Beach Chalet is the place to watch the waves
break on the shore and the sun set over the Pacific Ocean. The fine
microbrewery beers run the gamut from a light pilsner to a pale ale,
but the eclectic dinner menu seldom produces more than okay food.
At midday, the prices are lower, the food simpler, and the view, minus
the sunset, better. ⊠ *1000 Great Hwy., Outer Sunset,* ☎ *415/386–8439.
MC, V.*

$ ✕ **Park Chow.** After a morning or afternoon in Golden Gate Park, this
contemporary yet homey spot is just what your appetite ordered. In the
mood for spaghetti and meatballs? That's here. Prefer Thai noodles with
rock shrimp and chicken? That's also here. Or what about a big Amer-
ican burger, a pizza straight from the wood-burning oven, or an order
of iron-skillet mussels? They are all here, too, along with Sicilian can-
noli and southern pecan pie. There's another branch in the Castro. ⊠
1240 9th Ave., Inner Sunset, ☎ *415/665–9912;* ⊠ *215 Church St., Cas-
tro,* ☎ *415/552–2469. Reservations not accepted. MC, V.*

Chinese

$ ✕ **San Tung No. 2.** Many of the best chefs in Beijing's imperial kitchens
hailed from China's northeastern province of Shandong; this modest
but bright Shandong restaurant is a good introduction to the region's
cuisine. Specialties include steamed dumplings and hand-pulled noo-
dles either in soup or stir-fried. Among the typical accompaniments are
a salad of jellyfish, seaweed, or cucumber and a plate of cold poached
chicken marinated in Shaoxing wine. ⊠ *1031 Irving St., Inner Sun-
set,* ☎ *415/242–0828. MC, V.*

Union Square

Contemporary

$$–$$$ ✕ **Postrio.** There's always a chance to catch a glimpse of some
celebrity at this legendary eatery, including Postrio's owner, superchef
Wolfgang Puck, who periodically commutes here from Los Angeles.
A stunning three-level bar and dining area is highlighted by palm trees
and museum-quality contemporary paintings. The lunch and dinner
menus are Californian with Mediterranean and Asian overtones,
while the substantial breakfast and late-night bar menus (great piz-
zas) guarantee that regulars are kept happy at all hours. ⊠ *545 Post
St., Union Square,* ☎ *415/776–7825. Reservations essential. AE, D,
DC, MC, V. No lunch Sun.*

$–$$ ✕ **Grand Café.** In the heart of the theater district, this inviting combination dining room and bar is a magnet for folks seeking everything
from an early morning breakfast to a late-night snack. The dining room
menu includes elements of California, French, and Italian cooking, while

the bar serves hearty sandwiches and thin-crust pizzas. The spacious dining room, formerly a hotel ballroom, has fanciful sculptures of human figures and eye-catching murals. The smaller bar area has dozens of pen-and-ink cartoons to keep you amused. ⊠ *Hotel Monaco, 501 Geary St., Union Square,* ☎ *415/292–0101. AE, D, DC, MC, V.*

French

$$$$ ✕ **Fleur de Lys.** The creative cooking of French chef-partner Hubert Keller has brought every conceivable culinary award to this romantic spot. The menu changes constantly, but such dishes as sea bass with ratatouille crust and quail stuffed with wild mushrooms are among the possibilities. Perfectly smooth service adds to the overall enjoyment of eating here. There are tasting menus for both omnivores and vegetarians, and the elaborately canopied dining room is reminiscent of a sheikh's tent. ⊠ *777 Sutter St., Union Square,* ☎ *415/673–7779. Reservations essential. Jacket required. AE, DC, MC, V. Closed Sun. No lunch.*

$$$–$$$$ ✕ **Campton Place Restaurant.** This elegant, ultrasophisticated small hotel helped put new American cooking on the local culinary map in the 1980s. Today, the kitchen is in the talented hands of Gascony-born Laurent Manrique, who prepares a fine southern French menu that puts foie gras at center stage but still keeps a homespun *poule au pot* (poached chicken) as an option. The dining room, done up in peach and crystal, remains as elegant as ever, and the small side bar is a comfortable spot for sipping a martini while waiting for a table. ⊠ *340 Stockton St., Union Square,* ☎ *415/955–5555. Reservations essential. AE, D, DC, MC, V.*

Italian

$$ ✕ **Scala's Bistro.** Smart leather-and-wood booths, an extravagant mural along one wall, and an appealing menu of Italian plates make this one of downtown's most attractive destinations. A large open kitchen stands at the rear of the fashionable dining room, where regulars and out-of-towners alike sit down to breakfast, lunch, and dinner. Grilled octopus on fingerling potatoes and spaghetti carbonara are among the savory choices, while lovers of cream, chocolate, and calories will want to try "Bostini," Scala's signature dessert. ⊠ *432 Powell St., Union Square,* ☎ *415/395–8555. AE, D, DC, MC, V.*

Seafood

$$$ ✕ **Farallon.** Outfitted with sculpted jellyfish lamps, kelp-covered
★   columns, and sea urchin chandeliers, this swanky Pat Kuleto–designed restaurant is loaded with style *and* customers. Chef Mark Franz, who gained his fame at Stars, cooks up exquisite seafood that draws serious diners from coast to coast. When the restaurant opened in the late 1990s, Franz whipped up very rich—and quite delicious—sauces for much of his food, but he has since tempered his enthusiasm for butter, to the delight of anyone watching his or her diet. ⊠ *450 Post St., Union Square,* ☎ *415/956–6969. AE, D, DC, MC, V. No lunch Sun. and Mon.*

Vietnamese

$$ ✕ **Le Colonial.** The stamped tin ceiling, period photographs, slow-moving fans, and tropical plants re-create a 1920s French colonial setting for the upscale Vietnamese food. Le Colonial draws the local blue bloods for its spring rolls, beef tenderloin infused with chili-lime marinade, bass with ginger and lemongrass, and other Southeast Asian flavors. Upstairs, a suave lounge is the ideal place to sip a cocktail before dinner or a nightcap at the end of the evening. ⊠ *20 Cosmo Pl., Union Square,* ☎ *415/931–3600. AE, MC, V. Closed Sun. No lunch Sat.*

Van Ness/Polk

Italian

$$$ ✕ **Acquerello.** This elegant restaurant—white linens, fresh flowers, exquisite china—is one of the most romantic spots in town. Both the service and the food are exemplary, and the menu covers the full range of Italian cuisine. The gnocchi, especially pumpkin gnocchi with sage and truffles, and green onion fettuccine with crab and wine are memorable, as are the fish dishes. Chef-owner Suzette Gresham is responsible for the kitchen's high standards, while co-owner Giancarlo Paterlini oversees a superb list of Italian vintages. ⊠ *1722 Sacramento St., Van Ness/Polk,* ☎ *415/567–5432. AE, D, MC, V. Closed Sun. and Mon. No lunch.*

Steak

$$–$$$$ ✕ **Harris'.** Ann Harris knows her beef. She grew up on a Texas cattle
★   ranch and was married to the late Jack Harris of Harris Ranch fame. In her own large, New York–style restaurant she serves some of the best dry-aged steaks in town, including some truly pricey Japanese beef, but don't overlook the starter of spinach salad or the entrée of grilled California lamb chops. Be sure to include a side of the fine creamed spinach. If you're a martini drinker, take this opportunity to enjoy an artful example of the cocktail. ⊠ *2100 Van Ness Ave., Russian Hill,* ☎ *415/673–1888. AE, D, DC, MC, V. No lunch.*

4 LODGING

San Francisco's accommodations are as
diverse as its neighborhoods and its people.
There are luxury hotels, bed-and-breakfasts
housed in Victorian mansions, and stylish
motels with offbeat attitudes. Hotels here are
more than hotels: they are part of the scenery,
and whether they are upholding rich traditions
or hatching new ideas, they are beloved by
loyal customers and newcomers alike.

Revised by
Andy Moore

F EW CITIES IN THE UNITED STATES can rival San Francisco's variety in lodging. There are plush hotels ranked among the finest in
the world, renovated older buildings with a European flair, and
the popular chain hotels found in most American cities. One of the bright-
est spots in the lodging picture is the presence of many small bed-and-
breakfasts housed in elegant Victorian edifices, where evening hors
d'oeuvres and wine service are common practice. Another intriguing
trend is the growing number of ultradeluxe hotels with a bold fine arts
bent, such as Clift, Hotel Monaco, Hotel Palomar, and Hotel Triton,
each with a dynamic and playfully artsy style that says "look at me!"

The **San Francisco Convention and Visitors Bureau** (☎ 415/283–0177
or 888/782–9673, WEB www.sfvisitor.org) publishes a free lodging guide
with a map and listings of San Francisco and Bay Area hotels; or call
☎ 415/283–0177 or 888/782–9673 to reserve a room at more than
60 visitors bureau–recommended hotels in the city or near the airport.
San Francisco Reservations (☎ 800/677–1500, WEB www.hotelres.com)
handles advance reservations at more than 300 Bay Area hotels, often
at special discounted rates. Although there are about 31,000 hotel rooms
available on any given day, San Francisco is one of the top destinations
in the United States for tourists as well as business travelers and convention goers. Reservations are always advised, especially during the
peak seasons (May–October and weekends in December). Don't be concerned about air-conditioning; though some hotels have it, it rarely gets
warm enough in San Francisco to need it.

San Francisco's geography makes it conveniently compact. No matter
what their location, the hotels listed below are on or close to public
transportation lines. Several properties on Lombard Street and in the
Civic Center area have free parking, while hotels in the Union Square
and Nob Hill areas almost invariably charge $22–$40 a day for a spot
in their garage.

San Francisco hotel prices may come as a not-so-pleasant surprise. Weekend rates for double rooms start at about $75 but average about $165
per night citywide (slightly less on weekdays and off-season). Adding
to the expense is the city's 14% transient occupancy tax, which can
significantly boost the cost of a lengthy stay. The good news is that because of the hotel building boom of the late 1980s and 1990s, there is
now an oversupply of rooms, which has led to frequent discounts. Check
for special rates and packages when making reservations. If you're in
search of true budget accommodations (under $70), try the **YMCA
Central Branch** (✉ 220 Golden Gate Ave., Civic Center, ☎ 415/885–
0460). The **San Remo** (✉ 2237 Mason St., North Beach, ☎ 415/776–
8688 or 800/352–7366) is a great deal at $60 to $90.

An alternative to hotels and motels are private homes and apartments,
available through **American Family Inn/Bed & Breakfast San Francisco**
(✉ Box 420009, San Francisco 94142, ☎ 415/899–0060 or 800/452–
8249, FAX 415/899–9923, WEB www.bbsf.com). **Absolutely Accommodations** (✉ Box 330298, San Francisco 94133, ☎ 415/732–7959, FAX
415/252–7055, WEB www.lodgingincalifornia.com) represents private
residences—as well as hotels—statewide. **Bed & Breakfast California**
(✉ Box 2247, Saratoga 95070, ☎ 408/867–9662 or 800/872–4500,
FAX 408/867–0907, WEB www.bbintl.com) has, since 1978, specialized
in placing travelers in small B&B inns as well as cottages and rooms
in private homes. Lodging on private yachts at Pier 39 can be obtained
through **Dockside Boat & Bed** (✉ 489 Water St., Oakland 94607, ☎

415/392–5526 or 800/436–2574, FAX 510/444–0420, WEB www. boatandbed.com).

CATEGORY	COST*
$$$$	over $300
$$$	$200–$300
$$	$100–$200
$	under $100

*All prices are for a standard double room, excluding 14% tax.

Union Square/Downtown

The largest variety and greatest concentration of hotels is in the city's downtown hub, Union Square, where you can find the best shopping, the theater district, and convenient transportation to every spot in San Francisco. If the grand hotels right on Union Square are beyond your budget, consider the more modest establishments west of Mason Street—but be careful when walking there late at night.

$$$$ **Campton Place.** Highly attentive service is the hallmark of this
★ small, top-tier hotel behind a simple brownstone facade. The pampering—from unpacking assistance to nightly turndown—begins the moment the uniformed doormen greet you outside the marble lobby. Although many rooms are smallish, all are elegant in a contemporary Italian style, with light earth tones and handsome pearwood panelling and cabinetry. The large modern baths have deep soaking tubs, and double-paned windows keep city noises out (a plus in this active neighborhood). The Campton Place Restaurant is famed for its lavish breakfasts and country French dinners, and the hotel's lounge is popular at cocktail time with the downtown crowd. ⌧ *340 Stockton St., Union Square 94108,* ☎ *415/781–5555 or 800/235–4300,* FAX *415/955–5536,* WEB *www.camptonplace.com. 101 rooms, 9 suites. Restaurant, room service, in-room data ports, in-room safes, minibars, some microwaves, gym, bar, lobby lounge, dry cleaning, laundry service, concierge, business services, meeting room, parking (fee), some pets allowed (fee), no-smoking floors. AE, DC, MC, V.*

$$$$ **Clift.** Behind its stately beige brick facade, the venerable Clift has been totally transformed by entrepreneur Ian Schrager and artist/designer Philippe Starck into a "hotel as art" showplace. The cavernous lobby contains groupings of whimsical art objects meant to encourage a dreamlike, surreal mood. Spacious rooms, in shades of ivory, gray, and lavender, are furnished sparely with blond wood and transparent orange acrylic furniture, plus two huge mirrors on otherwise-empty (and acoustically rather thin) walls. The renowned Art Deco Redwood Room bar, paneled with wood from a single 2,000-year-old tree, now sports flat video screens showing digital artwork and is packed nightly with a young, fashionable crowd. Asia de Cuba restaurant fuses Asian and Latino cuisines and serves them with very loud (but cool) music. ⌧ *495 Geary St., Union Square 94102,* ☎ *415/775–4700 or 800/652–5438,* FAX *415/441–4621,* WEB *www.clifthotel.com. 293 rooms, 80 suites. 2 restaurants, room service, in-room data ports, in-room safes, minibars, in-room VCRs, gym, bar, lobby lounge, dry cleaning, laundry service, concierge, Internet, business services, meeting room, parking (fee), no-smoking floors. AE, D, DC, MC, V.*

$$$$ **Hotel Nikko.** The vast marble lobby of this Japan Airlines–owned
★ hotel is airy and serene, and its rooms are some of the most handsome in the city. They have inlaid cherrywood furniture with clean, elegant lines; gold drapes; wheat-color wall coverings; and ingenious window shades which screen the sun while allowing views of the city. Service throughout the hotel is attentive and sincere, and the staff is multilin-

Downtown San Francisco Lodging

Chestnut St.
Lombard St.
Octavia St.
Gough St.
Franklin St.
Van Ness Ave.
Polk St.
Larkin St.
Hyde St.
Leavenworth St.

RUSSIAN HILL

Green St.
Vallejo St.
Broadway
Broadway Tunnel
Pacific St.
Jackson St.

PACIFIC HEIGHTS

Lafayette Park

Washington St.
Clay St.
Sacramento St.
California St.

Pine St.
Bush St.
Sutter St.
Post St.
Geary St.
O'Farrell St.
Ellis St.
Eddy St.
Turk St.
Golden Gate Ave.
McAllister St.

Alta Plaza

Scott St.
Pierce St.
Steiner St.
Fillmore St.
Webster St.
Buchanan St.
Laguna St.
Octavia St.
Gough St.
Franklin St.
Van Ness Ave.
Polk St.
Larkin St.
Hyde St.
Leavenworth St.
Jones St.

JAPANTOWN

Alamo Square

Fulton St.
Market St.
8th St.
7th St.
Grove St.
Hayes St.

CIVIC CENTER

Abigail Howard
Johnson Hotel **21**
The Andrews **17**
The Archbishop's
Mansion **19**
The Argent **71**
Bed and
Breakfast Inn **10**
Bel-Aire
Travelodge **2**
Bijou **66**
Campton Place **53**
Chancellor Hotel
on Union Square . . .**51**

Clarion Hotel
San Francisco
Airport **78**
Clarion Bedford
Hotel **18**
Clift **57**
Commodore
International **44**
Coventry
Motor Inn **5**
Cow Hollow Motor
Inn and Suites **3**
Embassy Suites San
Francisco Airport—
Burlingame **73**
The Fairmont **29**

Four Seasons
Hotel San
Francisco **70**
Galleria Park **54**
Golden Gate
Hotel **48**
Grant Plaza
Hotel **42**
Harbor Court **39**
Hotel Bohème **28**
Hotel Del Sol **4**
Hotel Diva **58**
Hotel Drisco **13**
Hotel Majestic **15**
Hotel Milano **67**

Hotel Monaco **64**
Hotel Nikko **65**
Hotel Palomar **68**
Hotel Rex **47**
Hotel Sofitel–San
Francisco Bay **74**
Hotel Triton **43**
The Huntington
Hotel **30**
Hyatt at Fisherman's
Wharf **24**
Hyatt Regency **38**
Hyatt Regency San
Francisco Airport . . .**75**
Inn at the Opera . . .**22**

Inn at Union
Square **60**
Jackson Court **12**
King George **63**
La Quinta
Motor Inn **79**
Mandarin
Oriental **37**
Marina Inn **6**
Mark Hopkins
Inter–Continental . . .**31**
Marriott at
Fisherman's
Wharf **23**
The Maxwell **59**

Nob Hill Lambourne . .**41**
Omni San Francisco
Hotel **35**
Pacific Heights Inn . .**11**
Palace Hotel **61**
Pan Pacific Hotel . . .**50**
Park Hyatt **36**
Petite Auberge **45**
Phoenix Hotel **20**
Prescott Hotel **49**
Presidio Travelodge . . .**1**
Radisson Hotel
at Fisherman's
Wharf **26**

Radisson
Miyako Hotel **14**
Red Roof Inn **76**
Renaissance
Stanford Court **32**
Ritz–Carlton,
San Francisco **34**
San Francisco
Marriott **69**
San Francisco
Residence Club **33**
San Remo **27**
Savoy Hotel
& Brasserie **55**

Shannon Court
Hotel **56**
Sherman House **9**
Sir Francis Drake
Hotel **52**
Town House Motel . . .**7**
Tuscan Inn **25**
Union Street Inn **8**
Vintage Court **40**
W San Francisco . .**72**
The Westin **77**
Westin St. Francis . .**62**
White Swan Inn **46**
York Hotel **16**

gual. Don't miss the excellent fifth-floor fitness facility ($6 fee), which has traditional *ofuros* (Japanese soaking tubs), a *kamaburo* (Japanese sauna), and a glass-enclosed swimming pool and whirlpool. Restaurant Anzu serves prime beef dishes and sushi. ⊠ *222 Mason St., Union Square 94102,* ☎ *415/394–1111 or 800/645–5687,* FAX *415/421–0455,* WEB *www.nikkohotels.com. 510 rooms, 22 suites. Restaurant, room service, in-room data ports, some in-room hot tubs, some kitchenettes, some microwaves, minibars, indoor pool, gym, hair salon, Japanese baths, massage, sauna, bar, dry cleaning, laundry service, concierge, concierge floor, business services, meeting rooms, car rental, parking (fee), some pets allowed, no-smoking floors. AE, D, DC, MC, V.*

$$$$ 🏨 **Pan Pacific Hotel.** Exotic flower arrangements and Asian touches set this business-oriented hotel apart from others. A graceful Matisse-inspired bronze sculpture by Elbert Weinberg, *Joie de Danse,* encircles the fountain in the 21-story lobby atrium. Guest rooms, with soft green and beige color schemes and black-and-gold quilted bedspreads with Asian block-print designs, have elegant bathrooms lined with terra-cotta Portuguese marble. Complimentary personal valet service, a "pillow preference program" (the opportunity to choose from a dozen kinds, from soft down to firm foam), and a fleet of luxury cars that drop you at nearby destinations free of charge add up to a pampering experience. The hotel's restaurant, PACIFIC, is well regarded for its California cuisine. ⊠ *500 Post St., Union Square 94102,* ☎ *415/771–8600 or 800/327–8585,* FAX *415/398–0267,* WEB *www.panpac.com. 311 rooms, 19 suites. Restaurant, room service, in-room data ports, in-room safes, some in-room hot tubs, minibars, refrigerator, some in-room VCRs, gym, bar, lobby lounge, piano, dry cleaning, laundry service, concierge, Internet, business services, meeting room, parking (fee), some pets allowed (fee), no-smoking floor. AE, D, DC, MC, V.*

$$$$ 🏨 **Prescott Hotel.** Although not as famous as many hotels in the
★   area, the Prescott has several advantages: the relatively small size means personalized service, and its relationship with Postrio, the Wolfgang Puck restaurant attached to its lobby, means you get preferred reservations. Rooms are traditional, with a rich hunter-green theme. Bathrooms have marble-top sinks and gold and pewter fixtures. Complimentary coffee service and evening wine receptions are held by the fireplace in the hunting lodge–style living room. The more expensive Club Level rooms include complimentary expanded Continental breakfast and afternoon cocktails with Puck's pizza. ⊠ *545 Post St., Union Square 94102,* ☎ *415/563–0303 or 800/283–7322,* FAX *415/563–6831,* WEB *www.prescotthotel.com. 155 rooms, 9 suites. Restaurant, room service, in-room data ports, some in-room hot tubs, minibars, some in-room VCRs, gym, bar, lobby lounge, concierge, concierge floor, business services, meeting room, parking (fee), some pets allowed, no-smoking floors. AE, D, DC, MC, V.*

$$$$ 🏨 **Westin St. Francis.** Fatty Arbuckle got into trouble here; Al Jolson died here while playing poker; President Gerald Ford was shot at by Sara Jane Moore here (she missed). Since it opened in 1904, Emperor Hirohito, Queen Elizabeth II, and other U.S. presidents have also stayed at the St. Francis (albeit more quietly). Its imposing facade, black-marble lobby, and gold-top columns make it look more like a great public building than a hotel, but the Compass Rose bar and restaurant softens the effect to provide a retreat from the bustle of Union Square. Rooms in the modern 32-story tower have Asian-style lacquered furniture; ask for a room above the 15th floor for a spectacular view of the city. Rooms in the original building are smaller but have Empire-style furnishings and retain their Victorian-style moldings and glass doorknobs. ⊠ *335 Powell St., Union Square 94102,* ☎ *415/397–7000,* FAX *415/774–0124,* WEB *www.westin.com. 1,108 rooms, 84 suites.*

2 restaurants, café, room service, in-room data ports, in-room safes, some in-room hot tubs, some kitchenettes, health club, massage, steam room, bar, nightclub, dry cleaning, laundry service, concierge, Internet, business services, meeting room, travel services, parking (fee), some pets allowed (fee), no-smoking floors; no air-conditioning. AE, D, DC, MC, V.

$$$–$$$$
★ **Hotel Monaco.** A cheery yellow 1910 beaux-arts facade and snappily dressed doormen welcome you into the Monaco's plush lobby, with its grand marble staircase, French inglenook fireplace, and a high vaulted ceiling with murals of WWI planes and hot-air balloons. The hotel hosts a complimentary evening wine and appetizer hour in this delightful space. Guest rooms, with Chinese-inspired armoires, canopy beds, and high-back upholstered chairs, are full of flair with vivid stripes and colors. In the outer rooms, bay-window seats overlook the bustling theater district. There are special amenities for pets, and if you didn't bring a pet, ask for one of the "companion goldfishes" available. The on-site spa, Equilibrium, has massages, manicures, facials, and other services (for humans). The ornate Grand Café and Bar, in which you get preferred seating, serves French-California fare. ⊠ *501 Geary St., Union Square 94102,* ☎ *415/292–0100 or 800/214–4220,* FAX *415/292–0111,* WEB *www.monaco-sf.com. 181 rooms, 20 suites. Restaurant, room service, in-room data ports, in-room fax, in-room safes, some in-room hot tubs, minibars, some in-room VCRs, gym, massage, sauna, spa, steam room, bar, dry cleaning, laundry service, business services, Internet, parking (fee), some pets allowed, no-smoking floors. AE, D, DC, MC, V.*

$$$
★ **Hotel Rex.** Literary and artistic creativity are celebrated at the stylish Hotel Rex, where thousands of books, largely antiquarian, line the 1920s-style lobby. Original artwork adorns the walls, and the proprietors even host book readings and round-table discussions in the common areas. Upstairs, quotations from works by California writers are painted on the terra-cotta–color walls near the elevator landings. Good-size rooms have writing desks and lamps with whimsically hand-painted shades. Muted check bedspreads, striped carpets, and restored period furnishings upholstered in deep, rich hues may evoke the spirit of 1920s salon society, but the rooms also have modern amenities like voice mail and CD players. ⊠ *562 Sutter St., Union Square 94102,* ☎ *415/433–4434 or 800/433–4434,* FAX *415/433–3695,* WEB *thehotelrex.com. 92 rooms, 2 suites. Room service, in-room data ports, minibars, bar, lobby lounge, dry cleaning, laundry service, concierge, Internet, business services, meeting room, parking (fee), no-smoking floors. AE, D, DC, MC, V.*

$$$
Hotel Triton. A playfully conceived lobby of three-legged furniture, star-patterned carpeting, and inverted gilt pillars hints at the zaniness to come: the small rooms are decked out with pink and gold paint, S-curve chairs, and oddball light fixtures. Baths are split; the sink is often in the entry hall of your room. The fashion, entertainment, music, and film-industry types who frequent this place (from Lily Tomlin to the Psychedelic Furs) often ask for one of the deluxe theme suites like the Carlos Santana, Joe Boxer, or Jerry Garcia. Twenty-four "environmentally sensitive" rooms have water and air filtration systems and biodegradable soaps. ⊠ *342 Grant Ave., Union Square 94108,* ☎ *415/394–0500 or 888/364–2622,* FAX *415/394–0555,* WEB *www.hotel-tritonsf.com. 133 rooms, 7 suites. Café, dining room, room service, in-room data ports, 1 in-room hot tub, minibars, some in-room VCRs, gym, dry cleaning, laundry service, Internet, business services, meeting room, parking (fee), some pets allowed, no-smoking floors. AE, D, MC, V.*

$$$
Inn at Union Square. The tiny but captivating lobby of this small hotel has trompe l'oeil wallpaper depicting a window's "view" of a

genteel town square. The comfortable rooms—some decorated in Georgian style with fireplaces, some in a lighter, more contemporary style—all have nice touches like goose-down pillows, fresh flowers, and morning newspapers. Bathrooms have attractive granite vanities. You can lounge by the wood-burning fireplaces in each floor's tiny sitting area, where evening wine and hors d'oeuvres are served, followed by tea and cookies. Tips are not accepted, the hotel is completely no-smoking, and you have free access to a Club One health club a block away. ⊠ *440 Post St., Union Square 94102,* ☎ *415/397–3510 or 800/288–4346,* FAX *415/989–0529,* WEB *www.unionsquare.com. 23 rooms, 7 suites. In-room data ports, 1 in-room hot tub, massage, parking (fee); no air-conditioning; no-smoking. AE, DC, MC, V. CP.*

$$$ 🏨 **Sir Francis Drake Hotel.** Beefeater-costumed doormen welcome you into the regal lobby of this 1928 landmark property, decked out with boldly striped banners, plush velvet furniture, wrought-iron balustrades, chandeliers, and Italian marble. The guest rooms have deep green carpeting with gold stars, wide-striped green and yellow walls, and mahogany and cherrywood furniture. Harry Denton's Starlight Room, one of the city's plushest skyline bars, is on the top floor. The hotel's surprisingly affordable restaurant, Scala's Bistro, serves excellent food in its dramatic though somewhat noisy bi-level dining room. ⊠ *450 Powell St., Union Square 94102,* ☎ *415/392–7755 or 800/227–5480,* FAX *415/391–8719,* WEB *www.sirfrancisdrake.com. 412 rooms, 5 suites. 2 restaurants, in-room data ports, minibars, gym, nightclub, dry cleaning, laundry service, concierge, Internet, business services, meeting room, parking (fee), no-smoking floors. AE, D, DC, MC, V.*

$$–$$$ 🏨 **Hotel Diva.** Step across footprints, handprints, and autographs that stage stars have embedded in the sidewalk, as you step through the black granite and green glass entrance into the Diva's small lobby. Two major theaters, the Curran and American Conservatory Theater (A.C.T.), are right across Geary Street, and actors, musicians, and others of an artistic bent often stay here. Cobalt-blue carpets and brushed-steel headboards echoing the shape of ocean waves lend the white-walled rooms a nautical touch, and silver bedspreads, grey window shades and steel light fixtures are cool and sleek. Bathrooms are tiny but well equipped. A complimentary Continental breakfast, included in the room rate, is delivered to your room. ⊠ *440 Geary St., Union Square 94102,* ☎ *415/885–0200 or 800/553–1900,* FAX *415/346–6613,* WEB *www.hoteldiva.com. 88 rooms, 23 suites. Restaurant, room service, in-room data ports, in-room fax, in-room safes, minibars, in-room VCRs, gym, dry cleaning, laundry service, concierge, Internet, business services, meeting room, parking (fee), some pets allowed, no-smoking floor. AE, D, DC, MC, V. CP.*

$$–$$$ 🏨 **The Maxwell.** Behind dramatic black-and-red curtains, the Maxwell's lobby makes an impression with boldly patterned furniture in rich velvets and brocades. The hotel is handsome, stylish, and just a block from Union Square. Rooms have a clubby, retro look, with deep jewel tones, classic Edward Hopper prints on the walls, and drawings by bellman Jack Keating. Windows open fully, and the closets are nice and big. Pedestal sinks and white porcelain faucet handles contribute to a 1920s feel in the tiny bathrooms. Max's on the Square serves American breakfast, lunch, and dinner as well as after-theater dinner and drinks. ⊠ *386 Geary St., Union Square 94102,* ☎ *415/986–2000 or 888/734–6299,* FAX *415/397–2447,* WEB *www.maxwellhotel.com. 150 rooms, 3 suites. Restaurant, room service, in-room data ports, bar, laundry service, concierge, meeting room, parking (fee), no-smoking floor. AE, D, DC, MC, V.*

$$–$$$ 🏨 **Shannon Court Hotel.** Passing through the elaborate wrought-iron and glass entrance into the marble-tiled lobby, with its Spanish-style arches and Oriental carpets, evokes the days when guests arrived here with steamer trunks in tow. This hotel has some of the most spacious standard rooms in the Union Square area; many have sofa beds for families. Two of the luxury suites on the 16th floor have rooftop terraces with lofty city views. Complimentary morning coffee and afternoon tea and cookies are served in the lobby area. ⊠ *550 Geary St., Union Square 94102,* ☎ *415/775–5000 or 800/228–8830,* FAX *415/928–6813,* WEB *www.shannoncourt.com. 168 rooms, 4 suites. Restaurant, refrigerators, bar, dry cleaning, laundry service, concierge, meeting rooms, parking (fee), no-smoking floor. AE, D, DC, MC, V.*

$$ 🖭 **The Andrews.** Two blocks west of Union Square, this Queen Anne–style abode with a gold-and-buff facade and a huge Elliott grandfather clock in the lobby began its life in 1905 as the Sultan Turkish Baths. Today Victorian antique reproductions, old-fashioned flower curtains with lace sheers, iron bedsteads, ceiling fans, and large closets more than make up for the diminutive size of guest rooms (the scrupulously clean bathrooms—most with showers only—are even smaller). Complimentary wine is served each evening in the lobby. Fino, the hotel restaurant, has been praised for its pizza and carbonaras. ⊠ *624 Post St., Union Square 94109,* ☎ *415/563–6877 or 800/926–3739,* FAX *415/928–6919,* WEB *www.andrewshotel.com. 48 rooms. Restaurant, fans, some in-room VCRs, concierge, parking (fee); no smoking. AE, DC, MC, V. CP.*

$$ 🖭 **Bijou.** This hotel is a nostalgic tribute to 1930s cinema. The lobby's tiny theater, Le Petit Theatre Bijou, treats you to screenings from the hotel's collection of 65 San Francisco–theme films—from *The Maltese Falcon* to *What's Up Doc?* The smallish but cheerful rooms are decorated with black-and-white movie stills. For those who want to be in pictures, the hand-crafted chrome ticket booth in the lobby has a hot line with information on current San Francisco film shoots seeking extras. Complimentary coffee and pastries are served mornings in the lobby. ⊠ *111 Mason St., at Eddy St., Union Square 94102,* ☎ *415/771–1200 or 800/771–1022,* FAX *415/346–3196,* WEB *www.hotelbijou.com. 65 rooms. Laundry service, concierge, meeting rooms, parking (fee), no-smoking floor; no air-conditioning. AE, D, DC, MC, V. CP.*

$$ 🖭 **Chancellor Hotel on Union Square.** Built for the 1915 Panama Pacific International Exposition, the Chancellor was the tallest building in San Francisco when it opened. Although not as grand as some of its new neighbors, this busy hotel is one of the best buys on Union Square for comfort without extravagance. Floor-to-ceiling windows in the modest lobby overlook cable cars on Powell Street en route to Union Square or Fisherman's Wharf. The moderate-size Edwardian-style rooms have high ceilings and blue, cream, and rose color schemes. Bathrooms are small but modern; deep bathtubs are a treat, and a rubber ducky is provided. Connecting rooms are available for families, and the Chancellor Café is a handy place for meals. ⊠ *433 Powell St., Union Square 94102,* ☎ *415/362–2004 or 800/428–4748,* FAX *415/362–1403,* WEB *www.chancellorhotel.com. 135 rooms, 2 suites. Restaurant, room service, fans, in-room safes, bar, laundry service, concierge, meeting room, car rental, parking (fee); no air-conditioning, no smoking. AE, D, DC, MC, V.*

$$ 🖭 **Clarion Bedford Hotel.** You'll pass under Art Nouveau arches carved with grapevines and birds upon entering the bright yellow lobby of this handsome 1929 building. Avant-garde film posters from 1920s Russia adorn the walls. The light and airy rooms have white furniture, canopied beds, and vibrant floral bedspreads. Most rooms in this 17-story hotel (it's the tallest building on the block) have gorgeous bay and city views, but the baths are small. Business-class guest rooms have special desk lighting and an ergonomic chair. There is an evening wine

reception in the lobby, which is also the home of a small café. ⊠ *761 Post St., Union Square 94109,* ☎ *415/673–6040 or 800/227–5642,* FAX *415/563–6739,* WEB *www.hotelbedford.com. 137 rooms, 7 suites. Café, room service, in-room data ports, minibars, some microwaves, some refrigerators, bar, dry cleaning, laundry service, Internet, business services, parking (fee), some pets allowed, no-smoking floors. AE, D, DC, MC, V.*

$$ 🏨 **Commodore International.** Entering the fanciful and colorful lobby through the Commodore's big glass double doors is like stepping onto the main deck of an ocean liner of yore: neo-Deco chairs look like the backdrop for a film about transatlantic crossings; steps away is the Titanic Café, where goldfish bowls and bathysphere-inspired lights add to the maritime mood. The fairly large rooms with monster closets are painted in soft yellows and golds and display photographs of San Francisco landmarks. If red is your color, you may find yourself glued to a seat in the hotel's Red Room, a startlingly scarlet cocktail lounge filled with well-dressed hipsters bathed in crimson. ⊠ *825 Sutter St., Union Square 94109,* ☎ *415/923–6800 or 800/338–6848,* FAX *415/923–6804,* WEB *thecommodorehotel.com. 112 rooms, 1 suite. Restaurant, in-room data ports, nightclub, dry cleaning, laundry service, concierge, parking (fee), no-smoking floors; no air-conditioning. AE, D, MC, V.*

$$ 🏨 **King George.** The staff at the King George has prided itself on service and hospitality since the hotel's opening in 1914, when guest rooms started at $1 a night. Prices are still relatively low compared to other hotels in the neighborhood, and local and toll-free calls are free. The front desk and concierge staff are adept at catering to your every whim: they'll book anything from a Fisherman's Wharf tour to a dinner reservation. Rooms are compact but nicely furnished in classic English style, with walnut furniture and a crimson and green color scheme. High tea or a glass of ale in the mezzanine pub is an authentic English treat. ⊠ *334 Mason St., Union Square 94102,* ☎ *415/781–5050 or 800/288–6005,* FAX *415/391–6976,* WEB *www.kinggeorge.com. 141 rooms, 1 suite. Tea shop/wine bar, room service, fans, in-room data ports, in-room safes, 1 kitchenette, dry cleaning, laundry service, concierge, Internet, business services, meeting room, parking (fee), no-smoking floors; no air-conditioning in some rooms. AE, D, DC, MC, V.*

$$ 🏨 **Petite Auberge.** The dozens of teddy bears in the reception area may seem a bit precious, but the provincial decor of the rooms in this re-creation of a French country inn never becomes too cutesy. Rooms are small, and each has bright flowered wallpaper, an old-fashioned writing desk, and a much-needed armoire—there's little or no closet space. Many rooms have gas fireplaces; the suite has a whirlpool tub. Afternoon tea, wine, and hors d'oeuvres are served in the lobby by the fire, and a full breakfast buffet can be found downstairs each morning. ⊠ *863 Bush St., Union Square 94108,* ☎ *415/928–6000 or 800/365–3004,* FAX *415/775–5717,* WEB *www.foursisters.com. 25 rooms, 1 suite. Fans, 1 in-room hot tub, 1 in-room VCR, parking (fee); no air-conditioning, no smoking. AE, DC, MC, V. BP.*

$$ 🏨 **The Savoy Hotel & Brasserie.** A little slice of Paris on Theater Row, this mahogany and marble-fronted boutique hotel three blocks west of Union Square also houses Savoy Brasserie, which serves a mix of French and American dishes. Charming touches are complimentary afternoon sherry, tea, and cookies in the lobby, complimentary overnight shoe shine, and rooms with French Provençal–style furnishings and puffy feather beds with goose-down pillows. All rooms have coffeemakers, hair dryers, and voice mail. Suites have "parlor" rooms with a plush sofa and chair and marble-topped coffee table, as well as a large desk. ⊠ *580 Geary St., Union Square 94102,* ☎ *415/441–2700 or 800/227–*

4223, FAX 415-441-0124, WEB www.savoyhotel.net. 70 rooms, 13 suites. Restaurant, fans, in-room data ports, minibars, bar, dry cleaning, laundry service, concierge, business services, meeting rooms, parking (fee), no-smoking floor; no air-conditioning. AE, D, DC, MC, V.

$$ ⌖ **White Swan Inn.** A library with book-lined walls and a crackling fire is the heartbeat of the White Swan. Wine, cheese, and afternoon tea are served in the lounge, where comfortable chairs and sofas encourage lingering. Each of the good-size rooms in this warm and inviting inn has a gas fireplace with interesting old books on the mantle, private bath, refrigerator, and reproduction Edwardian furniture. Bedspreads and upholstery are in plaids of deep reds and greens; the carpeting and wallpaper are vibrantly floral. The breakfasts (included in the room rate) are famous, and you can buy the inn's cookbook and take a crack at crab-and-cheese soufflé toasts or artichoke pesto puffs. ⊠ *845 Bush St., Union Square 94108,* ☎ *415/775–1755 or 800/999–9570, FAX 415/775–5717, WEB www.foursisters.com. 23 rooms, 3 suites. Fans, in-room data ports, refrigerators, some in-room VCRs, gym, dry cleaning, laundry service, concierge, meeting room, parking (fee); no smoking, no air-conditioning. AE, MC, V. BP.*

$$ ⌖ **York Hotel.** Hitchcock fans may recognize the exterior of this reasonably priced, family-owned hotel five blocks west of Union Square. It's the building where Kim Novak as Judy Barton stayed in *Vertigo*. Inside, the ornate, high-ceiling lobby gives the hotel a touch of elegance. The moderate-size rooms—all with huge closets—are a tasteful mix of Mediterranean styles, with a terra-cotta, burgundy, and forest-green color scheme. The Plush Room cabaret, where well-known entertainers perform four to five times a week, is the York's drawing card. The surrounding neighborhood is a bit edgier than some, so be alert when walking here at night. ⊠ *940 Sutter St., Van Ness/Polk 94109,* ☎ *415/885–6800 or 800/808–9675, FAX 415/885–2115, WEB www.yorkhotel.com. 91 rooms, 5 suites. Fans, in-room data ports, in-room safes, minibars, some in-room VCRs, gym, bar, nightclub, laundry service, concierge, Internet, business services, meeting rooms, parking (fee); no smoking. AE, D, DC, MC, V.*

$–$$ ⌖ **Golden Gate Hotel.** Captain Nemo, a 25-pound cat who must live very well indeed, serves as the unofficial doorman for this homey, family-run B&B. Built in 1913 as a hotel, the four-story Edwardian has a yellow-and-cream facade with black trim, and bay windows front and back. The original "birdcage" elevator lifts you to hallways lined with historical photographs and guest rooms individually decorated with antiques, wicker pieces, and Laura Ashley bedding and curtains. Fourteen rooms have private baths, some with claw-foot tubs. Continental breakfast and afternoon tea and cookies are served in the cozy parlor by a fire. ⊠ *775 Bush St., Union Square 94108,* ☎ *415/392–3702 or 800/835–1118, FAX 415/392–6202, WEB www.goldengatehotel.com. 25 rooms, 14 with bath. Parking (fee); no smoking. AE, DC, MC, V. CP.*

$ ⌖ **Grant Plaza Hotel.** Amazingly low room rates for this part of town
★ make the Grant Plaza a find for budget travelers wanting to look out their window at the striking architecture and fascinating street life of Chinatown. The small rooms, all with private baths, are very clean and modern. Rooms on the top floor are newer, slightly brighter, and a bit more expensive; for a quieter stay ask for one in the back. The two large, beautiful stained-glass windows near the top-floor elevator area are worth a look. ⊠ *465 Grant Ave., Chinatown 94108,* ☎ *415/434–3883 or 800/472–6899, FAX 415/434–3886, WEB www.grantplaza.com. 71 rooms, 1 suite. Some in-room VCRs, concierge, business services, parking (fee); no air-conditioning. AE, DC, MC, V.*

Financial District

High-rise growth in San Francisco's Financial District has turned it into a mini-Manhattan and a spectacular sight by night. Shoppers and sightseers enjoy easy access to nearby Union Square, the Embarcadero, Pier 39 at Fisherman's Wharf, Market Street's shops, and the burgeoning South of Market (SoMa) area with its many restaurants and nightclubs. Don't expect much nightlife in the Financial District itself, though. Many restaurants and bars in the neighborhood close soon after the last commuters catch their BART train home.

$$$$ ☆ **Hyatt Regency.** The 20-story gray concrete Hyatt, at the foot of Mar-
★ ket Street, is the focal point of the Embarcadero Center, where more than 100 shops and restaurants cater to the Financial District. The spectacular 17-story atrium lobby (the world's largest) is a wonder of sprawling trees, a running stream, and a huge fountain. Glass elevators whisk you up to the Equinox restaurant, the city's only revolving rooftop restaurant. Rooms, some with bay-view balconies and all with city or bay views, have a handsome, contemporary look with blond-wood furniture and a grayish yellow-green color scheme. Ergonomic desk chairs are a relief for the hard-working businessperson. ⌧ *5 Embarcadero Center, Embarcadero 94111,* ☎ *415/788–1234 or 800/233–1234,* FAX *415/398–2567,* WEB *www.hyatt.com. 760 rooms, 45 suites. 2 restaurants, in-room data ports, in-room safes, some in-room hot tubs, some in-room VCRs, room service, gym, bar, lobby lounge, concierge, business services, meeting rooms, parking (fee), no-smoking floors. AE, D, DC, MC, V.*

$$$$ ☆ **Mandarin Oriental.** Since the Mandarin comprises the top 11 floors
★ of San Francisco's third-tallest building, all rooms provide panoramic vistas of the city and beyond. The glass-enclosed sky bridges connecting the two towers are almost as striking as the views. And the windows in the rooms actually open, unlike in many modern buildings, so you can hear the "ding ding" of the cable cars 48 floors below as you peer into the distant horizon (the hotel provides binoculars). Bowls of fruit and shoe-shine are complimentary for all, and those staying in the Mandarin Rooms can enjoy a decadent bathing experience in the extra deep bathtubs right next to picture windows. The second-floor restaurant, Silks, earns rave reviews for its innovative California cuisine with Asian touches. ⌧ *222 Sansome St., Financial District 94104,* ☎ *415/276–9888 or 800/622–0404,* FAX *415/433–0289,* WEB *www.mandarinoriental.com. 154 rooms, 4 suites. Restaurant, lobby lounge, room service, in-room data ports, in-room safes, minibars, some in-room VCRs, gym, dry cleaning, laundry service, concierge, Internet, business services, meeting room, parking (fee), some pets allowed (fee), no-smoking floors. AE, D, DC, MC, V.*

$$$$ ☆ **Omni San Francisco Hotel.** Twinkling crystal chandeliers, dark ma-
hogany paneling, and an elaborate iron staircase in the lobby may evoke an old-fashioned gentility, but this 1926 redbrick and stone edifice now houses a modern luxury hotel (opened in early 2002 after a $100 million renovation). Rooms, in either warm sunset shades or green and gold color schemes, have 9-ft ceilings with crown molding, and elegant carved mahogany furniture. Sliding doors lead to marble-floored baths with handsome green and black Chinese granite basins and fine toiletry items. L-shape suites at the corners of the building have six tall windows apiece, and are named after legendary local authors like Dashiell Hammett and John Steinbeck. Bob's Steak and Chop House, more elegant than it may sound, is just off the lobby. ⌧ *500 California St., Financial District 94104,* ☎ *415/677–9494,* FAX *415/273–3038,* WEB *www.omnisanfrancisco.com. 347 rooms, 15 suites. Restaurant, in-room data ports, some in-room faxes, in-room safes, minibars, some*

in-room VCR's, gym, bar, dry cleaning, laundry service, concierge, Internet, business services, meeting rooms, parking (fee), some pets allowed (fee), no-smoking floors. AE, D, DC, MC, V.

$$$$ ⊡ **Park Hyatt.** Contemporary in design but with a touch of old-world style, the Park Hyatt is a well-managed property in the Financial District across Battery Street from the Embarcadero Center. The hotel's public areas have large floral displays and fine artwork on the walls. The good-size rooms have Australian lacewood paneling, polished granite sinks, stylish contemporary furniture, and fresh flowers. The Park Grill restaurant serves excellent upscale California cuisine, and an elegant afternoon tea is served in the lobby lounge. Complimentary car service is available within downtown San Francisco. ⊠ *333 Battery St., Financial District 94111,* ☎ *415/392–1234 or 800/492–8822,* ℻ *415/421–2433,* 🖷 *www.hyatt.com. 323 rooms, 37 suites. Restaurant, 2 bars, room service, in-room data ports, some in-room hot tubs, some in-room VCRs, minibars, gym, dry cleaning, laundry service, Internet, business services, parking (fee), no-smoking floors. AE, D, DC, MC, V.*

$$$ ⊡ **Galleria Park.** Two blocks east of Union Square in the Financial Dis-
  ★   trict, this hotel with a black-marble facade is close to the Chinatown Gate and Crocker Galleria, one of San Francisco's most elegant shopping complexes. Guest rooms are comfortable, and each one has a floral bedspread, cream-colored striped wallpaper, and blond-wood furniture including a large writing desk. In the lobby, dominated by a massive hand-sculpted Art Nouveau fireplace and brightened by a restored 1911 skylight, complimentary coffee and tea are served in the mornings, wine in the evenings. The third-floor rooftop Cityscape Park has an outdoor jogging track. ⊠ *191 Sutter St., Financial District 94104,* ☎ *415/781–3060; 800/792–9639; 800/792–9855 in CA;* ℻ *415/433–4409,* 🖷 *www.galleriapark.com. 169 rooms, 8 suites. Room service, air conditioning, in-room data ports, in-room fax, 1 in-room hot tub, minibars, gym, dry cleaning, laundry service, concierge, Internet, business services, meeting room, parking (fee), no-smoking floors. AE, D, DC, MC, V.*

$$$ ⊡ **Harbor Court.** Overlooking the Embarcadero and within shouting
  ★   distance of the Bay Bridge, this cozy hotel, formerly an Army/Navy YMCA, is noted for the exemplary service of its friendly staff. Some guest rooms, with double sets of soundproof windows, overlook the bay. Rooms are smallish but have fancy touches like partially canopied, plushly upholstered beds; tastefully faux-textured walls; and fine reproductions of late-19th-century nautical and nature prints. In the evening complimentary wine is served in the lounge, sometimes accompanied by live guitar music, and coffee and tea are served in the morning. There is free access to adjacent YMCA facilities and limousine service to the Financial District. ⊠ *165 Steuart St., Embarcadero 94105,* ☎ *415/882–1300 or 800/346–0555,* ℻ *415/882–1313,* 🖷 *www.harborcourthotel.com. 130 rooms, 1 suite. Room service, in-room data ports, minibars, dry cleaning, laundry service, Internet, business services, parking (fee), some pets allowed, no-smoking floors. AE, D, DC, MC, V.*

South of Market (SoMa)

This up-and-coming area is a convenient spot for leisure and business travelers to bed down. The San Francisco Museum of Modern Art and the Yerba Buena Gardens complex are nearby, among other attractions.

$$$$ ⊡ **The Argent.** Rising 36 stories over the bustling downtown and South of Market areas, the Argent revels in its views, with floor-to-ceiling picture windows in the bright and airy guest rooms. About half of the rooms overlook Yerba Buena Gardens and the city, bay, and hills beyond. The others peer through the various tall buildings of the Financial District, some with a glimpse of the Golden Gate Bridge, the bay, or Alcatraz. Come back down to earth in the luxuriously appointed lobby and enjoy live music every evening but Sunday in the handsome, clublike lounge. ⊠ *50 3rd St., South of Market 94103,* ☎ *415/974–6400 or 877/222–6699,* 𝖥𝖠𝖷 *415/543–8268,* 𝖶𝖤𝖡 *www.argenthotel.com. 641 rooms, 26 suites. Restaurant, room service, in-room data ports, in-room safes, some kitchenettes, refrigerators, some in-room VCRs, health club, massage, bar, lobby lounge, dry cleaning, laundry service, concierge, Internet, business services, convention center, meeting rooms, parking (fee), no-smoking floor. AE, D, DC, MC, V.*

$$$$ 🛏 **Four Seasons Hotel San Francisco.** Sharing a skyscraper with multi-million dollar condos above and a huge sports and fitness complex below, this luxurious hotel inhabits Floors 6–13, with rooms overlooking either Yerba Buena Gardens or other parts of the nearby cityscape. Rooms are elegant in cream, gold, and soft green colors with contemporary artwork and fine linens. Some also have floor-to-ceiling windows and deep soaking tubs in addition to glass-enclosed showers. Fitness fans will appreciate free access to the vast and magnificently equipped Sports Club/LA, with a 25-yard lap pool, an aerobics room with a spring-cushioned floor, and dozens of classes and spa services available. The hotel's restaurant, Seasons, serves upscale American cuisine. ⊠ *757 Market St., South of Market 94103,* ☎ *415/633–3000,* 𝖥𝖠𝖷 *415/633–3009,* 𝖶𝖤𝖡 *www.fourseasons.com. 231 rooms, 46 suites. Restaurant, room service, in-room data ports, in-room safes, some in-room hot tubs, minibars, some in-room VCRs, indoor pool, health club, sauna, spa, steam room, basketball, volleyball, bar, dry cleaning, laundry service, concierge, concierge floor, Internet, business services, meeting rooms, parking (fee), some pets allowed, no-smoking floors. AE, D, DC, MC, V.*

$$$$ 🛏 **Hotel Palomar.** The top five floors of the green-tiled and turreted
★   1908 Pacific Place Building have been transformed by Bill Klimpton into an urbane and luxurious oasis above the busiest part of the city. A dimly lit lounge area with plush sofas gives way to restaurant Fifth Floor where modern French cuisine is served. Rooms have muted leopard-pattern carpeting and bold navy and cream striped drapes. The sleek furniture echoes a 1930s moderne sensibility. In the sparkling baths, a "tub menu" (with various herbal and botanical infusions) tempts adventurous bathers. In-room spa services such as massage, manicures, and body wraps are arranged through Hotel Monaco's Spa Equilibrium. ⊠ *12 Fourth St., South of Market 94103,* ☎ *415/348–1111 or 877/294–9711,* 𝖥𝖠𝖷 *415/348–0302,* 𝖶𝖤𝖡 *www.hotelpalomar.com. 182 rooms, 16 suites. Restaurant, room service, in-room data ports, in-room fax, some in-room hot tubs, minibars, some in-room VCRs, gym, massage, bar, lobby lounge, dry cleaning, laundry service, concierge, Internet, business services, meeting room, parking (fee), some pets allowed (fee), no-smoking floors. AE, D, DC, MC, V.*

$$$$ 🛏 **Palace Hotel.** This landmark hotel was the world's largest and most luxurious when it opened in 1875. Completely rebuilt after the earthquake and fire of 1906 (which sent Italian opera star Enrico Caruso into the street wearing nothing but a towel and vowing never to return to San Francisco), the splendid hotel has a stunning entryway and the fabulous Belle Epoque Garden Court restaurant, with its graceful chandeliers and stained-glass domed ceiling. Rooms, with twice-daily maid service and nightly turndown, have high ceilings, antique reproduction furnishings, and marble bathrooms. The hotel's Kyo-ya restaurant is widely considered the city's best Japanese restaurant. The Pied Piper Bar is named for its delightful 1909 Maxfield Parrish mural. ⊠ *2 New Montgomery St., South of Market, 94105,* ☎ *415/512–1111,* 𝖥𝖠𝖷 *415/543–0671. 518 rooms, 34 suites. 3 restaurants, room service,* *some in-room VCRs, indoor lap pool, health club, bar, laundry service, parking (fee), no-smoking floors. AE, D, DC, MC, V.*

$$$$ 🏨 **San Francisco Marriott.** When this 40-story hotel opened in 1989, critics either raved about or condemned its distinctive design (it's been compared to a parking meter and a jukebox). The flashy lobby has a mirrored ceiling and a 40-ft beaded crystal chandelier. An adjacent five-story, glass-topped atrium encloses a dining court lush with palm trees, tropical plants and a cascading fountain. If you are an art buff, you're in good company: a heavy-hitter art collection is installed throughout, and the hotel is very close to the San Francisco Museum of Modern Art and the Yerba Buena Gardens complex. The pastel rooms are small and plain but functional. Conventioneers often stay here. ⊠ *55 4th St., South of Market 94103,* ☎ *415/896–1600 or 800/228–9290,* FAX *415/896–6177,* WEB *www.marriott.com. 1,366 rooms, 134 suites. 3 restaurants, 2 piano bars, sports bar, room service, in-room data ports, some in-room hot tubs, minibars, some in-room VCRs, indoor pool, gym, hot tub, sauna, bar, dry cleaning, laundry service, concierge, Internet, business services, convention center, meeting rooms, car rental, parking (fee), no-smoking floors. AE, D, DC, MC, V.*

$$$$ 🏨 **W San Francisco.** Epitomizing cool modernity and urban chic both in its design and in the clientele it attracts, the 31-story W San Francisco owes part of its cache to its prime location next door to SFMOMA. Dimly lit hallways lead to smallish guest rooms, each with either a cozy corner sitting area or an upholstered window seat. The luxurious beds have pillow-top mattresses and goose-down comforters and pillows. Baths are handsomely elegant and have Aveda bath products. A glass-roofed pool and hot tub area is open 24 hours. Restaurant XYZ is popular with the trendy set. ⊠ *181 3rd St., South of Market 94103,* ☎ *415/777–5300 or 877/946–8357,* FAX *415/817–7823,* WEB *www.whotels.com. 418 rooms, 5 suites. Restaurant, café, room service, in-room data ports, in-room safes, minibars, refrigerators, in-room VCRs, indoor pool, gym, hot tub, massage, bar, dry cleaning, laundry service, concierge, business services, meeting room, parking (fee), some pets allowed (fee), no-smoking floors. AE, D, DC, MC, V.*

$$–$$$ 🏨 **Hotel Milano.** Adjacent to the San Francisco Shopping Centre and Nordstrom and a stone's throw from all the museums and attractions south of Market Street, this hotel is a shopper's and culture maven's delight. The eight-story hotel's stately 1913 neoclassic facade gives way to a warm and stylish lobby with a large Alexander Calder–style mobile over the lounge area. Guest rooms are spacious and handsomely decorated in warm earth tones with contemporary Italian furnishings. Weary shoppers and museum goers can soak, steam, or bake away fatigue in the split-level fitness center on the seventh and eighth floors. ⊠ *55 5th St., South of Market 94103,* ☎ *415/543–8555 or 800/398–7555,* FAX *415/543–5885,* WEB *hotelmilano.citysearch.com. 108 rooms. Restaurant, sushi bar, room service, in-room data ports, in-room safes, some in-room hot tubs, minibars, gym, hot tub, sauna, steam room, bar, dry cleaning, laundry service, concierge, business services, meeting room, parking (fee), no-smoking floors. AE, D, DC, MC, V.*

Nob Hill

Synonymous with San Francisco's high society, Nob Hill contains some of the city's best-known luxury hotels. All have spectacular views and noted restaurants. Cable car lines that cross Nob Hill should help you avoid the short but very steep trek from Union Square.

$$$$ 🏨 **The Fairmont.** Commanding the top of Nob Hill like a European
★ palace, the Fairmont has experienced plenty of drama including its triumph over the 1906 earthquake and the creation of the United Na-

tions Charter here in 1945. Architect Julia Morgan's 1907 lobby design includes alabaster walls and gilt-embellished ceilings supported by Corinthian columns. Gracious guest rooms, in pale color schemes, all have high ceilings, fine dark-wood furniture and colorful Chinese porcelain lamps. Rooms in the Tower are generally larger and have better views; all rooms have handsome marble baths. An array of amenities and services (including free chicken soup if you're under the weather) keep loyal (and royal) guests coming back. ⊠ *950 Mason St., Nob Hill 94108,* ☎ *415/772–5000 or 800/527–4727,* FAX *415/837–0587,* WEB *www.fairmont.com. 531 rooms, 65 suites. 2 restaurants, 2 bars, room service, in-room data ports, in-room fax, minibars, health club, hair salon, nightclub, baby-sitting, dry cleaning, laundry service, concierge, business services, meeting room, car rental, parking (fee), some pets allowed (fee), no-smoking floors. AE, D, DC, MC, V.*

$$$$ ▦ **Mark Hopkins Inter-Continental.** The circular redbrick drive of this towering Nob Hill architectural landmark leads to a graceful mirrored and marble-floored lobby. The rooms glow with gold, cream, and yellow tones, and the very elegant bathrooms are lined with multicolor Italian marble. Rooms on the upper floors have views of either the Golden Gate Bridge or the downtown cityscape. A motion-detection system alerts Housekeeping so they can do their work while you're away. The venerable yet vibrant rooftop lounge, the Top of the Mark, has cocktails, live music, and dancing, with an almost 360° view of the city and an elaborate weekend brunch to die for. ⊠ *999 California St., Nob Hill 94108,* ☎ *415/392–3434 or 800/662–4455,* FAX *415/421–3302,* WEB *www.markhopkins.net. 342 rooms, 38 suites. Restaurant, 2 bars, room service, some in-room hot tubs, some in-room VCRs, gym, dry cleaning, laundry service, concierge, Internet, business services, meeting room, car rental, parking (fee), some pets allowed. AE, D, DC, MC, V.*

$$$$ ▦ **Ritz-Carlton, San Francisco.** This world-class hotel is a stunning trib-
★ ute to beauty and warm, sincere service. Beyond the 17 Ionic columns of the neoclassic facade, crystal chandeliers in the lobby illuminate Georgian antiques and museum-quality 18th- and 19th-century paintings. The fitness center is a destination in its own right, with an indoor swimming pool, steam baths, saunas, and a whirlpool. All rooms have feather beds with 300-count Egyptian cotton sheets and down comforters. Club Level rooms include use of the Club Lounge with its dedicated concierge and several elaborate complimentary food presentations daily. The renowned Dining Room has a seasonal menu with modern French accents by celebrated chef Sylvain Portay. Afternoon tea in the Lobby Lounge—overlooking the beautifully landscaped garden courtyard—is a San Francisco institution. ⊠ *600 Stockton St., at California St., Nob Hill 94108,* ☎ *415/296–7465 or 800/241–3333,* FAX *415/986–1268,* WEB *www.ritzcarlton.com. 294 rooms, 42 suites. 2 restaurants, 3 bars, lobby lounge, in-room data ports, some in-room VCRs, indoor pool, health club, hot tub, sauna, dry cleaning, laundry service, concierge, concierge floor, Internet, business services, meeting room, parking (fee), no-smoking floors. AE, D, DC, MC, V.*

$$$–$$$$ ▦ **The Huntington Hotel.** The redbrick, ivy-covered Huntington Hotel has provided stately and gracious personal service to everyone from Bogart and Bacall to Picasso and Pavarotti. Rooms and suites, many of which have great views of Grace Cathedral, the bay, or the city skyline, are large because they used to be residential apartments. Most rooms have wet bars, all have large antique desks. A sunny indoor/outdoor spa area with panoramic city views has an indoor pool and 10 rooms for massages, facials, and body wraps. The hotel's famous Big 4 Restaurant serves contemporary American cuisine in a clubby room with green leather booths and an interesting collection of San Francisco and western memorabilia. ⊠ *1075 California St., Nob Hill 94108,* ☎ *415/474–5400 or*

800/227–4683, FAX 415/474–6227, WEB *www.huntingtonhotel.com. 100 rooms, 35 suites. Restaurant, room service, in-room data ports, in-room safes, some in-room hot tubs, some kitchenettes, indoor pool, massage, sauna, spa, steam room, bar, dry cleaning, laundry service, concierge, meeting room, parking (fee), no-smoking floors. AE, D, DC, MC, V.*

$$$–$$$$ ⛒ **Renaissance Stanford Court.** The lobby of this stately yet comfortable hotel is dominated by a stained-glass dome and a dramatic 360° mural depicting scenes of early San Francisco and the gold rush. Rooms achieve understated elegance with a mix of English country manor–style furnishings accented with Asian artwork and accessories. Perks include Egyptian cotton sheets, heated towel racks, plush robes, and nightly turndown service. Fournou's Ovens—known for its Provençal decor, 54-square-ft roasting oven, and world-class wine cellar—is usually packed. ✉ *905 California St., Nob Hill 94108,* ☎ *415/989–3500; 800/227–4736; 800/622–0957 in CA,* FAX *415/986–8195,* WEB *www.renaissancehotels.com. 385 rooms, 8 suites. Restaurant, room service, in-room data ports, gym, bar, lobby lounge, piano, dry cleaning, laundry service, concierge, Internet, business services, meeting room, parking (fee), some pets allowed, no-smoking floors. AE, D, DC, MC, V.*

$$$ ⛒ **Nob Hill Lambourne.** Designed as an urban retreat for traveling executives, this small, quiet hotel takes pride in providing both tools of the trade (personal computers, fax machines, personalized voice mail) and an escape from the job (spa treatment room with massages, body scrubs, manicures, and pedicures). Prepare for a good night's sleep, thanks to white-noise machines and rice-hull pillows, not to mention the vitamins and chamomile tea that arrive with turndown service. Rooms have soft lighting, queen-size beds with hand-sewn mattresses, silk-damask bedding, and contemporary furnishings in muted colors. Evening wine service is complimentary. ✉ *725 Pine St., at Stockton St., Nob Hill 94108,* ☎ *415/433–2287 or 800/274–8466,* FAX *415/433–0975,* WEB *www.nobhilllambourne.com. 14 rooms, 6 suites. In-room data ports, kitchenettes, in-room VCRs, exercise equipment, massage, spa, business services, parking (fee), no-smoking floor; no air-conditioning. AE, D, DC, MC, V. CP.*

$$$ ⛒ **Vintage Court.** This bit of the Napa Valley two blocks from Union Square has inviting rooms—some with sunny window seats—all with large writing desks, dark wood venetian blinds, and old fashioned steam heat. Baths are small, some with tub-showers and some with stall showers. Each room is named after a California winery, and the Wine Country theme extends to complimentary local vintages served nightly in front of the lobby fireplace, where long couches invite lingering. For fine food you need go no farther than to adjoining Masa's, one of the city's most celebrated French restaurants. ✉ *650 Bush St., Nob Hill 94108,* ☎ *415/392–4666 or 800/654–1100,* FAX *415/433–4065,* WEB *www.vintagecourt.com. 107 rooms, 1 suite. Restaurant, bar, minibars, parking (fee), some pets allowed; no smoking. AE, D, DC, MC, V. CP.*

$–$$ ⛒ **San Francisco Residence Club.** In contrast to the neighboring showplace hotels, the S. F. Residence Club is a humble guest house with million-dollar views, a money-saving meal plan, and a pleasant garden patio. The building has seen better days, and most of the modest rooms share baths, but many have sweeping bay views. The international clientele ranges from leisure travelers and business professionals to longer-term residents who take advantage of the full American breakfast *and* dinner included in the daily, weekly, or monthly room rate. A $100 advance deposit via check is required. ✉ *851 California St., Nob Hill 94108,* ☎ *415/421–2220,* FAX *415/421–2335. 84 rooms. Dining room, some refrigerators, laundry facilities; no TV in some rooms. No credit cards. MAP.*

Fisherman's Wharf/North Beach

All accommodations in Fisherman's Wharf are within a few blocks of restaurants, shops, and cable car lines. Because of city ordinances, no hotel exceeds four stories, so this is not the area for fantastic views of the city or the bay. Reservations are always necessary, sometimes weeks in advance during peak summer months, when rates rise by as much as 30%. Some street-side rooms can be noisy. Nearby North Beach has surprisingly few lodgings. A few small B&Bs, however, hide in unassuming Victorians on the neighborhood's side streets.

$$$–$$$$ ☆ **Hyatt at Fisherman's Wharf.** Location is the key to this hotel's popularity: it's within walking distance of Ghirardelli Square, the Cannery, Pier 39, Aquatic Park, and docks for Alcatraz ferries and bay cruises. It's also across the street from a cable car turnaround. The moderate-size guest rooms, decorated in shades of gold and cream with dark-wood furniture, have double-pane windows to keep out the often considerable street noise. Each floor has a laundry room. In the North Point Lounge, a lovely domed Tiffany skylight with a seashore motif crowns a large, comfy lounge area with a fireplace and fountain. ⊠ *555 N. Point St., Fisherman's Wharf 94133,* ☎ *415/563–1234 or 800/233–1234,* FAX *415/563–2218,* WEB *www.fishermanswharf.hyatt.com. 305 rooms, 8 suites. Restaurant, room service, in-room data ports, in-room safes, some in-room hot tubs, 1 kitchenette, some in-room VCRs, pool, gym, outdoor hot tub, sauna, sports bar, laundry facilities, Internet, business services, meeting rooms, parking (fee), no-smoking floors. AE, D, DC, MC, V.*

$$$–$$$$ ☆ **Marriott at Fisherman's Wharf.** Behind an unremarkable sand-color facade, the Marriott strikes a grand note with its lavish, low-ceiling lobby with marble floors, a double fireplace, and English club–style furniture. Rooms, all with forest-green, burgundy, and cream color schemes, have either a king-size bed or two double beds. One hundred of the rooms are specially designed for business travelers. Restaurant Spada serves breakfast, lunch, and dinner. Complimentary limo service to the Financial District is available each morning. ⊠ *1250 Columbus Ave., Fisherman's Wharf 94133,* ☎ *415/775–7555 or 800/228–9290,* FAX *415/474–2099,* WEB *www.marriott.com. 269 rooms, 16 suites. Restaurant, lobby lounge, room service, in-room data ports, some in-room fax, minibars, gym, sauna, bar, piano, dry cleaning, laundry service, concierge, business services, meeting rooms, parking (fee), some pets allowed (fee), no-smoking floor; no air-conditioning. AE, D, DC, MC, V.*

$$$ ☆ **Tuscan Inn.** The major attraction here is the friendly, attentive staff. The condolike exterior of the hotel—reddish brick with white concrete—gives little indication of the charm of the relatively small, Italian-influenced guest rooms, with their white-pine furniture and floral bedspreads and curtains. One entire wall in each room is mirrored. Room service is provided by Cafe Pescatore, the Italian seafood restaurant off the lobby. Morning coffee, tea, and biscotti are complimentary, and wine is served in the early evening. The oak-panel lobby is watched over by two impressive wooden lions flanking the large fireplace. Complimentary limousine service to the Financial District is available. ⊠ *425 N. Point St., at Mason St., Fisherman's Wharf 94133,* ☎ *415/561–1100 or 800/ 648–4626,* FAX *415/561–1199,* WEB *www.tuscaninn.com. 209 rooms, 12 suites. Restaurant, room service, minibars, some in-room VCRs, dry cleaning, laundry service, Internet, meeting room, parking (fee), some pets allowed (fee); no-smoking floors. AE, D, DC, MC, V.*

$$–$$$ ☆ **Radisson Hotel at Fisherman's Wharf.** Occupying an entire city ★ block, and part of a complex including 25 shops and restaurants, this is the only bayfront hotel at Fisherman's Wharf and the nearest to Pier 39 and the bay cruise docks. The medium-size lobby has plenty of comfortable couches and chairs. Eighty percent of the rooms have views of the bay and overlook a landscaped courtyard and pool. Rooms are contemporary, cleanly designed and bright, with tan carpeting, black-and-tan striped drapes, and cherrywood furniture. ⊠ *250 Beach St., Fisherman's Wharf 94133,* ☎ *415/392–6700 or 800/333–3333,* FAX *415/ 986–7853,* WEB *www.radisson.com. 355 rooms. 3 restaurants, in-room data ports, some refrigerators, pool, gym, concierge, parking (fee), no-smoking rooms. AE, D, DC, MC, V.*

$$ 🗹 **Hotel Bohème.** The Bohème, in the middle of historic North Beach and near many Italian restaurants and cafés, takes you back in time with coral-color walls, bistro tables, and memorabilia recalling the Beat generation. Allen Ginsberg, who stayed here many times, could in his later years be seen sitting in a window tapping away on his laptop computer. Screenwriters from Francis Ford Coppola's nearby American Zoetrope studio stay here often, as do poets and other artists. Beds have unnecessary but fun mosquito netting and baths have cheerful yellow tiles. Rooms in the rear are quieter. Complimentary sherry is served in the lobby. ⊠ *444 Columbus Ave., North Beach 94133,* ☎ *415/433–9111,* FAX *415/ 362–6292,* WEB *www.hotelboheme.com. 16 rooms. In-room data ports, Internet; no air-conditioning, no smoking. AE, D, DC, MC, V.*

$ 🗹 **San Remo.** This three-story 1906 Italianate Victorian just a few blocks
★ from Fisherman's Wharf was once home to longshoremen and Beats. A narrow stairway from the street leads to the front desk, and labyrinthine hallways to the small but charming rooms with lace curtains, forest-green wooden floors, brass beds, and other antique furnishings. The upper floors are brighter, being closer to the skylights that provide sunshine to the many potted plants in the brass-banistered hallways. About a third of the rooms have sinks; all rooms, except a charming penthouse cottage, share scrupulously clean black-and-white tile shower and toilet facilities with pull-chain toilets. ⊠ *2237 Mason St., North Beach 94133,* ☎ *415/776–8688 or 800/352–7366,* FAX *415/ 776–2811,* WEB *www.sanremohotel.com. 62 rooms, 1 suite. Laundry facilities, Internet, parking (fee); no room phones, no room TVs, no smoking. AE, DC, MC, V.*

Pacific Heights, Cow Hollow, and the Marina

Lombard Street, a major traffic corridor leading to the Golden Gate Bridge, stretches past San Francisco's poshest neighborhoods: Pacific Heights, Cow Hollow, and the Marina. The cheapest accommodations are along Lombard Street. If you prefer to be out of the hustle and bustle, opt for lodgings on smaller side streets. Wherever you stay in this area, it's a short walk to the Marina, where sailboats bob on the bay and park goers fly kites.

$$$$ 🗹 **Sherman House.** This magnificent Italianate mansion at the foot of
★ residential Pacific Heights is San Francisco's most luxurious small hotel. Rooms are individually decorated with Biedermeier, English Jacobean, or French Second Empire antiques. The decadent mood is enhanced by tapestry-like canopies over four-poster feather beds, wood-burning fireplaces with marble mantels, and sumptuous bathrooms, all with whirlpool baths. The six romantic suites attract honeymooners from around the world, and the elegant in-house dining room serves superb French-inspired cuisine. Room rates include valet parking, a full breakfast, and evening wine and hors d'oeuvres in the Gallery, an upstairs sitting room. ⊠ *2160 Green St., Pacific Heights 94123,* ☎ *415/563–3600 or 800/424–5777,* FAX *415/563–1882,* WEB *www.theshermanhouse.com. 8 rooms, 6 suites. Dining room, room service, in-room VCRs, piano, concierge, Internet, 1 meeting room, free parking; no air-conditioning, no smoking. AE, D, DC, MC, V. BP.*

$$$ **Hotel Drisco.** In one of the wealthiest and most beautiful residential neighborhoods in San Francisco, this understated, elegant 1903 Edwardian is a quiet haven for anyone overwhelmed by the busier parts of the city. The hotel serves as a celebrity hideaway from time to time; Ethan Hawke and Ashley Judd recently stayed here. Pale yellow and white rooms are outfitted with genteel furnishings and luxury amenities. Some rooms have sweeping city views. There is a lovely sitting room off the lobby where wine is set out every evening and coffee and tea is available day and night. ✉ 2901 Pacific Ave., Pacific Heights 94115, ☎ 415/346–2880 or 800/634–7277, FAX 415/567–5537, WEB www.hoteldrisco.com. 33 rooms, 15 suites. In-room data ports, minibars, in-room VCRs, gym, dry cleaning, laundry service, concierge; no smoking. AE, D, DC, MC, V. CP.

$$–$$$ **Jackson Court.** On a quiet residential block in tony Pacific Heights, Jackson Court is a converted brownstone mansion built in 1900, now a B&B and time-share. The light, spacious rooms have a mixture of antique and contemporary furnishings amid fresh flowers. The centerpiece of the parlor is an unusual hand-carved fireplace with gentle spiritlike faces said to be the original owners'. Afternoon tea and cookies are served here. The adjacent wood-paneled Game Room is a resource center for local information, books, and games. Some guest rooms have fireplaces and window seats. ✉ 2198 Jackson St., Pacific Heights 94115, ☎ 415/929–7670, FAX 415/929–1405, WEB www.jacksoncourt.com. 10 rooms. Recreation room, no-smoking floor; no air-conditioning. AE, MC, V. CP.

$$–$$$ ★ **Union Street Inn.** With the help of many precious family antiques and unique artwork, the innkeepers—Jane Bertorelli and David Coyle, who was once a chef for the Duke and Duchess of Bedford—made this green and cream colored 1902 Edwardian a delightful B&B inn. Equipped with candles, fresh flowers, and wineglasses, rooms are popular with honeymooners and romantics. The Carriage House, with its own hot tub, is set off from the main house by an old-fashioned English garden with lemon trees. An elaborate breakfast is included, as are afternoon tea and evening hors d'oeuvres. ✉ 2229 Union St., Cow Hollow 94123, ☎ 415/346–0424, FAX 415/922–8046, WEB www.unionstreetinn.com. 6 rooms. Parking (fee); no smoking. AE, MC, V. BP.

$$ **Bed and Breakfast Inn.** Hidden in an alley off Union Street between Buchanan and Laguna, this ivy-covered Victorian (San Francisco's first B&B) contains English country–style rooms in pastel colors with lace curtains and wicker furniture. Though the rooms with shared baths are quite small, the other rooms and two suites have ample space. The Mayfair, a bi-level apartment above the main house, has a living room, kitchenette, and a sleeping loft. The Garden Suite, a larger, more deluxe apartment, has a cozy country kitchen, whirlpool bath, and plenty of room for six people. ✉ 4 Charlton Ct., at Union St., Cow Hollow 94123, ☎ 415/921–9784, FAX 415/921–0544, WEB www.thebandb.com. 8 rooms, 3 with shared bath; 2 suites. Some in-room hot tubs, 1 kitchen, 1 kitchenette, some in-room VCRs, parking (fee); no TV in some rooms, no smoking. MC, V. CP.

$$ **Coventry Motor Inn.** Among the many motels on busy Lombard Street, this is one of the better built and one of the quietest, especially in the rooms not facing Lombard. Its handsome oak-paneled lobby has leather furniture and photographs of historic San Francisco. The unusually spacious rooms—with cheery yellow wallpaper and oak furniture—all have well-lit dining-working areas. Many rooms have bay windows; some on the upper floors have partial views of the Golden Gate Bridge. Covered parking is under the building, reached by elevator. ✉ 1901 Lombard St., Cow Hollow 94123, ☎ 415/567–1200, FAX 415/921–8745, WEB www.coventrymotorinn.com. 69 rooms. Free parking; no smoking. AE, DC, MC, V.

$$ 🏨 **Cow Hollow Motor Inn and Suites.** Built by the same family that runs it, this large, modern motel has interior corridors and rooms that are more spacious than average, with sitting-dining areas, dark-wood traditional furniture, floral wallpaper, and blue carpeting and bedspreads. Some rooms have views of the Golden Gate Bridge. The large suites ($195–$245) seem like typical San Francisco apartments with their hardwood floors, Oriental carpets, antique furnishings, marble fireplaces, and fully equipped kitchens. Covered parking is under the building. ✉ *2190 Lombard St., Cow Hollow 94123,* ☎ *415/921–5800,* FAX *415/922–8515,* WEB *www.cowhollowmotorinn.com. 117 rooms, 12 suites. Restaurant, some kitchens, some kitchenettes, some in-room VCRs, meeting room, free parking; no smoking. AE, DC, MC, V.*

$$ 🏨 **Hotel Del Sol.** Once a typical '50s-style motor court, the Del Sol is
★ now an anything-but-typical artistic statement. The sunny yellow and blue, three-story building and courtyard are a riot of stripes and bold colors. Rooms open onto the courtyard's heated pool and hammock under towering palm trees, and evoke a beach-house mood with plantation shutters, tropical-stripe bedspreads, and rattan chairs; some have brick fireplaces. The baths are small with bright-yellow tiling. Family suites have child-friendly furnishings and games for the kiddies, and the hotel maintains a "pillow library" with about 15 different kinds. ✉ *3100 Webster St., Cow Hollow 94123,* ☎ *415/921–5520 or 877/ 433–5765,* FAX *415/931–4137,* WEB *www.thehoteldelsol.com. 47 rooms, 10 suites. In-room data ports, in-room safes, some kitchenettes, pool, sauna, laundry service, concierge, free parking, no-smoking rooms. AE, D, DC, MC, V.*

$$ 🏨 **Presidio Travelodge.** After most of the west-bound traffic on Lombard Street veers off onto the Golden Gate Bridge approach, the street continues for two much quieter blocks leading up to one of the entrance gates of the Presidio, a former army base, now woodsy national parkland. It's a terrific location for this gray-and-blue three-story motel. Rooms have blond-wood furniture and standard motel amenities such as coffeemakers and cable TV. One room, the Bear's Den, has a VCR and library of children's videos. ✉ *2755 Lombard St., Cow Hollow 94123,* ☎ *415/931–8581,* FAX *415/776–0904,* WEB *www.travelodge.com. 27 rooms. Refrigerators, free parking, no-smoking rooms. AE, D, DC, MC, V.*

$–$$ 🏨 **Bel-Aire Travelodge.** Made up of twin white-and-blue buildings built in the mid-1950s across Steiner Street from each other, this cute motel is a block away from busy Lombard Street and much quieter than many motels on the main drag. The rooms have contemporary motel-style blond-wood furniture, with pale mauve walls and blue carpeting. Bathrooms have showers only, and there is a mirrored vanity table in each room. Other amenities are coffeemakers, cable TV, a daily newspaper, and free local calls. ✉ *3201 Steiner St., Cow Hollow 94123,* ☎ *415/921–5162 or 800/280–3242,* FAX *415/921–3602,* WEB *www.the. travelodge.com/sanfrancisco09664. 32 rooms. Fans, in-room data ports, airport shuttle, free parking, no-smoking rooms; no air-conditioning,. AE, D, DC, MC, V.*

$–$$ 🏨 **Marina Inn.** Five blocks from the Marina, this four-story hotel, built in 1924, feels a little like a B&B, but is priced like a motel. English country–style rooms are simply appointed, with a queen-size two-poster bed, private bath, small pinewood writing desks, nightstands, and armoires; the wallpaper and bedspreads are vividly floral. Some rooms facing Octavia and Lombard streets have bay windows with window seats, but they are noisier than the inside rooms. A simple complimentary Continental breakfast and afternoon sherry are served in the central sitting room. ✉ *3110 Octavia St., at Lombard St., Cow Hollow 94123,* ☎ *415/928–1000 or 800/274–1420,* FAX *415/928–*

5909, WEB *www.marinainn.com. 40 rooms. Coffee shop, in-room data ports, hair salon; no smoking. AE, DC, MC, V. CP.*

$–$$ 🏨 **Pacific Heights Inn.** One of the most genteel-looking motels in town, this two-story motor court near the busy intersection of Union and Van Ness is dressed up with wrought-iron railings and benches, hanging plants, and pebbled exterior walkways facing onto the parking lot. Rooms, with floral bedspreads and brass beds, are on the small side; however, most of the units are suites, some with full kitchens, some with extra bedrooms. Morning pastries and coffee are served in the lobby. ⊠ *1555 Union St., Van Ness/Polk 94123,* ☎ *415/776–3310 or 800/523–1801,* FAX *415/776–8176,* WEB *www.pacificheightsinn.com. 15 rooms, 25 suites. Some kitchens, some kitchenettes, free parking, some pets allowed, no-smoking rooms. AE, D, DC, MC, V. CP.*

$–$$ 🏨 **Town House Motel.** What this family-oriented motel lacks in luxury and atmosphere, it makes up for in value. The simple rooms, in blue tones with contemporary lacquered-wood furniture, all have refrigerators, irons and ironing boards, and hair dryers. Plantation shutters cover the windows. A light Continental breakfast in the lobby is complimentary. ⊠ *1650 Lombard St., Cow Hollow 94123,* ☎ *415/885–5163 or 800/255–1516,* FAX *415/771–9889,* WEB *www.sftownhousemotel.com. 24 rooms. Some microwaves, refrigerators, free parking, no-smoking rooms; no air-conditioning. AE, D, DC, MC, V. CP.*

Civic Center/Van Ness

Though many of the grand civic buildings here were hidden under scaffolding during the late 1990s, major projects like a massive renovation of City Hall, construction of the new San Francisco Public Library (the old library is being transformed into the new Asian Art Museum), and renovation of the War Memorial Opera House have all been completed, and the neighborhood is experiencing a renaissance of sorts. Fine restaurants flank Van Ness Avenue, and smaller, hipper places have opened west of Van Ness Avenue on Hayes Street.

$$$ 🏨 **The Archbishop's Mansion.** Everything here is extravagantly ro-
★ mantic, starting with the cavernous common areas, where a chandelier used in the movie *Gone with the Wind* hangs above a 1904 Bechstein grand piano once owned by Noël Coward. The 15 guest rooms, each named for a famous opera, are individually decorated with intricately carved antiques; many have whirlpool tubs or fireplaces (there are 16 fireplaces in the mansion). Though not within easy walking distance of many restaurants or attractions, its perch on the corner of Alamo Square near the Painted Ladies—San Francisco's famous Victorian homes—makes for a scenic, relaxed stay. ⊠ *1000 Fulton St., Western Addition 94117,* ☎ *415/563–7872 or 800/543–5820,* FAX *415/885–3193,* WEB *www.thearchbishopsmansion.com. 10 rooms, 5 suites. Some fans, in-room data ports, some in-room hot tubs, in-room VCRs, piano, meeting room, free parking, no-smoking rooms; no air-conditioning. AE, MC, V. CP.*

$$$ 🏨 **Hotel Majestic.** One of San Francisco's original grand hotels, and once the decade-long residence of screen stars Joan Fontaine and Olivia de Havilland, this five-story white 1902 Edwardian has an elegant lobby replete with glistening granite stairs, antique chandeliers, plush Victorian chairs, and a white-marble fireplace. Glass cases in the bar house a stunning collection of rare butterflies from Africa and New Guinea. At press time, the guest rooms, most of which have gas fireplaces, are undergoing a total conversion from their antique-laden past to a lighter and more contemporary look. ⊠ *1500 Sutter St., Pacific Heights 94109,* ☎ *415/441–1100 or 800/869–8869,* FAX *415/ 673–7331,* WEB *www.thehotelmajestic.com. 49 rooms, 9 suites. Restau-*

rant, bar, room service, dry cleaning, laundry service, meeting rooms, parking (fee); no smoking. AE, DC, MC, V.

$$$ ⊞ **Radisson Miyako Hotel.** Adjacent to the Japantown complex and three blocks from Fillmore Street and Pacific Heights, this pagoda-style hotel is popular with business travelers. Some guest rooms are in the tower building; others are in the garden wing, which has a traditional Japanese garden with a waterfall. Japanese-style rooms have futon beds with tatami mats, while Western rooms have traditional beds with mattresses; all have gorgeous Asian furniture and original artwork. Most have their own soaking rooms with a bucket and stool and a Japanese tub (1 ft deeper than Western tubs), and in-room shiatsu massages are available. ⊠ *1625 Post St., at Laguna St., Japantown 94115,* ☎ *415/922–3200 or 800/533–4567,* ℻ *415/921–0417,* ⓦ *www.miyakohotel.com. 211 rooms, 17 suites. Restaurant, in-room data ports, some in-room hot tubs, minibars, gym, massage, bar, dry cleaning, laundry service, Internet, business services, meeting rooms, no-smoking floors. AE, D, DC, MC, V.*

$$–$$$ ⊞ **Inn at the Opera.** Within a block or so of Davies Symphony Hall and the War Memorial Opera House, this hotel and time-share has hosted the likes of Pavarotti and Baryshnikov, as well as other lights of the music, dance, and opera worlds. Behind the marble-floor lobby are rooms of various sizes with creamy pastels and dark-wood furnishings. All rooms have queen-size beds, though the standard rooms are a bit cramped. Suites are sometimes available, when unoccupied by time-share owners. The bureau drawers are lined with sheet music, and every room has terry robes, a microwave oven, and a coffeemaker. Stars often congregate in the Ovation restaurant before and after performances. ⊠ *333 Fulton St., Hayes Valley 94102,* ☎ *415/863–8400 or 800/325–2708,* ℻ *415/861–0821,* ⓦ *www.innattheopera.com. 30 rooms, 18 suites. Restaurant, lobby lounge, room service, microwaves, concierge, business services, Internet, parking (fee); no air-conditioning, no smoking. AE, DC, MC, V. CP.*

$$ ⊞ **Phoenix Hotel.** From the piped-in, poolside jungle music to the aquatic-theme, ultrahip Backflip restaurant and lounge immersed in shimmering hues of blue and green, the Phoenix evokes the tropics—or at least a fun, kitschy version of it. Although probably not the place for a traveling executive seeking peace and quiet—or anyone put off by its location on the fringes of the seedy Tenderloin District—celebrities, including such big-name bands as R.E.M. and Pearl Jam have stayed here. Rooms are simple, with handmade bamboo furniture, tropical-print bedspreads, and original art by local artists. All rooms face the courtyard pool and sculpture garden. A hairstylist is on call if you want to look like a rock star. ⊠ *601 Eddy St., Civic Center 94109,* ☎ *415/776–1380 or 800/248–9466,* ℻ *415/885–3109,* ⓦ *www.thephoenixhotel. com. 41 rooms, 3 suites. Restaurant, room service, pool, massage, bar, nightclub, laundry service, free parking; no air-conditioning. AE, D, DC, MC, V. CP.*

$–$$ ⊞ **Abigail Howard Johnson Hotel.** This hotel, built in 1926 and a former B&B, retains its Art Deco–tiled lobby floor, faux-marble front desk, vintage gated elevator, and old-fashioned telephone booth in the lobby. Smallish rooms have hissing steam radiators and antiques. Room 211—the hotel's only suite—is the most elegant and spacious. The hotel caters to artists performing at nearby theaters. Complimentary Continental breakfast is served. Millennium Restaurant, right off the lobby, serves food so delicious it's hard to believe it's vegan (no meat or dairy). ⊠ *246 McAllister St., Civic Center 94102,* ☎ *415/626–6500,* ℻ *415/ 626–6580. 60 rooms, 1 suite. Restaurant, fans, dry cleaning, business services, laundry service, parking (fee), no-smoking floors; no air-conditioning. AE, D, DC, MC, V.*

The Airport

Construction booms near San Francisco International Airport during the mid-1980s and late-1990s brought several new luxury hotels to this rather bleak-looking area, where rates are about 20% less than those at their in-town counterparts. Airport shuttle buses are provided by all of the following hotels. Because they cater primarily to midweek business travelers, airport hotels often cut weekend prices; be sure to inquire.

$$$$ ★ 🏨 **Hotel Sofitel–San Francisco Bay.** Parisian boulevard lampposts, a métro sign, and a kiosk covered with posters bring an unexpected bit of Paris to this bay-side hotel. The French-theme public spaces—the Gigi Brasserie and La Terrasse bar—have a light, open, airy feeling that extends to the rooms, each of which has pale earth toned walls, a minibar and writing desk. ✉ *223 Twin Dolphin Dr., Redwood City 94065,* ☎ *650/598–9000 or 800/763–4835,* ℻ *650/598–0459,* ⓦⒺⒷ *www.hotelsofitelsfbay.com. 379 rooms, 42 suites. Restaurant, lobby lounge, minibars, gym, bar, laundry service, concierge, Internet, business services, meeting room, airport shuttle, free parking, some pets allowed (fee), no-smoking floors. AE, DC, MC, V.*

$$$$ 🏨 **The Westin.** This bay-front hotel, with an elegant, palm tree–lined entrance and a sparkling fountain, is geared toward business travelers and conventioneers. The medium-size guest rooms have cherry-wood furnishings with Asian touches and gold, green, and rose colors. All baths have double-headed showers and special no-cling shower curtains, and all beds have pillow-top mattresses. There is an atrium-enclosed swimming pool if you want to splash about. The rich, dark paneled restaurant, Alfiere, is in the lobby and has a Mediterranean-influenced menu. ✉ *1 Old Bayshore Hwy., Millbrae 94030,* ☎ *650/692–3500 or 800/937–8461,* ℻ *650/872–8111,* ⓦⒺⒷ *www.westin.com. 390 rooms, 3 suites. Restaurant, room service, in-room data ports, some in-room hot tubs, minibars, indoor pool, gym, business services, meeting rooms, airport shuttle, parking (fee), some pets allowed, no-smoking floors. AE, DC, MC, V.*

$$–$$$$ 🏨 **Embassy Suites San Francisco Airport–Burlingame.** With excellent service and facilities, this California Mission–style hostelry is one of the most lavish in the airport area. Set on the bay with up-close views of planes taking off and landing, it consists entirely of two-room suites that open onto a nine-story atrium and tropical garden replete with ducks, parrots, fish, and a waterfall. Living rooms all have a work area, sleeper sofa, wet bar, television, microwave, and refrigerator. Rates include a full breakfast and evening cocktails. ✉ *150 Anza Blvd., Burlingame 94010,* ☎ *650/342–4600 or 800/362–2779,* ℻ *650/343–8137,* ⓦⒺⒷ *www. embassyburlingame.com. 340 suites. Restaurant, room service, kitchenettes, minibars, indoor pool, gym, hot tub, sauna, bar, concierge, Internet, business services, meeting rooms, airport shuttle, free parking, some pets allowed (fee), no-smoking floors. AE, DC, MC, V. BP.*

$$–$$$$ ★ 🏨 **Hyatt Regency San Francisco Airport.** A spectacular 10-story lobby atrium encompasses 29,000 square ft of this dramatic hotel 2 mi south of the airport. This is the largest airport convention hotel in northern California, and almost every service and amenity you could think of is here, including athletic facilities and several dining and entertainment options. Rooms, in warm earth tones with traditional dark-wood furniture and floral bedspreads, are modern and well equipped. ✉ *1333 Bayshore Hwy., Burlingame 94010,* ☎ *650/347–1234,* ℻ *650/696–2669,* ⓦⒺⒷ *www.sanfrancisco.hyatt.com. 767 rooms, 26 suites. Restaurant, snack bar, café, sports bar, room service, in-room data ports, some in-room faxes, pool, gym, outdoor hot tub, lobby lounge, piano bar, dry cleaning, laundry service, concierge, Internet, business services,*

convention center, meeting room, airport shuttle, car rental, parking (fee), no-smoking floors. AE, D, DC, MC, V.

$$-$$$ ⊞ **Clarion Hotel San Francisco Airport.** This busy hotel just south of the airport has a gigantic, glass-front lobby and an adjoining garden area, where wrought-iron benches, a heated pool, and a whirlpool tub are set among pine trees. The newer Tower rooms have the best views and comfortable pillow-top beds, plus coffeemakers, irons, and ironing boards. Rooms in the older Garden Building are slightly larger but have fewer amenities. A popular jogging trail runs alongside the bay. ⊠ *401 E. Millbrae Ave., Millbrae 94030,* ☏ *650/692–6363 or 800/ 223–7111,* FAX *650/697–8735,* WEB *www3.choicehotels.com. 440 rooms, 6 suites. Restaurant, room service, in-room data ports, some in-room hot tubs, minibars, pool, gym, outdoor hot tub, bar, Internet, business services, meeting rooms, airport shuttle, parking (fee), some pets allowed (fee), no smoking floors. AE, DC, MC, V.*

$$ ⊞ **La Quinta Motor Inn.** Literally a stone's throw from U.S. 101, this motel with weathered-wood balconies and a red-tile roof provides quiet, well-insulated accommodations. Baths are bright and sparkling. A complimentary Continental breakfast, which includes a juice bar, is served in the lobby until 10 daily; there's also a restaurant next door. ⊠ *20 Airport Blvd., South San Francisco 94080,* ☏ *650/583–2223,* FAX *650/589–6770,* WEB *www.laquinta.com. 169 rooms, 3 suites. In-room data ports, some microwaves, some refrigerators, pool, gym, hot tub, dry cleaning, laundry service, laundry facilities, airport shuttle, some pets allowed, no-smoking floors. AE, D, DC, MC, V. CP.*

$–$$ ⊞ **Red Roof Inn.** Rooms in this five-story hotel, which attracts families and business travelers, are plain but very clean, with light-wood furnishings and free local phone calls. Upper floors facing the airport and San Francisco have better views but are noisier when planes start flying early in the morning. ⊠ *777 Airport Blvd., Burlingame 94010,* ☏ *650/342–7772,* FAX *650/342–2635,* WEB *www.redroof.com. 213 rooms. Restaurant, pool, business services, airport shuttle, free parking, some pets allowed, no-smoking rooms. AE, D, DC, MC, V.*

5 NIGHTLIFE AND THE ARTS

A spirit of playfulness has pervaded San Francisco's arts, entertainment, and nightlife scenes ever since its days as a rowdy sailors' port. Perhaps nothing is more purely San Franciscan than *Beach Blanket Babylon* at Club Fugazi, a hilarious cabaret that parodies local moods and mores. In addition, the San Francisco Opera, the San Francisco Symphony, and the San Francisco Ballet are all nationally renowned, while dozens of alternative groups represent everything from gay and lesbian performance art to family circus and mime.

NIGHTLIFE

Updated by
Sharron Wood

S AN FRANCISCO HAS A TREMENDOUS VARIETY of evening entertainment, from ultrasophisticated piano bars to come-as-you-
are dives that reflect the city's gold-rush past. Although it's hard
to generalize about this compact city where the prevailing influences
of some neighborhoods spill into others, the following regional categories should help you find the kind of entertainment you're looking
for. **Nob Hill** is noted for its plush hotel bars and panoramic skyline
lounges. **North Beach,** though it still has a short stretch of strip clubs
along Broadway, has cleaned up its image considerably, and it is now
known for historic bars that invoke the city's beatnik past as well as
sleek cocktail lounges. **Fisherman's Wharf,** although touristy, is great
for people-watching and is convenient to many hotels. Tony **Union Street**
and the nearby **Marina** are where you'll find singles bars that attract
well-dressed crowds in their twenties and thirties. South of Market—
SoMa, for short—is a hub of nightlife, with a bevy of popular dance
clubs, bars, and supper clubs, as well as a few excellent venues for live
music. The gay and lesbian scenes center on the **Castro District** and the
clubs and bars along **Polk Street.** Twentysomethings and alternative
types should check out the ever-funky **Mission District** and **Haight
Street** scenes, though even these two neighborhoods have more upscale
cocktail lounges and fewer dive bars every year.

For information on who is performing where, check out the *San Francisco Chronicle*'s pink "Datebook" insert—or consult the *San Francisco Bay Guardian,* free and available in racks around the city, listing
neighborhood, avant-garde, and budget-priced events. The *SF Weekly*
is also free and packed with information on arts events around town.
Another handy reference is the weekly magazine *Where,* offered free
in most major hotel lobbies and at Hallidie Plaza (Market and Powell Sts.).

Except at some hotel lounges, dressing up is not expected, though at
most nightspots jeans are the exception and stylish dress is the norm.
Of course, stylish means a sleek black designer outfit at one place and
a vintage jacket and motorcycle boots at another, so you'll have to use
your judgment. A 1998 state law banned smoking in any indoor place
of work—including all bars and clubs. Though bartenders in many bars
tolerate smoking, the police, officially, do not, and anyone caught
smoking may be fined. Bars generally close between midnight and 2
AM, though those in the Financial District, which cater to an after-work
crowd, may stop serving as early as 10 PM. Bands and other performers usually begin between 8 PM and 11 PM. The cover charge at smaller
clubs ranges from $3 to $10, and credit cards are rarely accepted. At
the larger venues the cover may go up to $30, and tickets can often be
purchased through **Tickets.com** (☎ 415/776–1999 or 510/762–2277).

No-Fault Nightspots
Detailed descriptions of the following clubs can be found within listings for each category.

Cabaret: Club Fugazi's *Beach Blanket Babylon* revue has been going
strong for more than 20 years. Judging by the sellout crowds nearly
every night, they must be doing something right.

Comedy: Go where your favorite comics are. Cobb's Comedy Club is
a good bet.

Dancing Emporiums: El Rio dances to a world beat on Fridays and other genres throughout the week. Serious swing and ballroom dancers attend weekend events at Metronome Ballroom.

Jazz: Sophisticated acts perform in a romantic atmosphere at Jazz at Pearl's. The very biggest names in jazz, though, are at Yoshi's, in Oakland.

Piano Bars: The clubby Big Four Bar is a romantic spot to listen to a piano player over a snifter of fine brandy.

Rock/Pop/Folk/Blues: Slim's, which books the top artists in each of these areas, is one of SoMa's most popular nightclubs. For more cutting-edge rock, Bottom of the Hill is a popular spot in Potrero Hill, while the Fillmore and Warfield grab the lion's share of touring national acts.

Singles Bars: Gordon Biersch is the spot for a beer and a flirt.

Skyline Bars: Harry Denton's Starlight Room is *the* romantic room with a view.

Cabarets

San Francisco's modest cabaret scene tends toward the outlandish, with the cross-dressing, lip-synching waitresses at asiaSF as a case in point. The only traditional cabaret is to be found at the Plush Room, where the sultry Paula West often sings to appreciative crowds.

asiaSF (⊠ 201 9th St., at Howard St., South of Market, ☎ 415/255–2742) is the hottest place in town for saucy, sexy fun. The entertainment, as well as gracious food service, is provided by "gender illusionists." These gorgeous men don daring dresses and strut in impossibly high heels on top of the bar, which serves as a catwalk, vamping to such tunes as *Cabaret* and *Big Spender*. The creative Asian-influenced cuisine is excellent.

Club Fugazi (⊠ 678 Green St., at Powell St., North Beach, ☎ 415/421–4222) is famous for *Beach Blanket Babylon,* a wacky musical revue that has become the longest-running show of its genre. A send-up of San Francisco moods and mores, *Beach Blanket* has run since 1974. Although the choreography is colorful, the singers brassy, and the songs witty, the real stars are the comically exotic costumes and famous ceiling-high "hats"—worth the price of admission in themselves. Order tickets as far in advance as possible. The revue has been sold out up to a month in advance. Those under 21 are admitted only to the Sunday matinee.

The **Marsh** (⊠ 1062 Valencia St., near 22nd St., Mission, ☎ 415/826–5750) books an eclectic mix of alternative and avant-garde theater, performance art, comedy, and the occasional musical act, with an emphasis on solo performances and seldom-staged plays. The room is homey and dimly lighted, and you can purchase freshly baked treats and excellent coffee at intermission.

Plush Room (⊠ 940 Sutter St., between Leavenworth and Hyde Sts., Tenderloin, ☎ 415/885–2800), in the York Hotel, is an intimate cabaret space that began in the 1920s as a speakeasy. The luster may have faded a bit, but the 120-seat room still books some excellent talent, such as Bay Area favorites Paula West and Wesla Whitfield. While the edges may be tattered, the crowd that frequents the Plush Room likes to put on the Ritz and quaff a martini or two. Cover charges range from $20 to $25, and there is a two-drink minimum.

Comedy Clubs

Despite San Francisco's diverse arts and entertainment scene, its comedy scene is rather limp. Big-name acts, however, often perform at its two main comedy clubs.

As well as teaching workshops in improvisation, **Bay Area Theatresports** (✉ Fort Mason, Bldg. B, Fisherman's Wharf, ☎ 415/474–8935) stages performances like "Improvised Shakespeare" and "Spontaneous Broadway." You never know quite what you're going to get, but tickets are reasonably priced.

Cobb's Comedy Club (✉ 2801 Leavenworth St., at Beach St., Fisherman's Wharf, ☎ 415/928–4320), in the Cannery, books such stand-up comics as Greg Proops, Will Durst, and Janeane Garofalo.

Punch Line (✉ 444 Battery St., between Clay and Washington Sts., Financial District, ☎ 415/397–7573), a launching pad for the likes of Jay Leno and Whoopi Goldberg, has some of the area's top talents. Recent headliners have included Margaret Cho and Jay Mohr. Those 18 and over are admitted.

Dance Clubs

Many of the rock, blues, and jazz clubs listed below have active dance floors. Some also have DJ dancing when live acts aren't performing.

El Rio (✉ 3158 Mission St., between Cesar Chavez and Valencia Sts., Mission, ☎ 415/282–3325) is a casual Mission District spot with a range of acts, from an open mike Tuesday to Arab dance music on Thursday and a packed world music dance party on Friday. Live bands play on Saturday. No matter what day you attend, expect to find a diverse crowd.

Metronome Ballroom (✉ 1830 17th St., at De Haro St., Potrero Hill, ☎ 415/252–9000), where lessons in all sorts of ballroom dance are given every day, is at its most lively on weekend nights, when ballroom, Latin, and swing dancers come for lessons and revelry. This alcohol-free spot is lively but mellow.

Rawhide II (✉ 280 7th St., between Howard and Folsom Sts., South of Market, ☎ 415/621–1197), formerly a gay country-and-western bar, has been transformed into a venue for a rotating lineup of DJ dance events, each attracting a different crowd. Low cover charges and an intimate atmosphere make it a popular spot.

Roccapulco (✉ 3140 Mission St., between Precita and Cesar Chavez Sts., Mission, ☎ 415/648–6611), a cavernous Mission District Dance hall and restaurant that brings in crowds, has live music and salsa dancing on Friday and Saturday. Look for salsa lessons on Wednesday, gay and lesbian dancing on Thursday.

330 Ritch Street (✉ 330 Ritch St., between 3rd and 4th Sts., South of Market, ☎ 415/541–9574), a popular SoMa nightclub with a stylish modern look, has an extensive tapas menu, a dance floor, and extremely varied music lineup; soul, R&B, salsa, and Brit pop music are only some of the styles you'll hear here. The club is closed on Monday and Tuesday nights.

Jazz

Though not as renowned for its jazz clubs as cities like New York or Paris, San Francisco has a respectable jazz scene, with local artists pushing the borders between jazz, swing, hip-hop, and funk. Check the Rock, Pop, Folk, and Blues venues below for special jazz events. Other op-

134

Above Paradise 77
asiaSF 53
Backflip 44
Balboa Cafe 88
Bay Area
Theatresports 1
Beach Chalet 81
Big Four Bar 18
Bimbo's 365 Club . .6
Bix 26
Blue Bar 24
Boom Boom Room . .85
Bubble Lounge 27
Buena Vista Café 2
Carnelian Room 30
The Cinch 12
Cityscape 65
A Clean
Well-Lighted
Place for Books 45
Club Fugazi 9
Club Q 71
Cobb's Comedy
Club 4
Curran Theater 62
Davies Symphony
Hall 51
Divas 57
Eagle Tavern 74
Edinburgh Castle 58
Embarcadero
Center Cinemas 39
Enrico's 20
Equinox 38
Exit Theatre 66
The Fillmore 84
Geary Theater 63
Girl Spot/End Up . . .73
Golden Gate
Theater 56
Gordon Biersch
Brewery and
Restaurant 42
Grand Views 37
Great American
Music Hall 43
Harrington's 41
Harry Denton's
Rouge 11
Harry Denton's
Starlight Room 36
Hayes and Vine 50
Herbst Theatre 47
Holding
Company 40
Hollywood
Billiards 55
Jazz at Pearl's 21
Justice League 80
Kimo's 16
Last Day Saloon 86
London Wine Bar . . .29

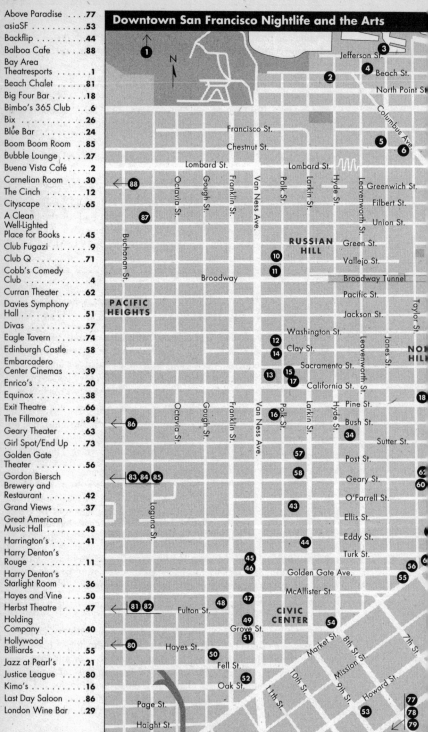

Downtown San Francisco Nightlife and the Arts

Lorraine Hansberry
Theatre 35
Lou's Pier 47 3
Lumière 17
Marines Memorial
Theatre 59
Moose's 8
N Touch 15
New Conservatory
Theatre 52
Old First
Presbyterian
Church 13
Opera Plaza
Cinemas 46
Orpheum Theater . . .54
Ovation 48
Paradise Lounge 79
Perry's 87
Phineas T.
Barnacle 83
Pier 23 7
Plush Room 34
Punch Line 28
Rawhide II 76
Red Devil Lounge . . .14
Redwood Room 60
Ritz-Carlton 31
Royal Oak 10
The Saloon 19
San Francisco
Art Institute 5
Seasons Bar 68
Slim's 78
Specs' 23
Stage Door
Theater 64
Storyville 82
The Stud 75
Theatre on the
Square 61
330 Ritch Street 72
The Tonga Room 33
Top of the Mark 32
Tosca Café 25
Vesuvio Café 22
View Lounge 69
The Warfield 67
War Memorial
Opera House 49
Yerba Buena
Center for the
Arts 70

tions run the gamut from mellow restaurant cocktail lounges to hip SoMa venues.

Blue Bar (✉ 501 Broadway, at Columbus Ave., North Beach, ☎ 415/981–2233), tucked beneath the retro Beat-generation restaurant Black Cat, finds thirty- and fortysomethings lounging in funky aqua armchairs around Formica tables. A dreamy blue light infuses the intimate space. Live jazz bands play nightly, and a scaled-down version of Black Cat's menu is available until 12:15 AM.

Bruno's (✉ 2389 Mission St., at 20th St., Mission, ☎ 415/648–7701) serves Italian food in one room while local jazz bands perform in its two lounges. The long bar and the plush red booths are both comfortable spots to indulge in a swanky cocktail.

Cafe du Nord (✉ 2170 Market St., between Church and Sanchez Sts., Castro, ☎ 415/861–5016) hosts some of the coolest jazz, blues, rock, and alternative sounds in town. The basement poolroom bar is "speakeasy hip." The music, provided mostly by local talent, is strictly top-notch. DJ events take place a few nights a week.

Elbo Room (✉ 647 Valencia St., between 17th and 18th Sts., Mission, ☎ 415/552–7788) is a convivial spot to hear up-and-coming jazz acts upstairs, or to relax in the dark, moody bar downstairs. DJ mixes, Brazilian jazz, world music, and the occasional funk band round out the musical offerings.

Enrico's (✉ 504 Broadway, at Kearny St., North Beach, ☎ 415/982–6223) was the city's hippest North Beach hangout after its 1958 opening. Following the retirement of famed owner Enrico Banducci—who also brought Woody Allen, Barbra Streisand, and Lenny Bruce to his late, lamented "hungry i" in the early 1960s—the luster faded. Today it's hip once again, with an indoor-outdoor café, a fine menu (tapas and Italian), and mellow nightly jazz combos.

Jazz at Pearl's (✉ 256 Columbus Ave., near Broadway, North Beach, ☎ 415/291–8255) is one of the few reminders of North Beach's heady beatnik days. With mostly straight-ahead jazz acts and dim lighting, this club has a mellow feel. The talent level is remarkably high, especially considering that there is rarely a cover—though there is a two-drink minimum.

Kimball's East (✉ 5800 Shellmound St., Emeryville, ☎ 510/658–2555), in an East Bay shopping complex just off I–80, hosts such jazz, soul, and R&B talents as Regina Belle and Mose Allison. This supper club has an elegant interior and serves fine food.

Moose's (✉ 1652 Stockton St., near Union St., North Beach, ☎ 415/989–7800), one of North Beach's most popular restaurants, also has great music in its small but stylish bar area. Combos play classic jazz nightly from 8 PM, as well as during Sunday brunch.

Storyville (✉ 1751 Fulton St., between Central and Masonic Sts., Western Addition, ☎ 415/441–1751) is a dressy club showcasing hiphop, soul, funk, and progressive jazz, among other eclectic styles. The occasional live act breaks up the DJ dance nights. The kitchen serves up California-Creole cuisine.

Yoshi's (✉ 510 Embarcadero St., between Washington and Clay Sts., Oakland, ☎ 510/238–9200) is one of the area's best jazz venues. Dr. John and Charlie Hunter are just a few of the musicians who play here when they're in town.

Piano Bars

You only have eyes for her . . . or him. Five quiet spots are perfect for holding hands and making plans.

The **Big Four Bar** (✉ 1075 California St., Nob Hill, ☎ 415/474–5400), on the ground floor of the Huntington Hotel, is a quietly opulent spot for piano music daily from 5:30 PM to around 11:30. The elegant, dimly lit spot has polished wood and brass, green leather chairs, and a carved ceiling.

Grand Views (✉ 345 Stockton St., at Sutter St., Union Square, ☎ 415/398–1234), on the 36th floor of the Grand Hyatt, has piano music Tuesday–Saturday from 7 PM, and a view of North Beach and the bay.

Ovation (✉ 333 Fulton St., near Franklin St., Hayes Valley, ☎ 415/553–8100), in the Inn at the Opera hotel, is a popular spot for a romantic rendezvous, especially weekends, when the pianist is playing. The focal point of this tastefully appointed, intimate restaurant-lounge is a crackling fireplace. The menu has American grill specialties with an emphasis on seafood.

The **Ritz-Carlton** (✉ 600 Stockton St., at Pine St., Nob Hill, ☎ 415/296–7465) has a tastefully appointed lobby lounge where a harpist plays during high tea (roughly 3–4:30) and a jazz trio or a pianist plays Thursday to Sunday evenings.

Seasons Bar (✉ 757 Market St., between 3rd and 4th Sts., South of Market, ☎ 415/633–3000) echoes the muted tones and elegant furnishings of the coolly minimalist Four Season Hotel, opened in 2001. Discreet staff in dark suits serve cocktails and salty nibbles like olives, while a piano player entertains, usually Tuesday through Sunday evenings.

Rock, Pop, Folk, and Blues

In the hip SoMa neighborhood and elsewhere, musical offerings range from straight-up rock to retro jazz to utter cacophony.

Bimbo's 365 Club (✉ 1025 Columbus Ave., at Chestnut St., North Beach, ☎ 415/474–0365), in the same location since 1951, has a plush main room and an adjacent lounge that retain a retro vibe perfect for the "Cocktail Nation" programming that keeps the crowds hopping.

Boom Boom Room (✉ 1601 Fillmore St., at Geary Blvd., Japantown, ☎ 415/673–8000) continues to attract old-timers and hipsters alike with top-notch blues acts. It's hard to go wrong no matter which night you show up. Live bands play nightly.

Bottom of the Hill (✉ 1233 17th St., at Texas St., Potrero Hill, ☎ 415/621–4455) showcases some of the city's best local alternative rock. Though it's ultra-low-key, the occasional blockbuster act—Alanis Morissette, Pearl Jam—has been known to hop on stage.

The **Fillmore** (✉ 1805 Geary Blvd., at Fillmore St., Western Addition, ☎ 415/346–6000), San Francisco's most famous rock music hall, serves up a varied menu of national and local acts: rock, reggae, grunge, jazz, folk, acid house, and more. Most tickets range from $20 to $30, and some shows are all-ages. Avoid steep service charges by buying tickets at the Fillmore box office on Sunday between 10 and 4.

Freight and Salvage Coffee House (✉ 1111 Addison St., Berkeley, ☎ 510/548–1761), one of the finest folk houses in the country, is worth a trip across the bay. Some of the most talented practitioners of folk,

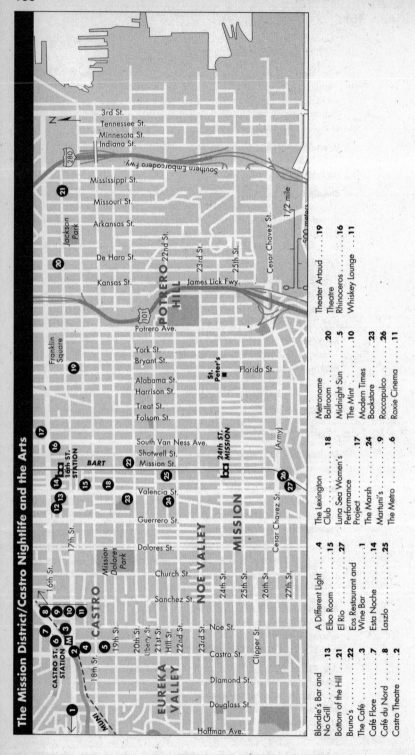

blues, Cajun, and bluegrass perform in this alcohol-free space, where most tickets range from $15.50 to $18.50.

Great American Music Hall (⊠ 859 O'Farrell St., between Polk and Larkin Sts., Tenderloin, ☎ 415/885–0750) is a great eclectic nightclub. Here you can find top-drawer entertainment, with acts running the gamut from the best in blues, folk, and jazz to alternative rock. The colorful marble-pillared emporium (built in 1907 as a bordello) also accommodates dancing at some shows. Pub grub is available most nights.

At the **Justice League** (⊠ 628 Divisadero St., near Hayes St., Western Addition, ☎ 415/289–2038), you'll find live jazz, hip-hop, funk, and world grooves, as well as DJ-driven dance nights. Hipsters of many ages relax in the decidedly urban interior, hand-painted by local graffiti artist Twist.

Last Day Saloon (⊠ 406 Clement St., between 5th and 6th Aves., Richmond, ☎ 415/387–6343) hosts major entertainers and rising local bands performing blues, Cajun, funk, country, or jazz.

Lou's Pier 47 (⊠ 300 Jefferson St., at Jones St., Fisherman's Wharf, ☎ 415/771–0377) is the place for jazz, blues, and hot Cajun seafood on the waterfront nightly. Bands typically start playing in the late afternoon and continue until midnight.

Paradise Lounge (⊠ 1501 Folsom St., at 11th St., South of Market, ☎ 415/621–1912), a quirky lounge with three stages for eclectic live music, DJ events, and dancing, also has beyond-the-fringe performances at the adjoining Transmission Theatre. It's a long-favored hangout for San Francisco's alternative scenesters, 21 and over only.

Pier 23 (⊠ Pier 23, at the Embarcadero, Fisherman's Wharf, ☎ 415/362–5125), a waterfront restaurant by day, turns into a packed club Wednesday through Saturday nights, with a musical spectrum ranging from Caribbean and salsa to Motown and reggae. Look for salsa dance classes on Wednesday.

Red Devil Lounge (⊠ 1695 Polk St., at Clay St., Van Ness/Polk, ☎ 415/921–1695) is a plush lounge where local and up-and-coming funk, rock, and jazz acts perform. There's also DJ dancing and the occasional open-mike night. Intimate tables line the narrow balcony overlooking the dance floor.

The **Saloon** (⊠ 1232 Grant Ave., near Columbus Ave., North Beach, ☎ 415/989–7666) is a favorite blues and rock spot among North Beach locals in the know.

Slim's (⊠ 333 11th St., between Harrison and Folsom Sts., South of Market, ☎ 415/522–0333), one of SoMa's most popular nightclubs, specializes in national touring acts—mostly classic rock, blues, jazz, and world music. Co-owner Boz Scaggs helps bring in the crowds and famous headliners.

The **Warfield** (⊠ 982 Market St., at 6th St., Civic Center, ☎ 415/775–7722), once a movie palace, is one of the city's largest rock-and-roll venues. There are tables and chairs downstairs and theater seating upstairs. Performers range from Porno for Pyros to Suzanne Vega to Nick Cave and the Bad Seeds.

Singles Bars

Ever notice how everyone looks so much better when you're visiting another town? Here's where the magic may happen for you.

Balboa Cafe (⊠ 3199 Fillmore St., at Greenwich St., Marina, ☎ 415/ 921–3944), a jam-packed hangout for the young and upwardly mobile crowd, is famous for its burgers and its single clientele.

Gordon Biersch Brewery and Restaurant (⊠ 2 Harrison St., at the Embarcadero, South of Market, ☎ 415/243–8246) is a favorite of the swinging under-thirty set on Friday. The upstairs dining room and microbrewery beer is a nightly draw for adults of all ages.

Harry Denton's Rouge (⊠ 1500 Broadway, at Polk St., Russian Hill, ☎ 415/346–7683) is the newest of bon vivant Harry Denton's nightspots. A mostly older, out-of-town set, dressed to the nines, fills the booths at dinnertime, though the crowd gets younger as the dancing begins later in the evening. Dramatic red curtains, dozens of sparkling chandeliers, and Vegas-style showgirls create a glitzy scene.

Holding Company (⊠ 2 Embarcadero Center, at Front and Clay Sts., Financial District, ☎ 415/986–0797), one of the most popular weeknight Financial District watering holes, is where scores of office workers gather to enjoy friendly libations. Open weekdays only, the Holding Company stays busy from lunch through early evening but tends to empty out by 9 PM.

Perry's (⊠ 1944 Union St., at Laguna St., Cow Hollow, ☎ 415/922– 9022), one of San Francisco's oldest singles bars, is usually jam-packed. You can dine here on great hamburgers as well as more substantial fare.

Royal Oak (⊠ 2201 Polk St., at Vallejo St., Russian Hill, ☎ 415/928– 2303) has a comfortable, clubby feel, with Tiffany-style lamps and ferns cascading down the walls. Arrive early to snag a seat on one of the red velvet couches.

Skyline and Ocean-view Bars

San Francisco is a city of spectacular vistas. Enjoy drinks, music, and sometimes dinner with views of the city or the Pacific Ocean at any of the bars below.

The **Beach Chalet** (⊠ 1000 Great Hwy., near Martin Luther King Jr. Dr., Outer Sunset, ☎ 415/386–8439), in a historic building filled with Works Project Administration murals, brews its own beers, like its golden Playland Pale Ale. Enjoy them with American bistro food and a stunning view overlooking the Pacific Ocean. If possible, time your visit to coincide with the sunset.

Carnelian Room (⊠ 555 California St., at Kearny St., Financial District, ☎ 415/433–7500), on the 52nd floor of the Bank of America Building, has what is perhaps the loftiest view of San Francisco's magnificent skyline. Enjoy dinner or cocktails at 779 ft above the ground; reservations are a must for dinner. The dress code requires jackets, but ties are optional.

Cityscape (⊠ 333 O'Farrell St., at Mason St., Union Square, ☎ 415/ 771–1400), on the 46th floor of the Hilton Hotel, serves dinner nightly until around 10 PM, then has dancing to tunes from the 1970s, '80s, and '90s until 12:30 or 1 AM.

Equinox (⊠ 5 Embarcadero Center, Embarcadero, ☎ 415/788–1234), an expensive restaurant and cocktail lounge on the 22nd floor of the Hyatt Regency, is popular with out-of-towners despite spotty service and mediocre cocktails because of its revolving platform with 360° views of the city. You can sightsee, eat, and drink, all from the comfort of your own chair.

Grand Views (☞ Piano Bars, *above*).

Harry Denton's Starlight Room (✉ 450 Powell St., between Post and Sutter Sts., Union Square, ☎ 415/395–8595), on the 21st floor of the Sir Francis Drake Hotel, re-creates the 1950s high life with rose-velvet booths and romantic lighting. DJ events during the week are replaced by Harry Denton's Starlight Orchestra Thursday through Saturday nights. Jackets are preferred for gentlemen.

Phineas T. Barnacle (✉ 1090 Point Lobos Ave., at the western end of Geary Blvd., Richmond, ☎ 415/666–4016), inside the Cliff House, provides a close-up view of the Pacific Ocean and the Marin Headlands.

Top of the Mark (✉ 999 California St., at Mason St., Nob Hill, ☎ 415/616–6916), in the Mark Hopkins Inter-Continental, was immortalized by a famous magazine photograph as a hot spot for World War II servicemen on leave or about to ship out. Bands play a mix of jazz, swing, and blues. There's an entertainment charge of $5, $10 on Friday and Saturday nights.

View Lounge (✉ 55 4th St., between Mission and Market Sts., South of Market, ☎ 415/896–1600), on the 39th floor of the San Francisco Marriott, has superb views through art deco–influenced windows. There's live piano music Monday–Thursday, and bands play Friday and Saturday.

Spoken Word

Nearly every night of the week, aspiring and established writers, poets, and performers step up to the mike and put their words and egos on the line. Check the listings section of the free alternative weekly papers and the *San Francisco Sunday Chronicle* "Book Review" section for more exhaustive options.

Above Paradise (✉ 308 11th St., at Folsom St., South of Market, ☎ 415/621–1912), on the top floor of SoMa's Paradise Lounge, hosts poetry readings every Sunday at 9.

City Arts and Lectures (☎ 415/392–4400) hosts more than 20 fascinating conversations a year with writers, composers, actors, politicians, and others. Events are usually held at the **Herbst Theatre** (✉ 401 Van Ness Ave., Civic Center). Past speakers include Jane Goodall, Salman Rushdie, Oliver Sacks, Ken Burns, and Joan Didion.

A Clean Well-Lighted Place for Books (✉ 601 Van Ness Ave., between Turk St. and Golden Gate Ave., Civic Center ☎ 415/441–6670) has free author readings and signings four to five times a week, ranging from strictly literary figures to such celebrities as Tony Bennett and luminaries like Jimmy Carter.

A Different Light (✉ 489 Castro St., between 18th and Market Sts., Castro, ☎ 415/431–0891) is host to a multitude of literary events each month, including author readings and book-release parties. Most of the material is by or about the gay and lesbian community. All are welcome. Flyers at the store announce the occasional open-mike nights.

Luna Sea Women's Performance Project (✉ 2940 16th St., No. 216C, between Capp St. and S. Van Ness Ave., Mission, ☎ 415/863–2989), a gallery and theater space amid the burgeoning Mission District arts scene, has an ever-changing lineup of women-themed projects, including visual arts displays, performance art, and readings. Some events are for women only.

Modern Times Bookstore (✉ 888 Valencia St., at 20th St., Mission, ☎ 415/282–9246), in the heart of the Mission District, hosts writers about six times a month for readings, question-and-answer sessions, and book signings.

West Coast Live (✉ 915 Cole St., Cole Valley, ☎ 415/664–9500), billed as "San Francisco's Live Radio Show to the World," invites an audience to the weekly live broadcasts, many at Fort Mason's Cowell Theater. The ever-changing guest list regularly includes author Anne Lamott, monologuist Josh Kornbluth, and improvisational theater troupe True Fiction Magazine, as well as appearances by various celebs passing through town.

Wine Bars

Why not forgo that frothy pint of beer for the more sedate pleasures of the vine? These spots offer tasting "flights," wines grouped together by type for contrast and comparison.

Bubble Lounge (✉ 714 Montgomery St., at Washington St., North Beach, ☎ 415/434–4204), an upscale yet comfortable champagne bar, attracts a Financial District crowd. Upstairs, young executives nestle into wing chairs and overstuffed couches, while downstairs a lively atmosphere surrounds the pool table and another bar. Champagne is this lounge's raison d'être and the selection is excellent, with more than 300 types to choose from. A full bar is also available, as are sushi, caviar, and other delicate nibbles.

Eos Restaurant and Wine Bar (✉ 901 Cole St., at Carl St., Haight, ☎ 415/566–3063) is a cozy space with more than 400 wines by the bottle and more than 40 by the glass. Guest speakers introduce the week's new wine flight every Wednesday 6:30 PM–8:30 PM. The adjoining restaurant's full menu of excellent East-West fusion cuisine is available at the bar.

Hayes and Vine (✉ 377 Hayes St., at Gough St., Hayes Valley, ☎ 415/626–5301) has a warm lounge, dominated by a stunning white-onyx bar, where you can relax and taste a few of the 1,100 wines available by the bottle or the 40 selections served by the glass. Cheeses, pâtés, and caviar are served.

London Wine Bar (✉ 415 Sansome St., between Clay and Sacramento Sts., Financial District, ☎ 415/788–4811), open on weekdays only, seems more a cozy pub than a snooty wine bar. Bartenders pour 30 to 40 wines by the glass from their extensive cellar, especially strong in wines from small California wineries.

San Francisco's Favorite Bars

Locals patronize many of the places listed above, but there are several joints they hold near and dear.

Backflip (✉ 601 Eddy St., at Larkin St., Civic Center, ☎ 415/771–3547), attached to the hipster Phoenix Hotel near the sketchy Tenderloin, is a clubhouse for a space-age rat pack—a combination of aqua-tiled retro and Jetsons-attired waitresses and bartenders. The mixed crowd circling the round bar is definitely trendy, but the mood remains friendly. Take in the funky details, such as the waterfall behind the glass wall in the restaurant and the pool and cabana on the patio.

Bix (✉ 56 Gold St., off Montgomery St., North Beach, ☎ 415/433–6300) is a spirited, elegant supper club with live jazz combos. A densely packed crowd in the small bar area is a mix of nattily dressed diners waiting for their table and small groups who have just stopped in to enjoy one of Bix's famous martinis.

Blondies' Bar and No Grill (⊠ 540 Valencia St., near 16th St., Mission, ☎ 415/864–2419) hosts a mix of DJ grooves and live jazz and swing. A rare enclosed "smoking lounge" in the back makes it a favorite of those who like to light up. Monster martinis are a specialty.

Buena Vista Café (⊠ 2765 Hyde St., at Beach St., Fisherman's Wharf, ☎ 415/474–5044), the wharf area's most popular bar, introduced Irish coffee to the New World—or so it says. Because it has a fine view of the waterfront, it's usually packed with tourists.

Edinburgh Castle (⊠ 950 Geary St., between Larkin and Polk Sts., Tenderloin, ☎ 415/885–4074) is a dark, cavernous spot with several seating areas. You can work off your fish-and-chips and Scottish brews with a turn at the dartboard or pool table. Live music alternates with spoken-word events and even Scottish cultural events (January's Robert Burns celebration is a favorite).

Harrington's (⊠ 245 Front St., near Sacramento St., Financial District, ☎ 415/392–7595), a comfortable family-owned Irish saloon, is a no-attitude place for an after-work drink. The restaurant, open Monday through Saturday, serves American fare.

Attached to the restaurant Foreign Cinema, **Laszlo** (⊠ 2532 Mission St., between 21st and 22nd Sts., Mission, ☎ 415/401–0810), with its bilevel design, dim lighting, and candles on each table, is a great spot for a romantic tête-à-tête over a classy cocktail or single malt whisky. DJs spin most nights after 9 PM.

The venerable **Redwood Room** (⊠ 495 Geary St., at Taylor St., Union Square, ☎ 415/929–2372) reopened in 2001 after extensive renovations by über-hip designer Philippe Starck. Bizarre video installations, sleek (though not necessarily comfortable) seating, a lush monochromatic look, and a host of glamorous patrons in the arts and entertainment mean it's tough to get in many nights.

Specs' (⊠ 12 Saroyan Pl., off Columbus Ave., North Beach, ☎ 415/421–4112), a hidden hangout for artists, poets, and other heavy drinkers, is worth looking for. It's an old-fashioned watering hole, conveying a sense of the North Beach of days gone by.

The **Tonga Room** (⊠ 950 Mason St., at California St., Nob Hill, ☎ 415/772–5278), on the Fairmont hotel's terrace level, has given San Francisco a taste of high Polynesian kitsch for more than 50 years. Fake palm trees, grass huts, a lagoon (three-piece combos play pop standards on a floating barge), and faux monsoons—courtesy of sprinkler-system rain and simulated thunder and lightning—grow more surreal as you quaff some fruity cocktails. The weekday happy hour (5 PM–7 PM) includes a $6 buffet of Asian finger foods.

Tosca Café (⊠ 242 Columbus Ave., near Broadway, North Beach, ☎ 415/391–1244), like Specs' and Vesuvio nearby, holds a special place in San Francisco lore. It has an Italian flavor, with opera, big band, and Italian standards on the jukebox, plus an antique espresso machine that's nothing less than a work of art. Celebrities are known to stop by when they're in town.

Vesuvio Café (⊠ 255 Columbus Ave., at Broadway, North Beach, ☎ 415/362–3370), near the legendary City Lights Bookstore, is little altered since its 1960s heyday. The second-floor balcony is a fine vantage point for watching the colorful Broadway-Columbus intersection. Another part of its appeal is its always-mixed clientele, from neighborhood regulars to young couples on dates to groups celebrating special occasions.

Gay and Lesbian Nightlife

In the days before the gay liberation movement, bars were more than mere watering holes. They also served as community centers where members of a mostly undercover minority could network and socialize. In the 1960s they became hotbeds of political activity. The Tavern Guild of San Francisco, comprising the town's major gay establishments, achieved several of the community's first political victories, waging and winning a legal and public relations battle to end police harassment. Even teetotaling gays benefited from the confrontation. By the 1970s other social opportunities became available to gay men and lesbians, and the bars' importance as centers of activity decreased.

Old-timers may wax nostalgic about the vibrancy of pre-AIDS, 1970s bar life, but you can still have plenty of fun today. The one difference is the one-night-a-week operation of some of the best clubs, which may cater to a different (sometimes straight) clientele on other nights. This type of club tends to come and go, so it's best to pick up one of the two main gay papers. The **Bay Area Reporter** (☎ 415/861–5019) is a biweekly newspaper that lists gay and lesbian events in its calendar. The **San Francisco Bay Times** (☎ 415/626–0260) is an award-winning paper aimed at gay and lesbian readers.

Of course, there's more to gay nightlife than the bars. Most nights **Theatre Rhinoceros** (☎ 415/861–5079) has plays and solo shows on two stages. Check the gay papers for other cultural and miscellaneous activities, such as sports clubs, social groups, and readings.

Gay Male Bars

"A bar for every taste, that's the ticket" was how the curious "documentary" *Gay San Francisco* described late-1960s nightlife here. Leather bars, drag-queen hangouts, piano bars, and bohemian cafés were among the many options for gay men back then. The scene remains just as versatile today. Unless otherwise noted, there is no cover charge at the following establishments.

IN THE CASTRO

The **Café** (✉ 2367 Market St., at 17th St., Castro, ☎ 415/861–3846) is in the heart of the Castro. Always comfortable and often packed with a mixed gay, lesbian, and straight crowd, it's a place where you can chat quietly or dance, as you please. The rare outdoor deck means it's a favorite destination for smokers.

Café Flore (✉ 2298 Market St., at Noe St., Castro, ☎ 415/621–8579), more of a daytime destination, attracts a mixed crowd including poets, punks, and poseurs. You can mingle day and night at open-air tables or inside the glass walls over beer, wine, excellent coffee, or tea. A separate concessionaire serves surprisingly tasty food until 10 PM; breakfast is popular.

The **Metro** (✉ 3600 16th St., at Market St., Castro, ☎ 415/703–9750) is a semi-upscale bar with a balcony overlooking the intersection of Noe, 16th, and Market streets. Guppies (gay yuppies) love this place, especially since it has a fairly good restaurant adjoining the bar. Tuesday, Thursday, and Sunday are karaoke nights.

Midnight Sun (✉ 4067 18th St., at Castro St., Castro, ☎ 415/861–4186), one of the Castro's longest-standing and most popular bars, has riotously programmed giant video screens, showing a mix of old sitcoms, *Will* *and Grace* episodes, and musicals and show tunes. Don't expect to be able to hear yourself think.

Whiskey Lounge (✉ 4063 18th St., at Castro St., Castro, ☎ 415/255–2733), upstairs from the Red Grill, is a relative newcomer to the Castro bar scene. A faux fireplace and comfy leather chairs make this lounge far cozier than the many other bars along the block.

ON/NEAR POLK STREET

The **Cinch** (✉ 1723 Polk St., between Washington and Clay Sts., Van Ness/Polk, ☎ 415/776–4162), a Wild West–theme neighborhood bar with pinball machines and pool tables, is one of several hosts of the gay San Francisco Pool Association's weekly matches. It's not the least bit trendy, which is part of its charm for those who regularly drink here.

Divas (✉ 1002 Post St., at Larkin St., Tenderloin, ☎ 415/928–6006), around the corner from the Polk Street bars in the rough-and-tumble Tenderloin, is *the* place for transvestites, transsexuals, and their admirers, with frequent stage performances.

Kimo's (✉ 1351 Polk St., at Pine St., Van Ness/Polk, ☎ 415/885–4535), a laid-back club, has floor-to-ceiling windows that provide a great view of Polk Street. On Friday and Saturday nights drag, cabaret, and comedy shows are held upstairs.

N Touch (✉ 1548 Polk St., at Sacramento St., Van Ness/Polk, ☎ 415/441–8413), a tiny dance bar, has long been popular with Asian–Pacific Islander gay men. Dancing, whether to '70s or '80s hits or contemporary house, is usually accompanied by go-go dancers. An amateur strip show during which patrons are encouraged to compete for prizes is held on Tuesday, and Monday is karaoke night.

THE SOMA SCENE

Eagle Tavern (✉ 398 12th St., at Harrison St., South of Market, ☎ 415/626–0880) is one of the few SoMa bars that remain from the days before AIDS and gentrification. Bikers are courted with endless drink specials. The Sunday-afternoon "Beer Busts" (3 PM–6 PM) are a social high point and benefit charitable organizations.

The **Stud** (✉ 399 9th St., at Harrison St., South of Market, ☎ 415/252–7883) is still going strong seven days a week more than 35 years after its opening in 1966. Each night's music is different—from funk, soul, and hip-hop to '80s tunes to favorites from the glory days of disco. On Tuesday, Trannyshack, a drag cabaret show, is held at midnight, and Friday brings an ever-changing lineup of women's events.

AROUND TOWN

Esta Noche (✉ 3079 16th St., near Valencia St., Mission, ☎ 415/861–5757), a longtime Mission District establishment, draws a steady crowd of Latino gays, including some of the city's wildest drag queens.

Martuni's (✉ 4 Valencia St., at Market St., Mission, ☎ 415/241–0205), an elegant, low-key bar at the intersection of the Castro, the Mission, and Hayes Valley, draws a mixed crowd that enjoys cocktails in a refined environment; variations on the martini are a specialty. In the back room, a pianist plays nightly; occasionally he's joined by cast members of musicals in town, who belt out favorites to an appreciative crowd in the intimate space.

The **Mint** (✉ 1942 Market St., between Duboce and Laguna Sts., Hayes Valley, ☎ 415/626–4726) attracts a mixed crowd that's very serious about its karaoke. Regulars sing everything from Simon and Garfunkel songs to disco classics in front of an attentive crowd, which gets straighter on the weekends.

Lesbian Bars

For a place known as a gay mecca, San Francisco has always suffered a surprising drought of seven-days-a-week women's bars. The meager selection is augmented by a few reliable one-nighters; call ahead to verify scheduling. Younger lesbians and gays don't segregate themselves quite as much as the older set. You'll find mixed crowds at a number of the bars listed under Gay Male Bars, *above*.

Club Q (⌧ 174 King St., at 3rd St., South of Market, ☎ 415/647–8258), a monthly (first Friday of every month) dance party from Paige Hodel's One Groove Productions, is the largest lesbian dance event in the Bay Area and is always packed. At press time the event was in a temporary location while they looked for a more permanent spot, but it's worth calling to see where the event has landed.

Hollywood Billiards (⌧ 61 Golden Gate Ave., near Taylor St., Tenderloin, ☎ 415/252–9643), a macho pool hall six nights a week, has become the unlikely host of a smoldering lesbian scene every Wednesday during its ladies' night.

Girl Spot (⌧ 401 6th St., at Harrison St., South of Market, ☎ 415/337–4962), at SoMa's End Up club, is held the third Saturday of every month. Call for information about the month's DJs and special events.

The **Lexington Club** (⌧ 3464 19th St., at Lexington St., Mission, ☎ 415/863–2052) is where, according to its slogan, "Every night is ladies' night." This all-girl club is geared toward the younger lesbian set.

Wild Side West (⌧ 424 Cortland Ave., between Mission and Bayshore Sts., Bernal Heights, ☎ 415/647–3099), though a bit out of the way, is a mellow neighborhood hangout where all are welcome and there's always a friendly pool game going on. It was once voted as the "Best Lesbian Bar for Everybody" by the *San Francisco Bay Guardian*.

THE ARTS

The best guide to arts and entertainment events in San Francisco is the "Datebook" section, printed on pink paper, in the *San Francisco Sunday Chronicle*. Also consult any of the free alternative weeklies.

Half-price, same-day tickets to many local and touring stage shows go on sale (cash only) at 11 AM from Tuesday through Saturday at the **TIX Bay Area** (☎ 415/433–7827) booth, inside the Geary Street entrance of the Union Square Garage, between Stockton and Powell streets. TIX is also a full-service ticket agency for theater and music events around the Bay Area (open Tuesday, Wednesday, and Thursday from 11 AM until 6 PM and Friday and Saturday until 7 PM).

The city's charge-by-phone ticket service is **Tickets.com** (☎ 415/776–1999 or 510/762–2277). **City Box Office** (⌧ 180 Redwood St., Suite 100, off Van Ness Ave. between Golden Gate Ave. and McAllister St., Civic Center, ☎ 415/392–4400) has a charge-by-phone service for many concerts and lectures. You can also buy tickets in person at its downtown location. The opera, symphony, the San Francisco Ballet's *Nutcracker,* and touring hit musicals are often sold out in advance. Tickets are usually available within a day of the performance for other shows.

Dance

Cal Performances and San Francisco Performances are the area's leading importers of world-class dance troupes.

More than 30 of the Bay Area's ethnic dance companies and soloists perform at the **Ethnic Dance Festival** (⌧ Palace of Fine Arts Theatre,

Bay and Lyon Sts., Marina, ☎ 415/474–3914), which takes place over three weekends in June. Prices are modest.

Oakland Ballet. Though its productions tend to be less extravagant than those of the San Francisco Ballet, the Oakland Ballet has earned an outstanding reputation for reviving and preserving masterworks from the early 20th century by re-creating historic dances by choreographers like Sergei Diaghilev and Bronisłava Nijinska. The company's fall season ends with its own *Nutcracker* in December. All performances are held at Oakland's **Paramount Theatre** (✉ 2025 Broadway, Oakland, ☎ 510/ 465–6400), near the 19th Street BART station. ☎ *510/452–9288.*

The **San Francisco Ballet** (✉ 301 Van Ness Ave., Civic Center, ☎ 415/ 865–2000) has regained much of its luster under artistic director Helgi Tomasson, and both classical and contemporary works have won admiring reviews. The company's primary season runs from February through May. Its repertoire includes such full-length ballets as *Swan Lake* and *Sleeping Beauty*; its annual December presentation of the *Nutcracker* is one of the most spectacular in the nation. The company also performs bold new dances from such star choreographers as William Forsythe and Mark Morris, alongside modern classics by George Balanchine and Jerome Robbins. Tickets and information are available at the **War Memorial Opera House** (✉ 301 Van Ness Ave., Civic Center).

The **Margaret Jenkins Dance Company** (☎ 415/826–8399) is a nationally acclaimed modern troupe. **Smuin Ballets/SF** (☎ 415/495–2234), founded by former San Francisco Ballet Director Michael Smuin, is renowned for its fluidity and excitement. The company regularly integrates pop music into its performances. **ODC/San Francisco** (☎ 415/ 863–6606) mounts an annual Yuletide version of *The Velveteen Rabbit* at the Center for the Arts. **Alonzo King's Lines Contemporary Ballet** (☎ 415/863–3360) has been performing in San Francisco since 1982, staging King's fluid ballets, sometimes in collaboration with musicians such as tabla master Zakir Hussain and saxophonist Pharoah Sanders. **Joe Goode Performance Group** (☎ 415/648–4848) is known for its physicality and high-flying style.

Film

The San Francisco Bay Area, including Berkeley and Marin County, is considered one of the nation's most important movie markets. Films of all sorts find an audience here. The area is also a filmmaking center: documentaries and experimental works are produced on modest budgets, feature films and television programs are shot on location, and some of Hollywood's biggest actors (including Robin Williams, Sharon Stone, and Danny Glover) live in the city. In San Francisco about a third of the theaters regularly show foreign and independent films.

The **Castro Theatre** (✉ 429 Castro St., near Market St., Castro, ☎ 415/ 621–6120), designed by Art Deco master Timothy Pfleuger, is worth visiting for its appearance alone. It hosts revivals as well as foreign and independent engagements. Extensive renovations completed in 2001 have made the city's most dramatic movie theater more comfortable, as well. Across the bay, the spectacular Art Deco **Paramount Theatre** (✉ 2025 Broadway, near 19th St. BART station, Oakland, ☎ 510/465– 6400) occasionally screens vintage flicks when it's not occupied by live music performances or the Oakland Ballet.

Foreign and Independent Films
Bridge (✉ 3010 Geary Blvd., at Blake St., Western Addition, ☎ 415/ 352–0810). **Clay** (✉ 2261 Fillmore St., at Clay St., Pacific Heights, ☎ 415/352–0810). **Embarcadero Center Cinemas** (✉ 1 Embarcadero

Center, Promenade level, Embarcadero, ☎ 415/352–0810). **Lumière** (⌧ 1572 California St., between Polk and Larkin Sts., Van Ness/Polk, ☎ 415/352–0810). **Opera Plaza Cinemas** (⌧ 601 Van Ness Ave., between Turk St. and Golden Gate Ave., Civic Center, ☎ 415/352–0810).

The **Roxie Cinema** (⌧ 3117 16th St., between Valencia and Guerrero Sts., Mission, ☎ 415/863–1087) specializes in film noir and new foreign and indie features. The avant-garde **Red Vic Movie House** (⌧ 1727 Haight St., between Cole and Shrader Sts., Haight, ☎ 415/668–3994) screens an adventurous lineup of contemporary and classic American and foreign titles in a funky setting. The **San Francisco Cinematheque** (☎ 415/822–2885) splits its experimental film and video schedule between the **San Francisco Art Institute** (⌧ 800 Chestnut St., at Jones St., Russian Hill) and the **Yerba Buena Center for the Arts** (⌧ 701 Mission St., at 3rd St., South of Market, ☎ 415/978–2787).

The **Pacific Film Archive** (⌧ 2575 Bancroft Way, near Bowditch St., Berkeley, ☎ 510/642–1124) screens a comprehensive mix of old and new American and foreign films.

Festivals

The **San Francisco International Film Festival** (☎ 415/931–3456) takes over several theaters for two weeks in late April and early May, primarily the Castro Theatre, the Pacific Film Archive, the Palace of Fine Arts, and the AMC Kabuki 8 Theatre at Post and Fillmore streets. The festival schedules about 150 films from around the globe, many of them American premieres. Marin County's **Mill Valley Film Festival** (☎ 415/383–5256), in early October, is also renowned.

The **Film Arts Festival of Independent Cinema** (☎ 415/552–8760), in early November, showcases Bay Area documentary and independent film talent. The **San Francisco International Lesbian and Gay Film Festival** (☎ 415/703–8650), the world's oldest and largest of its kind, takes place for two weeks in late June at various venues. The **San Francisco Jewish Film Festival** (☎ 415/621–0556) is held in late July. Look for the **San Francisco International Asian American Film Festival** (☎ 415/863–0814) in March. The **Festival Cine Latino** (☎ 415/553–8140) takes place in September. The **American Indian Film Festival** (☎ 415/554–0525), in November, is held at various venues, including the Palace of Fine Arts Theater.

Music

San Francisco's symphony, opera, and ballet all perform in the Civic Center area, where you'll also find the smaller, 928-seat Herbst Theater, host to many fine soloists and ensembles. Musical ensembles can be found all over the city: in churches and museums, in restaurants and parks, not to mention in Berkeley and on the peninsula. Each October, concert halls, clubs, and churches throughout the city host the acclaimed **San Francisco Jazz Festival** (☎ 415/398–5655), where both jazz legends and world-class up-and-comers perform.

Berkeley Symphony Orchestra. This East Bay ensemble has risen to considerable prominence under artistic director Kent Nagano's baton. The emphasis is on 20th-century composers, from Messiaen to Zappa, but more traditional pieces are also performed. The orchestra plays a handful of concerts each year from November through June, mostly in Zellerbach Hall. ⌧ *Zellerbach Hall, Telegraph Ave. and Bancroft Way, U.C. Berkeley campus, Berkeley,* ☎ 510/841–2800.

Cal Performances. This series, running from September through May at various U.C. Berkeley campus venues, offers the Bay Area's most varied bill of internationally acclaimed artists in all disciplines, from classical soloists to the latest jazz, world music, theater, and dance ensembles. The campus venues are the only Bay Area spots where you'll see performances by the wildly acclaimed Mark Morris Dance Group, which performs Zellerbach Hall several times a year. ⊠ *Zellerbach Hall, Bancroft Way and Telegraph Ave., Berkeley,* ☎ *510/642–9988.*

Chanticleer. This all-male a cappella ensemble is a Bay Area treasure. Lively and technically flawless performances show off a repertoire that ranges from sacred medieval music to show tunes to contemporary avant-garde works. ☎ *415/252–8589.*

42nd Street Moon Productions. This group produces delightful "semi-staged" revivals of rare chestnuts from Broadway's musical comedy golden age at the Eureka Theatre. Mini-seasons are irregularly scheduled throughout the year. ⊠ *215 Jackson St., between Front and Battery Sts., Financial District,* ☎ *415/255–8207.*

Kronos Quartet. Twentieth-century works and a number of premieres make up the programs for this always entertaining group. ☎ *415/731–3533.*

Old First Concerts. This well-respected Friday evening and Sunday afternoon series includes chamber music, choral works, vocal soloists, new music, and jazz. Phone for the reasonably priced tickets or visit the TIX booth in Union Square. ⊠ *Old First Presbyterian Church, 1751 Sacramento St., at Van Ness Ave., Van Ness/Polk,* ☎ *415/474–1608.*

Philharmonia Baroque. This ensemble has been called a local baroque orchestra with a national reputation and the nation's preeminent group for performances of early music. Its season of concerts, from fall through spring, celebrates composers of the 17th and 18th centuries, including Handel, Vivaldi, and Bach. ☎ *415/252–1288.*

San Francisco Performances. San Francisco's equivalent to Cal Performances brings an eclectic array of topflight global music and dance talents to various venues—mostly Yerba Buena Center for the Arts, Davies Symphony Hall, and Herbst Theatre. Recent artists include the Los Angeles Guitar Quartet, Anne-Sophie Mutter, and the Turtle Island String Quartet. ☎ *415/398–6449.*

San Francisco Symphony. The symphony performs from September through May, with additional summer performances of light classical musical and show tunes. Michael Tilson Thomas, who is known for his innovative programming of 20th-century American works, is the music director, and he and his orchestra often perform with soloists of the caliber of Andre Watts, Midori, and Renée Fleming. Tickets run $12–$100. ⊠ *Davies Symphony Hall, 201 Van Ness Ave., at Grove St., Civic Center,* ☎ *415/864–6000.*

St. Patrick's Catholic Church. This Gothic Revival building, completed in 1872 and rebuilt after the 1906 earthquake, hosts a notable chamber-music series on Wednesday at 12:30; suggested donation is $5. ⊠ *756 Mission St., between 3rd and 4th Sts., South of Market,* ☎ *415/777–3211.*

Stern Grove. The nation's oldest continual free summer music festival hosts Sunday afternoon performances of symphony, opera, jazz, pop music, and dance. The amphitheater is in a beautiful eucalyptus grove below street level, perfect for picnicking before the show. Dress for cool weather. ⊠ *Sloat Blvd. at 19th Ave., Sunset,* ☎ *415/252–6252.*

Summer in the City. Many members of the San Francisco symphony perform in the Summer in the City series in the 2,400-seat Davies Hall.

The schedule includes light classics and Broadway, country, and movie music. ✉ *Davies Symphony Hall, 201 Van Ness Ave., at Grove St., Civic Center,* ☎ *415/864–6000.*

Opera

Lamplighters. This operatic alternative specializes in Gilbert and Sullivan but presents other light operas as well. The troupe performs at various venues including the Yerba Buena Center for the Arts. ☎ *415/227–4797.*

Pocket Opera. This lively, modestly priced alternative to grand opera aims to bring opera to a broad audience. The concert performances of popular and seldom-heard works are mostly in English. Offenbach's operettas are frequently on the bill during the February–June season. Concerts are held at various locations. ☎ *415/972–8930.*

San Francisco Opera. Founded in 1923, this world-renowned company has resided in the Civic Center's War Memorial Opera House since it was built in 1932. Over its season, the opera presents approximately 70 performances of 10 to 12 operas from September through January and June through July. The opera uses supertitles: translations are projected above the stage during almost all non-English operas. Long considered a major international company and the most important operatic organization in the United States outside New York, the opera frequently embarks on coproductions with European opera companies. Ticket prices range from about $23 to $165. Standing-room tickets ($10) are sold at 10 AM for same-day performances, and patrons often sell extra tickets on the Opera House steps just before curtain time at face value or less. The full-time box office is at 199 Grove Street, at Van Ness Avenue. ✉ *301 Van Ness Ave., at Grove St., Civic Center,* ☎ *415/864–3330.*

Theater

San Francisco's theaters are concentrated on Geary Street west of Union Square, but a number of additional commercial theaters, as well as resident companies that enrich the city's theatrical scene, are within walking distance of this theater row. The three major commercial theaters are operated by the Shorenstein-Nederlander organization, which books touring plays and musicals, some before they open on Broadway.

The most venerable commercial theater is the **Curran** (✉ 445 Geary St., at Mason St., Union Square, ☎ 415/551–2000). The **Golden Gate** (✉ Golden Gate Ave. at Taylor St., Tenderloin, ☎ 415/551–2000) is a stylishly refurbished movie theater, now primarily a musical house. The gorgeously restored 2,500-seat **Orpheum** (✉ 1192 Market St., at Hyde St., Tenderloin, ☎ 415/551–2000) is used for the biggest touring shows.

The city's major nonprofit theater company is the **American Conservatory Theater (ACT),** which was founded in the mid-1960s and quickly became one of the nation's leading regional theaters. During its season from the early fall to the late spring, ACT presents approximately eight plays, from classics to contemporary works, often in rotating repertory. In December ACT stages a much-loved version of Charles Dickens's *A Christmas Carol.* The ACT ticket office is at 405 Geary Street (☎ 415/749–2228). Next door to ACT ticket office is its home, the **Geary Theater.**

The leading producer of new plays is the **Magic Theatre** (✉ Fort Mason Center, Bldg. D, Laguna St. at Marina Blvd., Marina, ☎ 415/441–8822).

Once Sam Shepard's favorite showcase, the Magic presents works by the latest rising American playwrights, such as Matthew Wells, Karen Hartman, and Claire Chafee.

Marines Memorial Theatre (✉ 609 Sutter St., at Mason St., Union Square, ☎ 415/441–7444) hosts touring shows plus some local performances. The **Stage Door Theater** (✉ 420 Mason St., between Post and Geary Sts., Union Square, ☎ no phone) is small but dependable. **Theatre on the Square** (✉ 450 Post St., between Mason and Powell Sts., Union Square, ☎ 415/433–9500) is a popular smaller venue. For commercial and popular success, nothing beats *Beach Blanket Babylon,* the zany revue that has been running since 1974 at North Beach's **Club Fugazi.** Conceived by the late San Francisco director Steve Silver, it is a hilarious mix of cabaret, show-biz parodies, and tributes to local landmarks.

The **Lorraine Hansberry Theatre** (✉ 620 Sutter St., at Mason St., Union Square, ☎ 415/474–8800) specializes in plays by black writers such as August Wilson and Langston Hughes. The **Asian American Theatre Company** (✉ 1840 Sutter St., Suite 207, between Buchanan and Webster Sts., Japantown, ☎ 415/440–5545) is dedicated to working with local actors. **A Traveling Jewish Theatre** (✉ 470 Florida St., between 17th and Mariposa Sts., Mission, ☎ 415/399–1809) creates and stages performances, often with Jewish themes, that explore the human condition. **Theatre Rhinoceros** (✉ 2926 16th St., at Mission St., Mission, ☎ 415/861–5079) showcases gay and lesbian performers. The two-stage **New Conservatory Theatre** (✉ 25 Van Ness Ave., between Fell and Oak Sts., Hayes Valley, ☎ 415/861–8972) hosts the annual Pride Season, focusing on contemporary gay- and lesbian-themed works, as well as other plays and events, including educational plays for young people. The **San Francisco Shakespeare Festival** (☎ 415/422–2222) offers free weekend performances in September in Golden Gate Park. A uniquely Bay Area summertime freebie is the Tony Award–winning **San Francisco Mime Troupe** (☎ 415/285–1717), whose politically leftist, barbed satires are hardly mime in the Marcel Marceau sense; they perform afternoon musicals at area parks from July 4 weekend through September.

Avant-garde theater, dance, opera, and performance art turn up in many locations, not all of them theaters. **Theater Artaud** (✉ 450 Florida St., Mission, ☎ 415/621–7797) is housed in a huge, converted machine shop. The **Yerba Buena Center for the Arts** (✉ 3rd and Howard Sts., South of Market, ☎ 415/978–2787) schedules contemporary theater events in addition to dance and music.

Intersection for the Arts (✉ 446 Valencia St., between 15th and 16th Sts., Mission, ☎ 415/626–2787) is a notable venue for small-scale plays.

The **Marsh** (✉ 1062 Valencia St., at 22nd St., Mission, ☎ 415/826–5750) stages experimental works. Ground zero for absurdist theater is the **Exit Theatre** (✉ 156 Eddy St., between Mason and Taylor Sts., Union Square, ☎ 415/673–3847), which also presents the annual **Fringe Festival** in September.

Tony Award–winning **Berkeley Repertory Theatre** (☎ 510/845–4700), across the bay, is the American Conservatory Theatre's major rival for leadership among the region's resident professional companies. It performs an adventurous mix of classics and new plays from fall to spring in a recently expanded theater complex at 2025 Addison Street, near BART's downtown Berkeley station. **California Shakespeare Festival** (☎ 510/548–9666), the Bay Area's largest outdoor summer theater event, performs in an amphitheater east of Oakland on Gateway Boulevard, just off state Route 24.

Nonprofit, acrobatically inclined **Make-A-Circus** (☎ 415/242–1414), which tours statewide in the summer and usually makes an appearance at Golden Gate Park, invites kids to learn circus skills at intermission then perform with the professionals during the second act. The new-vaudeville-style **New Pickle Circus** (☎ 415/487–7940) generally performs at indoor locales around Christmas time.

6 OUTDOOR ACTIVITIES AND SPORTS

In San Francisco, stockbrokers go surfing at noon, sailors navigate the chilling waters lapping at the legendary island called Alcatraz, and children flock to the Marina Green to fly kites in the shadow of the Golden Gate Bridge. Perhaps best of all, temperatures rarely drop below 50°F, so there are plenty of opportunities to enjoy the parks, beaches, and open spaces that abound.

W HEN YOU ARRIVE IN SAN FRANCISCO, the beautiful views alone will likely captivate you. On the best of days, when the fog burns off early, even veteran residents marvel at the sun sparkling on the bay and the cool, crisp air, which couldn't seem much cleaner. These are the makings for memorable, adrenaline-pumping fun against a magnificent backdrop.

Updated by
John Andrew
Vlahides

Whether you want to explore by land or water, in San Francisco you've got options. Bikers and hikers traverse the majestic Golden Gate Bridge, the winding trails of the Presidio, and the one-of-a-kind paths of Golden Gate Park. Bay explorers hop cruises and ferries or feed an addiction for adventure with a kayak tour or sailboat rental. If your first love is golf, horseback riding, ice or in-line skating, or even rock climbing, not to worry. And if you're up for a more traditional workout at a gym, or a yoga class, no problem. In San Francisco, it all can be yours.

PARTICIPANT SPORTS AND THE OUTDOORS

Since there's no reason not to go outside, physical fitness and outdoor activities are a way of life in the Bay Area. Joggers, bicyclists, and aficionados of virtually all sports can often enjoy their favorite pastimes within walking distance of downtown hotels. Golden Gate Park has numerous paths for runners, strollers, in-line skaters, and cyclists. Hiking trails with incredible ocean and bay views are abundant throughout the **Golden Gate National Recreation Area** (☎ 415/556–0560 National Parks Information Line), which encompasses the San Francisco coastline, the Marin Headlands, and Point Reyes National Seashore. Lake Merced in San Francisco and Lake Merritt in Oakland are among the most popular areas for joggers, and Berkeley's sprawling Tilden Park is great for hiking and mountain biking.

For a listing of running races, tennis tournaments, bicycle races, and other participant sports, check the monthly issues of *City Sports* magazine, available free at sporting goods stores, tennis centers, and other recreational sites.

The most important running event of the year is the *San Francisco Examiner*'s **Bay-to-Breakers race** on the third Sunday in May. Up to 100,000 serious and not-so-serious runners dress up in crazy costumes—an adult version of Halloween, but twice the fun—and make their way from the Embarcadero to the Pacific Ocean. For race information and entry forms, call ☎ 415/359–2600.

The **Chronicle Marathon** is held annually on the second Sunday in July. It starts and finishes at Speedway Meadow in Golden Gate Park, and up to 7,000 runners pass through downtown and up and over some of the city's milder hills. Related events include a four-person marathon relay, a 5K run, and a half-marathon run with a partner. For entry forms and race information, call ☎ 800/698–8699.

Bicycling

San Francisco has a number of scenic routes of varied terrain. With its legendary hills, the city offers countless cycling challenges—but also plenty of level ground. To avoid the former, look for a copy of the *San Francisco Biking/Walking Guide* ($3). Sold in select bookstores, the folding guide indicates street grades and delineates biking routes that avoid major hills and heavy traffic.

EMBARCADERO

A completely flat route, the Embarcadero gives you a clear view of open waters and the Bay Bridge on the pier side and sleek high-rises on the other. Rent a bike ($6 per hour, $27 per day) at **Adventure Bicycle Co.** (⊠ 968 Columbus Ave., between Chestnut and Lombard Sts., North Beach, ☎ 415/771–8735), pick up a complimentary map, and ride down Taylor Street to Beach Street. Turn right, and ride to the Embarcadero. Pedal along the waterfront on the dock-side promenade, along with fellow bikers, joggers, and walkers. Continue south past the Ferry Building, at the foot of Market Street, and pedal under the Bay Bridge to Pier 40. On your return trip, pass Beach Street and continue on the Embarcadero through Fisherman's Wharf to Aquatic Park. (Crowds here can be dense on the weekends.) Travel time is anywhere from 30 minutes to an hour; the round-trip tour is approximately 3 mi long.

GOLDEN GATE PARK

Golden Gate Park is a beautiful maze of roads and hidden bike paths, with rose gardens, lakes, waterfalls, museums, horse stables, bison, and, ultimately, a spectacular view of the Pacific Ocean. On Sundays, John F. Kennedy Drive is closed to motor vehicles, making it a popular and crowded route for those on people-powered wheels. Rent a bike for about $40 per day at **Golden Gate Cyclery** (⊠ 672 Stanyan St., Haight, ☎ 415/379–3870) and take a 20- to 30-minute ride down John F. Kennedy Drive through the park to the Great Highway, where land meets ocean. You may extend your ride another couple of miles by turning left, riding a few blocks, and connecting with a raised bike path that runs parallel to the Pacific, winding through fields of emerald-green ice plant and, after 2 mi, leading to Sloat Boulevard and the San Francisco Zoo.

MARINA GREEN

The Marina Green is a picturesque lawn stretching along Marina Boulevard, adjacent to Fort Mason. It's also the starting point of a well-trod route to the Golden Gate Bridge and beyond. Rent a bike ($5 per hour or $19 per day) at **Holiday Adventure Sales and Rentals** (⊠ 1937 Lombard St., at Webster St., Marina, ☎ 415/567–1192) and take Lombard Street west for eight blocks until you reach the Presidio and hit Lincoln Boulevard. Turn right and Lincoln Boulevard will eventually bring you to the base of the bridge, a 45-minute ride round-trip. If you're feeling ambitious, head across the bridge (signs indicate on which side cyclists must ride) and turn off on the first road leading northeast (Alexander Ave.). After a 15-minute (downhill) ride, you'll arrive on Bridgeway in downtown Sausalito, where you can rest in a café. From there take your bike aboard the Blue & Gold Fleet's ferry (the ferry terminal is at the end of Bridgeway) for a half-hour ride back to San Francisco's Fisherman's Wharf.

Boat Cruises and Ferries

One of the most memorable ways to explore San Francisco's natural beauty is by water. But if sailing and kayaking aren't for you, consider taking one of the city's numerous ferries and cruises. They're not just a mode of transportation, they also give you a chance to see the city from a new perspective and to breathe in the fresh air. And don't miss the sunset as it lights up the city's skyline.

Blue & Gold Fleet (☎ 415/705–5555 for advance tickets; 415/773–1188 for recorded schedule) offers daily service to Angel Island, a former military garrison and a beautiful wildlife preserve, where you can also bike, hike, relax on the beach, or tour historic buildings. Bike rentals are available on the island, or you can bring your own. You can also take ferries to the infamous Alcatraz Island (a 10-minute ride, which should be booked as far in advance as possible), the redwood haven of Muir Woods (a 20-minute ferry to Tiburon and a 20-minute van ride to the towering trees), and quaint Sausalito (a 30-minute trip), where you can enjoy strolling, window-shopping, and dining on the bay. The Blue & Gold Fleet offers frequent departures from Pier 39 and Pier 41 to these and other destinations. But if you're looking for romance, opt for an evening cruise. Relax with a cocktail and soak up beautiful views of the Golden Gate Bridge, Alcatraz, and Angel Island without ever leaving the deck.

On the **Alameda/Oakland Ferry** (☎ 510/522–3300), you can sail from Pier 39 or the Ferry Building to Oakland's Jack London Square. The trip lasts 30 to 45 minutes, depending on your departure point, and leads to the heart of Oakland's gentrified shopping and restaurant district. On your return to San Francisco the views may be more welcoming than during your departure, but arriving in Oakland by boat conveys a historic sense of this East Bay city's heyday as a World War II–era shipbuilding center.

Boating and Sailing

San Francisco Bay offers year-round sailing, but tricky currents and strong winds make the bay hazardous for inexperienced navigators. Boat rentals and charters are available throughout the Bay Area and are listed under "Boat Renting" in the Yellow Pages.

A Day on the Bay (☎ 415/922–0227) is in San Francisco's small-craft marina, just minutes from the Golden Gate Bridge and open waters. **Cass' Marina** (✉ 1702 Bridgeway, at Napa St., ☎ 415/332–6789), in Sausalito, will rent you 22- to 35-ft sailboats, as long as there's a qualified sailor in your group.

Stow Lake (☎ 415/752–0347), in Golden Gate Park, has rowboat, pedal boat, and electric boat rentals. The lake is open daily for boating, weather permitting, but call for seasonal hours.

Fishing

Numerous fishing boats leave from San Francisco, Sausalito, Berkeley, Emeryville, and Point San Pablo. They go for salmon and halibut outside the bay or striped bass and giant sturgeon within. San Franciscans cast lines from the Municipal Pier, Fisherman's Wharf, Baker Beach, and Aquatic Park. Trout fishing is possible at San Francisco's Lake Merced. You can rent rods and boats, purchase permits and licenses (up to $5 for a permit and $11 for a two-day license), and buy bait at the **Lake Merced Boating & Fishing Company** (✉ 1 Harding Rd., Lake Merced, ☎ 415/681–3310). One-day **licenses**, good for ocean fishing only, are available for $7 on charters, or you can pick up a California State Fishing License at the Lake Merced facility. Some selected sportfishing charters are listed below. Most depart daily from Fisherman's Wharf during the salmon-fishing season, which is from March through October.

Lovely Martha's Sportfishing (✉ Fisherman's Wharf, Berth 3, Fisherman's Wharf, ☎ 650/871–1691) offers salmon-fishing excursions as well as bay cruises.

Wacky Jacky (✉ Fisherman's Wharf, Pier 45, Fisherman's Wharf, ☎ 415/586–9800) will take you salmon fishing in a sleek, fast, and comfortable 50-ft boat.

Fitness Clubs and Day Spas

Thanks to the law of supply and demand, the number of fitness clubs in downtown San Francisco has soared. Although some clubs still retain private membership status, many facilities provide day passes for charges ranging from $10 to $20. Several hotels have arrangements with neighborhood health clubs, but some operate gyms of their own. Try the swanky club at the **Ritz-Carlton Hotel** (✉ 600 Stockton St., at Pine St., Nob Hill, ☎ 415/296–7465), which charges $20 for the public and is free to hotel guests. The **Fairmont Hotel's Club One** (✉ 950 California St., at Mason St., Nob Hill, ☎ 415/834–1010) costs $20 for the public and $15 for Fairmont guests; Club One also operates fitness centers at eight other locations within San Francisco, some of which have spa and salon services.

Various branches of **24 Hour Fitness Centers** (✉ 1200 Van Ness Ave., Van Ness/Polk, ☎ 415/776–2200; ✉ 350 Bay St., North Beach, ☎ 415/395–9595; ✉ 100 California St., Financial District, ☎ 415/434–5080; ✉ 303 2nd St., at Folsom St., Marathon Plaza, South of Market, ☎ 415/543–7808) are open to the public for a $15 day-use fee. Facilities and services vary, but most of the clubs have saunas, hot tubs, and steam rooms, as well as aerobics classes and fitness equipment. The **Embarcadero YMCA** (✉ 169 Steuart St., South of Market, ☎ 415/957–9622), one of the finest facilities in San Francisco, has racquetball, a 25-m swimming pool, and aerobics classes. The $12 drop-in fee includes use of the sauna, steam room, and whirlpool; padlocks are not provided for a guest's locker, so bring your own or use the tiny coin lockers. **Pinnacle Fitness** has two locations in the heart of the Financial District (✉ 61 New Montgomery St., South of Market, ☎ 415/543–1110; ✉ 1 Post Plaza, at Market St., Financial District, ☎ 415/781–6400). Both offer day passes for $15 ($10 for guests at local hotels), which include use of the lap pool at the Post Plaza location and access to aerobics and fitness classes at each; call for class times. The **World Gym** (✉ 290 De Haro St., at 16th St., Potrero Hill, ☎ 415/703–9650), though a bit off the beaten path, is a must-see for bodybuilding enthusiasts; a lack of extensive spa facilities is a fair trade-off for the extensive weight-training and aerobics equipment. The day rate of $15 includes aerobics classes.

When your body says "no more," day spas provide the necessary indulgences, including pampering wraps, scrubs, facials, manicures, pedicures, and, of course, massages. The signature treatment at the posh **Elizabeth Arden Red Door Salon & Spa** (✉ 126 Post St., between Grant Ave. and Kearny St., Union Square, ☎ 415/989–4888) is a thorough, nourishing facial. Or, for something you won't find elsewhere in town, try the $95 Ceramide Firm Lift Massage, a deep tissue rubdown using this well-known Elizabeth Arden product. Treatments designed especially for men are also available. Upon request, women can receive a complimentary makeup application. Swimmers and sauna addicts will love the elegant facilities at the **Ritz-Carlton** (✉ 600 Stockton St., at California St., Nob Hill, ☎ 415/296–7465), where you can also luxuriate with an intense sports massage and complimentary eucalyptus steam. If you've forgotten your swimsuit, purchase one at the check-in and enjoy the beautiful lap pool and Jacuzzi.

Traditional sit-down Japanese showers and communal bathing are two unique features of **Kabuki Hot Springs** (✉ 1750 Geary St., at Fillmore St., Japantown, ☎ 415/922–6000). For a real treat, try the renowned $115 Javanese Lulur Treatment: a combination massage with jasmine oil, exfoliation with tumeric and ground rice, yogurt application, and a soak by candlelight with rose petals while you sip tea or cucumber-infused water.

When society ladies want a day-spa experience, they visit **Mister Lee Beauty, Hair & Health Spa** (✉ 834 Jones St., at Sutter St., Union Square, ☎ 415/474–6002). After ascending the grand staircase you'll find the semblance of an Egyptian temple awaiting you. Mister Lee's offers all the usual spa options, such as exfoliating massage and facials, as well as cellulite treatments, lymphatic drainage, hydrotherapy tubs with underwater massage, and manicures and pedicures with algae wraps and paraffin. Day packages combining several treatments offer a 15% discount.

77 Maiden Lane Salon & Spa (⊠ 77 Maiden La., 2nd floor, Union Square, ☎ 415/391–7777) is an excellent downtown option, with a complete menu of spa services and treatments. It's also open on Sunday. **Spa Nordstrom** (⊠ San Francisco Center, 5th and Market Sts., 5th floor, Union Square, ☎ 415/977–5102) offers a $366 package, up to 6½ hours long, including a body wrap, manicure, pedicure, facial, lunch, and massage. Tea and the use of robes and slippers are complimentary, as they are at all of these spas.

If you love aromatherapy, visit the **Zendo Urban Retreat Center** (⊠ 256 Sutter St., at Grant Ave., Union Square, ☎ 415/788–3404), which relies on fragrant Aveda products in a luxurious living-room setting with antiques and Oriental rugs. You can have your entire body exfoliated and massaged, your toes pedicured and polished, and your hair cut and styled before enjoying a complimentary makeup application, complete with mint-scented lipstick.

Golf

Golfers putt to their hearts' content in San Francisco. Call the automated **golf information line** (☎ 415/750–4653) to get detailed directions to the city's public golf courses or to reserve a tee time ($1 reservation fee per player) up to seven days in advance. **Glen Eagles Golf Course** (⊠ 2100 Sunnydale Ave., Excelsior/Visitacion Valley, ☎ 415/587–2425) is a challenging 9-hole, par-36 course in McLaren Park. **Golden Gate** (⊠ 47th Ave. between Fulton St. and John F. Kennedy Dr., Golden Gate Park, ☎ 415/751–8987) is a 9-hole, par-27 course in Golden Gate Park just above Ocean Beach. **Harding Park Golf Course** (⊠ Harding Rd. and Skyline Blvd., Lake Merced, ☎ 415/661–1865) has an 18-hole, par-72 course. Inside the second 9 is the par-32 Jack Fleming Golf Course, with all the characteristics of a championship course, only this one is designed to be less difficult. **Lincoln Park** (⊠ 34th Ave. and Clement St., Richmond, ☎ 415/221–9911) has an 18-hole, par-68 course. The **Presidio Golf Course** (⊠ 300 Finley Rd., at Arguello Blvd., Presidio, ☎ 415/561–4661) is an 18-hole, par-72 course managed by Arnold Palmer's company. **Sharp Park,** in Pacifica (⊠ off Rte. 1 at the Sharp Park Rd./Fairway Dr. exit, Pacifica, ☎ 650/359–3380), has 18 holes and a par of 72.

Horseback Riding

Along the coast, through the vineyards, and along dusty country roads, the Bay Area has miles of trails that are great for western-style horseback riding. In Half Moon Bay, you can gallop along the beach with a horse from **Sea Horse Friendly Acres Ranch** (⊠ 1828 N. Cabrillo Hwy., Half Moon Bay, ☎ 650/726–8550).

Olema, a small town near Point Reyes, has horses for rent at **Five Brooks Ranch** (⊠ 8001 Rte. 1, Olema, ☎ 415/663–1570). Trails lead through the Point Reyes National Park all the way to the sea.

Ice-Skating

One of the best places from which to enjoy an impressive view of San Francisco's skyline is the skating rink at the **Yerba Buena Ice Skating & Bowling Center** (⊠ 750 Folsom St., at 3rd St., South of Market, ☎ 415/777–3727), open year-round. Magnificent floor-to-ceiling windows border the NHL-regulation rink, providing a view of the city's twinkling lights by night and bathing the rink in natural light by day. If you visit San Francisco during winter, you can enjoy outdoor ice-skating at the **Holiday Ice Skating Rink at Embarcadero Center** (✉ Justin Herman Plaza, at the foot of Market St., behind the Embarcadero Center, Embarcadero, ☎ 415/956–2688), particularly beautiful at sunset, from mid-November through early winter. **Berkeley Iceland** (✉ 2727 Milvia St., 4 blocks from the Ashby BART station, Berkeley, ☎ 510/843–8800) provides year-round skating at an indoor rink.

In-Line Skating

Golden Gate Park is one of the country's best places for in-line skating, with smooth surfaces, manageable hills, and lush scenery. John F. Kennedy Drive, which extends almost to the ocean, is closed to traffic on Sunday, when it seems that an enormous segment of the city's population heads to the park to blade. **Skates on Haight** (✉ 1818 Haight St., Haight, ☎ 415/752–8375), near the Stanyan Street entrance to the park, offers free lessons (with rentals) on Sunday morning at 9 AM and rents recreational in-line or roller skates for $6 per hour and $24 overnight.

For beginners, the path along the **Marina** offers a 1½-mi (round-trip) easy route on a flat, well-paved surface, with glorious views of San Francisco Bay. In summer, **FTC Sports** (✉ 1586 Bush St., Western Addition, ☎ 415/673–8363) rents and sells in-line skates and protective gear. Advanced skaters may want to experience the challenge and take in the brilliant views of **Tilden Park** (☎ 510/525–2233), in the Berkeley Hills. Follow signs to the parking lot at Inspiration Point. There you'll find the trailhead for Nimitz Way, a nicely paved 8-mi (round-trip) recreational path that stretches along a ridge with spectacular views of San Francisco and the bay.

Skaters with a competitive edge can take part in the nightly pickup in-line hockey games at **Bladium** (✉ 800 West Tower Ave., Bldg. 40, on the site of the former naval base, Alameda, ☎ 510/814–4999), where a pickup game costs $9 per person and gear can be rented for $3–$10.

Kayaking

Surrounded by water on three sides, San Francisco offers plenty of opportunities for all levels of kayaking enthusiasts, and shops and organizations to equip and lead them. Specializing in sea kayaking, **Sea Trek Ocean Kayaking Center** (✉ Schoonmaker Point Marina, Sausalito, ☎ 415/488–1000) provides guided trips to Angel Island for beginners ("starlight" and "full moon" paddles are particularly popular). Kayakers of all levels can tackle a guided coastal paddle, from Muir Beach to Sausalito, or under the Golden Gate Bridge, past the Marin Headlands. If you'd like to rent a kayak and strike out on your own, the friendly and knowledgeable folks at **Harbor Dive & Kayak Center** (✉ 200 Harbor Dr., Sausalito, ☎ 415/331–0904) will suit you up and recommend routes based on current conditions and your ability and interests.

Racquetball

Most racquetball clubs in San Francisco are private and require that drop-in guests be accompanied by a member. However, a few fitness centers offering day passes have racquetball courts on the premises. Some clubs allow nonmembers to make advance reservations; if you're going to play during peak periods, be sure to call before you go. The **Embarcadero YMCA** charges $12 for a day pass that includes use of the racquetball courts. At the University of San Francisco's **Koret Health and Recreation Center** (✉ Parker Ave. at Turk St., Inner Richmond, ☎ 415/422–6821), use of the courts is available to guests before 2 PM for $10. The San Francisco Recreation and Park Department maintains two free racquetball courts at the **Mission Recreation Center** (⊠ 2450 Harrison St., Mission, ☎ 415/695–5012). Reservations may be placed over the phone 90 minutes in advance. If you want to play squash for $20, head to **Club One** (⊠ The Fillmore Center, 1755 O'Farrell St., Fillmore, ☎ 415/776–2260).

Rock Climbing

Mission Cliffs Rock Climbing Center (⊠ 2295 Harrison St., at 19th St., Mission, ☎ 415/550–0515) is one of the largest indoor climbing facilities in the country, with a 14,000-square-ft gym and a 2,000-square-ft bouldering area. Day passes cost $20; shoes and harness rental, $5. You can climb the outside bouldering wall at **Club One Citicorp** (⊠ 1 Sansome St., Financial District, ☎ 415/399–1010) for a $20 day pass. The 24-ft-high wall, with 800 square ft of climbing terrain, is closed during inclement weather, so call ahead. **Berkeley Iron Works** (⊠ 800 Potter St., off 7th St., near the Ashby Ave. exit off I–80, Emeryville, ☎ 510/981–9900) is—depending on traffic—a quick drive across the Bay Bridge. Classes are available for beginners for $27. Experienced climbers must pass a safety test before climbing. Day passes cost $16. Another $6 rents shoes and a harness.

Swimming

The **San Francisco Recreation and Park Department** (☎ 415/831–2700) manages one outdoor swimming pool and seven indoor pools ($3 admission) throughout the city. The **Sava Pool** (⊠ 19th Ave. and Wawona St., Sunset, ☎ 415/753–7000) is one of the more popular—and consequently crowded—pools. **Hamilton Pool** (⊠ 1900 Geary Blvd., at Steiner St., Western Addition, ☎ 415/292–2001) is a favorite among swimmers. The **Embarcadero YMCA** has a 25-m pool, a gym, and spa facilities for a $12 day fee. The University of San Francisco's **Koret Health and Recreation Center,** a few blocks from the Golden Gate Park Panhandle, has an especially well maintained Olympic-size pool as well as an exercise room. You can have access to the facilities before 2 PM daily for a $10 fee. The small lap pool at **Pinnacle Fitness** is two blocks from Union Square.

Even if you're not a guest at the **Sheehan Hotel** (⊠ 620 Sutter St., Union Square, ☎ 415/775–6500), which is just a few blocks from Union Square, you can use its pool for a $10 fee.

Tennis

San Francisco tennis clubs are private and require membership. However, the San Francisco Recreation and Park Department maintains 132 public tennis courts throughout the city. All courts are free, except those in Golden Gate Park. The six courts at **Mission Dolores Park** (⊠ 18th and Dolores Sts., Castro) are available on a first-come, first-served basis. The 21 courts in **Golden Gate Park** (☎ 415/753–7001) are the only public ones for which you can make advance reservations. Fees range from $5 to $10, but kids and seniors play for free. For gorgeous views, head up to the steeply sloped **Buena Vista Park** (⊠ Buena Vista Ave. and Haight St., Lower Haight, ☎ 415/831–2700). Popular with Marina locals, the four lighted courts at the **Moscone Recreation Center** (⊠ 1800 Chestnut St., at Buchanan St., Marina, ☎ 415/292–2006) are free, but sometimes require a wait of one set or 30 to 40 minutes. Let the players know you're next and follow the posted etiquette rules. In the southeast corner of the beautiful Presidio, **Julius Kahn Playground** (⊠ W. Pacific Ave., between Spruce and Locust Sts., Presidio Heights, ☎ 415/753–7001) has four free courts; the park is a great distraction in case they're not free when you arrive.

Windsurfing and Gliding

In this city of powerful ocean gusts and adventurous souls, windsurfing and gliding are popular pastimes. The **San Francisco School of Windsurfing** (✉ Candlestick Point, ☎ 415/753–3235) offers lessons for beginners and more advanced surfers. **City Front Boardsports** (✉ 2936 Lyon St., at Lombard St., Marina, ☎ 415/929–7873), near Crissy Field, has a beginner's instruction package as well as a full line of equipment. Adventurous types should head to the **San Francisco Hang Gliding Center** (✉ Mt. Tamalpais State Park, Marin County, ☎ 510/528–2300), one of the few licensed schools in Northern California. (Others abound, but many are not insured or licensed.) This school specializes in tandem hang-gliding flights and aqua-gliding. It also offers tandem paragliding instruction on Mt. Tamalpais, with flights landing at picturesque Stinson Beach. Believe it or not, no experience is necessary.

Yoga

If you're missing the peace of mind of your yoga classes back home, don't let that send your heart racing. San Francisco's yoga institutes tailor weekend and evening classes for even the busiest traveler. And most welcome drop-ins with no advance registration required. Wear loose, comfortable clothing; avoid eating one to two hours prior to class; and arrive with more than just a few minutes to spare.

The **Integral Yoga Institute** (✉ 770 Dolores St., at 21st St., Mission, ☎ 415/821–1117) offers daily classes in four levels of Hatha yoga, which emphasizes breathing, posture, and meditation. Cost is $9, $6 for first-time participants and senior citizens. The **Iyengar Yoga Institute of San Francisco** (✉ 2404 27th Ave., at Taraval St., Sunset, ☎ 415/753–0909) offers more than 30 classes of all levels of Iyengar yoga, which emphasizes integration of body, mind, and spirit. Drop-ins pay about $15 per 90-minute session. The oldest established yoga school in San Francisco, **Magana & Walt Baptiste Yoga Center** (✉ 730 Euclid Ave., between Palm and Jordan Sts., Inner Richmond, ☎ 415/387–6833) offers Wednesday-evening and Saturday-morning classes in Baptiste yoga, focusing on muscular strength and toning. The cost for drop-ins is $15; private instruction is available. The school also holds classes in Middle Eastern dance. At the nonprofit **Yoga Society of San Francisco** (✉ 2872 Folsom St., at 25th St., Mission, ☎ 415/285–5537), Hatha yoga classes with a spiritual and meditative component are $12 per session, ranging from 90 to 120 minutes. A free hour-long fire-meditation session takes place weekdays at 6 AM and 7:30 PM, Saturday at 8 AM, and Sunday at 6:30 AM.

SPECTATOR SPORTS

For a local perspective on Bay Area sports, pick up a copy of the *San Francisco Chronicle* or *Examiner,* which lists game schedules and scores. If you can't wait until the ink is dry to learn game scores, log onto www.sfgate.com/sports or dial ☎ 800/555–8355.

Auto Racing

Sears Point Raceway (✉ Rte. 121 at Rte. 37, Sonoma, ☎ 707/938–8448 or 800/870–7223), in the Wine Country north of San Francisco, hosts drag races and other motor-sports events.

Baseball

The **San Francisco Giants** have moved from their former home at Candlestick Park to a new downtown bay-front stadium, Pacific Bell Park (✉ 24 Willie Mays Plaza, between 2nd and 3rd Sts., China Basin, ☎ 415/972–2000 or 800/734–4268). To avoid traffic jams, take one of the city buses or Muni lines that run nearby; call **Muni** (☎ 415/673–6864) for the stop nearest you.

The **Oakland A's** play at the Network Associates Coliseum (formerly the Oakland Coliseum) (⊠ 7000 Coliseum Way, off I–880, north of Hegenberger Rd., Oakland, ☎ 510/638–0500). To get to the game, take a BART train to the Coliseum stop. Same-day tickets can usually be purchased at the stadium, but advance purchase is recommended. Call the **Tickets.com Baseball Line** (☎ 510/762–2255). There's a per-call processing charge of $2.50, and per-ticket handling fees may also apply.

Basketball

The **Golden State Warriors** play NBA basketball at the Oakland Arena (⊠ 7000 Coliseum Way, off I–880, north of Hegenberger Rd., Oakland, ☎ 510/986–2200) from November through April. Tickets are available through **Tickets.com** (☎ 510/762–2277). BART trains whisk passengers away from the traffic jams, right to the Coliseum station and the entrance to the Arena.

Football

The NFC West's **San Francisco 49ers** play at 3Com Park (⊠ 3Com Park at Candlestick Point, Jamestown Ave. and Harney Way, Candlestick Point, ☎ 415/656–4900). Tickets are almost always sold out far in advance. The AFC West's **Oakland Raiders** play at the Network Associates Coliseum (formerly the Oakland Coliseum) (⊠ 7000 Coliseum Way, off I–880, north of Hegenberger Rd., Oakland). Except for high-profile games, tickets, sold through **Tickets.com** (☎ 510/762–2277), are usually available.

Hockey

Tickets for the NHL's **San Jose Sharks** are available from **Tickets.com** (☎ 510/762–2277). Games are held at the Compaq Center at San Jose (formerly the San Jose Arena).

Horse Racing

Depending on the season, horse racing takes place at the Golden Gate Fields or Bay Meadows Racecourse. Check local newspapers to find out which tracks are operating. The admission at **Golden Gate Fields** (⊠ 1100 Eastshore Hwy., off I–80), Albany, ☎ 510/559–7300, in the East Bay, is $3. **Bay Meadows Racecourse** (⊠ 2600 S. Delaware St., off Rte. 92, San Mateo, ☎ 650/574–7223), on the Peninsula, charges $3. Admission is free at both locations for ages 17 and under.

Rodeo

San Francisco relives its western heritage every October with the **Grand National Rodeo, Horse, and Stock Show.** The Grand National Rodeo is held at the **Cow Palace** (⊠ 2600 Geneva Ave., Daly City, ☎ 415/404–4111), just south of the city limits, in Daly City. (From downtown take U.S. 101 south to the Cow Palace/3rd Street exit; follow signs to Geneva Avenue, then head west seven blocks. Or take BART to the Balboa Park Station and transfer to Muni Bus 15.)

Soccer

The **San Jose Earthquakes** (⊠ 1257 S. 10th St., at Alma Dr., San Jose, ☎ 408/985–4625) play major-league soccer at Spartan Stadium.

Tennis

In February, the stars of men's tennis square off at the **Sybase Open Tennis Tournament** at the Compaq Center (formerly the San Jose Arena) (⊠ Santa Clara St. at Autumn St., San Jose). To avoid clogged highways, consider taking a free shuttle from the Santa Clara Street light-rail station. For individual tickets, call **Ticketmaster** (☎ 415/421–

8497). For ticket information, call the **San Jose Arena box office** (☎ 408/287–9200). Ticket packages are also available. The **Bank of the West Women's Tennis Tour** visits Palo Alto in the summer. Tickets are available through **Tickets.com** (☎ 510/762–2277).

BEACHES

San Francisco's beaches are perfect backdrops for romantic sunsets, but frequently icy temperatures and treacherous currents make most waters too dangerous for swimming. On occasional summer days when the coastal fog gets blown out to sea and the mercury rises, crowds do head for the shore. Always bring a sweater; even the sunniest of days can become cold and foggy without warning.

Aquatic Park
Nestled in a quiet cove between the lush hills adjoining Fort Mason, Ghirardelli Square, and the crowds at Fisherman's Wharf, Aquatic Park has a tiny, ¼-mi-long sandy beach with gentle water. Its cove and manicured lawns are part of the San Francisco Maritime National Historic Park. Keep an eye out for members of the **Dolphin Club** (☎ 415/441–9329), who come every morning for a dip in these ice-cold waters. An especially large and raucous crowd braves the cold on New Year's Day. There are no grills, but you will find rest rooms and showers.

Baker Beach
Baker Beach is a local favorite, with gorgeous views of the Golden Gate Bridge and the Marin Headlands. The pounding surf makes swimming a dangerous prospect, but the mile-long shoreline is ideal for fishing, building sand castles, or watching sea lions at play. On warm days, the entire beach is packed with bodies—including nudists at the north end—tanning in the sun. The first weekend of every month, rangers provide tours of the 95,000-pound cannon at Battery Chamberlin, overlooking the beach. Although the 1904 weapon is, of course, no longer used to defend the city, it can still spring into firing position. You'll find Baker Beach on the Presidio's Gibson Road, off Bowley Street. Picnic tables, grills, rest rooms, and drinking water are available.

China Beach
One of the city's safest swimming beaches, China Beach was named for the poor Chinese fishermen who once camped here. (You may also find it marked on maps as James D. Phelan Beach.) This 600-ft strip of sand, just south of the Presidio, has gentle waters as well as changing rooms, rest rooms, and showers. You'll also find grills, drinking water, and picnic tables. Despite its humble beginnings, today China Beach is bordered by the multimillion-dollar homes of the Seacliff neighborhood, including a massive pink structure owned by actor Robin Williams.

Marin Beaches
The beaches at the Marin Headlands are not safe for swimming. The giant cliffs are steep and unstable, and hiking down them can be dangerous. Farther north along the Marin coast, however, Muir and Stinson beaches beckon picnickers and sunbathers. Tucked in a rocky cove, **Muir Beach** is a tiny, picturesque beach usually filled with kids, dogs, families, and cuddling couples. Swimming is recommended only at the wide, flat expanse of **Stinson Beach,** and only from early May through September, when lifeguards are on duty, as shark sightings here—although not frequent—are not unusual. If possible, visit these areas during the week. Both beaches, and the roads leading to them, are crowded on sunny weekends.

Ocean Beach

South of the Cliff House, Ocean Beach is certainly not the city's cleanest shore, but its wide, sandy expanse stretches for miles, making it ideal for long walks and runs. You may spot sea lions sunning themselves atop the stony nearby islands, or daredevil surfers riding the roiling waves. Because of extremely dangerous currents, swimming is not recommended. After the sun sets, bonfires typically form a string of lights along the beach. No permits are required for fires, but they are only permissible south of Fulton Street. For particulars, call the **United States Park Police** at ☎ 415/561–5505. Rest rooms are available.

San Mateo County Coast

Less than an hour's drive south on scenic Route 1 brings you to the popular, 2-mi-long **Half Moon Bay State Beach,** a great spot for picnics. After lunch, explore the tide pools of **Fitzgerald Marine Life Refuge** (☎ 650/728–3584), near Montara, a few miles north. And for a faster trip back to the city during non–rush hour periods, take Route 92 east over the mountains to I–280 northbound.

7 SHOPPING

From fringe fashions in the Haight to leather chaps in the Castro, San Francisco's many distinctive neighborhoods offer consumers a bit of everything. There are ginseng health potions in Chinatown, fine antiques and art in Jackson Square, handmade kimonos in Japantown, and bookstores throughout the city, specializing in everything from Beat poetry to radical politics. For those who prefer the mainstream, there are high-end boutiques on Union Street and fine department stores in Union Square.

S HOPPING IN SAN FRANCISCO means much more than driving
to the local mall. Major department stores, swank fashion boutiques, vintage clothing stores, bath and body boutiques, and specialty stores for crafts, housewares, and more are scattered among the
city's diverse neighborhoods. San Francisco's creative side is revealed
in the number of art galleries, both upscale and fringe, as well as in its
terrific variety of CD and bookstores. Most stores accept at least Visa
and MasterCard, and many also accept American Express and Diners
Club. Very few accept cash only, and policies vary on traveler's checks.
The *San Francisco Chronicle* and *San Francisco Examiner* advertise
sales. For smaller shops check the two free weeklies, the *San Francisco
Bay Guardian* and *SF Weekly,* which can be found on street corners
every Wednesday.

Updated by
Sharron Wood

Major Shopping Districts

The Castro/Noe Valley

The Castro, often called the gay capital of the world, is also a major
shopping destination for nongay travelers. The Castro is filled with men's
clothing boutiques, home accessory stores, and various specialty stores.

Especially notable is **A Different Light,** one of the country's premier gay
and lesbian bookstores. **Under One Roof** (⊠ 549 Castro St., between
18th and 19th Sts., Castro, ☎ 415/252–9430) donates the profits
from its home and garden items, gourmet foods, bath products, books,
frames, and cards to Northern California AIDS organizations.

Just south of the Castro on 24th Street, largely residential Noe Valley
is an enclave of gourmet food stores, used-CD shops, clothing boutiques,
and specialty gift stores. Its dense cluster of cafés and casual restaurants makes it a great place to while away an afternoon. At **Panetti's**
(⊠ 3927 24th St., between Noe and Sanchez Sts., Noe Valley, ☎ 415/
648–2414) you'll find offbeat novelty items, whimsical picture frames,
journals, and more.

Chinatown

The intersection of Grant Avenue and Bush Street marks the gateway
to Chinatown. The 24 blocks of shops, restaurants, and markets are
a nonstop tide of activity. Dominating the exotic cityscape are the sights
and smells of food: crates of bok choy, tanks of live crabs, and hanging whole chickens. Racks of Chinese silks, toy trinkets, colorful pottery, baskets, and carved figurines are displayed chockablock on the
sidewalks, alongside fragrant herb shops. The **Great China Herb Co.**
(⊠ 857 Washington St., between Grant Ave. and Stockton St., Chinatown, ☎ 415/982–2195), where your bill might be tallied on an aba-
cus, is one of the biggest herb stores around.

Embarcadero Center

Five modern towers of shops, restaurants, offices, and a popular movie
theater—plus the Hyatt Regency hotel—make up the Embarcadero Center, downtown at the end of Market Street. Most of the stores are
branches of upscale national chains, like Ann Taylor, Banana Republic, and housewares giant Pottery Barn. It's one of the few major shopping centers with an underground parking garage and is a popular spot
for Financial District workers running errands on their lunch breaks.

Fisherman's Wharf

A constant throng of sightseers crowds Fisherman's Wharf, and with
good reason: Pier 39, the Anchorage, Ghirardelli Square, and the Cannery are all here, each with shops and restaurants, as well as outdoor

entertainment—musicians, mimes, and magicians. Best of all are the wharf's view of the bay and its proximity to cable car lines, which can shuttle shoppers directly to Union Square.

The Haight

Haight Street is a perennial attraction for visitors, if only to see the sign at Haight and Ashbury streets—the geographic center of the Flower Power movement during the 1960s. These days chain stores like the Gap and Ben and Jerry's have taken over large storefronts near the famous intersection, but it's still possible to find high-quality vintage clothing, funky jewelry, folk art from around the world, and used records and CDs galore in this always-busy neighborhood.

Hayes Valley

Hayes Valley, just west of the Civic Center, is packed with art galleries and such unusual stores as **Worldware,** where everything from clothing to furniture to candles is made of organic materials.

Jackson Square

Elegant Jackson Square is home to a dozen or so of San Francisco's finest retail antiques dealers, many of which occupy Victorian-era buildings.

Japantown

Unlike the other ethnic enclaves of Chinatown, North Beach, and the Mission, the 5-acre **Japan Center** (⌧ between Laguna and Fillmore Sts. and Geary Blvd. and Post St., Japantown) is under one roof. The three-block complex includes an 800-car public garage and three shops-filled buildings. Especially worthwhile are the Kintetsu and Kinokuniya buildings, where shops and showrooms sell electronics, tapes and records, jewelry, antique kimonos, *tansu* chests, paintings, colorful glazed dinnerware and teapots, and more.

The Marina District

Chestnut Street, one block north of Lombard Street and stretching from Fillmore to Broderick Street, caters to the shopping whims of Marina District residents, many of whom go for sporty clothing, fine shoes, and quality housewares.

The Mission

A large Latino population, plus young artists and musicians from various nations, lives in the diverse Mission District. Bargain hunters come to shop its many used-clothing, vintage furniture, and alternative book stores. Shoppers can unwind with a cup of coffee at one of dozens of cafés.

North Beach

Sometimes compared to New York City's Greenwich Village, North Beach is only a fraction of the size, clustered tightly around Washington Square and Columbus Avenue. Most of its businesses are small eateries, cafés, and shops selling clothing, antiques, and vintage wares. Once the center of the Beat movement, North Beach still has a bohemian spirit that's especially apparent at rambling **City Lights Bookstore,** where Beat poetry lives on.

Pacific Heights

Pacific Heights residents seeking fine items for their luxurious homes head straight for Fillmore Street between Post Street and Pacific Avenue, and Sacramento Street between Lyon and Maple streets, where private residences alternate with fine clothing and gift shops and housewares stores. A local favorite is the **Sue Fisher King Company,** whose quality home accessories fit right into this upscale neighborhood.

South of Market

High San Francisco rents mean that there aren't many **discount outlets** in the city, but a few do exist in the semi-industrial zone south of Market Street, called SoMa; most are along the streets and alleyways bordered by 2nd, Townsend, Howard, and 10th streets. At the other end of the spectrum is the gift shop of the **San Francisco Museum of Modern Art,** which sells books, handmade ceramics, art-related games, and other great gift items.

So-called "Multimedia Gulch," the few blocks encircling SoMa's South Park, between Bryant and Brannan and 2nd and 3rd streets, is the home of much of the city's multimedia industry. In recent years the area has seen a proliferation of restaurants, cafés, designer boutiques, and specialty shops.

Union Square

Serious shoppers head straight to Union Square, San Francisco's main shopping area and the site of most department stores, including **Macy's, Neiman Marcus,** and **Saks Fifth Avenue.** Also here are the **Virgin Megastore, F.A.O. Schwarz,** the **Disney Store,** and **Borders Books and Music.** Nearby are the pricey international boutiques of Alfred Dunhill, Cartier, Emporio Armani, Gucci, Hermès of Paris, Louis Vuitton, and Versace. The streets around Union Square recently experienced a building boom, with upscale retailers like BCBG, **Frette,** and Kate Spade opening new stores seemingly every week. The latest buzz has been about Prada, which at press time planned to construct a building designed by Rem Koolhaas for a boutique at Post and Grant streets.

The **San Francisco Shopping Centre** (✉ 865 Market St., between 4th and 5th Sts., Union Square, ☎ 415/495–5656), across from the cable car turnaround at Powell and Market streets, is distinguished by spiral escalators that wind up through the sunlit atrium. Inside are more than 35 retailers, including **Nordstrom. Godiva Chocolatier** (☎ 415/543–8910) displays its decadent treats, like toffee carré bonbons and gift boxes of chocolate truffles, on two floors. At Post and Kearny streets, the **Crocker Galleria** (✉ 50 Post St., Financial District, ☎ 415/393–1505) is a complex of 40 or so mostly upscale shops and restaurants housed beneath a glass dome. The rooftop garden has a view of the hectic streets and sidewalks below.

Union Street

Out-of-towners sometimes confuse Union Street—a popular stretch of shops and restaurants on the north side of the city—with downtown's Union Square. Nestled at the foot of a hill between Pacific Heights and the Marina District, the street is lined with high-end clothing, antiques, and jewelry shops, along with a few art galleries.

Department Stores

Since most of San Francisco's department stores cluster around Union Square and the San Francisco Shopping Centre, shoppers can hit all the major players without driving or walking from one end of town to the other.

Gump's (✉ 135 Post St., between Grant Ave. and Kearny St., Union Square, ☎ 415/982–1616) sometimes looks more like a museum than a department store, stocked as it is with large decorative vases, ornate Asian-inspired furniture, and extravagant jewelry. Luxurious bed linens are tucked away upstairs.

Macy's (✉ Stockton and O'Farrell Sts., Union Square, ☎ 415/397–3333) two downtown locations are behemoths. One branch—with entrances on Geary, Stockton, and O'Farrell streets—houses the women's, children's, furniture, and housewares departments. The men's department occupies its own building across Stockton Street.

Neiman Marcus (✉ 150 Stockton St., at Geary Blvd., Union Square, ☎ 415/362–3900), with its Philip Johnson–designed checkerboard facade, gilded atrium, and stained-glass skylight, is one of the city's most luxurious shopping experiences. Although its high-end prices may raise an eyebrow or two, its biannual "Last Call" sales—in January and July—draw a crowd.

Nordstrom (✉ 865 Market St., between 4th and 5th Sts., Union Square, ☎ 415/243–8500), the store that's known for service, is housed in a stunning building with spiral escalators circling a four-story atrium. Designer fashions, accessories, cosmetics, and most notably shoes are specialties.

Saks Fifth Avenue (✉ 384 Post St., at Powell St., Union Square, ☎ 415/ 986–4300) feels like an exclusive multilevel mall, with a central escalator ascending past a series of designer boutiques. With its extensive lines of cosmetics and jewelry, this branch of the New York–based store caters mostly to women. The restaurant on the fifth floor overlooks Union Square.

Outlets and Discount Stores

San Francisco is not a bargain hunter's mecca, but seasonal sales, usually in late January and late August, often offer deep discounts on fashionable clothing.

Christine Foley (✉ 430 9th St., between Harrison and Bryant Sts., South of Market, ☎ 415/621–8126) offers discounts of up to 50% on sweaters for men, women, and children. In the small storefront showroom, pillows, stuffed animals, and assorted knickknacks sell at retail prices.

Cut Loose (✉ 1218 Valencia St., at 23rd St., Mission, ☎ 415/282–0695) specializes in loose, flowing, casual clothing for women at discounted prices. Cotton and washable wool separates are available at modest markdowns—often about 25%.

Esprit (✉ 499 Illinois St., at 16th St., Potrero Hill, ☎ 415/957–2550), a San Francisco–based company, makes hip sportswear, shoes, and accessories, primarily for young women and children. Housed in a building as big as an airplane hangar, its bare-bones, glass-and-metallic interior feels somewhat sterile, but discounts of 30%–70% keep customers happy.

Jeremy's (✉ 2 South Park Rd., at 2nd St., South of Market, ☎ 415/ 882–4929), near the businesses and restaurants of South Park, specializes in top-notch merchandise, for both men and women, including Prada and Jil Sander, at drastic discounts—sometimes up to 50%. Look for a collection of stunning evening wear in the back.

Loehmann's (✉ 222 Sutter St., at Kearny St., Union Square, ☎ 415/ 982–3215), with its drastically reduced designer labels, is for fashion-conscious bargain hunters. Chaos reigns on the racks and in the dressing room, but savvy shoppers will find astounding bargains.

Nordstrom Rack (✉ 555 9th St., between Bryant and Brannan Sts., South of Market, ☎ 415/934–1211), opened in 2001, sells the department store's products at a discount of 30% to 75%. You'll find fragrances, cosmetics, and a few housewares, as well as a good selection of men's and women's clothing displayed on well-organized racks.

170

Abitare 48
Alexander Book Co. . .129
American Rag 63
Another Time 112
Art Options 119
Asakichi Antiques 2
ATYS 32
Barnes & Noble 43
BeneFit 11, 38
Billy Blue 72
Biordi Art Imports . . .52
Birkenstock 98
Body Time 28
Borders 88
Boretti Amber 70
Buffalo Exchange . . .62
Candelier 67
Catharine Clark 77
Chinatown Kite Shop . .60
Christine Foley 106
Church's English
Shoes Ltd. 75
City Lights Bookstore .53
A Clean Well-Lighted
Place for Books 103
Cookin': Recycled Gourmet
Appurtenances 113
CrossroadsTrading Co. . . .6
Crown Point Press . .126
Disney Store 88
Dottie Doolittle 11
Dragon House 81
Eleonore Austerer . . .86
Enchanted Crystal . . .24
Evolution 105
The Exploratorium Store .39
F. Dorian 118
F.A.O. Schwarz . . .96
Folk Art International .70
Fraenkel 77
Frette 66
G&M Sales 111
Gimme
Shoes 15, 78, 117
Gordon Bennett 40
Graffeo Coffee 44
Grand Central Station
Antiques 115
Green Apple Books . . .7
Gump's 74
Hackett Freedman . . .91
Hang 87
Hespe 30
Hunt Antiques 57
Imaginarium 10
Interior Visions 21
Jade Empire 59
Japonesque 54
Jeremy's 132
John Berggruen 95
John Pence 64
Just Desserts 56
K&L Wine Merchants .125
Kiehl's 14
Kinokuniya Bookstore . .1
Kozo Arts 26
Lang Antiques 89
La Tulipe Noir 22
Loehmann's 92

Downtown San Francisco Shopping

N

Jefferson St.

Beach St.

North Point St.

Columbus Ave.

Francisco St.

Chestnut St.

Lombard St.

Lombard St.

Greenwich St.

Filbert St.

Union St.

Octavia St.

Gough St.

Franklin St.

Van Ness Ave.

Polk St.

Larkin St.

Hyde St.

Leavenworth St.

RUSSIAN HILL

Green St.

Vallejo St.

Broadway

Broadway Tunnel

Pacific St.

Jackson St.

Taylor St.

PACIFIC HEIGHTS

Washington St.

Clay St.

Sacramento St.

California St.

Jones St.

NOB HILL

Pine St.

Bush St.

Octavia St.

Gough St.

Franklin St.

Van Ness Ave.

Polk St.

Larkin St.

Hyde St.

Leavenworth St.

Sutter St.

Post St.

Geary St.

O'Farrell St.

Ellis St.

Eddy St.

Turk St.

Buchanan St.

Laguna St.

Golden Gate Ave.

McAllister St.

CIVIC CENTER

Fulton St.

Grove St.

Hayes St.

Fell St.

Oak St.

Page St.

Haight St.

Market St.

Mission St.

Howard St.

8th St.

9th St.

10th St.

11th St.

7th St.

Lombardi's 18
Lucca Delicatessen . .37
MAC 23
Macy's 69
Ma·Shi'·Ko Folk Craft 4
Meyerovich 71
Mix 80
Modern Artifacts . . .110
Molinari Delicatessen . .51
Mudpie 31
Neiman Marcus . . .68
Niketown 84
Nile Trading Co. 5
Nordstrom 101
Nordstrom Rack 107
North Beach Leather 93
North Face 94, 109
Old and New Estates . . .33
Paper Source 9
Patagonia 42
PlumpJack Wines . . .36
Polanco 114
Rand McNally 130
Real Food Company . .19
Robert Koch 77
Rolo 108
Rosalie's New Look . .45
Saks Fifth Avenue 85
San Francisco
Camerawork 128
San Francisco Museum
of Modern Art 127
San Francisco Rock Art . .46
San Francisco Women
Artists Gallery 121
Sanrio 100
Scheuer Linen 82
Sephora 102
Shapiro 79
Sharper Image . . . 41,55,76
Shreve & Co. 90
Soko Hardware 3
Songlines 65
Spencer Smyth 58
Stacey's 131
Sue Fisher King . . .12, 83
Sur la Table 73
Thomas Reynolds 8
Three Bags Full 34
Thursday Showcase . . .104
Tilt 49
A Touch of Asia 29
Tower Records Outlet . .133
Twig 35
Union St. Goldsmith . .25
Victoria Pastry Co. . .50
Virgin Megastore . . .97
Virginia Breier 13
Vorpal 120
Wholesale Jeweler
Exchange 99
Wine Club 124
Wok Shop 61
Worldware 122
Xanadu Tribal Arts . .70
Yone 47
Yountville 16
Z Gallerie 27
Zeitgeist Timepieces . .123
Zonal 20, 116

Tower Records Outlet (⊠ 660 3rd St., between Townsend and Brannan Sts., South of Market, ☎ 415/957–9660), the city's most prolific record chain, has found a ready-made market in the burgeoning SoMa neighborhood. Always crowded, the outlet has new and used CDs (mostly remainders), videotapes, and magazines at discount prices.

Specialty Stores

Antique Furniture and Accessories

The most obvious place to look for antiques is Jackson Square. Another option is the San Francisco Design Center, where three buildings and more than 100 showrooms display furnishings and other home design items. The showrooms are open to the public, though many sell to design professionals only.

Asakichi Japanese Antiques (⊠ 1730 Geary Blvd., Japan Center, Japantown, ☎ 415/921–2147) carries antique blue-and-white Imari porcelains and handsome *tansu* chests. Upstairs, **Shige Antique Kimonos** (⊠ 1730 Geary Blvd., Japan Center, Japantown, ☎ 415/346–5567) has antique hand-painted, silk-embroidered kimonos as well as cotton *yukatas* (lightweight summer kimonos), *obis* (sashes worn with kimonos), and other kimono accessories.

Dragon House (⊠ 455 Grant Ave., between Pine and Bush Sts., Chinatown, ☎ 415/781–2351; ⊠ 315 Grant Ave., at Sutter St., Chinatown, ☎ 415/421–3693), unlike many other Chinatown stores that peddle cheap reproductions of Chinese art, sells genuine antiques and Asian fine arts. Its collection of ivory carvings, ceramics, and jewelry dates back 2,000 years and beyond—a fact that's especially evident in the prices.

Grand Central Station Antiques (⊠ 1632-A Market St., between Franklin and Gough Sts., Hayes Valley, ☎ 415/252–8155) knows that San Franciscans are looking for small, practical pieces they can put to good use in their small apartments. Mostly 19th- and early 20th-century European and American furniture include lots of storage pieces like armoires, highboys, buffets, and the occasional barrister bookcase. Service is affable.

Hunt Antiques (⊠ 478 Jackson St., between Montgomery and Sansome Sts., Financial District, ☎ 415/989–9531) feels like an English town house in the heart of Jackson Square. It is full of fine 17th- to 19th-century period English furniture, porcelains, Staffordshire pottery, and paintings.

Interior Visions (⊠ 2206 Polk St., between Vallejo and Green Sts., Russian Hill, ☎ 415/771–0656) has a welcoming proprietor who's happy to tell you about her collection of mostly 19th- and early 20th-century pieces. A French gold velvet chaise longue from the 1930s or a turn-of-the-20th-century Belgian oak armoire is among the treasures you could come away with. The store also carries a few contemporary items, like whimsical lamps crafted from papier mâché.

La Tulipe Noire Antiques (⊠ 2418 Polk St., at Union St., Russian Hill, ☎ 415/922–2000) will make Francophiles swoon over its hodgepodge of French decorative items. A charming French proprietor and his dog preside over colorful Parisian street signs, kitchen cannisters, and unusual items like an enamel umbrella stand.

X-21 Modern (⊠ 890 Valencia St., at 20th St., Mission, ☎ 415/647–4211) is packed with furniture and decorative items of the mid-20th century. Their wacky and not-too-expensive items might include a chair of molded plastic shaped like a human hand. Stainless steel desks and bookshelves are popular items.

Art Galleries

Art galleries are ubiquitous in San Francisco. While most surround Union Square, Hayes Valley near the Civic Center has become another gallery enclave. Pick up a copy of the free *San Francisco Bay Area Gallery Guide* at almost any gallery for addresses and a handy map of galleries throughout the city. For a quick overview, stop by **49 Geary Street,** which houses several of the city's best galleries. Most galleries are closed on Sunday and Monday.

Art Options (✉ 372 Hayes St., between Franklin and Gough Sts., Hayes Valley, ☎ 415/252–8334) specializes in contemporary glass crafts and one-of-a-kind nonprecious jewelry from local and nationally known artists. A variety of affordable pieces is available.

Catharine Clark Gallery (✉ 49 Geary St., between Kearny St. and Grant Ave., Union Square, ☎ 415/399–1439) focuses on the works of emerging artists with a Bay Area connection, though nationally known artists also display their sculpture, paintings, photographs, and installation artwork here.

Crown Point Press (✉ 20 Hawthorne St., between 2nd and 3rd Sts., South of Market, ☎ 415/974–6273) began in 1962 as a print workshop and has since expanded into its current quarters, where studios share the building with a large gallery. Etchings, intaglio prints, engravings, and aquatints by both local and internationally renowned artists are displayed in the airy space.

Eleonore Austerer Gallery (✉ 540 Sutter St., between Mason and Powell Sts., Union Square, ☎ 415/986–2244) is blessed with a charming space, complete with graceful archways and high ceilings, which shows the contemporary European art to great effect. Viennese owner Austerer stocks works by blue-chip artists like Chagall, Matisse, Renoir, and Miró, plus more recent works by lesser-known American and European artists.

Fraenkel Gallery (✉ 49 Geary St., between Kearny St. and Grant Ave., Union Square, ☎ 415/981–2661), one of the city's preeminent photography galleries, shows 19th-century to contemporary works by local and international artists like Richard Avedon in exhibits that rotate every few months.

Hackett Freedman Gallery (✉ 250 Sutter St., Suite 400, between Grant Ave. and Kearny St., Union Square, ☎ 415/362–7152) prides itself on its friendly staff, who will educate you about the art or leave you alone—whichever you prefer. Contemporary realist works, including still lifes, landscapes, and figurative paintings, compose the core of its collection.

Hang (✉ 556 Sutter St., between Mason and Powell Sts., Union Square, ☎ 415/434–4264) imbues gallery-going with a spirit of fun. Emerging artists display their typically affordable works in an industrial chic spot. A rental program lets you take a piece home before buying it.

Hespe Gallery (✉ 1764 Union St., between Gough and Octavia Sts., Cow Hollow, ☎ 415/776–5918) is filled with paintings and sculpture by emerging Bay Area artists. Styles include figurative, abstract, and realist. Owner Charles Hespe is an instantly likable art enthusiast who equally delights buyers and browsers.

John Berggruen Gallery (✉ 228 Grant Ave., at Post St., Union Square, ☎ 415/781–4629) is a well-respected dealer in American and European art of the 20th century, plus Latin American paintings of the 19th and 20th centuries.

John Pence Gallery (⊠ 750 Post St., between Leavenworth and Jones Sts., Tenderloin, ☎ 415/441–1138) uses its spacious 8,000-square-ft facility to display more than a hundred works, many of them by important contemporary academic realists. Drawings, paintings, and sculpture are all represented.

Meyerovich Gallery (⊠ 251 Post St., 4th floor, between Stockton St. and Grant Ave., Union Square, ☎ 415/421–7171) attracts art fans with works on paper and sculpture by well-known masters such as Picasso, Chagall, Motherwell, and Henry Moore. Colorful, whimsical sculptures by contemporary artist Ron Tatro attract browsers from across the room.

Robert Koch Gallery (⊠ 49 Geary St., between Kearny St. and Grant Ave., Union Square, ☎ 415/421–0122) displays photographic works from the 19th century to the present, with an emphasis on Russian and Eastern European artists.

San Francisco Camerawork (⊠ 1246 Folsom St., between 8th and 9th Sts., South of Market, ☎ 415/863–1001), recently relocated to the New Langon Arts building South of Market, is not just a gallery with frequently changing thematic exhibits but also an excellent photography resource center. Call for info about lectures, or browse through the well-stocked bookstore or library.

San Francisco Women Artists Gallery (⊠ 370 Hayes St., between Franklin and Gough Sts., Hayes Valley, ☎ 415/552–7392) is run and staffed by the women artists whose work is on display. It continues the tradition of the sketch clubs that began in the 1880s, in which groups of women artists shared and critiqued each other's work. The SFWA displays sculptures, paintings, mixed-media pieces, and video installations, and each month there is a different themed show.

Shapiro Gallery (⊠ 760 Market St., Suite 248, at Grant St., Union Square, ☎ 415/398–6655) specializes in 20th-century photography, especially the black-and-white works of Ansel Adams and Imogene Cunningham.

Songlines Aboriginal Art (⊠ 619 Post St., at Taylor St., Tenderloin, ☎ 415/614–1223) seeks to educate art lovers about Aboriginal art and culture. Special exhibits may include bark sculptures, Aboriginal-made didgeridoos, or contemporary paintings inspired by ritual body decorations.

Southern Exposure (⊠ 401 Alabama St. Mission, ☎ 415/863–2141) an artist-run, nonprofit space, is one of the city's most established venues for cutting-edge art. Juried shows and accompanying lectures and films change frequently in their spacious, high-ceilinged galleries.

Spencer Smyth Gallery (⊠ 495 Jackson St., Suite 110, at Montgomery St., Financial District, ☎ 415/391–5969) has stacks of vintage European poster art. These original lithographs, many advertising products like Orangina and fountain pens, date back to 1880s.

Thomas Reynolds Gallery (⊠ 2291 Pine St., at Fillmore St., Pacific Heights, ☎ 415/441–4093) specializes in California realism and works inspired by the Arts and Crafts movement. Many of its paintings depict Bay Area locales and are influenced by the Bay Area Figurative Movement, a movement dating back to the 1950s that incorporates both realist and abstract elements.

Vorpal Gallery (⊠ 393 Grove St., between Franklin and Gough Sts., Hayes Valley, ☎ 415/397–9200), a nationally acclaimed gallery with a sister space in New York, carries old and new masters (Rembrandt and Picasso, for example), as well as Latin American art and works by emerging artists. Its collection of works by M. C. Escher is one of the largest in the world.

Beauty

BeneFit (✉ 2117 Fillmore St., between California and Sacramento Sts., Pacific Heights, ☎ 415/567–0242; ✉ 2219 Chestnut St., between Scott and Pierce Sts., Marina, ☎ 415/567–1173; ✉ 1831 4th St., between Virginia St. and Hearst Ave., Berkeley, ☎ 510/981–9858; ✉ 35 Throckmorton, Mill Valley, ☎ 415/383–5577) sells its cosmetics and skin-care products at Macy's, but it's much more fun to come to one of its own retail locations. No-pressure salespeople will dab you with whimsical products like shimmery talcum powder or the lip and cheek stain Tinted Love.

Body Time (✉ 2509 Telegraph Ave., at Dwight Way, Berkeley, ☎ 510/ 548–3686; ✉ 2072 Union St., between Buchanan and Webster Sts., Cow Hollow, ☎ 415/922–4076; ✉ 1932 Fillmore St., between Bush and Pine Sts., Pacific Heights, ☎ 415/771–2431; ✉ 1465 Haight St., at Ashbury St., Haight, ☎ 415/551–1070) was founded in Berkeley in 1970 with a focus on premium-quality ingredients in natural perfumes, skin-care products, and aromatherapy products. This local minichain specializes in sustainably harvested essential oils that you can combine and dilute to create your own personal fragrances. The shop's practice of offering a discount to customers who bring back their empty bottles for a refill reflects its commitment to the environment.

Kiehl's (✉ 2360 Fillmore St., between Washington and Clay Sts., Pacific Heights, ☎ 415/359–9260) attracts an avid following for its high-quality and simply packaged skin- and hair-care products, produced since 1851. This spacious store with a wide selection of their products is only the second freestanding Kiehl's store in the United States.

MAC (✉ 1833 Union St., between Laguna and Octavia Sts., Cow Hollow, ☎ 415/771–6113) sells the sort of makeup that inspires a loyal following. Peppy salespeople are happy to show you creamy lipsticks, glittery powders, and dramatic eye shadows.

Sephora (✉ 1 Stockton St., at Market St., Union Square, ☎ 415/392– 1545), the Paris-based chain, is a wonderland of cosmetics, fragrances, and skin-care products. Two floors are packed with all the major brands, including Lorac, Stila, Chanel, Cargo, Urban Decay, and many, many more. Come to look for a red lipstick and you may never emerge from the many rows of makeup.

Booksellers

All the major chains are represented in San Francisco. **Barnes & Noble** (✉ 2550 Taylor St., between Bay and N. Point Sts., Fisherman's Wharf, ☎ 415/292–6762) is near Fisherman's Wharf. **Borders Books and Music** (✉ 400 Post St., at Powell St., Union Square, ☎ 415/399–1633) has four floors of books and magazines, as well as a café where you can read while sipping a cappuccino. Beyond the chains, countless small specialty bookstores delight bibliophiles.

Alexander Book Co. (✉ 50 2nd St., between Market and Mission Sts., South of Market, ☎ 415/495–2992), with three floors of titles, is stocked with literature, poetry, and children's books, with a focus on hard-to-find works by men and women of color.

Black Oak Books (✉ 630 Irving St., Sunset, between 7th and 8th Aves., ☎ 415/564–0877; ✉ 1491 Shattuck Ave., at Vine St., Berkeley, ☎ 510/486–0698), long one of Berkeley's favorite new- and used-book stores, has finally set up shop in San Francisco. A great number of author events, a large selection of scholarly books, and a knowledgeable staff are its hallmarks.

Booksmith (✉ 1644 Haight St., between Cole and Clayton Sts., Haight, ☎ 415/863–8688) is the place to shop for current releases, children's titles, international newspapers, and offbeat periodicals.

Bound Together Anarchist Book Collective (✉ 1369 Haight St., at Masonic Ave., Haight, ☎ 415/431–8355), collectively run since 1976, is an old-school anarchist entity staffed entirely by volunteers, with profits contributed to anarchist projects. Books and magazines are divided into sections with such headings as Conspiracies, Drugs, Film & Media, Magick & Spirit, and Syndicalist Periodicals. There's also a small Spanish-language section.

City Lights Bookstore (✉ 261 Columbus Ave., at Broadway, North Beach, ☎ 415/362–8193), the city's most famous and historically interesting bookstore, is where the Beat movement of the 1950s was born, grew up, flourished, and then faltered. Poet Lawrence Ferlinghetti still remains active in the workings of his wooden three-story building in the heart of North Beach. Best known for poetry, contemporary literature and music, and translations of Third World literature, City Lights also carries books on nature, the outdoors, and travel.

A Clean Well-Lighted Place for Books (✉ 601 Van Ness Ave., at Golden Gate Ave., Civic Center, ☎ 415/441–6670), in Opera Plaza, is a great place to while away the hours before or after a performance. Paperback literature and books on opera and San Francisco history are particularly well stocked.

A Different Light (✉ 489 Castro St., between Market and 18th Sts., Castro, ☎ 415/431–0891), San Francisco's most extensive gay and lesbian bookstore, has books by, for, and about lesbians, gay men, bisexuals, and the transgendered. Subjects run the gamut from sci-fi and fantasy to religion and film criticism. There's also a large magazine section, and a rack in front is chock-full of flyers for local events.

Get Lost Travel Books, Maps & Gear (✉ 1825 Market St., at Guerrero St., Mission, ☎ 415/437–0529) carries travel guides from the standard to the obscure, including an array of language-instruction materials. Luggage and travel accessories by Eagle Creek and others round out the selection.

Green Apple Books (✉ 506 Clement St., at 6th Ave., Sunset, ☎ 415/387–2272), a local favorite since 1967, has one of the largest used-book departments in the city as well as new books in every field. It's known for its comic books, history room, and rare-books collection. Two doors down, at 520 Clement Street, you'll find a fiction annex that also sells CDs.

Kinokuniya Bookstore (✉ Kinokuniya Bldg., 1581 Webster St., 2nd floor, Japantown, ☎ 415/567–7625), in the heart of the Japan Center, may have the nation's finest selection of English-language books on Japanese culture—everything from medieval history to lessons for making sushi. It's also the city's biggest seller of Japanese-language books.

Modern Times Bookstore (✉ 888 Valencia St., between 19th and 20th Sts., Mission, ☎ 415/282–9246), named after Charlie Chaplin's politically subversive film, carries quality literary fiction and nonfiction, much of it with a political bent. It also has a Spanish-language section and a variety of magazines. Author readings and public forums are held on a regular basis.

Rand McNally Map & Travel Store (✉ 595 Market St., at 2nd St., Financial District, ☎ 415/777–3131) will help you get from Tiburon to Tanzania, with travel books and accessories, maps, and gift items. Check out the topographical maps of California's state and national parks, as well as one of the largest collections of San Francisco–related books in the city.

Stacey's (✉ 581 Market St., between 1st and 2nd Sts., Financial District, ☎ 415/421–4687) has evolved from purely a professional-books specialist to include a large selection of general-interest books.

Tall Stories (✉ 2141 Mission St., between 17th and 18th Sts., Mission, ☎ 415/255–1915), hidden away on the second floor of an unassuming building, stocks an eclectic assortment of collectible books. Histories and twentieth-century first editions are particularly well represented. The store keeps limited open hours, so call ahead.

Children's Clothing

Dottie Doolittle (✉ 3680 Sacramento St., at Spruce St., Pacific Heights, ☎ 415/563–3244) is where Pacific Heights mothers buy Florence Eiseman dresses for their little girls. Less pricey clothes for boys and girls, from infants to age 14, are also sold.

Mudpie (✉ 1694 Union St., at Gough St., Cow Hollow, ☎ 415/771–9262) is filled with children's special-occasion wear, such as velvet dresses and handmade booties. Quilts, toys, and overstuffed child-size furniture make this a fun store for browsing.

Small Frys (✉ 4066 24th St., between Castro and Noe Sts., Noe Valley, ☎ 415/648–3954), in the heart of Noe Valley, carries colorful cottons, mainly for infants but also for older children, including Oshkosh and many California labels.

Yountville (✉ 2416 Fillmore St., between Jackson and Washington Sts., Pacific Heights, ☎ 415/922–5050), an upscale store for children up to age eight, carries Californian and European designs, like tiny silk sweaters for three-month-old infants and flouncy pink swimsuits for little girls.

Clothing for Men and Women

True to its reputation as the most European of American cities, San Francisco is sprinkled liberally with stores that sell traditional and trendy clothes by local designers. Shoppers eager to roam off the beaten track will find plenty of options.

Billy Blue (✉ 54 Geary Blvd., between Grant Ave. and Kearny St., Union Square, ☎ 415/781–2111) may be tiny but it stocks some big-time fashion, including luxurious camel-hair coats and cashmere sweaters, and impeccably tailored Italian suits. Prices are high but the quality and service are unbeatable, inspiring a devoted clientele.

Designers Club (✉ 3899 24th St., at Sanchez St., Noe Valley, ☎ 415/648–1057) specializes in local and national designers who use natural fibers and luxurious fabrics. In addition to clothing, there's a wide selection of hats and handbags.

Mix (✉ 309 Sutter St., at Grant Ave., Union Square, ☎ 415/392–1742) carries knock-out casual and dressy outfits that stand out from the rest. The difference is the creative use of fabrics, from wildly patterned tropical-looking silks to textured linen that has been sculpted into unusual shapes. Many works are by local designers.

North Beach Leather (✉ 224 Grant Ave., between Post and Sutter Sts., Union Square, ☎ 415/362–8300) is one of the city's best sources for high-quality leather garments, including skirts, jackets, pants, dresses, and accessories.

Rolo (✉ 2351 Market St., at Castro St., Castro, ☎ 415/431–4545; ✉ 450 Castro St., between 17th and 18th Sts., Castro, ☎ 415/626–7171; ✉ 1301 Howard St., at 9th St., South of Market, ☎ 415/861–1999; ✉ 25 Stockton St., between Ellis and O'Farrell Sts., Union Square, ☎ 415/989–7656) is a San Francisco favorite, with men's and women's designer-brand denim, sportswear, shoes, and accessories that reveal a distinct European influence. The Market and Castro street locations carry menswear only. The Howard Street location is Rolo's discount outlet.

Solo Mia (✉ 1599 Haight St., at Clayton St., Haight, ☎ 415/621–0342) sells luxurious women's clothing, much of it designed in-house. One-of-a-kind pieces, custom work, and diaphanous evening wear are offered along with jewelry, hats, and scarves.

Three Bags Full (✉ 2181 Union St., at Fillmore St., Cow Hollow, ☎ 415/567–5753; ✉ 500 Sutter St., at Powell St., Union Square, ☎ 415/398–7987; ✉ 3314 Sacramento St., near Fillmore St., Pacific Heights, ☎ 415/923–1454) sells beautiful sweaters and other knit items. Prices reflect the fact that they are hand-knitted from luxurious yarns of such fibers as silk, mohair, and cashmere.

Worldware (✉ 336 Hayes St., between Gough and Franklin Sts., Hayes Valley, ☎ 415/487–9030) is San Francisco's most ecologically correct store, with men's, women's, and children's clothing made from organic hemp, wool, and cotton. It also carries a potpourri of essential oils, skin-care products, and aromatherapy candles.

Gourmet Food

Faerie Queene Rococoa Chocolates (✉ 415 Castro St., between Market and 18th Sts., Castro, ☎ 415/252–5814) is barely large enough for two shoppers to stand in at the same time, but the whimsical decor makes it the city's most charming chocolate shop. The shopkeepers dole out samples of fudge while you try to decide among the extravagant choices.

Graffeo Coffee Roasting Company (✉ 735 Columbus Ave., at Filbert St., North Beach, ☎ 415/986–2420) is one of the best-loved coffee stores in a city that really loves its coffee. Open since 1938, this North Beach emporium sells Italian-roast beans in a variety of blends.

Harvest Market (✉ 2285 Market St., between Sanchez and Noe Sts., Castro, ☎ 415/626–0805) is the perfect place to pick up picnic fixings on your way to the park. Prepared foods like pasta salads, bean soups, and California rolls are ready to eat, or you can go your own way with a superb collection of crusty breads, cheeses, fruits, and vegetables.

Joseph Schmidt Confections (✉ 3489 16th St., between Church and Sanchez Sts., Castro, ☎ 415/861–8682) may not be the city's most famous chocolatier (Ghirardelli wins that prize), but it *is* the classiest. Egg-shape truffles, which come in more than 30 flavors, are Schmidt's best-selling product. The store's real specialty is edible, often seasonal, sculptures—from chocolate windmills to life-size chocolate turkeys. Try the unique line of creme-filled chocolate rounds called slicks.

Just Desserts (✉ 248 Church St., at Market St., Castro, ☎ 415/626–5774; ✉ 3 Embarcadero Center, Financial District, ☎ 415/421–1609; ✉ 3735 Buchanan St., at Marina St., Marina, ☎ 415/922–8675; ✉ Sony Metreon, 101 4th St., at Mission St., South of Market, ☎ 415/

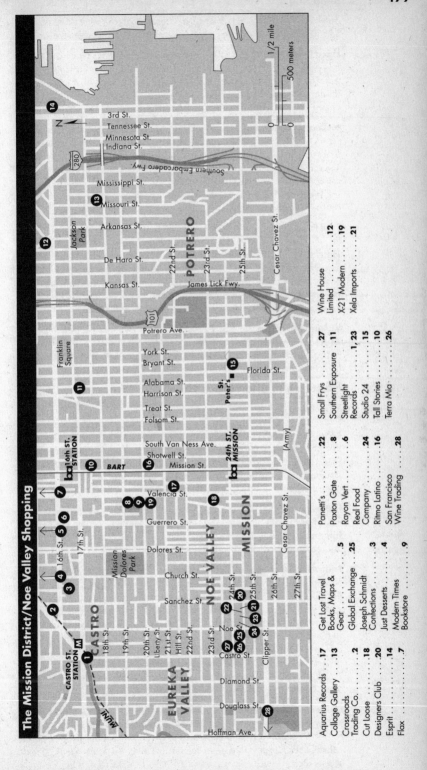

369–6137), a Bay Area favorite, carries chocolate velvet mousse cake, San Franciscans' favorite carrot cake, and other decadent treats.

Lucca Delicatessen (✉ 2120 Chestnut St., at Steiner St., Marina, ☎ 415/921–7873) is a bit of old Italy in the upscale Marina District. Take a number and wait your turn to choose from imported olive oils, homemade pastas and Italian sausages, and a wide selection of imported cheeses and prepared salads.

Molinari Delicatessen (✉ 373 Columbus Ave., at Vallejo St., North Beach, ☎ 415/421–2337), billing itself as the oldest delicatessen west of the Rockies, has been making its own salami, sausages, and cold cuts since 1896. Other homemade specialties include meat and cheese ravioli, tomato sauces, and fresh pastas. In-the-know locals like to stop by for lunch, eating a made-to-order sandwich at one of the two tables on the sidewalk outside.

Real Food Company (✉ 2140 Polk St., between Broadway and Vallejo St., Russian Hill, ☎ 415/673–7420; ✉ 1023 Stanyan St., at Carl St., Haight, ☎ 415/564–2800; ✉ 3939 24th St., between Noe and Sanchez Sts., Noe Valley, ☎ 415/282–9500; ✉ 3060 Fillmore St., at Filbert St., Marina, ☎ 415/567–6900), one of the city's most successful health food purveyors, sells some of the freshest produce outside the farmers' markets, as well as a full line of fresh fish, meat, and wines.

Victoria Pastry Co. (✉ 1362 Stockton St., at Vallejo St., North Beach, ☎ 415/781–2015), in business since the early 1900s, is a throwback to the North Beach of old, with its display cases full of Italian pastries, cookies, and St. Honoré cakes.

Handicrafts and Folk Art

Small galleries throughout the city sell crafts, pottery, sculpture, and jewelry from countries around the world.

Collage Gallery (✉ 1345 18th St., between Missouri and Texas Sts., Potrero Hill, ☎ 415/282–4401) is a studio-gallery that showcases the work of 80 Bay Area artists, including such handmade crafts as mosaic mirrors, handblown glass objects, jewelry, and more. The gallery's open hours are limited, so call ahead before making the trip.

F. Dorian (✉ 388 Hayes St., at Gough St., Hayes Valley, ☎ 415/861–3191) has cards, jewelry, and crafts from Mexico, Japan, Italy, Peru, Indonesia, the Philippines, Africa, and Sri Lanka, as well as the glass and ceramic works of local craftspeople.

Folk Art International/Boretti Amber/Xanadu Tribal Arts (✉ 140 Maiden La., between Stockton St. and Grant Ave., Union Square, ☎ 415/392–9999), three collections in one alluring space, displays a dazzling selection of Baltic amber jewelry, Latin American folk art, Oaxacan wood carvings, and tribal art from Africa, Oceania, and Indonesia. Items include both utilitarian and ritual objects, such as masks, sculptures, woven baskets, tapestries and textiles, tribal jewelry, and books on art and culture. If nothing else, the shop is worth a visit to see its Frank Lloyd Wright–designed home, where a spiral ramp recalls New York City's Guggenheim Museum.

Global Exchange (✉ 4018 24th St., between Noe and Castro Sts., Noe Valley, ☎ 415/648–8068; ✉ 2840 College Ave., at Russell St., Berkeley, ☎ 510/548–0370), a branch of the well-known nonprofit organization, sells handcrafted items from more than 40 countries. The staff works directly with village cooperatives and workshops: when you buy a Nepalese sweater, a South African wood carving, or a Pakistani cap, employees will explain the origin of your purchase.

Japonesque (✉ 824 Montgomery St., between Jackson and Pacific Sts., Financial District, ☎ 415/391–8860), at Jackson Square, specializes in handcrafted wooden boxes, sculpture, paintings, and handmade glass from Japan and the United States.

Ma-Shi'-Ko Folk Craft (✉ Kinokuniya Bldg., 1581 Webster St., at Post St., 2nd floor, Japantown, ☎ 415/346–0748) carries handcrafted pottery from Japan, including *mashiko,* the style that has been in production longer than any other. There are also masks and other antique and hand-crafted goods, all from Japan.

Nile Trading Co. African Art Gallery (✉ 1856 Fillmore St., between Sutter and Bush Sts., Pacific Heights, ☎ 415/776–2233) is packed floor to ceiling with masks, sculpture, baskets, jewelry, and other African arts and crafts.

Polanco (✉ 393 Hayes St., between Franklin and Gough Sts., Hayes Valley, ☎ 415/252–5753), a gallery that's devoted to showcasing the arts of Mexico, sells everything from antiques to traditional folk crafts to fine contemporary works. Brightly painted animal figures and a virtual village of Day of the Dead figures share space with religious statues and modern linocuts and paintings.

Soko Hardware (✉ 1698 Post St., at Buchanan St., Japantown, ☎ 415/931–5510), run by the Ashizawa family in Japantown since 1925, still specializes in beautifully crafted Japanese tools for gardening and woodworking. In addition to the usual hardware store items you'll also find books on topics like making shoji screens and seeds for Japanese plants.

Studio 24 (✉ 2857 24th St., at Bryant St., Mission, ☎ 415/826–8009), the gift shop of the acclaimed Galería de la Raza, sells crafts from Mexico and Central and South America. Prints by Latino artists, Days of the Dead folk art, and masks and wood carvings from Latin America are only a few of things you'll find in this colorful shop.

Twig (✉ 2162 Union St., between Webster and Fillmore Sts., Cow Hollow, ☎ 415/928–8944) is stocked with colorful and creative items, many handcrafted in California. Look for everything from glassware and pottery to jumbo multicolored birthday candles.

Virginia Breier (✉ 3091 Sacramento St., between Baker and Broderick Sts., Pacific Heights, ☎ 415/929–7173), a colorful gallery of contemporary and traditional North American crafts, represents mostly emerging artists. Every piece in the store is one-of-a-kind, from jewelry to light fixtures to Japanese *tansus.*

Xela Imports (✉ 3925 24th St., between Sanchez and Noe Sts., Noe Valley, ☎ 415/695–1323), pronounced "Shay-La," carries merchandise from Africa, central Asia, and Bali, including jewelry, religious masks, fertility statuary, and decorative wall hangings. There are also textiles and jewelry from India.

Housewares and Accessories

Abitare (✉ 522 Columbus Ave., between Union and Green Sts., North Beach, ☎ 415/392–5800) has an eclectic mix of goods, including soaps and bath supplies, candleholders, artsy picture frames, lamps, and one-of-a-kind furniture.

Biordi Art Imports (✉ 412 Columbus Ave., at Vallejo St., North Beach, ☎ 415/392–8096), a family-run business since 1946, imports hand-painted pottery directly from Italy—mainly Tuscany and Umbria—and ships it worldwide. Dishware sets can be ordered in any combination.

Candelier (✉ 33 Maiden La., between Grant Ave. and Kearny St., Union Square, ☎ 415/989–8600), a fragrant little shop on tony Maiden Lane, sells tapers, votives, pillars, and any other sort of candle you can conceive. Luxury bath products and small decorative items also fill the shelves.

Cookin': Recycled Gourmet Appurtenances (✉ 339 Divisadero St., between Oak and Page Sts., Western Addition, ☎ 415/861–1854) stacks the jumble of used cookware ceiling-high in some places; if you can't make sense of the system, ask the helpful owner for guidance. The merchandise runs the gamut from high-quality kitchen items like hand-hammered French copper pots to a bewildering selection of garlic presses.

Evolution (✉ 1271 9th St., between Folsom and Howard Sts., South of Market, ☎ 415/861–6665; ✉ 805 University Ave., at 6th St., Berkeley, ☎ 510/665–0200) carries furniture that is beautiful in its simplicity. Amish, Shaker, and Arts and Crafts reproductions typically come in solid hardwoods, like a warm cherry. Both stores also carry a small collection of pillows, desk accessories, and other decorative knickknacks.

Frette (✉ 124 Geary St., between Grant Ave. and Stockton St., Union Square, ☎ 415/981–9504), Italian purveyor of some of the world's finest linens, opened its first San Francisco store in 2000. Trademark sheets and duvet covers share space with bath linens and a small collection of women's clothing made from luxurious cashmere, silk, and linen.

Gordon Bennett (✉ Ghirardelli Sq., 900 N. Point St., Fisherman's Wharf, ☎ 415/351–1172) carries housewares and ceramics made by local artists. The artfully designed wrought-iron garden sculptures and furniture, garden tools, and whimsical topiaries will tempt any homemaker.

Modern Artifacts (✉ 1639 Market St., between Franklin and Gough Sts. Mission, ☎ 415/255–9000) has all the accoutrements necessary for a stylish modernist apartment, from Eames chairs to a Hans Wegner sofa covered in a nubby fabric and a sensuous lamp designed by renowned Italian architect Gae Aulenti. Swiss bike messenger bags and backpacks by Freitag are all the rage.

Paxton Gate (✉ 824 Valencia St., between 19th and 20th Sts., Mission, ☎ 415/824–1872) elevates gardening to an art. This serene shop displays beautiful earthenware pots, amaryllis and narcissus bulbs, garden decorative items, and coffee-table books like *An Inordinate Fondness for Beetles*.

Rayon Vert (✉ 3187 16th St., between Valencia and Guerrero Sts., Mission, ☎ 415/861–3516), an artful boutique on the Mission's most stylish stretch of sidewalk, sells refurbished furniture and housewares with a unique rustic look. Items range from imposing armoires in metal and glass to such smaller items as antique candleholders and Christmas ornaments. They also deliver their stylish and unusual floral arrangements throughout the city.

Scheuer Linen (✉ 340 Sutter St., at Stockton St., Union Square, ☎ 415/392–2813), a Union Square fixture since 1953, draws designers and everyday shoppers with luxurious linens for the bed, the bath, and the dinner table. Fragrant candles, soaps, and bath accessories make good gifts.

Sue Fisher King Company (✉ 3067 Sacramento St., between Baker and Broderick Sts., Pacific Heights, ☎ 415/922–7276; ✉ 375 Sutter St., between Stockton St. and Grant Ave., Union Square, ☎ 415/398–2894) has an assortment of decorative pillows and luxurious throws,

Italian dinnerware, fine linens for the bedroom and kitchen, books on gardening and home decoration, and an extravagant selection of French and Italian products for the bath and body. Out back at the Sacramento Street location is a tiny, charming garden area chock-full of plants.

Sur la Table (✉ 77 Maiden La., between Grant Ave. and Kearny St., Union Square, ☎ 415/732–7900) stocks everything the home chef could need, plus some things most have never heard of—like round aspic cutters and larding needles. Cooking classes and demonstrations are often held downstairs.

Terra Mia (✉ 1314 Castro St., at 24th St., Noe Valley, ☎ 415/642–9911) lets you create ceramic pieces of your own design using the store's art supplies and kiln. Teapots, mugs, goblets, and tiles are among the items that can be fired and ready to use within a week.

The Wok Shop (✉ 718 Grant Ave., at Sacramento St., Chinatown, ☎ 415/989–3797) carries woks, of course, but also anything else you could need for Chinese cooking, from bamboo steamers to ginger graters to wicked-looking Chinese cleavers. You'll also find accessories for Japanese cooking, like sushi paraphernalia and tempura racks.

Jewelry and Collectibles

Enchanted Crystal (✉ 1895 Union St., at Laguna St., Cow Hollow, ☎ 415/885–1335) has a large collection of glass jewelry, ornaments, and other art pieces, many crafted by Bay Area artists.

Jade Empire (✉ 826 Grant Ave., at Clay St., Chinatown, ☎ 415/982–4498), one of the many fine jewelry stores in Chinatown, has uncut and pre-set jade, diamonds, and other gems as well as freshwater pearls, beads, porcelain dolls, and lanterns.

San Francisco Museum of Modern Art Museum Store (✉ 151 3rd St., between Mission and Howard Sts., South of Market, ☎ 415/357–4035) is famous for its exclusive line of watches and jewelry, as well as its artists' monographs, Picasso dishes, and other dinnerware. Posters, calendars, children's art-making sets and books, and art books for adults round out the merchandise.

Shreve & Co. (✉ 200 Post St., at Grant Ave., Union Square, ☎ 415/421–2600) is one of the city's most elegant jewelers and the oldest retail store in San Francisco. Along with gems in dazzling settings, the store carries Lalique crystal and Limoges porcelain figurines.

Union Street Goldsmith (✉ 1909 Union St., at Laguna St., Cow Hollow, ☎ 415/776–8048), a local favorite since 1976, prides itself on its wide selection of such rare gemstones as golden sapphires and violet tanzanite. You'll also find black Tahitian South Seas pearls. Custom work is a specialty.

Wholesale Jeweler Exchange (✉ 121 O'Farrell St., between Powell and Stockton Sts., Union Square, ☎ 415/788–2365), with more than 20 independent jewelers displaying their own merchandise, is the place to find gems and finished jewelry at less-than-retail prices.

ANTIQUE JEWELRY

Brand X Antiques (✉ 570 Castro St., at 18th St., Castro, ☎ 415/626–8908) has vintage jewelry from the early part of the century, including a wide selection of estate jewelry and objets d'art.

Lang Antiques and Estate Jewelry (✉ 323 Sutter St., at Grant Ave., Union Square, ☎ 415/982–2213) carries vintage jewelry and small antique objects, including fine glass, amber, silver, and a large assortment of engagement rings.

Amoeba 2
Ashbury
Market 11
Bead
Store 16
Body Time . . .7
Booksmith . . .4
Bound Together
Anarchist Book
Collective . .10
Brand X
Antiques . .20
Buffalo
Exchange . . .8
A Different
Light 17
Faerie Queene
Rococoa
Chocolates .15
Harvest
Market 12
Held Over . . .6
John
Fluevog 3
Recycled
Records 9
Revival of the
Fittest 1
Rolo . .14, 18
Solo Mia 5
Uncle
Mame 13
Under One
Roof 19

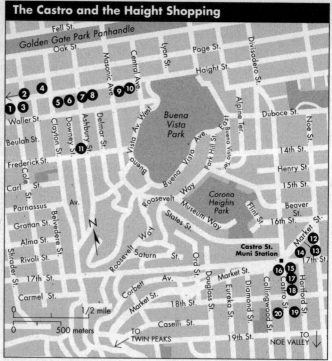

The Castro and the Haight Shopping

Old and New Estates (⊠ 2181-A Union St., at Fillmore St., Cow Hollow, ☎ 415/346–7525) has antique and estate jewelry, crystal, objets d'art, vintage watches, and silver.

Zeitgeist Timepieces and Jewelry (⊠ 437-B Hayes St., at Gough St., Hayes Valley, ☎ 415/864–0185) is the city's best spot for vintage timepieces, with a large selection of mechanical wristwatches and pocket watches from the 1930s to 1960s, ranging from the modestly priced to the extravagant. There's also a collection of dainty jeweled watches, which the owners prefer to think of as "jewelry that tells time."

BEADS

The **Bead Store** (⊠ 417 Castro St., at Market St., Castro, ☎ 415/861–7332) has a daunting collection—more than a thousand kinds of strung and unstrung beads, including such stones as lapis and carnelian, Czech and Venetian glass, African trade beads, Buddhist and Muslim prayer beads, and Catholic rosaries. Premade silver jewelry is another specialty, along with religious masks, figurines, and statuary from India and Nepal.

Yone (⊠ 478 Union St., at Grant Ave., North Beach, ☎ 415/986–1424), in business since 1965, carries so many types of beads that the owner has lost track (somewhere between 5,000 and 10,000, he thinks). Individual beads, made of glass, wood, plastic, bone, sterling silver, and countless other materials, cost up to $100.

Music

Amoeba (⊠ 1855 Haight St., between Stanyan and Shrader Sts., Haight, ☎ 415/831–1200; ⊠ 2455 Telegraph Ave., at Haste St., Berkeley, ☎ 510/549–1125), a longtime Berkeley favorite for new and used CDs, records, and cassettes at truly bargain prices, opened its doors to music-rich Haight Street in 1997. Both locations stock thousands of titles, from punk and hip-hop to jazz and classical.

Aquarius Records (✉ 1055 Valencia St., between 21st and 22nd Sts., Mission, ☎ 415/647–2272) began as *the* punk rock store in the 1970s. Owner Windy Chien carries on the tradition in this Mission District space, opened in 1996, which carries a large selection of dance music and experimental electronica.

Recycled Records (✉ 1377 Haight St., between Masonic and Central Aves., Haight, ☎ 415/626–4075), a Haight Street landmark, buys, sells, and trades a vast selection of used records, including obscure alternative bands and hard-to-find imports. It carries a small collection of CDs, but vinyl is the real reason to come here.

Ritmo Latino (✉ 2401 Mission St., at 20th St., Mission, ☎ 415/824–8556) is San Francisco's best bet if you're looking for Latin music. Friendly staffers will help you navigate the store's wide selection of salsa, *ranchero,* Latin jazz, *conjunto,* mariachi, and more.

Streetlight Records (✉ 3979 24th St., between Noe and Sanchez Sts., Noe Valley, ☎ 415/282–3550; ✉ 2350 Market St., at Castro St., Castro, ☎ 415/282–8000), a Noe Valley staple since 1973 with a branch on Market Street, buys and sells thousands of used CDs, with an emphasis on rock, jazz, soul, and R&B. There is plenty of vinyl for purists.

Virgin Megastore (✉ 2 Stockton St., at Market St., Union Square, ☎ 415/397–4525), the huge, glitzy music store near Union Square, has hundreds of listening stations, a classical music room, and an extensive laser disc department, as well as a bookstore and a café overlooking Market Street.

Paper and Postcards

Flax (✉ 1699 Market St., near Valencia St., Mission, ☎ 415/552–2355), an art supply giant in mid-Market, gets the creative juices flowing. In addition to cards and handmade paper, Flax has one-of-a-kind photo albums and journals, fine pens and pencils, crafts kits, drafting tables and easels, and inspiring doodads for kids.

Kozo Arts (✉ 1969-A Union St., between Buchanan and Laguna Sts., Cow Hollow, ☎ 415/351–2114) brings the art of papermaking to new levels. In addition to housing specialty papers made of materials like bark, silk, and bird's nest, Kozo imports hand-silk-screened papers from Japan, Korea, and Italy. Also for sale are hand-bound photo albums and journals.

Paper Source (✉ 1925 Fillmore St., at Pine St., Pacific Heights, ☎ 415/409–7710) has one of the city's widest selections of fine papers; beautiful handmade varieties line the walls of this little shop. The back room is stocked with stationery in many colors and textures. Look for occasional classes in paper making and related arts.

Shoes

Birkenstock Natural Footwear (✉ 42 Stockton St., between Market and O'Farrell Sts., Union Square, ☎ 415/989–2475) has come a long way since it produced just one style of sandal. Its famously comfortable shoes now come in more styles, including clogs and sandals that could almost be considered fashionable. Custom work on some types of shoes is available.

Church's English Shoes Ltd. (✉ Crocker Galleria, 50 Post St., between Montgomery and Kearny Sts., Financial District, ☎ 415/433–5100) is where well-dressed men find high-quality Church's English shoes to go with their Hugo Boss suits. Italian shoes of luxurious leather are also a specialty.

Gimme Shoes (✉ 416 Hayes St., Hayes Valley, at Gough St., ☎ 415/864–0691; ✉ 2358 Fillmore St., at Washington St., Pacific Heights, ☎ 415/441–3040; ✉ 50 Grant Ave., between O'Farrell and Geary Sts., Union Square, ☎ 415/434–9242) stocks top-notch European-designed shoes from the chunky to the sleek. And if $400 seems a little steep for a pair of sandals, perhaps you haven't seen the classic styles by designer Robert Clergerie.

John Fluevog (✉ 1697 Haight St., Haight, at Cole St., ☎ 415/436–9784) has one of the city's best selections of trendy footwear. A huge selection of chunky, square-toed shoes and shiny, knee-high boots by New Romantics is popular with club kids.

Sporting Goods

G&M Sales (✉ 1667 Market St., at Gough St., Mission, ☎ 415/863–2855), a local institution since 1948, has one of the city's best selections of camping gear, with dozens of pitched tents on display, not to mention outerwear, hiking boots, ski goods, and fishing gear. You can also rent gear here.

Lombardi's (✉ 1600 Jackson St., at Polk St., Russian Hill, ☎ 415/771–0600) has been serving its clientele since 1948, with sports clothes and equipment, outerwear, camping goods, fitness equipment, and athletic footwear. Ski rentals are also available.

Niketown (✉ 278 Post St., at Stockton St., Union Square, ☎ 415/392–6453) is more a glitzy multimedia extravaganza than a sporting-goods store, but it's still the best place in town to find anything and everything with that famous swoosh.

North Face (✉ 180 Post St., between Kearny St. and Grant Ave., Union Square, ☎ 415/433–3223; ✉ 1325 Howard St., between 9th and 10th Sts., South of Market, ☎ 415/626–6444), a Bay Area–based company, is famous for its top-of-the-line tents, sleeping bags, backpacks, and outdoor apparel, including rugged Gore-Tex jackets and pants. The Howard Street store, an outlet, sells overstocked and discontinued items along with occasional seconds.

Patagonia (✉ 770 N. Point St., at Hyde St., Fisherman's Wharf, ☎ 415/771–2050) specializes in technical wear for serious outdoors enthusiasts. Along with sportswear and casual clothing, it carries body wear for backpacking, fly-fishing, kayaking, and the like.

Toys and Gadgets

ATYS (✉ 2149-B Union St., between Fillmore and Webster Sts., Cow Hollow, ☎ 415/441–9220), with its roly-poly vases and corkscrew people, adds humor and design savvy to practical tools. Whimsical gadgets for the home and office are imported from Scandinavia, Italy, Germany, and Japan.

Chinatown Kite Shop (✉ 717 Grant Ave., between Clay and Sacramento Sts., Chinatown, ☎ 415/989–5182), a family-owned business since 1969 provides everything from basic diamond-shaped kites to box, stunt, and animal-shaped kites. Colorful dragon kites make great Chinatown souvenirs.

The **Disney Store** (✉ 400 Post St., at Powell St., Union Square, ☎ 415/391–6866; ✉ Pier 39, Fisherman's Wharf, ☎ 415/391–4210), with its colorful walls and gargoyle-shape pillars, sells a potpourri of books, toys, clothing, and Disney collectibles. You'll also find Disney-oriented table- and glassware for sale.

The **Exploratorium Store** (✉ 3601 Lyon St., at Marina Blvd., Marina, ☎ 415/561–0360) sells educational gadgets and gizmos so much fun your kids won't know they're learning while they're playing with them. Space- and dinosaur-related games are popular, as are science videos and CD-ROMs.

F.A.O. Schwarz (⊠ 48 Stockton St., at O'Farrell St., Union Square, ☎ 415/394–8700), the San Francisco branch of the famed American institution, is every child's dream, with games, stuffed toys, motorized cars, model trains, and more.

Imaginarium (⊠ 3535 California St., between Laurel and Spruce Sts., Pacific Heights, ☎ 415/387–9885), a California-based company, manufactures its own learning-oriented games and gadgets and imports European brands rarely found in larger stores.

Sanrio (⊠ 39 Stockton St., at Market St., Union Square, ☎ 415/981–5568) is devoted to pop icon Hello Kitty and all her friends. You'll find a plethora of items ranging from lunch boxes to huge plush toys here.

Sharper Image (⊠ 680 Davis St., at Broadway, Financial District, ☎ 415/445–6100; ⊠ 253 Post St., at Stockton St., Union Square, ☎ 415/986–1244; ⊠ Ghirardelli Sq., 900 N. Point St., Fisherman's Wharf, ☎ 415/776–1443) carries high-end gadgets that bring out the child in everyone. Marvel over ultraslim CD players, pneumatic pogo sticks, tiny digital cameras, and more.

Vintage Fashion, Furniture, and Accessories

FASHION

American Rag (⊠ 1305 Van Ness Ave., between Sutter and Bush Sts., Western Addition, ☎ 415/474–5214) stocks a huge selection of new and used men's and women's clothes from the United States and Europe, all in excellent shape. It also carries shoes and such accessories as sunglasses, hats, belts, and scarves.

Buffalo Exchange (⊠ 1555 Haight St., between Clayton and Ashbury Sts., Haight, ☎ 415/431–7733; ⊠ 1800 Polk St., between Washington and Jackson Sts., Van Ness/Polk, ☎ 415/346–5726), part of a national chain, sells fashionable, high-quality used clothing for both men and women. A wide selection of Levi's, leather jackets, sunglasses, and vintage lunch boxes are among the items you'll find here. Some new clothes are available as well.

Crossroads Trading Company (⊠ 1901 Fillmore St., at Bush St., Pacific Heights, ☎ 415/775–8885; ⊠ 2231 Market St., between Sanchez and Noe Sts., Castro, ☎ 415/626–3162) buys, sells, and trades men's and women's new and used clothing, some of it vintage. Used contemporary sportswear is the specialty. Ties, belts, hats, and purses are also in stock.

Held Over (⊠ 1543 Haight St., between Ashbury and Clayton Sts., Haight, ☎ 415/864–0818) carries an extensive collection of clothing, accessories, shoes, handbags, and jewelry from the 1940s to 1970s.

Rosalie's New Look (⊠ 782 Columbus Ave., at Greenwich St., North Beach, ☎ 415/397–6246) has a huge selection of wigs and a full-service salon that specializes in 1960s updos and extensions.

FURNITURE AND ACCESSORIES

Another Time (⊠ 1586 Market St., at Franklin St., Hayes Valley, ☎ 415/553–8900), an Art Deco lover's delight, carries furniture and accessories by Heywood Wakefield and others. It's within a few blocks of numerous other stores that stock vintage collectibles.

ANTIQUING AROUND TOWN

THOSE WHO TAKE PLEASURE in hunting down antiques will have a field day in San Francisco. Though sky-high rents mean that real bargains are rare, the variety is terrific. Antiques stores of a feather flock together in the same neighborhood, which means that unless you're looking for an American Art Deco lamp, Japanese *tansu* chest, and 17th-century French table, you can probably focus on a single area and cover the shops by foot.

The city's preeminent antiques neighborhood is tree-lined **Jackson Square,** centered on Jackson Street between Montgomery and Sansome streets. Antiques stores here, in the city's earliest surviving commercial area, are housed primarily in charming buildings that date to the 1850s, which miraculously survived the big earthquakes of both 1906 and 1989. Don't be intimidated by the fact that you have to ring the bell and get buzzed in and out of most of the stores; the proprietors are almost unfailingly friendly and happy to discuss the origin of that Italian tilt-top table with you.

Almost all the shops in Jackson Square are worth a visit, but while you're here stop by **Antonio's Antiques** (⊠ 701 Sansome St., at Jackson St., Financial District, ☎ 415/781–1737), where the two stories of furniture and objets d'art might include an 18th-century French harp or delicate tortoiseshell miniatures. If you like the shop's pieces, which lean toward French and Italian items from the 17th and 18th centuries, you'll also want to visit its warehouse store (⊠ 701 Bryant St., South of Market, ☎ 415/781–1737).

In sharp contrast to Antonio's, busily packed with ornate pieces, is the uncluttered **Dillingham & Company** (⊠ 431 Jackson St., between Montgomery and Sansome Sts., Financial District, ☎ 415/989–8777), where the 17th- to 19th-century, mostly English pieces are displayed with particularly informative placards.

If the extravagant items in Jackson Square are out of your reach, consider a stroll down Market Street near Franklin Street, where American and European antiques of the late 19th and early 20th centuries appeal to a broader crowd. Though some of the pieces found in these stores can be a bit tatty, reasonable prices make the shops worth a visit. Particularly popular with young San Franciscans outfitting stylish retro apartments is **Another Time** (⊠ 1586 Market St., at Franklin St., Hayes Valley, ☎ 415/553–8900), where Art Deco vanities, armoires, and cocktail cabinets are all the rage.

Japanese antiques are found primarily in Japantown, especially in the three-block Japan Center, convenient for browsing during foul weather. Particularly unusual is **Shige Antique Kimonos** (⊠ 1730 Geary Blvd., on Webster St. bridge, Japantown, ☎ 415/346–5567), where hand-painted, silk-embroidered kimonos are the specialty.

The occasional antiques store can also be found in almost any other shopping neighborhood of the city. In ritzy Cow Hollow you'll find a few antiques shops on Union Street, including some with Asian antiques. You might want to stop by **Fumiki** (⊠ 2001 Union St., at Buchanan St., Cow Hollow, ☎ 415/922–0573; ⊠ 272 Sutter St., between Grant Ave. and Kearny St., Union Square, ☎ 415/362–6677), where Asian antiques from the 17th through 20th centuries include Korean interpretations of Japanese *tansu* chests and Chinese tea pots. In Potrero Hill, **Forgotten Shanghai** (⊠ 1301 17th St., Potrero Hill, ☎ 415/701–7707) sells Asian antiques that are both beautiful and practical. Camphor wood trunks and beautifully aged leather boxes are among the treasures you might find. And in Russian Hill the stores sell everything from Victoriana to simple pine furniture to trendy depression-era decorative items.

— Sharron Wood

Revival of the Fittest (✉ 1701 Haight St., at Cole St., Haight, ☎ 415/ 751–8857) carries reproductions of such antique collectibles as clocks and vases along with cards, calendars, clothing, and jewelry.

San Francisco Rock Art Posters and Collectibles (✉ 1851 Powell St., between Filbert and Greenwich Sts., North Beach, ☎ 415/956–6749) takes you back to the 1960s with its huge selection of rock-and-roll memorabilia, including posters, handbills, and original art. Also available are posters from more recent shows—many at the legendary Fillmore Auditorium—with such musicians as George Clinton, Porno for Pyros, and Johnny Cash.

Zonal (✉ 568 Hayes St., at Laguna St., Hayes Valley, ☎ 415/255– 9307; ✉ 2139 Polk St., between Broadway and Vallejo St., Russian Hill, ☎ 415/563–2220) looks like the garage of a rich and eccentric old uncle, and the sign on the window reads ALWAYS REPAIR, NEVER RE-STORE. Depression-era American country furniture bumps up against old apothecary jars and stainless steel operating lights. The Polk Street store specializes in larger furniture items.

Wine and Spirits

Ashbury Market (✉ 205 Frederick St., at Ashbury St., Haight, ☎ 415/ 566–3134) is a quirky neighborhood market popular with the city's serious wine lovers. Debbie Zachareas, wine director of Bacar and formerly of Eos and Vertigo, made a name for herself as wine buyer of this shop, which stocks the shelves with an eclectic selection of wines, emphasizing California's Rhône-style producers. Ashbury Market also sells fine foods.

K&L Wine Merchants (✉ 766 Harrison St., between 3rd and 4th Sts., South of Market, ☎ 415/896–1734), a spacious, well-stocked, and reasonably priced showroom, has friendly staffers who promise not to sell what they don't taste themselves.

PlumpJack Wines (✉ 3201 Fillmore St., at Greenwich St., Cow Hollow, ☎ 415/346–9870) has a well-priced, well-stocked collection of hard-to-find California wines, along with a small selection of imported wines. Gift baskets—like the Italian market basket filled with wine, Italian foods, and a cookbook—are popular hostess gifts.

San Francisco Wine Trading (✉ 250 Taraval St., at Funston Ave., Forest Hill, ☎ 415/731–6222) is the only place to find well-known Bay Area importer Kermit Lynch's line of wines. Owner Gary Marcaletti is a well-respected wine expert. It also has Saturday afternoon tastings.

The **Wine Club** (✉ 953 Harrison St., between 5th and 6th Sts., South of Market, ☎ 415/512–9086) is nothing much to look at, but it makes up for its bare-bones feel with a huge selection of wines at some of the best discount prices in the city. There's also wine paraphernalia, including glasses, books, openers, and decanters, along with caviar and cigars.

At **Wine House Limited** (✉ 129 Carolina St., between 16th and 17th Sts., Potrero Hill, ☎ 415/355–9463), a highly informed and friendly sales staff is willing to help you find the perfect wine for any occasion. This Potrero Hill store has especially good burgundy, Bordeaux, and Rhône selections and a small but well-chosen assortment of California wines, all at reasonable prices.

Flea Markets and Farmers' Markets

The **San Francisco Farmers Market/Ferry Plaza** (☎ 415/353–5650) is the more upscale of the city's farmers' markets, with fancy pots of jam and baked goods placed next to the organic basil and heirloom toma-

toes. The Saturday market takes place on the Embarcadero at Green
Street. There's an additional market on Tuesday at Justin Herman Plaza.

The **San Francisco Farmers Market/United Nations Plaza** (⊠ United
Nations Plaza, Civic Center, ☎ 415/558–9455), every Sunday and
Wednesday near the Civic Center, sells heaps of cheap produce, along
with occasional baked goods, potted herbs, and even live chickens. This
is the best place in the city for ingredients for Asian cooking.

Thursday Showcase (⊠ United Nations Plaza, Civic Center, ☎ 415/
255–1923), Thursday and Friday roughly 8 to 5:30, is a covered outdoor market selling antiques, collectibles, and local and imported
crafts items. During summer there is free live entertainment at noon.

8 SIDE TRIPS FROM SAN FRANCISCO

One of San Francisco's best assets is its surroundings. To the north are the Mediterranean-style waterfronts, redwood-shaded communities, and vast parklands of idyllic Marin County. To the east are Berkeley and Oakland—one a colorful university town and the other a multifaceted port. South of the city are Silicon Valley and the peninsula, where cattle ranches and California Mission architecture coexist with modern industry. Point your car north, east, or south, and you're bound to discover what makes the Bay Area such a coveted place to live.

Updated by
Marty
Olmstead

BEYOND THE ASPHALT-COVERED HILLS and pastel-painted neigh-borhoods of the City by the Bay, in the towns that surround San Francisco, lies a host of diversions as enchanting as those found in the city. To the north is Marin County, where the lively waterfront town of Sausalito has charming homes that hug narrow, winding streets. From the air, most of the county appears to be open space, intersected with medium-size cities and dotted with mansions and marinas. The highest peak in the Bay Area, Mt. Tamalpais, beckons, too, with mile after mile of hiking and biking trails; beach towns nestle at the foot of the mountain, and to the west is Muir Woods. Hugging the coast, the Golden Gate National Recreation Area extends from the Golden Gate Bridge up to the 66,500-acre Point Reyes National Seashore, where there's plenty of space to hike, bike, camp, and go horseback riding.

Across San Francisco Bay, the town often referred to as the "People's Republic of Berkeley" still retains its liberal image, though it's drasti-cally tamer than it was in the late 1960s. Formerly radical Berkeley has grown up and is now as famous for the free-range chicken at Chez Panisse as it is for having been the birthplace of the Free Speech Move-ment. Its neighbor to the south, Oakland, is shaking off its image as San Francisco's poor relation, with a successful port and a revitalized downtown, now easily accessible by ferry from San Francisco.

The massive infusion of capital that fueled the dot-com boom also sent Silicon Valley real-estate prices skyrocketing from Palo Alto to San Jose. Though the boom is now bust, many excellent restaurants that flour-ished during the high-tech heyday survived the turmoil, with relatively fewer closings than in nearby San Francisco.

Also south of San Francisco is a wonderful section of the Coast High-way, Route 1, which runs almost the length of the state. San Mateo County claims some of the most beautiful and most accessible beaches in all of California, interspersed with a handful of visitor-friendly towns.

Dining and lodging price ranges in this chapter refer to the charts in Chapters 3 and 4.

MARIN COUNTY

Anchored by San Francisco Bay on the south and east and the ocean on the west, Marin County is the prettiest spot of any of the nine Bay Area counties. Add to that landscape the peak of Mount Tamalpais and thousands of acres of protected open spaces, and you have a re-gion tailor-made for outdoors enthusiasts. The territory ranges from chaparral, grassland, and coastal scrub to broadleaf and evergreen for-est, redwood, salt marsh, and beach, leaving relatively little room for human habitation. The people who live here face the highest real es-tate prices north of San Francisco.

Marin's laid-back reputation has been supplanted by its image as one of the most health-conscious counties in America, a place where yoga and aerobics classes, as well as windsurfing and mountain biking, have been popular since the 1970s.

Sausalito is inarguably the best-known town, but its neighbor to the north, Mill Valley, has emerged as the better place for dining. The wealthy enclaves of Tiburon and especially Belvedere have grand homes that regularly appear on fund-raising circuits. Larkspur and San Anselmo have walkable downtown areas, each with its own share of good restaurants and shops. West Marin is another story. Separated from the inland county by the slopes and ridges of the mountain, this territory beckons to mavericks, artists, ocean-lovers, and other free spirits. Stinson Beach is the county's main beach town, but reclusive Bolinas, nearby, would just as soon you not know where it is.

San Rafael is Marin's most populous city, with more restaurants, fewer hotels, and less charm than elsewhere. County business—including the courts, the chambers of the board of supervisors, and the main library—is headquartered in a landmark Frank Lloyd Wright building clearly visible from U.S. 101. The **Marin Civic Center** (✉ 3501 Civic Center Dr., on San Pedro Rd., ☎ 415/499–4122) is a wonder of arches, circles, and skylights. Surrounded by open space, this was Wright's last major architectural undertaking. Call the center for information on frequent docent tours.

Sausalito

Sausalito's bougainvillea-covered hillsides, expansive yacht harbor, and aura of an artists' colony make it feel like a resort on the Adriatic. Luckily you don't need a passport or an airplane ticket to enjoy Sausalito's superb views and laid-back charm. The town rests on the bay less than 10 mi north of San Francisco and is easily accessible by ferry. Mild weather encourages strolling and outdoor dining, although morning fog and afternoon winds can roll over the hills from the ocean, funneling through the central part of town once known as Hurricane Gulch.

Like much of San Francisco, Sausalito had a raffish reputation before it went upscale. Discovered in 1775 by Spanish explorers and named Sausalito (Little Willow) for the trees growing around its springs, the town served as a port for whaling ships during the 19th century. By the mid-1800s wealthy San Franciscans were making Sausalito their getaway across the bay. They built lavish Victorian summer homes in the hills, many of which still stand today. In 1875 the railroad from the north connected with ferryboats to San Francisco, bringing the merchant and working classes with it. This influx of hardworking, fun-loving folk polarized the town into "wharf rats" and "hill snobs," and the waterfront area grew thick with saloons, gambling dens, and bordellos. Bootleggers flourished during Prohibition, and shipyard workers swelled the town's population during the 1940s.

Sausalito developed its bohemian flair in the 1950s and '60s, when a group of artists, led by a charismatic Greek portraitist named Varda, established an artists' colony and a houseboat community here. Since then Sausalito has also become a major yachting center, and restaurants attract visitors for fresh seafood as well as spectacular views. The town remains friendly and casual, although summer traffic jams can fray nerves. If possible, visit on a weekday—and take the ferry.

Snaking between the bay and the hills is **Bridgeway,** Sausalito's main thoroughfare, crowded with shops, restaurants, and people. South on Bridgeway, toward San Francisco, an esplanade along the water is lined with restaurants on piers, all with picture-perfect views of the bay. Stairs along the west side of Bridgeway climb the hill to wooded neighborhoods filled with both opulent and rustic homes.

NEED A BREAK?

Judging by the crowds gathered outside **Hamburgers** (✉ 737 Bridgeway, ☎ 415/332–9471), you'd think someone was juggling flaming torches out front. They're really gaping at the juicy hamburgers sizzling on a rotating grill. Brave the line (it moves fast), get your food to go, and head for the esplanade to enjoy the sweeping views and the tastiest burger this side of the Golden Gate Bridge.

Northern California

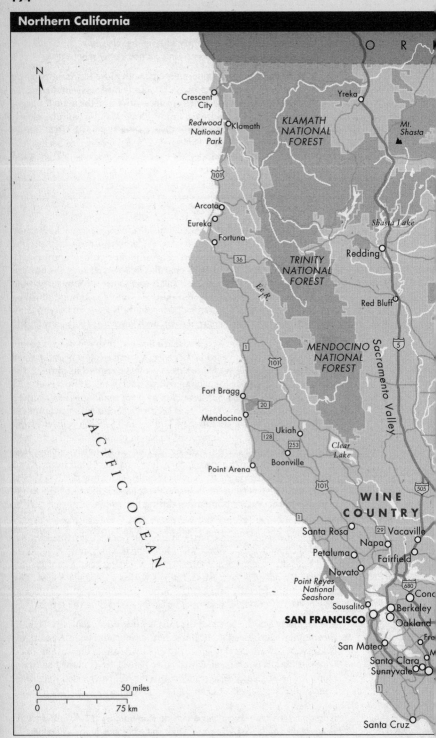

N

Crescent City

Yreka

Redwood National Park Klamath

KLAMATH NATIONAL FOREST

Mt. Shasta

[101]

Arcata

Eureka

Fortuna

Shasta Lake

[36]

TRINITY NATIONAL FOREST

Redding

Ee R

Red Bluff

[5]

[1]

MENDOCINO NATIONAL FOREST

Sacramento Valley

[101]

Fort Bragg

[20]

Mendocino

[128]

Ukiah

[253]

Clear Lake

Boonville

Point Arena

[101]

[505]

WINE

COUNTRY

[1]

Santa Rosa

[29] Vacaville

Napa

Petaluma

Fairfield

Novato

[680]

Point Reyes National Seashore

Conc

Sausalito

Berkeley

SAN FRANCISCO

Oakland

Fre

San Mateo

M

Santa Clara

Sunnyvale

[1]

PACIFIC OCEAN

0   50 miles
0   75 km

Santa Cruz

O R
R

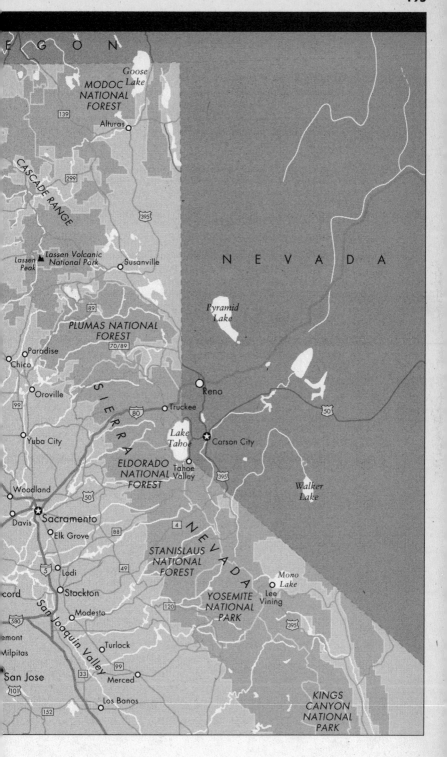

196

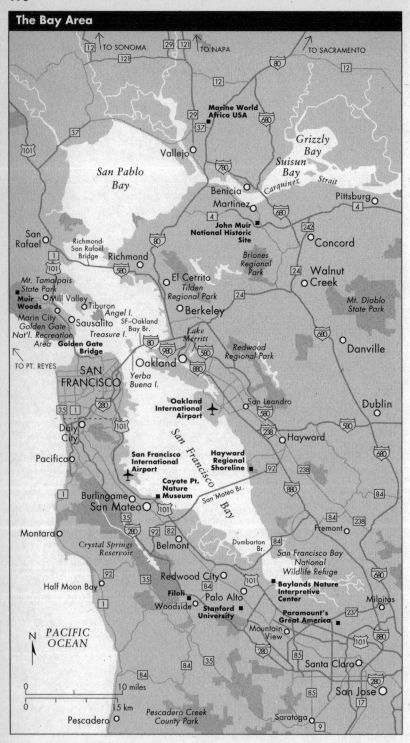

The Bay Area

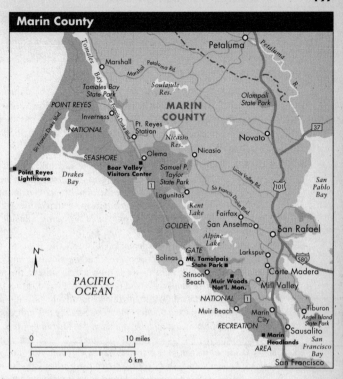

Marin County

The handkerchief-size park in the center of town is the landmark **Plaza Viña del Mar,** named for Sausalito's sister city in Chile. The park has a fountain and two somber 14-ft-tall elephant statues created for the 1915 Panama-Pacific International Exposition in San Francisco.

On the waterfront, between the Hotel Sausalito and the Sausalito Yacht Club, is an unusual historic landmark—a **drinking fountain** inscribed with HAVE A DRINK ON SALLY. It's in remembrance of Sally Stanford (no relation to the university), the former San Francisco madam who later became the town's mayor. Although, as suggested by a sidewalk-level bowl that reads HAVE A DRINK ON LELAND, the fountain may actually be in remembrance of her dog.

The U.S. Army Corps of Engineers uses the **Bay Model,** a 400-square-ft replica of the entire San Francisco Bay and the San Joaquin–Sacramento River delta, to reproduce the rise and fall of tides, the flow of currents, and the other physical forces at work on the bay. The model is housed in a former World War II shipyard building, along with a display on shipbuilding history. ✉ *2100 Bridgeway, at Marinship Way,* ☎ *415/332–3871.* 🎟 *Free.* ☉ *Labor Day–Memorial Day, Tues.–Sat. 9–4; Memorial Day–Labor Day, Tues.–Fri. 9–4, weekends 10–5.*

Some of the more than 450 **houseboats** that make up Sausalito's floating-homes community line the shore of Richardson Bay. The sight of these colorful, quirky abodes is one of Marin County's most famous views. For a close-up view of the houseboats, head north on Bridgeway from downtown, turn right on Gate 6 Road, and park where it dead-ends at the public shore.

The **Bay Area Discovery Museum** fills five former military buildings with entertaining and enlightening hands-on exhibits related to science and the arts. Kids and their families can fish from a boat at the indoor wharf, explore the skeleton of a house, and make multitrack recordings. From San Francisco take the Alexander Avenue exit from U.S. 101 and follow signs to East Fort Baker. ⊠ *557 McReynolds Rd., at East Fort Baker,* ☎ *415/487–4398.* ⌘ *$7.* ☉ *Tues.–Fri. 9–4; weekends 10–5.*

The **Sausalito Art Festival** (☎ 415/332–3555), held during Labor Day weekend, attracts more than 50,000 people to the northern waterfront area; Blue & Gold ferry service to Sausalito is extended during the festival.

Dining and Lodging

$–$$$$ ✕ **Spinnaker.** Spectacular bay views are the prime attraction in this contemporary building on a point beyond the harbor near the yacht club—but you can fuel up on a passable menu of homemade pastas and various seafood specialties as you gaze out at the remarkable scene. You might find a stately pelican perched on one of the pilings outside. ⊠ *100 Spinnaker Dr.,* ☎ *415/332–1500. AE, D, DC, MC, V.*

$$–$$$ ✕ **Mikayla at Casa Madrona.** Although the food at this longtime Sausalito hilltop dining room (reached by elevator and then a flower-decked walkway) is better some nights than others, the view is superb. The California menu is based on grilled fish and meats treated simply but elegantly. Bamboo furniture and handsome animal designs on the walls give the space a tropical feel. The Sunday buffet brunch with champagne is popular. ⊠ *801 Bridgeway,* ☎ *415/331–5888. Reservations essential. AE, D, DC, MC, V. No lunch.*

$$–$$$ ✕ **Ondine.** Jutting out into the bay with clear views of San Francisco and Angel Island, this second-story restaurant is extremely romantic for dinner or Sunday brunch. However, some diners never look up from the dazzling displays on their plates. Star dishes include sautéed halibut cheeks, seared scallops, and roast lamb with figs and fingerling potatoes. ⊠ *558 Bridgeway Ave.,* ☎ *415/331–1133. Reservations essential. AE, DC, MC, V. No lunch.*

$$ ✕ **Alta Mira.** This Sausalito landmark, in a Spanish-style hotel a block above Bridgeway, has unparalleled views of the bay from both the heated front terrace and the windowed dining room. It's a favored destination Bay Area–wide for Sunday brunch (try the famed eggs Benedict and Ramos Fizz), alfresco lunch, or cocktails at sunset. Though the California-Continental cuisine is forgettable, the view never fails. ⊠ *125 Bulkley Ave.,* ☎ *415/332–1350. AE, DC, MC, V.*

$$ ✕ **Christophe.** Small and very French, this charming dining room is one of the few bargains in town. The early bird dinners, which change seasonally, are a penny-pincher's delight. A four-course meal costs $15, and the choices include veal cheeks, braised oxtail, onion tart, and lamb stew, among others. Prices rise reasonably as the night goes on. ⊠ *1919 Bridgeway,* ☎ *415/332–9244. MC, V. Closed Mon. No lunch Sun.*

$ ✕ **Bayside Cafe.** Just a few steps from the bay, this dependable coffee shop is regularly patronized by members of the nearby houseboat community. Dozens of egg dishes, waffles, pancakes, and combos are on the long breakfast menu; all kinds of sandwiches, salads, pastas, and burgers constitute the lunch listings, available until 4 PM. ⊠ *1 Gate Six Rd.,* ☎ *415/331–2313. AE, D, DC, MC, V. No dinner.*

$$$–$$$$ ▣ **Casa Madrona.** What began as a small inn with a handful of historic accommodations in a 19th-century landmark house has expanded over the decades to incorporate five cottages and a variety of accommodations that cascade down the hill from Bulkley Avenue to Bridgeway. The design in these rooms and suites ranges from the cuteness of the Artist's Loft to elegant Mediterranean and Asian-inspired motifs. In early 2002, the inn added 22 rooms and 9 suites in an adjacent three-story building that once housed a complex of shops. These are

uniformly contemporary, with wet bars and bay windows; some have balconies overlooking Richardson Bay. Casa Madrona also opened a full-service spa with eight treatment rooms. ✉ *801 Bridgeway, 94965,* ☎ *415/332–0502 or 800/567–9524,* FAX *415/332–2537,* WEB *casamadrona.com. 34 rooms. Restaurant, hot tub, spa. AE, D, DC, MC, V. CP.*

$$–$$$ 🎬 **Hotel Sausalito.** Soft yellow, green, and orange tones create a warm, Mediterranean feel at this well-run inn with handmade furniture and tasteful original art and reproductions. The rooms, some of which have harbor or park views, range from small ones that are good for budget-minded travelers to commodious suites. Continental breakfast is included. ✉ *16 El Portal, 94965,* ☎ *415/332–0700 or 888/442–0700,* FAX *415/332–8788,* WEB *www.hotelsausalito.com. 14 rooms, 2 suites. In-room data ports, concierge, no-smoking room. 2-night minimum weekends. AE, DC, MC, V. CB.*

Tiburon

On a peninsula called Punta de Tiburon (Shark Point) by the Spanish explorers, this beautiful Marin County community still feels like a village, despite the encroachment of commercial establishments concentrated in the downtown area. The harbor faces Angel Island across Raccoon Strait, and San Francisco is directly south, 6 mi across the bay—which makes the view from the decks of restaurants on the harbor a major attraction. Slightly more low-key than Sausalito, Tiburon has centered on the waterfront ever since the town's incarnation in 1884, when ferries from San Francisco connected here with a railroad to San Rafael. Whenever the weather is pleasant and particularly during the summer, the ferry is the most relaxing way to visit and avoid traffic and parking problems.

Tiburon's **Main Street** is lined on the bay side with restaurants with outdoor decks that jut out over the harbor, giving diners a bird's-eye view of San Francisco. Sunday brunch is popular here. On the other side of the narrow street are shops and galleries that sell casual clothing, jewelry, posters, and paintings.

At the end of the block, Main Street turns into **Ark Row,** a tree-shaded walk lined with antiques and specialty stores. Look closely and you'll see that some of the buildings are actually old houseboats that once floated in Belvedere Cove before being beached and transformed into stores.

Windsor Vineyards (✉ 72 Main St., ☎ 415/435–3113, WEB www. windsorvineyards.com) has free tastings in a converted 19th-century rooming house on Ark Row.

The stark-white **Old St. Hilary's Landmark and Wildflower Preserve,** an 1886 Carpenter's Gothic church barged over from Strawberry Point in 1957, stands overlooking the town from its hillside perch. Operated by the Landmarks Society, the church is surrounded by a wildflower preserve that is spectacular in May and June, when the rare black jewel flower is in bloom. ✉ *Esperanza St. off Mar West St.,* ☎ *415/435–2567.* ✉ *$2 suggested donation.* ☉ *Apr.–Oct., Wed. and Sun. 1–4 and by appointment.*

In a wildlife sanctuary on the route into Tiburon is the 1876 **Lyford House,** a pale yellow Victorian fantasy that was saved from demolition by the Audubon Society, barged across Richardson Bay, furnished with period decor, and installed on the grounds of the Bay Audubon Center and Sanctuary. Although it is open only for private events, the center offers programs on area birds; call in advance for specific times and topics. The center is located off Greenwood Cove Rd., ½ mi east of the Tiburon/Blythedale exit off Hwy. 101. ✉ *376 Greenwood Beach Rd., off Tiburon Blvd.,* ☎ *415/388–2524.* ✉ *$2 suggested donation.* ☉ *Nov.–Apr., Sun. 1–4.*

Dining

$–$$ ✗ **Guaymas.** This festive Mexican restaurant claims a knockout view of the bay, handsome whitewashed adobe walls, tile floors, and a heated terrace bar that serves a margarita to match the best Puerto Vallarta has to offer. The large open kitchen churns out a long list of such authentic Mexican dishes as ceviche, *carnitas ropa* (slowly roasted pork with salsa and black beans), mesquite-grilled fish, and tamales. Sunday brunch is popular, so reserve in advance. ✉ *5 Main St., at the ferry terminal,* ☎ *415/435–6300. AE, D, DC, MC, V.*

$–$$ ✗ **Sam's Anchor Cafe.** Sam's is a major draw for tourists and old salts who flock to its deck for bay views, beer, seafood, and Ramos Fizzes. The informal restaurant with mahogany wainscoting has been a college hangout since 1921. Burgers, sandwiches, soups, seafood, and salads are standards, but the food pales next to the atmosphere. Stick to the simpler dishes and watch for the low-flying gulls; they know no restraint. ✉ *27 Main St.,* ☎ *415/435–4527. AE, D, DC, MC, V.*

$ ✗ **Sweden House Bakery & Café.** This dollhouse-like painted-wood café is a cozy place for pastries and coffee, breakfast, or sandwiches (chicken salad with walnuts and Swedish meat loaf are good choices). A morning order of the delicious Swedish pancakes with lingonberries may prompt you to book a flight to Stockholm. The secluded deck outside is nice on sunny days (it's open until 5 weekdays, 6 on weekends and one hour later between Memorial Day and Labor Day. ✉ *35 Main St.,* ☎ *415/435–9767. Reservations not accepted. MC, V. No dinner.*

Mill Valley

Shaded by dense redwood groves, Mill Valley has an idyllic, woodsy location and a friendly neighborhood mood. Big-name attractions here are few. People come to enjoy the town's leisurely pace, to browse through the stores, or just to lose themselves in the misty confines of the nearby forest. Lying at the base of Mt. Tamalpais, the Bay Area's tallest mountain, Mill Valley is virtually surrounded by parklands and traversed by creeks and streams. If it weren't for its very American coffee bars, organic food stores, and new-age establishments, this could be a village in Europe.

Mill Valley's rustic village flavor is no modern conceit but a holdover from the town's early days as a logging camp. In 1896 the Mill Valley and Mt. Tamalpais Scenic Railroad, "the crookedest railroad in the world," began transporting visitors from Mill Valley to the top of Mt. Tam and down to Muir Woods, and the town soon became a vacation retreat for joyriding city slickers. The trains stopped running in the 1940s, but you can still see the old railway depot, now transformed into the popular Depot Bookstore & Cafe.

The small **downtown area,** no more than five blocks square, is a collection of small, somewhat pricey boutiques selling everything from gourmet cookware to lacy pajamas. In the center of it all is Lytton Square, at the corner of Miller and Throckmorton avenues, where locals and visitors congregate on weekends to socialize in the many surrounding coffeehouses.

To see one of the many outdoor oases that make Mill Valley so appealing, follow Throckmorton Avenue ¼ mi south from Lytton Square to **Old Mill Park,** a shady patch of redwoods that shelters a playground, a reconstructed sawmill, and a replica passenger car from the Mt. Tam railway. From the park, Cascade Drive winds its way past creek-side homes to the trailheads of several forest paths.

NEED A BREAK?	The central spot for people-watching, book browsing, and coffee sipping is the **Depot Bookstore & Cafe** (⊠ 87 Throckmorton Ave., ☎ 415/383–2665), in the center of Lytton Square. Built in 1924, the building originally served as the depot for the Mt. Tam railway, as evidenced by its tall arched windows and unique design.

Dining and Lodging

$–$$$ ✕ **Buckeye Roadhouse.** This is a blast from the past with a 1990s twist. There is mahogany paneling, a huge stone fireplace, hunting-lodge details, and a partial view of Richardson Bay. Traditional American fare, prepared with a modern hand, includes crisp onion rings with house-made ketchup, brisket, baby-back ribs with mashed sweet potatoes, and baked pudding. Although the bar and dining room are usually jammed with diners, the service is generally first-rate. ⊠ *15 Shoreline Hwy.,* ☎ *415/331–2600. D, DC, MC, V.*

$–$$ ✕ **Frantoio.** Late fall into early winter—during the olive harvest—is the ideal time to visit this enormous trattoria, whose dining room is dominated by an authentic olive oil mill. Here is the opportunity to taste freshly pressed olive oil in a salad, drizzled over pasta, or as a dip for bread. The sight of the great granite grinding stones at work is a marvel—and certainly worth a visit. ⊠ *152 Shoreline Hwy.,* ☎ *415/289–5777. AE, D, DC, MC, V. No lunch.*

$–$$ ✕ **Gira Polli.** Rosemary-laced roast chicken is the specialty here, slowly spun on a monumental Italian-imported rotisserie over an aromatic wood fire. The crisp-skinned birds come with herb-dusted roast potatoes and bread. Good sides include a salad of sliced tomatoes and milky fresh mozzarella and a dessert of lemony cheesecake. If the dining room is crowded, takeout is encouraged. ⊠ *590 E. Blithedale Ave.,* ☎ *415/383–6040. AE, MC, V. No lunch.*

$–$$ ✕ **Piazza D'Angelo.** A huge bar area holds diners waiting for a table in the skylit recesses of Marin's premier Italian restaurant. In the heart of downtown, D'Angelo's is known for outstanding osso buco and veal saltimbocca (when they're available), as well as pastas and an unsurpassed crème brûlée. ⊠ *22 Miller Ave.,* ☎ *415/388–2000. AE, MC, V.*

$ ✕ **Thep Lela.** All the Thai classics are here—curries in a rainbow of colors; lemongrass-scented chicken soup; fish cakes dotted with green beans; and noodles tossed with bean sprouts. Be prepared for a wait. ⊠ *411 Strawberry Village,* ☎ *415/383–3444. MC, V. No lunch Sun.*

$$–$$$$ ★ ⬚ **Mill Valley Inn.** Mill Valley's only downtown hotel has rooms in its main building, as well as two cottages in the redwoods and the six-room Creek House, which includes a penthouse apartment. Tuscan colors of ocher and olive, handcrafted beds, armoires and lamps by local artisans, and balconies and verandas make each room distinctive. ⊠ *165 Throckmorton Ave., 94941,* ☎ *415/389–6608 or 800/595–2100,* ⅎⅈⅹ *415/389–5051,* ⓦⒺⒷ *www.millvalleyinn.com. 25 rooms. Meeting room. AE, D, DC, MC, V. CP.*

$$ ⬚ **Acqua Hotel.** Color schemes of jade and celadon befit a hotel named after the Italian word for water. Sleek and contemporary inside and out, this three-story boutique hotel opened in 1999 on Richardson Bay between Sausalito and Mill Valley. Soundproofing quells almost all the noise from the nearby highway. ⊠ *555 Redwood Hwy., 94941,* ☎ *415/380–0400 or 888/662–9555,* ⅎⅈⅹ *415/380–9696,* ⓦⒺⒷ *www.marinhotels.com. 50 rooms. Gym, laundry service, concierge, meeting room. AE, D, DC, MC, V. CP.*

The Marin Headlands

The term "Golden Gate" may now be synonymous with the world-famous bridge, but it originally referred to the grassy, poppy-strewn hills flanking the passageway into San Francisco Bay. To the north side of the gate lie the Marin Headlands, part of the Golden Gate Recreation Area and the most dramatic scenery in the area. If you've just come from the enclosed silence of the nearby redwood groves, you'll be struck by the headlands' raw beauty. Windswept hills plunge down to the ocean, and creek-fed thickets shelter swaying wildflowers.

Photographers flock here for shots of the city, with the Golden Gate Bridge in the foreground and the city skyline on the horizon. Equally remarkable are the views north along the coast and out to sea, where the Farallon Islands are visible on clear days. The headlands are the only break in the Coast Range Mountains, providing access to the ocean for the rivers of California's 400-mi-long Central Valley.

The headlands' strategic position at the mouth of the bay made them a logical site for World War II military installations. Today you can explore the crumbling concrete batteries where naval guns once protected the approaches from the sea. The headlands' main attractions are centered on Forts Barry and Cronkhite, which lie just across Rodeo Lagoon from each other. Fronting the lagoon is Rodeo Beach, a dark stretch of sand that attracts sand-castle builders and dog lovers. The **Marin Headlands Visitor Center** (⊠ Fort Barry, Field and Bunker Rds., Bldg. 948, 94965, ☎ 415/331–1540) sells a useful guide to historic sites and wildlife and has exhibits on the area's history and ecology. ⊙ Daily 9:30–4:30.

For a look at a more recent episode in the area's military history, head to the now-defunct **Nike Missile Site** (☎ 415/331–1453), above Fort Barry, the only one remaining in the United States. The site is open Wednesday through Sunday from 12:30 to 4, giving you a firsthand view of menacing Hercules missiles and missile-tracking radar. On the first Sunday of each month informative tours are conducted at both the missile site and the military barracks at Fort Cronkhite.

Most people only come for the day, but hearty types can take advantage of any of the 15 **campsites** (☎ 415/331–1540 reservations) that dot the headlands. The excellent **Marin Headlands Hostel** (☎ 415/331–2777) charges $13 a night in the old military infirmary.

At the end of Conzelman Road is the **Point Bonita Lighthouse,** a recently restored beauty that is still guiding ships to safety with its original 1855 refractory lens. Half the fun of a visit is the ½-mi walk from the parking area down to the lighthouse, which takes you through a rock tunnel and across a suspension bridge. Signposts along the way detail the bravado of surfmen, as the early lifeguards were called, and the tenacity of the "wickies," the first keepers of the light. ⊠ End of Conzelman Rd., ▣ Free. ⊙ Weekends 12:30–3:30.

Craggy **Hawk Hill** is the best place on the West Coast to watch the migration of eagles, hawks, and falcons as they fly south for the winter. As many as a thousand have been sighted in a single day. The viewing area is about 2 mi up Conzelman Road from U.S. 101; look for a Hawk Hill sign. In September and October, on rain- and fog-free weekends at noon, you'll find the folks from the Golden Gate Raptor Observatory (☎ 415/331–0730) at the hill giving lectures about the birds, followed at 1 by a raptor banding demonstration.

Muir Woods

One hundred fifty million years ago ancestors of redwood and sequoia trees grew throughout the United States. Today the *Sequoia semper-virens* can be found only in a narrow, cool coastal belt from Monterey

★ to Oregon. **Muir Woods National Monument,** 17 mi northwest of San Francisco, 12 mi north of the Golden Gate Bridge, is a 550-acre park that contains one of the most majestic redwood groves in the world. Some redwoods in the park are nearly 250 ft tall and 1,000 years old. This grove was saved from destruction in 1905. Three years later it was named after naturalist John Muir, whose environmental campaigns helped to establish the national park system. His response: "This is the best tree lover's monument that could be found in all of the forests of the world. Saving these woods from the ax and saw is in many ways the most notable service to God and man I have heard of since my forest wandering began."

Muir Woods is a pedestrian's park; no cars are allowed in the redwood grove itself. Beginning from the park headquarters, a 2-mi, wheelchair-accessible **loop trail** crosses streams and passes ferns and azaleas, as well as magnificent stands of redwoods. Among the most famous are **Bohemian Grove** and the circular formation called **Cathedral Grove.** On summer weekends the trail is lined with visitors oohing and ah-hing in a dozen languages about the trees. If you'd prefer a little more serenity, the challenging **Dipsea Trail** climbs west from the forest floor to soothing views of the ocean and the Golden Gate Bridge.

The weather in Muir Woods is usually cool and often wet, so dress warmly and wear shoes appropriate for damp trails. No picnicking or camping is allowed, and pets are not permitted. The park is open daily from 8 until sunset. Parking can be difficult here, so try to come early in the morning or late in the afternoon. The **Muir Woods Visitor Center** has a wide selection of books and exhibits on redwood trees and the history of Muir Woods. ⊠ *Panoramic Hwy. off Rte. 1,* ☎ *415/388–2595.* ▣ *$2.* ☉ *Daily 8 AM–sunset.*

Dining

$–$$$ ✕ **Pelican Inn.** Hearty English fare—from fish-and-chips to prime rib and Yorkshire pudding—is served with a fine selection of imported beers and ales in this supremely inviting inn. Shepherd's pie, beef Wellington, roast salmon, and duck breast are recommended. Old farm tools hang above a large, open hearth in the wood-paneled dining room, and the bar is as convivial as a Tudor-style pub in the Cotswolds. Join in a game of darts to further the mood. ⊠ *10 Pacific Way (off Rte. 1), Muir Beach,* ☎ *415/383–6000. MC, V. Limited menu on Mon. in winter.*

$–$$ ✕ **Sand Dollar.** This is the oldest bar in town, so you're sure to meet lots of locals lingering inside by the fire on foggy days or out on the deck when the sun breaks through. It has an all-American menu: burgers and fries, salads, and sandwiches for lunch; fresh fish and pastas for dinner; and a mud pie for dessert. Sunny Sunday lunchtimes are like impromptu parties. ⊠ *3458 Rte. 1, Stinson Beach,* ☎ *415/868–0434. AE, MC, V.*

$–$$ ✕ **Stinson Beach Grill.** An extensive selection of beer and wine and outdoor seating on a heated deck are the big draws here. Several types of oysters, as well as other seafood, are served at lunch and dinner, while the evening menu lists pasta, lamb steak, chicken, and Mexican and Japanese specialties. ⊠ *3465 Rte. 1, Stinson Beach,* ☎ *415/868–2002. MC, V.*

Mt. Tamalpais State Park

Although the summit of Mt. Tamalpais is only 2,571 ft high, the mountain rises practically from sea level, dominating the topography of Marin County. About 18 mi northwest of San Francisco and adjacent to Muir Woods National Monument, Mt. Tamalpais affords views of the entire Bay Area and the Pacific Ocean to the west. The mountain was sacred to the Native Americans, who saw in its profile—as you can see today—the silhouette of a sleeping Indian maiden. Locals fondly refer to it as the "Sleeping Lady." For years this 6,300-acre park has been a favorite destination for hikers. There are more than 200 mi of trails, some rugged but many developed for easy walking through meadows, grasslands, and forests and along creeks. Mt. Tam, as it's called by locals, is also the reputed birthplace of mountain biking in the 1970s, as evidenced by the many Spandex-clad bikers whizzing down the park's winding roads.

The park's major thoroughfare, the **Panoramic Highway,** snakes its way up from U.S. 101 to the Pan Toll Ranger Station before dropping down to the town of Stinson Beach. Pan Toll Road branches off the Panoramic Highway at the ranger station, connecting up with Ridgecrest Boulevard. Along these roads are numerous parking areas, picnic spots, scenic overlooks, and trailheads. Parking is free along the roadside, but there is a fee at the ranger station and other parking lots.

The **Mountain Theater,** also known as the Cushing Memorial Theater, is a natural amphitheater just off Ridgecrest Boulevard. Constructed in the 1930s, the theater has enough terraced stone seats for 3,750 people. Every May and June such popular plays as *The Music Man* and *My Fair Lady* attract hundreds of locals who tote overstuffed picnic baskets up the short trail to the theater.

The Rock Spring Trail starts at the Mountain Theater and gently climbs about 1¾ mi to the **West Point Inn,** once a stop on the Mt. Tam railroad route. Relax at a picnic table and stock up on water before forging ahead to Mt. Tam's Middle Peak, about 2 mi uphill.

Starting from the Pan Toll Ranger Station, the precipitous **Steep Ravine Trail** brings you past stands of coastal redwoods and, in the springtime, numerous small waterfalls. Take the connecting Dipsea Trail to reach the town of Stinson Beach and its swath of golden sand. If you're too weary to make the 2½-mi trek back up, Golden Gate Transit Bus 63 will carry you from Stinson Beach back to the ranger station.

Point Reyes National Seashore

★   A triangular peninsula jutting out into the Pacific, **Point Reyes** is the only national seashore on the West Coast and one of the Bay Area's most spectacular treasures. When Francis Drake sailed down the California coast in 1579, he missed the Golden Gate and San Francisco Bay, but he did land at what he described as a convenient harbor, now thought to be Drake's Bay. Today Point Reyes's hills and dramatic cliffs attract other kinds of explorers: hikers, whale-watchers, and solitude seekers.

The **Bear Valley Visitors Center** houses some fine exhibits on park wildlife and the evocative *Enchanted Shore* slide show. Rangers provide information on beaches, whale-watching, hiking trails, and backcountry camping. A ½-mi path from the visitor center leads to **Kule Loklo,** a brilliantly reconstructed Miwok Indian village that sheds light on the daily lives of the region's first inhabitants. Trails to the park's free campgrounds also depart from here. ⊠ *Bear Valley Rd. west of Rte. 1,* ☎ *415/663–1092.* ☜ *Free.* ☉ *Weekdays 9–5, weekends 8–5.*

You'll experience the diversity of Point Reyes's ecosystems on the scenic **Coast Trail,** which starts just outside the nearby town of Bolinas, at the Palomarin Trailhead. From here it's a 3-mi trek through eucalyptus groves and pine forests and along seaside cliffs to beautiful Bass Lake. On hot summer days you'll find locals from the nearby town of Bolinas making use of the *Tarzan*-esque rope swing. To reach the Palomarin Trailhead, take Bolinas–Olema Road toward Bolinas, follow signs to the Point Reyes Bird Observatory, and then continue until the road dead-ends.

The **Point Reyes Lighthouse,** in operation since December 1, 1870, is one of the park's premier attractions. The lighthouse originally cast a rotating beam lit by four wicks that burned lard oil. Keeping the wicks lit and the lens free of soot in Point Reyes's perpetually foggy climate was a constant struggle that reputedly drove the early attendants to alcoholism and insanity. On busy whale-watching weekends (late December–March), parking at the forged-iron-plate lighthouse may be restricted by park staff; on these days buses ($3) shuttle people to the lighthouse. If you don't want to walk down—and up—the 308 steps, you may want to skip the descent to the lighthouse itself (the whales are also visible from the cliffs above the lighthouse), but the view from the bottom is worth the effort. Wildlife enthusiasts should make a stop at Drake's Beach (watch for signs) on the way to the lighthouse. A colony of elephant seals established themselves here in 1997, and their numbers have been growing ever since. The lighthouse lies 22 mi from the Bear Valley Visitors Center at the end of the point, a scenic 45-minute drive over hills dotted with old cattle ranches. ☎ *415/669–1534.* ✉ *Free. ☉ Thurs.–Mon. 10–4:30, except in very windy weather.*

Just off the southern end of Point Reyes, the tiny town of **Bolinas** wears its 1960s idealism on its sleeve, attracting potters, poets, and peace lovers to its quiet streets. The main thoroughfare, Wharf Road, looks like a hippie-fied version of Main Street U.S.A. A funky gallery, a general store selling organic produce, a café, and an offbeat saloon line the street. Although privacy-seeking locals have torn down signs to the town, Bolinas isn't difficult to find: heading north from Stinson Beach on Route 1, make a left at the first road just past the Bolinas Lagoon (Bolinas–Olema Road) and then turn left at the stop sign.

OFF THE BEATEN PATH
AUDUBON CANYON RANCH – Here budding ornithologists have the chance to view the nests of great blue herons and egrets. Five miles of hiking trails crisscross the 1,000-acre bird sanctuary off the marshy Bolinas Lagoon. There is also a small museum with displays on local geology and natural history that is open year-round. ✉ *4900 Rte. 1, north of Stinson Beach,* ☎ *415/868–9244.* ✉ *$10 suggested donation. ☉ Mid-Mar.–mid-July, weekends 10–4.*

Dining

$$$$ ✕ **Manka's.** Regional cuisine emphasizing fresh fish and game is served with style in this renovated 1917 hunting lodge. Handsome wood-paneled walls, a large fireplace, and candlelight create a wonderful setting for dinner. Chef-owner Margaret Grade focuses on local seafood, game, vegetables, greens, and dairy goods, with an eye to simplicity, which fits right in with the West Marin County lifestyle. Five-course dinners (six-course on Saturday) are prix-fixe, and the short menu changes daily. ✉ *30 Calendar Way, at Argyll Way, Inverness,* ☎ *415/669–1034. MC, V. Closed Tues. and Wed., and Sun.–Thurs. Jan.– Mar. No lunch.*

$–$$ ✕ **Station House Cafe.** In good weather hikers fresh from the park fill the adjoining garden to enjoy alfresco dining. Local ingredients dominate the menu. Steamed mussels, grilled salmon, and barbecued oysters are all predictable hits. ✉ *11180 Rte. 1, Point Reyes Station,* ☎ *415/663–1515.*

$ ✕ **Café Reyes.** In a triangular, semi-industrial room with glazed concrete floors and ceilings high enough to accommodate several full-size market umbrellas, people dine on a blend of California, Mexican, and Thai dishes. A torte of baked eggplant and goat cheese, a fish burrito with salsa, baby back ribs, and a baby shrimp and vegetable stir-fry burrito with ginger sauce and chutney are dished out with efficiency. Try the spacious patio on nice days. ✉ *11101 Rte. 1, Point Reyes Station,* ☎ *415/663–9493. No credit cards.*

Camping

Within Point Reyes's 66,500 acres are four free campgrounds in isolated wilderness areas. Reservations are essential one to two months in advance; to reserve call ☎ 415/663–8054 weekdays between 9 and noon. All have barbecue pits, picnic tables, pit toilets, and food-storage lockers; the water is not potable and must be treated before drinking.

An 8-mi hike from the Bear Valley Visitors Center leads to ⚠ **Coast Camp,** with 14 oceanfront campsites. ⚠ **Glenn Camp,** a 5-mi trek from the nearest road, has 12 campsites in a quiet valley. The most popular place for campers to sleep is at ⚠ **Sky Camp,** a 2½-mi hike from the visitor center. It has two group and a dozen individual sites. ⚠ **Wildcat Camp** has seven sites on a bluff that is a rugged 6½-mi trek from the nearest road and a short walk from the ocean.

Marin County A to Z

To research prices, get advice from other travelers, and book travel arrangements, visit www.fodors.com.

BOAT AND FERRY TRAVEL

Golden Gate Ferry (☎ 415/923–2000) crosses the bay to Sausalito from the south wing of the Ferry Building at Market Street and the Embarcadero; the trip takes 30 minutes. **Blue & Gold Fleet** ferries (☎ 415/705–5555, 🕸 www.telesails.com) depart daily for Sausalito and Tiburon from Pier 41 at Fisherman's Wharf. Commuter ferries also depart to Tiburon weekdays only from the Ferry Building. The trip to Sausalito takes 30 minutes. Direct ferries travel to Tiburon in 20 minutes, but those making multiple stops can take up to an hour. The **Angel Island–Tiburon Ferry** (☎ 415/435–2131, 🕸 www.angelislandferry.com) sails from Tiburon across the strait to Angel Island, daily April–September and weekends October–March.

BUS TRAVEL

Golden Gate Transit buses (☎ 415/923–2000) travel to Sausalito, Tiburon, and Mill Valley from 1st and Mission streets and from other points in San Francisco. For Mt. Tamalpais State Park, take Bus 20 to Marin City; in Marin City transfer to Golden Gate Transit Bus 63 (weekends and holidays only) to reach the park.

San Francisco Muni Bus 76 (☎ 415/673–6864) runs hourly from 4th and Townsend streets to the Marin Headlands Visitor Center on Sunday and major holidays only. The trip takes 45 minutes one-way.

CAR TRAVEL

Take U.S. 101 north across the Golden Gate Bridge. For Sausalito, take the first exit, Alexander Avenue, just past Vista Point; follow signs to Sausalito and then go north on Bridgeway to the municipal parking lot near the center of town. For Tiburon, exit at Tiburon Boulevard.

For Mill Valley, exit at East Blithedale, continue west on East Blithedale to Throckmorton Avenue, and turn left to reach Lytton Square. All three trips take from 30 to 45 minutes one-way, depending on traffic.

The Marin Headlands are a logical stop en route to Sausalito, but reaching them can be tricky. After exiting on Alexander Avenue, take the first left turn through a tunnel under the highway and look for signs to Fort Barry and Fort Cronkhite. Conzelman Road follows the cliffs that face the ocean; Bunker Road is a less spectacular inland route through Rodeo to Fort Barry and Fort Cronkhite.

For Muir Woods and Mt. Tamalpais, take the Route 1–Stinson Beach exit off U.S. 101 and follow Route 1 west and then north. Both trips may take from 45 minutes to over an hour, depending on traffic; allow plenty of extra time on summer weekends.

SIGHTSEEING GUIDES

Blue & Gold Fleet (☎ 415/705–5555, WEB www.telesails.com) has one-hour narrated tours of the San Francisco Bay with frequent daily departures from Pier 39 in San Francisco for $18. **Gray Line** (☎ 415/558–9400, WEB www.graylinesanfrancisco.com) offers daily four-hour bus tours of Muir Woods, with a stop in Sausalito en route, departing the Transbay Terminal at 425 Mission St. at 9 AM, for $37 with 24-hour advance reservations required. **Great Pacific Tour Co.** (☎ 415/626–4499) gives morning and afternoon four-hour tours of Muir Woods and Sausalito for $39, with hotel pick-up in 13-passenger vans.

VISITOR INFORMATION

➤ TOURIST INFORMATION: **Mill Valley Chamber of Commerce** (✉ 85 Throckmorton Ave., 94941, ☎ 415/388–9700). **Sausalito Visitor Center** (✉ 780 Bridgeway, 94965, ☎ 415/332–0505). **Tiburon Peninsula Chamber of Commerce** (✉ 96-B Main St., 94920, ☎ 415/435–5633, WEB www.tiburon.citysearch.com).

THE EAST BAY

Since the late 1980s, especially, growth in the Silicon Valley has blurred the lines between "South Bay" and "East Bay," as towns in both areas have become bedroom communities for workers in the high-tech industry. The East Bay, when San Franciscans refer to it, often means nothing more than what you can see across the bay from the city, chiefly, Oakland and Berkeley, both of which are in Alameda County. In fact, east of Alameda, Contra Costa County has emerged as a powerful business nexus. It includes several small towns as well as upscale Walnut Creek, where most of the county's fine restaurants and shopping centers are found. South of Alameda and Contra Costa counties, the towns begin to run into one another, reaching critical mass on the edge of the Silicon Valley.

Berkeley

Although the **University of California** dominates Berkeley's history and contemporary life, the university and the town are not synonymous. The city of 100,000 facing San Francisco across the bay has other interesting attributes. Berkeley is culturally diverse and politically adventurous, a breeding ground for social trends, a continuing bastion of the counterculture, and an important center for Bay Area writers, artists, and musicians. Some longtime residents will point out that the city has lost its renegade 1960s spirit, but most visitors will still be struck by Berkeley's liberal bent and the way it embraces all things offbeat.

Named for George Berkeley, an Irish philosopher and clergyman who crossed the Atlantic to convert Native Americans to Christianity, Berkeley grew with its university. The state legislature chartered the school in 1868 as the founding campus of the state university system and established it five years later on a rising plain of oak trees split by Strawberry Creek. Frederick Law Olmsted, who designed New York's Central Park, proposed the first campus plan. University architects over the years have included Bernard Maybeck as well as Julia Morgan, who designed Hearst Castle at San Simeon. The central campus occupies 178 acres, bound by Bancroft Way to the south, Hearst Avenue to the north, Oxford Street to the west, and Gayley Road to the east. With more than 30,000 students and a full-time faculty of 1,400, the University of California is one of the nation's leading intellectual centers and a major site for scientific research.

The **Berkeley Visitor Information Center** (⊠ University Hall, Room 101, 2200 University Ave., at Oxford St., ☎ 510/642–5215) is the starting point for weekday 1½-hour student-guided tours of the campus starting at 10. The tours leave from Sather Tower at 10 on Saturday and 1 on Sunday. Dozens of **cafés** surround the campus. Students, faculty, and other Berkeley residents spend hours nursing coffee concoctions of various persuasions while they read, discuss, and debate—or eavesdrop on others doing the same.

Northwest of campus, **Walnut Square** houses upscale boutiques and restaurants at Shattuck and Vine streets. Around the corner is Chez Panisse Café and Restaurant, at the heart of what is locally known as the Gourmet Ghetto, a three-block stretch of specialty shops and eateries.

South of campus, along College Avenue near Ashby Avenue, the area known as **Elmwood** has many shops for browsing. Shingled houses line the tree-shaded streets near College and Ashby avenues. You can see hillside homes with spectacular views on the winding roads near the intersection of Ashby and Claremont avenues. At the opposite side of the city, on **4th Street** north of University Avenue, an industrial area has been converted into a pleasant shopping street with a few popular eateries, several trendy home furnishings stores, and a couple of shops selling handcrafted and ecoconscious goods. Those looking for inexpensive lodging should investigate **University Avenue,** west of campus. The area is noisy, congested, and somewhat dilapidated, but there are a couple of decent motels.

Telegraph Avenue is Berkeley's student-oriented thoroughfare and the best place to get a dose of the city's famed counterculture. On any given day you might encounter a troop of chanting Hare Krishnas or a naked man walking down the street. Telegraph is first and foremost a place for shopping and socializing. Cafés, bookstores, poster shops, and street vendors line the avenue. T-shirt vendors and tarot card readers come and go on a whim, but a few establishments are neighborhood landmarks. **Cody's Books** (No. 2454) is one of the best bookstores in a city that reveres them. **Moe's Books** (No. 2476) carries a huge selection of used titles. **Amoeba Music** (No. 2455) has one of the Bay Area's largest and cheapest selections of new and used CDs and tapes. **Rasputin Music** (No. 2401) offers good prices on new CDs and a wide selection of used ones. Allen Ginsberg wrote his acclaimed poem "Howl" at **Caffe Mediterraneum** (No. 2475), a relic of 1960s-era café culture.

Numbers in the text correspond to numbers in the margin and on the Berkeley map.

❶ **Sproul Plaza,** just inside the U.C. Berkeley campus at Telegraph Avenue and Bancroft Way, was the site of several free speech and civil

Lawrence Hall
of Science . . .6

Phoebe
Hearst
Museum of
Anthropology .3

Sather
Tower 2

Sproul
Plaza 1

U.C. Berkeley
Art Museum . .4

U.C. Botanical
Garden 5

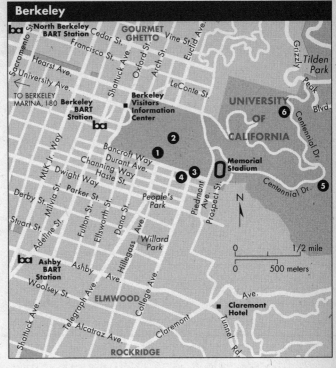

Berkeley

rights protests in the 1960s. Today a lively panorama of political and social activists, musicians, and students show off Berkeley's flair for the bizarre. Preachers orate atop milk crates, amateur entertainers bang on makeshift drum sets, and protesters distribute leaflets on everything from marijuana to the Middle East.

2 **Sather Tower,** the campus landmark popularly known as the Campanile, can be seen for miles. The 307-ft structure was modeled on St. Mark's Tower in Venice and completed in 1914. The carillon is played weekdays at 7:50, noon, and 6, Saturday at noon and 6, and for an extended 45-minute concert Saturday and Sunday at 2. Take the elevator 175 ft up, then walk another 38 steps to the observation deck for a view of the campus and a close-up look at the iron bells, which each weigh up to 10,500 pounds. 🎫 $2. 🕐 *Weekdays 10–4, weekends 10–5.*

3 The **Phoebe Hearst Museum of Anthropology,** in Kroeber Hall, has a collection of more than 4,000 artifacts, only a small fraction of which are on display at any time. In 2002 the museum opened its new "Celebrating the Diversity of California Indian Culture" and, as part of its centennial, "A Century of Collecting," featuring more than 3,000 pieces. Changing exhibits may cover the archaeology of ancient America or the crafts of Pacific Islanders. ☎ *510/642–3682.* 🎫 $2. 🕐 *Wed.–Sun. 10–4:30.*

4 The **U.C. Berkeley Art Museum** houses a surprisingly interesting collection of works spanning five centuries, with an emphasis on contemporary art. Changing exhibits line the spiral ramps and balcony galleries. Don't miss the series of vibrant paintings by abstract expressionist Hans Hofmann. On the ground floor, the **Pacific Film Archive** has programs of historic and contemporary films. The reception desk and library of the archive remain at the museum, but the exhibition theater has been moved to a new space at 2575 Bancroft Way near Bowditch. ⊠ *2626 Bancroft Way,* ☎ *510/642–0808; 510/642–1124 film-program information.* ☎ *$6.* ☉ *Wed. and Fri.–Sun. 11–5, Thurs. 11–9.*

❺ More than 13,500 species of plants from all over the world flourish in the 34-acre **U.C. Botanical Garden**—thanks to Berkeley's temperate climate. Informative tours of the garden are given weekends at 1:30. Benches and shady picnic tables make this a relaxing alternative to the busy main campus. ⊠ *Centennial Dr.,* ☎ *510/642–3343.* ☎ *$3.* ☉ *Daily 9–5. Closed first Tues. of each month.*

OFF THE
BEATEN PATH

INDIAN ROCK – An outcropping of nature in a sea of north Berkeley homes, this is an unbeatable spot for a sunset picnic. Grab a take-out meal on nearby Solano Avenue; then pick up Indian Rock Path where Solano Avenue hits the Alameda. You'll know you've reached the rock when you see amateur rock climbers clinging precariously to its side. At the top you'll join after-work walkers and cuddling couples, all watching the sun sinking beneath the Golden Gate Bridge.

❻ The fortresslike **Lawrence Hall of Science,** a dazzling hands-on science center, lets kids look at insects under microscopes, solve crimes using chemical forensics, and explore the physics of baseball. On weekends there are special lectures, demonstrations, and planetarium shows. On clear Saturday nights the museum sets up telescopes on its outdoor plaza for the popular Saturday Night Stargazing from 8 to 11. ⊠ *Centennial Dr., near Grizzly Peak Blvd.,* ☎ *510/642–5132,* WEB *www.lawrencehallofscience.org.* ☎ *$7.* ☉ *Daily 10–5.*

Tilden Park (☎ *510/562–7275*), an oasis in the midst of the city, has a botanical garden, an 18-hole golf course, and an environmental education center. You'll find picnic sites and 31 mi of paths on its 2,000 acres. Both kids and kids at heart will love the park's miniature steam trains, pony rides, and the vintage menagerie-style carousel. Swimming is permitted at Lake Anza.

Outdoorsy types will enjoy the **Berkeley Marina,** with its spectacular views of San Francisco and Angel Island (from a ¼-mi wooden pier) and its picnic-friendly grassy expanses. At the northern tip of the marina, the 92-acre **Cesar E. Chavez Park** fills with kite fliers on sunny days. ⊠ *University Ave., ½ mi west of I–80.*

NEED A
BREAK?

Of all the coffeehouses in latte-crazed Berkeley, the one that deserves a pilgrimage is **Peet's** (⊠ *2124 Vine St.,* ☎ *510/841–0564*). When this, the original, opened at Vine and Walnut in 1966, the coffee was roasted in the store and brewed by the cup. Peet's—it's the Dutch last name of the founder—has since expanded with stores in San Francisco, Walnut Creek, Marin County, and elsewhere. This isn't a café where you can sit on sofas or order quiche. It's strictly coffee, tea, and sweets. Peet's coffee is unparalleled, and the company is so confident you'll like it that it now has mail-order service for people who live in Peet-less places like Hawaii.

Dining and Lodging

$$$$ ✕ **Chez Panisse Café & Restaurant.** The downstairs portion of Alice
  ★   Waters's legendary eatery is noted for its formality and personal service. Here, the daily-changing multi-course dinners are prix-fixe and pricey—although the cost is lower on weekdays. Upstairs, in the informal café, the crowd livelier, the prices lower, and the ever-changing menu à la carte. The food is simpler, too: penne with new potatoes, arugula, and sheep's-milk cheese; fresh figs with Parmigiano-Reggiano

BERKELEY IN THE 1960S: STUDENT ACTIVISM RISES UP

THOSE LOOKING FOR TRACES of Berkeley's politically charged past need go no farther than Sather Gate. Both the Free Speech Movement and the fledgling political life of actor-turned-politician Ronald Reagan have their roots here. It was next to Sather Gate, September 30, 1964, that a group of students directly defied the U.C. Berkeley chancellor's order that all organizations advocating "off-campus issues" (e.g., civil rights, nuclear disarmament) keep their information tables off campus. Citation of the tablers brought more than 400 sympathetic students into Sproul Hall that afternoon. They stayed until 3 AM the following morning, setting a precedent of protest that would be repeated in the coming months, with students jamming Sproul Hall in greater numbers each time.

Conservative U.C. president Clark Kerr eventually backed down and allowed student groups to pass out information on campus. By then, the Free Speech Movement had gathered momentum, and the conflict had made a national hero of student leader Mario Savio. Political newcomer Ronald Reagan played on Californians' unease about the unruly Berkeley students in his successful 1966 bid for governor, promising to reign in the "unwashed kooks." Try as he might, the movement continued to grow.

By the end of the 1960s, however, the cohesion of the groups making up the Free Speech Movement had begun to fray. Some members began questioning the efficacy of sit-ins and other nonviolent tactics that had, until then, been the hallmark of Berkeley student protests. The Black Panthers, headquartered just over the border in Oakland, were ascending into the national spotlight, and their "take no prisoners" approach appealed to some of the Berkeley activists who had seen little come of their efforts to affect national policy.

By 1969 things seemed particularly bleak. Both Robert Kennedy and Martin Luther King Jr. were dead. The student idealism that had worked so well in overpowering administration resistance to free speech on campus seemed powerless to stop the flow of troops heading to Vietnam.

When the university brought in police units to repossess People's Park, a university-owned plot of land at Telegraph Avenue and Haste Street that students and community members had adopted as a park, Berkeley exploded. In the afternoon of May 15, 1969, nearly 6,000 students and residents moved to reclaim the park. In the ensuing riot, police and sheriff's deputies fired both tear gas and buckshot, blinding one observer and killing another. Governor Ronald Reagan, making good on his campaign promises from three years previous, ordered the National Guard into Berkeley. Despite a ban on public assembly, crowds continued to gather and march in the days following the first riot. The park changed hands several times in the following tear gas–filled months, with the fence coming down for final time in 1972.

A large, colorful mural on the side of Amoeba Records (at Haste and Telegraph) offers the protestors' version of park history. Although the area around People's Park and Sather Gate may seem quiet now—with tie-dye T-shirt vendors on Telegraph Avenue providing one of the few visible links to Berkeley's more clamorous past—issues such as affirmative action and tuition fee increases still bring protests to the steps of Sproul.

— Chris Baty

cheese and arugula; and grilled tuna with savoy cabbage. ☒ *1517 Shattuck Ave., north of University Ave.,* ☏ *510/548–5525 restaurant; 510/548–5049 café. Reservations essential. AE, D, DC, MC, V. Closed Sun.*

$–$$$ ✕ **Café Rouge.** You can recover from shopping in this spacious two-story bistro, complete with zinc bar, skylights, and festive lanterns. The short, seasonal menu runs the gamut from the sophisticated—rack of lamb, juniper berry-cured pork chops—to the homey—spit-roasted chicken or pork loin or a hamburger topped with cheddar. Begin your meal with Dungeness crab, a Provençal fish stew, or a plate of the house-made charcuterie, and cap it off with the crème brûlée. ☒ *1782 4th St.,* ☏ *510/525–1440. AE, MC, V. No dinner Mon.*

$$ ✕ **Lalime's.** In this charming, flower-covered house, the cuisine reflects the entire Mediterranean region. Prix-fixe and à la carte menus are offered, both of them in constant flux. Choices can range from grilled ahi tuna to creamy Italian risotto to seared duck foie gras. The dining room, on two levels, is done in light colors, creating a cheerful mood that makes this the perfect spot for any special occasion. Add your name to the mailing list and receive the restaurant newsletter, which includes upcoming menus. ☒ *1329 Gilman St.,* ☏ *510/527–9838. Reservations essential. AE, DC, MC, V. No lunch.*

$$ ✕ **Mazzini.** Simple, unpretentious food is what you'll find in this trattoria outfitted with marble-topped tables and trompe l'oeil murals of Tuscan landscapes. Opened in late 1998 to almost instant acclaim, Mazzini has a lunch menu of straightforward dishes such as *orecchiette* (ear-shape pasta) with rapini and chili. At dinnertime, the menu expands to include authentic trattoria dishes such as steak tagliata and a Tuscan seafood stew. ☒ *2826 Telegraph Ave., near Ashby Ave.,* ☏ *510/848–5599. AE, MC, V.*

$–$$ ✕ **Rivoli.** Italian-inspired dishes using fresh, mostly organic California ingredients star on a menu that changes frequently. Typical meals include fresh line-caught fish, pastas, and inventive dishes such as its trademark Portobello mushroom fritters with aioli and Parmesan with arugula. Desserts can range from a pear granita with gingersnaps to a refreshing Meyer lemon tart. Attentive service adds to the overall appeal, and the lovely garden is cheerful. ☒ *1539 Solano Ave.,* ☏ *510/526–2542. Reservations essential. AE, D, DC, MC, V. No lunch.*

$ ✕ **Bette's Oceanview Diner.** Buttermilk pancakes that you'll never forget are just one of the specialties at this 1930s-inspired diner, complete with checkered floors and burgundy booths. There are also *huevos rancheros* (Mexican-style scrambled eggs) and lox and eggs for breakfast, and kosher franks and a slew of sandwiches for lunch. The wait for a seat can be long. If you're starving, Bette's to Go, next door, offers takeout. ☒ *1807 4th St.,* ☏ *510/644–3230. MC, V. No dinner.*

$ ✕ **Picante Cocina Mexicana.** A no-nonsense, barnlike place, Picante is a find for anyone in search of good Mexican food for a song. The *masa* (flour) is freshly ground for the tortillas and tamales, the salsas are complex, and the combinations are inventive. Try tamales filled with butternut squash and chilies or a simple taco of roasted *poblanos* (peppers) and sautéed onions. Order at the counter and pick up your meal when your number is called. ☒ *1328 6th St.,* ☏ *510/525–3121. MC, V.*

$$–$$$$ 🏨 **Hotel Durant.** Long the mainstay of parents visiting their children at U.C. Berkeley, the Hotel Durant is a good option for those who want to be a short walk from campus and from the restaurants and shops of Telegraph Avenue. Rooms, accented with dark woods set against neutral shades of green and mauve, are small without feeling cramped. The hotel's bar, Henry's, is *the* place for U.C. Berkeley sports fans to congregate after football games. ☒ *2600 Durant Ave., 94704,* ☏ *510/845–8981,* 🖷 *510/486–8336,* 🕸 *www.hoteldurant.com. 135 rooms, 5 suites. Restaurant, bar, room service, dry cleaning, laundry service,* *business services, meeting room, parking (fee), no-smoking room. AE, D, DC, MC, V.*

$–$$ ⌂ **French Hotel.** The only hotel in north Berkeley, this three-story brick structure has a certain *pensione* feel. Its 18 rooms have pastel or brick walls and modern touches such as white wire baskets in lieu of actual dressers. Balconies make the rooms seem larger than their modest dimensions. Top-of-the-line is the three-bedroom penthouse, with enviable views of San Francisco Bay. A ground-floor café buzzes day and night with students and other denizens of the Gourmet Ghetto; Chez Panisse is across the street. ✉ *1538 Shattuck Ave., 94709,* ☎ *510/548–9930,* ℻ *510/548–9930. 18 rooms. Room service, concierge; no air-conditioning. AE, D, DC, MC, V.*

Oakland

Often overshadowed by San Francisco's beauty and Berkeley's offbeat antics, Oakland's allure lies in its amazing diversity. Here you can find a Nigerian clothing store, a beautifully renovated Victorian home, a Buddhist meditation center, and a lively salsa club, all within the same block. Oakland's multifaceted nature reflects its colorful and often tumultuous history. Once a cluster of Mediterranean-style homes and gardens that served as a bedroom community for San Francisco, the city became a hub of shipbuilding and industry almost overnight when the United States entered World War II. New jobs in the city's shipyards and factories attracted thousands of new workers, including some of the first female welders, and the city's neighborhoods were imbued with a proud but gritty spirit. In the 1960s and '70s this intense community pride gave rise to such militant groups as the Black Panther Party and the Symbionese Liberation Army, but they were little match for the economic hardships and racial tensions that plagued Oakland. In many neighborhoods the reality was widespread poverty and gang violence—subjects that dominated the songs of such Oakland-bred rappers as the late Tupac Shakur.

Today Oakland is a mosaic of its past. The affluent have once again flocked to the city's hillside homes as a warmer and more spacious alternative to San Francisco, while a constant flow of new residents—many from Central America and Asia—ensures continued diversity, vitality, and growing pains. Many neighborhoods to the west and south of downtown remain run-down and unsafe, but a renovated downtown area and the thriving Jack London Square have injected new life into the city. The national visibility from the 1998 election of former California governor Jerry Brown as Oakland mayor further invigorated the city's rising spirits. Despite economic disparities between its separate parts, Oakland is held together by a strong sense of community. Everyday life here revolves around the neighborhood, with a main business strip attracting both shoppers and socializers. Some areas, like Piedmont and Rockridge, are perfect places for browsing, eating, or just relaxing between sightseeing trips to Oakland's architectural gems, rejuvenated waterfront, and numerous green spaces.

Numbers in the text correspond to numbers in the margin and on the Oakland map.

★ ❶ One of Oakland's top attractions, the **Oakland Museum of California,** is an inviting series of landscaped buildings that display the state's art, history, and natural wonders. The museum is the best possible introduction to a tour of California, and its detailed exhibits can help fill the gaps on a brief visit. The Hall of California Natural Sciences lets you walk through the state's myriad ecosystems, beginning with the screeching gulls and sand dunes of the Pacific Ocean and ending with the coyotes and brush of the Nevada border. A breathtaking film, *Fast Flight,* condenses the trip into five minutes. The museum's rambling Cowell Hall of California History includes everything from Spanish-era armor to a gleaming fire engine that battled the flames in San Francisco in 1906. The Gallery of California Art has an eclectic collection of modern works and early landscapes. Of particular interest are paintings by Richard Diebenkorn, Joan Brown, Elmer Bischoff, and David Park, all members of the Bay Area Figurative School, which flourished here after World War II. The museum also has a bookstore, a pleasant café, and a sculpture garden with a view of the Oakland and Berkeley hills in the distance. ⊠ *1000 Oak St., at 10th St.,* ☎ *510/238–2200,* WEB *www.museumca.org.* ⊡ *$6.* ☉ *Tues.–Thurs. and Sat. 10–5, Fri. 10–9, Sun. noon–5.*

❷ A proud reminder of the days when Oakland was a wealthy bedroom community, the **Camron-Stanford House** exudes dignity from its foundation up to its ornate widow's walk. Built in 1876, the Victorian served as the home of the Oakland Museum from 1910 to 1967, and a room containing documents and original artifacts chronicles the museum's history. Six painstakingly redecorated period rooms occupy the upper floor—a tribute to the craftsmanship and dedication that went into the 1978 restoration. ⊠ *1418 Lakeside Dr.,* ☎ *510/444–1876,* WEB *www. lakemerritt.org.* ⊡ *$4.* ☉ *Wed. 11–4, Sun. 1–5.*

❸ **Lake Merritt** is a 155-acre oasis surrounded by parks, with several outdoor attractions on its north side. Joggers and power-walkers charge along the 3-mi path that encircles the lake, and crew teams often glide across the water. Come at sunset to see a string of lanterns create a necklace of golden light along the lakeshore.

❹ On the north shore of Lake Merritt, the **Rotary Nature Center and Waterfowl Refuge** is the nesting site of herons, egrets, geese, and ducks in the spring and summer. Migrating birds pass through from September through February, and you can watch the birds being fed daily at 3:30 year-round. ⊠ *Perkins St. at Bellevue Ave.,* ☎ *510/238–3739.* ⊡ *Free.* ☉ *Daily 10–5.*

Given the city's reputation for Victorian and Craftsman homes, newcomers are generally surprised by the profusion of Art Deco architecture in the downtown neighborhood around the 19th Street BART station. Some of these buildings have fallen into disrepair, but the

★ ❺ **Paramount Theatre** (⊠ 2025 Broadway, ☎ 510/465–6400), perhaps the most glorious example of Art Deco architecture in the city if not all the Bay Area, remains open and operating as a venue for concerts and performances of all kinds. For $1 you can take a two-hour tour of the building, departing near the box office on 21st Street at 10 AM on the first and third Saturday of each month. When classic films come to the Paramount, the theater stages a live organ performance, shows vintage newsreels and cartoons, and offers the chance to win prizes during the "Deco-Win Spin."

❻ In the midst of Oakland's downtown area, **Preservation Park** is a surprisingly idyllic little business community made up of 14 restored Victorians with tidy, bright green lawns. Wooden benches surrounding a bubbling fountain provide an excellent place to enjoy the architecture and a brief respite from the busy city center.

OFF THE BEATEN PATH   **ELI'S MILE HIGH CLUB –** Reputedly the birthplace of West Coast blues, this small, basic club harks back to the years just after World War II, when Oakland gave birth to its version of that gritty, hurts-so-bad-I-think-I'm-gonna-die music. Today Eli's continues to bring in live blues bands, with

Camron-
Stanford
House 2

Jack London
Square 7

Lake Merritt . . . 3

Oakland
Museum of
California 1

Paramount
Theatre 5

Preservation
Park 6

Rotary Nature
Center and
Waterfowl
Refuge 4

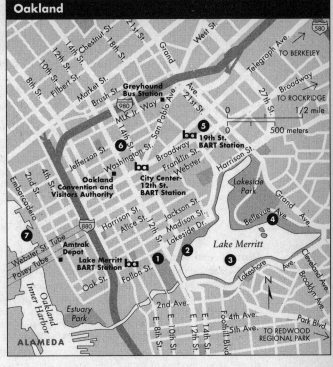

Oakland

cover charges that range from free to about $8. A pool table and soul food are additional draws. ⊠ *3629 Martin Luther King Jr. Way,* ☎ *510/655–6661.* ⊙ *Thurs.–Sat. 8 PM–2 AM.*

⑦ When the author Jack London lived in Oakland, he spent many a day boozing and brawling in the waterfront area now called **Jack London Square** (⊠ Embarcadero at Broadway, ☎ 510/814–6000). Lined with shops, restaurants, small museums, and historic sites, the square contains a bronze bust of London, author of *The Call of the Wild, The Sea Wolf, Martin Eden,* and other books. Jack London once spent a summer in the nearby **Klondike Cabin,** which was reassembled after being sent from Alaska. Even if you're not a London fan, the square is one of Oakland's livelier areas, particularly on Sunday, when community events like the morning farmers' market take place.

The tiny, wonderful **Heinold's First and Last Chance Saloon** (⊠ 56 Jack London Sq., ☎ 510/839–6761), one of Jack London's old haunts, has been serving since 1883, although it's a little worse for the wear since the 1906 earthquake.

The best local collection of biographical information on Jack London (including letters and photographs) resides in the **History Room** at the Oakland Main Library (⊠ 125 14th St., ☎ 510/238–3134).

Sequoia sempervirens, or coastal redwoods, grow to more than 100 ft tall in **Redwood Regional Park** (☎ 510/562–7275), one of the few spots in the Bay Area that escaped timber-hungry loggers during the 19th century. The park has forested picnic spots and dozens of hiking trails, including the 31-mi **National Skyline Trail,** which links Redwood to four other parks in the Berkeley–Oakland hills. From downtown Oakland take Interstate 580 east toward Hayward, exit at 35th Avenue/MacArthur Boulevard, and then take 35th Avenue east (it will become Redwood Road). Watch for the park entrance on the left, about 3–4 mi down the road.

The upscale neighborhood of **Rockridge** is one of Oakland's most desirable places to live. Explore the tree-lined streets that radiate out from College Avenue just north and south of the BART station for a look at California bungalow architecture at its finest. **College Avenue** is the main shopping drag in Rockridge. By day it's crowded with shoppers buying fresh flowers, used books, and clothing; by night the same folks are back for dinner and home-brewed ales in the numerous restaurants and pubs. The hub of College Avenue life is **Market Hall** (⊠ 5655 College Ave., ☎ 510/652–4680), an airy European-style marketplace where eight specialty food shops sell meat, fish, wine, pasta, bread, flowers, tea, coffee, and organic produce. At the end of College Avenue is the shady campus of the **California College of Arts and Crafts** (⊠ 5212 Broadway, ☎ 510/594–3600). Art students and the general public gather at the college's **Steven Oliver Arts Center**—open Monday–Saturday 11–5, Wednesday until 9—for cutting-edge exhibits of sculpture, paintings, and mixed media.

Dining and Lodging

$$–$$$ ✕ **Oliveto.** Standing smack dab in the heart of Rockridge, this locally renowned restaurant, with respected chef Paul Bertolli at its helm, combines a first-class dining room and casual café. Upstairs, in a sea of subtle Mediterranean tones, you're treated to imaginative yet restrained Italian cuisine. The menu changes daily, but representative fare includes house-made duck prosciutto, pan-seared swordfish, and spit-roasted leg of lamb. Downstairs, in the terra-cotta-walled café, everything from an espresso to a pizza to a full-blown Italian meal can be enjoyed at one of the small tables or at the bar. ⊠ *5655 College Ave.,* ☎ *510/ 547–5356 restaurant; 510/547–4382 café. AE, DC, MC, V. No lunch in restaurant weekends.*

$–$$ ✕ **Autumn Moon Café.** Home-style American café food is served in this friendly spot in a century-old house. Enjoy such tantalizing items as roast chicken hash with poached eggs for breakfast; salmon teriyaki with rice and fresh vegetables for lunch; and pan-seared halibut with griddled corn polenta and roasted wild mushrooms for dinner. A root beer float makes for a delightful finish. ⊠ *3909 Grand Ave.,* ☎ *510/ 595–3200. AE, MC, V. No lunch Mon. and Tues.*

$ ✕ **Le Cheval Restaurant.** A longtime favorite among the city's many Vietnamese restaurants, Le Cheval is known for big parties and family-style dining. Try the *pho* (Hanoi-style beef noodle soup fragrant with star anise). Other entrées include lemon chicken, cubed beef steak, claypot snapper and shark in coconut milk. It's hard to spend more than $20 for an entire meal unless you order the special crab at about $30. At midday, everyone seems to be downing bowls of noodles topped with marinated grilled meats and chili-laced fish sauce. ⊠ *1007 Clay St.,* ☎ *510/763–8495. AE, D, DC, MC, V. No lunch Sun.*

$$$–$$$$ ⊡ **Claremont Resort and Spa.** Straddling the Oakland-Berkeley bor-
★ der, the Claremont Hotel beckons like a gleaming white castle in the hills. Traveling executives come for the business amenities, including 40 rooms outfitted with computer terminals, T-1 Internet connections, guest E-mail addresses, and oversize desks. The Claremont also shines for leisure travelers, drawing in honeymooners and families alike with its luxurious suites, therapeutic massages, and personalized yoga workouts at the on-site spa. ⊠ *41 Tunnel Rd., at Ashby and Domingo Aves., 94705,* ☎ *510/843–3000 or 800/323–7500,* ℻ *510/843–6629.* ⓦⓔⓑ *www.claremontresort.com. 282 rooms. 3 restaurants, 2 bars, in-room data ports, tennis courts, 2 pools, spa, dry cleaning, concierge, meeting rooms, parking (fee), no-smoking floor. AE, D, DC, MC, V.*

$$–$$$$ ⊞ **Waterfront Plaza Hotel.** The waterfront views and Jack London
★ Square's vibrant collection of shops and restaurants make the neigh-
borhood one of the most appealing in Oakland. Yet even without the
lively surroundings, this thoroughly modern hotel would rank among
the best in the city. Despite its large size, the ever-friendly staff and man-
agement put immense effort into making your stay comfortable—
perks include VCRs, hair dryers, twice-daily housekeeping, and ironing
essentials in every room. ⊠ *10 Washington St., in Jack London Square,
94607,* ☎ *510/836–3800 or 800/729–3638,* FAX *510/832–5695,* WEB
*www.waterfrontplaza.com. 144 rooms. Restaurant, room service, in-
room data ports, in-room VCRs, pool, gym, dry cleaning, laundry ser-
vice, concierge, business services, meeting room, parking (fee),
no-smoking rooms. AE, D, DC, MC, V.*

$$–$$$ ⊞ **Lake Merritt Hotel.** Built in 1927, this Clarion Suites property has
been restored to its original Mediterranean Art Deco splendor. Hid-
den behind an unassuming entryway are a stunning lobby and lounge,
with 16-ft ceilings, mohair and velvet sofas, and walls in period shades
of pewter, ivory, cobalt, and crimson. Beyond the lounge lies Madi-
son's, a spacious dining area with unparalleled views of Lake Merritt.
Unfortunately, the rooms are less splendid than the lobby and lounge,
though many come equipped with a kitchenette and a well-stocked desk.
⊠ *1800 Madison St., 94612,* ☎ *510/832–2300 or 800/933–4683,* FAX
510/832–7150, WEB *www.lakemerritthotel.com. 51 rooms. Restaurant,
in-room data ports, kitchenettes (some), dry cleaning, laundry service,
business services, parking (fee), no-smoking rooms. AE, D, MC, V.*

$$ ⊞ **Executive Inn at Embarcadero Cove.** Though north-facing rooms have
a freeway view and a noise problem, the hotel is convenient to both
the Oakland airport and downtown Oakland. To make up for its re-
moved location, the Executive Inn provides complimentary shuttle
service to the Oakland airport, BART stations, and Jack London
Square. The generic pastel pink-and-green rooms are nothing special,
but all south-facing rooms have peaceful views overlooking the waters of the Oakland Estuary. ⊠ *1755 Embarcadero (off I–880 at 16th
St. exit), 94606,* ☎ *510/536–6633 or 800/346–6331,* FAX *510/536–6006.
146 rooms. Pool, gym, outdoor hot tub, dry cleaning, laundry service,
business services, meeting room, airport shuttle, free parking, no-
smoking rooms. AE, D, DC, MC, V.*

East Bay A to Z

BOAT AND FERRY TRAVEL

The Oakland/Alameda Ferry (☎ 510/522–3300, WEB www.eastbayferry.
com) runs several times daily between San Francisco's Ferry Building,
Alameda, and the Clay Street dock near Jack London Square. Purchase
tickets on board.

CAR TRAVEL

Take Interstate 80 east across the Bay Bridge. For Berkeley, take the
University Avenue exit through downtown Berkeley to the campus or
take the Ashby Avenue exit and turn left on Telegraph Avenue to the
traditional campus entrance; there is a parking garage on Channing
Way. For Oakland, take Interstate 580 off the Bay Bridge to the Grand
Avenue exit for Lake Merritt. To reach downtown and the waterfront,
take Interstate 980 from Interstate 580 and exit at 12th Street. Both
trips take about 30 minutes, longer during rush hour.

TRAIN TRAVEL

BART trains (☎ 510/465–2628) make stops in downtown Berkeley
and in several parts of Oakland, including Rockridge. Use the Lake

Merritt station for the Oakland Museum and southern Lake Merritt, the Oakland City Center–12th Street station for downtown, and the 19th Street station for the Paramount Theatre and the north side of Lake Merritt. From the Berkeley (not North Berkeley) station it's a five-minute walk on Center Street to the western edge of campus. Both trips take from 30 to 45 minutes one-way.

VISITOR INFORMATION

➤ TOURIST INFORMATION: **Berkeley Convention and Visitors Bureau** (⊠ 2015 Center St., 94704, ☎ 510/549–8710, WEB www.berkeleycvb.com). **Oakland Convention and Visitors Bureau** (⊠ 475 14th St., Suite 120, 94612, ☎ 510/839–9000, WEB www.oaklandcvb.com).

THE INLAND PENINSULA

Less glamorous than so-called "marvelous Marin" and the colorful East Bay cities of Berkeley and Oakland, the Inland Peninsula is often passed over by visitors to the Bay Area. Many associate the area with the blandness and urban sprawl that have long been synonymous with Silicon Valley. Such associations are justified only in part. Much of the area between Santa Clara County and San Francisco *is* clogged with modern office complexes and strip-mall shopping centers, but the peninsula also has lovely hills, redwood forests, and historic mansions.

Palo Alto is home to Stanford University, which occupies 8,200 acres of former farmland. Downtown, a hub of upscale restaurants and shops caters to a new class of high-tech elite as well as the university crowd. The wealthy residential community of Woodside harbors one of California's few remaining grand country houses, Filoli, as well as countless hiking and biking trails. Throughout the rest of the inland peninsula, former country estates built by the mining and transportation "bonanza kings" of the 19th century lie hidden in the hills, waiting to be discovered by those who care to look.

Much of your first impression of this area will depend on where and when you enter. Take the 30-mi stretch of U.S. 101 from San Francisco along the eastern side of the peninsula and you'll see office complex after shopping center after business tower—and you'll likely get caught in horrific morning and evening commuter traffic. On the west side, however, the less-crowded Interstate 280 takes you past picturesque hills, lakes, and reservoirs.

Palo Alto

Palo Alto's main attraction is the Eden-like campus of Stanford University, an 8,200-acre expanse of grass-covered hills that was once part of founder Leland Stanford's farm. Downtown Palo Alto is now a hotbed of trendy restaurants, shops, and attractions catering to the glut of high-income peninsula residents as well as the university crowd. Wander up and down University Avenue and the surrounding side streets and you'll discover Wolfgang Puck's star-studded Spago, the historic Stanford Theatre, a 1920s-style movie palace founded and financed by David Packard Jr., and even a Barbie Hall of Fame. Just down the road, the Stanford Shopping Center is one of the Bay Area's best. A bit farther afield, the Stanford Linear Accelerator and the Hewlett-Packard garage attract those who hope to learn the secrets of high-tech success by osmosis.

Stanford University, 30 mi south of San Francisco, has its roots among the peninsula's great estates. Originally the property was former California governor Leland Stanford's farm for breeding horses. For all its stature as one of the nation's leading universities, Stanford is still known as "The Farm." Founded and endowed by Leland and Jane Stanford in 1885 as a memorial to their son, Leland Jr., who died of typhoid fever, the university opened in 1891. Frederick Law Olmsted conceived the plan for the grounds and Romanesque sandstone buildings, joined by arcades and topped by red-tile roofs. Variations on this style persist in newer buildings, which, along with playing fields, cover about 1,200 acres of the 8,200-acre campus. The center of the university is the inner quadrangle, a group of 12 original classroom buildings later joined by Memorial Church, whose facade and interior walls are covered with mosaics of biblical scenes.

The university is organized into seven schools made up of 70 departments. In addition, there are several institutes on campus, including the Hoover Institution on War, Revolution, and Peace, which is a research center and library. The 285-ft **Hoover Tower** is a landmark and tourist attraction; an elevator ($2) leads to an observation deck that provides sweeping views of the area.

Except for the central cluster of buildings, the Stanford campus is remarkably uncongested—enrollment is only about 14,000—although certain areas, such as the Clock Tower and White Plaza, are a constant stream of students on bicycles and in-line skates. Free one-hour **walking tours** leave daily at 11 and 3:15 from the Visitor Information Center (☎ 650/723–2560 or 650/723–2053) in front of Memorial Hall on Serra Street, opposite Hoover Tower. The main campus entrance, Palm Drive, is an extension of University Avenue from Palo Alto. Lined with majestic palm trees and leading directly to the main quadrangle, this entrance will give you a full perspective of Stanford's unique California Mission–Romanesque architecture and its western Ivy League ambience.

★ **Iris and B. Gerald Cantor Center for Visual Arts.** A major repository for one of the most comprehensive and varied art collections in the Bay Area, this museum's works span the centuries as well as the globe, from pre-Columbian to modern. Included is the world's largest collection—180—of Rodin sculptures outside of Paris, many of them displayed in the outdoor sculpture garden. (Don't miss the awe-inspiring complete reproductions of the *Gates of Hell*.) Other highlights include a bronze Buddha from the Ming dynasty, wooden masks and carved figurines from 18th- and 19th-century Africa, paintings by Georgia O'Keeffe, and sculpture by Willem de Kooning and Bay Area artist Robert Arneson. ⊠ *328 Lomita Dr. and Museum Way, off Palm Dr. at Stanford University,* ☎ *650/723–4177,* WEB *www.stanford.edu/dept/ccva.* ⊠ *Free.* ☉ *Wed. and Fri.–Sun. 11–5, Thurs. 11–8. Rodin Sculpture Garden tours Sat. at 11, Sun. at 3.*

Papua New Guinea Sculpture Garden. Tucked into a small, heavily wooded plot of land are examples of some very untraditional art. The inconspicuous garden is filled with tall, ornately carved wooden poles; drums; and carved stones—all created on location by 10 artists from Papua New Guinea who spent six months here in 1994. A Stanford anthropology professor proposed the idea for the garden. Detailed plaques explain the concept and the works themselves. ⊠ *Santa Teresa St. and Lomita Dr., at Stanford University.* ⊠ *Free.*

Hewlett-Packard garage. Though it doesn't look like much, this a good place to get a sense of the humble origins of one of the world's largest technology companies. It all started in this one-car garage, where former Stanford freshman roommates William Hewlett and David Packard put their heads together back in the 1930s. The rest is history. Today, the Hewlett-Packard garage is a California State Landmark. ⊠ *Behind 367 Addison Ave.*

Two-hour tours of the **Stanford Linear Accelerator Center (SLAC)** reveal the workings of the 2-mi-long electron accelerator, which is used for elementary-particle research. Call for reservations and times. ⊠ *Sand Hill Rd., 2 mi west of main campus,* ☎ 650/926–2204.

Dining and Lodging

$$–$$$ ✕ **Evvia.** An innovative Greek menu and a stunning interior ensure that
★ Evvia always packs in a crowd. A large fireplace, hand-painted pottery, and a big bar area with colorful backlit glassware make this one of Palo Alto's most inviting restaurants. Though the menu is written out in Greek (with English translations), there's an unmistakable California influence in dishes like wild mushroom risotto and *psari sta karvouna* (mesquite-grilled striped bass with herbs and braised greens). ⊠ *420 Emerson St.,* ☎ *650/326–0983. Reservations essential. AE, D, DC, MC, V. No lunch weekends.*

$$–$$$ ✕ **Il Fornaio Cucina Italiana.** In the gorgeous, Italianate Garden Court Hotel, Il Fornaio has a casually rustic look, with food as the visual focus. You can sample superb antipasti and pasta, or pizzas and calzones baked to perfection in a wood-burning oven. The café area near the front door is a nice stop for coffee and snacks, and counter service makes for quick meals while watching the cooking. Early each month, the restaurant presents Italian regional dinners for two weeks. ⊠ *520 Cowper St.,* ☎ *650/853–3888. AE, DC, MC, V.*

$$–$$$ ✕ **L'Amie Donia.** Chef-owner Donia Bijan, who made a name for herself at San Francisco's Sherman House and Brasserie Savoy, has decorated her utterly charming French bistro in sunny yellow and soothing blue. Her menus, which reflect the seasons, focus on the rustic, flavorful fare that one might find in the French countryside: roast beets with warm goat cheese and walnuts, rabbit with mustard sauce, or pan-roasted veal chop with an almond crust. ⊠ *530 Bryant St.,* ☎ *650/323–7614. Reservations essential. AE, D, MC, V. Closed Sun. and Mon. and late Dec.–mid-Jan. No lunch.*

$$–$$$ ✕ **Spago.** Silicon Valley's best and brightest have made a hit out of Wolfgang Puck's splashy, dashing Spago. The fare is inventive Californian, the service flawless. Flat breads, bread sticks, and specialty loaves will tide you over until the real food arrives. Dinner might include grilled lamb T-bone or grilled quail with a white bean cassoulet. The tasty desserts are artistically presented. ⊠ *265 Lytton Ave.,* ☎ *650/833–1000. Reservations essential. AE, D, DC, MC, V. No lunch weekends.*

$–$$ ✕ **Nola.** With a lantern-lit central courtyard and a whimsical, folk art–filled interior, this New Orleans–inspired restaurant has a festive mood. The food is California-Cajun: grilled Cajun pork chop on garlic mashed potatoes with braised red chard and sweet apple coulis; and jambalaya and shrimp étouffée. Almost all the wines are served by the glass as well as by the bottle. Save room for the house-made beignets. ⊠ *535 Ramona St.,* ☎ *650/328–2722. AE, DC, MC, V. No lunch weekends.*

$–$$ ✕ **Perry's Palo Alto.** An offshoot of Perry's, which made a name for itself in San Francisco as the premier singles bar in the 1970s, this one replicates the menu and much of the fun-loving clientele. It's a little removed from the liveliest part of University Avenue, but locals find it worth the detour for some of the best hamburgers on the peninsula. Grilled fish and filet mignon are among the top dishes, but dinner can be as simple as a vegetarian burger and classic fried onion rings. Lobster is served Saturday night. ⊠ *546 University Ave.,* ☎ *650/326–0111. AE, D, DC, MC, V.*

$–$$ ✕ **Zibibbo.** This lively restaurant's eclectic menu includes selections from
★ an oak-fired oven, rotisserie, grill, and oyster bar. Large platters are
placed in the center of the table so you can share dishes like skillet-
roasted mussels, Swiss chard tart with goat cheese and currants, leg of
lamb with chickpea-tomato tagine, and more. The menu changes seasonally in this two-story Victorian, where you can sit in the garden,
glassed-in atrium, upstairs loft, or middle dining room, or cozy up to
the exhibition kitchen counter or high-ceilinged bar. ⊠ *430 Kipling
St.,* ☎ *650/328–6722. AE, DC, MC, V.*

$ ✕ **Pasta?** The most expensive of the many pastas here is $9. This is
good food at any price—nothing fancy, but made with fresh seasonal
ingredients and presented with care. In addition to such standard pasta
dishes as salmon fettuccine, there are always a few lighter selections
served with light oil and no cheese or salt. A handful of meat and fish
entrées, such as pork medallions with Chianti sauce, are priced well
below $10. Naturally, the place does a brisk business with students.
⊠ *326 University Ave.,* ☎ *650/328–4585. MC, V.*

$ ✕ **Pluto's.** The space-age name and design have nothing to do with the
earthly pleasures of this loud and lively restaurant's fresh, custom-made
salads, sandwiches, and hot meals. Service is quasi-buffet-style. Grab
a menu, make your choices from any of the food stations, and the server
will determine how much you owe. Choose greens with a choice of
eight fixings such as grilled fennel or roasted peppers, or build your
own sandwich with a base of marinated flank steak or grilled eggplant,
and add extras like caramelized onions or garlic mayo. ⊠ *482 University Ave.,* ☎ *650/853–1556. MC, V.*

$$$$ ☷ **Garden Court Hotel.** From the outside this boutique hotel looks like
★ an Italian villa, complete with columns and arches, a dormer roof, and
balconies dressed up with bougainvillea. The inside is even more appealing, with tasteful, sunlight-filled rooms outfitted with a two- or
four-poster bed with comforter. Some rooms overlook a lush central
courtyards; all suites have private terraces. Ground floor shops and
restaurants include Il Fornaio. ⊠ *520 Cowper St., 94301,* ☎ *650/322–
9000 or 800/824–9028,* ℻ *650/324–3609.* Ⱳ ᴱ ᴮ *www.gardencourt.com.
50 rooms, 12 suites. Restaurant, bar, room service, in-room data ports,
in-room pay-per-view TV, gym, laundry service, concierge, business services. AE, D, DC, MC, V.*

$$$–$$$$ ☷ **Sheraton Hotel Palo Alto.** This business hotel provides one of Palo
Alto's loveliest havens of tranquillity: a koi pond winds its elaborate
course all the way from the pool area through landscaped gardens. (Re-
quest an even-numbered room for a better view of the pond.) The hotel
is amazingly quiet considering its site on a busy intersection one block
from the Stanford Shopping Center. Rooms are standard-issue busi-
ness style, with typical amenities. ⊠ *625 El Camino Real, 94301,* ☎
650/328–2800 or 800/874–3516, ℻ *650/327–7362. 350 rooms.
Restaurant, room service, in-room data ports, pool, gym, lounge, laun-
dry service, laundry facilities, concierge, business services, meeting
room, no-smoking floor. AE, D, DC, MC, V.*

$$$–$$$$ ☷ **Stanford Park Hotel.** The original oil paintings, antiques, tapestries,
and forest-green color scheme make this stately hotel feel more like an
English hunt club than a hotel in Silicon Valley. Rooms are welcoming,
with fireplaces, vaulted ceilings, English yew-wood armoires, and framed
hunting scenes. The Duck Club Restaurant carries on the hunting motif
with a regional American menu with a fair share of game. ⊠ *100 El
Camino Real, 94025,* ☎ *650/322–1234 or 800/368–2468,* ℻ *650/322–
0975.* Ⱳ ᴱ ᴮ *www.woodsidehotels.com. 163 rooms. Restaurant, bar, lobby
lounge, in-room data ports, minibars, pool, gym, laundry service, con-
cierge, business services, meeting room. AE, DC, MC, V.*

$$-$$$ 🏨 **The Victorian on Lytton.** Only a block from downtown Palo Alto, this inn caters to business travelers who want comfort and amenities without teddy bears and lace. Innkeepers Susan and Maxwell Hall gutted the building—a former apartment building—and completely configured the interior to accommodate spacious rooms, some with canopy beds. Complimentary breakfast is ordered the night before and brought to your room in the morning. ⊠ *555 Lytton Ave., 94301,* ☎ *650/322–8555,* FAX *650/322–7141,* WEB *www.victorianonlytton.com. 10 rooms. No-smoking rooms; no air-conditioning. AE, MC, V. BP.*

$-$$ 🏨 **Cowper Inn.** In a quiet, residential neighborhood five minutes from downtown Palo Alto, this former Victorian home is one of the least expensive lodging options in the area, and it's charming to boot. One very small shared-bath room goes for $80. The cozy parlor has a brick fireplace, piano, and a big window looking out on tree-lined Cowper Street. Breakfast includes homemade muffins and granola and fresh-squeezed orange juice. ⊠ *705 Cowper St., 94301,* ☎ *650/327–4475,* FAX *650/329–1703,* WEB *www.cowperinn.com. 14 rooms, 2 with shared bath. Piano. AE, MC, V. CP.*

Shopping

The **Stanford Shopping Center,** one of the Bay Area's first shopping centers, remains one of its best. In addition to an excellent selection of such upscale stores as Ralph Lauren, Smith & Hawken, Crate & Barrel, and Bloomingdale's, you'll find some irresistible eateries here. ⊠ *180 El Camino Real, take Sand Hill Rd. east off I–280 or Embarcadero Rd. west off U.S. 101,* ☎ *650/617–8585.*

Woodside

Just west of Palo Alto, Woodside is a tiny, rustic town where weekend warriors stock up on espresso and picnic fare before charging off on their mountain bikes. Blink once and you're past the town center. The main draw here is the wealth of surrounding lush parks and preserves.

One of the few great country houses in California that remains intact is ★**Filoli,** in Woodside. Built between 1915 and 1917 for wealthy San Franciscan William B. Bourn II, it was designed by Willis Polk in a Georgian Revival style, with redbrick walls and a tile roof. The name is Bourn's acronym for "fight, love, live." As interesting as the house—the setting of the television series *Dynasty*—are the 16 acres of formal gardens. These were planned and developed over a period of more than 50 years and preserved for the public when the last private owner, Mrs. William P. Roth, deeded Filoli to the National Trust for Historic Preservation.

The gardens rise south from the mansion to take advantage of the natural surroundings of the 700-acre estate and its vistas. Among the designs are a sunken garden. In the middle of it all is a charming teahouse designed in the Italian Renaissance style. From June through September Filoli hosts a monthly series of Sunday afternoon jazz concerts. Bring a picnic or buy a box lunch; Filoli provides tables, sodas, wine, fruit, and popcorn. In December the mansion is festively decorated for a series of holiday events: brunches, afternoon teas, Christmas concerts, and more. ⊠ *Cañada Rd. near Edgewood Rd.,* ☎ *650/364–2880,* WEB *www.filoli.org.* 🖾 *$10.* ☺ *Mid-Feb.–Oct., Tues.–Sat. 10–3 for guided and self-guided tours. Reservations essential for guided tours.*

One peninsula oddity unknown even to most residents is the **Pulgas Water Temple,** where exquisitely groomed grounds surround a Romanesque temple and a reflecting pool. Walk past the temple up the steps of the columned circular temple to feel the power of the water as it thunders deafeningly under your feet. Look up to the top of the columns and read the inscription from the Bible's Isaiah: I GIVE WATER IN THE WILDERNESS AND RIVERS IN THE DEEP, TO GIVE DRINK TO MY PEOPLE. The temple commemorates the massive underground pipeline project of the early 1930s that channeled water from Hetch Hetchy near Yosemite to the Crystal Springs Reservoir on the peninsula. ⊠ *Cañada Rd., 1½ mi north of Edgewood Rd.,* ☎ *650/872–5900.* 🎟 *Free.* ⊙ *Weekdays 9:30–4.*

Dining

$–$$ ✕ **Bucks in Woodside.** You'll either be amused or turned off by the eccentric decor of this casual restaurant. Giant plastic alligators, Elvis paintings, a human-size Statue of Liberty model, and framed computer chips on the walls make a not-so-subtle aesthetic statement. The menu is a grab bag of crowd pleasers: basic soups, sandwiches, burgers, and salads. For breakfast there's a "U-do-it" omelet in addition to other more standard choices. ⊠ *3062 Woodside Rd.,* ☎ *650/851–8010. AE, D, MC, V.*

$–$$ ✕ **Woodside Bakery and Café.** Stop by the bakery section for a cup of hot cocoa and a fresh-baked pastry, or sit in the café for a glass of wine and a light meal. Everything is fresh and well presented. The menu tends toward light, seasonal dishes such as fresh pastas and salads. But you'll also find more substantial entrées like oven-braised lamb shank and baked Dijon chicken. ⊠ *3052 Woodside Rd.,* ☎ *650/851–0812. AE, MC, V.*

Inland Peninsula A to Z

CAR TRAVEL

By car the most pleasant direct route down the peninsula is Interstate 280, the Junipero Serra Freeway, which passes along Crystal Springs Reservoir. For Stanford University, exit at Sand Hill Road and drive east. Turn right on Arboretum Drive, then right again on Palm Drive, which leads to the center of campus. U.S. 101, also known as the Bayshore Freeway, is more direct but also more congested; from there take University Avenue or Embarcadero Road west to Stanford. For Woodside take the Woodside Road exit and drive west.

TRAIN TRAVEL

CalTrain (☎ 800/660–4287) runs from 4th and Townsend streets to Palo Alto ($4 each way); from there take the free **Marguerite shuttle bus** (☎ 650/723–9362) to the Stanford campus and the Palo Alto area. Buses run about every 15 minutes 6 AM–7:45 PM and are timed to connect with trains and public transit buses.

VISITOR INFORMATION

➤ TOURIST INFORMATION: **Palo Alto Chamber of Commerce** (⊠ 325 Forest Ave., 94301, ☎ 650/324–3121). **Woodside Town Hall** (⊠ 2955 Woodside Rd., 94062, ☎ 650/851–6790).

SAN MATEO COUNTY COAST

Although the San Mateo County Coast is only a few miles from the inland peninsula and San Francisco, its undeveloped hills, rugged coastline, and quaint towns and inns are worlds away from urban sprawl, strip shopping centers, and traffic congestion. Set out from San Francisco down scenic Route 1, hugging the twists and turns of the coast, or venture 11 mi west from Interstate 280 near San Mateo, over hilly Route 92. As you wind your way past Christmas tree farms, pumpkin patches, and rural flower growers, you'll find that the pace of life is slower here than in the rest of the Bay Area.

The towns along the coast were founded in 1769 when Spanish explorer Gaspar de Portola arrived. After the Mexican government gained control, the land was used for agriculture by ranchers who provided food to San Francisco's Mission Dolores. Soon, lighthouses and ships were being built to facilitate the transport of goods to San Francisco. You can still visit the short, squat Point Montara Lighthouse in Montara, 8 mi north of Half Moon Bay, or the 115-ft Pigeon Point Lighthouse, one of the tallest on the West Coast, 7 mi south of Pescadero.

Most towns that dot the coast are no more than a few blocks long, with just enough room for a couple of B&Bs, restaurants, and boutiques or galleries. Beyond the towns are the beautiful coastal beaches—the area's lifeblood.

Half Moon Bay

The largest and most visited of the coastal communities, Half Moon Bay is nevertheless a tiny town with a population of fewer than 10,000. The town's hub, **Main Street,** is lined with five blocks of small crafts shops, art galleries, and outdoor cafés, many housed in renovated 19th-century structures. Half Moon Bay comes to life on the third weekend in October, when 300,000 people gather for the **Half Moon Bay Art and Pumpkin Festival** (☎ 650/726–9652).

The 4-mi stretch of **Half Moon Bay State Beach** (⊠ Rte. 1, west of Main St., ☎ 650/726–8819) is perfect for long walks, kite flying, and picnic lunches, though the 50°F water and dangerous currents discourage swimming.

The coastal communities can easily be explored on two wheels. The **Bicyclery** (⊠ 101 Main St., ☎ 650/726–6000) has bike rentals and will provide information on organized rides up and down the coast. If you prefer to go it alone, try the 3-mi bike trail that leads from Kelly Avenue in Half Moon Bay to Mirada Road in Miramar.

Built in 1928 after two horrible shipwrecks on the point, the **Point Montara Lighthouse** still has its original lightkeeper's quarters from the late 1800s. Gray whales pass this point during their migration from November through April, so bring your binoculars. The lighthouse is also a youth hostel known for its outdoor hot tub at ocean's edge. ⊠ *16th St. at Rte. 1, Montara,* ☎ *650/728–7177. Call for hrs, tours, and lodging rates.*

Dining and Lodging

$$ ✕ **Pasta Moon.** The sight of the wood-burning oven tips you off to the thin-crust pizzas that are served in this small restaurant. The kitchen also turns out handmade pastas, a wonderful crisp-skinned roast chicken, grilled quail, and marinated flank steak. ⊠ *315 Main St.,* ☎ *650/726–5125. AE, D, DC, MC, V.*

$$ ✕ **San Benito House.** Tucked inside a historic inn in the heart of Half Moon Bay, this ground-floor restaurant serves a limited dinner menu that changes weekly and often includes bouillabaisse, roasted quail, sea bass or other fresh fish, a vegetarian meal, and house-made ravioli or other pastas. By day the kitchen prepares memorable sandwiches with bread baked in the restaurant's oven and sells them, deli style, for a picnic by the sea. ⊠ *356 Main St.,* ☎ *650/726–3425. AE, DC, MC, V. No dinner Mon.–Wed.*

$–$$ ✕ **Two Fools.** The kitchen tosses together big organic salads and packs contemporary burritos with a healthy mix of ingredients. A slice of old-fashioned American meat loaf topped with caramelized onions is sandwiched in a house-made bun at lunchtime, when takeout is popular with locals. Dinnertime brings fresh fish, a daily risotto, roasted chicken, and a house-made nut loaf for vegetarians. Weekend brunch draws people touring the coast. ✉ *408 Main St.,* ☎ *650/712–1222. AE, D, MC, V. No dinner Mon.*

$$$–$$$$ ⊞ **Mill Rose Inn.** Pampering touches include in-room fireplaces, brass beds stacked high with down comforters, decanters of sherry and brandy on the tables, in-room coffee and cocoa, and baskets of fruit and candies. The stunning gardens are planted extensively with roses and climbing sweet peas. Room rates include a lavish champagne breakfast and afternoon snacks. ✉ *615 Mill St., 94019,* ☎ *650/726–8750 or 800/900–7673,* FAX *650/726–3031,* WEB *www.millroseinn.com. 4 rooms, 2 suites. Refrigerators, in-room VCRs; no smoking. AE, D, DC, MC, V. BP.*

$$–$$$ ⊞ **Old Thyme Inn.** Rooms in this charming 1898 Princess Anne Victorian are named for herbs, such as mint, and are decorated accordingly. The more expensive rooms have fireplaces and whirlpool tubs. Antiques, fresh flower bouquets, a homemade breakfast, complimentary sherry, and afternoon snacks make this a lovely place to spend a relaxing weekend. ✉ *779 Main St., 94019,* ☎ *650/726–1616 or 800/720–4277,* FAX *650/726–6394,* WEB *www.oldthymeinn.com. 7 rooms. In-room data ports, no-smoking rooms. AE, D, MC, V. BP.*

$$ ⊞ **The Goose and Turrets.** Artifacts from the international travels of innkeepers Raymond and Emily Hoche-Mong fill the shelves of this inn 8 mi north of Half Moon Bay. A full home-cooked breakfast, afternoon goodies, and homemade chocolate truffles are sure to make anyone feel at home. ✉ *835 George St., Montara 94037,* ☎ *650/728–5451,* FAX *650/728–0141,* WEB *goose.montara.com. 5 rooms. Boccie, no-smoking room. AE, D, DC, MC, V. BP.*

Pescadero

As you walk down Stage Road, Pescadero's main street, it's hard to believe you're only 30 minutes from Silicon Valley. The few short blocks that compose the downtown area could almost serve as the backdrop for a western movie, with Duarte's Tavern serving as the centerpiece. In fact, Pescadero, some 16 mi south of Half Moon Bay, was reportedly larger in the late 19th century than it is today. This is a good place to stop for a bite or to browse for antiques housed in what looks like a converted barn. The town's real attraction, though, is its proximity to beaches and spectacular hiking.

If a quarantine is not in effect (watch for signs), from November through April you can look for mussels at **Pescadero State Beach,** where sandy expanses, tidal pools, and rocky outcroppings form one of the coast's more scenic beaches. Barbecue pits and tables attract many picnicking families. Across U.S. 101 at the **Pescadero Marsh Natural Preserve,** hikers can spy on birds and other wildlife by following any of the trails that crisscross 600 acres of marshland. Early spring and fall are the best times to visit. ☎ *650/879–2170.* ▨ *Free, parking $5.* ☉ *Daily 8–sunset.*

If you prefer mountain trails to sand dunes, head for **Pescadero Creek County Park,** a 7,500-acre expanse of shady, old-growth redwood forests, grasslands, and mountain streams. The park is actually composed of three smaller ones: Heritage Grove Redwood Preserve, Sam McDonald Park, and San Mateo Memorial County Park. At 6½ mi, the Old Haul Road Trail runs the length of the park. Campsites cost $15 per night. ☎ *650/879–0238.* ▨ *$4 per vehicle.*

OFF THE
BEATEN PATH

SAN GREGORIO – In addition to beautiful scenery and expansive state beaches, this area is home to the idiosyncratic **San Gregorio General Store** (✉ Rte. 84 at Stage Rd., 1 mi east of Rte. 1, ☎ 650/726–0565). Part old-time saloon, part hardware store, part grocery, the store has been a fixture in town since the late 1800s; the current Spanish-style structure replaced the original wood building when it burned down in 1930. Come to browse through the hodgepodge items—camp stoves, books, and boots, to name just a few—or to listen to Irish music and bluegrass on weekend afternoons.

Dining

$–$$ ✗ **Duarte's Tavern.** This 19th-century roadhouse serves simple American fare, with locally grown vegetables and fresh fish as standard items. If you really want a treat and can afford to splurge, order the abalone, for $45. Don't pass up the famed house artichoke soup or the old-fashioned berry pie à la mode. Breakfasts of eggs, bacon, sausage, and hotcakes are hearty here. ✉ 202 Stage Rd., ☎ 650/879–0464. AE, MC, V.

En Route   At the south end of the coast is the 115-ft **Pigeon Point Lighthouse,** one of the tallest on the West Coast. Built in 1872, it has been used as a backdrop in numerous TV shows and commercials. The light from the 8,000-pound Fresnel lens can be seen 20 mi at sea. The former coast guard quarters now serve as a youth hostel. ✉ Pigeon Point Rd. and Rte. 1, ☎ 650/879–2120. ⬛ $2. ⊙ Weekends 11–4, guided tours 10:30–3.

Año Nuevo State Reserve

At the most southerly point of the San Mateo County Coast, Año Nuevo is the world's only approachable mainland rookery for elephant seals. If you know you'll be in the area between mid-December and March, make reservations early for a 2½-hour guided walking tour to view the huge (up to 3 tons), fat, furry elephant seals mating or birthing, depending on the time of year. Tours proceed rain or shine, so dress for anything. From April through November there's less excitement, but you can still watch the seals lounging on the beach. The visitor center has a fascinating film and exhibits, and there are plenty of hiking trails in the area. ✉ Rte. 1 south of Pigeon Point, take Rte. 1 south from Pescadero, ☎ 650/879–0227; 800/444–4445 tour reservations. ⬛ $4, parking $5. ⊙ Tours leave every 15 mins 8:45–3.

San Mateo County Coast A to Z

BUS TRAVEL

SamTrans (☎ 800/660–4287) buses travel to Half Moon Bay from the Daly City BART station. Another bus connects Half Moon Bay with Pescadero. Each trip takes approximately one hour. Call for schedules, since departures are infrequent.

CAR TRAVEL

Public transportation to this area is limited, so it's best to drive. To get to Half Moon Bay, take Route 1, also known as the Coast Highway, south along the length of the San Mateo coast. A quicker route is via Interstate 280, the Junipero Serra Freeway; follow it south as far as Route 92, where you can turn west toward the coast. To get to Pescadero, drive south 16 mi on Route 1 from Half Moon Bay. For Año Nuevo continue south on Route 1 another 12 mi.

VISITOR INFORMATION

➤ Tourist Information: **California State Parks Bay Area District Office** (✉ 250 Executive Park Blvd., Suite 4900, San Francisco 94134, ☎

415/330–6300). **Half Moon Bay Chamber of Commerce** (⊠ 520 Kelly Ave., 94019, ☎ 650/726–8380, WEB www.halfmoonbaychamber.org).

ON AND AROUND THE BAY

Around the bay are miles of shoreline parks and wildlife refuges, easily accessible but almost never seen by travelers on the busy Bayshore and East Shore freeways. Yerba Buena Island provides the center anchorage for the Bay Bridge. It is connected by a causeway to man-made Treasure Island, which has a military museum and relics of the island's 1939 Golden Gate International Exposition. Excursions are available to the Farallon Islands, 23 mi outside the Golden Gate, where wildlife is abundant. Other boating excursions explore the bay and the delta's maze of waterways as far as Stockton and Sacramento. Back on land, about an hour's drive northeast of San Francisco, the town of Benicia, once the state capital, has been meticulously restored. Across Carquinez Strait is the former home of naturalist John Muir.

Yerba Buena and Treasure Islands

Every day 250,000 people pass through **Yerba Buena Island** on their way across the San Francisco–Oakland Bay Bridge, yet the island remains a mystery to most of them. Yerba Buena and the adjacent Treasure Island are primarily military bases, but they are accessible to the public. **Treasure Island** provides a superb bay-level view of the San Francisco skyline.

Wildlife Refuges

Wildlife refuges provide welcome access to the bay's shore, which can appear to be a congested commercial strip from surrounding freeways. Among the best of the public parks is **Coyote Point Nature Museum** (☎ 650/342–7755), just off U.S. 101 south of San Francisco Airport, open Tuesday–Saturday 10–5 and Sunday noon–5. The **Palo Alto Baylands Nature Interpretive Center** (☎ 650/329–2506), open Tuesday–Wednesday 10–5, Thursday–Friday 2–5, and weekends 1–5, is in the marshes at the east end of Embarcadero Road in Palo Alto. The **San Francisco Bay National Wildlife Refuge** (☎ 510/792–0222) is on Marshlands Road off Thornton Avenue in Fremont, at the east end of Dumbarton Bridge/Route 84; it is open daily from 7 to 6. On West Winton Avenue, at the east end of San Mateo Bridge/Route 92, the **Hayward Regional Shoreline** contains the Cogswell Marsh—the largest marsh restoration project on the West Coast. It is open daily 6 AM–sunset; for guided walks call the **Interpretive Center** (☎ 510/670–7270), open weekends 10–5.

A major wildlife center outside the bay is the **Gulf of the Farallones National Marine Sanctuary.** Though the islands are off-limits to visitors, rare nesting birds and passing seals and whales are visible from cruise boats. The Oceanic Society Expeditions (☎ 415/474–3385) operates cruises on weekends and on select weekdays from June through November. The fare for the eight-hour trip is $67.

Benicia and Martinez

The historic port city of **Benicia** is worth a detour for travelers on Interstate 80 between San Francisco and Sacramento. The old town center is on 1st Street, and at the foot of the street there is a fishing pier with a view through Carquinez Strait to San Pablo Bay. Benicia was named for the wife of General Mariano Vallejo, who owned the surrounding 99,000 acres. It was the state capital in 1852 and 1853. The handsome brick Greek Revival **capitol** has been splendidly restored. ⊠ *1st and W. G Sts.,* ☎ *707/745–3385.* 🎫 *$2.* ☉ *Daily 10–5.*

The Federal-style **Fischer-Hanlon Home,** next door to the capitol, is closed to the public, but you're invited to wander through the home's gardens. Nearby are scattered historic buildings, art galleries, crafts workshops, and antiques stores. The **Chamber of Commerce** (⊠ 601 1st St., ☎ 707/745–2120) distributes a guide to the old waterfront district—including a list of former brothels. The **Union Hotel** (⊠ 401 1st St., ☎ 707/746–0100) has been brilliantly restored; its restaurant is among the area's finest.

Just across Carquinez Strait from Benicia is **Martinez,** another historic port city that has become increasingly industrial. Martinez is said to be the birthplace of the martini, which according to legend was first called the "Martinez cocktail" and was later slurred into its present designation.

Atop a hill and surrounded by orchards and gardens is the **John Muir National Historic Site,** the carefully restored Victorian-era residence of conservationist John Muir. ⊠ *Alhambra Ave. at Rte. 4,* ☎ *925/228–8860.* 🎫 *$3.* ☉ *Wed.–Sun. 10–4:30.*

Six Flags Marine World

One of northern California's most popular attractions, this 160-acre wildlife and theme park has been a phenomenal success since moving in 1986 from a crowded site south of San Francisco to Vallejo, about an hour's drive northeast. Animals of the sea, air, and land perform in shows, roam in natural habitats, and stroll among park visitors with their trainers. Among the animal stars are killer whales, dolphins, camels, elephants, sea lions, chimpanzees, and a troupe of human water-skiers (April–October). The 1998 addition of roller coasters, water rides, and bumper cars has further added to the huge crowds of kids and their tired parents trekking to the park from San Francisco and its suburbs.

Owned by the Marine World Foundation, a nonprofit organization devoted to educating the public about the world's wildlife, the park is a family attraction, with entertaining but informative shows and close-up looks at exotic animals. For additional sightseeing, you can reach the park on a high-speed ferry from San Francisco, a trip that offers unusual vistas through San Francisco and San Pablo bays. ⊠ *Marine World Pkwy., Vallejo,* ☎ *707/643–6722,* 🌐 *www.sixflags.com.* 🎫 *$43.* ☉ *Hrs vary per season. Call for info.*

On and Around the Bay A to Z

BOAT AND FERRY TRAVEL

During Marine World's operating season, high-speed **Blue & Gold Fleet** (☎ 415/705–5444) ferries depart throughout the day for Marine World from Pier 39 at Fisherman's Wharf; the trip takes one hour. One-way tickets cost $9.

BUS TRAVEL

You can use public transportation to get to Marine World; for all other destinations you'll need a car. **Greyhound** (☎ 800/231–2222) runs buses from downtown San Francisco to Vallejo.

CAR TRAVEL

To get to Treasure Island, take the Bay Bridge to the Treasure Island exit. For Benicia, take the Interstate 780 exit in Vallejo, then Benicia's

East 2nd Street exit. For Marine World, take Interstate 80 east to Marine World Parkway in Vallejo. The trip takes an hour each way. Parking is $5 at the park.

TRAIN TRAVEL

You can use public transportation to get to Marine World; for all other destinations you'll need a car. You can take a **BART** train (☎ 650/992–2278) to the El Cerrito Del Norte station and transfer to the **Vallejo Transit line** (☎ 707/648–4666) to reach Marine World.

VISITOR INFORMATION

➤ TOURIST INFORMATION: **Benicia Chamber of Commerce** (✉ 601 1st St., 94510, ☎ 707/745–2120). **Martinez Area Chamber of Commerce** (✉ 603 Marina Vista, 94553, ☎ 925/228–2345).

9 THE WINE COUNTRY

You don't have to be a wine enthusiast to appreciate the mellow beauty of Napa and Sonoma counties, whose hills and verdant vineyards resemble those of Tuscany and Provence. Here, among state-of-the-art wineries, fabulous restaurants, and luxury hotels where aromatherapy and massage are daily rituals, you just might discover that life need have no nobler purpose than enjoying the fruits of the earth.

Updated by
Marty
Olmstead

I N 1862, AFTER AN EXTENSIVE TOUR of the wine-producing areas of Europe, Count Agoston Haraszthy de Mokcsa reported a promising prognosis about his adopted California: "Of all the countries through which I passed, not one possessed the same advantages that are to be found in California. . . . California can produce as noble and generous a wine as any in Europe; more in quantity to the acre, and without repeated failures through frosts, summer rains, hailstorms, or other causes."

The "dormant resources" that the father of California's viticulture saw in the balmy days and cool nights of the temperate Napa and Sonoma valleys have come to fruition today. The wines produced here are praised and savored by connoisseurs throughout the world. The area also continues to be a proving ground for the latest techniques of grape growing and wine making.

Ever more competitive, vintners constantly hone their skills, aided by the scientific expertise of graduates of the nearby University of California at Davis and by the practical knowledge of the grape growers. They experiment with high-density vineyard planting, canopy management (to control the amount of sunlight that reaches the grapes), and filtration of the wine.

For many, wine making is a second career. Any would-be wine maker can rent the cumbersome, costly machinery needed to stem and press the grapes. Many say making wine is a good way to turn a large fortune into a small one, but that hasn't deterred the doctors, former college professors, publishing tycoons, art dealers, and others who come here to try their hand at it.

In 1975 Napa Valley had no more than 20 wineries; today there are more than 240. In Sonoma County, where the web of vineyards is looser, there are well over 150 wineries, and development is now claiming the cool Carneros region, at the head of the San Francisco Bay, deemed ideal for growing the chardonnay grape. Within these combined regions of the Wine Country, at least 120 wineries have opened in the last eight years alone. Nowadays many individual grape growers produce their own wines instead of selling their grapes to larger wineries. As a result, smaller "boutique" wineries harvest excellent, reasonably priced wines that have caught the attention of connoisseurs and critics, while the larger wineries consolidate land and expand their varietals.

This state-of-the-art viticulture has also given rise to a gastronomic renaissance. Inspired by the creative spirit that produces the region's great wines, esteemed chefs are opening restaurants in record numbers, making culinary history in the process.

In addition to great food and wine, you'll find a wealth of California history in the Wine Country. The town of Sonoma is filled with remnants of Mexican California and the solid, ivy-covered, brick wineries built by Haraszthy and his followers. Calistoga is a virtual museum of Steamboat Gothic architecture, replete with the fretwork and clapboard beloved of gold-rush prospectors and late-19th-century spa goers. A later architectural fantasy, the beautiful art nouveau mansion of the Beringer brothers, is in St. Helena, and the postmodern extravaganza of Clos Pegase is in Calistoga.

The area's natural beauty draws a continuous flow of tourists—from the spring, when the vineyards bloom yellow with wild mustard, to the fall, when the grapes are ripe. Haraszthy was right: this is a chosen place.

Pleasures and Pastimes

Dining

Many star chefs from urban areas throughout the United States have migrated to the Wine Country, drawn by the area's renowned produce and world-class wines—the products of fertile soil and near-perpetual sun during the growing season. As a result of this marriage of imported talent and indigenous bounty, food now rivals wine as the principal attraction of the region.

Higher quality has, of course, meant higher prices. However, those on a budget will also find appealing inexpensive eateries. High-end delis offer superb picnic fare, and brunch is a cost-effective strategy at pricey restaurants.

With few exceptions (which are noted in individual restaurant listings), dress is informal. Where reservations are indicated as essential, you may need to reserve a week or more ahead. During the summer and early fall harvest seasons you may need to book several months ahead. For dining price ranges, *see* Chapter 3.

Galleries and Museums

More and more artists and art dealers are discovering the Napa Valley as a showplace for original works of art. Internationally famous artists and local artists exhibit their work side by side in galleries that showcase artistic styles to suit every taste. Shows at most galleries are scheduled throughout the year, and exhibitions change frequently.

Hot-Air Ballooning

Day after day, colorful balloons fill the morning sky high above the Wine Country's valleys. To aficionados, peering down at vineyards from the vantage point of the clouds is the ultimate California experience. Balloon flights take place soon after sunrise, when the calmest, coolest conditions offer maximum lift and soft landings. Prices depend on the duration of the flight, number of passengers, and services. Some companies provide such extras as pickup at your lodging or champagne brunch after the flight. Expect to spend at least $175 per person.

Lodging

In a region where first-class restaurants and wineries attract connoisseurs from afar, it's no surprise that elegant lodgings have sprung up. Ranging from quaint to utterly luxurious, the area's many inns, hotels, and spas are usually exquisitely appointed. Most local bed-and-breakfasts have historic Victorian and Spanish architecture and serve a full breakfast highlighting local produce. The newer hotels and spas include state-of-the-art buildings offering such comforts as massage treatments or spring water–fed pools. Many house world-class restaurants or are a short car ride away from gastronomic bliss.

All of this luxury does come with a hefty price tag. As the cost of vineyards and grapes has risen, so have prices. Since Santa Rosa is the largest population center in the area, it has the widest selection of moderately priced rooms. Try there if you've failed to reserve in advance or have a limited budget. Many B&Bs are fully booked long in advance of the summer and fall seasons, and small children are often discouraged as guests. For all accommodations in the area, rates are lower on weeknights and about 20% less in the winter. For lodging price ranges, *see* Chapter 4.

Spas and Mud Baths

Mineral water soaks, mud baths, and massage are rejuvenating local traditions. Calistoga, known worldwide as the Hot Springs of the West, is famous for its warm, spring water–fed mineral tubs and mud baths full of volcanic ash. Sonoma, St. Helena, and other towns also have full-service spas.

Wine Tasting

Wine tasting can be an educational, fascinating, and even mysterious ritual. The sight of polished glasses and uniquely labeled bottles lined up in a row, the tour guide's commentary on the character of each wine, the decadent mood of the vineyards with their full-to-bursting grapes— all combine to create an anticipation that's gratified with the first sip of wine. Learning about the origin of the grapes, the terraces on which they're grown, the weather that nurtured them, and the methods by which they're transformed into wine will give you a new appreciation of wine—and a great afternoon (or all-day) diversion. For those new to the wine tasting game, Robert Mondavi and Korbel Champagne Cellars give general tours geared toward teaching novices the basics on how wine and champagne are made and what to look for when tasting.

There are more than 400 wineries in Sonoma and Napa, so it pays to be selective when planning your visit. Better to mix up the wineries with other sights and diversions—a picnic, trips to local museums, a ride in a hot-air balloon—than attempt to visit too many in one day. Unless otherwise noted, the wineries in this chapter are open daily year-round and charge no fee for admission, tours, or tastings.

Exploring the Wine Country

Numbers in the text correspond to numbers in the margin and on the Wine Country map.

Great Itineraries

The Wine Country is composed of two main areas: the Napa Valley and the Sonoma Valley. Five major paths cut through both valleys: U.S. 101 and Routes 12 and 121 through Sonoma County, and Route 29 north from Napa. The 25-mi Silverado Trail, which runs parallel to Route 29 north from Napa to Calistoga, is a more scenic, less crowded route with a number of distinguished wineries.

Because the Wine Country is expansive, it's best to plan smaller, separate trips over the course of several days. You can get a feel for the area's towns and vineyards by taking to the open road over a weekend. Along the way you can stop at a winery or two, have a picnic lunch, and watch the countryside glide past your windshield. With four or five days you'll be able to explore more towns and wineries and also indulge in dining adventures. You might even bike the Silverado Trail or fish the Russian River. A full week will allow time for all of the above, plus pampering at the region's hot springs and mud baths, a round of golf, and a hot-air balloon ride.

IF YOU HAVE 2 DAYS

Start at the circa-1857 **Buena Vista Carneros Winery** ㉟ just outside of Sonoma. From there, take Route 12 north to the Trinity Road/Oakville Grade. Drive east over the Mayacamas Mountains, taking time to admire the views as you descend into the Napa Valley. Take Route 29 north into historic ⛫ **St. Helena** for lunch. After lunch in St. Helena, take the 30-minute tour of **Beringer Vineyards** ㉖. The next day continue up 29 North to **Calistoga** for an early morning balloon ride, an afternoon trip to the mud baths, and a visit to **Clos Pegase** ㉚ before heading back to St. Helena for dinner at Greystone—the Culinary Institute of America's beautiful West Coast campus and highly acclaimed restaurant.

234

Arrowood
Vineyards 37
Artesa 5
Beaulieu Vineyard . .21
Benziger Family
Winery 38
Beringer
Vineyards 26
Buena Vista
Carneros Winery . .35
Caymus Vineyards . .19
Charles Krug
Winery 25
Château
Montelena 33
Chateau Potelle 7
Clos du Val 10
Clos Pegase 30
Copia 8
Cuvaison 29
Domaine Carneros . . .4
Domaine Chandon . .14
Dry Creek
Vineyard 46
Dutch Henry
Winery 32
Ferrari-Carano
Winery 49
Freemark Abbey
Winery 27
Frog's Leap 20
Gloria Ferrer
Champagne Caves . .2
Hess Collection
Winery and
Vineyards 6
Joseph Phelps
Vineyards 24
Kenwood
Vineyards 40
Kunde Estate
Winery 39
Landmark
Vineyards 41
Luna 9
Matanzas Creek
Winery 42
Michel-
Schlumberger 47
Mumm Napa
Valley 17
Niebaum-Coppola
Estate 22
Opus One 15
Pine Ridge 11
Quivira 48
Ravenswood 36
RMS Brandy
Distillery 3
Robert Mondavi . . .16
Robert Sinskey 13
Rochioli Vineyards
and Winery 43
Rodney Strong
Vineyards 44
Rutherford Hill
Winery 18
St. Supéry 23
Schramsberg 31
Sebastiani
Vineyards 34
Simi Winery 45
Stag's Leap
Wine Cellars 12
Sterling
Vineyards 28
Viansa 1

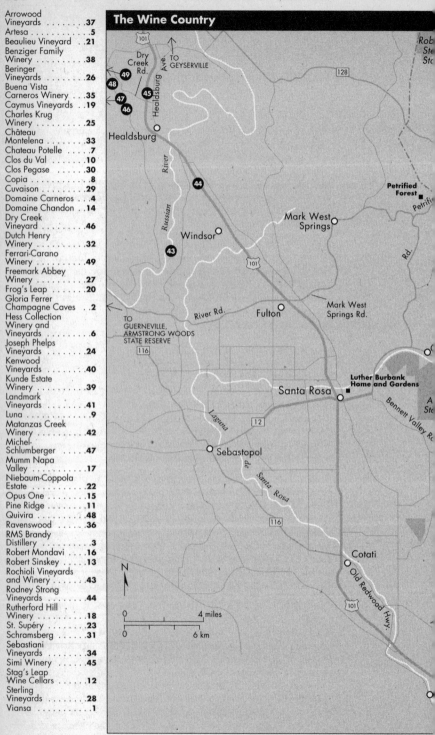

The Wine Country

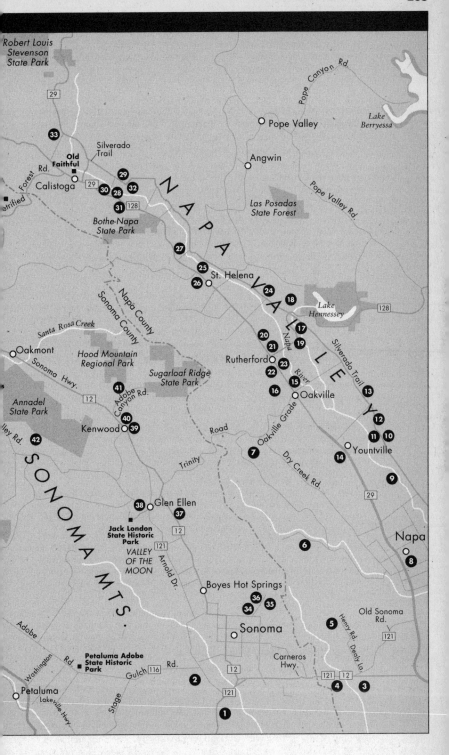

IF YOU HAVE 4 DAYS

Concentrate on the Napa Valley, starting at Yountville and traveling north to Calistoga. Make your first stop in **Oakville,** where the circa-1880s Oakville Grocery—once a Wells Fargo Pony Express stop—is indisputably the most popular place for picnic supplies. Enjoy the picnic grounds at **Robert Mondavi** ⑯ before touring the winery and tasting the wine. If time permits, spend the night in the town of 🏨 **Rutherford** and visit either **Rutherford Hill Winery** ⑱ or the **Niebaum-Coppola Estate** ㉒, or continue north to 🏨 **St. Helena.** Take a look at the Silverado Museum and visit the shopping complex surrounding the **Freemark Abbey Winery** ㉗. On the third day drive to 🏨 **Calistoga** for a balloon ride before heading north to Old Faithful Geyser of California; then continue on to Robert Louis Stevenson State Park, which encompasses the summit of Mount St. Helena. On the fourth day take Route 29 just north of Calistoga proper, head west on Petrified Forest Road, and then go south on Calistoga Road, which runs into Route 12. Follow Route 12 southeast to **Glen Ellen** for a taste of the Sonoma Valley. Visit Jack London State Historic Park, and then loop back north on Bennett Valley Road to beautiful **Matanzas Creek Winery** ㊷ in Santa Rosa.

IF YOU HAVE 7 DAYS

Begin in the town of **Sonoma,** whose colorful plaza and mission evoke early California's Spanish past. Afterward, head north to 🏨 **Glen Ellen** and the Valley of the Moon. Picnic and explore the grounds at Jack London State Historic Park. Next morning visit **Kenwood Vineyards** ㊵ before heading north to 🏨 **Healdsburg** in Dry Creek Valley via Santa Rosa and U.S. 101. In this less-trafficked haven of northern Sonoma County, a host of "hidden" wineries—including **Ferrari-Carano Winery** ㊾—lie nestled in the woods along the roads. Spend the night in 🏨 **Healdsburg.** On the third day cross over into Napa Valley—take Mark Springs Road east off U.S. 101's River Road exit and follow the signs on Porter Creek Road to Petrified Forest Road to Route 29. Spend the day (and the night) in the quaint western-style town of 🏨 **Calistoga,** noted for its mud baths and mineral springs. Wake up early on the fourth day for a balloon ride. If you're feeling energetic, take to the Silverado Trail for a bike ride with stops at **Cuvaison** ㉙, **Stag's Leap Wine Cellars** ⑫, and **Clos du Val** ⑩. On day five, visit the galleries, shops, and eateries of St. Helena before heading to Oakville for the Oakville Grocery, a must-see (and must-taste) landmark. Spend the night and visit the wineries in 🏨 **Rutherford.** On day six, explore nearby **Yountville,** stopping for lunch at one of its many acclaimed restaurants before heading up the hill to the **Hess Collection Winery and Vineyards** ⑥, on Mt. Veeder, where a brilliant art collection and excellent wines may keep you occupied for hours. Splurge on dinner at Domaine Chandon. On your last day return to the town of Sonoma via the Carneros Highway, stopping for a look at how brandies are made at the **RMS Brandy Distillery** ③, then moving on to the landmark **Buena Vista Carneros Winery** ㉟, or **Gloria Ferrer Champagne Caves** ②.

When to Tour the Wine Country

"Crush," the term used to indicate the season when grapes are picked and crushed, usually takes place in September or October, depending on the weather. From September until December the entire Wine Country celebrates its bounty with street fairs and festivals. The Sonoma County Harvest Fair, with its famous grape stomp, is held the first weekend in October. The Napa Valley Wine Festival takes place the first weekend in November. Golf tournaments, wine auctions, and art and food fairs occur throughout the fall.

In season (April–October), Napa Valley draws crowds of tourists, and traffic along Route 29 from St. Helena to Calistoga is often backed up on weekends. The Sonoma Valley, Santa Rosa, and Healdsburg are less crowded. In season and over holiday weekends it's best to book lodging, restaurant, and winery reservations well in advance. Many wineries give tours at specified times and require appointments.

To avoid crowds, visit the Wine Country during the week and get an early start (most wineries open around 10). Pack a sun hat, since summer is usually hot and dry and autumn can be even hotter.

CARNEROS REGION

One of the most important viticultural areas in the Wine Country straddles southern Sonoma and Napa counties. The Carneros region has a long, cool growing season tempered by maritime breezes and lingering fogs off the San Pablo Bay—optimum slow-growing conditions for pinot noir and chardonnay grapes. So exotic-looking are the misty Carneros marshlands that Francis Ford Coppola chose them as the location for scenes of the Mekong Delta in his 1979 movie *Apocalypse Now.* When the sun is shining, however, Carneros looks like a sprawling and scenic expanse of quintessential Wine Country, where wildflower meadows and vineyards stretch toward the horizon.

Southern Sonoma County

36 mi from San Francisco, north on U.S. 101, east on Rte. 37, and north on Rte. 121.

❶ Sam Sebastiani, of the famous Sebastiani family, and his wife, Vicki, established their own hilltop winery, **Viansa.** Reminiscent of a Tuscan villa, the winery's ocher-color building is surrounded by olive trees and overlooks the valley. The varietals produced here depart from the traditionally Californian and include muscat canelli and nebbiolo. The Italian Marketplace on the premises sells delicious specialty sandwiches and salads to complement Viansa's Italian-style wines. The adjacent Wine Country Visitor Center has brochures and information. ✉ *25200 Arnold Dr., Sonoma County,* ☎ *707/935–4700,* WEB *www. viansa.com.* ⊘ *Daily 10–5. Tours by appointment.*

❷ The sparkling and still wines at **Gloria Ferrer Champagne Caves** originated with a 700-year-old stock of Ferrer grapes. The method here is to age the wines in a "cava," or cellar, where several feet of earth maintain a constant temperature—an increasingly popular alternative to temperature-controlled warehouses. ✉ *23555 Carneros (Rte. 121),* ☎ *707/ 996–7256,* WEB *www.gloriaferrer.com.* ⊞ *Tasting fees vary.* ⊘ *Daily 10:30–5:30. Tours daily between 11 and 4.*

Southern Napa County

7 mi east of Rte. 121/116 junction on Rte. 121/12.

❸ Learn the history and folklore of rare alembic brandy at the **RMS Brandy Distillery.** Tours include an explanation of the double-distillation process, which eliminates all but the finest spirits for aging; a view of the French-built alembic distillation pots that resemble Aladdin's lamp; a trip to the atmospheric oak barrel house, where taped chants create an otherworldly mood; and a sensory evaluation of vintage brandies (no tasting allowed, by law). ✉ *1250 Cuttings Wharf Rd., Napa (from Domaine Carneros, head 1 mi east on Carneros Hwy.),* ☎ *707/253–9055,* FAX *707/253–0116,* WEB *www.rmsbrandy.com.* ⊘ *Apr.– Oct., daily 10–5; Nov.–Mar., daily 10:30–4:30. Tours every hr.*

4 Domaine Carneros occupies a 138-acre estate dominated by a classic château inspired by Champagne Taittinger's historic Château de la Marquetterie in France. Carved into the hillside beneath the winery, Domaine Carneros's cellars produce sparkling wines reminiscent of the Taittinger style and using only Carneros grapes. At night the château is a glowing beacon rising above the dark vineyards. By day activity buzzes throughout the visitor center, the touring and tasting rooms, and the kitchen and dining room, where private luncheons and dinners emphasize food and wine pairings. Complimentary appetizers are served with wines. ⊠ *1240 Duhig Rd., Napa,* ☎ *707/257–0101,* ℻ *707/257–3020,* WEB *www.domainecarneros.com.* ▧ *Tasting fees vary.* ☾ *Daily 10:30–6:30. Tours daily at 11, noon, 1, 2, 3, and 4, Apr.–Oct.; Mon.–Thurs. at 11, 1, and 3 and Fri.–Sun. hourly 11–4, Nov.–Mar.*

5 Artesa is bunkered into a scenic Carneros hilltop, formerly the site of Codorniu Napa. The Spanish owners are now producing primarily still wines under the talented wine maker Don Van Staaveren (formerly of Chateau St. Jean). ⊠ *1345 Henry Rd., north off Old Sonoma Rd. and Dealy La.,* ☎ *707/224–1668,* ℻ *707/224–1672,* WEB *www. artesawinery.com.* ▧ *Tasting fees vary.* ☾ *Daily 10–5. Tours daily; times vary.*

THE NAPA VALLEY

The Napa Valley is the undisputed capital of American wine production, with more than 240 wineries. Famed for its unrivaled climate and neat rows of vineyards, the area is made up of small, quirky towns whose Victorian Gothic architecture—narrow, gingerbread facades and pointed arches—is reminiscent of a distant world. Calistoga feels like an Old West frontier town, with wooden-plank storefronts and people in cowboy hats. St. Helena is posh, with tony shops and elegant restaurants. Yountville is compact and redolent of American history, yet fast becoming an up-to-the-minute culinary hub.

With long country roads winding through the region, bicycling is a popular pastime. For rentals try **Napa Valley Bike Tours and Rentals** (⊠ 4080 Byway E, Napa, ☎ 707/255–3377, ℻ 707/255–3380).

Napa

46 mi from San Francisco, east and north on I–80 to Rte. 37 west to Rte. 29 north.

The city of Napa is undergoing quite a metamorphosis, especially since the 2001 opening of Copia: The American Center for Wine, Food and the Arts. New restaurants and inns also opened at about the same time, and the resurrection of the Napa Valley Opera House was scheduled to be completed in 2002. The oldest town in the Napa Valley—established in 1848—it also claims an advantageous location. Most destinations in both the Napa and Sonoma valleys are easily accessible from here. For those seeking an affordable alternative to the hotels and B&Bs in the heart of the Wine Country, Napa is a good option. But choose lodgings right downtown or on the north side of town near Yountville, as parts of Napa are downright seedy.

★ **6** The **Hess Collection Winery and Vineyards** is a delightful discovery on a hilltop 9 mi northwest of Napa (don't give up; the road leading to the winery is long and winding). Within the simple, rustic limestone structure, circa 1903, you'll find Swiss owner Donald Hess's personal art collection, including works by such contemporary European and American artists as Robert Motherwell, Francis Bacon, and Frank

Stella. Cabernet sauvignon is the real strength here, though Hess also produces some fine chardonnays. The winery and the art collection are open for self-guided tours. ⊠ *4411 Redwood Rd., west off Rte. 29,* ☎ *707/255–1144,* FAX *707/253–1682,* WEB *www.hesscollection.com.* ⊡ *Tasting fee $3.* ⊙ *Daily 10–4.*

❼ Chateau Potelle, on the slopes of Mt. Veeder, produces acclaimed estate zinfandel, chardonnay, and cabernet sauvignon, all of which thrive in the poor soil at nearly 2,000 ft above the valley floor. Jean Noel and Marketta Fourneaux du Sartel were official tasters in Bordeaux and the Rhône before establishing this winery in 1998. It's a quiet, out-of-the-way spot for a picnic. ⊠ *3875 Mt. Veeder Rd. (5 mi west of Rte. 29 off the Oakville Grade),* ☎ *707/255–9440,* WEB *www.chateaupotelle.com.* ⊙ *Thurs.–Mon. 11–5.*

❽ Copia: The American Center for Wine, Food and the Arts is a two-story complex that celebrates American cultural contributions to wine and food and offers related exhibitions, demonstrations and classes, as well as dining at Julia's Kitchen, named for the legendary Julia Child. Tours of seasonal gardens are also available. ⊠ *2921 Silverado Trail,* ☎ *707/ 259–1600,* WEB *www.copia.org.* ⊡ *Tasting fee: $7.* ⊙ *Daily 10–5. Tours by appointment.*

❾ Luna, the southernmost winery on the Silverado Trail, was established in 1996 by three veterans of the Napa wine industry intent on making less-conventional wines, particularly Italian varieties. They've planted pinot gris on the historic property and also make sangiovese and merlot. ⊠ *2921 Silverado Trail,* ☎ *707/255–5862,* WEB *www.lunavineyards.com.* ⊡ *Tasting fee: $7.* ⊙ *Daily 10–5. Tours by appointment.*

❿ Clos du Val, founded by French owner Bernard Portet, produces a celebrated reserve cabernet. It also makes zinfandel, pinot noir, merlot, sangiovese, and chardonnay. Although the winery itself is austere, the French-style wines age beautifully. ⊠ *5330 Silverado Trail,* ☎ *707/259–2200,* WEB *www.closduval.com.* ⊡ *Tasting fee $5.* ⊙ *Daily 10–5. Tours by appointment.*

⓫ Small **Pine Ridge** makes estate-bottled wines, including chardonnay, cabernet, and merlot, as well as a first-rate chenin blanc. Tours include barrel tastings in the winery's caves. ⊠ *5901 Silverado Trail,* ☎ *707/253–7500,* FAX *707/253–1493,* WEB *www.pineridgewinery.com.* ⊡ *Tasting fees vary.* ⊙ *Daily 10:30–4:30. Tours by appointment at 10:15, 1, and 3.*

Dining and Lodging

$$–$$$ ✕ **Bistro Don Giovanni.** Even in winter, the valley views from the covered patio are extraordinary. The wine list at the restaurant of Giovanni and Donna Scala is as locally representative as the menu is eclectic. Don't miss the individual pizzas cooked in a wood-burning oven, the handmade pastas, or the focaccia sandwiches encasing grilled vegetables. The terra-cotta tile floors and high ceilings create a casual Mediterranean feel. ⊠ *4110 St. Helena Hwy. (Rte. 29),* ☎ *707/224–3300. AE, D, DC, MC, V.*

$$–$$$ ✕ **Foothill Cafe.** On the less glamorous side of Route 29, this low-key restaurant is a big favorite with locals, who may or may not know that the chef is an alumnus of Masa's in San Francisco. Typical dishes include oak-roasted prime rib with a potato-Stilton gratin and salmon crusted with ginger and peppercorns. ⊠ *2766 Old Sonoma Rd.,* ☎ *707/252–6178. MC, V. No lunch. Closed Mon.–Tues.*

$$–$$$ ✕ **Silverado Country Club.** There are two restaurants and a bar and grill at this large, famous resort. The elegant Vintner's Court, with California–Pacific Rim cuisine, serves dinner only (à la carte dining is available on Wednesday, Thursday, and Saturday); there is a seafood buffet

240

All Seasons Café . . .22
Auberge du Soleil 13
The Big 3 Diner 32
Bistro Don Giovanni 4
Bistro Jeanty 7
Bistro Ralph 40
Bouchon 8
Brix 10
Café Citti 36
Cafe La Haye 27
Café Lolo 37
Calistoga Inn 19
Catahoula Restaurant and Saloon 23
Celadon 2
Chez Marie 45
Della Santina 26
Foothill Café 1
French Laundry 9
The Girl and the Fig 29
The Glen Ellen Inn . .34
Inn at the Tides 43
John Ash & Co. . . .41
Kenwood Restaurant & Bar . . .35
La Casa 28
La Salette 31
La Toque 12
Livefire 6
Martini House 16
Meadowood Resort 14
Meritage 25
Mixx 38
Mustards Grill 11
Pacifico 20
Ristorante Piatti 30
River's End 44
Saddles 24
Sante 33
Sassafras 39
Silverado Country Club 5
Sonoma Mission Inn & Spa 33
Terra 17
Tra Vigne 15
Wappo Bar Bistro 21
Willow Wood Market Café 42
Wine Spectator Greystone Restaurant 18
ZuZu 3

Napa and Sonoma Dining

242

Applewood Inn **38**
Auberge du
Soleil **18**
Beltane Ranch . . . **16**
Best Western
Dry Creek Inn **31**
Brannan
Cottage Inn **23**
Calistoga Spa
Hot Springs **25**
Chateau Hotel **9**
Cottage Grove
Inn **26**
El Bonita Motel . . . **19**
El Dorado Hotel **2**
The Farmhouse Inn . **37**
Fort Ross Lodge . . . **33**
Fountaingrove Inn . . **29**
Gaige House Inn . . . **14**
Glenelly Inn **15**
Harvest Inn **20**
Healdsburg Inn
on the Plaza **34**
The Honor
Mansion **35**
Hotel Healdsburg . . **36**
The Inn at
Occidental **39**
Inn at the Tides . . . **41**
La Résidence **10**
Los Robles Lodge . . **28**
MacArthur Place . . . **4**
Madrona Manor . . **32**
Meadowlark
Country House **27**
Meadowood
Resort **21**
Milliken Creek Inn . . **8**
Mount View Hotel . . **24**
Napa River Inn **6**
Napa Valley
Lodge **13**
Petit Logis Inn **11**
Rancho Caymus
Inn **17**
Silverado
Country Club
and Resort **7**
Sonoma Coast
Villa Inn and Spa . . **40**
Sonoma Mission
Inn & Spa **5**
Thistle Dew Inn **3**
Vineyard Inn **1**
Vintage Inn **12**
Vintner's Inn **30**
Wine Country Inn . . **22**

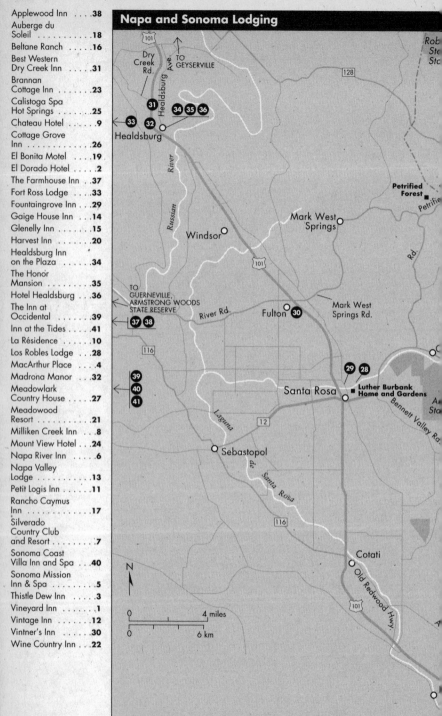

Napa and Sonoma Lodging

Robert Louis Stevenson State Park

29

Silverado Trail

Old Faithful

Forest Rd.

27

Calistoga

29

23 – 26

128

Petrified

Bothe-Napa State Park

Pope Canyon Rd.

Pope Valley

Lake Berryessa

Angwin

Pope Valley Rd.

Las Posadas State Forest

N A P A

Napa County

Sonoma County

Santa Rosa Creek

Oakmont

Hood Mountain Regional Park

Sonoma Hwy.

12

Annadel State Park

ley Rd.

Adobe Canyon Rd.

Sugarloaf Ridge State Park

Kenwood

Road

Trinity

16

15 **14** Glen Ellen

Jack London State Historic Park

12

VALLEY OF THE MOON

121

Arnold Dr.

5 Boyes Hot Springs

2 **3** **4**

Sonoma

Petaluma Adobe State Historic Park

Gulch 116 Rd.

Stage

Petaluma

Lakeville Hwy.

12

121

Adobe

Washington Rd.

Carneros Hwy.

121 12

Old Sonoma Rd.

121

Henry Rd. Dealy La.

22 **21**

St. Helena

20

19

18

Lake Hennessey

128

17

Rutherford

Napa River

Oakville

Oakville Grade

Silverado Trail

V A L L E Y

11 **12** **13**

Yountville

Dry Creek Rd.

10

29

7

8

9

6

Napa

S O N O M A   M T S.

on Friday night and a champagne brunch on Sunday. Royal Oak serves steak and seafood nightly. The bar and grill is open for breakfast and lunch year-round. ⊠ *1600 Atlas Peak Rd. (follow signs to Lake Berryessa),* ☏ *707/257–0200 or 800/532–0500. Reservations essential. AE, D, DC, MC, V. Vintner's Court closed Mon.–Tues. No dinner Sun.*

\$–\$\$ ✕ **Celadon.** Venture into downtown Napa for chef-owner Greg Cole's creative and enticing food. Dishes like flash-fried calamari with a chipotle chili and ginger glaze and small tasting plates such as a large crab cake laced with whole-seed mustard sauce make this an ideal place to sample contemporary cuisine accompanied by any of a dozen wines available by the glass. ⊠ *1040 Main St.,* ☏ *707/254–9690. AE, MC, V. Closed Sun. No lunch Sat.*

\$ ✕ **ZuZu.** Spanish glass lamps, a carved-wood Latin American goddess and hammered-tin ceiling panels set the tone for a menu composed almost entirely of tapas. These little dishes so common in Spain are a rarity in the Wine Country and this upbeat place was immediately adopted by the in-crowd. White anchovies with endive, ratatouille, grilled tuna, and lamb sausage are typical fare. ⊠ *829 Main St.,* ☏ *707/224–8555. AE, D, DC, MC, V. No lunch weekends.*

\$\$\$–\$\$\$\$ ⌑ **Milliken Creek Inn.** This lavishly landscaped inn opened in 2001 on the banks of the Napa River. The understated interiors have pale green walls, rattan furniture, water views, and lots of palm and elephant motifs. The 3-acre property is a short drive from Copia: The American Center for Wine, Food and the Arts. ⊠ *1815 Silverado Trail, 94558,* ☏ *707/255–1197, 888/622–5775,* WEB *www.millikencreekinn.com. 277 condo units. Massage, Internet. AE, D, DC, MC, V.*

\$\$\$–\$\$\$\$ ⌑ **Napa River Inn.** This waterfront inn opened in 2000 as part of a 2½-acre project including restaurants, shops, and a spa. Accommodations in the 1884 Hatt Building maintain some of the original architectural details, including maple hardwood floors; some have canopy beds, fireplaces, and artwork depicting an 1880s river town. Brighter colors dominate in the adjacent Embarcadero building, where some rooms have small balconies. ⊠ *500 Main St., 94559,* ☏ *707/251–8500 or 877/251–8500,* FAX *707/251–8504,* WEB *www.napariverinn.com. 65 rooms, 1 suite. Restaurant, in-room data ports, refrigerators. AE, D, DC, MC, V.*

\$\$–\$\$\$\$ ⌑ **Silverado Country Club and Resort.** This luxurious if somewhat staid 1,200-acre property in the hills east of Napa has cottages, kitchen apartments, and one- to three-bedroom condominiums, many with fireplaces. With multiple golf courses, pools, and tennis courts, it's a place for serious sports enthusiasts and anyone who enjoys the conveniences of a full-scale resort. ⊠ *1600 Atlas Peak Rd. (6 mi east of Napa via Rte. 121), 94558,* ☏ *707/257–0200 or 800/532–0500,* FAX *707/257–2867,* WEB *www.silveradoresort.com. 277 condo units. 3 restaurants, bar, kitchenettes, 2 18-hole golf courses, 23 tennis courts, 9 pools, bicycles. AE, D, DC, MC, V.*

\$\$ ⌑ **Chateau Hotel.** Despite the name, this is a pretty simple motel with only the barest nod to France. Clean rooms, its location at the entrance to the Napa Valley, Continental breakfast, and discounts for senior citizens make up for its lack of charm. ⊠ *4195 Solano Ave. (west of Rte. 29, exit at Trower Ave.), 94558,* ☏ *707/253–9300; 800/253–6272 in CA,* FAX *707/253–0906,* WEB *www.napavalleychateauhotel.com. 115 rooms. Refrigerators, pool, hot tub. AE, D, DC, MC, V.*

Nightlife and the Arts

In 1995, former telecommunications tycoon and vintner William Jarvis and his wife transformed a historic stone winery building in downtown Napa into the **Jarvis Conservatory,** an excellent venue for baroque French ballet and Spanish operetta known as zarzuela. Performances open to the public are held in conjunction with workshops and festivals centered on these two art forms. The conservatory presents opera nights featuring local talent the first and third Saturday of each month. ⊠ *1711 Main St.,* ☎ *707/255–5445.* ☉ *Regular shows 1st and 3rd Sat. of month; call for ticket prices and listing of other shows.*

Outdoor Activities and Sports

FISHING

You can fish from the banks of the Napa River at **John F. Kennedy Park** (⊠ 2291 Streblow Dr., ☎ 707/257–9529). There are also picnic facilities and barbecue pits. Call ahead for river conditions.

GOLF

The 18-hole **Chardonnay Club** (⊠ 2555 Jameson Canyon Rd., ☎ 707/257–8950) course is a favorite among Bay Area golfers. The greens fee, $55 weekdays and $70 weekends, includes a cart. Within the vicinity of the Silverado Trail, the **Silverado Country Club** (⊠ 1600 Atlas Peak Rd., ☎ 707/257–0200) has two challenging 18-hole courses with a beautiful view at every hole. The greens fee for hotel guests is $130, including a cart; the reciprocal rate for members of other clubs is $150.

TENNIS

Vintage High School (⊠ 1375 Trower Ave.) maintains eight public tennis courts. **Napa High School** (⊠ 2474 Jefferson St.) maintains six tennis courts with coin-operated night lights. Call the Napa Valley School District (☎ 707/253–3715) for information.

Yountville

13 mi north of the town of Napa on Rte. 29.

Yountville has become the valley's boomtown. No other small town in the entire Wine Country has as many inns, restaurants, or shops—and new ones seem to open every few months. A popular Yountville attraction is **Vintage 1870** (⊠ 6525 Washington St., ☎ 707/944–2451), a 26-acre complex of boutiques, restaurants, and gourmet stores. The vine-covered brick buildings were built in 1870 and housed a winery, livery stable, and distillery. The original mansion of the property is now the popular Mexican-style **Compadres Bar and Grill.** Nearby is the **Pacific Blues Café,** housed in the train depot Samuel Brannan built in 1868 for his privately owned Napa Valley Railroad. At **Yountville Park** there's a picnic area with tables, barbecue pits, and a view of grapevines.

At the intersection of Madison and Washington streets is Yountville's **Washington Square.** It is now a complex of boutiques and restaurants. **Pioneer Cemetery,** the final resting place of the town's founder, George Yount, is nearby, on the far side of Washington Street.

⑫ In 1995, the World Wine Championships gave **Stag's Leap Wine Cellars** a platinum award for its 1990 reserve chardonnay, designating it the highest-ranked premium chardonnay in the world. But it was the 1973 cabernet sauvignon that put the winery—and the California wine industry—on the map by placing first in the famous Paris tasting of 1976. Today, Stag's Leap makes five cabernets as well as a hard-to-find petite sirah. ⊠ *5766 Silverado Trail,* ☎ *707/944–2020,* WEB *www.cask23.com.* 🖃 *Tasting fee $5.* ☉ *Daily 10–4:30. Tours by appointment.*

⑬ **Robert Sinskey** makes estate-bottled wines, including chardonnay, cabernet, and merlot, but is best known for its pinot noir. ⊠ *6320 Silverado Trail,* ☎ *707/944–9090,* FAX *707/994–9092,* WEB *www.robertsinskey.com.* 🖃 *Tasting fees vary.* ☉ *Daily 10–4:30. Tours by appointment.*

⑭ French-owned **Domaine Chandon** claims one of Yountville's prime pieces of real estate, on a knoll west of downtown. Tours of the sleek, modern facilities on the beautifully maintained property include sample flutes of the méthode champenoise sparkling wine. Champagne is $3.75–$12 per glass, hors d'oeuvres are available, and an elegant restaurant beckons. ⊠ *California Dr., west of Rte. 29,* ☎ *707/944–2280,* WEB *www.chandon.com.* ☉ *Daily 10–6; closed Mon.–Tues. Dec.–Mar. Tours on the hr 11–5.*

Dining and Lodging

$$$$ ✕ **French Laundry.** Napa Valley's most acclaimed restaurant can be found
★ inside an old converted stone building on a residential street corner. The prix-fixe menus, one of which is vegetarian, include five or nine courses and usually have two or three additional surprises—little bitefuls such as a tiny ice cream cone filled with salmon tartare. Chef Thomas Keller, with two coveted James Beard awards on his mantel, doesn't lack for admirers. A full three hours will likely pass before you reach dessert. Reservations are hard won and not accepted more than two months in advance, but lunch is a little easier to come by. ⊠ *6640 Washington St.,* ☎ *707/944–2380. Reservations essential. AE, MC, V. Closed 1st 2 wks in Jan. No lunch Mon.–Thurs.*

$$–$$$ ✕ **Brix.** This spacious dining room has artisan glass, fine woods, and an entire wall of west-facing windows that overlooks vineyards and the Mayacamas Mountains. Mains include tamari-glazed Atlantic salmon, spicy ahi on a futomaki roll, as well as New York strip with a goat cheese–potato gratin. A wood-burning oven is used for cooking pizzas. Desserts receive an Asian accent as well, with a ginger crème brûlée among the offerings. ⊠ *7377 St. Helena Hwy. (Rte. 29),* ☎ *707/944–2749. AE, D, DC, MC, V.*

$$–$$$ ✕ **Livefire.** Fred Halpert's rustic restaurant opened in 1998 on
★ Yountville's expanding restaurant row. This is a cozy spot warmed with earthy colors like mustard and terra-cotta. Fish, ribs, and poultry come piping hot out of a French rotisserie or a Chinese smoker. Service is top-notch. ⊠ *5518 Washington St., 1 mi north of Yountville,* ☎ *707/944–1500. AE, D, DC, MC, V.*

$$–$$$ ✕ **Mustards Grill.** Everyone's favorite Napa Valley restaurant attracts
★ wine makers and other locals as well as hungry tourists. Grilled fish, steak, local fresh produce, and an impressive wine list are the trademarks of this boisterous bistro with a black-and-white marble floor and upbeat artwork. The thin, crisp, golden onion rings are addictive. ⊠ *7399 St. Helena Hwy. (Rte. 29), 1 mi north of Yountville,* ☎ *707/944–2424. Reservations essential. D, DC, MC, V.*

$$ ✕ **Bistro Jeanty.** In 1998 Philippe Jeanty opened his own restaurant with a menu inspired by the cooking of his French childhood. His traditional cassoulet will warm those nostalgic for bistro cooking, while classic coq au vin rises above the ordinary with the infusion of a spicy red wine sauce. The scene here is Gallic through and through with a small bar and a handful of tables in a crowded room. ⊠ *6510 Washington St.,* ☎ *707/944–0103. MC, V.*

$–$$ ✕ **Bouchon.** The team that brought the French Laundry to its current pinnacle opened a second restaurant nearby in 1998. French country fare—*steak frites,* leg of lamb, and sole meunière—is served amid elegant antique chandeliers and a snazzy zinc bar. Late-night diners are pleased it's open until at least 1 AM. ⊠ *6534 Washington St.,* ☎ *707/944–8037. AE, MC, V.*

$$$–$$$$ ⌂ **La Résidence.** Romantic and secluded in extensive landscaping, these deluxe accommodations are in two buildings: the Mansion, a renovated 1870s Gothic Revival manor house built by a riverboat captain from New Orleans; and the French Barn. Towering oaks bathe

the entire property in shade. The spacious rooms have period antiques, fireplaces, and double French doors opening onto verandas or patios. ⊠ *4066 St. Helena Hwy. (Rte. 29, 4 mi south of Yountville),* ☎ *707/253–0337,* FAX *707/253–0382,* WEB *www.laresidence.com. 20 rooms. Dining room, pool, hot tub, business services. AE, D, DC, MC, V. BP.*

$$$–$$$$　🏨 **Napa Valley Lodge.** The balconies, covered walkways, and red-tile roof are reminiscent of a hacienda. The large pool area is landscaped with lots of greenery. Many spacious second-floor rooms have vineyard views, and five suites are available. Fresh brewed coffee, Continental breakfast, and the morning paper are complimentary. ⊠ *2230 Madison St., at Rte. 29,* ☎ *707/944–2468 or 800/368–2468,* FAX *707/944–9362,* WEB *www.woodsidehotels.com/napa. 55 rooms. Refrigerators, pool, gym, hot tub, sauna. AE, D, DC, MC, V. CP.*

$$$–$$$$　🏨 **Vintage Inn.** Accommodations in this luxurious inn are arranged in two-story villas throughout the 3½-acre property. All the spacious rooms were revamped in 2001, adding French fabrics and 19th-century antiques as well as whirlpools to all the bathrooms. Some private patios have vineyard views. You're treated to a bottle of wine, Continental breakfast with champagne, and afternoon tea. ⊠ *6541 Washington St., 94599,* ☎ *707/944–1112 or 800/351–1133,* FAX *707/944–1617,* WEB *www.vintageinn.com. 80 rooms. Refrigerators, tennis court, pool, hot tub, bicycles. AE, DC, MC, V. CP.*

$$　🏨 **Petit Logis Inn.** In 1997 Jay and Judith Caldwell remodeled a row of shops into a small, charming one-story inn. Murals and 11-ft ceilings infuse each unique room with a European elegance. Breakfast, included in the room rate, is offered at one of two nearby restaurants. ⊠ *6527 Yount St., 94599,* ☎ *707/944–2332,* WEB *www.petitlogis.com. 5 rooms. Refrigerators, hot tubs. AE, MC, V. CP.*

Outdoor Activities and Sports

HOT-AIR BALLOONING

Balloons Above the Valley (⊠ Box 3838, Napa 94558, ☎ 707/253–2222; 800/464–6824 in CA) is a reliable organization; rides are $185 per person. **Napa Valley Balloons** (⊠ Box 2860, Yountville 94599, ☎ 707/944–0228; 800/253–2224 in CA) charges $175 per person.

Oakville

2 mi west of Yountville on Rte. 29.

There are three reasons to visit the town of Oakville: its grocery store, its scenic mountain road, and its magnificent, highly exclusive winery. The **Oakville Grocery** (⊠ 7856 St. Helena Hwy. [Rte. 29]), built in the late 1880s to serve as a grocery store and Wells Fargo Pony Express stop, carries gourmet foods and difficult-to-find wines. Custom-packed picnic baskets are a specialty. Along the mountain range that divides Napa and Sonoma, the **Oakville Grade** is a twisting half-hour route with breathtaking views of both valleys. Though the surface of the road is good, it can be difficult to negotiate at night, and trucks are advised not to attempt it at any time.

⓯ Opus One, the combined venture of California wine maker Robert Mondavi and French baron Philippe Rothschild, is famed for its vast (1,000 barrels side by side on a single floor), semicircular cellar modeled on the Château Mouton Rothschild winery in France. The futuristic building is the work of the same architects responsible for San Francisco's Transamerica Pyramid. The state-of-the-art facilities produce about 20,000 cases of ultrapremium Bordeaux-style red wine from grapes grown in the estate's own vineyards and in the surrounding Oakville appellation. ⊠ *7900 St. Helena Hwy. (Rte. 29),* ☎ *707/963–1979,* FAX

707/944–1753, WEB *www.opusonewinery.com.* ⊠ *Tasting fee $25.* ⊙ *Daily 10–3:30. Tasting and tours by appointment.*

🔟 At **Robert Mondavi,** the most famous winery in the nation, you're encouraged to take the 60-minute production tour with complimentary tasting, before trying the reserve reds ($1–$5 per glass). In-depth three- to four-hour tours and gourmet lunch tours are also popular. Afterward, visit the art gallery, or stick around for a summer concert. ⊠ *7801 St. Helena Hwy. (Rte. 29),* ☎ *707/259–9463,* WEB *www.robertmondavi.com.* ⊙ *Daily 9–5. Tours by appointment.*

Rutherford

1 mi northwest of Oakville on Rte. 29.

From a fast-moving car, Rutherford is a quick blur of dark forest, a rustic barn or two, and maybe a country store. But don't speed by this tiny hamlet. With its singular microclimate and soil, this is an important viticultural center.

🔢 A joint venture of Mumm—the French champagne house—and Seagram, **Mumm Napa Valley** is considered one of California's premier sparkling-wine producers. Its Napa Brut Prestige and ultrapremium Vintage Reserve are the best known. The excellent tour and comfortable tasting room are two more good reasons to visit. An art gallery contains a permanent exhibit of photographs by Ansel Adams that record the wine-making process. ⊠ *8445 Silverado Trail,* ☎ *707/942–3434,* WEB *www.mummnapavalley.com.* ⊠ *Tasting fees vary.* ⊙ *Daily 10–5. Tours daily on the hour 10–3.*

🔢 The wine at **Rutherford Hill Winery** is aged in French oak barrels stacked in more than 44,000 square ft of caves—one of the largest such facilities in the nation. Tours of the caves can be followed by a picnic in oak, olive, or madrone orchards. ⊠ *200 Rutherford Hill Rd., off the Silverado Trail,* ☎ *707/963–7194,* WEB *www.rutherfordhill.com.* ⊠ *Tasting fees vary.* ⊙ *Daily 10–5. Tours 11:30, 1:30, and 3:30.*

🔢 **Caymus Vineyards** is run by wine master Chuck Wagner, who started making wine on the property in 1972. His family, however, had been farming the land (grapes and plums) since 1906. Today a 100% cabernet sauvignon special selection is the winery's claim to fame. Caymus also turns out a superior white, the Conundrum Proprietary, made of an unusual blend of grapes—sauvignon blanc, semillon, chardonnay, muscat canelli, and viognier. ⊠ *8700 Conn Creek Rd.,* ☎ *707/963– 4204.* ⊙ *Daily 10–4. Tours and complimentary sit-down tastings by appointment.*

🔢 **Frog's Leap** is the perfect place for wine novices to begin their education. Owners John and Julie Williams maintain a sense of humor and a humble attitude that translates into an informative and satisfying experience. They also happen to produce some of the finest zinfandel, cabernet sauvignon, and sauvignon blanc in the Wine Country. Call ahead for directions. There is no tasting room. ⊠ *8815 Conn Creek Rd.,* ☎ *707/963–4704,* FAX *707/963–0242,* WEB *www.frogsleap.com.* ⊙ *Tours and tasting by appointment.*

🔢 **Beaulieu Vineyard** utilizes the same wine-making process, from crush to bottle, as it did the day it opened in 1900. The winery's cabernet is a benchmark of the Napa Valley. The Georges du Latour Private Reserve consistently garners high marks from major wine publications. ⊠ *1960 St. Helena Hwy. (Rte. 29),* ☎ *707/963–2411,* WEB *www. bvwines.com.* ⊠ *Tasting fee $5, $25 in Reserve Room.* ⊙ *Daily 10– 5. Tours daily at 11, 1, 2, 3, and 4, and on Sat. on the half-hr.*

In the 1970s, filmmaker Francis Ford Coppola bought the old Niebaum estate, a part of the world-famous Inglenook estate. He resurrected an early Inglenook-like quality red with his first bottle of Rubicon, released in 1985. Since then, **Niebaum–Coppola Estate** has consistently received high ratings, and in 1995 Coppola purchased the other half of the Inglenook estate, the ancient, ivy-covered château, and an additional 95 acres of land. When you're through touring the winery, take a look at the Coppola movie memorabilia, which includes Don Corleone's desk and chair from *The Godfather* and costumes from *Bram Stoker's Dracula*. ⊠ *1991 St. Helena Hwy. (Rte. 29),* ☎ *707/963–9099,* WEB *www.niebaum-coppola.com.* ☞ *Tasting fee $7.50.* ☉ *Daily 10–5. Tours daily at 10:30 and 2:30.*

㉓ **St. Supéry** makes such excellent sauvignon blanc that it often sells out, but you can usually sample that variety as well as chardonnay, several red wines, and two kosher wines in the tasting room. This winery's unique discovery center allows you to inhale distinct wine aromas and match them with actual black pepper, cherry, citrus, and the like. A restored 100-year-old Victorian house is part of the excellent winery tour. ⊠ *8440 St. Helena Hwy. S (Rte. 29),* ☎ *707/963–4507,* WEB *www.stsupery.com.* ☞ *Tasting fee $5 (lifetime).* ☉ *Daily 10–5. Tours at 11, 1, and 3.*

Dining and Lodging

$$$$ ✕ **La Toque.** This understated restaurant, housed in the Rancho Cay-
★   mus Inn, gives Yountville's French Laundry its toughest competition for diners' haute cuisine dollar. Chef-owner Ken Frank specializes in intense flavors in his changing prix-fixe menu that may include braised chanterelles, ravioli with chestnuts and rabbit, and cannellini-cranberry ragout. His cheese courses and desserts are worth saving some room for. A special truffle menu is added from mid-Jan. to mid-Feb. ⊠ *1140 Rutherford Rd.,* ☎ *707/963–9770. Reservations essential. AE, MC, V. Closed Mon.–Tues. and first 2 wks in Jan. No dinner Sun.*

$$$$ ✕🏠 **Auberge du Soleil.** This stunning property, terraced on a hill stud-
★   ded by olive trees, has some of the valley's best views. The hotel's renowned restaurant is reclaiming its original glory with an award-winning wine list and dishes like raw yellowfin tuna with baby beets and Florida red snapper with pureed cauliflower, and the moderately priced bar menu is almost as good. Guest rooms, except for the most expensive ones, run a bit small; all are decorated with a nod to the spare side of southwestern style. ⊠ *180 Rutherford Hill Rd., off Silverado Trail just north of Rte. 128, 94573,* ☎ *707/963–1211 or 800/348–5406,* FAX *707/963–8764,* WEB *www.aubergedusoleil.com. 50 rooms. Restaurant, 3 tennis courts, pool, gym, hot tub, massage, steam room. AE, D, DC, MC, V. EP.*

$$–$$$$ 🏠 **Rancho Caymus Inn.** California-Spanish in style, this cozy inn has well-maintained gardens and large suites with kitchens and whirlpool baths. Well-chosen details include beehive fireplaces, tile murals, stoneware basins, and Ecuadorean llama-hair blankets. ⊠ *1140 Ruther-ford Rd., junction of Rtes. 29 and 128, 94573,* ☎ *707/963–1777 or 800/845–1777,* FAX *707/963–5387,* WEB *www.ranchocaymus.com. 26 rooms. Restaurant, some kitchenettes, refrigerators. AE, DC, MC, V. 2-night minimum on weekends. CP.*

St. Helena

2 mi northwest of Oakville on Rte. 29.

By the time pioneer winemaker Charles Krug planted grapes in St. Helena around 1860, quite a few vineyards already existed. Today the town greets you with its abundant selection of wineries—many of which lie along the route from Yountville to St. Helena—and restaurants, including Greystone on the West Coast campus of the Culinary Institute of America. Many Victorian and false-front buildings dating from the late 19th and early 20th centuries distinguish the downtown area. Arching sycamore trees bow across Main Street (Route 29) to create a pleasant, shady drive.

㉔ Bordeaux blends, Rhône varietals, and a cabernet sauvignon are the house specialties at **Joseph Phelps Vineyards.** One of Napa's top wineries, it first hit the mark with Johannisberg riesling. ✉ *200 Taplin Rd.,* ☎ *707/963–2745,* WEB *www.jpvwines.com.* 🎫 *Tasting fee $5.* ☉ *Mon.–Sat. 9–5, Sun. 10–4. Tours and tastings by appointment only.*

㉕ **Charles Krug Winery** opened in 1861 when Count Haraszthy loaned Krug a small cider press. Today, it is run by the Peter Mondavi family. The gift shop stocks everything from gourmet food baskets with grape-shape pasta to books about the region and its wines. The joint tasting and tour fee is $3. ✉ *2800 N. Main St.,* ☎ *707/963–5057.* ☉ *Daily 10:30–5:30. Tours at 11:30, 1:30, and 3:30.*

㉖ Arguably the most beautiful winery in the Napa Valley, the 1876 **Beringer Vineyards** is also the oldest continuously operating one. In 1883 the Beringer brothers, Frederick and Jacob, built the Rhine House Mansion, where tastings are now held among Belgian Art Nouveau hand-carved oak and walnut furniture and stained-glass windows. ✉ *2000 Main St. (Rte. 29),* ☎ *707/963–4812,* WEB *www.beringerblass.com.* 🎫 *Tasting fees vary.* ☉ *Daily 9:30–4. Tours daily.*

㉗ **Freemark Abbey Winery** was originally called the Tychson Winery after Josephine Tychson, the first woman to establish a winery in California. It has long been known for its cabernets, whose grapes come from the fertile Rutherford Bench. All other wines are estate grown, including a much-touted late-harvest riesling. ✉ *3022 St. Helena Hwy. N (Rte. 29),* ☎ *707/963–9694,* WEB *www.freemarkabbey.com.* ☉ *Daily 10–4:30. Tour daily at 2.*

Grape-seed mud wraps and Ayurvedic-inspired massages performed by two attendants are among the trademarks of the upscale **Health Spa Napa Valley** (✉ 1030 Main St., ☎ 707/967–8800), which has a pool and a health club. Should your treatments leave you too limp to operate your car, you can walk to Tra Vigne and other St. Helena restaurants.

For some nonalcoholic sightseeing, visit the **Silverado Museum,** next door to the public library. Its Robert Louis Stevenson memorabilia consists of more than 8,000 artifacts, including first editions, manuscripts, and photographs. ✉ *1490 Library La.,* ☎ *707/963–3757.* 🎫 *Free.* ☉ *Tues.–Sun. noon–4.*

The **Culinary Institute of America,** the country's leading school for chefs, set up its West Coast headquarters in the Greystone Winery, the former site of the Christian Brothers Winery and a national historic landmark. The CIA campus consists of 30 acres of herb and vegetable gardens, a 15-acre merlot vineyard, and a Mediterranean-inspired restaurant, which is open to the public. Also on the property are a well-stocked culinary store, a quirky corkscrew and winepress museum, and a culinary library. Cooking demonstrations are occasionally scheduled for nonstudents. ✉ *2555 Main St.,* ☎ *707/967–2600 or 800/333–9242,* FAX *707/967–1113,* WEB *www.ciachef.edu.*

Dining and Lodging

$$–$$$ ✕ **Terra.** A romantic restaurant housed in an 1888 stone foundry, Terra is especially known for its exquisite Mediterranean-inspired dishes, many with Asian touches. The sweetbreads ragout, grilled squab, and sake-marinated Chilean sea bass are memorable. Save

room for dessert. ⊠ *1345 Railroad Ave.,* ☎ *707/963–8931. Reservations essential. DC, MC, V. Closed Tues. No lunch.*

$$–$$$ ✕ **Tra Vigne.** Made famous by TV chef Michael Chiarello, this field-
★   stone building has been transformed into a striking trattoria with a huge wood bar, high ceilings, and plush banquettes. Homemade mozzarella, olive oil, and vinegar, and house-cured pancetta and prosciutto contribute to a mouthwatering tour of Tuscan cuisine. The outdoor courtyard in summer and fall is a sun-splashed Mediterranean vision of striped umbrellas and awnings, crowded café tables, and rustic pots overflowing with flowers. ⊠ *1050 Charter Oak Ave., off Rte. 29,* ☎ *707/963–4444. Reservations essential. D, DC, MC, V.*

$$–$$$ ✕ **Wine Spectator Greystone Restaurant.** This restaurant, housed in the handsome old Christian Brothers' winery, is run by the Culinary Institute of America. Century-old stone walls house a large and bustling restaurant, with cooking, baking, and grilling stations in full view. The menu has a Mediterranean spirit and emphasizes such small plates as bruschetta topped with wild mushrooms and *muhammara* (a spread of roasted red peppers and walnuts). Typical main courses include Alaska halibut and grilled ahi. ⊠ *2555 Main St.,* ☎ *707/967–1010. AE, DC, MC, V.*

$$$$ ✕⊡ **Meadowood Resort.** Secluded at the end of a semiprivate road, this 256-acre resort has accommodations in a rambling country lodge and several bungalows. The elegant dining room specializes in California Wine Country cooking, either à la carte or as part of a prix-fixe menu. Seating is also available outdoors on a terrace overlooking the golf course. The Grill, a less formal, less expensive restaurant, serves a lighter menu of pizzas and spa food for breakfast and lunch (and early dinners on Friday and Saturday). ⊠ *900 Meadowood La., 94574,* ☎ *707/963–3646 or 800/458–8080,* FAX *707/963–5863,* WEB *www.meadowood.com. 40 rooms, 45 suites. 2 restaurants, bar, room service, 9-hole golf course, 7 tennis courts, 2 pools, health club, hot tub, massage, sauna, steam room, croquet. AE, D, DC, MC, V.*

$$$–$$$$ ⊡ **Harvest Inn.** Many of the larger-than-average rooms in this Tudor-esque inn on lushly landscaped grounds were renovated and brightened in 2000. Most rooms have wet bars, antique furnishings, and fireplaces. Pets are allowed in certain rooms for a $75 fee. Complimentary breakfast is served in the breakfast room and on the patio overlooking the vineyards. ⊠ *1 Main St., 94574,* ☎ *707/963–9463 or 800/950–8466,* FAX *707/963–4402,* WEB *www.harvestinn.com. 55 rooms. Room service, refrigerators, 2 pools, 2 hot tubs. AE, D, DC, MC, V. CP.*

$$–$$$$ ⊡ **Wine Country Inn.** Surrounded by a pastoral landscape of hills, old
★   barns, and stone bridges, this is a peaceful New England–style retreat. Rural antiques fill all the rooms, most of which overlook the vineyards with either a balcony, patio, or deck. Most rooms have fireplaces, and some have private hot tubs. A hearty country breakfast is served buffet style in the sun-splashed common room, and wine tastings are scheduled in the afternoon. ⊠ *1152 Lodi La. (off Rte. 29), 94574,* ☎ *707/963–7077,* FAX *707/963–9018,* WEB *www.winecountryinn.com. 24 rooms. Pool, hot tub. MC, V. BP.*

$$–$$$ ⊡ **El Bonita Motel.** This cute motel with such pleasant touches as window boxes and landscaped grounds has relatively elegant furnishings with muted pastel walls and floral upholstery. Some rooms have whirlpool spas. ⊠ *195 Main St. (Rte. 29), 94574,* ☎ *707/963–3216 or 800/541–3284,* FAX *707/963–8838,* WEB *www.elbonita.com. 41 rooms. Pool. AE, MC, V. 2-night minimum weekends.*

Shopping

Handcrafted candles made on the premises are for sale at the **Hurd Beeswax Candle Factory** (⊠ 3020 St. Helena Hwy. N (Rte. 29), ☎

707/963–7211). Bargain hunters will delight in the many designer labels at the **Village Outlet Stores** complex on St. Helena Highway, across the street from Freemark Abbey Winery. **On the Vine** (⊠ 1234 Main St., ☎ 707/963–2209) sells wearable art and unique jewelry with food and wine themes.

At **I. Wolk Gallery** (⊠ 1235 Main St., ☎ 707/963–8800) you'll find works by established and emerging artists from New York, Chicago, Los Angeles, and Santa Fe—everything from abstract and contemporary realist paintings to high-quality works on paper and sculpture. **Art on Main** (⊠ 1359 Main St., ☎ 707/963–3350), one of the oldest galleries in the region, sells oils, watercolors, ceramics, and etchings by northern California artists. **Dean & Deluca** (⊠ 607 St. Helena Hwy. S [Rte. 29], ☎ 707/967–9980), a branch of the famous Manhattan store, is crammed with everything you need in the kitchen—including terrific produce and deli items—as well as a huge wine selection. The **Campus Store** (⊠ at the Culinary Institute of America, 2555 Main St., ☎ 888/424–2433) is the place to shop for preparing and cooking food, from chef's pants to fish stock to cutlery.

Vanderbilt & Company (⊠ 1429 Main St., ☎ 707/963–1010), the prettiest store in town, is filled with Italian ceramics, tabletop decor, and other high-quality home accessories.

Calistoga

3 mi northwest of St. Helena on Rte. 29.

In addition to its wineries, Calistoga is noted for its mineral water, hot mineral springs, mud baths, steam baths, and massages. The Calistoga Hot Springs Resort was founded in 1859 by maverick entrepreneur Sam Brannan, whose ambition was to found "the Saratoga of California." He tripped up the pronunciation of the phrase at a formal banquet—it came out "Calistoga"—and the name stuck.

The **Sharpsteen Museum** has a magnificent diorama of the Calistoga Hot Springs Resort in its heyday. Other exhibits document Robert Louis Stevenson's time in the area and the career of museum founder Ben Sharpsteen, an animator at the Walt Disney studio. ⊠ *1311 Washington St.,* ☎ *707/942–5911.* ⊞ *$3 donation.* ☉ *Daily 11–4.*

Indian Springs, an old-time spa, has been pumping out 212°F water from its three geysers since the late 1800s. The place offers some of the best bargains on mud bathing and short massages and has a large mineral-water pool. The spa has 16 cottages with studio or one-bedroom units and a larger structure with three bedrooms. ⊠ *1712 Lincoln Ave.,* ☎ *707/942–4913.* ☉ *Daily 9–7. Reservations recommended for spa treatments.*

㉘ **Sterling Vineyards** sits on a hilltop 1 mi south of Calistoga, its pristine white Mediterranean-style buildings reached by an aerial tramway from the valley floor. The view from the tasting room is superb, and the gift shop is one of the best in the valley. ⊠ *1111 Dunaweal La.,* ☎ *707/942–3300,* WEB *www.sterlingvineyards.com.* ⊞ *Tram $6.* ☉ *Daily 10:30–4:30.*

㉙ **Cuvaison** specializes in chardonnay, merlot, and cabernet sauvignon for the export market. Two small picnic areas on the grounds look out over Napa Valley. ⊠ *4550 Silverado Trail,* ☎ *707/942–6266,* WEB *www.cuvaison.com.* ⊞ *Tasting fees vary.* ☉ *Daily 10–5. Tours at 10:30 and by appointment.*

★ ③⓪ Designed by postmodern architect Michael Graves, **Clos Pegase** is a one-of-a-kind structure packed with unusual art objects from the collection of art-book publisher and owner Jan Shrem. Works of art even appear in the underground wine tunnels. ✉ *1060 Dunaweal La.,* ☎ *707/942-4981,* WEB *www.clospegase.com.* ⊙ *Daily 10:30–5. Tours at 11 and 2.*

③① **Schramsberg,** perched on a wooded knoll on the southeast side of Route 29, is one of Napa's most historic wineries, with caves that were dug by Chinese laborers in 1880. The winery makes sparkling wines in several styles, in several price ranges. ✉ *1400 Schramsberg Rd.,* ☎ *707/942-4558,* WEB *www.schramsberg.com.* ☞ *Tasting and tour $7.50.* ⊙ *Daily 10–4. Tours by appointment only.*

③② It's worth taking a slight detour off the main artery to find **Dutch Henry Winery,** a small winery whose wines are available only on-site or through mail order. Free tastings are held in a working winery, where winemakers also explain the winemaking process. This is a good place to try sauvignon blanc and syrah. ✉ *4310 Silverado Trail,* ☎ *707/942-5771,* WEB *www.dutchhenry.com.* ⊙ *Daily 10–4:30. Tours by appointment only.*

③③ **Château Montelena** is a vine-covered stone French château constructed circa 1882 and set amid Chinese-inspired gardens, complete with a man-made lake with gliding swans and islands crowned by Chinese pavilions. Château Montelena produces chardonnays and cabernet sauvignons. ✉ *1429 Tubbs La.,* ☎ *707/942-5105,* WEB *www.montelena.com.* ☞ *Tasting fees vary: $10.* ⊙ *Daily 10–4. Tours by appointment at 11 and 2.*

🄲 Many families bring children to Calistoga to see **Old Faithful Geyser of California** blast its 60-ft tower of steam and vapor about every 40 minutes (the pattern is disrupted during heavy rains or if there's an earthquake in the offing). One of just three regularly erupting geysers in the world, it is fed by an underground river that heats to 350°F. The spout usually lasts three minutes. Picnic facilities are available. ✉ *1299 Tubbs La. (1 mi north of Calistoga),* ☎ *707/942-6463,* WEB *www.oldfaithfulgeyser.com.* ☞ *$6.* ⊙ *Apr.–Sept., daily 9–6; Oct.–Mar., daily 9–5.*

🄲 The **Petrified Forest** contains the remains of the volcanic eruptions of Mount St. Helena 3.4 million years ago. The force of the explosion uprooted the gigantic redwoods, covered them with volcanic ash, and infiltrated the trees with silica and minerals, causing petrifaction. Explore the museum, and then picnic on the grounds. ✉ *4100 Petrified Forest Rd. (5 mi west of Calistoga),* ☎ *707/942-6667.* ☞ *$5.* ⊙ *Late Apr.–early Sept., daily 10–6; early Sept.–late Apr., daily 10–5.*

🄲 **Robert Louis Stevenson State Park,** on Route 29, 3 mi northeast of Calistoga, encompasses the summit of Mount St. Helena. It was here, in the summer of 1880, in an abandoned bunkhouse of the Silverado Mine, that Stevenson and his bride, Fanny Osbourne, spent their honeymoon. The stay inspired Stevenson's "The Silverado Squatters," and Spyglass Hill in *Treasure Island* is thought to be a portrait of Mount St. Helena. The park's approximately 3,600 acres are mostly undeveloped except for a fire trail leading to the site of the bunkhouse—which is marked with a marble tablet—and to the summit beyond.

Dining and Lodging

$$–$$$ ✕ **Catahoula Restaurant and Saloon.** This sleek restaurant, named after
★ Louisiana's state dog, is the brainchild of chef Jan Birnbaum, whose credentials include stints at the Quilted Giraffe in New York and Campton Place in San Francisco. Using a large wood-burning oven, Birnbaum turns out such dishes as spicy gumbo with rooster and pork porterhouse. The large barroom opposite the dining room has its own

menu of small plates, which are ideal for sampling Birnbaum's kitchen wizardry. ⊠ *Mount View Hotel, 1457 Lincoln Ave.,* ☎ *707/942–2275. Reservations essential. MC, V. Closed Tues. and Jan.*

$$ ✕ **All Seasons Café.** Bistro cuisine takes a California spin in this sun-filled space with marble tables and a black-and-white checkerboard floor. The seasonal menu includes organic greens, wild mushrooms, local game birds, and house-smoked beef, as well as homemade breads, desserts, and freshly made ice cream. The café shares space with a well-stocked wineshop. ⊠ *1400 Lincoln Ave.,* ☎ *707/942–9111. D, DC, MC, V. No lunch Mon.–Wed.*

$$ ✕ **Calistoga Inn.** Grilled meat and fish for dinner and soups, salads, and sandwiches for lunch are prepared with flair at this microbrewery with a tree-shaded outdoor patio. ⊠ *1250 Lincoln Ave.,* ☎ *707/942–4101. AE, MC, V.*

$–$$ ✕ **Wappo Bar Bistro.** This colorful restaurant is an adventure in international dining with a menu ranging from Asian noodles and Thai shrimp curry to chiles rellenos to Turkish meze. ⊠ *1226 S. Washington St.,* ☎ *707/942–4712. AE, MC, V. Closed Tues. and first 2 wks. in Dec.*

$ ✕ **Pacifico.** Technicolor ceramics and subtropical plants adorn this Mexican restaurant, which serves Oaxacan and other fare. Fajitas and moles are among the specialties. ⊠ *1237 Lincoln Ave.,* ☎ *707/942–4400. MC, V.*

$$–$$$$ ⊡ **Mount View Hotel.** Listed on the National Register of Historic Places, the Mount View is the largest Napa Valley hotel north of St. Helena. A full-service European spa provides state-of-the-art pampering, and three cottages are each equipped with a private redwood deck, Jacuzzi, and wet bar. Catahoula's saloon adds to the allure. ⊠ *1457 Lincoln Ave., 94515,* ☎ *707/942–6877,* FAX *707/942–6904,* WEB *www.mountviewhotel.com. 32 rooms. Restaurant, pool, spa. AE, D, MC, V.*

$$$ ⊡ **Cottage Grove Inn.** Sixteen elegant and contemporary cottages are shaded by elm trees. Rooms have skylights and plush furnishings. Fireplaces, CD players, two-person hot tubs, and porches with wicker rocking chairs add to the coziness. Spas and restaurants are within walking distance. Rates include Continental breakfast and afternoon wine and cheese. ⊠ *1711 Lincoln Ave., 94515,* ☎ *707/942–8400 or 800/799–2284,* FAX *707/942–2653,* WEB *www.cottagegrove.com. 16 rooms. Refrigerators, in-room VCRs. AE, D, DC, MC, V. 2-night minimum weekends. CP.*

$$–$$$ ⊡ **Meadowlark Country House.** Decidedly laid-back and sophisticated, this inn is surrounded by 20 hillside acres just north of downtown Calistoga. Innkeeper Kurt Stevens prides himself on being helpful but not intrusive. The main house, built in 1886, and a newer building, added in the 1990s, hold unfussy but country-stylish rooms. Rates include a full breakfast. ⊠ *601 Petrified Forest Rd., 94515,* ☎ *707/942–5651 or 800/942–5651,* FAX *707/942–5023,* WEB *www.meadowlarkinn.com. 7 rooms. Pool, hot tub, sauna. AE, MC, V. BP.*

$$ ⊡ **Brannan Cottage Inn.** This pristine Victorian cottage with lacy white fretwork, large windows, and a shady porch is the only one of Sam Brannan's 1860 resort cottages still standing on its original site. Rooms have private entrances, and elegant stenciled friezes of stylized wildflowers cover the walls. A full breakfast is included. ⊠ *109 Wapoo Ave., 94515,* ☎ *707/942–4200,* WEB *www.brannancottageinn.com. 6 rooms. MC, V. CP.*

$$ ⊡ **Calistoga Spa Hot Springs.** No-nonsense motel-style rooms have kitchenettes stocked with utensils and coffeemakers, which makes them popular with families and travelers on a budget. (There's a supermarket a block away.) The on-premises spa includes mineral baths, mud baths, swimming pools, and a hot tub. ⊠ *1006 Washington St., 94515,* ☏ *707/942–6269,* FAX *707/942–4214,* WEB *www.calistogaspa.com. 57 rooms. Snack bar, kitchenettes, 2 pools, wading pool, hot tub, spa, meeting room. MC, V. 2-night minimum weekends, 3-night minimum holiday weekends.*

Outdoor Activities and Sports

BIKING

Getaway Adventures and Bike Shop (⊠ 1117 Lincoln Ave., ☏ 707/942–0332 or 800/499–2453) rents bikes and conducts winery and other bike tours. It's closed Wednesday.

GLIDING, HOT-AIR BALLOONING

The **Calistoga Ballooning** (☏ 707/944–2822) charters early morning flights (exact times vary) out of Calistoga or, depending on weather conditions, St. Helena, Oakville, or Rutherford. The company's deluxe balloon flight ($175–$210 per person, depending on the optional activities) may include a picnic or a breakfast at the Meadowood Resort. Pilots are well versed in Napa Valley lore.

TENNIS

Near the center of town, at the intersection of **Stevenson and Grant streets,** are four courts with night lighting.

Shopping

For connoisseurs seeking extraordinary values, the **All Seasons Café Wine Shop** (⊠ 1400 Lincoln Ave., ☏ 707/942–6828) is a true find. A wineshop inside the **Calistoga Wine Stop** (⊠ 1458 Lincoln Ave., ☏ 707/942–5556), California's second-oldest existing train depot, carries 500 vintages.

THE SONOMA VALLEY

Unlike its upscale neighbor, Sonoma Valley is rustic and unpretentious. Its name is Miwok Indian for "many moons," but Jack London's nickname for the region—Valley of the Moon—is more fitting. The scenic valley, bounded by the Mayacamas Mountains on the east and Sonoma Mountain on the west, extends north from San Pablo Bay nearly 20 mi to the eastern outskirts of Santa Rosa. The varied terrain, soils, and climate (cooler in the south because of the bay influence and hotter towards the north) allow grape growers to raise cool-weather varietals such as chardonnay and pinot noir as well as merlot, cabernet sauvignon, and other heat-seeking vines. There are some three dozen wineries in the valley, most of them on or near Route 12, a California Scenic Highway that runs the length of the valley. In addition to wineries, you can find a few tasting rooms on the historic plaza in the town of Sonoma.

Sonoma

14 mi west of Napa on Rte. 12; 45 mi from San Francisco, north on U.S. 101, east on Rte. 37, and north on Rte. 121/12.

Sonoma is the oldest town in the Wine Country. Its historic town plaza is the site of the last and the northernmost of the 21 missions established by the Franciscan order of Father Junípero Serra. The **Mission San Francisco Solano,** whose chapel and school were used to bring Christianity to the Native Americans, is now a museum with a fine collection of 19th-century watercolors. ⊠ *114 Spain St. E,* ☏ *707/938–9560.* ⊡ *$1 (includes same-day admission to Sonoma Barracks on the central plaza and General Vallejo's home, Lachryma Montis).* ☉ *Daily 10–5.* Sonoma's central plaza also includes the largest group of old adobes north of Monterey.

WINE TASTING 101

IF ONE OF YOUR REASONS for visiting the Wine Country is to learn about wine, your best friend should be the person who is pouring in a winery tasting room. The people who do this are only too happy to share their knowledge. Though wine bars and shops abound, many of them offering tastings at certain times, the best way to learn about wines is to visit the wineries themselves. True, you'll only get to taste one product line, but since most wineries make 5 or 10 or even more types, you can make a lot of headway after visiting one or two wineries.

Why do people make such a big deal about tasting wine? Because it's the only way to learn the differences among varieties of wines and styles of wine making. The more you know, the more you will get out of the experience. Certainly, you can pick up any decent bottle of chardonnay to have with tonight's chicken dinner without making a major production of it. But if you love wine, or think you might, you'll have a lot of fun doing some comparison tasting. You can learn why you like what you like and how to find similar wines anywhere in the world.

Contrary to the cartoon image, tasting wine is by no means an effete exercise. As long as you don't act pretentious—say, by tilting your glass with your pinkie finger in the air—you won't look silly.

So how do you go about tasting wine? You start by looking at it. Usually the pourer will give you between 1 and 1½ ounces of each wine you try. You can hold the glass by the stem or by the bowl; the former grip will keep the wine from heating up, but the latter is a good idea if the tasting room is so crowded you fear getting jostled. If you can hold the glass to the light, all the better. You're looking for clues to the grape variety as well as to the wine's age. Connecting the color with the wine grape is part of the sensory experience and is likely to help you remember the aromas and flavors better. As for how old the wine is, remember that red wines pale as they age, while white wines get darker.

Sniff once or twice to see if you smell anything recognizable. Next, swirl the wine gently in the glass. Aerating the wine this way releases more aromas. (This step works with just about every type of wine except the sparkling kind, which tends to go flat when the bubbles are crushed in the process.) Don't be afraid to stick your nose in the glass. The idea is get close enough to the liquid to pick up subtle scents. The receptor nerve cells in your nose can pick up every scent and forward them to the brain's olfactory bulb. Those cells tire quickly, however, so be sure to assess the aromas as quickly as possible.

At this point, it is time to taste. While smell plays an enormous role in taste memory, so can "mouth-feel," or the weight of the wine on your tongue. Is it light or watery? Is it rich like milk? Mentally record these impressions, along with any other tactile sensations such as smoothness or silkiness. Hold the wine in your mouth for a few seconds to give your taste buds a chance to pick up as many flavors as possible. Wines carry an almost infinite range of flavors, from butter to olives, mint to chocolate, pineapple to vanilla, or cherry, blackberry, or even violets.

Finally, if you can still perceive flavor well after you've swallowed the wine, you can say it has a long finish. And you can be assured that it's a wine you will remember.

— Marty Olmstead

Originally planted by Franciscans of the Sonoma Mission in 1825, the ③④ **Sebastiani Vineyards** were bought by Samuele Sebastiani in 1904. Red wine is king here. To complement it, Sylvia Sebastiani has recorded her good Italian home cooking in a family recipe book, *Mangiamo*. The winery was closed for more than a year for seismic upgrading, during which time the main tasting room was totally remodeled and expanded, and reopened in 2001. The winery also operates a **tasting room** (⊠ 103 W. Napa St.) on the plaza, which has the same phone number and is open daily. ⊠ *483 4th St. E,* ☎ *707/938–5532.* ⊙ *Daily 10–5. Tours 10:30–4.*

③⑤ **Buena Vista Carneros Winery** is the oldest continually operating winery in California. It was here, in 1857, that Count Agoston Haraszthy de Mokcsa laid the basis for modern California wine making, bucking the conventional wisdom that vines should be planted on well-watered ground by instead planting on well-drained hillsides. Chinese laborers dug tunnels 100 ft into the hillside, and the limestone they extracted was used to build the main house. The winery, which is surrounded by redwood and eucalyptus trees, has a specialty food shop, an art gallery, and picnic areas. ⊠ *18000 Old Winery Rd., off Napa Rd. (follow signs from the plaza),* ☎ *707/938–1266 or 800/ 678–8504,* WEB *www.buenavistawinery.com.* ⊙ *Daily 10:30–4:30. Tour daily at 2.*

③⑥ **Ravenswood,** literally dug into the mountains like a bunker, is famous for its zinfandel. The merlot should be tasted as well. On weekends from late May through Labor Day the winery serves barbecued chicken and ribs ($7–$10) in the vineyards to complement its hearty reds. ⊠ *18701 Gehricke Rd., off E. Spain St.,* ☎ *707/938–1960,* WEB *www.ravenswood-wine.com.* ⊠ *Tasting fee: $4.* ⊙ *Daily 10–4:30. Tours by appointment at 10:30.*

A tree-lined driveway leads to **Lachryma Montis,** which General Mariano G. Vallejo, the last Mexican governor of California, built for his large family in 1851; the state purchased the home in 1933. The Victorian Gothic house is secluded in the midst of beautiful gardens. Opulent furnishings, including a white-marble fireplace in every room, are particularly noteworthy. ⊠ *W. Spain St., near 3rd St. E,* ☎ *707/938– 9559.* ⊠ *$1.* ⊙ *Daily 10–5. Tours by appointment.*

Dining and Lodging

$$–$$$ ✕ **Santé.** The latest incarnation of the Sonoma Mission Inn's formal restaurant re-launched in 2001 with a renewed focus on spa cuisine. Dishes such as ahi tuna and scallop dumplings reflect chef Toni Robertson's Asian background, but the California influence dominates in choices like carrot and pumpkin seed ravioli and roasted beets with a soufflé of Sonoma goat cheese. ⊠ *Sonoma Mission Inn, 18140 Sonoma Hwy. (2 mi north of Sonoma on Rte. 12 at Boyes Blvd.), Boyes Hot Springs,* ☎ *707/938–9000. AE, DC, MC, V.*

$–$$$ ✕ **Meritage.** A fortuitous blend of southern French and northern Italian cuisine is the backbone of this restaurant, where chef Carlo Cavalli works wonders with house-made pastas, particularly *gemelli.* An oyster bar augments extensive seafood choices and breakfast is available Wednesday through Sunday. The wine list includes blends from the major players in both Napa and Sonoma. ⊠ *522 Broadway,* ☎ *707/938–9430. AE, MC, V.*

$$ ✕ **The Girl and the Fig.** In late 2000, this popular Glen Ellen restaurant migrated to the Sonoma Hotel and revitalized the historic barroom with cozy banquettes and an inventive cuisine. A seasonally changing menu may include something with figs, a fillet of turbot on beet risotto, steak frites, or cassoulet. The wine list is notable for its inclusion of

Rhône and other less-common varietals. ⊠ *110 W. Spain St., Sonoma Plaza,* ☎ *707/938–3634. AE, D, DC, MC, V.*

\$\$ ✕ **La Salette.** Chef-owner Manny Azevedo, born in the Azores and raised in Sonoma, found culinary inspiration in his travels. The flavors of his dishes, such as Mozambique prawns with tomatoes and grilled plantains and salt cod baked with white onions, stand strong while complementing each other. The house-made Portuguese bread is addictive. Paintings and sculpture enliven the off-white walls in this restaurant, which has patio seating for balmy evenings. ⊠ *18625 Rte. 12, Boyes Hot Springs,* ☎ *707/938–1927. MC, V. Closed Mon.–Tues.*

\$\$ ✕ **Ristorante Piatti.** A beautiful room opens onto one of the finest patios in the valley at this restaurant, the first in a minichain of California trattorias. Pizza from the wood-burning oven and northern Italian specials (spit-roasted chicken, ravioli with lemon cream) are served in a rustic space with an open kitchen and pastel images of vegetables on the walls, or on the terrace. ⊠ *El Dorado Hotel, 405 1st St. W,* ☎ *707/996–2351. AE, MC, V.*

\$–\$\$ ✕ **The Big 3 Diner.** Overstuffed booths, ceiling fans, and an open kitchen give this corner bistro an informal feel. Country breakfasts, pizza from the wood-burning oven, and mostly straightforward American fare are the specialties. The limited menu includes several spa cuisine items. ⊠ *Sonoma Mission Inn, 18140 Sonoma Hwy. (2 mi north of Sonoma on Rte. 12 at Boyes Blvd.), Boyes Hot Springs,* ☎ *707/938–9000. AE, DC, MC, V.*

\$–\$\$ ✕ **Cafe La Haye.** In a postage-stamp-size kitchen, skillful chefs turn out a half dozen main courses that star on a small but worthwhile menu. Chicken, beef, pasta, fish, and risotto get a deluxe treatment without fuss or fanfare. This offbeat café turns out some of the best food in the Wine Country. ⊠ *140 E. Napa St.,* ☎ *707/935–5994. MC, V. Closed Mon. No dinner Sun. No lunch.*

\$–\$\$ ✕ **Della Santina.** This longstanding favorite is a world unto itself, with the most authentic Italian food in town and a charming enclosed brick patio in back. Daily fish and veal specials offer an alternative to other menu choices of classic northern Italian pastas and rotisserie meats. Of special note are the gnocchi and, when available, petrale sole and sand dabs. ⊠ *133 E. Napa St.,* ☎ *707/935–0576. AE, D, MC, V.*

\$–\$\$ ✕ **La Casa.** Whitewashed stucco and red tiles evoke Old Mexico at this restaurant just around the corner from Sonoma's plaza. There's bar seating, a patio, and an extensive menu of traditional Mexican food: chimichangas and snapper Veracruz for entrées, sangria to drink, and flan for dessert. The food is not the world's best, but locals love the casual atmosphere and the margaritas. ⊠ *121 E. Spain St.,* ☎ *707/996–3406. AE, DC, MC, V.*

\$–\$\$ ✕ **Saddles.** True to its name, this haven for beef lovers is decorated with things horsey, from saddles to boots. Ten dishes employ midwestern corn-fed USDA prime beef, in addition to pork chops, chicken, fish, and a black Angus burger. Side dishes include a sinful potato au gratin as well as green vegetable selections. Appetizers can be ordered in the bar, in case you want to sample from the martini list. ⊠ *29 E. MacArthur St., at MacArthur Pl.,* ☎ *707/938–2942. AE, D, DC, MC, V.*

\$\$\$\$ 🏨 **MacArthur Place.** Chic country colors like olive and lemon distinguish the accommodations at this sprawling complex. Rooms are in a remodeled historic mansion as well as in contemporary two-story structures tucked into the back of the property. Beyond the extensively landscaped grounds is a full-service spa, adjacent to the pool. ⊠ *29 E. MacArthur St., 95476,* ☎ *707/938–2929 or 800/722–1866,* FAX *707/933–9833,* WEB *www.macarthurplace.com. 64 rooms. Restaurant, pool, hot tub, spa. AE, D, MC, V.*

$$$–$$$$ ✕🏠 **Sonoma Mission Inn & Spa.** A $21 million upgrade in 1999 transformed the cramped spa at this turn-of-the-20th-century resort into a fittingly world-class venue. The beautifully landscaped Mission-style property also has an Olympic-size pool supplied, as are the spa facilities, by warm mineral water pumped up from wells beneath the property. Gourmet and classic spa food is served at the Sante restaurant. Thirty suites in a secluded, tree-shaded area have verandas or patios, whirlpools, and fireplaces. ✉ *18140 Rte. 12 (2 mi north of Sonoma at Boyes Blvd.), Box 1447, Boyes Hot Springs 95476,* ☏ *707/938–5358,* 𝖥𝖠𝖷 *707/996–5358. 168 rooms, 60 suites. 2 restaurants, coffee shop, 2 bars, 2 pools, hot tub, spa. AE, DC, MC, V.*

$$$ 🏠 **El Dorado Hotel.** A modern hotel in a remodeled old building, this
★ place has unusually spare and simple accommodations. Rooms reflect Sonoma's Mission era, with Mexican-tile floors and white walls. The best rooms are Nos. 3 and 4, which have larger balconies that overlook the Sonoma Plaza. ✉ *405 1st St. W, 95476,* ☏ *707/996–3030 or 800/289–3031,* 𝖥𝖠𝖷 *707/996–3148,* 𝖶𝖤𝖡 *www.hoteleldorado.com. 27 rooms. Restaurant, pool. AE, MC, V.*

$$–$$$ 🏠 **Thistle Dew Inn.** The public rooms of this turn-of-the-20th-century Victorian home a half block from Sonoma Plaza are filled with collector's-quality Arts and Crafts furnishings. Four of the six rooms have private entrances and decks, and all have queen-size beds with antique quilts, private baths, and air-conditioning. Some rooms have fireplaces; some have whirlpools. Welcome bonuses include a hot tub and free use of the inn's bicycles. ✉ *171 W. Spain St., 95476,* ☏ *707/938–2909; 800/382–7895 in CA,* 𝖥𝖠𝖷 *707/996–8413,* 𝖶𝖤𝖡 *www.thistledew.com. 6 rooms. Hot tub, bicycles. AE, MC, V. BP.*

$–$$ 🏠 **Vineyard Inn.** Built as a roadside motor court in 1941, this B&B inn with red-tile roofs brings a touch of Mexican village charm to an otherwise lackluster and somewhat noisy location at the junction of two main highways. It's across from two vineyards and is the closest lodging to Sears Point Raceway. Rooms have queen-size beds, and Continental breakfast is included. ✉ *23000 Arnold Dr., at junction of Rte. 116 and 121, 95476,* ☏ *707/938–2350 or 800/359–4667,* 𝖥𝖠𝖷 *707/938–2353,* 𝖶𝖤𝖡 *www.sonomavineyardinn.com. 17 rooms, 7 suites. AE, MC, V. CP.*

Nightlife and the Arts

The **Sebastiani Theatre** (☏ 707/996–2020), on historic Sonoma Square, schedules first-run movies. Every Sunday in August and September **Shakespeare at Buena Vista** (☏ 707/938–1266) brings the Bard to Sonoma. Performances are best enjoyed with a picnic lunch and a bottle of wine. Small blues and jazz bands play Friday and Saturday nights at **Cucina Viansa** (☏ 707/935–5656) on the plaza, where the crowd is a mix of young to middle-aged fans.

Shopping

Several shops in the four-block **Sonoma Plaza** attract food lovers from miles around. The **Sonoma Cheese Factory** (✉ Sonoma Plaza, 2 Spain St., ☏ 707/996–1000), run by the same family for four generations, makes Sonoma Jack cheese and the tangy Sonoma Teleme. Great swirling baths of milk and curds are visible through the windows, along with flat-pressed wheels of cheese. **Shushu Fufu** (✉ Sonoma Plaza, 452 1st St. E, ☏ 707/938–3876) is a chic shoe boutique with labels including Cole-Haan and Arche, makers of fine French walking shoes. **Half-Pint** (✉ Sonoma Plaza, 450 1st St. E, ☏ 707/938–1722) carries fashionable clothing and accessories for infants and children.

Glitzy it's not, but the **Total Living Company** (✉ 5 E. Napa St., ☏ 707/939–3900) is great for full-spectrum lightbulbs, well-designed household utensils, and clever items that make daily life easier.

Glen Ellen

7 mi north of Sonoma on Rte. 12.

Jack London lived in the Sonoma Valley for many years. The craggy, quirky, and creek-bisected town of Glen Ellen commemorates him with place-names and nostalgic establishments. The **Jack London Bookstore** (⊠ 14300 Arnold Dr., ☎ 707/996–2888) carries many of the namesake author's books. Built in the early 1900s, **London Lodge** (⊠ 13740 Arnold Dr., ☎ 707/996–3100, WEB www.jacklondonlodge.com) is tucked out of sight down the hill from the Jack London State Historic Park. The **Olive Press** (⊠ 14801 Arnold Dr., ☎ 707/939–8900) not only carries many local olive oils, serving bowls, books, and dining accessories, it also presses fruit for a number of local growers, usually in the late fall. It is in the Jack London Village complex.

In the hills above Glen Ellen—known as the Valley of the Moon—lies **Jack London State Historic Park.** London's collection of South Seas and other artifacts are on view at the House of Happy Walls, a museum of London's effects. The ruins of Wolf House, which London designed and which mysteriously burned down just before he was to move in, are close to the House of Happy Walls. Also restored and open to the public are a few farm outbuildings and the cottage where London lived and wrote. London is buried on the property. ⊠ 2400 London Ranch Rd., ☎ 707/938–5216. ☞ Parking $3. ☉ Park daily 9:30–5, museum daily 10–5.

㊲ **Arrowood Vineyards** is neither as old nor as famous as some of its neighbors, but wine makers and critics are quite familiar with the excellent handcrafted wines produced here. The winery's harmonious architecture overlooking the Valley of the Moon earned it an award from the Sonoma Historic Preservation League, and the wine-making equipment is state-of-the-art. A spacious new tasting room was added in 1999. The winery was purchased by Robert Mondavi in 2000, but wine maker Richard Arrowood has stayed on. ⊠ 14347 Sonoma Hwy., ☎ 707/938–5170, WEB www.robertmondavi.com. ☞ Tasting fees vary. ☉ Daily 10–4:30. Tours by appointment.

As you drive along Route 12, you'll see orchards and rows of vineyards flanked by oak-covered mountain ranges. One of the best-㊳ known local wineries is **Benziger Family Winery,** which specializes in premium estate and Sonoma County wines. Among the first wineries to identify certain vineyard blocks for particularly desirable flavors, Benziger is noted for its merlot, pinot blanc, chardonnay, and fumé blanc. Free, educational tram tours through the vineyards depart several times a day, weather permitting. ⊠ 1883 London Ranch Rd., ☎ 707/935–3000, WEB www.benziger.com. ☞ Tasting fees for reserve wines vary. ☉ Daily 10–4:30. Tours every ½ hr Mar.–Sept. 9:30–5, Oct.–Feb. 9:30–4.

Dining and Lodging

$$ ✕ **The Glen Ellen Inn.** Recommended for romantic evenings, this dinner-only restaurant adjusts its seafood and pasta offerings according to seasonal availability, but roasted meats like venison and chicken and house specials such as a "fire and ice" salad—with cold lettuce and spicy dressing—remain constants. ⊠ 13670 Arnold Dr., ☎ 707/996–6409. AE, MC, V. Closed Wed. No lunch.

$$$–$$$$ 🏠 **Gaige House Inn.** This glamorous country inn blends the comfort of a 19th-century residence with contemporary, uncluttered furnishings accented with Asian details such as prints and bamboo and rattan woods. The newest and largest accommodations are behind the house overlooking Calabazas Creek. A large pool surrounded by a green lawn, striped awnings, white umbrellas, and magnolias conjures a manicured Hamptons-like glamour in the midst of rustic Glen Ellen. ✉ *13540 Arnold Dr., 95442,* ☎ *707/935–0237 or 800/935–0237,* FAX *707/935–6411,* WEB *www.gaige.com. 15 rooms. Pool, outdoor hot tub. AE, D, MC, V. BP.*

$$–$$$ 🏨 **Beltane Ranch.** On a slope of the Mayacamas range on the eastern side of the Sonoma Valley lies this 100-year-old house built by a retired San Francisco madam. The Wood family, who have lived on the premises since 1936, have stocked the comfortable living room with dozens of books on the area. The rooms, furnished with antiques, open onto the building's wraparound porch. The cottage apartment, created out of the gardener's quarters, has a sitting room. ✉ *11775 Sonoma Hwy. (Rte. 12), 95442,* ☎ *707/996–6501.* WEB *www.beltaneranch.com. 6 rooms. Tennis court, hiking. No credit cards. BP.*

$$ 🏨 **Glenelly Inn.** On the outskirts of Glen Ellen, this sunny little establishment, built as an inn in 1916, offers all the comforts of home—plus a hot tub in the garden. Innkeeper Kristi Hallamore serves breakfast in front of the common room's cobblestone fireplace and provides local delicacies in the afternoon. On sunny mornings you can eat outside under the shady oak trees. ✉ *5131 Warm Springs Rd., 95442,* ☎ *707/ 996–6720,* FAX *707/996–5227,* WEB *www.glenelly.com. 8 rooms. Outdoor hot tub. MC, V. BP.*

Kenwood

3 mi north of Glen Ellen on Rte. 12.

Kenwood has a historic train depot and several restaurants and shops that specialize in locally produced goods. Its inns, restaurants, and winding roads nestle in soothing bucolic landscapes.

㊴ **Kunde Estate Winery** lies on 2,000 acres and is managed by the fourth generation of Kunde family grapegrowers and winemakers. The standard tour of the grounds includes its extensive caves. A tasting and dining room lies 175 ft below a chardonnay vineyard. Tastings usually include viognier, chardonnay, cabernet sauvignon, and zinfandel. ✉ *10155 Rte. 12,,* ☎ *707/833–5501.* WEB *www.kunde.com.* ☉ *Daily 10:30–4:30. Tours 11–3 Apr.–Dec., Fri.–Mon.; Jan.–Mar., Fri.–Sun.*

㊵ The beautifully rustic grounds at **Kenwood Vineyards** complement the attractive tasting room and artistic bottle labels. Although Kenwood produces all premium varietals, the winery is best known for its Jack London Vineyard reds—pinot noir, zinfandel, merlot, and a unique Artist Series cabernet. Most weekends the winery offers a free food-and-wine pairing. ✉ *9592 Sonoma Hwy.,* ☎ *707/833–5891,* WEB *www. kenwoodvineyards.com.* ☉ *Daily 10–4:30. No tours.*

㊶ **Landmark Vineyards.** The landscaping and design of this winery, established by the heirs of John Deere, are as classical as its wine-making methods. Those methods include two fermentations in French oak barrels and the use of the yeasts present in the skins of the grapes rather than the addition of manufactured yeasts to create the wine. Landmark's Damaris Reserve and Overlook chardonnays have been particularly well received, as has the winery's Grand Detour pinot noir. The winery's first claret was introduced in 1998. ✉ *101 Adobe Canyon Rd., off Sonoma Hwy.,* ☎ *707/833–1144 or 800/452–6365,* WEB *www. landmarkwine.com.* ☉ *Daily 10–4:30. Horse-drawn carriage vineyard tours Sat. 11:30–3:30 Apr.–Sept.*

Dining

$$–$$$ ✕ **Kenwood Restaurant & Bar.** One of the enduring favorites in an area known for fine dining, this is where Napa and Sonoma chefs eat on their nights off. You can indulge in California country cuisine in the

sunny, South of France–style dining room or head through the French doors to the patio for a memorable view of the vineyards. ✉ *9900 Rte. 12,* ☎ *707/833–6326. MC, V. Closed Mon.*

$–$$ ✕ **Café Citti.** The aroma of garlic envelops the neighborhood whenever the Italian chef-owner is roasting chickens at this homey roadside café. Deli items, hot pastas, and soups makes this an excellent budget stop. ✉ *9049 Rte. 12,* ☎ *707/833–2690. MC, V.*

ELSEWHERE IN SONOMA COUNTY

At nearly 1,598 square mi, Sonoma is far too large a county to cover in one or two days. The land mass extends from San Pablo Bay south to Mendocino County and from the Mayacamas Mountains on the Napa side west to the Pacific Ocean. One of the fastest-growing counties in northern California, Sonoma is still rather sparsely populated; even the county seat, Santa Rosa, has fewer than 120,000 residents.

Within this variegated terrain are hills and valleys, rivers, creeks, lakes, and tidal plains that beg to be explored. Wineries can be found from the cool flatlands of the south to the hot interior valleys to the foggy coastal regions. To be sure, Sonoma offers much more than wine, though the county, with 60,000 acres of vineyards, contributes to the North Coast's $4 billion–a-year wine industry. And Sonoma, though less famous than Napa, in fact has more award-winning wines.

In addition to the Sonoma Valley, the major grape-growing appellations include the Alexander Valley and the Dry Creek Valley close to Healdsburg, and the Russian River Valley to the west of U.S. 101. The latter has been gaining an international reputation for its pinot noir, which thrives in the valley climate cooled by the presence of morning and evening fog.

Guerneville, which is a very popular summer destination for gays and lesbians, and neighboring Forestville are in the heart of the Russian River valley. Dozens of small, winding roads and myriad wineries make this region a delight to explore, as do small towns like Occidental.

After meandering for miles, the Russian River arrives at its destination at Jenner, one of several towns on Sonoma's 62 mi of coastline. A number of state beaches offer tide-pooling and fishing. While less dramatic than the beaches on the far north coast, those along Sonoma's coast offer cooling summer winds and plenty of restaurants serving ocean-fresh seafood.

Santa Rosa

8 mi northwest of Kenwood on Rte. 12.

Santa Rosa is the Wine Country's largest city and a good bet for moderately priced hotel rooms, especially for those who have not reserved in advance.

The **Luther Burbank Home and Gardens** commemorates the great botanist who lived and worked on these grounds for 50 years, single-handedly developing the modern techniques of hybridization. Arriving as a young man from New England, he wrote: "I firmly believe . . . that this is the chosen spot of all the earth, as far as nature is concerned." The Santa Rosa plum, Shasta daisy, and lily of the Nile agapanthus are among the 800 or so plants he developed or improved. In the music room of his house, a Webster's Dictionary of 1946 lies open to a page on which the verb "burbank" is defined as "to modify and improve plant life." ✉ *Santa Rosa and Sonoma Aves.,* ☎ *707/*

524–5445, WEB *www.lutherburbank.org.* ⊠ *Gardens free, guided tours of house and greenhouse $3.* ◎ *Gardens daily 8–dusk. Tours Apr.–Oct., Tues.–Sun. 10–4.*

★ ㊷ **Matanzas Creek Winery** specializes in three varietals—sauvignon blanc, merlot, and chardonnay—and makes a hard-to-find sparkling wine. All three varietals have won glowing reviews from various magazines. Huge windows in the visitor center overlook a field of 3,100 tiered and fragrant lavender plants. Acres and acres of gardens planted with unusual grasses and plants from all over the world have caught the attention of horticulturists. After you taste the wines, ask for the self-guided garden tour book before taking a stroll. ⊠ *6097 Bennett Valley Rd.,* ☎ *707/528–6464 or 800/590–6464,* WEB *www.matanzascreek.com.* ⊠ *Tasting fees vary.* ◎ *Daily 10–4:30, Apr.–Dec. Tours weekdays at 10:30 and 3, weekends at 10:30.*

Dining and Lodging

$$–$$$ ✕ **Café Lolo.** This casual but sophisticated spot is the territory of chef and co-owner Michael Quigley, who has single-handedly made downtown Santa Rosa a culinary destination. His dishes stress fresh ingredients and an eye to presentation. Don't pass up the chocolate kiss, an individual cake with a wonderfully soft, rich center. ⊠ *620 5th St.,* ☎ *707/576–7822. AE, MC, V. Closed Sun. No lunch Sat.*

$$–$$$ ✕ **John Ash & Co.** The first Wine Country restaurant to tout locally grown ingredients in the 1980s, John Ash has maintained its status despite the departure of its namesake chef in 1991. A total interior redecoration in 2001 made the rooms look less Californian and more Italian. With patio seating outside and a cozy fireplace indoors, the slightly formal restaurant looks like a villa amid the vineyards. A café menu offers bites between meals. ⊠ *4330 Barnes Rd. (River Rd. exit west from U.S. 101),* ☎ *707/527–7687. Reservations essential. AE, DC, MC, V. No lunch Mon.*

$–$$ ✕ **Mixx.** Great service and an eclectic mix of dishes made with locally grown ingredients define this small restaurant with large windows, high ceilings, and Italian blown-glass chandeliers. House-made ravioli, grilled Cajun prawns, and grilled leg of lamb are among the favorites of the many regulars. The wine list, which won the 2000 Harvest Fair gold medal for being the best in the county, includes 20 choices by the glass and some highly sought selections from Williams-Selyem (pinot noir) and Dutton-Goldfield. ⊠ *135 4th St., at Davis St. (behind the mall on Railroad Sq.),* ☎ *707/573–1344. AE, D, MC, V. Closed Sun. No lunch Sat.*

$–$$ ✕ **Sassafras.** Opened in 2001 on the site of the former Mistral, this restaurant focuses on regional American cuisine, with a largely North American wine list. Dishes that sound familiar get a contemporary twist, as in a pizza with Creole-style ingredients, a meatloaf-with-ketchup that's really a venison-and-pork terrine with cranberry sauce, or a pecan pie served with a lavender custard. ⊠ *1229 N. Dutton Ave.,* ☎ *707/578–7600. AE, D, DC, MC, V. No lunch weekends.*

$$–$$$$ ▥ **Vintner's Inn.** Set on 50 acres of vineyards, this French provincial inn has large rooms, many with wood-burning fireplaces, and a trellised sundeck. Breakfast is complimentary, and the close-by John Ash & Co. restaurant is tempting for other meals. Discount passes to an affiliated health club are available, and VCRs can be rented for a small fee. ⊠ *4350 Barnes Rd., River Rd. exit west from U.S. 101, 95403,* ☎ *707/575–7350 or 800/421–2584,* FAX *707/575–1426,* WEB *www.vintnersinn.com. 44 rooms. Restaurant, hot tub. AE, DC, MC, V. CP.*

$$–$$$ ▥ **Fountaingrove Inn.** A redwood sculpture and a wall of cascading water
★ distinguish the lobby at this elegant, comfortable hotel and conference center. A buffet breakfast is complimentary, and an elegant restaurant

has piano music and a stellar menu. For an additional fee you'll have access to a nearby 18-hole golf course, a tennis court, and a health club. ✉ *101 Fountaingrove Pkwy., near U.S. 101, 95403,* ☎ *707/578–6101 or 800/222–6101,* ⨍⨍ *707/544–3126,* WEB *www.fountaingroveinn.com. 124 rooms, 6 suites. Restaurant, room service, in-room data ports, pool, hot tub, meeting room. AE, D, DC, MC, V. CP.*

$–$$ 🏨 **Los Robles Lodge.** This pleasant, relaxed motel overlooks a pool that's set into a grassy landscape. Pets are allowed, except in executive rooms. Some rooms have whirlpools. ✉ *1985 Cleveland Ave., Steele La. exit west from U.S. 101, 95401,* ☎ *707/545–6330 or 800/255–6330,* ⨍⨍ *707/575–5826. 100 rooms. Restaurant, coffee shop, pool, outdoor hot tub, lounge, laundry facilities. AE, DC, MC, V.*

Nightlife and the Arts

The **Luther Burbank Center for the Arts** (✉ 50 Mark West Springs Rd., ☎ 707/546–3600) presents concerts, plays, and other performances by locally and internationally known artists. For symphony, ballet, and other live theater performances throughout the year, call the **Spreckels Performing Arts Center** (☎ 707/584–1700 or 707/588–3434) in Rohnert Park. **SRT** (Summer Repertory Theatre; ✉ 1501 Mendocino Ave., ☎ 707/527–4307) presents classic and contemporary plays during the summer months.

Outdoor Activities and Sports

GOLF

The **Fountaingrove Country Club** (✉ 1525 Fountaingrove Pkwy., ☎ 707/579–4653) has an 18-hole course. The greens fee, which includes an optional cart and range balls, runs $75–$95 depending on the time of week. **Oakmont Golf Club** (✉ west course: 7025 Oakmont Dr., ☎ 707/539–0415; ✉ east course: 565 Oak Vista Court, ☎ 707/538–2454) has two 18-hole courses. The greens fee is $30–$45, plus $26 for an optional cart.

HOT-AIR BALLOONING

For views of the ocean coast, the Russian River, and San Francisco on a clear day, **Above the Wine Country** (☎ 707/829–9850 or 888/238–6359) operates out of Santa Rosa, although many flights actually originate outside Healdsburg. The cost is $195 per person, including a champagne brunch.

Russian River Valley

5 mi northwest of Santa Rosa.

The Russian River flows all the way from Mendocino to the Pacific Ocean, but in terms of winemaking, the Russian River Valley is centered on a triangle with points at Healdsburg, Guerneville, and Sebastopol. Tall redwoods shade many of the two-lane roads that access this scenic area where, thanks to the cooling marine influence, pinot noir and chardonnay are the king and queen of grapes. For a free map of the area, contact **Russian River Wine Road** (✉ Box 46, Healdsburg 95448, ☎ 707/433–6782, WEB www.wineroad.com).

Topolos at Russian River Vineyards. Rustic woods and a homey tasting room await you at this unusual winery in a hop kiln–style building. Michael Topolos is a leader in biodynamic farming, and he will gladly talk about environmental-friendly practices over a taste of port, alicante bouschet, or other unusual varieties. ✉ *5700 Gravenstein Hwy. N (Hwy. 116),* ☎ *707/887–1575,* WEB *www.topolos.com.* ⊙ *11–5:30.*

Iron Horse. Tucked into Green Valley, this showplace estate is equally successful at making still wine as the sparkling type. You should allow time to meander around the gardens, which are planted to bloom practically all year round, thanks to the winery's proximity (12 mi) to the ocean. ⊠ *9786 Ross Station Rd. (near Sebastopol),* ☏ *707/433–2305,* WEB *www.ironhorsevineyards.com.* ☉ *Feb.–Nov., daily 10–5; Dec.–Jan., daily 11–4.*

㊸ **Rochioli Vineyards and Winery** claims one of the prettiest picnic sites in the area, with tables overlooking vineyards. The winery makes one of the county's best chardonnays, but is particularly known for its pinot noir and sauvignon blanc. ⊠ *6192 Westside Rd.,* ☏ *707/433–2305.* ☉ *Feb.–Nov., daily 10–5; Dec.–Jan., daily 11–4.*

Hop Kiln. You can easily spot the triple towers of the old hop kiln, a California state historical landmark. One of the friendliest wineries in the Russian River area, Hop Kiln has a vast tasting room just steps away from a duck pond where you can picnic. This is a good place to try light wines such as riesling or A Thousand Flowers, but be sure to try some of the big-bodied reds as well. ⊠ *6050 Westside Rd.,* ☏ *707/433–6491,* WEB *www.hopkilnwinery.com.* ☉ *Daily 10–5.*

㊹ Old Vine zinfandel, along with chardonnay and pinot noir, is top of the line at **Rodney Strong Vineyards.** Picnic areas overlook the vineyards. ⊠ *11455 Old Redwood Hwy.,* ☏ *707/433–6511,* WEB *www.rodneystrong.com.* ☉ *Daily 10–5. Tours daily 11 and 3.*

OFF THE
BEATEN PATH

KORBEL CHAMPAGNE CELLARS – In order to be called champagne, a wine must be made in the French region of Champagne or it's just sparkling wine. But despite the objections of the French, champagne has entered the lexicon of California wine makers, and many refer to their sparkling wines as champagne. Whatever you call it, Korbel produces a tasty, reasonably priced wine as well as its own beer, which is available at a brewpub on the premises. The wine tour, one of the best in Sonoma County, clearly explains the process of making sparkling wine. The winery's 19th-century buildings and gorgeous rose gardens are a delight in their own right. ⊠ *13250 River Rd., Guerneville,* ☏ *707/824–7000,* WEB *www.korbel.com.* FAX *707/869–2981.* ☉ *Oct.–Apr., daily 9–4:30; May–Sept., daily 9–5. Tours on the hr 10–3.*

Dining and Lodging

$–$$ ✕ **Chez Marie.** It took a New Orleans chef to turn this tiny restaurant into a California auberge. Forestville is light on places to eat, so the place fills up with locals familiar with the jambalaya and gumbos and sprinkling of French specialties. ⊠ *6675 Front St., Forestville,* ☏ *707/887–7503. Closed Mon.–Wed. No lunch.*

$$–$$$
★ 🏠 **Applewood Inn.** On a knoll in the shelter of towering redwoods, this hybrid inn has two distinct types of accommodations. Those in the original Belden House are comfortable but modest in scale. Most of the 10 accommodations in the newer buildings, both salmon-pink stucco, are larger and airier, particularly the second-floor rooms and the penthouse minisuite. The buildings cluster around a Mediterranean-style courtyard complete with gurgling fountains. ⊠ *13555 Rte. 116, Guerneville 95421,* ☏ *707/869–9093,* FAX *707/869–9170,* WEB *www.applewoodinn.com. 19 rooms. Restaurant, pool, outdoor hot tub. AE, MC, V.*

$$–$$$ 🏠 **The Farmhouse Inn.** Members of a longtime Guerneville family bought this property in 2001, reconfigured the restaurant and lobby in the 1873 farmhouse and upgraded the adjacent guest cottages. These deluxe accommodations have feather beds, wood-burning fireplaces, and private saunas. The restaurant ($$–$$$), open for dinner Thursday–Sunday, relies largely on seasonal local products and fresh

seafood. ⊠ *7871 River Rd., Forestville 95436,* ☎ *707/887–3300 or 800/464–6642,* WEB *www.farmhouseinn.com. 8 rooms. Restaurant, refrigerators, pool, massage, saunas. AE, MC, V.*

Healdsburg

17 mi north of Santa Rosa on U.S. 101.

The countryside around Dry Creek Valley and Healdsburg is a fantasy of pastoral bliss—beautifully overgrown and in constant repose. Alongside the relatively untrafficked roads, country stores offer just-plucked fruits and vine-ripened tomatoes. Wineries here are barely visible, tucked behind groves of eucalyptus or hidden high on fog-shrouded hills.

Healdsburg itself is centered on a fragrant plaza surrounded by shady trees, appealing antiques shops, and restaurants. A whitewashed bandstand is the venue for free summer concerts, where the music ranges from jazz to bluegrass.

Dining and Lodging

$$ ✕ **Bistro Ralph.** In a town where good restaurants rarely seem to last, Ralph Tingle has sustained success with his California home-style cuisine, serving up a small menu that changes weekly. The stark industrial space includes a stunning wine rack of graceful curves fashioned in metal and wood. Take a seat at the bar and chat with the locals, who love this place just as much as out-of-towners do. ⊠ *109 Plaza St., off Healdsburg Ave.,* ☎ *707/433–1380. Reservations essential. MC, V. No lunch weekends.*

$$$$ 🏨 **Hotel Healdsburg.** Healdsburg's first luxury downtown hotel opened late in 2001. Although it rises three stories, its green facade blends in nicely with the plaza across the street. The attention to detail is striking, from the sleek decor to the wide, uncarpeted hallways, not to mention lots of "HH" motifs, a la Gucci. ⊠ *25 Matheson St., 95448,* ☎ *707/431–2800 or 800/889–7188,* FAX *707/431–0414,* WEB *www.hotelhealdsburg.com. 49 rooms, 6 suites. Restaurant, bar, room service, refrigerator, pool, spa, Internet. AE, D, DC, MC, V.*

$$$$ 🏨 **Madrona Manor.** The oldest continuously operating inn in the area, this 1881 Victorian mansion, surrounded by eight acres of wooded and landscaped grounds, is straight out of a storybook. Sleep in the splendid three-story mansion, the carriage house, or one of two separate cottages. Mansion rooms are recommended: all nine have fireplaces, and five contain the antique furniture of the original owner. ⊠ *1001 Westside Rd. (take central Healdsburg exit from U.S. 101, turn left on Mill St.), Box 818, 95448,* ☎ *707/433–4231 or 800/258–4003,* FAX *707/433–0703,* WEB *www.madronamanor.com. 22 rooms. Restaurant, pool. MC, V.*

$$–$$$$ 🏨 **The Honor Mansion.** This photogenic 1883 Italianate Victorian has won rave reviews for its interior design. Antiques, feather beds, and fancy water bottles are luxurious touches found in the rooms in the main house. A separate cottage is available in the rear and an adjacent water tower has a suite. Full breakfast is included. ⊠ *14891 Grove St., 95448,* ☎ *707/433–4277 or 800/554–4667,* FAX *707/431–7173,* WEB *www.honormansion.com. 7 rooms. Pool, hot tub. D, MC, V. BP.*

$$$ 🏨 **Healdsburg Inn on the Plaza.** This 1900 brick building on the town plaza has a bright solarium and a roof garden. The rooms, most with fireplaces, are spacious, with quilts and pillows piled high on antique beds. In the bathrooms claw-foot tubs are outfitted with rubber ducks; six rooms have whirlpool baths. Full champagne breakfast, afternoon coffee and cookies, and early evening wine and hors d'oeuvres are included. ⊠ *110 Matheson St., Box 1196, 95448* ☎ *707/433–6991,* FAX *707/433–9513,* WEB *www.healdsburginn.com. 11 rooms. D, MC, V. CP.*

Shopping

Oakville Grocery (⊠ 124 Matheson St., ☎ 707/433–3200) has a bustling Healdsburg branch filled with wine, produce, condiments, and deli items. For a good novel, children's literature, and books on interior design and gardening, head to **Levin & Company** (⊠ 306 Center St., ☎ 707/433–1118), which also stocks a lot of CDs and tapes. **Tip Top Liquor Warehouse** (⊠ 90 Dry Creek Rd., ☎ 707/431–0841) has a large selection of local wines, including some hard-to-find labels.

Every Saturday morning from early May through October, Healdsburg locals gather at the open-air **Farmers' Market** (⊠ North Plaza parking lot, North and Vine Sts., ☎ 707/431–1956) to pick up supplies from local producers of vegetables, fruits, flowers, cheeses, and olive oils.

Dry Creek and Alexander Valleys

On the west side of Hwy. 101, Dry Creek Valley remains one of the least developed appellations in Sonoma. The valley made its name on the zinfandel grapes that flourish on the benchlands, while the gravelly, well-drained soil of the valley floor is better known for chardonnay and, in the north, sauvignon blanc. The wineries in this region tend to be smaller and clustered in bunches.

The Alexander Valley, which lies east of Healdsburg, has a number of family-owned wineries. Most can be found right on Hwy. 28, which runs through this scenic, diverse appellation where zinfandel and chardonnay grow particularly well.

45 **Simi Winery.** Giuseppe and Pietro Simi, two brothers from Italy, began growing grapes in Sonoma in 1876. Though their winery's operations are strictly high-tech these days, its tree-studded entrance area and stone buildings recall a more genteel era. The tour highlights the winery's rich history. ⊠ *16275 Healdsburg Ave. (take Dry Creek Rd. exit off U.S. 101), Alexander Valley,* ☎ *707/433–6981,* WEB *www.simiwinery.com.* ☉ *Tours Mar.–Dec., daily 11, 1, and 3; Jan.–Feb., daily 11 and 2.*

46 **Dry Creek Vineyard,** whose fumé blanc is an industry benchmark, is also earning notice for its reds, especially zinfandels and cabernets. Picnic beneath the flowering magnolias and soaring redwoods. ⊠ *3770 Lambert Bridge Rd., Dry Creek Valley,* ☎ *707/433–1000,* WEB *www. drycreekvineyard.com.* ☉ *Daily 10:30–4:30. Tours by appointment.*

47 Housed in a California Mission–style complex off the main drag, **Michel-Schlumberger** produces ultrapremium wines including chardonnay, merlot, pinot blanc, and syrah, but its reputation is based on the exquisite cabernet sauvignon. ⊠ *4155 Wine Creek Rd., Dry Creek Valley,* ☎ *707/ 433–7427 or 800/447–3060,* WEB *www.michelschlumberger.com.* ☉ *Tastings and tours at 11 and 2 by appointment.*

48 An unassuming winery in a wood and cinder-block barn, **Quivira** produces some of the most interesting wines in Dry Creek Valley. Though it is known for its exquisitely balanced and fruity zinfandel, it also makes a superb blend of red varietals called Dry Creek Cuvée. ⊠ *4900 W. Dry Creek Rd., Dry Creek Valley,* ☎ *707/431–8333,* WEB *www.quivirawine.com.* ☉ *Daily 10–4:30. Tours by appointment.*

Noted for its beautiful Italian villa–style winery and visitor center (the breezy courtyard is covered with just about every kind of flower imag-
49 inable), **Ferrari-Carano Winery** produces chardonnays, fumé blancs, and merlots. Tours take you between the rows of grapevines right into the vineyards themselves. ⊠ *8761 Dry Creek Rd., Dry Creek Valley,* ☎ *707/433–6700,* WEB *www.ferrari-carano.com.* ☒ *Tasting fee $2.50.* ☉ *Daily 10–5. Tours by appointment.*

OFF THE
BEATEN PATH

CLOS DU BOIS – Five miles north of Healdsburg on Route 116, these vineyards produce the fine estate chardonnays of the Alexander and Dry Creek valleys that have been mistaken for great French wines. ✉ *19410 Geyserville Ave., Geyserville,* ☎ *707/857–3100 or 800/ 222–3189,* WEB *www.closdubois.com.* ☉ *Daily 10–4:30. No tours.*

Lodging

$$ 🖬 **Best Western Dry Creek Inn.** Continental breakfast and a bottle of wine are complimentary at this three-story Spanish Mission–style motel. Midweek discounts are available. A coffee shop is next door. ✉ *198 Dry Creek Rd., 95448,* ☎ *707/433–0300 or 800/222–5784,* FAX *707/433–1129. 102 rooms. Pool, hot tub, laundry facilities. AE, D, DC, MC, V. CP.*

Occidental

10 mi from Valley Ford, north on Rte. 1, east on Rte. 12 (Bodega Hwy.), and north on Bohemian Hwy.

A village surrounded by the redwood forests, orchards, and vineyards of western Sonoma County, Occidental is so small that you might drive right through the town and barely take notice. A 19th-century logging hub with a present-day bohemian feel, Occidental has a top-notch B&B, good eats, and a handful of art galleries and crafts and clothing boutiques, all of which make the town an ideal base for day trips to Sonoma Coast beaches, Bodega Bay, Armstrong Redwoods Reserve, and Point Reyes National Seashore.

Dining and Lodging

$–$$ ✕ **Willow Wood Market Café.** About 5 mi east of Occidental in the village of Graton is one of the best-kept secrets in the Wine Country. Tucked among the market merchandise are a number of tables and a counter where casually dressed locals sit down to order freshly made soups and salads or heartier American fare like a roasted half-chicken served with mashed potatoes. ✉ *9020 Graton Rd., Graton,* ☎ *707/ 823–0233. Reservations not accepted. MC, V. Closed Sun.*

$$–$$$ 🖬 **The Inn at Occidental.** Jack Bullard had to open an inn to have a
★   place to show off his collections, such as the antique English and Irish cut glass jars that fill the Glass Room. Antiques, quilts and original artwork fill the guest rooms. A fireplace and fine Asian rugs create a cozy but dignified mood in the ground-floor living room of the original house. Full breakfast is included. For a longer stay, you might consider the Sonoma Cottage, which goes for $540 to $600 a night. ✉ *3657 Church St., Box 857, 95465,* ☎ *707/874–1047 or 800/522– 6324,* FAX *707/874–1078. 14 rooms, 2 suites. Concierge. AE, D, DC, MC, V. BP.*

OFF THE
BEATEN PATH

OSMOSIS ENZYME BATHS – The tiny town of Freestone, 3 mi south of Occidental and 7½ mi east of Bodega Bay off Route 12 (Bodega Highway), is famous regionally as the home of the unique Osmosis Enzyme Baths. This spa, in a two-story clapboard house on extensive grounds, specializes in several treatments, including a detoxifying "dry" bath in a blend of enzymes and fragrant wood shavings. After 20 minutes in the tub, opt for a 75-minute massage in one of the free-standing Japanese-style pagodas near the creek that runs through the property. ✉ *209 Bohemian Hwy., Freestone,* ☎ *707/823–8231.*

SPA TREATMENT IN THE WINE COUNTRY

THE WINE COUNTRY was in the forefront of the long-simmering American love affair with hot springs, mud baths, and spa treatments. Blessed with natural mineral ash from nearby volcanoes and mineral springs, areas around Calistoga and Sonoma were popular with Native Americans long before the stressed-out white man arrived. Today you can find spas of every stripe throughout the Wine Country.

Dr. Wilkinson's is the oldest spa in Calistoga. Best known for its mud baths, it is perhaps the least chic of the bunch. ⊠ *1507 Lincoln Ave., Calistoga,* ☎ *707/ 942–4102,* WEB *drwilkinson.com.*

Lincoln Avenue Spa occupies a 19th-century bank building, a history suggested by elegant woodwork and a tiled steam room. House specialties include mint and green tea wraps ($55). ⊠ *1339 Lincoln Ave., Calistoga,* ☎ *707/942–5296.*

The **Mount View Spa** is the most elegant in town, though like most other Calistoga spas, it could be larger. You won't find mud baths at this retreat at the rear of the Mount View Hotel lobby, but it is one of the best places for facials. ⊠ *1457 Lincoln Ave., Calistoga,* ☎ *707/ 942–5789.*

Nance's Hot Springs has rows of cot-like beds that practically beg you to take a nap after a treatment. The spa area offers mud baths, a mineral whirlpool bath, and mineral steam baths. You can find good bargains here if you arrive mid-week; a hot mineral bath followed by a half-hour massage costs $50 (with hour-long massage, $70). ⊠ *1614 Lincoln Ave., Calistoga,* ☎ *707/942–6211.*

Calistoga Spa Hot Springs is the best choice if you have several hours to lounge around. A house special is "The Works" ($102), a two-hour marathon of mud bath, mineral whirlpool, steam bath, blanket wrap, and hour-long massage. If you're booking any treatment, you can pay $5 and get all-day pool access as well. You can try relaxing in four pools of varying size and temperature until you decide on a favorite. This spa dates to the 1920s, an era depicted in photographs lining the hallway. ⊠ *1006 Washington St., Calistoga,* ☎ *707/942–6269,* WEB *www.calistogaspa.com.*

Lavender Hill Spa is in a country cottage on the edge of town. The nicest treatment rooms are in the rear, with views of the lavender garden. ⊠ *1015 Foothill Blvd., Calistoga,* ☎ *707/942–4495.*

Health Spa Napa Valley is in a complex shared with an inn and a restaurant. The house specialty is Ayurvedic treatments; for an unforgettable experience, you should book the Abhyanga, which is performed by two practitioners ($160). ⊠ *1030 Main St., St. Helena,* ☎ *707/ 967–8800,* WEB *www.napavalleyspa.com.*

The **Sonoma Mission Inn and Spa** is the best-known sybarite hot spot in the Wine Country. A multi-million-dollar upgrade in the late 1990s transformed the resort's facilities into a destination spa. You'll want to arrive at least 45 minutes in advance of your appointment to spend some time in the bathing ritual room. ⊠ *18140 Sonoma Hwy., Sonoma,* ☎ *707/ 938–9000.*

Facilities at **Kenwood Inn & Spa** claim the prettiest spa setting in the Wine Country, thanks to the vineyards across the road and the Mediterranean style of the inn. Pool privileges are granted with the booking of any body or beauty treatment. ⊠ *10400 Sonoma Hwy., Kenwood,* ☎ *707/833–1293.*

The **The Garden Spa** has larger-than-life floral murals and the nicest, most expensive gift shop of all the Wine Country spas. The treatments are based on herbs, flowers, or minerals, rather than a blend of two or three. The two-hour Rose Garden treatment ($194) includes a bath in rose petals, a rose-petal body polish and essential oil massage. This spa, part of an inn, also has a small pool and co-ed steam rooms. ⊠ *29 E. MacArthur St., Sonoma,* ☎ *707/933–3193.*

— Marty Olmstead

Bodega Bay

8 mi from Valley Ford on Rte. 1, 65 mi north of San Francisco via U.S. 101 and Rte. 1.

Bodega Bay (where Alfred Hitchcock's *The Birds* took place) is one of the busiest harbors on the Sonoma County coast. Commercial boats pursue fish as well as the famed Dungeness crabs. T-shirt shops and galleries line both sides of Route 1; a short drive around the harbor leads to the Pacific. This is the last stop, town-wise, before Gualala, and a good spot for stretching your legs and taking in the salt air. For a closer look at Bodega Bay, visit the **Bodega Marine Laboratory** (☎ 707/875–2211 directions), on a 326-acre reserve on nearby Bodega Head. The lab gives free one-hour tours and peeks at intertidal invertebrates, such as sea stars and sea anemones, departing on the quarter-hour Friday from 2 to 3:30 PM (suggested donation of $2).

Dining and Lodging

$$$ ✕▦ **Inn at the Tides.** The condominium-style buildings at this complex have spacious rooms with high ceilings and an uncluttered look. All rooms have views of the harbor, and some have fireplaces. The inn's two restaurants ($$–$$$) serve both old-style and more adventurous seafood dishes. In season you can buy a slab of salmon or live or cooked crab at a seafood market across the highway and have the kitchen prepare it for you. ⊠ *800 Rte. 1, Box 640, 94923,* ☎ *707/875–2751 or 800/541–7788,* FAX *707/875–2669,* WEB *www.innatthetides.com. 86 rooms. 2 restaurants, room service, refrigerators, pool, hot tub, sauna, bar, laundry facilities. AE, D, MC, V.*

$$$–$$$$ ▦ **Sonoma Coast Villa Inn and Spa.** This secluded oasis in the coastal hills between Valley Ford and Bodega Bay is a most unusual inn. Founded as an Arabian horse ranch in 1976, the 60-acre property has a single-story row of accommodations beside a swimming pool. Red-tile roofs, a stucco exterior, and two courtyards create a European feel. Rooms have slate floors, French doors, beamed ceilings, and wood-burning fireplaces. The dining room serves complimentary full breakfast as well as a light buffet Friday and Saturday evenings. ⊠ *16702 Rte. 1, Bodega 94922,* ☎ *707/876–9818 or 888/404–2255,* FAX *707/ 876–9856,* WEB *www.scvilla.com. 18 rooms. Pool, hot tub, spa. AE, MC, V. CP.*

Outdoor Activities and Sports

Bodega Bay Sportfishing (⊠ Bay Flat Rd., ☎ 707/875–3344) charters ocean-fishing boats and rents equipment. The operators of the 400-acre **Chanslor Guest Ranch** (⊠ 2660 Rte. 1, ☎ 707/875–3333) lead guided horseback rides.

Shopping

The **Ren Brown Gallery** (⊠ 1781 Rte. 1, ☎ 707/875–2922) in the north end of town is renowned for its selection of Asian arts, crafts, furnishings, and design books. This two-floor gallery also displays works of a number of local artists worth checking out.

Jenner

10 mi north of Bodega Bay on Rte. 1.

The Russian River empties into the Pacific Ocean at Jenner. The town has a couple of good restaurants and some shops. South of the Russian River is windy **Goat Rock State Beach,** where a colony of sea lions (walk north from the parking lot) resides most of the year. The beach is open daily from 8 AM to sunset; there's no day-use fee.

Dining

$$$–$$$$ ✕ **River's End.** At the right time of year, diners at this rustic restaurant
★ can view sea lions lazing on the beach below. The creative fare is eclec-
tic, ranging from Continental to Indonesian, with seafood, venison, and
duck dishes. ⊠ *Rte. 1, north end of Jenner,* ☎ *707/865–2484. MC, V.
Closed most weekdays Nov.–Mar.*

Fort Ross State Historic Park

9 mi north of Jenner on Rte. 1.

Fort Ross, completed in 1821, became Russia's major fur-trading out-
post in California. The Russians brought Aleut sea-otter hunters down
from Alaska. By 1841 the area was depleted of seals and otters, and
the Russians sold their post to John Sutter, later of gold-rush fame. After
a local Anglo rebellion against the Mexicans, the land fell under U.S.
domain, becoming part of California in 1850. The state park service
has reconstructed Fort Ross, including its Russian Orthodox chapel,
a redwood stockade, the officers' barracks, and a blockhouse. The ex-
cellent museum here documents the history of the fort and some of the
North Coast. ⊠ *Rte. 1,* ☎ *707/847–3286.* ⊑ *$3 per vehicle (day use).*
☉ *Daily 10–4:30. No dogs allowed past parking lot.*

Lodging

$–$$$ ⊞ **Fort Ross Lodge.** Conveniently located about 1½ mi north of its name-
sake fort, this lodge has a wind-bitten feel to it. Some of the rooms have
views of the shoreline; others have private hot tubs. Six hill units have
saunas, hot tubs, and fireplaces. ⊠ *20705 Rte. 1, 95450,* ☎ *707/847–
3333 or 800/968–4537,* ℻ *707/847–3330,* ⓦ *www.fortrosslodge.com.
22 rooms. Refrigerators. AE, MC, V.*

Outdoor Activities and Sports

Take a swim at the outdoor pool, or rent a canoe for a trip down the
Russian River at **Memorial Beach Park,** open from Memorial Day to
Labor Day. **Burke's Canoe Trips** (⊠ Mirabel Rd. at River Rd., Forestville,
☎ 707/887–1222, ⓦ www.burkescanoetrips.com) rents kayaks and
canoes for cruising down the Russian River; the best time to go is from
May through October.

WINE COUNTRY A TO Z

*To research prices, get advice from other travelers, and book travel ar-
rangements, visit www.fodors.com.*

BUS TRAVEL
Greyhound (☎ 800/231–2222) runs buses from the Transbay Termi-
nal at 1st and Mission streets in San Francisco to Sonoma and Santa
Rosa.

CAR RENTAL
Although traffic on the two-lane country roads can be heavy, the best
way to get around the sprawling Wine Country is by private car.
Rentals are available at the airports and in San Francisco, Oakland,
Sonoma, Santa Rosa, and Napa.

CAR TRAVEL
From San Francisco, cross the Golden Gate Bridge, go north on U.S.
101, east on Route 37, and north and east on Route 121. For Sonoma
wineries, head north at Route 12; for Napa, turn left (to the northwest) when Route 121 runs into Route 29.

From Berkeley and other East Bay towns, take Interstate 80 north to Route 37 west to Route 29 north, which will take you directly up the middle of the Napa Valley. To reach Sonoma county, take Route 121 west off Route 29 south of the city of Napa. From points north of the Wine Country, take U.S. 101 south to Geyserville and take Route 128 southeast to Calistoga and Route 29. Most Sonoma County wine regions are clearly marked and accessible off U.S. 101; to reach the Sonoma Valley, take Route 12 east from Santa Rosa.

EMERGENCY SERVICES

➤ CONTACTS: **Ambulance** (☎ 911). **Police** (☎ 911).

LODGING

B & BS

The **Bed & Breakfast Association of Sonoma Valley** (✉ 3250 Trinity Rd., Glen Ellen 95442, ☎ 707/938–9513 or 800/969–4667, WEB www. sonomabb.com). **Bed & Breakfast Exchange** (✉ 15 Angwin Plaza, Box 762, Angwin 94508, ☎ 707/965–3400, WEB www.apollotravel.net). **The Wine Country Inns of Sonoma County** (☎ 707/433–4667; 800/354–4743 brochure). **Wine Country Reservations** (☎ 707/257–7757).

TOURS

Full-day guided tours of the Wine Country usually include lunch and cost about $60 per person. The guides, some of whom are winery owners themselves, know the area well and may show you some lesser-known cellars. Reservations are usually required.

Gray Line (✉ 350 8th St., San Francisco 94103, ☎ 415/558–9400) has buses that tour the Wine Country. **Great Pacific Tour Co.** (✉ 518 Octavia St., Civic Center, San Francisco 94102, ☎ 415/626–4499, WEB www.greatpacifictour.com) operates full-day tours of Napa and Sonoma, including a restaurant lunch, in passenger vans that seat 14. **HMS Travel Group** (✉ 707 4th St., Santa Rosa 95404, ☎ 707/526–2922 or 800/367–5348) offers customized tours of the Wine Country for six or more people, by appointment only. The **Napa Valley Wine Train** (✉ 1275 McKinstry St., Napa 94559, ☎ 707/253–2111 or 800/427–4124, WEB www.winetrain.com) allows you to enjoy lunch, dinner, or weekend brunch on one of several restored 1915 Pullman railroad cars that run between Napa and St. Helena. Dinner costs $79, lunch $70, brunch $59.50; per-person prices include train fare, meals, tax, and service. On weekend brunch trips and weekday lunch trips you can ride a special "Deli" car for $29.50. In winter service is sometimes limited to Thursday through Sunday; call ahead.

TRANSPORTATION AROUND THE WINE COUNTRY

Sonoma County Area Transit (☎ 707/585–7516 or 800/345–7433) offers daily bus service to points all over the county. The **VINE** (Valley Intracity Neighborhood Express; ☎ 707/255–7631) provides bus service within the city of Napa and between other Napa Valley towns.

VISITOR INFORMATION

➤ TOURIST INFORMATION: **Napa Valley Conference and Visitors Bureau** (✉ 1310 Napa Town Center, Napa 94559, ☎ 707/226–7459, WEB www. napavalley.com). The **North Coast Visitors Bureau** (✉ The Cannery, 2801 Leavenworth St., 2nd floor, Fisherman's Wharf, San Francisco 94133, ☎ 415/394–5991). **Sonoma County Tourism Program** (✉ 520 Mendocino Ave., Suite 210, Santa Rosa 95401, ☎ 707/565–5383 or 800/576–6662, WEB www.sonomacounty.com). **Sonoma Valley Visitors Bureau** (✉ 453 1st St. E, Sonoma 95476, ☎ 707/996–1090, WEB www.sonomavalley.com).

BOOKS AND MOVIES

Books

While many novels have San Francisco settings, they don't come any better than *The Maltese Falcon,* by Dashiell Hammett, the founder of the hard-boiled school of detective fiction. First published in 1930, Hammett's books continue to be readily available in new editions, and the details about the fog, the hills, and the once-seedy offices south of Market continue to be accurate.

Another standout is Vikram Seth's *Golden Gate,* a novel in verse about life in San Francisco and Marin County in the early 1980s. Others are John Gregory Dunne's *The Red White and Blue,* Stephen Longstreet's *All or Nothing* and *Our Father's House,* and Alice Adams's *Rich Rewards.* Many of the short stories in Adams's collection, *To See You Again,* have Bay Area settings. *The Joy Luck Club* by Bay Area writer Amy Tan is a novel about four generations of Chinese American women in San Francisco.

Two books that are filled with interesting background information on the city are Richard H. Dillon's *San Francisco: Adventurers and Visionaries* and *San Francisco: As It Is, As It Was,* by Paul C. Johnson and Richard Reinhardt.

For anecdotes, gossip, and the kind of detail that will make you feel almost like a native San Franciscan, get hold of any of the books by the late and much-loved San Francisco *Chronicle* columnist Herb Caen: *Baghdad-by-the-Bay, Only in San Francisco, One Man's San Francisco,* and *San Francisco: City on Golden Hills.* Armistead Maupin's gay-themed soap opera–style *Tales of the City* stories are set in San Francisco; you can read them or watch them on video.

Movies

Films shot in San Francisco in the 1990s include *Mrs. Doubtfire, Basic Instinct, The Rock, Metro, The Presidio,* and *The Game.* Among the older films about the city, *San Francisco,* starring Clark Gable and Spencer Tracy, re-creates the 1906 earthquake with outstanding special effects. In *Escape from Alcatraz,* Clint Eastwood plays the prisoner who allegedly escaped from the famous jail on a rock in the San Francisco Bay. Eastwood also starred in the Dirty Harry film series, which takes place around the Bay Area. *The Times of Harvey Milk,* about San Francisco's first openly gay elected official, won the Academy Award for best documentary feature in 1984. Alfred Hitchcock immortalized Mission Dolores and the Golden Gate Bridge in *Vertigo,* the eerie story of a detective with a fear of heights, starring Jimmy Stewart and Kim Novak. A few other noteworthy films shot in San Francisco are *Dark Passage,* with Humphrey Bogart; *Foul Play,* with Chevy Chase and Goldie Hawn; the 1978 remake of *Invasion of the Body Snatchers.*; and *Bullitt,* starring Steve McQueen, with a memorable car chase scene down San Francisco's infamous hills.

INDEX

Icons and Symbols

★ Our special recommen-
  dations
✕ Restaurant
▦ Lodging establishment
✕▦ Lodging establishment
  whose restaurant war-
  rants a special trip
♻ Good for kids (rubber
  duck)
☞ Sends you to another
  section of the guide for
  more information
⊠ Address
☎ Telephone number
☉ Opening and closing
  times
🎫 Admission prices

Numbers in white and black
circles ③ ❸ that appear on
the maps, in the margins, and
within the tours correspond
to one another.

A

A. P. Hotaling Company
  Whiskey Distillery, 27
Abigail Howard Johnson
  Hotel ▦, 127
Abitare (store), 181
Above Paradise (spoken
  word), 141
Absinthe ✕, 84
Absolutely Accommodations,
  106
Acqua Hotel ▦, 201
Acquerello ✕, 104
Addresses, viii
Adventure Bicycle Co., 155
Afghan restaurants, 96–97
Air travel, viii–x. ☞ Also
  Plane travel
Airport area lodging, 128–
  129
Airports and transfers, x–xi
Alameda/Oakland Ferry,
  156
Alcatraz Island, 50
Alexander Book Co. (store),
  175
Alexander Valley, 267–268
All Seasons Café ✕, 254
All Seasons Café Wine Shop,
  255
Alma ✕, 95
Alonzo King's Lines
  Contemporary Ballet, 147
Alta Mira ✕, 198
Alta Plaza Park, 42, 43
American Conservatory
  Theater (ACT), 150

American Family Inn/Bed &
  Breakfast San Francisco,
  106
American Indian Film
  Festival, 148
American Rag (store), 187
American restaurants, 86,
  87–88, 100, 102
Amoeba (store), 184
Amoeba Music (store), 208
Amusement parks, 228
Andalou ✕, 93
Andrews ▦, 113
Angel Island, 50, 52
Angel Island-Tiburon Ferry,
  206
Angkor Borei ✕, 93
Año Nuevo State Reserve,
  226
Another Time (store), 188,
  189
Anthropological museum,
  209
Antica Trattoria ✕, 100
Antique furniture and
  accessories, shopping for,
  172, 188
Antique jewelry, shopping
  for, 183–184
Antonio's Antiques, 188
Apartment rentals, xxiv
Applewood Inn ▦, 265
Aqua ✕, 89
Aquarium of the Bay, 53
Aquariums, 53, 59
Aquarius Records (store),
  185
Aquatic Park, 163
Archbishop's Mansion ▦,
  126
Argent ▦, 117–118
Ark Row (Tiburon), 199
Arrowood Vineyards, 260
Art galleries and museums,
  15, 22, 23, 25, 31, 41,
  47–48, 49, 55, 64, 68,
  70, 173–175, 209–210,
  213–214, 216, 219, 232,
  252
Art on Main (gallery), 252
Art Options (store), 173
Artesa (winery), 238
Arts, 146–152, 244–245,
  259, 264
Asakichi Japanese Antiques
  (store), 172
Ashbury Market, 189
Asian American Theatre
  Company, 151
Asian Art Museum, 47–48
AsiaSF (cabaret), 132
Atherton House, 43
ATMs, xxvi
ATYS (store), 186
Auberge du Soleil ✕, 249
Audubon Canyon Ranch, 205

Auto racing, 161
Autumn Moon Cafe ✕, 216
Axford House, 71, 72
Azie ✕, 101

B

B44 ✕, 7, 90
Backflip (bar), 142
Baker Beach, 163
Balboa Cafe (singles bar),
  140
Ballet, 146–147, 244–245
Ballooning, 232, 247, 255,
  264
Balmy Alley, 68
Bank of America Building, 28
Bank of the West Women's
  Tennis Tour, 162
Barbary Coast, 25–28
Barnes & Noble (store), 175
Bars, 140–141, 142–144
BART, xii
Baseball, 161–162
Basketball, 162
Bay Area, 228–229
Bay Area Discovery Museum,
  197–198
Bay Area Theatresports, 133
Bay Model, 197
Bayside Cafe ✕, 198
Bay-to-Breakers race, 154
Beach Blanket Babylon
  (cabaret revue), 8, 132,
  151
Beach Chalet, 59
Beach Chalet ✕, 66, 102,
  140
Beaches, 65–66, 163–164
San Mateo County, 164, 224,
  225
Sonoma County, 270
Bead Store, 184
Beads, shopping for, 184
Bear Valley Visitors Center,
  204
Beaulieu Vineyard, 248
Beauty, shopping for, 175
Bed and Breakfast Inn ▦,
  124
Bed & Breakfast California,
  106
Bed-and-breakfasts, xxiv,
  77–78, 106, 124, 272
Bel-Aire Travelodge ▦, 125
Beltane Ranch ▦, 261
BeneFit (store), 175
Benicia, 227–228
Benziger Family Winery, 260
Beringer Vineyards, 233,
  250
Berkeley, 207–213
Berkeley Marina, 210
Berkeley Repertory Theatre,
  151
Berkeley Symphony
  Orchestra, 148

Berkeley Visitor Information
Center, 208

Best Western Dry Creek Inn
☒, 268

Betelnut ✕, 86

Bette's Oceanview Diner ✕,
212

Bicycling, xi, 154–155, 224,
238, 255

Big Four Bar (piano bar),
137

Big 3 Diner ✕, 258

Bijou ☒, 113

Billy Blue (store), 177

Bimbo's 365 Club
(nightclub), 137

Biordi Art Imports (store),
181

Bird sanctuaries, 205, 214,
225

Birkenstock Natural
Footwear, 185

Bistro Don Giovanni ✕, 239

Bistro Jeanty ✕, 246

Bistro Ralph ✕, 266

Bix (bar), 142–143

Bizou ✕, 101

Black Cat ✕, 97

Black Oak Books (store),
175–176

Blondie's Bar and No Grill,
143

Blue and Gold Fleet, 52,
155–156, 206

Blue Bar (jazz club), 136

Blues music, 132, 137, 139

Boat cruises and ferries. ☞
See Ferries and boats

Boating, 156

Bodega Bay, 270

Bodega Marine Laboratory,
270

Body Time (store), 175

Bohemian Grove, 203

Bolinas, 205

Booksmith (store), 176

Bookstores, 175–177

Boom Boom Room
(nightclub), 137

Borders Books and Music
(store), 168, 175

Boretti Amber (gallery), 180

Bottom of the Hill
(nightclub), 137

Bouchon ✕, 246

Boulevard ✕, 87

Bound Together Anarchist
Book Collective (store),
176

Brand X Antiques, 183

Brannan Cottage Inn ☒, 254

Bridge (cinema), 147

Bridgeway, 193

Brix ✕, 246

Broadway and Webster
Street estates, 42, 43

Brocklebank Apartments, 39

Bruno's (jazz club), 136

Bubble Lounge (wine bar),
142

Buckeye Roadhouse ✕, 201

Bucks in Woodside ✕, 223

Buena Vista Café ✕, 52, 143

Buena Vista Carneros
Winery, 233, 236, 257

Buena Vista Park, 76, 77

Buffalo Exchange (store),
187

Buffalo Paddock, 59

Bus travel, xi–xii
Bay Area, 228
Marin County, 206
San Mateo County, 226
Wine Country, 271

Business hours, xi

C

Cabarets, 131, 132

Cable Car Museum, 38

Cable Car terminus, 11, 14

Cable cars, xii–xiii, 8, 18

Café (gay male bar), 144

Café Citti ✕, 262

Café Claude ✕, 89

Cafe du Nord (jazz club),
136

Café Flore ✕, 75, 144

Cafe La Haye ✕, 258

Cafe Lolo ✕, 263

Café Marimba ✕, 85–86

Café Niebaum-Coppola
(wine bar) ✕, 35

Café Reyes ✕, 206

Café Rouge ✕, 212

Caffe Mediterraneum ✕, 208

Caffe Sport ✕, 36

Caffe Trieste ✕, 36

Cal Performances, 146, 148–
149

Cal Train, xii

California Academy of
Sciences, 58, 59, 61

California College of Arts
and Crafts, 216

California Historical Society,
21, 22

California Palace of the
Legion of Honor, 63, 64

California Shakespeare
Festival, 151–152

California Welcome Center,
53

Calistoga, 233, 236, 252–
255

Calistoga Inn ✕, 254

Calistoga Spa Hot Springs
☒, 254–255, 269

Calistoga Wine Stop (store),
255

Cambodian restaurants, 93

Cameras and photography,
xiii

Camping, 202, 206

Campton Place ✕☒, 103,
107

Campus Store, 252

Camron-Stanford House, 214

Candelier (store), 182

Cannery, 50, 52

Canoeing, 271

Capitol (Benicia), 228

Capp's Corner ✕, 97–98

Car rental, xiii–xiv, xxii,
271

Car travel, xiv–xv, xxii
Bay Area, 228–229
East Bay, 217
Inland Peninsula, 223
Marin County, 206–207
San Mateo County, 226
Wine Country, 271–272

Carnelian Room (skyline
bar), 28, 140

Carneros region, 237–238

Carta ✕, 84

Cartoon Art Museum, 21, 22

Casa Madrona ☒, 198–199

Cassis Bistro ✕, 85

Castro district, 72, 74–76,
80–81, 131, 144–145,
166

Castro Theatre, 8, 72, 74,
147

Catahoula Restaurant and
Saloon ✕, 253–254

Cathedral Grove, 203

Catherine Clark Gallery, 173

Caymus Vineyards, 248

Celadon ✕, 244

Center for the Arts, 20, 22

Cesar E. Chavez Park, 210

Cha Cha Cha ✕, 78

Chamber of Commerce
(Benicia), 228

Chancellor Hotel ☒, 113

Chanticleer (a cappella
ensemble), 149

Charanga ✕, 95

Charles Krug Winery, 250

Chateau Hotel ☒, 244

Château Montelena (winery),
253

Chateau Potelle (winery),
239

Chez Marie ✕, 265

Chez Nous ✕, 93

Chez Panisse Café &
Restaurant ✕, 210, 212

Children, xv–xvi
clothing for, 177
what to see and do with, 14,
24–25, 52, 53, 55, 59, 61,
66, 75–76, 197, 210, 253

Children's Playground, 58,
61

China Beach, 164

Chinatown, 8, 29–33, 81,
166

Chinatown Gate, 29, 30

Chinatown Kite Shop (store),
186

Chinese American National
Museum and Learning
Center, 30, 31

Chinese Culture Center, 30,
31

Chinese restaurants, *81, 86–87, 88, 98, 102*

Chinese Six Companies, *30, 31*

Christian Science Church, *43*

Christine Foley (store), *169*

Christophe ✕, *198*

Chronicle Marathon, *154*

Churches, *32, 36, 39, 43, 46, 70, 199*

Church's English Shoes Ltd., *185*

Cinch (gay male bar), *145*

Circuses, *152*

City Arts and Lectures (spoken word), *141*

City Box Office, *146*

City Hall, *47, 48*

City Lights Bookstore, *34, 35, 167, 176*

Cityscape (skyline bar), *140*

Civic Center, *46–49, 81, 84–85, 126–127*

Claremont Resort and Spa ⌂, *216*

Clarion Bedford Hotel ⌂, *113–114*

Clarion Hotel San Francisco Airport ⌂, *129*

Clarke's Mansion, *74*

Clay (cinema), *147*

Clean Well-Lighted Place for Books (store), *141, 176*

Cliff House, *63, 64–65*

Clift Hotel ⌂, *107*

Climate, *xxxiii*

Clos du Bois (winery), *268*

Clos du Val (winery), *236, 239*

Clos Pegase (museum/winery), *233, 253*

Clothing, shopping for, *177–178, 187*

Club Fugazi (cabaret), *132, 151*

Club Q (lesbian bar), *146*

Coast Trail, *205*

Cobb's Comedy Club, *133*

Cody's Books (store), *208*

Coit Tower, *8, 34, 35*

Coleman House, *43*

Collage Gallery (store), *180*

College Avenue (Oakland), *216*

Comedy clubs, *131, 133*

Commodore International ⌂, *114*

Compadres Bar and Grill ✕, *245*

Compass Rose ✕, *19*

Concierges, *xvi*

Conservatory of Flowers, *57, 61*

Consulates and embassies, *xxii*

Consumer protection, *xvi*

Contemporary restaurants, *80–81, 84, 87, 88, 90,* *92, 93, 95, 97, 100–101, 102–103*

Cookin': Recycled Gourmet Appurtenances (store), *182*

Copia: The American Center for Wine, Food and the Arts, *239*

Cosmopolitan Cafe ✕, *100*

Cottage Grove Inn ⌂, *254*

Coventry Motor Inn ⌂, *124*

Cow Hollow, *85–86, 123–126*

Cow Hollow Motor Inn and Suites ⌂, *125*

Cow Palace, *162*

Cowper Inn ⌂, *222*

Coyote Point Nature Museum, *227*

Crafts
museum for, 55
shopping for, 180–181

Creativity Explored (art gallery), *67, 68*

Credit cards, *xxvi–xxvii*

Crocker Galleria, *168*

Crossroads Trading Company (store), *187*

Crown Point Press, *173*

Cucina Viansa (blues club), *259*

Culinary Institute of America, *250*

Curran (theater), *150*

Currency, *xxii*

Customs and duties, *xvi–xvii*

Cut Loose (store), *169*

Cuvaison (winery), *236, 252*

D

Dance, *146–147*

Dance clubs, *132, 133*

Dean and Deluca (store), *252*

Delfina ✕, *95*

Della Santina ✕, *258*

Department stores, *168–169*

Depot Bookstore and Café ✕, *201*

Designers Club (store), *177*

Different Light (bookstore), *141, 166, 176*

Dillingham and Company (store), *188*

Dine ✕, *101*

Dining, *xvii–xviii.* ☞ *Also* Restaurants

Dipsea Trail, *203*

Disabilities and accessibility, *xviii–xx*

Discount outlets, *169, 172*

Discounts and deals, *xx*

Disney Store, *168, 186*

Divas (gay male bar), *145*

Diving, *xx*

Dockside Boat and Bed, *106–107*

Dr. Wilkinson's (spa), *269*

Domaine Carneros (winery), *238*

Domaine Chandon (winery), *246*

Dominguez (bakery), *68*

Donahue Monument, *23–24*

Dottie Doolittle (store), *177*

Downtown area, *107, 110–115*

Dragon House (store), *172*

Drinking fountain (Sausalito), *197*

Dry Creek Valley, *267–268*

Dry Creek Vineyard, *267*

Duarte's Tavern ✕, *226*

Dutch Henry Winery, *253*

Dutch Windmill, *59, 61*

E

E & O Trading Co. ✕, *15*

Eagle Tavern (gay male bar), *145*

East Bay, *207–218*

Eclectic restaurants, *84*

Edinburgh Castle (bar), *143*

El Bonita Motel ⌂, *251*

El Dorado Hotel ⌂, *259*

El Rio (dance club), *133*

Elbo Room (jazz club), *136*

Electricity, *xxii*

Eleonore Austerer Gallery, *173*

Eli's Mile High Club (blues club), *214–215*

Elisabeth Daniel ✕, *88*

Elmwood (Berkeley), *208*

Embarcadero, *20–25, 86–87, 155*

Embarcadero Center, *21, 22, 166*

Embarcadero Center Cinemas, *147–148*

Embassy Suites San Francisco Airport-Burlingame ⌂, *128*

Emergencies, *xxii, 272*

Enchanted Crystal (store), *183*

Enrico's Sidewalk Cafe ✕, *97, 136*

Eos Restaurant & Wine Bar ✕, *90, 92, 142*

Equinox (skyline bar), *140*

Esprit (store), *169*

Esta Noche (gay male bar), *145*

Ethnic Dance Festival, *146–147*

Evolution (store), *182*

Evvia ✕, *220*

Excursions from San Francisco, *192–229*

Executive Inn at Embarcadero Cove ⌂, *217*

Exit Theatre, *151*

Exploratorium (museum), *54, 59, 186–187*

F

F.A.O. Schwarz (store), 14, 168, 187
F. Dorian (store), 180
Faerie Queene Rococoa Chocolates, 178
Fairmont Hotel ⌷, 38, 39, 119–120
Farallon ✕, 103
Farmers' Market (Healdsburg), 267
Farmers' markets, 189–190
Farmhouse Inn ⌷, 265–266
Ferrari-Carano Winery, 236, 267
Ferries and boats, xi, 8, 52, 155–156, 206, 217, 228
Ferry Building, 21, 22–23
Festival Cine Latino, 148
Festivals and seasonal events, xxxiii–xxxiv, 74, 146–147, 148, 149, 151–152, 198, 224, 259
Feusier House, 38, 39
Fifth Floor ✕, 100–101
Film, 147–148, 259
Film Arts Festival of Independent Cinema, 148
Fillmore (nightclub), 137
Filoli (estate), 222
Financial District, 87–90, 116–117
Fischer-Hanlon Home, 228
Fisherman's Wharf, 50, 52, 90, 122–123, 131, 166–167
Fishing, 156, 245, 270
Fitness, 156–158
Fitzgerald Marine Life Refuge, 164
Flag House, 41
Flatiron Building, 23
Flax (store), 185
Flea markets, 189–190
Fleur de Lys ✕, 103
Florio ✕, 92–93
Fog City Diner ✕, 86
Folk art, shopping for, 180–181
Folk Art International/Boretti Amber/Xanadu Tribal Arts (gallery), 180
Folk music, 132, 137, 139
Football, 162
Foothill Café ✕, 239
Foreign Cinema ✕, 95
Forgotten Shanghai (store), 188
Fort Mason Center, 54, 55
Fort Point, 54, 55–56
Fort Point Mine Depot, 56
Fort Ross Lodge ⌷, 271
Fort Ross State Historic Park, 271
49 Geary Street (galleries), 173
42nd Street Moon Productions, 149
42 Degrees ✕, 93

Fountaingrove Inn ⌷, 263–264
Fountains, 15, 23
Four Seasons Hotel San Francsico ⌷, 118
450 Sutter Street, 14
4th Street (Berkeley), 208
Fraenkel Gallery (store), 173
Franklin Street buildings, 42, 43
Frantoio ✕, 201
Freemark Abbey Winery, 236, 250
Freight and Salvage Coffee House (nightclub), 137, 138
French Hotel ⌷, 213
French Laundry ✕, 246
French restaurants, 85, 87, 88–89, 90, 92–93, 95, 96, 97, 99, 101, 103
Frette (store), 168, 182
Friends of Recreation and Parks, 57
Fringale ✕, 7, 101
Frog's Leap (winery), 248
Fumiki (store), 188
Furniture, shopping for, 172, 187, 189

G

G & M Sales (store), 186
Gaige House Inn ⌷, 260–261
Galeria de la Raza/Studio 24, 68
Galleria Park ⌷, 117
Garden Court ✕, 87
Garden Court Hotel ⌷, 221
Garden Spa, 269
Gardens and parks, 25, 37, 39, 43, 57–59, 61–63, 65, 66, 77, 197, 199, 200–201, 210, 214, 215–216, 253, 260, 262–263, 270, 271
Gary Danko ✕, 7, 90
Gay and lesbian nightlife, 144–146
Gay and lesbian travel, xx–xxi
Gaylord's ✕, 90
Geary Theater, 14, 15, 150
German restaurants, 84
Get Lost Travel Books, Maps and Gear, 176
Geyser, 253
Ghirardelli Chocolate Factory, 27
Ghirardelli Square, 50, 52
Gimme Shoes (store), 186
Gira Polli ✕, 201
Girl & the Fig ✕, 257–258
Girl Spot (lesbian bar), 146
Glen Ellen, 236, 260–261
Glen Ellen Inn ✕, 260
Glenelly Inn ⌷, 261
Gliding, 161, 255

Global Exchange (store), 180
Gloria Ferrer Champagne Caves, 236, 237
Goat Rock State Beach, 270
Golden fire hydrant, 71, 72
Golden Gate (theater), 150
Golden Gate Bridge, 8, 54, 56
Golden Gate Church, 43
Golden Gate Ferry, 206
Golden Gate Fortune Cookies Co., 30, 31
Golden Gate Hotel ⌷, 115
Golden Gate National Recreation Area, 154
Golden Gate National Recreation Area Visitors' Center, 65
Golden Gate Park, 57–59, 61–63, 155
Golden State Warriors, 162
Golf, 158, 245, 264
Goose and Turrets ⌷, 225
Gordon Bennett (store), 182
Gordon Biersch Brewery and Restaurant (singles bar), 140
Gourmet food, shopping for, 178, 180
Grace Cathedral, 38, 39
Graffeo Coffee Roasting Company, 178
Grand Café ✕, 102–103
Grand Central Station Antiques, 172
Grand National Rodeo, Horse, and Stock Show, 162
Grand Views (skyline piano bar), 137, 141
Grant Avenue, 34, 36
Grant Plaza Hotel ⌷, 115
Grateful Dead house, 77
Great American Music Hall (nightclub), 139
Great China Herb Co. (store), 166
Great Eastern ✕, 81
Greek restaurants, 87
Green Apple Books, 176
Greens ✕, 86
Greens to Go ✕, 55
Guaymas ✕, 200
Guidebooks, xxi
Guided tours
  Marin County, 207
  Palo Alto, 219
  Wine Country, 272
Gulf of the Farallones National Marine Sanctuary, 227
Gump's (store), 168

H

Haas-Lilienthal House, 42, 43
Hackett Freedman Gallery, 173

Haight-Ashbury intersection, 77

Haight district, 76–78, 90, 92, 131, 167

Half-Pint (store), 259

Half Moon Bay, 224–225

Half Moon Bay Art and Pumpkin Festival, 224

Half Moon Bay State Beach, 164, 224

Hallidie Building, 14, 15

Hamburgers ✕, 193

Hammersmith Building, 14, 15

Handicrafts, shopping for, 180–181

Hang (gallery), 173

Harbor Court ☒, 117

Harbor Village ✕, 86

Harrington's (bar), 143

Harris' ✕, 104

Harry Denton's Rouge (singles bar), 140

Harry Denton's Starlight Room (skyline bar), 141

Harvest Inn ☒, 251

Harvest Market, 178

Harvey Milk Plaza, 72, 74–75

Hawk Hill, 202

Hawthorne Lane ✕, 101

Hayes and Vine (wine bar), 142

Hayes Street Grill ✕, 84

Hayes Valley, 167

Hayward Regional Shoreline, 227

Healdsburg, 236, 266–267

Healdsburg Inn on the Plaza ☒, 266

Health Spa Napa Valley, 250, 269

Heinold's First and Last Chance Saloon, 215

Held Over (store), 187

Helmand ✕, 96–97

Herbst Theatre, 49

Hespe Gallery, 173

Hess Collection Winery and Vineyards, 236, 238–239

Hewlett-Packard garage, 220–221

Historical museums, 22, 23, 25, 28, 31, 38, 48, 53, 57, 213–214, 250, 252

History Room (Oakland Main Library), 215

Hobart Building, 23

Hockey, 162

Holding Company (singles bar), 140

Holiday Adventure Sales and Rentals, 155

Holidays, xxi

Hollywood Billiards (lesbian bar), 146

Home exchanges, xxiv

Honor Mansion ☒, 266

Hoover Tower, 219

Hop Kiln (winery), 265

Horse racing, 162

Horseback riding, 158, 270

Hostels, xxiv–xxv, 202

Hot Air Ballooning. ☞ See Ballooning

Hotel Bohème ☒, 123

Hotel Del Sol ☒, 125

Hotel Diva ☒, 112

Hotel Drisco ☒, 124

Hotel Durant ☒, 212–213

Hotel Healdsburg ☒, 266

Hotel Majestic ☒, 126–127

Hotel Milano ☒, 119

Hotel Monaco ☒, 7, 111

Hotel Nikko ☒, 107, 110

Hotel Palomar ☒, 118

Hotel Rex ☒, 7, 111

Hotel Sausalito ☒, 199

Hotel Sofitel-San Francisco Bay ☒, 128

Hotel Triton ☒, 111

Hotels, xxv. ☞ Also Lodging
- Benicia, 228
- Berkeley, 212–213
- Half Moon Bay, 225
- Mill Valley, 201
- Oakland, 216–217
- Palo Alto, 221–222
- price categories, 107
- Sausalito, 198–199
- Wine Country, 232, 244, 246–247, 251, 254–255, 258–259, 260–261, 263–264, 265, 266, 268, 270, 271

Houseboats (Sausalito), 197

Housewares and accessories, shopping for, 181–183

Hunt Antiques (store), 172

Huntington ☒, 120–121

Hurd Beeswax Candle Factory, 251–252

Hyatt at Fisherman's Wharf ☒, 122

Hyatt Regency Hotel ☒, 21, 23, 116

Hyatt Regency San Francisco Airport ☒, 128–129

Hyde Street Pier, 50, 52–53

I

I. Wolk Gallery, 252

Ice-skating, 158–159

Icons and symbols, vi, 274

Il Fornaio ✕, 87

Il Fornaio Cucina Italiana ✕, 220

Imaginarium (store), 187

Imperial Tea Court, 30

Ina Coolbrith Park, 38, 39

Indian Oven ✕, 92

Indian restaurants, 90, 92

Indian Rock, 210

Indian Springs (spa), 252

Inland Peninsula, 218–223

In-line skating, 159

Inn at Occidental ☒, 268

Inn at the Opera ☒, 127

Inn at the Tides ☒, 270

Inn at Union Square ☒, 111–112

Insurance, xxi, xxii–xxiii

Interior Visions, 172

International travelers, xxii–xxiii

Intersection for the Arts, 151

Iris and B. Gerald Cantor Center for Visual Arts, 219

Iron Horse (winery), 264–265

Isobune ✕, 46

Italian restaurants, 85, 87, 89, 93, 95, 97–98, 100, 103, 104

Izzy's Steak & Chop House ✕, 86

J

Jack London Bookstore, 260

Jack London Square, 215

Jack London State Historic Park, 260

Jackson Court ☒, 124

Jackson Square, 26, 27–28, 167, 188

Jade Empire (store), 183

Japan Center, 45–46, 167

Japan Center Mall, 45, 46

Japanese restaurants, 89, 92, 98–99

Japanese Tea Garden, 58, 62

Japantown, 44–46, 92, 167

Japonesque (store), 181

Jardinière ✕, 7, 81

Jarvis Conservatory, 244–245

Jazz, 132, 133, 136

Jazz at Pearl's (jazz club), 136

Jenner, 270–271

Jeremy's (store), 169

Jewelry and collectibles, shopping for, 183–184

Jianna ✕, 97

Joe Goode Performance Group, 147

John Ash & Co. ✕, 263

John Berggruen Gallery, 173

John Fluevog Shoes, 186

John Muir National Historic Site, 228

John Pence Gallery, 174

Joseph Phelps Vineyards, 250

Joseph Schmidt Confections (store), 178

Julius' Castle ✕, 35, 36

Just Desserts (store), 178, 180

Justice League (nightclub), 139

Justin Herman Plaza, 22

K

K & L Wine Merchants, 189

Kabuki Springs & Spa, 45, 46

Kabuto Sushi ✕, 98–99
Katia's ✕, 99
Kay Cheung Seafood
  Restaurant ✕, 32
Kayaking, 159
Kenwood, 261–262
Kenwood Inn & Spa, 269
Kenwood Restaurant & Bar
  ✕, 261–262
Kenwood Vineyards, 236,
  261
Kiehl's (store), 175
Kimball's East (jazz club),
  136
Kimo's (gay male bar), 145
King George ☶, 114
Kinokuniya Bookstore, 176
Klondike Cabin, 215
Kokkari ✕, 89
Kong Chow Temple, 30, 31
Korbel Champagne Cellars,
  265
Kozo (store), 185
Kronos Quartet, 149
Kule Loklo, 204
Kunde Estate Winery, 261
Kyo-ya ✕, 89

L
La Casa ✕, 258
La Folie ✕, 99
La Quinta Motor Inn ☶, 129
La Residence ☶, 246–247
La Salette ✕, 258
La Santenaca ✕, 95–96
La Taqueria ✕, 96
La Toque ✕, 249
La Tulipe Noire Antiques
  (store), 172
La Victoria (bakery), 68
La Vie ✕, 99
Lachryma Montis (house),
  257
Lafayette Park, 42, 43
Laguna Street Victorians, 44
Lake Merritt, 214
Lake Merritt Hotel ☶, 217
Lalime's ✕, 212
L'Amie Donia ☶, 220
Lamplighters (opera), 150
Land's End, 65
Landmark Vineyards, 261
Lang Antiques and Estate
  Jewelry (store), 183
Last Day Saloon (nightclub),
  139
Laszlo (bar), 143
Latin restaurants, 95–96
Laurel Court ✕, 39
Lavendar Hill Spa, 269
Lawrence Hall of Science,
  210
Le Central ✕, 88
Le Cheval Restaurant ✕, 216
Le Colonial ✕, 103
Le Soleil ✕, 99
Legion Café ✕, 64
Lesbian bars, 146

Levi Strauss headquarters,
  35, 36
Levin & Company (store),
  267
Lexington Club (lesbian bar),
  146
Libraries, 48–49, 72
Lighthouses, 202, 205, 224,
  226
Liguria Bakery ✕, 33
Lincoln Avenue Spa, 269
Lincoln Park, 63–66
Livefire ✕, 246
Lodging, xxiv–xxv, 106–
  129. ☞ Also Hotels
Loehmann's (store), 169
Lombard Street, 8, 38, 40
Lombardi's (store), 186
London Lodge, 260
London Wine Bar, 142
Lorraine Hansberry Theatre,
  151
Los Robles Lodge ☶, 264
L'Osteria del Forno ✕, 98
Lotta's Fountain, 21, 23
Louise M. Davies Symphony
  Hall, 47, 48
Lou's Pier 47 (nightclub),
  139
Lovejoy's Antiques & Tea
  Room ✕, 71, 72
Lucca Delicatessen, 180
Luggage, xxviii
LuLu ✕, 102
Lumière (cinema), 148
Luna (winery), 239
Luna Park ✕, 93, 95
Luna Sea Women's
  Performance Project
  (spoken word), 141
Luther Burbank Center for the
  Arts, 264
Luther Burbank Home and
  Gardens, 262–263
Lyford House, 199–200

M
MAC (store), 175
MacArthur Park ✕, 88
MacArthur Place ☶, 258
Macondray Lane, 38, 40
Macy's (store), 168–169
Madrona Manor ☶, 266
Magic Theatre, 150–151
Magnes Museum, 21, 23
Maiden Lane, 14, 15
Mail and shipping, xxiii,
  xxv–xxvi
Main Street (Half Moon
  Bay), 224
Main Street (Tiburon), 199
Make-A-Circus, 152
Mandarin Oriental ☶, 116
Manka's ✕, 205
Margaret Jenkins Dance
  Company, 147
Marin beaches, 163
Marin Civic Center, 193

Marin County, 192–193,
  197–207
Marin Headlands, 201
Marin Headlands Hostel ☶,
  202
Marin Headlands Visitor
  Center, 202
Marina District, 53–57, 85–
  86, 123–126, 131, 167
Marina Green, 155
Marina Inn ☶, 125–126
Marine Mammal Store &
  Interpretive Center, 53
Marines Memorial Theatre,
  151
Maritime museum, 53
Mark Hopkins Inter-
  Continental Hotel ☶, 38,
  40, 120
Market Hall, 216
Market Street, 21, 23–24
Marriott at Fisherman's
  Wharf ☶, 122
Marsh (cabaret/theater),
  132, 151
Martinez, 228
Martuni's (gay male bar),
  145
Masa's ✕, 96
Ma-Shí-Ko Folk Craft (store),
  181
Masonic Auditorium, 38, 40
Matanzas Creek Winery,
  236, 263
Maxwell ☶, 112
Maykadeh ✕, 98
Mazzini ✕, 212
McCormick and Kuleto's ✕,
  90
Meadowlark Country House
  ☶, 254
Meadowood Resort ✕☶, 251
Meal plan abbreviations,
  xxiv
Mecca ✕, 80
Media, xxvi
Mediterranean restaurants,
  84, 85, 102
Merenda ✕, 85
Meritage ✕, 257
Metreon (entertainment
  complex), 20, 24
Metro (gay male bar), 144
Metronome Ballroom (dance
  club), 133
Mexican restaurants, 85–86,
  96
Meyerovich Gallery, 174
Michel-Schlumberger
  (winery), 267
Middle Eastern restaurants,
  98
Midnight Sun (gay male
  bar), 144–145
Mifune ✕, 92
Mikayla at Casa Madrona ✕,
  198
Mill Rose Inn ☶, 225
Mill Valley, 200–201

Mill Valley Film Festival, *148*
Mill Valley Inn ☒, *201*
Millenium ✕, *84–85*
Milliken Creek Inn ☒, *244*
Mint (gay male bar), *145*
Mission District, *66–68, 70, 93, 95–96, 131, 167*
Mission Dolores, *67, 70*
Mission San Francisco Solano, *255*
Mix (store), *177*
Mixx ✕, *263*
Modern Artifacts (store), *182*
Modern Times Bookstore, *142, 176*
Moe's Books (store), *208*
Molinari Delicatessen, *180*
Momo's ✕, *100*
Money matters, *xxvi–xxvii*
Moose's ✕, *97, 136*
Morrison Planetarium, *61*
Mo's Grill ✕, *100*
Moscone Convention Center, *20, 24*
Mott Visitor Center, *54, 56*
Mt. Tamalpais State Park, *204*
Mount View Hotel and Spa ☒, *254, 269*
Mountain Theater, *204*
Mud baths, *232–233*
Mudpie (store), *177*
Muir Woods, *203*
Muir Woods National Monument, *203*
Muir Woods Visitor Center, *203*
Mumm Napa Valley (winery), *248*
Muni, *xii*
Murals, *24, 70*
Musée Mécanique, *65*
Museo Italo-Americano, *55*
Museum of the City of San Francisco, *48*
Music, *148–150.* ☞ *Also* Dance clubs; Opera
Music, shopping for, *184–185*
Mustard's Grill ✕, *246*

N

N Touch (gay male bar), *145*
Nance's Hot Springs, *269*
Napa, *238–239, 244–245*
Napa County, *237–238*
Napa River Inn ☒, *244*
Napa Valley, *238–239, 244–255*
Napa Valley Lodge ☒, *247*
National AIDS Memorial Grove, *58, 62*
National Maritime Museum, *50, 53*
National Park Store, *53*
National parks, *xxvii*
National Skyline Trail, *215*

Natural history museums, *59, 61*
Neiman Marcus (store), *168, 169*
New Asia ✕, *32*
New Conservatory Theatre, *151*
New Pickle Circus, *152*
Newspapers and magazines, *xxvi*
Niebaum-Coppola Estate (winery), *236, 249*
Nightlife, *131–133, 136–137, 139–146*
    Wine Country, 244–245, 259, 264
Nike Missile Site, *202*
Niketown (store), *186*
Nile Trading Co. Africa Art Gallery, *181*
1907 Firehouse, *39*
Nob Hill, *37–41, 96, 119–121, 131*
Nob Hill Lambourne ☒, *121*
Noe Valley, *70–72, 166*
Noe Valley Branch Library, *71, 72*
Nola ✕, *220*
Nordstrom (store), *169*
Nordstrom Rack (store), *169*
North Beach, *33–37, 96–98, 122–123, 131, 167*
North Beach Leather (store), *177–178*
North Face (store), *186*
Northern Waterfront, *49–50, 52–53*

O

Oakland, *213–217*
Oakland A's, *162*
Oakland Ballet, *147*
Oakland Museum of California, *213–214*
Oakland Raiders, *162*
Oakville, *236, 247–248*
Oakville Grade, *247*
Oakville Grocery, *247, 267*
Occidental, *268*
Ocean Beach, *63, 65–66, 164*
Ocean-view bars, *140–141*
Octagon House, *42, 44*
ODC/San Francisco (dance group), *147*
Old and New Estates (store), *184*
Old Chinese Telephone Exchange, *30, 32*
Old Faithful Geyser of California, *253*
Old First Concerts, *149*
Old Mill Park, *200–201*
Old St. Hilary's Landmark and Wildflower Preserve, *199*
Old St. Mary's Cathedral, *29, 32*
Old Thyme Inn ☒, *225*

Olive Press (store), *260*
Oliveto ✕, *216*
Omni San Francisco Hotel ☒, *116–117*
On the Vine (store), *252*
Ondine ✕, *198*
140 Maiden Lane, *15*
One Market ✕, *87*
Opera, *150*
Opera Plaza Cinemas, *148*
Opus One (winery), *247–248*
Orpheum (theater), *150*
Osmosis Enzyme Baths, *268*
Outdoor activities. ☞ *See* Sports and outdoor activities
Outlets, *169, 172*
Ovation (piano bar), *137*

P

PacBell Park, *8*
Pacific Blues Café ✕, *245*
Pacific Film Archive, *148, 209*
Pacific Heights, *42–44, 92–93, 123–126, 167*
Pacific Heights Inn ☒, *126*
Pacific Stock Exchange, *26, 28*
Pacific Union Club, *38, 40–41*
Pacifico ✕, *254*
Packing for the trip, *xxvii–xxviii*
Painted Ladies, *73*
Palace Hotel ☒, *21, 24, 118–119*
Palace of Fine Arts, *8, 54, 56*
Palio d'Asti ✕, *89*
Palo Alto, *218–222*
Palo Alto Baylands Nature Interpretive Center, *227*
Pan-Asian restaurants, *86*
Pan Pacific Hotel ☒, *110*
Pane e Vino ✕, *85*
Panetti's (store), *166*
Panoramic Highway, *204*
Paper, shopping for, *185*
Paper Source (store), *185*
Papua New Guinea Sculpture Garden, *219*
Paradise Lounge (nightclub), *139*
Paramount Theatre, *147, 214*
Parc Hong Kong Restaurant ✕, *98*
Parco Coffee and Tea ✕, *48*
Park Chow ✕, *102*
Park Hyatt ☒, *117*
Parking, *xiv–xv*
Parks. ☞ *See* Gardens
Passports and visas, *xxiii*
Pasta? ✕, *221*
Pasta Moon ✕, *224*
Pastis ✕, *87*
Patagonia (store), *186*

Paxton Gate (store), *182*
Peace Pagoda, *46*
Peet's ✕, *210*
Pelican Inn ✕, *203*
Perry's (singles bar), *140*
Perry's Palo Alto ✕, *220*
Pescadero, *225–226*
Pescadero Creek County
   Park, *225*
Pescadero Marsh Natural
   Preserve, *225*
Pescadero State Beach, *225*
Petit Logis ☒, *247*
Petite Auberge ☒, *114*
Petrified Forest, *253*
Pharmacies, *xi*
Philharmonia Baroque
   (orchestra), *149*
Phineas T. Barnacle (skyline
   bar), *140*
Phoebe Hearst Museum of
   Anthropology, *209*
Phoenix Hotel ☒, *127*
Piano bars, *132, 137*
Piazza D'Angelo ✕, *201*
Picante Cocina Mexicana ✕,
   212
Pier 39 (mall), *50, 53*
Pier 23 (nightclub), *139*
Pigeon Point Lighthouse, *226*
Pine Ridge (winery), *239*
Pioneer Cemetery, *245*
Planetariums, *61*
Plaza Viña del Mar, *197*
Plouf ✕, *88–89*
PlumpJack Café ✕, *85*
PlumpJack Wines (store),
   189
Plush Room (cabaret), *132*
Pluto's ✕, *221*
Pocket Opera, *150*
Point Bonita Lighthouse, *202*
Point Montara Lighthouse,
   224
Point Reyes Lighthouse, *205*
Point Reyes National
   Seashore, *204–206*
Polanco (store), *181*
Polk Street (gay nightlife),
   131, 145
Polk-Williams House, *41*
Pop music, *132, 137, 139*
Portals of the Past (mansion
   ruins), *62*
Portsmouth Square, *29, 32*
Postcards, shopping for, *185*
Postrio ✕, *102*
Precita Eyes Mural Arts and
   Visitors Center, *68, 70*
Prescott Hotel ☒, *110*
Preservation Park, *214*
Presidio, *54, 56–57*
Presidio Museum, *57*
Presidio Officers' Club, *57*
Presidio Travelodge ☒, *125*
Price categories
dining, 80
lodging, 107

Pulgas Water Temple, *222–
   223*
Punch Line (comedy club),
   133

Q

Quivira (winery), *267*

R

R & G Lounge ✕, *81*
Racquetball, *159–160*
Radio stations, *xxvi*
Radisson Hotel at
   Fisherman's Wharf ☒,
   122–123
Radisson Miyako Hotel ☒,
   127
Rancho Caymus Inn ☒, *249*
Rand McNally Map and
   Travel Store, *177*
Randall Museum, *74, 75–76*
Rasputin Music (store), *208*
Ravenswood (winery), *257*
Rawhide II (dance club),
   133
Rayon Vert (store), *182*
Real Food Company (store),
   180
Recycled Records (store),
   185
Red and White Fleet, *52*
Red Devil Lounge
   (nightclub), *139*
Red Roof Inn ☒, *129*
Red Vic Movie House, *148*
Red Victorian Peace Center
   Bed & Breakfast ☒, *77–78*
Redwood Regional Park,
   215–216
Redwood Room (bar), *143*
Ren Brown Gallery, *270*
Renaissance Stanford Court
   Hotel ☒, *38, 41, 121*
Rest rooms, *xxviii*
Restaurants, *80–104.* ☞
   Also specific cuisines
Benicia, 228
Berkeley, 210, 212
Half Moon Bay, 224–225
Mill Valley, 201
Muir Woods, 203
Oakland, 216
Palo Alto, 220–221
Pescadero, 226
Point Reyes, 205–206
price categories, 80
Sausalito, 193, 198
Tiburon, 200
*Wine Country, 232, 239, 244,
   246, 249, 250–251, 253–
   254, 258–259, 260, 261–
   262, 263, 265, 266, 268,
   270, 271*
Woodside, 223
Revival of the Fittest (store),
   189
Richmond district, *98–99*
Rincon Center, *21, 24*

Ripley's Believe It or Not
   (museum), *52*
Ristorante Ideale ✕, *97*
Ristorante Piatti ✕, *258*
Ritmo Latino (store), *185*
Ritz-Carlton, San Francisco
   ✕☒, *7, 41, 96, 120, 137*
River's End ✕, *271*
Rivoli ✕, *212*
RMS Brandy Distillery, *236,
   237*
Robert Koch Gallery, *174*
Robert Louis Stevenson State
   Park, *253*
Robert Mondavi (winery),
   236, 248
Robert Sinskey (winery),
   245
Roccapulco (dance club),
   133
Rochioli Vineyards and
   Winery, *265*
Rock climbing, *160*
Rock music, *132, 137, 139*
Rockridge, *216*
Rodeos, *162*
Rodney Strong Vineyards,
   265
Rolo (store), *178*
Rooftop @ Yerba Buena
   Gardens (entertainment
   complex), *20, 24–25*
Rosalie's New Look (store),
   187
Rose Pistola ✕, *7, 98*
Rose's Café ✕, *85*
Rotary Nature Center and
   Waterfowl Refuge, *214*
Roxie Cinema, *148*
Royal Oak (singles bar),
   140
Rubicon ✕, *88*
Russian Hill, *37–41, 99–100*
Russian restaurants, *99*
Russian River Valley, *264–
   266*
Russian River Wine Road,
   264
Ruth Asawa's fantasy
   fountain, *14, 15*
Rutherford, *236, 248–249*
Rutherford Hill Winery, *236,
   248*

S

SFMOMA Artists Gallery, *55*
SS *Jeremiah O'Brien*
   (historic ship), *23*
Saddles ✕, *258*
Safety, *xxviii*
Sailing, *156*
Saint Francis Fountain and
   Candy Store, *70*
St. Francis of Assisi Church,
   34, 36
St. Helena, *233, 236, 249–
   252*
St. Mary's Cathedral, *46*

St. Patrick's Catholic Church, 149

St. Supery (winery), 249

Saints Peter and Paul Catholic Church, 34, 36

Saks Fifth Avenue (store), 168, 169

Saloon (nightclub), 139

Sam's Anchor Cafe ✕, 200

San Benito House ✕, 224

San Francisco African-American Historical and Cultural Society, 55

San Francisco Art Institute, 3, 41

San Francisco Arts Commission Gallery, 49

San Francisco Ballet, 147

San Francisco Bay model, 197

San Francisco Bay National Wildlife Refuge, 227

San Francisco Brewing Company, 27, 28

San Francisco Camerawork, 174

San Francisco Cinematheque, 148

San Francisco Convention and Visitors Bureau, 106

San Francisco Craft and Folk Art Museum, 55

San Francisco Farmers' Market/Ferry Plaza, 189–190

San Francisco Farmers' Market/ United Nations Plaza, 190

San Francisco 49ers, 162

San Francisco Giants, 161–162

San Francisco International Asian American Film Festival, 148

San Francisco International Film Festival, 148

San Francisco International Jazz Festival, 148

San Francisco International Lesbian and Gay Film Festival, 74, 148

San Francisco Jewish Film Festival, 148

San Francisco Marriott ☉, 119

San Francisco Mime Troupe, 151

San Francisco Museum of Modern Art, 8, 20, 25, 168, 183

San Francisco Opera, 150

San Francisco Performances, 146, 149

San Francisco Performing Arts Library and Museum, 49

San Francisco Public Library, 47, 48–49

San Francisco Residence Club ☉, 121

San Francisco Rock Art Posters and Collectibles (store), 189

San Francisco Shakespeare Festival, 151

San Francisco Shopping Centre, 168

San Francisco Symphony, 149

San Francisco Visitors Information Center, 11, 15

San Francisco Wine Trading (store), 189

San Francisco Women Artists Gallery, 174

San Francisco Zoo, 63, 66

San Gregorio, 226

San Gregorio General Store, 226

San Jose Earthquakes, 162

San Jose Sharks, 162

San Mateo County Coast, 164, 223–227

San Remo ☉, 106, 123

San Tung No. 2 ✕, 102

Sand Dollar ✕, 203

Sante ✕, 257

Sanppo ✕, 92

Sanrio (store), 187

Santa Rosa, 262–264

Sassafras ✕, 263

Sather Tower, 209

Sausalito, 193, 197–199

Sausalito Art Festival, 198

Savoy Hotel & Brasserie ☉, 114–115

Scala's Bistro ✕, 103

Scheuer Linen (store), 182

Schramsberg (winery), 253

Science museums, 55, 59, 61, 197–198, 210, 213–214

Sculptures, 22, 23–24, 25

Sea Change (sculpture), 25

Seafood restaurants, 84, 89–90, 103

Seasons Bar, 137

Sebastiani Theatre, 259

Sebastiani Vineyards, 257

Senior citizen travel, xxviii

Sephora (store), 175

700 block of Montgomery Street, 27–28

1735 Franklin (house), 43

Seymour Pioneer Museum, 20, 25

Shakespeare at Buena Vista, 259

Shakespeare Garden, 58, 62

Shannon Court Hotel ☉, 112–113

Shapiro Gallery, 174

Sharper Image (store), 187

Sharpsteen Museum, 252

Sheraton Hotel Palo Alto ☉, 221

Sherman House ☉, 7, 123

Shige Antique Kimonos (store), 172, 188

Ships, historic, 23

Shoes, shopping for, 185–186

Shopping, 166–169, 172–178, 180–190

Palo Alto, 222

San Gregorio, 226

Wine Country, 251–252, 255, 259, 267, 270

Shreve & Co. (store), 183

Shushu Fufu (store), 259

Side trips from San Francisco, 192–193, 197–229

Sightseeing tours, xxviii–xxix. ☞ Also Guided tours

Silverado Country Club and Resort ✕☉, 239, 244

Silverado Museum, 250

Simi Winery, 267

Singaporean restaurants, 99

Singles bars, 132, 139–140

Sir Francis Drake Hotel ☉, 112

Six Flags Marine World, 228

Skyline bars, 132, 140–141

Slanted Door ✕, 96

Slim's (nightclub), 139

Small Frys (store), 177

Smuin Ballets/SF, 147

Soccer, 162

Soko Hardware (store), 181

Solo Mia (store), 178

SoMa (South of Market), 20–25, 100–102, 117–119, 131, 145, 168

Songlines Aboriginal Art, 174

Sonoma, 236, 255, 257–259

Sonoma Cheese Factory (store), 259

Sonoma Coast Villa Inn and Spa ☉, 270

Sonoma County, 237, 255, 257–271

Sonoma Mission Inn & Spa ✕☉, 259, 269

Sonoma Plaza (stores), 259

Sonoma Valley, 255, 257–262

South Park Café ✕, 101

Southern Exposure (store), 174

Spago ✕, 220

Spanish restaurants, 90, 93, 100

Spas, 46, 156–158, 232–233, 250, 252, 254–255, 259, 268, 269, 270

Specialty stores, 172–178, 180–190

Specs' (bar), 143

Spectator sports, 161–163

Spencer Smyth Gallery, 174

Spinnaker ✕, 198

Spoken word, 141–142

Sporting goods, shopping for, *186*

Sports and outdoor activities, *154–164*

Wine Country, 245, 247, 255, 264, 270, 271

Spreckels Mansion (Haight), *76, 78*

Spreckels Mansion (Pacific Heights), *42, 44*

Spreckels Performing Arts Center, *264*

Sproul Plaza (Berkeley), *208–209*

Stacey's (store), *177*

Stage Door Theater, *151*

Stag's Leap Wine Cellars, *236, 245*

Stanford Linear Accelerator Center (SLAC), *220*

Stanford Park Hotel ⌸, *221*

Stanford Shopping Center, *222*

Stanford University, *218–219*

Stars ✕, *81*

Station House Cafe ✕, *205–206*

Steak houses, *86, 104*

Steep Ravine Trail, *204*

Steinhart Aquarium, *59*

Sterling Vineyards, *252*

Stern Grove (festival), *149*

Steven Oliver Arts Center, *216*

Stevenson, Robert Lewis, *250, 252, 253*

Stinson Beach Grill ✕, *203*

Storyville (jazz club), *136*

Stow Lake, *59, 62*

Straits Café ✕, *99*

Streetlight Records (store), *185*

Strybing Arboretum & Botanical Gardens, *58, 62–63*

Stud (gay male bar), *145*

Students, *xxix*

Studio 24 (store), *181*

Sue Fisher King Company (store), *167, 182–183*

Summer in the City (music series), *149–150*

Sunset District, *102*

Suppenkuche ✕, *84*

Sur la Table (store), *183*

Sutro Heights Park, *63, 66*

Sweden House Bakery & Café ✕, *200*

Swensen's Ice Cream ✕, *39*

Swimming, *160, 271*

Sybase Open Tennis Tournament, *162*

Symbols and icons, *vi, 274*

T

Tadich Grill ✕, *90*

Tall Stories, *177*

Tattoo Art Museum, *36*

Taxes, *xxix*

Taxis, *xxix–xxx*

Tea House ✕, *62*

Telegraph Avenue (Berkeley), *208*

Telegraph Hill, *34, 36–37*

Telephones, *xxiii–xxiv*

Television stations, *xxvi*

Temples, *31, 32–33, 222–223*

Ten Ren Tea Company, *30*

Tennis, *160, 162–163, 245, 255*

Terra ✕, *250–251*

Terra Mia (store), *183*

Thai restaurants, *92*

Theater, *150–152*

Theater Artaud, *151*

Theatre on the Square, *151*

Theatre Rhinoceros, *144, 151*

Theme parks, *228*

Thep Lela ✕, *201*

Thep Phanom ✕, *92*

1360 Montgomery Street, *35, 37*

Thistle Dew Inn ⌸, *259*

Thomas Reynolds Gallery, *174*

Three Bags Full (store), *178*

388 Market Street, *23*

330 Ritch Street (dance club), *133*

Thursday Showcase (market), *190*

Ti Couz ✕, *95*

Tiburon, *199–200*

Tickets, *19, 131, 146, 162*

Tickets.com, *131, 146, 162*

Tilden Park, *210*

Time, *xxx*

Timing the visit, *xxxiii–xxxiv*

Tin How Temple, *30, 32–33*

Tip Top Liquor Warehouse (store), *267*

Tipping, *xxx*

TIX Bay Area (ticket service), *14, 19, 146*

Ton Kiang ✕, *98*

Tonga Room (bar), *39, 143*

Top of the Mark (skyline bar), *40, 140*

Topolos at Russian River Vineyards, *264*

Tosca Café (bar), *143*

Total Living Company (store), *259*

Tours and packages, *xxx–xxxi*

Tower Records Outlet, *172*

Town House Motel ⌸, *126*

Toys and gadgets, shopping for, *186–187*

Tra Vigne ✕, *251*

Train travel, *xxxi, 217–218, 223, 229*

Transamerica Pyramid, *26, 28*

Transportation, *xxxi, 272*

Travel agencies, *xxxi*

Traveling Jewish Theatre, *151*

Treasure Island, *227*

Trolley, *21*

Tuscan Inn ⌸, *122*

2151 Sacramento (condominium), *43*

2223 ✕, *80–81*

Twig (store), *181*

Twin Peaks, *76*

Two Fools ✕, *224–225*

U

U.C. Berkeley Art Museum, *209–210*

U.C. Botanical Gardens, *210*

USS *Pampanito* (submarine), *52*

Under One Roof (store), *166*

Union Hotel ✕⌸, *228*

Union Square, *11, 14–15, 19, 102–103, 107, 110–115, 168*

Union Street, *131, 168*

Union Street Goldsmith (store), *183*

Union Street Inn ⌸, *7, 124*

United Nations Plaza, *47, 49*

University Avenue (Berkeley), *208*

University of California, *207–208, 211*

V

Vallejo steps area, *38, 41*

Van Ness/Polk area, *104, 126–127*

Vanderbilt & Company (store), *252*

Vedanta Society, *42, 44*

Vegetarian restaurants, *84–85, 86*

Venetian Carousel, *53*

Vesuvio Café (bar), *143–144*

Veterans Building, *47, 49*

Viansa (winery), *237*

Victoria Pastry Co., *180*

Victorian houses, *44, 73, 199–200, 214*

Victorian on Lytton ⌸, *222*

Vietnamese restaurants, *96, 99, 103*

View Lounge (skyline bar), *141*

Village Outlet Stores, *252*

Vineyard Inn ⌸, *259*

Vintage Court ⌸, *121*

Vintage 1870 (shopping center), *245*

Vintage fashion, furniture, and accessories, shopping for, *187, 189*

Vintage Inn ⌸, *247*

Vintner's Inn ⌸, *263*

Virgin Megastore, *168, 185*

Virginia Breier (store), *181*

Visitor information, *xxxi–xxxii*
Bay Area, 229
East Bay, 218
Inland Peninsula, 223
Marin County, 207
San Mateo County Coast, 226–227
Wine Country, 272
Vivande Porta Via ✕, 93
Vorpal Gallery, 174–175

W

W San Francisco ⌂, 119
Walking, *xxix*
Walnut Square (Berkeley), 208
Walter/McBean Gallery, 41
Wappo Bar and Bistro ✕, 254
War Memorial Opera House, 47, 49
Warfield (nightclub), 139
Washington Square (San Francisco), 34, 37
Washington Square (Yountville), 245
Waterfront Plaza Hotel ⌂, 217
Wave Organ, 55
Wax Museum, 52
Web sites, *xxxii–xxxiii*
Wedding Houses, 42, 44
Wells Fargo Bank History Museum, 26, 28
West Coast Live (radio show), 142
West Point Inn, 204

Western Shoreline, 63–66
Westin ⌂, 128
Westin St. Francis Hotel ⌂, 14, 19, 110–111
Whiskey Lounge (gay male bar), 145
White Swan Inn ⌂, 115
Whittier Mansion, 42, 44
Wholesale Jewelers Exchange (store), 183
Wild Side West (lesbian bar), 146
Wildlife refuges, 225, 226, 227
Willow Wood Market Café ✕, 268
Windsor Vineyards, 199
Windsurfing, 161
Wine and spirits, shopping for, 189
Wine bars, 142
Wine Club (store), 189
Wine Country, 231–233, 236–272
Wine Country Inn ⌂, 251
Wine House Limited (store), 189
Wine Spectator Greystone Restaurant ✕, 251
Wine tasting, 233, 256
Wineries, 199, 233, 237, 238, 239, 245, 246, 247, 248, 249, 250, 252, 253, 257, 260, 261, 263, 264–265, 267, 268
Wok Shop (store), 183
Women's Building, 67, 70

Woodside, 222–223
Woodside Bakery and Café ✕, 223
Worldware (store), 167, 178

X

X-21 Modern (gallery), 172
Xanadu (gallery), 15, 180
Xela Imports (store), 181

Y

Yank Sing ✕, 88
Yerba Buena Center for the Arts, 151
Yerba Buena Gardens, 20, 25
Yerba Buena Island, 226
YMCA Central Branch, 106
Yoga, 161
Yone (store), 184
York Hotel ⌂, 115
Yoshi's (jazz club), 136
Yountville, 236, 245–247
Yountville (store), 177
Yountville Park, 245

Z

Zao Noodle Bar ✕, 81
Zarzuela ✕, 100
Zeitgeist Timepieces and Jewelry, 184
Zibibbo ✕, 221
Zonal (store), 189
Zoo, 66
Zuni Café & Grill ✕, 84
ZuZu ✕, 244

NOTES

Fodor's Key to the Guides

America's guidebook leader publishes guides for every kind of traveler. Check out our many series and find your perfect match.

Fodor's Gold Guides
America's favorite travel-guide series offers the most detailed insider reviews of hotels, restaurants, and attractions in all price ranges, plus great background information, smart tips, and useful maps.

Fodor's Road Guide USA
Big guides for a big country—the most comprehensive guides to America's roads, packed with places to stay, eat, and play across the U.S.A. Just right for road warriors, family vacationers, and cross-country trekkers.

COMPASS AMERICAN GUIDES
Stunning guides from top local writers and photographers, with gorgeous photos, literary excerpts, and colorful anecdotes. A must-have for culture mavens, history buffs, and new residents.

Fodor's CITYPACKS
Concise city coverage with a foldout map. The right choice for urban travelers who want everything under one cover.

Fodor's EXPLORING GUIDES
Hundreds of color photos bring your destination to life. Lively stories lend insight into the culture, history, and people.

Fodor's POCKET GUIDES
For travelers who need only the essentials. The best of Fodor's in pocket-size packages for just $9.95.

Fodor's To Go
Credit-card–size, magnetized color microguides that fit in the palm of your hand—perfect for "stealth" travelers or as gifts.

Fodor's FLASHMAPS
Every resident's map guide. 60 easy-to-follow maps of public transit, parks, museums, zip codes, and more.

Fodor's CITYGUIDES
Sourcebooks for living in the city: Thousands of in-the-know listings for restaurants, shops, sports, nightlife, and other city resources.

Fodor's AROUND THE CITY WITH KIDS
68 great ideas for family days, recommended by resident parents. Perfect for exploring in your own backyard or on the road.

Fodor's ESCAPES
Fill your trip with once-in-a-lifetime experiences, from ballooning in Chianti to overnighting in the Moroccan desert. These full-color dream books point the way.

Fodor's FYI
Get tips from the pros on planning the perfect trip. Learn how to pack, fly hassle-free, plan a honeymoon or cruise, stay healthy on the road, and travel with your baby.

Fodor's Languages for Travelers
Practice the local language before hitting the road. Available in phrase books, cassette sets, and CD sets.

Karen Brown's Guides
Engaging guides to the most charming inns and B&Bs in the U.S.A. and Europe, with easy-to-follow inn-to-inn itineraries.

Baedeker's Guides
Comprehensive guides, trusted since 1829, packed with A–Z reviews and star ratings.

At bookstores everywhere.   www.fodors.com/books